Wm. H. Taft

Charles E. Hughes

Harlan F. Stone

Fred M. Vinson

Earl Warren

Warren E. Burger

William H. Rehnquist

THE
SUPREME COURT
A to Z

CQ'S ENCYCLOPEDIA OF AMERICAN GOVERNMENT

THE
SUPREME COURT
A to Z

A READY REFERENCE ENCYCLOPEDIA
Revised Edition

ELDER WITT, *Advisory Editor*

CONGRESSIONAL QUARTERLY INC.
WASHINGTON, D.C.

Copyright © 1994 Congressional Quarterly Inc.
1414 22nd Street, N.W.
Washington, D.C. 20037

Book Design by Kachergis Book Design, Pittsboro, North Carolina.

Printed in the United States of America.

Acknowledgments

Photographs by Lee Troell Anderson originally appeared in *The Illustrated History of the Supreme Court of the United States* by Robert Shnayerson, published by Harry N. Abrams, Inc. Reprinted with permission.

Chart on page 16 originally appeared in *American Government: Freedom and Power*, second edition, by Theodore J. Lowi and Benjamin Ginsburg, published by W. W. Norton, 1992. Reprinted with permission.

cover images

1. Bank of the United States cartoon, Library of Congress
2. Supreme Court building pediment, R. Michael Jenkins
3. William H. Woodward, Dartmouth College
4. Cross of Gold speech cartoon, Library of Congress
5. Abortion demonstrators, R. Michael Jenkins
6. John Marshall, silhouette
7. William H. Rehnquist, Collection of the Supreme Court of the United States
8. *Jencks v. United States* cartoon, *Los Angeles Examiner*
9. Harriet Scott, Library of Congress
10. William Cushing, Library of Congress
11. Dred Scott, Library of Congress
12. Ronald Reagan and Sandra Day O'Connor, George Tames/*New York Times*
13. Oliver Wendell Holmes, Jr., Library of Congress

frontispiece Detail of Supreme Court building pediment, Rowland Scherman Photography

Library of Congress Cataloging-in-Publication Data
The Supreme Court A to Z : a ready reference encyclopedia / Elder Witt, advisory editor.—Rev. ed.
      p.   cm. — (CQ's encyclopedia of American government; v. 3)
      Includes bibliographical references and index.
      ISBN 1-56802-007-4 (paper)—1-56802-053-8 (cloth)
      1. United States. Supreme Court—Encyclopedias. 2. United States. Supreme Court—Biography. I. Witt, Elder. II. Series.
KF8742.A35S8   1994
347.73'26'03'—dc20   94-29912
[347.3073503]   CIP

Contents

Foreword

There's no right place to begin learning about the U.S. Supreme Court. You can begin anywhere—with a case, a justice, a year, an issue.

For me, it began with two cases. One, from Topeka, everyone knows: *Brown v. Board of Education* (1954).

I was a third-grader in Chattanooga, Tennessee. My father was a member of the school board, which announced quickly that it would comply with the Court's ruling and begin to dismantle segregation in our city's public schools. The community's response was angry and threatening. Our world changed dramatically, all because of a decision by the U.S. Supreme Court in Washington, D.C. Even an eight-year-old wondered at such power.

Fifteen years later, there was another case: *Tinker v. Des Moines Independent School District #1* (1969). School children have a First Amendment right to signify protest in a peaceful, nondisruptive manner. I was a freshman reporter in Washington, D.C. It was the first of a long line of Supreme Court decisions I would report over the next two decades.

The more I learned, the deeper my fascination with the people, the process, the institution, and the genius that had designed a system that has worked for so long under such different circumstances and pressures. That fascination culminated in two years of work on the book from which much in this book is drawn, *Guide to the U.S. Supreme Court,* first published in 1979, with the second edition published in 1989.

There is no single point of access to knowledge about the Court, no official beginning. Anywhere you begin, you will pick up a thread that will lead you into the tapestry of this institution.

The details may be complex, but the pattern is simple. The Supreme Court is more than 200 years old; it has had over 100 members; it has decided thousands of cases. Yet just as visitors to its courtroom are struck as much by its compactness as by its grandeur, so too should they notice the simplicity of its mode of operation, little changed from its first meeting.

The Court is in business to resolve real disputes between real people over real issues—and in the course of doing that, to interpret and illuminate the meaning of our nation's basic charter, the U.S. Constitution, and the laws enacted under it. The Court itself, the justices, resolves these disputes. Decisions are not made by committee or filtered through a bureaucracy. The outcome is announced publicly, along with a report of who voted how, and with written reasons backing those positions. In a political city where bureaucracy flourishes, decisions are often ducked, and positions obscured as often as they are clarified, the Court stands apart, independent and different.

Perhaps that is why the Court is seen as remote and mysterious when in fact its public sessions and its work are quite accessible. Lawyers are somewhat possessive about the Court and its work, but it is not just their Supreme Court. It is the nation's Court, the people's Court, if you will, and to the extent this volume enhances access to it and enlarges knowledge of it, it will have achieved its purpose.

So begin. What do you wish to know?

- What has the Court said about CONFESSIONS?
- What does JUDICIAL REVIEW mean anyway?
- What HISTORIC MILESTONES should you be aware of in the Court's history?
- What was the decision in *GIBBONS V. OGDEN*?
- What is the SCHEDULE OF TERMS AND DAYS?
- How many RESIGNATIONS have there been from the Court?

The answers are here. We hope that you find them illuminating.

Elder Witt

Preface

The Supreme Court A to Z is one of three comprehensive volumes from Congressional Quarterly offering quick and accurate answers to your questions about the United States government. This volume and its companions, Congress A to Z and The Presidency A to Z, make up CQ's Encyclopedia of American Government, a set we believe provides the most concise and accessible ready-reference information about the history, powers, and operations of the three branches of government.

In this volume you will find information about the nation's highest court, including the array of important legal decisions that have shaped contemporary interpretation of the U.S. Constitution and the fascinating but sometimes little-known individuals who, as justices, have decided the issues that affect every citizen. CQ editors and writers provide engaging, nontechnical answers to commonly asked questions about the Supreme Court and its rulings. This book and its companions are intended for anyone who has an interest in national government and politics. High school students researching term papers, political activists working on an issue or a campaign, and anyone following politics and government will find CQ's Encyclopedia of American Government useful.

The entries in The Supreme Court A to Z and the other two volumes are arranged alphabetically and are extensively cross-referenced to guide you to related information in each individual book. Each volume also has a detailed index.

The core of this volume is a series of essays that give overviews of many constitutional issues, such as freedom of speech and due process. Shorter entries cover related subjects. Brief biographies of all the justices are included.

This book is the product of many people at Congressional Quarterly now or in the past who have had a special interest in the Supreme Court and the constitutional and legal issues that have shaped our nation. The text was organized and prepared under the general direction of CQ reference editor Jeanne Ferris, who was assisted greatly by the continuing advice and wisdom of Elder Witt. Witt, who more than anyone else at CQ has been the custodian of CQ's historical coverage of the Court and its work, is the editor and principal writer of both the first and second editions of the award-winning Guide to the U.S. Supreme Court. The principal writers for this volume were Kenneth Jost and Martha Gottron, both of whom brought important strengths to the project—Jost as a lawyer and legal affairs journalist and Gottron as a major contributor to both editions of Guide to the U.S. Supreme Court. Bruce Maxwell also made important contributions to the text.

Nancy Lammers, assistant director of the Book Editorial Department, devised and executed the plan that turned the text into a finished book. Lys Ann Shore served as editor, adding her expert touch to clarify when needed and tighten when necessary. Carolyn Goldinger, with the able assistance of Laura Carter, selected and gathered the hundreds of images that bring this text to visual life. Carter also coordinated with dispatch the many details of this project. Joyce Kachergis and her talented staff are responsible for the book's design and production.

We hope this volume on the Supreme Court and the others on Congress and the presidency that comprise CQ's Encyclopedia of American Government will help readers understand, appreciate, and appraise—critically but fairly—the governmental institutions under which we live.

David R. Tarr
Editorial Director, CQ Books

A

Abortion

Beginning in the mid-1800s, many states enacted laws prohibiting abortion, mainly to protect women from unsafe medical procedures. In the 1960s, a movement grew to relax the laws against abortion, reflecting the drive to gain additional legal rights for women. By the early 1970s, several states had enacted abortion reform laws. In 1973, the Supreme Court transformed this political issue into a major legal controversy by ruling that the Constitution protects a woman's right to an abortion during most of her pregnancy. This ruling was made in a case called *ROE V. WADE*.

The decision was an unexpectedly broad victory for abortion rights advocates. It mobilized abortion opponents, who began trying to overturn the ruling by constitutional amendment or statute or to enact restrictive laws that at least limited its impact.

Over the next decade, the Court applied its ruling to strike down several restrictive laws that states enacted after *Roe*. In 1976 the Court struck down provisions of a Missouri law that required a husband's consent for a first-trimester abortion, required parental consent for unmarried women under age eighteen to have an abortion, and proscribed use of the most common procedure for performing abortions *(Planned Parenthood v. Danforth)*.

The Court upheld a provision in the Missouri law requiring a woman to certify that she had given her informed consent before undergoing an abortion. But in 1983 the Court struck down an Ohio law that enlarged on that requirement. The Ohio law listed specific information that a doctor must give a woman before an abortion, including a statement that a fetus is a human life from the moment of conception. The decision in that case *(Akron v. Akron Center for Reproductive Choice)* also invalidated a twenty-four-hour waiting period before an abortion. Three years later, the Court struck down a more limited Pennsylvania law that required doctors to inform women of the risks of an abortion and of the assistance available if the woman decided to complete her pregnancy.

During the same period, though, the Court sustained one legislative strategy adopted by abortion opponents: bans on the use of public funds to finance abortions for poor women. In *Maher v. Roe* (1977) the Court, by a 6–3 vote, upheld a Connecticut law that permitted state Medicaid assistance only for "medically necessary" abortions while it provided such aid for childbirth. The Court rejected arguments that the funding limitation violated either the right to privacy or the right to equal protection. Three years later, in *Harris v. McRae*, the Court voted 5–4 to uphold a stricter federal provision—the so-called Hyde Amendment—that barred federal funding even for medically necessary abortions.

The Reagan Era and After

Antiabortion activists gained an important political ally with the 1980 election of President Ronald Reagan, a strong opponent of abortion. Reagan's first appointee to the Court, Justice Sandra Day O'Connor, strongly criticized *Roe* in a dissenting opinion in the Akron case. She was joined in that opinion by *Roe's* two original dissenters, justices Byron R. White and William H. Rehnquist. By the end of his second term, Reagan had given abortion opponents further encouragement by elevating Rehnquist to chief justice and appointing two other justices—Antonin Scalia and Anthony M. Kennedy—who were thought likely to vote to overturn Roe.

The effect of the Reagan appointments was seen in a 1989 decision, *Webster v. Reproductive Health Services*. This ruling upheld by a 5–4 vote the major provisions of a restrictive Missouri abortion law. The law prohibited the use of public facilities or public employees to perform abortions. It also required physicians to test the viability of the fetus before permitting an abortion to be performed on a woman believed to be as much as twenty weeks pregnant.

3

Since the decision in Roe v. Wade, *the constitutionality of various state laws regulating abortion has been tested in the Supreme Court. The issue continues to provoke strong feelings on both sides.*
Source: R. Michael Jenkins

The decision fell short of what abortion opponents had hoped for. Rehnquist, White, and Kennedy wrote in a plurality opinion that they would permit restrictions on abortion if the restrictions had a rational basis; they would not require a compelling government interest in order to justify such regulations. Scalia went further and said he would have overruled *Roe*. But O'Connor declined to join either opinion, saying the case did not require the Court to reconsider *Roe*. Still, the decision drew an impassioned dissent from Justice Harry A. Blackmun, who had written the *Roe* opinion. Blackmun warned that the "right to reproductive choice" was imperiled.

In 1990 and 1991, President George Bush, who like Reagan was an avowed opponent of abortion, filled two more seats on the Court with David H. Souter and Clarence Thomas. Both sides of the abortion debate then braced for a watershed ruling when in late 1991 a case reached the Court that challenged a broad set of abortion restrictions adopted in Pennsylvania.

The Court upheld all but one of the restrictions in a decision, *Planned Parenthood v. Casey* (1992), that satisfied neither side. For the first time, four justices—Rehnquist, White, Scalia, and Thomas—voted to overrule *Roe*. But the Court's main opinion, authored by O'Connor, Kennedy, and Souter, reaffirmed the "essential holding" of *Roe* while setting forth a new "undue burden" test for determining the validity of abortion regulations. "An undue burden exists," the three justices wrote, ". . . if [a law's] purpose and effect is to place substantial obstacles in the path of a woman seeking an abortion before the fetus attains viability."

Using that test, O'Connor, Kennedy, and Souter cast the deciding votes with Rehnquist, White, Scalia, and Thomas to uphold a twenty-four-hour waiting period, specific information that doctors were to communicate to women before an abortion, and a requirement for a minor to obtain the consent of a parent or a judge before undergoing an abortion. But O'Connor, Kennedy, and Souter voted with Blackmun and John Paul Stevens—who continued to apply *Roe's* stricter standard—to strike down a provision that a woman must notify her husband before seeking an abortion.

The five-vote majority in support of retaining *Roe* deeply disappointed antiabortion groups. But abortion rights advocates said the new "undue burden" test represented a major retreat from *Roe* and would encourage states to enact additional restrictions.

Abortion rights supporters returned to the Court with new cases aimed at protecting abortion clinics from protests that involved violence, trespassing, or other unlawful activities.

In January 1993, the Court said clinics could not use a Reconstruction-era civil rights law to prevent blockades by antiabortion demonstrators. One year later, however, the Court unanimously ruled that clinics can bring civil damage suits under the federal antiracketeering law known as RICO against persons involved in criminal protests. And in its final decision of the 1993–1994 term, the Court upheld, 6–3, the power of judges to enjoin antiabortion protestors from demonstrating too close to clinics as long as the injunctions "burden no more speech than necessary to serve a significant government interest."

Administrative Assistant to the Chief Justice

In addition to strictly judicial functions, the CHIEF JUSTICE of the United States is responsible for an increasingly complex set of administrative duties. Since 1972 an administrative assistant has helped the chief justice with these extrajudicial activities.

Under Chief Justice Warren E. Burger the administrative assistant provided research and analysis for the chief justice to use in public speeches and statements, monitored the literature and developments in the fields of judicial administration and court improvement, stayed in close touch with groups and individuals working in those fields, and helped the chief justice in supervising the institutional operations of the Court. Other duties include helping the chief justice prepare the Court's budget and coordinate personnel policies. The administrative assistant also oversees the judicial fellows and internship programs.

The first administrative assistant was Mark Cannon; the second, Noel J. Augustyn; the third, Larry Averill; the fourth, Robb Jones. A fifth administrative assistant, Harvey Rishikof, was selected in 1994.

Administrative Office of the U.S. Courts

As its name implies, the Administrative Office of the U.S. Courts performs many support functions for the federal court system. Those duties and functions have expanded considerably over the half-century the office has been in existence.

The office prepares and submits to Congress the budget and legislative agenda for the federal courts. It provides administrative assistance to the clerical staffs of the courts, the probation officers, bankruptcy judges, magistrates, and other court personnel. It also audits and disburses funds for the operation of the courts.

The administrative office provides support to the committees of the JUDICIAL CONFERENCE of the United States. It compiles and publishes statistics on the work and workloads of the courts, as directed by the conference, and maintains liaison with various groups, including Congress and the executive branch. The director and the deputy director are appointed by the Supreme Court.

Created by Congress in 1939, the Administrative Office of the U.S. Courts operates under the direction of the Judicial Conference. The director prepares an annual report about the activities of the office and the situation of the federal courts, along with any recommendations for improvement. The report is submitted to the Judicial Conference at its annual meeting, to Congress, and to the attorney general.

In fiscal 1994 about 960 people worked in the administrative office. In fiscal 1994 the office had a budget of $44.9 million.

Affirmative Action

Affirmative action describes programs that give special consideration or preference to members of previously disadvantaged groups, most commonly African Americans, in such areas as university admissions, employment, and government contracting. The nation and the Supreme Court were sharply divided during the 1970s and 1980s on the wisdom and legality of such programs.

Supporters argued that "race-conscious remedies" were needed to compensate for the effects of past DISCRIMINATION and to achieve a more diverse, representative student body or work force. Opponents said minority preferences amounted to "reverse discrimination" against whites, or a race-based spoils system.

The Supreme Court ruled on thirteen affirmative action cases between 1974 and 1990, with seemingly confusing results. By 1987 the Court had struck down nearly as many affirmative action plans as it had upheld. With the agreement of never more than six justices, the Court had approved some use of affirmative action in school admissions, job training, contract set-asides, admission to union membership, and promotions. It had forbidden the use of affirmative action in layoffs to preserve the jobs of African Americans at the expense of more senior white employees.

In 1987 the Court came down firmly on the side of affirmative action, ruling that affirmative action, when carefully used, was an appropriate remedy violating neither the Constitution nor any federal CIVIL RIGHTS law.

The justices were still closely divided, however. Three years later the Court split 5–4 in upholding a congressionally mandated minority preference policy adopted by the Federal Communications Commission (FCC). The policy was aimed at increasing minority ownership of broadcast stations.

Two of the Court's most consistent supporters of affirmative action retired after the decision in the FCC case. William J. Brennan, Jr., retired in 1990, and Thurgood Marshall in 1991. They were succeeded by more conservative justices, David H. Souter and Clarence Thomas. By the end of the 1991–1992 Court term, neither had voted in an affirmative action case.

Admissions

When the affirmative action issue first reached the Court, the justices sidestepped it. In *DeFunis v. Odegaard* (1974) the Court, by a vote of 5 to 4, refused to rule on a white plaintiff's challenge to the use of racial preferences by the University of Washington law school in admitting students. The plaintiff had been admitted to the school under a court order and was due to graduate in the spring of 1974, only months after the Court heard arguments in the case. On that basis, the majority ruled the case moot—that is, no longer presenting a live controversy.

Four years later, in *University of California Regents v. Bakke* (1978), the Court established the rule that has gone unchanged since that time. By a 5–4 vote, the Court ruled that state universities cannot set aside a fixed quota of seats for minority group members; a different five-justice majority said race can be considered as one factor in admissions.

The plaintiff in the case, Allan Bakke, had twice been denied admission to the medical school at the University of California at Davis. He challenged the school's decision to set aside sixteen seats for minority applicants in each medical school class of one hundred students. Bakke claimed the practice violated both his right to equal protection of the laws and Title VI of the Civil Rights Act of 1964, which forbids discrimination in federally funded programs.

Four members of the Court—Chief Justice Warren E. Burger and justices Potter Stewart, William H. Rehnquist, and John Paul Stevens—said the set-aside violated Title VI and did not decide the constitutional issue. "Race cannot be the basis of excluding anyone from participation in a federally funded program," Stevens explained.

Four others—Brennan, Marshall, Byron R. White, and Harry A. Blackmun—found no violation of Title VI or of the Constitution. "Government may take race into account when it acts not to demean or insult any racial group, but to remedy disadvantages cast on minorities by past racial prejudice, at least when appropriate findings have been made by judicial, legislative, or administrative bodies with competence to act in this area," Brennan wrote.

Justice Lewis F. Powell, Jr., cast the decisive vote in the case. He provided the fifth vote to strike down the school's quota system, saying it violated both Title VI and the equal protection clause. But he also said universities could make limited use of minority preferences in situations where past discrimination had been proved.

Powell's vote effectively established the rule of the

Twice rejected for admission to the medical school at the University of California at Davis, Allan Bakke challenged the school's quota system for minority admissions. The Court struck down the university's system but said race may be considered in such decisions. Bakke received his degree in 1982.   Source: AP/Wide World Photo

case. Despite the fractured nature of the ruling, the Court has not decided another case involving university minority preference policies since Bakke.

Employment

The Court has allowed both private and government employers to establish voluntary affirmative action programs to benefit African Americans or women.

The key ruling came in *United Steelworkers of America v. Weber* (1979). In that case the Court held, 5–2, that such programs do not violate the JOB DISCRIMINATION provisions found in Title VII of the 1964 Civil Rights Act. Stewart joined the four justices who had endorsed race-conscious remedies in *Bakke* to form the majority in the case; Powell and Stevens did not participate.

The *Weber* decision upheld a training program established by Kaiser Aluminum and the steelworkers' union in 1974 that reserved half of all in-plant craft-training slots for members of minorities. In the Court's opinion Brennan said that Congress could not have intended the civil rights law to prohibit private employers from voluntarily taking steps to open opportunities for blacks in job areas traditionally closed to them. In sharp dissents, Burger and Rehnquist both accused the majority of twisting the legislative history to achieve a result directly opposed to the language of the act.

President Ronald Reagan strongly opposed affirmative action, and his administration urged the Court to reverse its course in several employment-related cases. In its next two such cases, the Court did limit use of affirmative action in layoff situations.

In *Firefighters Local Union No. 1784 v. Stotts* (1984) the Court voted 6–3 to overturn a judge's order that had protected the jobs of black firefighters who had been hired following a consent decree in a race discrimination suit. The judge's order had required the Memphis fire department to meet budget cutbacks by laying off more senior whites. In an opinion by Justice White, the Court agreed with the administration that Title VII protected the seniority system. Two years later the Court, by a vote of 5 to 4, extended the *Stotts* ruling by finding an equal protection violation in a school board's voluntary use of affirmative action plans to protect recently hired black workers in a similar layoff situation *(Wygant v. Jackson Board of Education* [1986]).

Justice Sandra Day O'Connor, named to the Court by Reagan in 1981, joined the majority in opposing the affirmative action plans in both *Stotts* and *Wygant*. But she distanced herself from the administration's position in a separate opinion in *Wygant*. "The Court is in agreement," she wrote, "[that] remedying past or present racial discrimination by a state actor is a sufficiently weighty state interest to warrant the remedial use of a carefully constructed affirmative action program."

Six weeks later, on July 2, 1986, the Court held in separate cases that neither court-ordered minority quotas for union admission nor race-based job promotions violated the 1964 Civil Rights Act.

In *Local #28 of the Sheet Metal Workers' International v. Equal Employment Opportunity Commission,* the Court, by a 5–4 vote, upheld an order requiring the union, which had refused to admit African Americans, to increase its nonwhite membership to 29.23 percent by August 1987. In *Local #93, International Association of Firefighters v. City of Cleveland,* the Court held, 6–3, that the Civil Rights Act did not prevent the city from resolving a bias complaint by agreeing to promote one black firefighter for every white promoted.

In February 1987 the Court upheld, by a vote of 5 to 4, another challenged affirmative action plan: a one-black-for-one-white promotion quota imposed on Alabama's state troopers by a federal judge. Dissenting in the case were Rehnquist (now the chief justice), White, O'Connor, and Antonin Scalia (at that time the Court's newest member).

The Court settled any remaining doubts about the legality of some affirmative action programs in March 1987 by upholding such a plan to benefit women. The 6–3 decision in *Johnson v. Transportation Agency, Santa Clara County, Calif.* stated that the voluntary plan by the county transportation department to move women into higher ranking positions did not violate Title VII—thereby extending the holding in *Weber* to public employers. Rehnquist, White, and Scalia dissented.

Government Programs

The Court has twice upheld the federal government's broad discretion to fashion minority preference policies, but it has given state and local governments less freedom to do so.

In *Fullilove v. Klutznick* (1980) the Court upheld, 6–3, Congress's decision in the Public Works Employment Act of 1977 to set aside a certain percentage of federal funds for contracts with minority-owned businesses. "In the continuing effort to achieve the goal of equality of economic opportunity," Burger wrote for the Court, "Congress has necessary latitude to try new techniques such as the limited use of racial and ethnic criteria to accomplish remedial objectives."

Following the *Fullilove* decision dozens of state and local governments adopted similar set-aside programs for minority-owned businesses. In 1989 the Court struck down, 6–3, an especially rigid plan adopted by Richmond, Virginia. The plan required the prime contractor on every city construction project to subcontract at least 30 percent of the dollar amount of the contract to minority-owned businesses.

Writing for the Court in *City of Richmond v. J. A. Croson Co.,* O'Connor said states can adopt race-conscious remedial programs "only when they possess evidence that their own spending practices are exacerbating a pattern of prior discrimination" and only if they "identify that discrimination, public or private—with some specificity." O'Connor's opinion was joined by Rehnquist, White, Stevens, and Anthony M. Kennedy (the last of the Reagan-appointed justices); Scalia concurred separately.

One year later the Court reaffirmed the federal government's power to adopt "benign race-conscious measures"—even a measure not adopted to compensate victims of past discrimination. The 5–4 decision in *Metro Broadcasting Inc. v. FCC* (1990) upheld an FCC policy that gave special credit to members of minority groups in applying for new broadcast licenses and required some radio and television stations to be sold only to minority-controlled companies. During the Reagan administration the FCC had tried to dismantle the policy, but Congress had ordered it kept in place.

In his opinion for the Court, Brennan emphasized the congressional finding that preferential programs were needed for broadcast diversity, which he described as an important government objective. As in *Fullilove,* he said, the Constitution grants deference to Congress; the strict scrutiny standard of *Croson* did not apply.

White and Stevens changed sides from *Croson* to create the majority. O'Connor led the four dissenters in calling the new decision a "departure" from the Court's previous rulings that racial classifications are not permitted "[e]xcept in the narrowest of circumstances."

Aliens

The Supreme Court has ruled that aliens—citizens of foreign countries residing in the United States—are entitled under the Fourteenth Amendment to equal protection of the laws. But the Court has applied that ruling unevenly. It has struck down some state and federal laws that limited opportunities or benefits for aliens while it has upheld others.

In two early decisions, the Court protected the right of aliens to earn a living. In *Yick Wo v. Hopkins* (1886) the Court invalidated San Francisco's system of enforcing a safety ordinance for laundries in such a way as prevent the operation of Chinese-owned laundries while white-owned laundries were permitted to operate. In a similar vein, the Court in 1915 nullified an Arizona law that limited the number of aliens who could be employed at most businesses.

Beginning in 1914, however, the Court upheld other state laws restricting aliens. The most significant of these were laws passed in several western states that barred aliens who were ineligible for citizenship from owning or leasing agricultural lands. The laws were intended to deter Japanese immigration. But the Court, in *Terrace v. Thompson,* said the state measures had a "reasonable basis" since Congress itself had recognized two classes of aliens—those who were eligible for citizenship and those who were not.

The Court's attitude toward aliens began to shift during World War II in cases upholding the wartime internment of Japanese-Americans living on the West Coast. The Court declared that distinctions based on race and ancestry warranted "close scrutiny" and could be justified only by "pressing public necessity," such as the war. After the war, this new attitude resulted in two rulings in 1948 that narrowed laws restricting alien ownership of land and overturned a California law preventing the Japanese from fishing in the state's coastal waters.

In 1971 the Court seemed to tighten its review of laws affecting aliens when it struck down an Arizona statute barring welfare benefits for most aliens. In *Graham v. Richardson* a unanimous Court said that laws based on alienage are "inherently suspect and subject to close judicial scrutiny."

Under that doctrine the Court struck down laws barring aliens from being lawyers, engineers, notaries public, or civil servants. But in 1978 and 1979, the Court upheld New York laws that barred aliens from being police officers or public school teachers, citing the importance of those jobs to the operation of state government.

The federal government has somewhat more latitude than the states in dealing with aliens. In 1976 the Court upheld a regulation denying some federally financed health benefits to most aliens. On the same day, however, it overturned a federal regulation excluding all aliens from the competitive federal civil service.

The Court's most recent major decision on the issue upset a Texas law that kept illegal alien children from attending public schools. In *Plyler v. Doe* (1982) the Court reiterated that aliens are entitled to equal protection of the laws. It found no national policy or state interest sufficient to justify denying aliens the right to a free public education.

Amending Process

The Constitution gives the Supreme Court no specific role in proposing or ratifying constitutional amendments. The Court's few substantive rulings on the amending process have generally supported the broad authority the Constitution grants to Congress on this subject.

Two procedures for proposing amendments are set out in Article V, but only one has ever been used. The process begins with Congress, which by two-thirds majority votes of the Senate and House of Representatives may submit amendments to the states for ratification. Under the second, untried method, amendments may be proposed by a constitutional convention, which Congress must convene if asked to do so by the legislatures of two-thirds of the states.

Under either method, a proposed amendment becomes part of the Constitution if it is ratified by three-fourths of the states, through state legislatures or state conventions, whichever Congress chooses. So far, in all but one instance Congress has specified ratification by state legislatures. The convention route was used to ratify the Twenty-first Amendment (repealing Prohibition).

The president is not required to sign and cannot block a congressional resolution proposing a constitutional amendment. The Bill of Rights was not submitted to the president, and in 1798 the Supreme Court specifically endorsed this interpretation of the amending process in a decision regarding the effect of the Eleventh Amendment.

Thirty-three amendments were submitted to the states through mid-1992. Twenty-seven were ratified, four of which were written to overturn Supreme Court decisions. (See REVERSALS OF RULINGS BY CONSTITUTIONAL AMENDMENT.)

The Twenty-seventh Amendment (prohibiting a pay raise for members of Congress from taking effect until after the next biennial congressional election) had the most curious history of any of the ratified amendments. It was submitted in 1789 as part of the Bill of Rights, but was ratified by just six states through 1791. After lying dormant for nearly two centuries, a new ratification drive began in the mid-1980s. This attempt led to approval by the needed thirty-eighth state on May 7, 1992.

After some speculation on the amendment's validity after such a long passage of time, the amendment was certified on May 18, 1992, by the archivist of the United States, who has responsibility for receiving notice of ratification from the states. Congress, seeking to have the final word on the issue, over the next two days adopted a joint resolution recognizing the amendment by a vote of 414 to 3 in the House and 99 to 0 in the Senate.

Four other proposed amendments were still technically pending in 1992. A resolution to invalidate these amendments was introduced in the Senate but was referred to committee.

Two other amendments proposed by Congress— the Equal Rights Amendment (ERA) for women and an amendment to give the District of Columbia voting representation in the House and Senate—failed to win ratification within the time period set by Congress.

The Supreme Court upheld Congress's power to set a deadline for ratification when the practice was first used, as part of what became the Eighteenth Amendment (national prohibition). In *Dillon v. Gloss* (1921), the Court said that "the fair inference or implication from Article V is that the ratification must be within some reasonable time after the proposal" and that Congress's power to specify a deadline was "an incident of its power to designate the mode of ratification."

In 1939 the time-limit issue reached the Court again in a case involving Kansas's attempt to withdraw its ratification of the proposed child labor amendment, which had been submitted to the states in 1924. In *Coleman v. Miller* the Court said that the decision on what constitutes a reasonable time limit was a political question to be decided by Congress, not by the Court.

In a concurring opinion four justices called into question the Court's earlier finding that ratification should occur within a reasonable time, calling it "an advisory opinion, given wholly without constitutional authority." The acceptance of the Twenty-seventh Amendment in 1992 left uncertain whether Congress

Ben Shahn's mural for the Public Works Administration captures the feeling of a New York speakeasy during Prohibition. The constitutional amendment prohibiting the manufacture, sale, and transportation of alcoholic beverages enjoyed only a brief life but engendered more Supreme Court cases testing its validity than any other amendment.   Source: Museum of the City of New York

has the power to disregard state ratifications because of the passage of time if the amendment itself contains no time limit. Similarly uncertain are the right of a state to rescind its ratification of a proposed amendment and the right of Congress to extend a deadline for ratification.

In *Coleman v. Miller* the Court strongly indicated that only Congress could decide the rescission issue. Congress never dealt with the question, however, because the child labor amendment had not been ratified by enough states.

Earlier decisions on rescission were inconsistent. At Congress's direction, the secretary of state counted the ratification of the Fourteenth Amendment by three states that had voted to withdraw their approval of the measure. But the secretary of state apparently accepted North Dakota's rescission of its ratification of the Twenty-fifth Amendment (the presidential disability amendment added to the Constitution in 1967).

Both the rescission and extension issues arose in October 1978 when Congress passed a thirty-nine-month extension for approval of the ERA, which needed ratification by three more states to be adopted. Opponents of the amendment challenged the exten-

sion, while supporters hoped to nullify the actions of four state legislatures in voting to rescind their previous ratification of the amendment.

In 1981 a federal judge in Idaho ruled that Congress had exceeded its power in extending the ratification deadline. He also ruled that states could rescind their approval of the amendment if they acted during the ratification period. Early in 1982, the Supreme Court agreed to hear an appeal from those rulings. After the ratification period expired on June 30, however, the Court dismissed the case as moot, leaving the questions unresolved.

Amicus Curiae

Amicus curiae is a Latin term meaning "friend of the court." An amicus curiae is a person or organization who volunteers or is invited to take part in matters before a court, but who is not a party in the case. An amicus curiae may file a brief, called an amicus brief, with the permission of the court or of the parties to the case. The brief may argue for or against hearing the case or address the merits of the case itself. The federal government, acting through the office of the SOLICITOR GENERAL, frequently files amicus briefs in Supreme Court cases, often at the invitation of the Court. The Court may permit an amicus to participate in oral argument as well. Invitations to file amicus briefs and permission to take part in oral argument are rarely granted, except to the federal government.

Amicus briefs are also frequently filed by interest groups seeking to influence the Court, particularly in cases being considered on the merits. According to one count, during the 1982 term more than 1,400 interest groups filed, either individually or in groups, more than 3,000 amicus briefs. Particularly important and controversial cases attract many amicus briefs. The Court, for example, received eighty amicus briefs in the case of *Webster v. Reproductive Health Services* (1989), which dealt with state regulation of abortion. These briefs were filed by private organizations and individuals, members of Congress, and state legislators, as well as state attorneys general and the federal government.

State governments are another leading source of amicus briefs, frequently joining together to express their views on issues affecting the states.

In its rule 37, the Court acknowledges that amicus briefs that bring new and relevant material to its attention are "of considerable help." The Court, however, has tried to discourage the filing of briefs that simply seek to register an opinion on the matter before the Court.

Antitrust

The industrial growth of the United States in the late nineteenth century brought with it the creation of "combinations" or "trusts" in many areas of business and industry. The trusts often eliminated all significant competition and drove smaller companies out of the market. By the turn of the twentieth century trusts dominated such industries as steel, oil, sugar, meat packing, leather, electrical goods, and tobacco.

This development posed a threat to the traditional concept of the free enterprise system. The unsavory methods the trusts frequently used to gain control of

and then to tighten their hold on an industry aroused considerable public outcry. In 1890 Congress responded to these concerns by passing the Sherman Antitrust Act, which made illegal "[e]very contract, combination in the form of trust or otherwise, or conspiracy, in restraint of trade or commerce among the several states, or with foreign nations."

Early Rulings

The Supreme Court's first rulings on the law indicated a greater willingness to apply its provisions to labor than to business. The Court in 1895 invoked its traditional distinction between "commerce" (subject to regulation by Congress) and "manufacturing" (an area for the states to govern) to reject the government's effort to use the law to break up the sugar trust. (See COMMERCE POWER.) In 1908, however, the Court ruled that the law did apply to boycotts organized by labor unions.

Although the Court later broadened the reach of the Sherman Act in business cases, it eased enforcement by ruling in 1911 that the statute applied only to unreasonable combinations or undue restraints of trade. The Court followed this "rule of reason" until the mid-1930s, when it shifted toward a more literal ("per se") application of the act. In the 1970s it returned to a rule of reason.

In 1914 Congress attempted to counter some of the Court's interpretations of the law by passing the Clayton Act and the Federal Trade Commission Act. The Clayton Act more specifically defined business practices prohibited by antitrust law; it also sought to establish an exemption for lawful labor union activities. The Federal Trade Commission Act created a new agency with rule-making and enforcement power over "unfair trade practices."

The body of antitrust law that has developed since 1914 encompasses additional statutes, many administrative rules and regulations, and a sometimes confusing collection of decisions by the Supreme Court and other federal courts. The federal government—chiefly the Justice Department and the Federal Trade Commission—has the major role in enforcing antitrust law through both civil and criminal actions. Private parties, either businesses or consumers, can also bring civil antitrust suits. If successful, they can recover

THE BOSSES OF THE SENATE.

The enormous power of big business in politics is captured in this 1889 cartoon by Joseph Keppler. Even when Congress attempted to curb the trusts with passage of the Sherman Antitrust Act in 1890, the Supreme Court was slow to back the law.
Source: Library of Congress

three times the damages resulting from the defendant's anticompetitive conduct.

In the 1970s and 1980s, antitrust law seemed to be in decline. Many political and economic conservatives urged a more permissive attitude toward business combinations in the interest of greater economic efficiency. The Court did relax its antitrust doctrine during this period, but not so far as antitrust critics urged.

Antitrust and Business

The Supreme Court's first antitrust ruling, *United States v. E.C. Knight Co.* (1895), was a stunning setback for supporters of the Sherman Act. The defendants in the suit were the American Sugar Refining Company and four smaller Philadelphia processors who, through stockholder agreements, established a trust controlling more than 90 percent of all the sugar processed in the United States. The federal government challenged the combination as an illegal restraint of trade in interstate commerce designed to raise sugar prices.

The Court rejected the suit by an 8–1 vote. Writing for the majority, Chief Justice Melville W. Fuller said that the combination in question related solely to the acquisition of refineries in Pennsylvania and to sugar processing in that state. Therefore, it did not involve interstate commerce and was not touchable by the Sherman Act. If federal antitrust law did apply to manufacturing combinations, Fuller added, "comparatively little of business operations and affairs would be left for state control."

Although the *Knight* ruling seriously limited the scope of the Sherman Act, the Court did not declare the law unconstitutional. In its next two cases the Court applied the law to strike down a combination of railway companies aimed at fixing freight rates and to upset a regional marketing agreement among six corporations that engaged in the manufacturing and interstate sale of iron pipe.

Nine years later the Court moved further away from the narrow view set out in the sugar ruling. *Northern Securities Co. v. United States* (1904) involved the government's challenge to a holding company set up by the major stockholders of two competing railroads to buy the controlling interest of the roads. By a 5–4 vote, the Court held that the holding company was clearly intended to eliminate competition between the two rail lines.

The opinion—written by Justice John Marshall Harlan, the lone dissenter in the sugar ruling—significantly modified the earlier decision by ruling that the holding company was, in fact, in commerce. The antitrust act, Harlan wrote, applied to "every combination or conspiracy which would extinguish competition between otherwise competing railroads engaged in interstate trade or commerce, and which would in that way restrain such trade or commerce."

A year later the Court turned its back decisively on the *Knight* ruling. *Swift & Co. v. United States* (1905) concerned the "beef trust"—meat-packing houses that had made extensive agreements among themselves to control livestock and meat prices in many of the nation's stockyards and slaughterhouses.

Swift claimed that its livestock was bought and sold locally and that it was therefore not engaged in interstate commerce. In his opinion for a unanimous Court, Justice Oliver Wendell Holmes, Jr., rejected that claim and adopted what came to be called the "stream of commerce" doctrine. The flow of cattle from one part of the state to another with the expectation that they will eventually be sold out of state, Holmes said, "is a current of commerce among the states, and the purchase of the cattle is a part and incident of such commerce."

While the holding company and beef trust cases revived the Sherman Act, the Court in 1911 introduced a more lasting change in antitrust law. The decision in *Standard Oil Co. v. United States* sustained the government's effort to break up the giant Standard Oil complex. In his opinion for the Court, Chief Justice Edward D. White said that the Sherman Act could not have been intended to apply to every business combination. Instead, he said, courts must apply a "rule of reason" to determine the legality of such arrangements. Two weeks later the Court again endorsed the rule in a decision breaking up the tobacco trust.

In later decisions the Court applied the rule of reason to block government antitrust cases. In 1913 it refused to break up a combination of shoemaking equipment manufacturers that controlled as much as 80 percent of the market. And in 1920 the Court ruled that U.S. Steel Corp. had not violated the an-

titrust act because the company had failed in its attempt to create a monopoly.

Opposition to the rule of reason contributed to passage of the Clayton and Federal Trade Commission acts during the Democratic administration of President Woodrow Wilson. Antitrust enforcement went into decline during the 1920s and became popular again only in the late 1930s. Over the next three decades the Court returned to a more literal interpretation of the antitrust laws. It applied per se rules not only to price fixing and agreements among competitors but also to market allocations between manufacturers and distributors.

The more conservative Court in the 1970s and 1980s reversed the trend. It adopted a more tolerant attitude toward mergers and distribution agreements and revived the rule of reason in some areas. But the Court has stopped short of the wholesale dismantling of antitrust law urged by some conservatives.

Antitrust and Labor

Efforts to include a specific exemption for labor unions in the Sherman Act failed. As a result, the act was used almost from its passage to justify orders halting strikes or boycotts by labor unions.

The Court first suggested that the Sherman Act could be applied to labor unions in 1895 when it affirmed the contempt conviction of labor leader Eugene V. Debs. In 1908 the Court made that position clear in the Danbury Hatters' case, which involved a labor-organized boycott designed to aid union organizing at the company. Speaking for the Court, Chief Justice Fuller said that the act applied to any combinations "aimed at compelling third parties and strangers involuntarily not to engage in the course of trade except on conditions that the combination imposes."

Congress responded in 1914 by including provisions in the Clayton Act that were intended to exempt labor from antitrust law and to prohibit federal court injunctions in labor cases unless "necessary to prevent irreparable injury to property, or to a property right." The Court, however, construed these provisions narrowly in the 1920s. In 1921 it upheld an injunction against a labor-organized secondary boycott and in 1925 sustained an injunction against an intrastate coal strike.

To force the Court to expand its interpretation of the labor exemption in the Clayton Act, Congress in 1932 passed the Norris-LaGuardia Act, which prohibited the issuance of injunctions by federal courts in labor disputes except where unlawful acts were threatened or committed. The Court in 1938 upheld the act on the ground that it was within congressional power to determine the jurisdiction of the federal courts. The Court maintained that ruling in several later challenges to the law. In 1941 the Court ruled further that strikes and secondary boycotts would not be considered violations of any federal law.

Antitrust and the States

In 1943 the Supreme Court held that the Sherman Antitrust Act was not intended to prevent states from adopting policies that restrained competition in some part of the state's economy.

The decision in *Parker v. Brown* upheld California's raisin-marketing program, which was aimed at promoting the state's raisin industry by virtually eliminating price competition among raisin growers. In his opinion for the Court, Chief Justice Harlan Fiske Stone said that the Sherman Act did not apply to state action and that the marketing scheme did not constitute an impermissible burden on interstate commerce.

The Court in 1978 ruled that local governments had the same antitrust immunity only if their anticompetitive conduct was undertaken to carry out state policy to replace competition with regulation or monopoly. But in 1991 the Court ruled more permissively that cities are protected from antitrust liability even if they have conspired with private business to enact regulations favoring one company over another.

Appeal

An appeal is a legal proceeding to ask a higher court to review or modify a lower court decision. The party filing an appeal is called the *appellant,* the opposing party the *appellee.*

In Supreme Court practice, the term *appeal* refers to cases that fall within the Court's MANDATORY JURISDICTION as opposed to cases that the Court agrees to review under the discretionary writ of CERTIORARI. Since the Court's mandatory jurisdiction was virtually eliminated by a 1988 judicial reform act, the Court hears almost no appeals anymore in the technical sense of the word. Petitions for certiorari are commonly referred to as appeals, although this use of the term is not legally precise.

In the federal court system, a case can be appealed from the trial-level district court to one of the thirteen circuit courts of appeals. Most states similarly have one or more intermediate-level courts of appeals (appellate courts) below the state's highest court. Generally, a party that loses in a trial court may appeal to the intermediate appellate court as a matter of right. If the party loses and continues the appeal, the higher court—either the state supreme court or the U.S. Supreme Court—usually has discretion in deciding whether to review the case. (See COURTS, LOWER.)

In a civil case, either the plaintiff or the defendant can appeal an adverse ruling. In criminal cases, a defendant can appeal a conviction, but the DOUBLE JEOPARDY clause prevents the government from appealing an acquittal. The prosecution, however, can appeal some pretrial rulings, such as a dismissal of an indictment on grounds of a legal defect.

In several cases between 1894 and 1903 the Court ruled that the Constitution does not require the states to provide an appeals procedure in criminal cases. But in *Frank v. Mangum* (1915) the Court ruled that DUE PROCESS does require a state to provide some "corrective procedure" to allow state convicts to pursue remedies for federal constitutional violations. This may be either an appeal or a HABEAS CORPUS proceeding. Today all states provide for appeals in criminal cases.

A defendant who wins a reversal of a conviction upon appeal can be tried again without violating the double jeopardy clause, although there are limits on the sentence the defendant can receive in a retrial. In

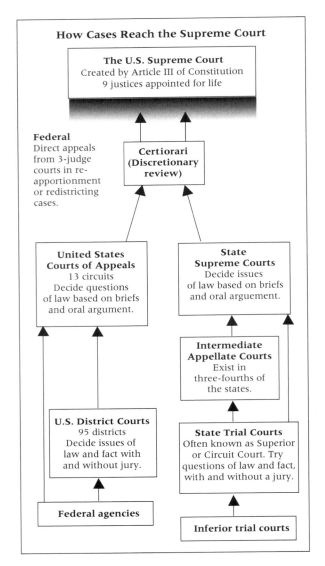

How Cases Reach the Supreme Court

The U.S. Supreme Court
Created by Article III of Constitution
9 justices appointed for life

Federal
Direct appeals
from 3-judge
courts in re-
apportionment
or redistricting
cases.

**Certiorari
(Discretionary
review)**

**United States
Courts of Appeals**
13 circuits
Decide questions
of law based on briefs
and oral argument.

**State
Supreme Courts**
Decide issues
of law based on briefs
and oral arguement.

**Intermediate
Appellate Courts**
Exist in
three-fourths of
the states.

U.S. District Courts
95 districts
Decide issues of
law and fact with
and without jury.

State Trial Courts
Often known as Superior
or Circuit Court. Try
questions of law and fact,
with and without a jury.

Federal agencies

Inferior trial courts

Source: Theodore J. Lowi and Benjamin Ginsburg, American Government: Freedom and Power, *2d ed. W.W. Norton, 1992. Used with permission.*

North Carolina v. Pearce (1969) the Court held that a judge cannot impose a greater sentence than the defendant received in the original trial except on the basis of objective reasons related to the defendant's conduct since the first trial. In 1973, however, the Court said that ruling did not limit the power of a jury to impose a longer sentence on retrial. Concerning capital cases, the Court ruled in *Bullington v. Missouri* (1981) by a 5–4 vote that the government cannot seek the death penalty in a retrial if the jury refused to impose a death sentence in the first trial.

In another 5–4 ruling, the Court in *United States v. DiFrancesco* (1980) upheld a new federal law authorizing the government to appeal the sentencing of certain "dangerous special offenders." This ruling also gave the appeals court power to affirm, reduce, or increase the sentence. The Court said the double jeopardy clause did not bar the sentencing appeal because the new sentence had to be within the range allowed by statute and the law gave defendants notice of the possibility of an increase.

Indigents and Appeals

The Court in 1956 began a line of cases based on the EQUAL PROTECTION clause to safeguard the right of indigent criminal defendants to an appeal.

In *Griffin v. Illinois* the Court ruled by a 5–4 vote that states must provide a free trial transcript to an indigent defendant in a felony case for use in preparing an appeal. In *Douglas v. California* (1963) the Court followed the same principle in striking down, by a vote of 6 to 2, a California law that provided court-appointed attorneys on appeal only when the appellate court decided legal counsel would be advantageous to the success of the appeal.

By 1971 the entire Court agreed that poverty alone should not bar a person from appealing a conviction. In *Mayer v. Chicago* the Court unanimously held that a state's refusal to provide a free transcript to a defendant so that he might appeal his misdemeanor conviction was a violation of equal protection. In *Ross v. Moffitt* (1974), however, the Court refused to require that an attorney be provided in discretionary appeals.

Two years later the Court limited the circumstances under which the federal government must provide transcripts at public expense. In *United States v. McCollum* the Court upheld a congressional provision that a transcript should be provided only after a judge found that the challenge to the conviction was not frivolous and that the transcript was necessary to resolve the issues presented.

The Court has twice ruled on issues related to the

right of indigents to appeal civil cases. In *Lindsey v. Normet* (1972) the Court struck down a state law requiring that a tenant appealing a ruling in an eviction action post a bond in twice the amount expected to accrue during the appeal. The Court based its decision on the grounds of equal protection, because no similar provision applied to other cases. But in *Bankers Life & Casualty Co. v. Crenshaw* (1988) the Court upheld the imposition of a 15 percent penalty on a party that unsuccessfully appeals from a money judgment. The Court said the requirement was rational because it applied to plaintiffs and defendants alike and did not single out one class of appellants.

Appellant

See APPEAL.

Appellee

See APPEAL.

Appointment and Removal Powers of the President

The president's power to appoint and remove subordinate officials complements his power to manage the executive branch. The Constitution, however, limits the president's power of appointment by requiring Senate confirmation for many offices. It also makes no specific mention of the power of removal.

In a 1926 decision the Supreme Court sustained the president's power to remove executive branch officials, but in a 1935 ruling it upheld Congress's right to provide job protection to members of independent regulatory agencies. More recently the Court also upheld a congressional statute authorizing judicial appointment of an "independent counsel" to investigate and prosecute wrongdoing within the executive branch.

Early Disputes

Article II, Section 2 of the Constitution provides that the president "shall nominate, and by and with the Advice and Consent of the Senate, shall appoint, Ambassadors, other public Ministers and Consuls, Judges of the supreme Court, and all other Officers of the United States, whose Appointments are not herein otherwise provided for, and which shall be established by Law." The Constitution authorizes Congress to vest the appointment of "inferior Officers" in the president alone, the courts, or heads of departments. Congress has construed "inferior officers" so narrowly that every officer of the armed forces, for example, receives a presidential appointment subject to Senate confirmation.

The First Congress in 1789 debated the president's removal power in connection with a bill to establish an executive department of foreign affairs. The bill originally provided that the principal officer was "to be removed from office by the President of the United States." However, in the final bill the removal clause was changed to read, "whenever the principal officer shall be removed by the President of the United States."

Chief Justice William Howard Taft, in the 1926 case, *Myers v. United States,* construed that change to mean that the First Congress believed the president had the sole power to remove executive branch officers. But some scholars question his interpretation.

Although President Andrew Jackson and the Senate argued over his power to remove the secretary of the treasury, the first major challenge to the president's removal power arose after the Civil War, in the dispute between Congress and President Andrew Johnson over control of Reconstruction policy.

In 1867 Congress passed the Tenure of Office Act, providing that any civil officer appointed by the president with Senate confirmation could be removed only with Senate approval. Johnson defied this law by removing his secretary of war without Senate approval, and this was one of the charges listed in the unsuccessful effort to remove him through impeachment. The law was later modified and then repealed in 1887 without any judicial ruling on its constitutionality.

Court Rulings

In the meantime, Congress passed a law in 1876 making removal of postmasters subject to Senate consent. That law was tested before the Supreme Court some fifty years later, in a case that arose from President Woodrow Wilson's decision to fire a postmaster named Myers without Senate approval.

In a 6–3 ruling in 1926—after both Myers and Wilson had died—the Supreme Court upheld the dismissal. Taft, a former president who had been named chief justice in 1921, wrote that the president enjoyed "unrestricted power to remove the most important of his subordinates." He held that the Constitution made no distinction between the removal of policy-making officials and removal of "executive officers engaged in the discharge of their normal duties." Taft suggested that the president's removal power extended even to officers appointed to independent regulatory commissions.

The dissenting justices—James C. McReynolds, Louis D. Brandeis, and Oliver Wendell Holmes—argued that Congress could set conditions for removal. They pointed out that Congress had created the position and retained the right to abolish the post altogether. They also argued that the power to remove an inferior administrative officer, as opposed to high political officers, was not indispensable to the president's power.

Less than a decade later, the Court adopted the dissenters' view to limit the removal power asserted in *Myers.* President Franklin D. Roosevelt touched off the dispute in October 1933 by trying to replace a member of the Federal Trade Commission (FTC), William E. Humphrey. Humphrey challenged the president's action, pointing out that the act establishing the FTC gave members fixed seven-year terms. Members could be removed by the president only for specified reasons, such as inefficiency, neglect of duty, or wrongdoing in office. After Humphrey's death, his heirs continued the case under the name *Humphrey's Executor v. United States.*

In a unanimous decision on May 27, 1935, the Court ruled against Roosevelt. Justice George Sutherland stated that because the FTC was both a quasi-judicial and a quasi-legislative body, it was not subject to the unlimited executive power of removal. Sutherland said that Congress's power "to require [regulatory agencies] to act independently of executive control cannot well be doubted." Key to the ruling was the distinction between executive duties, such as those in question in *Myers,* and the quasi-legislative and quasi-judicial duties of regulatory agencies.

Two recent rulings on the SEPARATION OF POWERS have further defined the limits of congressional and presidential power over appointing and removing officers.

In *Bowsher v. Synar* (1986) the Court ruled, in a 7–2 vote, that Congress had improperly given an enforcement role to the comptroller general as part of the Balanced Budget and Emergency Deficit Control Act of 1985. (The comptroller general is a legislative branch official.) Since Congress had the authority to remove the comptroller general from office, the Court said, executive power could not be delegated to him. "Congress in effect has retained control over the execution of the Act and intruded into the executive function," Chief Justice Warren E. Burger wrote in his opinion for the Court.

Two years later, however, the Court upheld Congress's 1978 decision to authorize a special judicial panel to appoint an "independent counsel" in cases of suspected executive branch wrongdoing. The decision was part of the post-Watergate Ethics in Government Act. The act permitted removal of the special prosecutor only by the attorney general and only for "good cause."

The Court's 7–1 ruling in this case, *Morrison v. Olson* (1988), relied on the constitutional provision for judicial appointment of "inferior officers." Writing for the Court, Chief Justice William H. Rehnquist rejected the claim that the act interfered with the president's ability to ensure the faithful execution of laws by denying him the power to appoint or remove the independent counsel. Justice Antonin Scalia was the lone dissenter.

Arguments

After the Supreme Court has agreed to review a specific case, the case is placed on the argument calendar. The justices hear oral argument on Monday, Tuesday, and Wednesday for seven two-week periods between the first week of October and the end of April or beginning of May.

The number of cases scheduled for oral argument has declined under Chief Justice William H. Rehnquist. The Court's schedule permits up to 168 arguments each term, but in the 1992–1993 term the Court heard arguments in only 116 cases.

Oral argument gives attorneys the opportunity to highlight the important points from their BRIEF, the written summary of their arguments and supporting laws. Briefs are circulated to the justices weeks, if not months, before oral argument takes place. Oral argument also gives the justices an opportunity to probe more deeply into a case.

Like many other aspects of the Court's operations, the time allotted for argument and the atmosphere in which arguments are heard have changed considerably over the years. In the early days of the Court, arguments in a single case often would continue for days.

For the spectators who crowded the courtroom, oral arguments provided high entertainment. In the nineteenth century Washington society flocked to hear great orators, such as Henry Clay and Daniel Webster, argue before the Court. On at least one occasion arguments were adjourned so that counsel could sober up.

Eventually the increasing number of cases required the Court to place strict time limits on arguments. Today each side has only thirty minutes to present its case, and much of that time may be taken up by questions from the justices.

The value of oral argument has long been disputed. Some view it as a very important step in helping justices come to a decision in each case. Others contend that most justices have already made up their minds by the time a case is argued.

Although justices usually do not comment publicly on the operations of the Court, a few have said publicly that oral argument serves a useful purpose. Chief Justice Charles Evans Hughes found that arguments saved him a great deal of time that he would otherwise have had to spend reviewing briefs and records. Justice William J. Brennan, Jr., said that his understanding of what a particular case was about often crystallized during oral argument, even though he had read the briefs beforehand.

Timing and Time Limits

Cases are argued roughly in the order in which they are granted review. At least three months usually elapse between the time the justices agree to hear a case and the argument itself. Under special circumstances, the scheduled time for an argument may be advanced or postponed.

A case of special significance to the nation may be heard and decided quite quickly. A prime example occurred in 1974, when the Supreme Court was asked to decide whether executive privilege shielded President Richard Nixon from turning over White House tapes to the special prosecutor in the case of the Watergate affair. Arguments were heard in an extraordinary summer session on July 8, and the Court rendered its ruling, which went against Nixon, on July 24.

The Court did not set time limits on oral arguments until 1849, when counsel for each party was allowed no more than two hours to present his argument. The two-hour allowance continued until the early twentieth century and was then reduced to one hour.

In 1970 the time was further reduced to thirty minutes for each side. Under the current rules of the Court, which were revised in 1990, an attorney may apply to the Court for more time before the case is heard, but such requests are rarely granted. The rules also stipulate that only one attorney for a side may argue the case unless special permission is granted.

An exception to the latter rule is occasionally made for an AMICUS CURIAE—a person or organization who participates in a case but is not a party to it. Counsel for an amicus curiae may participate in oral argument if the party supported by the amicus allows the amicus to use part of its argument time and if the Court agrees. The Court itself may grant a motion allowing argument by counsel for an amicus curiae. The Court rules stipulate that such a motion must state "why oral argument is thought to provide assistance to the Court not otherwise available." The rules also note that such motions are granted "only in the most extraordinary circumstances."

Questioning

Court rules also advise counsel that oral arguments should emphasize and clarify the written argument set out in the briefs. That same rule warns emphatically that "the Court looks with disfavor on oral argument read from a prepared text." During the 1974 term two justices interrupted an attorney who was reading from a prepared text and called his attention to the rule. Most attorneys appearing before the Court use an outline or notes to help them keep their arguments on track.

Attorneys may be frequently interrupted by the justices with questions. The frequency of questioning, as well as the manner in which questions are asked, depends on the style of a justice and his or her interest in a particular case. Of the members of the Court in the early 1990s, Justices Antonin Scalia and Ruth Bader Ginsburg were perhaps the most active questioners, along with Sandra Day O'Connor, Anthony M. Kennedy, and David H. Souter. By contrast, Justices Harry A. Blackmun and Clarence Thomas rarely asked questions.

Justices sometimes use questions to clarify the argument. Sometimes a justice tries to influence his or her colleagues by drawing attention to a weak argument or a particularly strong one.

Attorneys who do not respond immediately and directly to a question can find themselves in trouble. Several justices have made their annoyance clear when an attorney has promised to answer the inquiry later in the oral argument.

Circulating the Argument

Since 1955 the Supreme Court has tape-recorded oral arguments. The marshal of the Court keeps this tape throughout the term in which the argument is presented. Use of the tape during this time is usually limited to the justices and their law clerks. At the end of the term, the tapes are sent to the National Archives in Washington, D.C. People wishing to listen to the tape or buy a copy of the transcript can apply to the Archives for permission to do so.

Since 1968 the Court has also contracted with private firms to tape and transcribe all oral arguments. The transcriptions must be exact except that the letter Q must substitute for the names of the justices who ask questions. These transcripts are usually available the week after the argument is heard.

The Court has repeatedly rejected pleas from broadcast news organizations to permit radio or television coverage of arguments. In 1993, however, a law professor published a book and audio tape package consisting of excerpts from arguments in some of the Court's most dramatic cases since the 1960s. Radio and television stations played excerpts from the tapes in news stories about the book. The Court initially hinted at legal action against the professor on the grounds that he did not have permission from the National Archives to reproduce the tapes, but eventually backed down.

Arms, Right to Bear

The Second Amendment states: "A well regulated militia, being necessary to the security of a free state, the right of the people to keep and bear arms, shall not be infringed." Opponents of gun control laws maintain that the amendment protects personal possession of firearms, while gun control advocates contend that the amendment merely preserves the states' rights to maintain militias.

The Supreme Court accepted the latter view in its only ruling on the subject. In *United States v. Miller* (1939) the Court upheld federal registration of sawed-off shotguns by saying that the weapons were not "part of ordinary military equipment" and thus had no "reasonable relationship to the preservation or efficiency of a well regulated militia."

The interpretation of the amendment cannot be conclusively settled by textual or historical analysis. Gun control supporters argue that the reference to militias limits the meaning of the entire amendment. Opponents maintain that the "right of the people" denotes a personal right in addition to the authority to maintain militias.

Some evidence from the scanty congressional debate over the amendment suggests that the framers

The Boston Massacre of March 5, 1770, inflamed hostility to British rule of the colonies. By ratifying the Second Amendment to the Constitution, the young nation acknowledged that people may have to defend themselves against tyranny.
Source: Library of Congress

were solely concerned with preserving states' militias sufficient to prevent the establishment of a standing army. But during the earlier debate over ratification of the Constitution, critics—including Patrick Henry and Samuel Adams—argued for the need to construe the Constitution so as to protect the right of all peaceable citizens to keep their own arms.

The Court's decision in *Miller* sustained a registration requirement enacted as part of the National Firearms Act in 1934. After reciting the original provisions of the Constitution dealing with the militia, the Court said the Second Amendment had to be "interpreted and applied" in light of the "obvious purpose to assure the continuation and render possible the effectiveness of such forces."

Even if the Second Amendment does protect personal possession of firearms, a ruling of a federal appeals court, left standing by the Court in 1983, held

that it does not apply to state or local laws. In addition, the amendment would not necessarily prohibit all federal gun control laws. Courts might rule that the right was not infringed by some laws, such as registration and licensing requirements or limitations on ownership by minors, felons, or the mentally impaired. Despite the passage of additional federal gun control laws since 1968, however, there has been no authoritative resolution of the constitutional issue.

Arrests

The Fourth Amendment to the Constitution prohibits "unreasonable searches and seizures." Since 1806, this provision has been construed to apply to arrests; in recent years it has been considered to apply

The Supreme Court has been asked many times, especially during the twentieth century, to rule on the legality of an arrest by police.
Source: R. Michael Jenkins

also to limited detentions, such as investigatory stops. The Supreme Court has held that a full custodial arrest always requires PROBABLE CAUSE but does not necessarily require a warrant, at least in felony cases. Lesser detentions may be based merely on "reasonable suspicion," and some police-citizen encounters have been held not to be "seizures" at all.

An unlawful arrest or detention does not prevent a court from trying a defendant, nor does it invalidate a conviction. It may, however, affect the evidence that can be used against a defendant. In the case of a defendant who has been illegally arrested or detained, evidence found in a subsequent search or any statements given during later police interrogation might be suppressed—that is, the evidence could not be used in court. (See EXCLUSIONARY RULE.)

The Supreme Court has never applied the Fourth Amendment's warrant requirement as strictly to arrests as to searches. The Court has upheld the common law rule of arrests by approving warrantless arrests by law enforcement officers for crimes committed in their presence and for other crimes where there are reasonable grounds for arrest. The Court said in 1975 that to impose a warrant require-

ment on all arrests would "constitute an intolerable handicap for legitimate law enforcement."

In *United States v. Watson* (1976) the Court explicitly upheld the warrantless arrest of a felony suspect in a public place. The ruling left open the question of whether warrantless arrests in misdemeanor cases would also be upheld. Four years later, the Court ruled in *Payton v. New York* (1980) that police may not enter a home to arrest its occupant without either a warrant for the arrest or the consent of the occupant. In 1985 the Court further limited police practices by ruling, in a 6–3 vote, that police may not use deadly force to stop a fleeing felon unless they have reason to believe the person threatens the life of people nearby.

The Court's 1975 decision in *Gerstein v. Pugh* had made clear that a suspect arrested without a warrant must be given a prompt probable cause hearing before a magistrate in order to be kept in custody. In 1991 the Court upheld, by a 5–4 vote, a delay of up to forty-eight hours between an arrest and an initial court hearing. Writing for the Court in *County of Riverside, California v. McLaughlin,* Justice Sandra Day O'Connor said local courts need flexibility to combine the probable cause hearing with a bail hearing or arraignment.

Lesser Detentions

In recent decades the Court has grappled with the rules governing police detentions that fall short of an arrest. In *Terry v. Ohio* (1968), the Court upheld the right of a police officer to "stop and frisk" someone for weapons, provided that the police could point to "specific and articulable facts" that reasonably suggested possible criminal activity. Later rulings on the issue have not followed a consistent pattern. Generally they have made it easier for police to justify a stop and have given police greater leeway in searching a person during a stop.

Many of the rulings have involved police efforts to combat illegal drug traffic. A 1985 decision, for example, upheld the brief detention of a driver suspected of transporting drugs. The driver was detained for twenty minutes while police located a truck that had been traveling with the car and confirmed their suspicions that it carried narcotics. The Court has said that narcotics agents can hold a traveler's luggage at an airport long enough for a "canine sniff" to detect narcotics. Even greater leeway is allowed in border searches of international travelers. In 1985 the Court upheld a twenty-four-hour detention of a traveler suspected of smuggling drugs in her alimentary canal.

On the other hand, the Court in 1983 held that police had exceeded their authority in taking an airport traveler to an interrogation room on grounds short of probable cause, holding his ticket, and retrieving his luggage without permission. In 1969 and again in 1979 the Court had said that police cannot take a suspect to a stationhouse for fingerprinting without probable cause for an arrest.

Another important area of concern has been police roadblocks. In *Delaware v. Prouse* (1979) the Court ruled, 8–1, that police could not randomly stop motorists—without any probable cause—to check licenses and registrations. But in *Michigan Department of Police v. Sitz* (1990) the Court upheld, by a vote of 6 to 3, the use of "sobriety checkpoints" to check for evidence of drunken driving. Writing for the majority, Chief Justice William H. Rehnquist said that the checkpoints are not unreasonable "seizures." He pointed out that states have a strong interest in deterring drunken driving, the checkpoints further that interest, and the intrusion on motorists is "slight."

Two other recent rulings indicate the Rehnquist Court's tendency to be less restrictive toward police practices. In 1990 the Court ruled that police acted properly in stopping a suspect based on an anonymous tip that he was transporting drugs; this information fell far short of what would be needed to show probable cause. And in 1991 the Court refused to suppress as evidence drugs that a suspect dropped after a police squad car began trailing him along a street. The Court acknowledged that police had no basis to stop the suspect before they saw the drugs. But it ruled that the surveillance did not amount to a "seizure" because there was no physical force or submission to the officers' authority.

Assembly, Freedom of

The First Amendment to the Constitution prohibits any law "abridging . . . the right of the people to peaceably assemble." Along with the twin right of free speech, freedom of assembly protects people's right to parade or demonstrate to make their views known. (See SPEECH, FREEDOM OF.) Since events such as parades and demonstrations may prevent other people from using the same public places, the Supreme Court has allowed these forms of expression to be regulated more closely than speech. The Court has also permitted greater restrictions on labor picketing, on the ground that it combines protected speech with economic conduct that is subject to regulation.

The first Supreme Court decision involving freedom of assembly was *United States v. Cruikshank* (1876). In its ruling the Court said the right was a privilege of national citizenship only when it was exercised for the purpose of petitioning Congress or otherwise influencing the federal government. This narrow construction blocked the use of federal civil rights laws to protect blacks from anti-Reconstruction terrorism.

The Court took a broader view with two decisions in the 1930s. In *DeJonge v. Oregon* (1937) the Court held that freedom of assembly was on a par with the rights of free speech and free press. Further, it could be applied to the states under the DUE PROCESS clause of the Fourteenth Amendment. "Peaceable assembly for lawful discussion cannot be made a crime," the Court said as it overturned DeJonge's conviction for having conducted a meeting under the auspices of the Communist party.

Two years later, in *Hague v. C.I.O.* (1939), the Court held that an anti-union mayor could not deny a parade permit to labor organizers. Three justices said the right of assembly was protected by the privileges and immunities clause of the Fourteenth Amendment; two others found it protected under the due process clause. The "due process" view eventually prevailed. More important, Justice Owen J. Roberts's plurality opinion gave birth to what was later called the public forum doctrine. It protected the right to assemble and speak in places such as streets and parks that have "immemorially . . . [since] time out of mind" been open to the public for those purposes.

In *Cox v. New Hampshire* (1941), however, the Court made clear that state and local governments could still regulate the use of streets for parades and demonstrations. The Court held that a city could not deny a parade permit because the paraders' views might be unpopular. Still, a city could impose restrictions—"without unfair discrimination"—based on "time, place and manner in relation to the other proper uses of the streets."

The Civil Rights Movement

The Court expanded the right of assembly in the 1960s in cases arising out of the civil rights movement. In two cases—*Edwards v. South Carolina* (1963) and *Cox v. Louisiana* (1965)—the Court overturned breach-of-the-peace convictions of civil rights protesters. It ruled that the statutes could not be used to punish lawful exercise of the rights of assembly, free speech, and petition outside state capitol buildings. Cox also won a reversal of a second conviction arising out of the same incident for violating a state law that prohibited picketing or parading "in or near" a courthouse. In a 5–4 vote the Court upheld the law as a "precise, narrowly drawn regulatory statute" but ruled that Cox had reason to believe he was not violating any law. (He obeyed police orders to confine demonstrators to a sidewalk in front of the courthouse.)

Justice Hugo L. Black led the dissenters in *Cox II.* He dissented again in 1966 when the Court overturned the breach-of-the-peace convictions of five black men who staged a peaceful protest against racial segregation by refusing to leave a public library that was reserved for use by whites. Later that year Black won a majority for a narrower approach, when Justice Potter Stewart switched sides.

In that case, *Adderly v. Florida,* the Court sustained criminal trespass convictions of blacks for demonstrating outside a county jail to protest the arrest of other civil rights protesters. "Traditionally, state capitol grounds are open to the public," Black wrote to distinguish the previous cases. "Jails, built for security purposes, are not." Using analogous reasoning, the Court in 1976 upheld a ban on political speeches or demonstrations on a military base.

Public Forums

By the 1970s the Court had adopted a "public forum" analysis to define speech and assembly rights.

This could be applied to public properties ranging from streets and sidewalks to public transportation and internal mail systems. The rules that emerged allowed restrictions on "traditional" public forums or areas opened by the government only when the restrictions were necessary to serve a compelling governmental interest. Such areas were called designated public forums. Restrictions on nonpublic forums were judged only by a reasonableness test.

Under this doctrine, the Court in 1982 struck down a law barring demonstrations on the sidewalks adjacent to its own building, but in 1990 it upheld a ban on soliciting money on a sidewalk outside a post office. In 1988 the Court declared residential streets to be public forums but upheld a local ordinance forbidding picketing of an individual home. The decision cited the need to protect a "captive audience" from "offensive speech." In 1992 the Court held that public airports are not public forums. Then, by different majorities, it upheld a ban on solicitation within terminal buildings while striking down an accompanying ban on leafleting.

Labor picketing first received constitutional protection when the Court ruled, in *Thornhill v. Alabama* (1940), that states cannot completely forbid it. A series of decisions between 1949 and 1957, however, established that states can restrict picketing to prevent illegal conduct. Such conduct could range from violence and coercion to secondary boycotts and other unfair labor practices.

Assigning Opinions

After the justices have voted on a case, a justice who voted with the majority is assigned to write the majority opinion, or the opinion of the court. If the chief justice has voted with the majority, the chief justice makes the assignment. If the chief justice is in the minority, the senior associate justice voting with the majority assigns the job of writing the majority opinion. (See OPINIONS OF THE COURT.)

Several factors may influence the choice. The assigning justice may consider the points made by the majority justices during the conference discussion, the workloads of the justices, and the need to avoid the more extreme opinions within the majority. Expertise in the particular area of law involved may be a factor. For example, the writing of the majority opinion in *Roe v. Wade* (1973) and several other major abortion cases was assigned to Justice Harry A. Blackmun, who had developed an expertise in medical law during his legal career through work with the famous Mayo Clinic in Minnesota, his home state.

Chief Justice Charles Evans Hughes sometimes assigned conservative opinions to liberal justices and liberal opinions to conservative justices to avoid giving any impression that the Court was divided along ideological lines.

The assignment of opinions can create morale problems among members of the Court. Justices have become annoyed and even angered when they were not assigned to write opinions in cases of particular interest to them or when they were directed to write them in routine, uninteresting cases. One example of dissatisfaction involved a 1972 abortion case. Justice William O. Douglas was said to believe that Chief Justice Warren E. Burger voted with the majority so that he could assign the writing of the majority opinion even though, Douglas alleged, Burger's sympathies lay with the minority. Douglas threatened to file a scathing dissent on what he saw as Burger's misuse of the assignment power but was dissuaded from doing so by his colleagues, who argued that the Court's reputation would suffer if the dissent were publicized.

Associate Justices

See names of individual justices.

Association, Freedom of

The right of an individual to associate with others who share similar beliefs is not explicitly granted by the Constitution or the Bill of Rights. Instead the Supreme Court has found this right to be implicit within the freedoms of speech and assembly guaranteed in the First Amendment and in the concept of ordered liberty protected by the Fourteenth Amendment. (See ASSEMBLY, FREEDOM OF; SPEECH, FREEDOM OF.)

Judicial recognition of this right is of recent vintage. In 1927 the Supreme Court upheld a state law that prohibited associating with people in a organization that advocated overthrow of the government by unlawful means. (See SEDITION LAWS.) In 1928 the Court affirmed the conviction of an officer in the Ku Klux Klan who disobeyed a state law requiring certain organizations to file membership lists with the state. During the Cold War, the Court heard repeated challenges to laws restricting political activities in suspected subversive organizations. However, none of the Court's decisions during that period were based on a right of association. (See COMMUNISM.)

The Civil Rights Movement

The CIVIL RIGHTS movement late in the 1950s won judicial recognition of a constitutionally protected right of association. In a series of cases involving the National Association for the Advancement of Colored People (NAACP), the Court struck down state laws aimed at curtailing the group's activities. The rulings were based on a newly recognized right of association, which the Court viewed as equal to other First Amendment freedoms.

In *NAACP v. Alabama ex rel. Patterson* (1958) the Court unanimously reversed a contempt of court citation against the NAACP. The group had been cited for refusing to turn over its membership list under an Alabama registration law for out-of-state corporations. "It is beyond debate that freedom to engage in association for the advancement of beliefs and ideas is an inseparable aspect of the 'liberty' assured by the Due Process Clause of the Fourteenth Amendment," Justice John Marshall Harlan wrote in his opinion for the Court. Compelled disclosure of membership lists, he said, "may constitute [an] effective . . . restraint" on that right.

Two years later in *Shelton v. Tucker* (1960) the Court similarly struck down an Arkansas law requiring teachers in public schools to disclose organizations to which they had belonged or contributed in the previous five years. The law was widely understood to be

In a series of cases the National Association for the Advancement of Colored People defended itself against attempts by southern states to intimidate it. Arkansas NAACP chief Daisy Bates, center, was convicted for refusing to disclose membership lists. The Supreme Court reversed her conviction in 1960.
Source: Life Picture Service

aimed at exposing teachers who belonged to the NAACP. The Court said the law's "comprehensive interference with associational freedom" went beyond the state's legitimate need for information about the fitness or competence of its teachers.

In a third case, *NAACP v. Button* (1963), the Court struck down a provision of Virginia's ethics regulations for lawyers. The regulation forbade the solicitation of clients by advocacy groups, such as the NAACP, that litigated cases in which they had no direct interest. The Court held that the law infringed on the right of association. Writing for the Court, Justice William J. Brennan, Jr., said that civil rights litigation was "political expression" protected by the Constitution even though it did not fall within "a narrow, literal conception of freedom of speech, petition, or assembly."

Political Patronage and Private Clubs

In a series of decisions beginning in 1976, the Court expanded the right of association to limit the role of political patronage in the hiring or firing of rank-and-file government employees.

In 1947 the Court had rejected an attack, based on freedom of association, against the federal Hatch Act. The Hatch Act generally prohibits federal employees from taking active part in political campaigns or man-

aging political party activities. The 4–3 ruling in the case *(United Public Workers v. Mitchell)* found no constitutional objection to Congress's judgment that the act promoted an efficient public service. In *Civil Service Commission v. Letter Carriers* (1973) the Court, in a 6–3 vote, reaffirmed that stance in a decision upholding the Hatch Act limitations. In a companion case *(Broadrick v. Oklahoma State Personnel Board)* the Court, by a 5–4 vote, affirmed a similar state law.

In 1976, however, the Court ruled, 5–3, that government employees' rights of association were violated by a practice of the Cook County, Illinois, sheriff's office. The sheriff's office had been using political party membership as a basis for dismissing non-civil service employees whenever a new sheriff took office. Political association, the Court said in *Elrod v. Burns*, "could not . . . constitute adequate ground for denying public employment." Four years later, a fragmented Court found a similar violation in a local public defender's actions; the official had discharged assistant defenders because they did not have the support of the local Democratic party.

In 1990 the Court voted 5–4 to limit the use of patronage in hiring, promotion, and transfer policies as well. Writing for the Court in *Rutan v. Republican Party of Illinois*, Justice Brennan said that personnel decisions affecting low-level employees "based on political affiliation or support are an impermissible infringement on the First Amendment rights of public employees." Speaking for the four dissenters, Justice Antonin Scalia said the Court had no basis for striking down the historically recognized practice of political patronage.

In the 1980s the Court refused to expand the freedom of association to protect exclusionary membership policies of large private clubs. In two decisions involving all-male community service organizations—*Roberts v. United States Jaycees* (1984) and *Board of Directors of Rotary International v. Rotary Club of Duarte* (1987)—the Court unanimously ruled that freedom of association did not prevent the enforcement of state or local antidiscrimination laws.

The Court's rulings distinguished two kinds of association rights. The freedom of intimate association is the right to enter into and carry on "highly personal" relationships, such as marriage or family relationships. The freedom of expressive association is the right to associate with others of a like mind in order to further a particular goal. The first aspect of freedom of association was not involved in either of the club cases, the Court said, and any infringement of the second was outweighed by society's interest in assuring equal treatment of women and men.

Attainder, Bill of

A bill of attainder is a legislative act that inflicts punishment on designated individuals without judicial trial. In the eighteenth century this power was abused to punish political opponents in England and to punish Tories in revolutionary America. These abuses led the Constitutional Convention to flatly prohibit Congress or the states from passing any bill of attainder (Article I, Sections 9 and 10). The Supreme Court has struck down three acts of Congress and one state constitutional provision under the clauses relating to bills of attainder.

The Court's decisions in the *Test Oath Cases* in 1867 struck down a loyalty oath requirement passed by Congress that effectively barred former Confederates from practicing law in federal court *(Ex parte Garland)*

and a similar but broader Missouri provision *(Cummings v. Missouri)*. The 5–4 rulings stretched the definition of a bill of attainder to encompass after-the-fact disqualification of classes of persons, not just specifically named individuals. (See LOYALTY OATHS.)

The two other rulings involved acts aimed at keeping communist sympathizers out of government and labor unions. In *United States v. Lovett* (1946) the Court struck down a 1943 law that forbade paying three specific federal employees who had been identified as subversives in a legislative committee hearing. In *United States v. Brown* (1965) the Court voted 5–4 to strike down a section of the 1959 Labor-Management Reporting and Disclosure Act that barred people from holding union office if they were members of the Communist party or had been party members in the past five years.

The *Brown* decision contrasted with a 1950 ruling in which the Court upheld a section of the Taft-Hartley Act that required union officers to sign affidavits that they were not members of the Communist party. In his opinion for the Court in *Brown*, Chief Justice Earl Warren distinguished it from the earlier case by explaining that the newer law covered past membership in the party. Thus, it served as a permanent disqualification against designated individuals.

The *Brown* ruling appeared to raise questions about other after-the-fact disqualification statutes that had been upheld in the past. These included laws forbidding convicted felons to practice medicine or hold office in a labor union. But in a 1977 decision involving former president Richard Nixon the Court backed away from an expansive analysis of the concept of bill of attainder.

Nixon challenged an act of Congress giving the federal government custody of his records and papers, on the grounds of bill of attainder. But the Court found that even though the law applied only to Nixon, he "constituted a legitimate class of one" on whom Congress could "fairly and rationally focus."

Attorney General

The attorney general of the United States is the nation's chief legal officer, representing the federal gov-

As President Lyndon Johnson, left, Vice President Hubert Humphrey, second from right, and Justice Thurgood Marshall, right, look on, Justice Tom C. Clark swears in his son Ramsey Clark as attorney general in 1967. Justice Clark, who had served as Harry Truman's attorney general, resigned from the Court to avoid any possible conflict of interest.
Source: National Archives

ernment's interests in law courts throughout the nation. The attorney general is also the chief law enforcement officer.

As head of the Justice Department, the attorney general oversees the Office of the SOLICITOR GENERAL, as well as legal departments dealing with antitrust, civil and criminal law, civil rights, internal security, taxes, and natural resources. These legal departments in turn monitor the litigation by U.S. attorneys assigned to each of the federal district courts, handle cases in the courts of appeals, and help the Solicitor General prepare cases involving the United States that are argued before the Supreme Court. (See COURTS, LOWER.)

Typically the attorney general also helps the president screen and select judicial nominees to the federal courts, including the Supreme Court. Even before a vacancy exists on the Court, the attorney general, usually working with top aides in the White House, may have reviewed the background of and interviewed potential candidates. (See NOMINATION TO THE COURT.)

The position of attorney general was created by the Judiciary Act of 1789 to handle all lawsuits in which

the United States was involved and to advise the president on questions of law. Until 1870 the attorney general worked with only a small staff in association with U.S. attorneys in the states.

Congress created the Department of Justice in 1870, seemingly to avoid the costs of having to hire private attorneys to prosecute government cases. That law made the attorney general the head of the department and created the Office of the Solicitor General to help with the court work and caseload.

Throughout the nation's history, the attorney generalship has proved to be a springboard to the Supreme Court. Nine justices had prior service as attorney general. The first was Roger B. Taney of Maryland, appointed in 1835. The most recent was Tom C. Clark, appointed in 1949. Nine other justices, including two members of the 1993–1994 Court, served in other Justice Department posts. Chief Justice William H. Rehnquist and Justice Antonin Scalia served as assistant attorney general. The newest justice, Stephen G. Breyer, who was to take his place on the Court in the fall of 1994, also served as an assistant to the attorney general in 1965–1967. (See BACKGROUND OF JUSTICES.)

B

Background of Justices

In two hundred years the Supreme Court has had only 108 members, making it one of the most exclusive as well as enduring of the world's governing bodies. All but two of the justices have been men, all but two have been white, and all but a handful have been Protestant. Yet the Court has exhibited diversity in other ways—politically and geographically, and in the age, personality, and previous service of its individual members.

There are no constitutional or statutory qualifications at all for serving on the Supreme Court. There is no age limitation, no requirement that justices be native-born citizens, not even a requirement that appointees have a legal background—although all 108 justices have been lawyers.

Judge Tapping Reeve's house and one-room law school in Litchfield, Connecticut, where Justices Henry Baldwin, Levi Woodbury, and Ward Hunt studied law.
Source: ©1992 Robert Houser

Legal Experience

All of President George Washington's appointees were lawyers, and no president has deviated from this precedent. The nature of the justices' legal education, however, has changed radically over the years.

Until the mid-nineteenth century, it was traditional for aspiring lawyers to study privately in a law office until they had learned the law sufficiently to pass the bar. The first justice to receive a law degree from an American university was Benjamin Curtis, who obtained his from Harvard in 1832. Two of the earliest justices, John Rutledge and John Blair, received their legal education in England at the Inns of Court.

Not until 1957 was the Supreme Court composed entirely of law school graduates. Before that time many appointees had attended law school without receiving degrees. The last justice never to have attended law school was James F. Byrnes, who served on the Court from 1941 to 1942. The son of poor Irish immigrants, Byrnes never even graduated from high school. He left school at age fourteen, worked as a law clerk, and became a court stenographer. Byrnes read law in his spare time and passed the bar at age twenty-four.

The last justice not to have a law degree was Stanley F. Reed, who served from 1938 to 1957. He attended law school at both the University of Virginia and Columbia University but received no degree.

Judicial Experience

All justices have been lawyers, but only sixty-seven have had judicial experience before coming to the Supreme Court. Surprisingly, many more justices have had judicial experience at the state level (forty-four) than at the federal level (thirty-one). (The figures overlap because eight justices have held both federal and state judicial offices.)

All except two of Washington's appointees had state judicial experience. Robert Trimble, appointed to the Court in 1826, was the first federal judge to become a justice; he had served nine years on the federal bench. By 1880 only two other federal judges had been named to the Court.

After 1880, when federal circuit judge William B. Woods was appointed, the pace picked up, and federal judicial experience became an increasingly important factor in appointment. Seven of the nine justices in 1994 had been federal circuit judges; two had been state court judges (David Souter had been both). Only Chief Justice William H. Rehnquist had no prior judicial experience. Stephen G. Breyer, who was to join the Court in the fall of 1994, also was a federal circuit judge; he replaced retiring Justice Harry A. Blackmun, who came to the Court from the Eighth U.S. Circuit Court of Appeals.

Political Positions

Many justices have had political careers, serving in Congress, as governors, or as members of a cabinet. One president, William Howard Taft, was later appointed to the Court; he was named chief justice in 1921. More than one-fourth of all justices, twenty-seven in all, have held congressional office before being named to the Court. Six others sat in the Continental Congress in the 1770s or 1780s.

The first justice with congressional experience was William Paterson, who had served in the Senate from 1789 to 1790. A few justices have come directly from Congress to the Court. Only one incumbent House member, James M. Wayne in 1835, has been named to the Court. Five incumbent senators have been appointed to the Court: John McKinley in 1837, Levi Woodbury in 1846, Edward D. White in 1894, Hugo L. Black in 1937, and Harold H. Burton in 1945.

The last Supreme Court appointee with any congressional service was Sherman Minton, appointed in 1949. He served as a U.S. senator from Indiana from 1935 to 1941, then was appointed to a circuit court of appeals judgeship. Since Black's retirement in 1971, no Supreme Court member has had any congressional experience.

Since John Adams appointed his secretary of state,
John Marshall, chief justice in 1801, nineteen other cabinet members have become justices. Thirteen of them were appointed while still serving in the cabinet. Not surprisingly, more attorneys general have been named to the Court than holders of any other cabinet position. Nine attorneys general, including seven incumbents, have been appointed to the Court. Next in number come secretaries of the treasury (four), secretaries of state (three), and secretaries of the navy (three). One postmaster general, one secretary of the interior, one secretary of war, and one secretary of labor have also been appointed to the Court.

The first chief justice, John Jay, left that post to become governor of New York. Only six governors have been appointed to the Court after their gubernatorial terms. The first was William Paterson, who served as governor of New Jersey from 1790 to 1793. The most recent was California governor Earl Warren, appointed chief justice by President Dwight Eisenhower in 1953. Warren had a long political career behind him, having served as attorney general of California before winning three terms as governor. In 1948 he was the Republican nominee for vice president, and he ran a brief campaign for the presidential nomination in 1952.

Governor Charles Evans Hughes of New York was appointed to the Court by President Taft in 1910. Hughes had conducted investigations into fraudulent insurance practices in New York before being elected governor in 1906. He left the Court in 1916 to run for president on the Republican ticket, losing narrowly to Woodrow Wilson. Later he served as secretary of state under presidents Warren Harding and Calvin Coolidge. He returned to the Court in 1930 as chief justice.

The three other former governors appointed to the Supreme Court were Levi Woodbury of New Hampshire in 1846 (governor, 1823–1824), Salmon P. Chase of Ohio in 1864 (governor, 1856–1860), and Frank Murphy of Michigan in 1940 (governor, 1937–1939).

James Byrnes followed John Jay's path, leaving the Court in 1942 after only six months in the post. He moved on to other positions in federal and state government, including the governorship of South Carolina, to which he was elected in 1951.

Justices from the Executive Branch

Thirty-five justices of the Supreme Court—including ten chief justices—served as executive branch officials before their appointment to the Court. One served in the cabinet after leaving the Court. Twenty of the thirty-four held cabinet-level posts—nine of them were attorneys general—and another eight served in other posts in the Department of Justice.

Four justices, Roger B. Taney, Levi Woodbury, William H. Moody, and William Howard Taft, held more than one cabinet post. Taft held more high executive branch posts than any other justice. He is the only person to serve both as president and chief justice of the United States.

The following table lists the justices, the major executive branch positions they held, and their years of service.

Justice	Position	Court Service
John Jay*	Secretary for foreign affairs under the Articles of Confederation, 1784–1789; U.S. diplomat, 1794–1795	1789–1795
John Marshall*	Envoy to France, 1797–1798; secretary of state, 1800–1801	1801–1835
Smith Thompson	Secretary of the navy, 1818–1823	1823–1843
Gabriel Duvall	Comptroller of the treasury, 1802–1811	1811–1835
John McLean	Postmaster general, 1823–1829	1829–1861
Roger B. Taney*	Attorney general, 1831–1833; secretary of the treasury, 1833–1834	1836–1864
Levi Woodbury	Secretary of the navy, 1831–1834; secretary of the treasury, 1834–1841	1845–1851
Nathan Clifford	Attorney general, 1846–1848	1858–1881
Salmon P. Chase*	Secretary of the treasury, 1861–1864	1864–1873
Lucius Q. C. Lamar	Secretary of the interior, 1885–1888	1888–1893
Joseph McKenna	Attorney general, 1897–1898	1898–1925
William Rufus Day	Secretary of state, 1898	1903–1922
William H. Moody	Secretary of the navy, 1902–1904; attorney general, 1904–1906	1906–1910
Charles E. Hughes*	Secretary of state, 1921–1925	1910–1916, 1930–1941
Willis Van Devanter	Counsel, Interior Department, 1897–1903	1910–1937
James McReynolds	Attorney general, 1913–1914	1914–1941
William H. Taft*	U.S. solicitor general, 1890–1892; secretary of war, 1904–1908; president, 1908–1912	1921–1930
Edward T. Sanford	Assistant attorney general, 1907–1908	1923–1930
Harlan F. Stone*	Attorney general, 1924–1925	1925–1946
Owen J. Roberts	Prosecuting attorney, Teapot Dome scandal, 1924	1930–1945
Stanley Reed	Solicitor general, 1935–1938	1938–1957
William O. Douglas	Chairman, Securities and Exchange Commission, 1937–1939	1939–1975
Frank Murphy	Attorney general, 1938–1940	1940–1949
James F. Byrnes	Secretary of state, 1945–1947	1941–1942
Robert H. Jackson	Solicitor general, 1938–1939; attorney general, 1940–1941	1941–1954
Fred M. Vinson*	Secretary of the treasury, 1945–1946	1946–1953
Tom C. Clark	Attorney general, 1945–1949	1949–1967
Byron R. White	Deputy attorney general, 1961–1962	1962–1993
Arthur J. Goldberg	Secretary of labor, 1961–1962	1962–1965
Abe Fortas	Undersecretary of interior, 1942–1946	1965–1969
Thurgood Marshall	Solicitor general, 1964–1967	1967–1991
Warren E. Burger*	Assistant attorney general, 1953–1955	1969–1986
William H. Rehnquist*	Assistant attorney general, 1969–1971	1971–
Antonin Scalia	Assistant attorney general, 1974–1977	1986–
Clarence Thomas	Assistant secretary of education for civil rights, 1981–1982; chairman, Equal Employment Opportunity Commission, 1982–1990	1991–
Stephen G. Breyer	Assistant to attorney general 1965–1967; Watergate prosecutor, 1973	1994–

*Denotes chief justice.

Age

The age at which justices join the Court varies widely. The oldest person ever appointed to the Court was Horace H. Lurton, who was sixty-five when he became a justice in 1910. Two justices were older than that when they achieved the office of chief justice. When he was named chief justice in 1941, Harlan Fiske Stone was sixty-eight; Charles Evans Hughes was sixty-seven when he was elevated to chief justice in 1930.

The youngest justices were William Johnson and Joseph Story, who were both only thirty-two when they were appointed in 1804 and 1811, respectively. Story was younger than Johnson by about a month.

Only two other justices were under forty when appointed: Bushrod Washington, nephew of the president, was thirty-six when appointed in 1798; James Iredell was thirty-eight when appointed in 1790. Iredell was also the youngest justice to die on the Court; he died in 1799 at age forty-eight. The youngest twentieth-century justice was William O. Douglas, who was forty when appointed in 1939.

Religion

Every member of the Court was Protestant until 1835, when Andrew Jackson nominated Roger B. Taney, a Roman Catholic, for chief justice. Taney's religion seemed to raise no controversy at the time. Instead, the issue was Taney's close alliance to Jackson, whom Taney had served as attorney general and secretary of the treasury.

Another Catholic was not appointed to the Court until thirty years after Taney's death. In 1894 Grover Cleveland named Edward D. White of Louisiana an associate justice; White later became chief justice. Other Catholics appointed to the Court include Joseph McKenna (1897), Pierce Butler (1922), Frank Murphy (1939), William J. Brennan, Jr. (1956), Antonin Scalia (1986), and Anthony M. Kennedy (1988). Scalia is also the first Italian-American justice.

Much more controversial than any of the nominations of Catholics was that of Louis D. Brandeis, the first Jewish justice. Brandeis was named to the Court by Wilson in 1916. He was already a controversial fig-ure because of his views on social and economic matters. Conservatives bitterly fought his nomination, and an element of anti-Semitism tinged some of the opposition. When Brandeis took his seat on the Court, Justice James McReynolds refused to speak to him for three years and once refused to sit next to him for a Court picture-taking session.

Herbert Hoover's nomination of Benjamin Cardozo in 1932 established a so-called Jewish seat on the Supreme Court. Justice Felix Frankfurter replaced Cardozo in 1939. He in turn was replaced by Justice Arthur J. Goldberg in 1962. When Goldberg resigned in 1965 to become U.S. ambassador to the United Nations, President Lyndon Johnson chose Abe Fortas to replace him. But with Justice Fortas's resignation in 1969, President Richard Nixon broke the tradition of a "Jewish seat" by choosing a Protestant, Harry A. Blackmun. More than two decades passed before the appointment of another Jewish justice: Ruth Bader Ginsburg, named by President Bill Clinton in 1993. Clinton's second nominee, Stephen G. Breyer, also was Jewish.

Race and Gender

The first black justice, Thurgood Marshall, was appointed to the Court in 1967. Marshall had been counsel for the National Association for the Advancement of Colored People and one of the attorneys who successfully argued the 1954 case of *Brown v. Board of Education of Topeka,* in which the Court overturned the "separate but equal" doctrine of racial segregation. Marshall was solicitor general of the United States when Johnson named him to the Court.

When Marshall announced his retirement in 1991, President George Bush nominated another African American, Clarence Thomas, to the seat. Thomas was a circuit court judge and former chairman of the Equal Employment Opportunity Commission. A conservative who was opposed by many civil rights organizations, Thomas won confirmation on a 52–48 vote, the narrowest margin of any justice in the twentieth century.

During the 1980 presidential campaign, Republican candidate Ronald Reagan promised to name a woman to the Court. He did that in his first year in office by appointing Sandra Day O'Connor in 1981 as the first female justice. Clinton's selection of Ginsburg brought the number of women on the Court to two.

Geographical Representation

Justices have come from thirty-one of the fifty states, and states have not been represented in any particular appointment pattern. New York has been the home of sixteen justices, Pennsylvania of eleven. Eleven justices have come from Massachusetts, nine from Ohio, and six each from Virginia and Kentucky. No other states have been so frequently represented on the Court.

Early in the Court's history, geographical balance was a major consideration in selecting nominees. Because of the justices' function as circuit judges, it was popularly assumed that each region should have a spokesman on the Court. Until the Civil War this resulted in a "New England seat," a "Virginia seat," a "New York seat," and a "Pennsylvania seat." With the nation's post–Civil War expansion and the end of the justices' circuit-riding duties, this tradition faded.

Foreign-born Justices

Six justices were born outside the United States. James Wilson was born in 1742 in Caskardy, Scotland, and came to America as a young man. A signer of the Declaration of Independence and a member of the 1787 Constitutional Convention, Wilson was one of the original members of the Supreme Court.

James Iredell was born in 1751 in Lewes, England; he came to America at the age of seventeen and settled in North Carolina. William Paterson, born in County Antrim, Ireland, emigrated to America with his parents when he was two years old. David Brewer, born in 1837 in Smyrna, Turkey, was the son of an American missionary.

George Sutherland, born in 1852 in Buckinghamshire, England, came to the United States when his father, a convert to Mormonism, moved his family to the Utah Territory. Felix Frankfurter, born in 1882 in Vienna, Austria, came to the United States with his parents in 1894.

Bail

Bail is money or property pledged by an accused person to guarantee his appearance at trial. The Eighth Amendment states that "[e]xcessive bail shall not be required." The Supreme Court in 1895 held that the amendment reflected a presumption in favor of granting bail. Throughout U.S. history federal law has provided a right to bail for persons arrested for noncapital offenses.

In 1894 the Court ruled that the Eighth Amendment provision did not apply to the states. Court decisions extending provisions of the Bill of Rights to the states never dealt with the bail limitation. Still, in a 1971 ruling the Court appeared to assume that it does apply to the states.

The main Supreme Court decision on the question of excessive bail is *Stack v. Boyle* (1951). In that case the Court set aside as excessive bail fixed at $50,000 for twelve Communist leaders in California who had been indicted for conspiracy under the Smith Act. The Court found the bail "higher than an amount reasonably calculated" to ensure the defendants' presence at trial.

The following spring the Court held that the Eighth Amendment did not guarantee an absolute right to bail. In *Carlson v. Landon* (1952) the Court upheld, by a vote of 5 to 4, the attorney general's decision to deny bail to certain foreign Communists who had been detained pending deportation proceedings. The majority said the amendment merely provided that bail "shall not be excessive in those cases where it is proper to grant bail."

Twice in the 1980s the Court approved the denial of bail to certain suspects: dangerous juveniles *(Schall v. Martin* and *Abrams v. Martin* [1984]) and organized crime figures *(United States v. Salerno* [1987]).

Writing for the Court in *Salerno,* Chief Justice William H. Rehnquist reiterated that the Eighth Amendment "says nothing about whether bail shall be available at all." He stated that the amendment does not deny the government's power to regulate pretrial releases for reasons other than ensuring the appearance of the accused at trial. "We believe," he concluded, "that when Congress has mandated detention on the basis of a compelling interest other than prevention of flight . . . , the Eighth Amendment does not require release on bail."

Baker v. Carr

In 1962 the Supreme Court ruled that federal courts may entertain a challenge to a state legislature's failure to realign seats to take account of changing population. This decision, *Baker v. Carr,* set the stage for court-mandated REAPPORTIONMENT AND REDISTRICTING and affected legislative seats in virtually every state. Chief Justice Earl Warren considered the ruling the Court's most important decision during his tenure.

The Tennessee legislature had failed to reapportion itself since 1901 despite a state constitutional requirement to do so after every ten-year census. As a result, rural areas that had lost population to the cities and suburbs continued to enjoy vastly disproportionate representation.

Rural interests had blocked reapportionment in the legislature, and the state supreme court rejected a lawsuit to force the lawmakers to reapportion. A group of urban residents and officials—acting under the name of Charles W. Baker, chairman of the Shelby County (Memphis) governing body—then sued Tennessee's secretary of state, Joe Carr, in federal court to try to force the legislature to comply with the requirement.

A three-judge federal court dismissed the suit in late 1959, citing the Supreme Court's earlier refusal (1946) to hear a congressional redistricting case. After the Court agreed to hear the appeal in the Tennessee case, the Kennedy administration joined the plaintiffs in early 1961 in urging the justices to reinstate the suit.

After two rounds of arguments, the Supreme Court's 6–2 decision in March 1962 established only that there was no reason for federal courts to refuse to hear challenges to legislative malapportionment. "The right asserted [to equal representation] is within the reach of judicial protection under the Fourteenth Amendment," Justice William J. Brennan, Jr., wrote for the Court. The plaintiffs had standing "in order to protect or vindicate an interest of their own." The case did not present a "nonjusticiable" political question just because it sought "protection of a political right." Judicial standards for resolving the claim under the equal protection clause, Brennan said, were "well developed and familiar."

The narrow decision left the question of a remedy up to the district court. In a concurring opinion, Justice Tom C. Clark said he would have gone further and granted the plaintiffs relief.

In their dissents, justices Felix Frankfurter and John Marshall Harlan strongly criticized the majority for what Harlan called "an adventure in judicial experimentation." Frankfurter, who had written the main opinion in the 1946 case, added: "The Court overlooks the fact that there is not under our Constitution a judicial remedy for every political mischief, for every undesirable exercise of legislative power."

In later cases, the Court fleshed out the meaning of its decision. A 1963 case *(Gray v. Sanders)* gave birth to the "one person, one vote" requirement. The standards laid down by the Court forced every state legislature but one (Oregon) to reapportion to comply with the decision.

Bakke

See AFFIRMATIVE ACTION.

Baldwin, Henry

Henry Baldwin (1780–1844) was one of the most erratic justices who ever served on the Supreme Court. During his fourteen years on the Court, he suffered periods of mental illness, had screaming arguments with his colleagues, and was said to be occasionally violent.

Baldwin was born in New Haven, Connecticut. He grew up on the family farm near New Haven and graduated from Yale College in 1797. He then moved to Philadelphia to clerk in the office of Alexander Dal-

January 1830, Baldwin served until his death in 1844. Always eccentric, he missed a whole term of the Court after a mental breakdown in the winter of 1832–1833. He supported the Constitution above all, but his unpleasant behavior toward those around him weakened the persuasiveness of his arguments. When he died, Baldwin's friends were forced to take up a collection to pay for his funeral because he was heavily in debt.

Source: Library of Congress

las, one of the city's leading attorneys. After being admitted to the Philadelphia bar, Baldwin moved to Pittsburgh. It was a growing city "out west" that had lots of room for young men like Baldwin who sought to make names for themselves.

Though still in his mid-twenties, Baldwin quickly became a major figure in Pittsburgh's political and social affairs. He joined with two other men, Tarleton Bates and Walter Forward, in creating a law firm that became known as the "Great Triumvirate of Early Pittsburgh." Baldwin himself was called the "Idol of Pennsylvania" and the "Pride of Pittsburgh." Besides being deeply involved in political and legal activities, Baldwin also was active in business. He was part owner of at least three mills in Pennsylvania and one in Ohio.

Baldwin entered Congress in 1817 but resigned in 1822 because of health problems. After two years of rest, he resumed his political activities in Allegheny County. In 1823 he pressed Andrew Jackson to run for president, and he remained a close adviser to Jackson.

Nominated for the Supreme Court by Jackson in

Barbour, Philip P.

Philip Pendleton Barbour (1783–1841) wanted to run for vice president with Andrew Jackson in 1832. However, he dropped out of the race in favor of Jackson's choice, Martin Van Buren, because of Democratic fears that the election could be thrown into the Senate. Four years later, Jackson appointed Barbour to the Supreme Court.

Barbour was born into a prominent Virginia family. His father was a member of the Virginia house of burgesses and a wealthy planter in Orange County. His older brother served as Virginia's governor, U.S. senator, and secretary of war under President John Quincy Adams.

After largely educating himself in the law, Barbour started a practice in Kentucky. He attended one session at the College of William and Mary before resuming his law practice in Virginia. A long career of public service followed. He was a member of the Virginia house of delegates (1812–1814), a U.S. representative (1814–1825, 1827–1830), Speaker of the House (1821–1823), a state judge on the general court for the eastern district of Virginia (1825–1827), president of the Virginia Constitutional Convention (1829–1830), and judge of the Federal District Court for Eastern Virginia (1830–1836). While a member of Congress, Barbour argued that the Supreme Court should be able to declare a statute unconstitutional only if five of the seven justices concurred.

Barbour's loyalty as a Jacksonian Democrat did not go unnoticed. After passing him over for the cabinet in 1829 and persuading him to abandon his vice-pres-

Source: Library of Congress

GENERAL. Because the U.S. government is involved in so many of the cases that come to the Court, the solicitor general and staff appear there more than any other "law firm" in the country.

Origins

When the Supreme Court initially convened in February 1790, one of its first actions was to establish qualifications for lawyers who wished to practice before it. Those requirements—acceptable personal and professional character and qualification to practice before a state's or territory's highest court—have remained the same since 1790. In all, some 180,000 attorneys have been admitted to the Supreme Court bar. About 5,000 are now admitted each year.

Although some lawyers seek admission to the Supreme Court bar merely for personal prestige, membership does have a real function. Attorneys cannot process any case to completion by themselves unless they are members of the Supreme Court bar. A nonmember may work on a case, but at least one member of the Court bar must sponsor any case filed with the Court.

A lawyer who wishes to be admitted to the Supreme Court bar must submit two documents to the clerk of the court. The first is a certificate from the appropriate judicial official of the highest court in the state or territory stating that the attorney has been admitted to practice there for the past three years and is in good standing. The second is an executed form, furnished by the Court, containing a personal statement from the applicant and endorsements by two members of the Supreme Court bar who know the applicant personally and who affirm that he or she "is of good moral and professional character." There is also a $100 admission fee.

The clerk of the court screens all applications and notifies lawyers whose applications are in order.

Before 1970 attorneys could gain formal admission to the bar only through an oral motion in open court. The attorney selects a day when the Court is in public session and notifies the clerk. The applicant then finds a member of the Supreme Court bar who is able and willing to stand in Court with the applicant. When the Court convenes, the chief justice announces that admissions will be entertained. The clerk then calls

idential quest in 1832, Jackson nominated Barbour for the Supreme Court in 1836. In his most significant case, *Mayor of New York v. Miln,* Barbour argued that states had the right to monitor the health of foreigners arriving in their territory. Barbour had the shortest tenure of any of Jackson's appointees, dying of a heart attack in 1841.

Bar of the Supreme Court

The lawyers who argue before the Supreme Court do not work for the Court, but without them the Court would have no work. These lawyers counsel the clients, file the petitions, write the briefs, and argue the cases before the Court. They represent the federal government, the states, the individuals, and the businesses whose disputes come to the Court. Their skill—or lack of it—in presenting a client's claim and the issues it raises can make the Court's work easier or more difficult.

The Supreme Court bar is not an organized group, but it has an undisputed leader—the U.S. SOLICITOR

the sponsor to the rostrum, the sponsor requests that the applicant be admitted to the bar, and the chief justice announces that the motion is granted.

After all the motions have been made and granted, the chief justice welcomes the new members, and the clerk administers the oath of office to the group. Each newly admitted member of the bar is asked to "solemnly swear that as an attorney and counselor of this Court, you will conduct yourself uprightly and according to law, and that you will support the Constitution of the United States. So help you God." The applicants reply in unison, "I do."

In 1970, largely as a result of the increasing amount of time being spent on the oral motions in open session, the Court began to allow applicants to submit written motions without making a formal appearance. These so-called mail-order admissions now constitute 80 percent or more of all admissions to the Supreme Court bar.

Attorneys can be disbarred from the Supreme Court following disbarment in some other jurisdiction or "conduct unbecoming a member of the bar of this Court." An attorney may also resign from the bar; no reason need be given.

Changes in the Bar

To some observers modern members of the Supreme Court bar seem to lack the dramatic flair and oratorical genius of nineteenth-century advocates, such as DANIEL WEBSTER, HENRY CLAY, JOHN C. CALHOUN, and AUGUSTUS H. GARLAND.

In the nineteenth century attorneys sent their cases to attorneys in Washington who were experienced in arguing before the Supreme Court. Garland, as attorney general and a private attorney, argued 130 cases before the Court. JEREMIAH SULLIVAN BLACK argued sixteen cases before the court between 1861 and 1865 and won thirteen, including eight reversals of lower courts.

Today, however, attorneys travel to Washington to present their own briefs. It is a rare private attorney who has argued more than five cases before the Supreme Court.

Bill of Rights

The Bill of Rights consists of the first ten amendments to the Constitution. It originated from a campaign pledge made by supporters of the new charter during the debate over ratification in 1787 and 1788. When opponents depicted the more powerful national government as a threat to individual liberties, the Federalist supporters—including James Madison—promised to add a bill of rights once the Constitution was ratified. As a member of the House of Representatives, Madison played the major role in

From hundreds of suggestions from the states, James Madison created a list of seventeen constitutional amendments, which he presented to the House of Representatives. The Senate then whittled the number down to twelve, of which ten, known as the Bill of Rights, were ratified by the states.
Source: National Portrait Gallery, Smithsonian Institution

drafting the amendments and winning approval for them from the First Congress in 1789. Ratification by the necessary number of states was completed two years later, on December 15, 1791.

Provisions

The provisions, drawn in part from listings of rights contained in state constitutions, were wide-ranging. What became the First Amendment combined several provisions protecting freedom of expression. (See ASSEMBLY, FREEDOM OF; PETITION, RIGHT OF; PRESS, FREEDOM OF; RELIGION, FREEDOM OF; SPEECH, FREEDOM OF.) The Second Amendment safeguarded state militias; it has also been claimed by opponents of gun control as a protection for personal possession of firearms.

The next two amendments protected people in their homes. The Third Amendment prohibited peacetime quartering of troops in private homes—a hated practice of the British during the colonial era. Alone of the amendments, it has never been the subject of judicial interpretation. The Fourth Amendment prohibited "unreasonable" SEARCH AND SEIZURE and required PROBABLE CAUSE for warrants for ARRESTS or searches. These provisions have resulted in a host of sometimes technical rules governing police investigations.

The next four amendments related mostly to TRIALS and punishment. They protected the right to INDICTMENT by a GRAND JURY (Fifth Amendment), trial by "an impartial jury" in all criminal cases (Sixth Amendment), and trial by jury in civil cases involving more than twenty dollars (Seventh Amendment). (See JURIES.) To further safeguard criminal trials, the Fifth Amendment established a privilege against SELF-INCRIMINATION. The Sixth Amendment guaranteed defendants the right to an attorney and the right to compel witnesses to testify in their behalf. (See COUNSEL, RIGHT TO LEGAL.) The Eighth Amendment prohibited excessive BAIL, excessive fines, and CRUEL AND UNUSUAL PUNISHMENT.

The final two amendments established more general protection of rights. The Ninth Amendment was designed to quiet fears that any unlisted rights would be viewed as unprotected. It states that "[t]he enumeration in the Constitution, of certain rights, shall not be construed to deny or disparage others retained by the people." The Tenth Amendment safeguarded states' rights by providing that states retained all powers "not delegated to the United States by the Constitution, nor prohibited by it to the states. . . . "

Two other proposed amendments were also included, but failed to win ratification at the time. One would have fixed the ratio of population to members of the House of Representatives, increasing the size of the House as the nation grew. The other would have barred salary increases for members of Congress until after the next biennial election for House members. This last proposal was belatedly ratified in 1992, more than two centuries after it was submitted to the states. (See AMENDING PROCESS.)

Madison drafted and won House approval of another amendment that would have prohibited the states from infringing "the equal rights of conscience," freedom of the press, or the right to trial by jury in criminal cases. The Senate, however, rejected the amendment. The vote reveals how the First Congress viewed the various proposals as applying only to the new federal government and not to the states.

The States and the Bill of Rights

Despite that history, the Supreme Court was urged in the early nineteenth century to enforce provisions of the Bill of Rights against the states. In a series of decisions beginning with *Barron v. Baltimore* (1833), the Court refused. In *Barron* the owner of a wharf in Baltimore challenged city action that seriously impaired the value of his property by creating shoals and shallows around it. Barron argued that the action was a "taking" of his property without just compensation in violation of the Fifth Amendment. (See PROPERTY RIGHTS.)

In his final opinion for the Court, Chief Justice John Marshall said the issue in *Barron* was "one of great importance, but not of much difficulty." The Bill of Rights, Marshall said, was adopted to secure individual rights against the "apprehended encroachments of the general government—not against those of the local governments." He said the Court found no indication that Congress intended the Bill of Rights to apply to the states, and that it would not extend the provisions on its own.

Since the federal government had only limited powers during much of the nineteenth century, the Supreme Court's ruling meant that it had few occasions to interpret the Bill of Rights before the Civil War. In approving what became the Fourteenth Amendment, however, Congress appears to have intended to apply the Bill of Rights to the states through the DUE PROCESS clause. It provided that no state could "deprive any person of life, liberty, or property, without due process of law. . . . " (See CIVIL WAR AMENDMENTS.)

In its early rulings interpreting the Fourteenth Amendment, the Court eased the requirements of the Bill of Rights as they pertained to state criminal justice systems. In *Hurtado v. California* (1884) the Court held that due process did not require indictment by a grand jury in state criminal cases. In later rulings in 1900 and 1908, the Court similarly refused either to require twelve-person juries in state criminal cases or to strictly enforce the Fifth Amendment's privilege against self-incrimination in state cases.

Meanwhile the Court did hand down two rulings applying provisions of the Fourth and Fifth amendments more strictly in federal cases. In *Boyd v. United States* (1886) the Court said that the Fourth Amendment protected individuals against a subpoena of private business papers if it would require production of self-incriminating evidence. And in *Counselman v. Hitchcock* (1892) the Court held that the Fifth Amendment privilege against self-incrimination extended to grand jury proceedings, not just to trials. Two decades later, the Court first established the EXCLUSIONARY RULE barring the use at trial of evidence obtained in violation of the Fourth Amendment. The ruling was made in a federal criminal case, *Weeks v. United States* (1914).

Only later in the twentieth century did the Court have frequent occasion to interpret and enforce the Bill of Rights. Beginning in the 1920s, the Court ruled that the due process clause of the Fourteenth Amendment does encompass some of the provisions of the Bill of Rights. Under the INCORPORATION DOCTRINE, the Court by 1969 had required states to abide by virtually all the provisions of the First, Fourth, Fifth, Sixth, and Eighth amendments.

Black, Hugo L.

During his thirty-four years on the Supreme Court, Justice Hugo Lafayette Black (1886–1971) wrote some of the most important decisions in the nation's history. His opinions for the Court barred prayer in public schools; required states to provide legal counsel to defendants charged with serious crimes; established the rule of "one person, one vote"; and struck down laws making it difficult for blacks to vote. Black also was a great dissenter, and many of his dissenting viewpoints were later adopted by the Court.

Black was born in Harlan, Alabama. After trying medical college for one year, Black switched to the study of law. He received his law degree from the Uni-

Source: Library of Congress

versity of Alabama in 1906 and began practicing privately. Black's first major public office came in 1926, when he was elected to the U.S. Senate as the poor people's candidate. To make up for his lack of formal education, Black studied history and the classics at the Library of Congress.

Black was one of President Franklin D. Roosevelt's biggest supporters in the Senate. When Justice Willis Van Devanter retired in 1937, it was expected that Sen. Joseph T. Robinson, D-Ark., the Senate majority leader who had led the battle for Roosevelt's Court-packing plan, would get the nomination. Robinson died suddenly, however, and the nomination fell to Black, one of the few southern senators who had supported Roosevelt's plan. Black's nomination provoked strong opposition. Some senators felt he was unqualified for the Court and that his support of the Court-packing plan was wrong. Nonetheless, the Senate confirmed Black by a vote of 63 to 16.

Shortly after his confirmation, the media reported that Black had joined the Ku Klux Klan in the 1920s. Black made a dramatic radio address in which he admitted his past membership in the Klan but said he had resigned after only two years. The furor died down.

Black's appointment to the Court in 1937 helped propel its shift towards liberalism. At the time Black was appointed, the Court began emphasizing cases involving personal rights over those involving property rights. Black himself championed First Amendment rights. He was one of the few justices in the Court's history to believe that First Amendment rights were absolute and that the government could not curtail them in any way.

Perhaps Black's most famous opinion for the Court came in the case of *GIDEON V. WAINWRIGHT* (1963). In *Gideon* the Court unanimously ruled that states must provide counsel for criminal defendants charged with serious crimes who cannot afford to hire lawyers. In the Court's opinion, Black wrote that not only judicial precedents "but also reason and reflection require us to recognize that in our adversary system of criminal justice, any person haled into court, who is too poor to hire a lawyer, cannot be assured a fair trial unless counsel is provided for him. This seems to us to be an obvious truth."

After suffering a disabling stroke, Black retired from the Court on September 17, 1971. He died eight days later.

Black, Jeremiah S.

Jeremiah Sullivan Black (1810–1883) has the singular distinction of being the only person to have lost a seat on the Supreme Court by a single vote.

A distinguished lawyer, Black had been a judge on the Pennsylvania supreme court and had served as U.S. attorney general from 1857 to 1860. He was serving as President James Buchanan's secretary of state when Buchanan, a lame-duck Democrat, nominated him to a vacancy on the Supreme Court a month before Abraham Lincoln was to take office.

Republicans were loath to confirm Black because they wanted to give Lincoln the opportunity to fill the vacancy. The situation was further complicated by the slavery issue. Although he was a northerner who supported the Union, Black was not an abolitionist. This made him unacceptable to the antislavery faction in Congress. He was also opposed by Stephen A. Douglas, who had just lost the election to Lincoln.

Black went on to serve as the Supreme Court reporter in 1861–1862 and to argue many cases before the Court that he might have sat on under other circumstances. Between 1861 and 1865, he argued sixteen cases, winning thirteen of them, including eight reversals of lower court rulings.

The most famous case that Black participated in, however, was *Ex parte McCardle,* argued in 1869. Mississippian William H. McCardle was the intemperate editor of the *Vicksburg Times* who vigorously opposed in print the military rule the Reconstruction Act of 1867 had imposed on the South. McCardle was eventually arrested for libel, among other charges.

McCardle charged that his petition for release through a writ of habeas corpus had been wrongfully denied. He appealed to the Supreme Court, where he was represented by Black and by David Dudley Field, brother to Justice Stephen J. Field, who was sitting on the Court.

Fearing that the Court would take the opportunity to overturn the Reconstruction Act, Congress repealed the Supreme Court's JURISDICTION in habeas corpus cases. The Court then dismissed the case for lack of jurisdiction. This was the only time in the nation's history that Congress prevented the Court from deciding a pending case by removing its jurisdiction over the subject matter of the case.

Blackmun, Harry A.

Harry Andrew Blackmun (1908–   )will be remembered as author of the Supreme Court's landmark decision in *ROE V. WADE* (1973), which legalized abortion. President Nixon nominated Blackmun to the Court in 1970, as his third choice for filling the vacancy created by the resignation of Justice Abe Fortas. Nixon's first two choices—Clement F. Haynsworth, Jr., of South Carolina and G. Harrold Carswell of Florida—were rejected by the Senate. Nixon contended that rejection of his first two nominees showed that the Senate "as it is presently constituted" would not confirm a judicial conservative from the South. Nixon then nominated Blackmun, a judge on the Eighth Circuit Court of Appeals who had lived in Minnesota for most of his life.

Blackmun and Chief Justice Warren E. Burger were lifelong friends, whose relationship went back to their grade-school years in the Minneapolis-St. Paul area. Blackmun was born in Nashville, Illinois, but spent most of his youth in Minneapolis-St. Paul, where his father was an official of the Twin Cities Savings and Loan Company.

After graduating from high school, Blackmun received a scholarship to attend Harvard University. He majored in mathematics, and briefly considered becoming a physician. Instead, he entered Harvard Law School after graduating Phi Beta Kappa from Harvard and received his law degree in 1932.

Blackmun returned to St. Paul after law school to become a law clerk to U.S. circuit court judge John B. Sanborn. After a year and a half, he left the clerkship

Source: Library of Congress

to join a Minneapolis law firm, where he worked for sixteen years. In addition to practicing law, Blackmun also taught at the Mitchell College of Law in St. Paul and at the University of Minnesota Law School. Blackmun was hired as "house counsel" for the Mayo Clinic in Rochester, Minnesota, in 1950.

In 1959, President Dwight D. Eisenhower appointed him to the Eighth Circuit Court of Appeals. On the appeals court Blackmun developed a reputation for writing scholarly and thorough opinions.

When Blackmun joined the Supreme Court in 1970, he and Burger were frequently labeled the "Minnesota Twins" because it was believed that they thought and voted alike. However, within a few years Blackmun began moving in a liberal direction that distanced him from Burger, who throughout his tenure anchored the Court's conservative wing.

By 1991, after the retirements of Justices William J. Brennan, Jr., and Thurgood Marshall, Blackmun had become the Court's most liberal justice on many issues, including abortion, civil rights, and church-state relations. He announced in March 1994 that he would retire by the beginning of the Court's next term.

Blair, John, Jr.

John Blair, Jr. (1732–1800) was one of President George Washington's original appointees to the Supreme Court in 1789. While serving as a judge on Virginia's first court of appeals in 1782, he joined in a majority decision in *Commonwealth v. Caton*. The ruling held that the court could declare legislative acts unconstitutional. In 1803, just over two decades later, the U.S. Supreme Court adopted this same position in *MARBURY V. MADISON* when it declared that the Court could declare an act of Congress invalid if it violated the Constitution.

Blair was born in Williamsburg, Virginia, to one of the state's most prominent families. He graduated from the College of William and Mary in 1754, studied law at the Middle Temple in London, and then returned home to practice law. In 1766 he entered the Virginia house of burgesses at age thirty-four. Blair was a conservative who opposed the resolutions of Patrick Henry condemning the Stamp Act. Nonetheless, he joined with leading merchants in agreeing to boycott some British imports. Blair resigned his seat in 1770 to become clerk of the governor's council and held a succession of state offices and judgeships. He also participated in the Constitutional Convention in 1787, where he strongly supported ratification.

Appointed to the Supreme Court in 1789, Blair served for only seven years. His wife's illness and the Court's relative inactivity caused him to miss some sessions, and he resigned in January 1796. He suffered debilitating headaches in the last years of his life, possibly brought on by the hardships of riding circuit. (See CIRCUIT RIDING.) He died in August 1800 at his home in Williamsburg.

Source: Library of Congress

Blatchford, Samuel

Samuel Blatchford (1820–1893), a federal judge from New York, was President Chester Arthur's third choice for the Supreme Court seat vacated when Justice Ward Hunt retired in 1882. Arthur first chose Roscoe Conkling, a New York politician, but Conkling declined the appointment despite his confirmation by the Senate. Arthur's second choice, Sen. George F. Edmunds of Vermont, also turned down the job. Arthur then nominated Blatchford, who was confirmed by the Senate on a voice vote.

Blatchford was born into a prominent New York City family. His father was counsel for the Bank of England and the Bank of the United States and served in the New York legislature. Blatchford enrolled at Columbia College at age thirteen and graduated four years later at the top of his class.

Blatchford began his legal education in 1837 by serving as the private secretary for New York gover-

Source: Collection of the Supreme Court of the United States

Bradley, Joseph P.

Supreme Court justice Joseph P. Bradley (1813–1892) cast the deciding vote that made Rutherford B. Hayes president in 1877. The 1876 presidential election, which pitted the Republican Hayes against Democrat Samuel Tilden, ended in a dispute over voting in several southern states. To resolve it, Congress created a fifteen-member commission that included seven Republicans, seven Democrats, and Supreme Court justice David Davis, an independent who would cast the deciding vote.

Davis resigned from the commission, however, when the Illinois legislature elected him to the U.S. Senate. Bradley, a Republican who was considered the next least partisan justice, was appointed to replace him. Bradley voted with the Republicans on every issue. The Democratic press attacked Bradley, but he always maintained that he had voted strictly on legal and constitutional issues and that partisan politics had not influenced him.

Source: Library of Congress

nor William H. Seward, his father's friend. After passing the bar in 1842, he practiced with his father for three years and then joined Seward's law firm in Auburn, New York. He remained there for nine years before joining with Seward's nephew in forming a law firm in New York City. In 1855 Blatchford turned down a seat on the New York supreme court to continue practicing admiralty and international law.

Blatchford developed a reputation as a legal scholar because of his extensive reporting of federal court decisions. He was appointed district judge for southern New York in 1867 and a judge of the second circuit court of New York in 1872. After Blatchford had served for fifteen years on the federal bench, Arthur appointed him to the Supreme Court in 1882. Many of the cases he heard on the Court dealt with admiralty or patent law, and his experience in these fields was invaluable to his colleagues. He died in 1893.

Bradley was born in Berne, New York, and grew up in poverty on his parents' small farm. After attending a country school, where he was an excellent student, Bradley began teaching at age sixteen. A local minister befriended him and sponsored his enrollment at Rutgers University, from which he graduated in 1836. Bradley then studied law and passed the bar in 1839. He quickly built a thriving law practice based on specialties in patent, commercial, and corporate law, and became counsel for various railroads.

In the winter of 1860–1861 Bradley traveled to Washington, D.C., to work toward a compromise between the North and South. Once the Civil War had begun, he threw his full support behind the Union and Abraham Lincoln's administration. Although Bradley had never held any public office, President Ulysses S. Grant nominated him for the Supreme Court in February 1870. His opinions included declaring the 1875 Civil Rights Act unconstitutional, arguing that private discrimination on the basis of race was legal, and supporting the right of Illinois to deny a woman admission to the state bar. Bradley, who became known for the quality of his scholarship on the Court, continued serving until his death in January 1892.

Source: Collection of the Supreme Court of the United States

Brandeis, Louis D.

Intense opposition arose when President Woodrow Wilson nominated Louis Dembitz Brandeis (1856–1941) for the Supreme Court in 1916. A coalition of special interests—primarily industrial and business leaders whom Brandeis had vanquished in court during his career as a "people's attorney"—claimed he was a dangerous radical. An undercurrent of anti-Semitism was also evident in the battle against Brandeis, who was Jewish. After four months of hearings, however, the Senate confirmed Brandeis by a 47–22 vote.

Brandeis was born in Louisville, Kentucky. In 1877 he graduated from Harvard Law School with the highest grade point average in the school's history. After practicing law for a short time in St. Louis, Brandeis returned to Cambridge to open a law office with one of his Harvard classmates. Brandeis's practice flourished. Although he was earning more than $50,000 annually by the time he was thirty-five—a very large income at that time—Brandeis and his wife chose to live simply.

When corporate monopolies began dominating American business at the turn of the century, Brandeis devoted his energy to fighting them on behalf of the public. He often charged no fee for this work. Brandeis challenged rates charged by the Boston gas company, monopolistic practices of the New Haven Railroad, and wages paid by New York's garment industry. The press labeled him the "people's attorney."

Wilson had great respect for Brandeis and often asked his opinions, before nominating him for the Court in 1916. After the bruising confirmation battle,

Brandeis found that life on the Court was no easier. Justice James Clark McReynolds openly shunned Brandeis, the Court's first Jewish justice, and refused to speak to him for three years after Brandeis joined the Court.

On the Court the liberal Brandeis frequently dissented from the majority's conservative rulings. He was often joined in dissent by Justice Oliver Wendell Holmes, Jr. Some of Brandeis's most important dissents came in cases involving the First Amendment. Shortly after the end of World War I, Brandeis and Holmes dissented when the Court upheld convictions under the Espionage and Sedition acts. The majority held that a person could be convicted if his or her speech had a "bad tendency." In his dissent, Brandeis wrote that this test was improper because it ignored the speaker's intent and the likelihood that danger would result.

Brandeis and Holmes also dissented when the Court upheld the conviction of bootleggers in *Olmstead v. United States* (1928). The bootleggers claimed their Fourth Amendment rights were violated because the government had used wiretaps to gather its evidence. The Court majority rejected their claim, but Brandeis and Holmes embraced it. "In a government of laws, existence of the government will be imperiled if it fails to observe the law scrupulously," Brandeis wrote.

Despite his liberal social and political views, Brandeis favored JUDICIAL RESTRAINT rather than judicial activism. In a concurring opinion in *Ashwander v. Tennessee Valley Authority* (1936), Brandeis set forth a classic set of rules for the Court to use in deciding whether to accept a case. After serving twenty-two years on the Court, Brandeis resigned in 1939. He died in 1941.

Brennan, William J., Jr.

When President Dwight Eisenhower appointed William Joseph Brennan, Jr. (1906–   ), to the Supreme Court in October 1956, some charged that Eisenhower had chosen Brennan to help him win the next month's presidential election. Brennan was a Catholic, and some claimed that Eisenhower, a Republican, was trying to attract the votes of Catholics in large cities, who normally voted Democratic. Eisenhower insisted he had made the appointment solely based on Brennan's merit. However, he later said that appointing the liberal Brennan was one of the worst mistakes he made as president.

Brennan was born in Newark, New Jersey, in 1906, making him the first justice born in the twentieth century. He graduated from the University of Pennsylvania in 1928 and from Harvard Law School in 1931. Brennan then joined a prominent Newark law firm and served on the staff of the undersecretary of war during World War II. In 1949 Brennan was appointed to the newly created New Jersey superior court. The next year he moved to the appellate division of the superior court. In 1952 he was appointed

Source: Library of Congress

to the state supreme court, where he served for four years until his appointment to the Supreme Court.

Brennan was the author of some of the most important decisions issued by the Warren Court. He wrote opinions expanding the right to freedom of association, granting criminal defendants in state courts the right not to incriminate themselves, forcing school districts to desegregate, and expanding the appeal rights of state prisoners. Brennan also wrote decisions overturning the convictions of members of the Communist party who refused to register with the government and striking down New York state's teacher loyalty oath. Other decisions written by Brennan made it harder for public figures to collect libel damages, barred police line-ups conducted without the suspect's attorney being present, and required reapportionment of congressional districts to uphold the concept of "one person, one vote."

Brennan's string of important decisions continued under chief justices Warren Burger and William Rehnquist, although Brennan increasingly dissented as the Court grew more conservative. He wrote opinions for the Court forcing states to use the same standards in convicting juveniles as in convicting adults, overturning a state law that allowed only women to receive alimony in divorces, granting the right of equal protection to illegal aliens, and limiting school boards' power to remove books from libraries. Other Brennan opinions required the Jaycees to admit women, upheld various affirmative action plans, and overturned a Louisiana law requiring public schools that taught the theory of evolution to also teach "creation science."

Brennan was a staunch defender of the First Amendment. "The First Amendment bars the State from imposing upon its citizens an authoritative vision of truth," Brennan wrote in *Herbert v. Lando* (1979). "It forbids the State from interfering with the communicative processes through which its citizens exercise and prepare to exercise their rights of self-government. And the Amendment shields those who would censure the State or expose its abuses." Citing poor health, Brennan retired in July 1990 after serving on the Court for nearly thirty-four years.

Brewer, David J.

When David Josiah Brewer (1837–1910) took his seat on the Supreme Court in 1889, he joined his uncle, Justice Stephen J. Field. The two men were the only uncle-nephew combination in the Court's history. They served together until Field's retirement in 1897.

Brewer is one of only six justices who were born abroad. His father was a missionary in the part of Asia Minor that later became Turkey, and Brewer was born there. The family returned to the United States shortly after his birth. Brewer attended Wesleyan University, graduated from Yale in 1856, and received his law degree from Albany Law School in 1858. Shortly after obtaining his law degree, he headed west to Kansas.

In Kansas, Brewer served in a succession of public positions. He was U.S. commissioner of the circuit court in Leavenworth (1861–1862), judge of probate and criminal courts for Leavenworth County (1863–1864), judge of the first judicial district of

Source: Library of Congress

Kansas (1865–1869), justice on the Kansas supreme court (1870–1884), and judge of the eighth federal circuit (1884–1889).

When Justice Stanley Matthews died in 1889, Kansas senators Preston B. Plumb and John J. Ingalls asked President Benjamin Harrison to appoint Brewer to the seat. While Harrison was considering their proposal, he received a letter from Brewer himself urging the president to appoint his Yale classmate, Henry Billings Brown, then a Michigan district court judge. Harrison was impressed by Brewer's generous attitude toward Brown, and nominated Brewer to the Court.

Brewer was not afraid to express his opinions outside the Court. He publicly backed independence for the Philippines, the vote for women, and residency rights for Chinese aliens in America. On the Court, Brewer wrote the opinion in *Muller v. Oregon* (1908), ruling that a state could set limits on how many hours women could work—then a liberal position. However, his first major opinion, delivered in *Louisville, New Orleans and Texas Railway Co. v. Mississippi* (1890), upheld a state law that required railroads to provide separate seats for blacks and whites on trips within the state. Brewer's ruling foreshadowed the Court's decision six years later in *PLESSY V. FERGUSON* upholding the doctrine of "separate but equal" facilities for blacks and whites. Brewer died in 1910 after serving twenty years on the Court.

Breyer, Stephen G.

When President Bill Clinton introduced Stephen G. Breyer, his second Supreme Court nominee, at a White House ceremony on May 16, 1994, he described the federal appeals court judge as a "consensus-builder." The reaction to the nomination proved his point.

Senators from both parties quickly endorsed Breyer's nomination. So did legal experts from across the ideological spectrum. A handful of liberals and consumer advocates raised the only vocal dissents, criticizing Breyer as pro-business.

Breyer, chosen to replace the retiring liberal justice

Harry Blackmun, won a reputation as a centrist in his fourteen years on the federal appeals court in Boston and his two earlier stints as a staff member for the Senate Judiciary Committee. Breyer's work crossed ideological lines. He played a critical role in enacting airline deregulation in the 1970s and writing federal sentencing guidelines in the 1980s.

Born in 1938, Breyer graduated from Stanford University and Harvard Law School. He clerked for Supreme Court Justice Arthur Goldberg and helped draft Goldberg's influential opinion in the 1965 case establishing the right of married couples to use contraceptives. Afterward, he served two years in the Justice Department's antitrust division and then took a teaching position at Harvard Law School in 1967. His area of specialty included administrative law, antitrust, and economic regulation.

Breyer took leaves from Harvard to serve as an assistant prosecutor in the Watergate investigation in 1973, special counsel to the Judiciary Committee's Administrative Practices Subcommittee from 1974 to 1975, and the full committee's chief counsel from 1979 to 1980. He worked for Sen. Edward Kennedy,

Source: R. Michael Jenkins

D-Mass., but also established good relationships with Republican committee members.

Breyer's ties to senators paid off when Democratic President Jimmy Carter nominated him for the federal appeals court. Action on the nomination was not completed before Republican Ronald Reagan was elected president in November. But Republican senators allowed a vote on Breyer's nomination—the only one of Carter's judicial appointments cleared after his defeat.

As a judge, Breyer was regarded as scholarly, judicious, and open-minded with generally conservative views on economic issues and more liberal views on social questions. He wrote two books on regulatory reform that criticized economic regulations as anti-competitive and questioned priorities in some environmental and health rulemaking. He also served as a member of the newly created United States Sentencing Commission from 1985 to 1989. Later he defended the commission's guidelines against criticism from judges and others who viewed them as overly harsh and restrictive.

In his rulings, Breyer showed a sensitivity to First Amendment issues and mixed views on civil rights and criminal law questions. He never directly ruled on abortion, but did vote to strike down a controversial regulation barring abortion counseling by federally funded family planning clinics. The Supreme Court later upheld the rule. Breyer's opinions were described as well-written and free of rhetoric. His court also had a reputation for quick decision making. He told a bar association meeting in 1981 that the average turnaround on opinions was two to three days.

Breyer was confirmed by the Senate on July 29, 1994 by a vote of 87–9. He joined Ruth Bader Ginsburg as the Court's second Jewish member. The Court has had two Jewish members only once before, in the 1930s when Louis Brandeis and Benjamin Cardozo served together for six years.

Brief

A brief is the document an attorney prepares to serve as the basis for an argument in court. It sets outs the facts and legal arguments in support of the attorney's case. Briefs in Supreme Court cases must be filed with the Court weeks before the case is formally argued. Although Supreme Court rules state that counsel should assume that all the justices have read the briefs before argument, justices vary greatly in the attention they personally devote to briefs.

The form and organization of the brief are covered by the rules of the Supreme Court. The rules specify that briefs must contain the following elements:

- The questions presented for review
- A list of all parties to the proceeding
- A table of contents and table of relevant case law and other legal authorities
- Citations to the opinions and judgments delivered in the lower courts
- A statement showing that the case is within the jurisdiction of the Court
- The constitutional provisions, treaties, statutes, ordinances, and regulations involved
- A concise statement of the case
- A summary of the argument
- The argument itself, which must state "clearly the points of fact and of law being presented, citing the authorities and statutes relied upon"
- A conclusion stating the specific relief the party is seeking

The rules limit the number of pages in briefs, specifying that the major brief—the one that addresses the merits of the case—should not exceed fifty pages. The rules also advise that briefs "must be compact, logically arranged with proper headings, concise, and free from burdensome, irrelevant, immaterial, and scandalous matters."

Briefs that do not follow these rules may be disallowed. In a 1974 case, for example, the Court declared that one party's brief was not concise and gave unnecessary detail. Accordingly the Court directed counsel to file a brief complying with the rules within twenty days (*Huffman v. Pursue, Ltd.* [1974]).

The rules also set out a color code for the covers of different kinds of briefs. Petitions are white; motions opposing them are light orange. Petitioners' briefs on the merits are light blue, while those of respondents are light red. Reply briefs are yellow; amicus curiae briefs, green; and documents filed by the United

States, gray. All other documents are required to have a tan cover.

The brief of the petitioner or appellant must be filed within forty-five days of the Court's announced decision to hear the case. Except for *IN FORMA PAUPERIS* cases, forty copies of the brief must be filed with the Court. For *in forma pauperis* proceedings, in which a party to a case is too poor to pay the fees, one typed copy must be filed with the clerk and one typed copy sent to each of the other parties in the case.

The opposing brief from the respondent or appellee is to be filed within thirty days of receipt of the brief of the petitioner or appellant. Either party may petition the clerk for an extension of time.

During or after oral argument, the justices may ask counsel in the case to submit supplementary briefs on particular points of law or issues.

Brown, Henry B.

Henry Billings Brown (1836–1913) is best known as the author of the Supreme Court's opinion in *PLESSY V. FERGUSON* (1896), giving the Court's blessing to racial segregation. The decision upheld a Louisiana law that required railroads to provide separate accommodations for black and white passengers.

In the opinion, Brown wrote that the Louisiana law was a reasonable use of the state's police power to protect the comfort and peace of its citizens. "Legislation is powerless to eradicate racial instincts or to abolish distinctions based upon physical differences, and the attempt to do so can only result in accentuating the difficulties of the present situation," Brown wrote. "If the civil and political rights of both races be equal one cannot be inferior to the other civilly, or politically. If one race be inferior to the other socially, the Constitution of the United States cannot put them upon the same plane." In 1954 the Court overturned *Plessy* with its ruling in *BROWN V. BOARD OF EDUCATION OF TOPEKA*, holding that separate facilities were inherently unequal.

Brown was born in South Lee, Massachusetts, to a family headed by a prosperous merchant. His parents decided he should pursue a legal career, so they en-

rolled him in a private secondary school and later in Yale University. He graduated from Yale in 1856 and briefly attended Yale Law School and Harvard Law School. Brown moved to Detroit in 1859 and passed the bar within a year. When the Civil War broke out, he was wealthy enough to hire a substitute so that he did not have to serve in the army.

Shortly after Abraham Lincoln became president, Brown was appointed deputy U.S. marshal for Detroit. Two years later he became assistant U.S. attorney for the eastern district of Michigan, including Detroit. Brown developed expertise in admiralty law because Detroit was a busy Great Lakes port.

Governor Henry H. Crapo appointed Brown interim circuit judge for Wayne County in 1868, but Brown was defeated when he ran for election to a full term. He then resumed his private law practice, specializing in shipping cases. In 1872 Brown ran an unsuccessful congressional campaign.

Three years later President Ulysses S. Grant appointed Brown district judge of eastern Michigan, a position he held for fourteen years. As a district judge Brown developed a national reputation for his exper-

Source: Library of Congress

tise in admiralty law. When Supreme Court justice Samuel Miller died in 1890, Judge Howell Edmunds Jackson of the sixth federal circuit court urged President Benjamin Harrison to appoint Brown to the seat. Harrison followed the advice of Jackson, his former colleague in the Senate, and nominated Brown in December 1890. Three years later Brown returned Jackson's favor by recommending that Harrison appoint him to replace Justice Lucius Q. C. Lamar, who had died.

During his fifteen years on the Court, Brown often took a centrist position, espousing positions generally acceptable in his day. Like the majority of his colleagues, he voted in *Holden v. Hardy* (1898) to uphold states' rights to regulate the working conditions of miners. But he also voted in *Lochner v. New York* (1905) to overturn a state law setting hours for bakers.

In 1890, the same year he was appointed to the Court, Brown suffered an attack of neuritis that left him blind in one eye. Nonetheless, Brown served on the Court until his impaired vision finally forced him to retire in 1906. He died in 1913.

Linda Carol Brown in 1952 at age nine. Her father's suit against the Topeka, Kansas, board of education led to the 1954 decision that integrated the nation's schools.   Source: AP/Wide World Photo

Brown v. Board of Education of Topeka

The Supreme Court in 1954 made a historic decision to prohibit racial SEGREGATION in public schools. The ruling involved five cases in which parents of black children had asked lower courts to order school boards to stop enforcing laws requiring or permitting segregated schools.

Brown v. Board of Education of Topeka was brought in 1951 by Oliver Brown on behalf of his daughter Linda. Topeka had segregated its primary schools under an option permitted by Kansas law. A federal district court found Topeka's segregation detrimental to black children but found no constitutional violation because the black and white primary schools were substantially equal.

The other four cases involved similar challenges from Clarendon County, South Carolina; Prince Edward County, Virginia; New Castle County, Delaware; and the District of Columbia. All five cases were argued before the Court in December 1952. In June 1953 the Court requested reargument and asked the

attorneys specifically to address three main questions: whether the framers of the Fourteenth Amendment intended it to apply to segregation in public schools; whether the Court had the power to abolish segregation if the evidence of intent was inconclusive; and what approach the Court should take to end school segregation if it was found unconstitutional.

The cases were reargued in December 1953, with the new chief justice, Earl Warren, presiding over the Court. Warren had been appointed to succeed Fred M. Vinson, who had died in September.

Warren himself took on the task of writing the Court's opinion. He kept it short—just thirteen paragraphs—and free of accusatory rhetoric. He lobbied the other justices to obtain a unanimous decision with no separate opinions. All nine justices—including Robert H. Jackson, who had left a hospital bed to be present—were in Court on May 17, 1954, when the decision was announced.

Warren quickly disposed of the Court's first question, whether the framers of the Fourteenth Amendment intended it to bar school segregation. The evidence was inconclusive. Instead, Warren considered

On the steps of the U.S. Supreme Court are the NAACP Legal Defense Fund lawyers who argued the school segregation cases that overturned Plessy v. Ferguson *(1896). Fourth from the right is future justice Thurgood Marshall.   Source: NAACP*

the effects of segregation on public education. "Does segregation of children in public schools solely on the basis of race, even though the physical facilities and other 'tangible' factors may be equal, deprive the children of the minority group of equal educational opportunities?" Warren asked. "We believe that it does."

Separating children from others solely because of their race, Warren said, "generates a feeling of inferiority." This rejected part of the rationale for the Court's 1896 decision in PLESSY V. FERGUSON, upholding segregation under the "separate but equal" doctrine. As proof Warren cited, in a famous and controversial footnote, seven sociological studies on the detrimental effects of enforced racial segregation.

Warren then stated: "We conclude that in the field of public education the doctrine of 'separate but equal' has no place. Separate educational facilities are inherently unequal." On that basis he concluded that the plaintiffs had been deprived of the EQUAL PROTECTION of the laws as guaranteed by the Fourteenth Amendment. In the companion case from the District of Columbia, *Bolling v. Sharpe,* Warren reached the same result by reading an equal protection requirement into the Fifth Amendment due process clause.

Warren ended by saying that the Court wanted to hear a new round of arguments before fashioning remedies in the cases. A little over a year later, on May 31, 1955, Warren announced the Court's unanimous opinion in *Brown (II)*. The Court did not draw up specific decrees, require immediate compliance, or set deadlines. Instead, the cases were remanded to lower courts with directions that school officials "make a prompt and reasonable start toward full compliance" with the earlier decision and proceed to desegregate "with all deliberate speed." (See SCHOOL DESEGREGATION)

Burger, Warren E.

The nomination of Warren Earl Burger (1907–   ) to replace Earl Warren as chief justice of the United States signaled a turning point in the Court's history. Under Burger's direction, the Court gradually replaced the liberal, activist approach favored by the Warren Court with a conservative viewpoint that emphasized a narrow reading of the Constitution.

Burger was born in St. Paul, Minnesota. After attending the University of Minnesota, he graduated

presidential nomination in 1952. In 1953 he was appointed assistant attorney general in charge of the Justice Department's civil division. Burger continued in that post until 1956, when President Dwight Eisenhower named him to the U.S. court of appeals for the District of Columbia. On the appeals court, Burger became known as a conservative judge who took an especially hard line in criminal cases. Burger served on the appeals court for thirteen years until President Richard Nixon named him chief justice of the United States in 1969.

The Court's transition from liberalism to conservatism under Burger was gradual. This was primarily because in its early years the Burger Court was still dominated by liberal justices. In the first years after Burger became chief justice the Court upheld the use of several controversial means to remedy school segregation, ruled invalid a state law discriminating against women, and rejected, by a vote of 6 to 3, the Nixon administration's attempt to stop newspapers from publishing the classified Pentagon Papers. The Court also overturned every existing death penalty law, expanded defendants' right to counsel, and ruled that the government could not use electronic surveillance without obtaining a warrant.

The Court's most notable decision in this period came in 1974, when Nixon refused to turn over tapes of White House recordings subpoenaed by the special prosecutor investigating the Watergate scandal. Nixon asserted executive privilege in refusing to give up the tapes. But in a stunning blow that doomed Nixon's chance of remaining in office, the Supreme Court ruled 8–0 that the president had to surrender the tapes. (See EXECUTIVE PRIVILEGE AND IMMUNITY.)

As liberal justices began leaving the Court, Republican presidents replaced them with conservatives. In 1976 the Court upheld some new death penalty laws, allowing executions to resume after a four-year hiatus caused by the 1972 ruling striking down all death penalty laws. The conservative trend continued throughout Burger's tenure as chief justice. He retired in September 1986 to devote full time to directing the national commission on the bicentennial of the U.S. Constitution.

magna cum laude from the St. Paul College of Law (now Mitchell College of Law). For the next twenty-two years he practiced law with a respected Minnesota firm. Burger also taught part time at his alma mater from 1931 to 1948.

In addition to practicing law, Burger became active in Republican party politics. He attracted the attention of national party leaders while working on Harold Stassen's unsuccessful bid for the Republican

Source: Collection of the Supreme Court of the United States

Burton, Harold H.

Democratic president Harry S. Truman came under strong pressure to appoint a Republican to the Supreme Court when Justice Owen Roberts resigned in 1945. Only one Republican served on the Court at the time. Truman improved his standing with Republican congressional leaders by nominating Harold Hitz Burton (1888–1964), a Republican senator from Ohio who became Truman's friend when they were colleagues in the Senate.

Burton was born in Jamaica Plain, Massachusetts. He graduated from Bowdoin College in 1909 and received his law degree from Harvard in 1912. After holding several different jobs in Ohio and Idaho and serving in World War I, Burton went to Cleveland to practice law. He served in the Ohio legislature in 1929 and in that same year was named director of law for Cleveland. Running on a reform platform calling for ridding the city of gangsters, Burton was elected

mayor of Cleveland in 1935. He was twice reelected by the largest majorities in the city's history. In 1941 Burton was elected to the U.S. Senate, and four years later Truman appointed him to the Supreme Court.

Despite his friendship with Truman, Burton was not afraid to vote against the president. On April 8, 1952, the day before a nationwide steel strike was scheduled to begin, Truman ordered the Commerce Department to seize and operate the nation's steel mills. Truman said the order was justified by the need for continued steel production to support U.S. troops fighting in Korea. The steel companies appealed the order all the way to the Supreme Court. On June 2, 1952, the Court ruled 6–3 in *Youngstown Sheet and Tube Co. v. Sawyer* that the president had unconstitutionally overstepped his authority. Burton voted with the majority against the president.

Burton developed Parkinson's disease while serving on the Court, and its progression forced him to retire on October 13, 1958. He died in 1964.

Busing

The use of court-ordered busing to help achieve SCHOOL DESEGREGATION was approved by the Supreme Court in 1971. The ruling aroused strong opposition from many whites and a mixed reaction among African Americans and other minority groups. In later decisions the Court limited the use of busing between cities and suburbs and allowed school districts to be freed of busing orders once the vestiges of legally mandated SEGREGATION had been eliminated.

The school bus had long been a fixture of school systems in rural and urban areas alike. Controversy arose when lower federal courts required school districts to increase the use of busing to transport pupils outside their normal geographic school zones in order to achieve racial balance.

In one case a federal district court ordered extensive busing to desegregate the school system in the Charlotte–Mecklenburg area in North Carolina. The plan required about 42,000 pupils—nearly half the student population—to be bused in an effort to achieve a 71:29 white-black ratio in each school, which would reflect the system's overall white-black ratio.

In *Swann v. Charlotte-Mecklenburg County Board of Education* (1971) the Supreme Court unanimously upheld busing as one of several permissible remedial techniques to help achieve desegregation. Writing for the Court, Chief Justice Warren E. Burger said that objections to busing might be valid "when the time or distance of travel is so great as to either risk the health of the children or significantly impinge on the educational process." But, he continued, "all awkwardness and inconvenience cannot be avoided in the interim period when the remedial adjustments are being made to eliminate the dual school systems."

Three years later, however, in *Milliken v. Bradley* (1974), the Court struck down a lower court's effort to integrate the predominantly black schools in Detroit and the mostly white schools in the adjoining suburbs by requiring busing across district lines. Burger, writing for a 5–4 majority, said that school district boundary lines could be "bridged" only if all the districts had been responsible for fostering school segregation.

The Court's decisions in *Swann* and *Milliken* both relied on the distinction between de jure and de facto segregation. De jure segregation was imposed by law or fostered by official actions, such as the drawing of school zones, while de facto segregation resulted from residential patterns, economic status, or other factors outside the usual scope of the equal protection clause. Courts had power to order the dismantling of de jure segregation, but not of de facto segregation.

In addition, the Court in *Swann* and again in *Pasadena City Board of Education v. Spangler* (1976) emphasized that school systems could not be ordered to make annual adjustments to maintain a specific racial balance once a desegregation plan had been implemented. The effect of the decisions was to reduce the power of lower courts to counteract the effects of "white flight" resulting from court-ordered busing.

Source: *Library of Congress*

Butler, Pierce

Chief Justice William Howard Taft directed a massive campaign to have Minnesota corporate attorney Pierce Butler (1866–1939) appointed to the Supreme Court when Justice William Day retired in 1922.

Butler had impressed Taft when the two men worked on an arbitration in Canada the previous year. Taft, who was trying to create a conservative majority on the Court, also believed that Butler would align himself with the Court's conservative wing. To help secure the nomination for Butler, Taft launched a letter-writing campaign on his behalf and attacked the abilities of other potential nominees. He also obtained endorsements of Butler from the Minnesota congressional delegation, senior officials in the Catholic Church (Butler was a Roman Catholic), and local bar associations around the country. The lobbying effort was successful. President Warren G. Harding nominated Butler, and the Senate confirmed him by a 61–8 vote.

Butler was born in Northfield, Minnesota, and received two undergraduate degrees at Carleton College. He was admitted to the bar in 1888 at age twenty-two after studying law privately. Butler then practiced law and in 1891 was elected assistant attorney of Ramsey County. Two years later he became county attorney. He left that job in 1897 to resume private legal practice. Around 1910 he gained Harding's attention when he was chosen to represent the federal government in a series of antitrust cases. Butler's prosecution of those cases won him high praise from Attorney General George Wickersham.

As Taft had predicted, Butler became solidly aligned with the Court's conservative wing. Butler was a member of the four-justice bloc that consistently voted to overturn President Franklin D. Roosevelt's New Deal programs. He served on the Court for nearly seventeen years until his death in November 1939.

Byrnes, James F.

James Francis Byrnes (1879–1972) served the shortest term on the Supreme Court of any justice. President Franklin D. Roosevelt nominated him for the Court in June 1941, but Byrnes resigned just fifteen months later to become director of the Office of Economic Stabilization during World War II.

Byrnes was born in Charleston, South Carolina. His father died shortly before his birth. At age fourteen Byrnes left school to work as a law clerk in a Charleston firm. In 1900 he was named court reporter for the second circuit of South Carolina in Aiken, and he read law privately. Byrnes passed the bar in 1903, despite never having attended law school. In that same year he bought the Aiken newspaper, the *Journal and Review,* and became its editor. Five years later Byrnes became district attorney for South Carolina's second circuit, and in 1910 he was elected to the U.S. House. While serving seven terms in Congress Byrnes became friends with Roosevelt. Byrnes was elected to the U.S. Senate in 1930, and in 1932 served as a speechwriter and key strategist in

Roosevelt's campaign for the presidency. In later elections Roosevelt twice considered naming Byrnes his running mate, but both times chose other men instead.

Byrnes's appointment to the Supreme Court in 1941 was supposed to be a reward for his loyalty. He quickly grew restless, however, desiring to be actively involved in the war effort. He resigned from the Court in October 1942 to return to the administration as what Roosevelt called "assistant President." Byrnes served as director of the Office of Economic Stabilization from 1942 to 1943 and as director of the Office of War Mobilization the following two years. After Roosevelt died, Byrnes was secretary of state in the Truman administration. In 1950 Byrnes, who supported states' rights and separate-but-equal schools for blacks and whites, was elected governor of South Carolina. He died in 1972.

Source: Library of Congress

C

Calhoun, John C.

John C. Calhoun (1782–1850) of South Carolina was the leading spokesman for the South in the period leading up to the Civil War. A one-time nationalist, he changed his views in 1828 and became an advocate of the theory of nullification, which claimed that individual states had authority to annul any federal act they deemed illegal. Although he later abandoned nullification, Calhoun remained a fierce advocate of states' rights in the Senate until his death.

Calhoun entered the House of Representatives in 1811 as a nationalist, supporting efforts to strengthen the central government. In the House and later as secretary of war under President James Madison, he supported such nationalist programs as the second Bank of the United States, the protective tariff of 1816, and federal aid for internal improvements.

In 1824, Calhoun campaigned as an unabashed nationalist for the presidency. Instead he had to settle for the vice presidency under President John Quincy Adams. He was reelected vice president in 1828, this time under President Andrew Jackson. In the meantime, however, economic problems blamed on high tariffs had turned Calhoun's South Carolina allies into strong advocates of states' rights. Calhoun followed, now denouncing the tariff as unconstitutional and pushing nullification as the remedy.

Calhoun resigned as vice president in 1832 to return to the Senate as champion of his state's effort to nullify a new tariff act. Jackson asked for legislation to reaffirm the president's power to use the military to enforce federal law. Calhoun argued against the bill; after it was passed, South Carolina voted to nullify that act as well.

Calhoun then shifted from nullification to other strategies of sectional resistance to the national government. He became an apologist for slavery and fought efforts to prohibit slavery in new states or in the territories. Although he never favored secession, Calhoun's arguments in 1847 for protecting slavery in the territories deepened sectional divisions over the issue.

In his final speech in the Senate in March 1850—delivered by a colleague because Calhoun was too ill to speak—Calhoun argued against Henry Clay's last compromise to forestall secession. The plan permitted new territories to vote on allowing slavery and strengthened federal law regarding the return of fugitive slaves. Calhoun argued that the plan did not go far enough to restore sectional balance.

Calhoun's posthumous publication, *Discourse on the Constitution*, proposed several constitutional reforms. These included elimination of the Supreme Court's jurisdiction to hear appeals from state courts and creation of a dual executive—elected from the North and the South—each with a veto power.

Campaigns and Elections

Laws regulating political campaigns and elections may involve First Amendment rights to free speech and political association. (See SPEECH, FREEDOM OF; ASSOCIATION, FREEDOM OF.) In a variety of cases since the late 1960s, the Supreme Court has imposed limits on some aspects of campaigns and elections, based on constitutional grounds. These include campaign financing and ballot access.

Campaign Financing

Federal law had limited campaign spending for federal office since 1925. In the wake of the Watergate affair, Congress passed the Federal Election Campaign Amendments of 1974. These revised the limits on campaign spending and individual campaign contributions and established a system of public funding for presidential campaigns.

For many years the Supreme Court had avoided

ruling on the constitutionality of campaign spending limits. But in a challenge to the new law, the Court held that the spending limits infringed on constitutionally protected political speech. "[V]irtually every means of communicating ideas in today's mass society requires the expenditure of money," the Court said in *Buckley v. Valeo* (1976).

The ruling upheld the act's limits on campaign contributions, citing the government's interest in preventing corruption. It specified, however, that the limits could not be applied to a candidate's expenditures from his own funds. The Court also upheld public subsidies for presidential campaigns and said that the spending limits imposed on candidates who accepted public funds were constitutional.

Two years later the Court struck down a state law that forbade corporations to spend money to influence voters' decisions on referendum issues *(First National Bank of Boston v. Bellotti* [1978]). In 1981 the Court struck down a city ordinance setting a $250 limit on an individual's contribution to a group taking a position on a ballot issue *(Citizens Against Rent Control/Coalition for Fair Housing v. City of Berkeley).*

In *Bellotti* the Court said that laws forbidding corporations to contribute to candidates might still be justified in the interest of preventing corruption. On that basis, the Court ruled in *Austin v. Michigan Chamber of Commerce* (1990) that states can bar corporations from spending their own money on political campaigns rather than setting up a political action committee (PAC) for that purpose.

Political Parties

The Supreme Court in 1941 ruled that party primaries for federal office are subject to congressional regulation. That ruling *(United States v. Classic)* reversed a twenty-year-old precedent and permitted Congress to expand federal campaign finance laws to cover primary elections for the House and Senate.

Several rulings in the 1970s and 1980s dealt with the states' power to protect the integrity of the membership rolls and nominating procedures of political parties. The decisions reflected an effort to balance the rights of political parties to run their own affairs and the rights of voters to participate in party nominating decisions.

In one key decision *(Cousins v. Wigoda* [1975]) the Court barred an Illinois state court from stepping into a dispute involving rival sets of delegates to the 1972 Democratic National Convention. The Court also respected the autonomy of political parties in two decisions involving open and closed primaries. (Open primaries are those in which any registered voter can participate, while closed primaries are limited to registered party voters.) A 1981 decision allowed Wisconsin to require an open primary, but said the state could not require the national party to recognize the results. Five years later, the Court held that states could not compel political parties to hold closed primaries; parties could make those decisions themselves.

To protect voters' rights, the Court ruled in 1973 that states cannot impose unreasonable deadlines for party registration to vote in a primary. The case involved a law that forbade voting in a party primary if the voter had participated in a primary of another party within the last twenty-three months. But the next year the Court upheld a state law that banned people from running as independent or new-party candidates unless they had disaffiliated themselves from any other party at least one year before the election.

Regulation of Elections

The right to vote, called suffrage, was originally a matter for the states. It has become nationalized through constitutional amendments, federal legislation, and Supreme Court rulings striking down restrictions on suffrage. (See VOTING RIGHTS.) Beginning in the 1960s, the Court also set some limits on state laws imposing stiff requirements on minor political parties to gain access to the ballot.

In *Williams v. Rhodes* (1968) the Court struck down an Ohio law that effectively kept any minor-party candidates off the ballot. The Court held that the law violated voters' and candidates' rights under the equal protection clause. Since then the Court has treated several other such laws in similar fashion. For example, in 1992 the Court struck down an Illinois law that required a new political party in Chicago to gather 25,000 signatures in both the city and the suburbs in order to place candidates on a countywide ballot.

In two other cases in 1992, however, the Court rejected First Amendment challenges to election laws. The Court upheld a Hawaii law that forbade write-in votes in state elections. It also affirmed a Tennessee statute that prohibited electioneering within 100 feet of the entrance of a polling place.

Campbell, John A.

In the months before the outbreak of the Civil War, Justice John Archibald Campbell (1811–1889), a Georgia native, warned the southern states against dissolving the Union. Campbell opposed secession and thought that slavery would gradually die out if the South were left alone. When the war started, however, Campbell resigned from the Court and returned to the South to serve in the Confederate government.

Campbell was born in Washington, Georgia, and was considered a child prodigy. He enrolled at Franklin College (now the University of Georgia) at

Source: Library of Congress

age eleven, and graduated with first honors three years later. Immediately after graduating from Franklin, he received an appointment to the U.S. Military Academy at West Point. He withdrew after three years to return home to support his family after his father died. When Campbell was eighteen, the Georgia legislature passed a special measure admitting him to the bar.

In 1830 Campbell moved to Alabama to establish his legal practice. He quickly became one of the state's leading lawyers, and his reputation began to spread across the country. Following his election to the Alabama legislature in 1837, Campbell twice declined appointments to the Alabama supreme court.

His nomination to the U.S. Supreme Court was anything but routine. Whig President Millard Fillmore had nominated three different men to replace the late Justice John McKinley, but the Democratic Senate had refused to consider the nominations. That left the nomination to Democrat Franklin Pierce when he took office in March 1853. In an unprecedented move, the Supreme Court justices sent a committee to Pierce to ask that he choose Campbell. Pierce agreed, and Campbell joined the Court in 1853. His opinions addressed a wide variety of issues, including corporate liability and jurisdiction over rivers.

After resigning from the Court in April 1861, Campbell joined the Confederate government as assistant secretary of war in charge of administering the draft law. He remained in the job until the Confederacy fell in 1865. Following a few months of detention by the victorious Union forces, Campbell was freed and returned to New Orleans, where he developed a prosperous law practice. In the quarter-century before his death in 1889, Campbell frequently argued before the Supreme Court.

Capital Punishment

In a stunning and controversial decision, the Supreme Court in 1972 effectively nullified all existing death sentences in the United States. The Court ruled that capital punishment, as permitted by existing laws, violated the Eighth Amendment ban on CRUEL AND UNUSUAL PUNISHMENT. Four years later, however, the Court approved the reinstatement of capital punishment as long as the law guided the discretion of the sentencing judge or jury in choosing between a death sentence or prison term. Since then the Court has rejected most broad challenges to death penalty procedures and has shown increasing impatience with repeated legal challenges brought by death row inmates.

History of the Death Penalty

The Constitution recognizes capital punishment. The Fifth Amendment refers to "capital" crimes, bars double jeopardy "for life or limb," and requires due process before depriving anyone of "life, liberty, or property."

For most of U.S. history, courts imposed virtually no constitutional restraints on death penalty cases. The Supreme Court in 1890 upheld electrocution as a method of execution. In 1947 the Court permitted the execution of a Louisiana man after the state's first attempt to electrocute him failed.

During the nineteenth century, states began to adopt discretionary death penalty laws in place of laws that automatically imposed the death penalty. By the mid-twentieth century, many critics were complaining that such unguided discretion led to virtually random imposition of the death penalty—random, that is, except for the disproportionate number of black men given death sentences. But the Supreme Court in 1971 held, by a vote of 6 to 3, that such "untrammeled discretion" did not violate the due process clause of the Fourteenth Amendment.

The next year, however, the Court effectively reversed itself in a challenge brought under the Eighth Amendment. In *Furman v. Georgia* (1972) the Court voted 5–4 to invalidate all existing death penalty statutes. Each of the five justices in the majority wrote a separate opinion. Two—William J. Brennan, Jr., and Thurgood Marshall—said they considered the death penalty cruel and unusual punishment in all circumstances. The other three objected to the way capital punishment was being applied. William O. Douglas

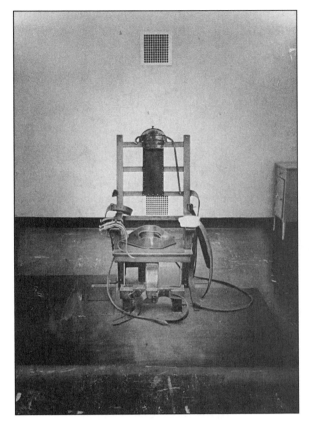

This electric chair once was used to carry out death sentences in Washington, D.C.   Copyright Washington Post; Reprinted by permission of the District of Columbia Public Library

found its operation "pregnant with discrimination." Potter Stewart said it was "so wantonly and so freakishly imposed." Byron R. White said it was carried out so rarely that it was "pointless and needless."

The four dissenting justices said that repealing capital punishment was a matter for state legislatures, not for the Court.

Mandatory and Discretionary Laws

States responded by reenacting death penalty laws. Ten sought to comply with *Furman* by making death the mandatory punishment for specified crimes. Twenty-five adopted discretionary statutes.

These laws provided for a separate death penalty hearing after conviction and typically listed specific aggravating and mitigating circumstances for the jury to weigh in choosing the sentence.

Challenges to both types of statutes reached the Court in 1976. Three justices—Stewart, Lewis F. Powell, Jr., and John Paul Stevens—provided the swing votes in upholding the discretionary death penalty laws and striking down the mandatory statutes.

In *Gregg v. Georgia* Stewart wrote the Court's opinion upholding the discretionary sentencing scheme. He wrote that "[n]o longer can a jury wantonly and freakishly impose the death sentence; it is always circumscribed by the legislative guidelines." Only Brennan and Marshall dissented.

In *Woodson v. North Carolina,* however, a 5–4 majority ruled that mandatory death penalty statutes do violate the Eighth Amendment. Individual consideration of the defendant's character and record and the circumstances of the particular offense, the justices said, was "a constitutionally indispensable part of the process of inflicting the penalty of death."

The Court has decided a steady stream of death penalty cases ever since. In these cases it has rejected broad-based challenges while occasionally tightening death penalty laws or sentencing procedures. A 1977 decision barred the death penalty for rape and, by implication, for any offense other than murder. The Court has forbidden mandatory death sentences for specific offenses, such as killing a police officer or a fellow prison inmate. It has allowed the death penalty for an accomplice to a felony murder only if the accomplice was a major participant in the crime and displayed "reckless indifference" to the value of human life. The Court has blocked the execution of people for crimes committed when they were under sixteen or of those who are insane and cannot understand the reason for their execution.

Challenges

The two broadest challenges to the use of the death penalty both failed. In *Pulley v. Harris* (1984) the Court held, in a 7–2 vote, that states need not ensure that any death sentence is proportional to the punishment imposed on others convicted of similar crimes. The case of *McCleskey v. Kemp* (1987) addressed the dispro-portionate imposition of the death penalty in cases where the victims were white. The Court ruled, 5–4, that this did not require striking down state death penalty laws.

In 1991 the Court reversed a 1987 decision that had been one of the few victories for death penalty opponents. In *Payne v. Tennessee* the Court permitted use of so-called victim impact statements during sentencing hearings for the death penalty.

The Court has shown impatience with death penalty challenges in other ways. In 1991 it used two death penalty cases to place new limits on HABEAS CORPUS. In 1993 it ruled that a death row inmate ordinarily is not entitled to a federal court hearing on a claim of innocence unless he also has an independent claim of constitutional error in his trial or other state court proceedings.

Brennan's and Marshall's retirements in 1990 and 1991 left the Court with no consistent opponent of capital punishment. In February 1994, Justice Harry A. Blackmun declared in a highly personal 7,000-word statement that he would no longer vote to uphold death sentences. Blackmun, who retired at the end of the 1993–1994 term, said it had proved impossible to administer capital punishment fairly and consistently. No other justice joined Blackmun's statement.

Cardozo, Benjamin N.

When Justice Oliver Wendell Holmes, Jr., retired in 1932, newspapers, legal scholars, and political leaders agreed almost unanimously that New York judge Benjamin Nathan Cardozo (1870–1938) should be appointed to replace him. President Herbert Hoover was less sure, however. Cardozo was a Jew from New York, and the Court already had two justices from New York and one Jew. Justice Harlan Fiske Stone, a New Yorker, thought so highly of Cardozo that he offered to resign to make a place for him. Hoover declined the offer but finally appointed Cardozo.

Cardozo was born in New York City. He received his undergraduate and master's degrees from Columbia University and studied at the Columbia Law

Source: Collection of the Supreme Court of the United States

School in 1891 without obtaining a degree. He was admitted to the bar that same year, after which he started practicing appellate law with his older brother. Cardozo practiced privately for twenty-three years before being elected to the New York supreme court in 1914. After serving very briefly, Cardozo was appointed to the New York court of appeals. Elevated to chief judge in 1926, Cardozo helped the court win a reputation as the top state court in the nation. He also wrote extensively on the law and developed a national reputation as a legal scholar.

Once appointed to the Supreme Court in 1932, Cardozo aligned himself with the Court's liberal wing on most issues. He consistently voted with this wing to uphold President Franklin D. Roosevelt's New Deal programs. Cardozo was also the first justice to express the view that First Amendment rights should have priority when balanced against competing rights and interests. In *Palko v. Connecticut* (1937) Cardozo wrote that freedom of "thought and speech . . . is the matrix, the indispensable condition, of nearly every other form of freedom." Thus, First Amendment rights were on a "different plane of social and moral values" than other rights protected by the Bill of Rights. The Court echoed this view in many later decisions. Following a long illness, Cardozo died in 1938 after serving six years on the Court.

Case Law

Case law is simply the law as found in previous cases—that is, the body of decisions written and developed by judges in the course of ruling on particular cases.

Case law is a fundamental element of the English and American COMMON LAW systems. It distinguishes them from so-called civil law systems, which set out basic law in statutory codes rather than court decisions. This reliance on judicial decisions helps make the law both stable and dynamic.

A judge is supposed to decide a particular dispute according to a general rule that covers a whole class of similar disputes. The rule is to be found in a previous case that serves as a PRECEDENT for deciding the new dispute. The new ruling in turn will serve as a binding precedent for judges to follow in deciding similar cases in the future.

At the same time the ability—indeed, the necessity—to adapt and apply precedents to new situations means that the law is constantly changing. Further, courts are only required to follow the central "holding" of a case—the rule of law that was necessary for the decision. Other statements, called dicta, are viewed as not binding. (See OBITER DICTUM.) But often the holding of a case can be stated in any of several ways.

The Supreme Court follows this method. Any decision by the Court—whether it involves a constitutional, statutory, or regulatory issue—relies heavily on the citation of previous cases as legal authority for the ruling. But the Court also reshapes the previous cases and, in doing so, may have considerable leeway in deciding what cases to follow and how to apply them to the new legal issue. Sometimes the Court goes so far as to overturn a prior ruling, establishing a new rule that will supposedly be a binding precedent for future cases. (See REVERSALS OF EARLIER RULINGS.)

The Court has particularly broad discretion in using this case law process in constitutional law. As a result, many precedent-setting constitutional rulings take seemingly erratic paths in later decisions. For example, the Court's 1964 decision to give constitutional protections to defendants in libel suits brought by public officials *(New York Times Co. v. Sullivan)* was applied in 1968 to suits brought by "public figures" as well. In 1974, however, the Court said the same protections did not apply to suits brought by "private figures." In later decisions the Court narrowed the definition of a public figure for purposes of deciding which rule to apply.

Another example is the Burger Court's abortion rights ruling, *Roe v. Wade* (1973). The decision was expanded over the next decade to invalidate some newly enacted restrictions on abortion procedures. At the same time the Court upheld federal and state laws that barred poor women from receiving Medicaid funds to pay for an abortion. Then in 1992 the Court shifted its position and overruled two of its earlier rulings to uphold restrictions much the same as those it had once struck down. At the same time the Court said it was reaffirming *Roe's* "core holding."

These twists and turns in constitutional law have led some people to believe that the justices decide cases on the basis of their personal and political views rather than on the basis of the law. The criticism has some truth but is overstated. The justices' legal views shape their decision making, but those views may not correspond to their personal convictions. For example, three justices—Harry A. Blackmun, Lewis F. Powell, Jr., and Potter Stewart—all voted to uphold capital punishment despite their personal opposition to the death penalty.

The case law process is one of the sources of discipline for the justices. When applying a precedent, a justice must explain and justify the decision in legal terms for it to command the support of other members of the Court. Most justices accept the view that a departure from precedent requires some special justification. At the same time, the case law process allows the justices to take account of new circumstances and evolving standards to adapt the laws to the needs of an ever-changing society.

Case or Controversy Rule

The single most basic restriction on the work of the federal courts is the requirement that they decide only "cases or controversies."

Article III of the Constitution states that federal judicial power extends to specified types of "cases" and "controversies," using the two terms interchangeably. (See JURISDICTION.) The Supreme Court has interpreted the words to limit federal courts to resolving disputes between adversary parties whose legal rights and interests are truly in collision, a collision for which federal courts may be able to impose a remedy.

The rule has practical value for the courts. It limits possible federal caseloads and helps protect judicial power by confining its exercise to true legal disputes. It also aids courts in making decisions by ensuring that parties with opposing interests have an incentive to frame their disputes in concrete terms and to present arguments exploring all aspects of the situation.

One of the earliest corollaries developed by the Supreme Court from the case or controversy rule was its decision that neither it nor lower federal courts would give advisory opinions.

In 1793 the justices declined to answer a set of questions submitted to them by Secretary of State Thomas Jefferson on behalf of President George Washington concerning neutrality and the interpretation of several major treaties with Britain and France. The Court indicated in correspondence that it found issuing advisory opinions contrary to the constitutional principle of SEPARATION OF POWERS.

More than a century later, the Court reaffirmed this stance by rejecting a congressionally authorized test case to determine the constitutionality of certain laws Congress had passed concerning Indian lands. When the case, *Muskrat v. United States,* reached the Court in 1911, the Court dismissed it on the ground that no actual dispute existed. All parties in the case were in reality working together to ascertain the constitutionality of the law and not attempting to resolve any actual conflict between legal rights or concrete interests.

Declaratory Judgments

In the early twentieth century state courts began to use declaratory judgments, rulings in which a court simply declares conclusively the rights and obligations of the parties in dispute. One of the main questions raised was whether the case or controversy rule allowed the use of this new remedy by the federal courts. In 1928 the Supreme Court seemed to say no. But five years later, in an apparent change of mind, the Court took jurisdiction over just such a case.

Congress then passed the Federal Declaratory Judgment Act of 1934, specifically authorizing federal courts to issue such judgments in "cases of actual controversy." The Supreme Court unanimously upheld the constitutionality of the law three years later. Writing for the Court in *Aetna Life Insurance Co. v. Haworth* (1937), Chief Justice Charles Evans Hughes said the act simply provided a new remedy for the courts to use in cases already within their jurisdiction.

Later rulings made clear that federal courts have broad discretion in deciding whether to grant requests for declaratory judgments. "The Declaratory Judgment Act was an authorization, not a command," the Court stated in 1962. "It gave the federal courts competence to make a declaration of rights; it did not impose a duty to do so."

Source: Collection of the Supreme Court of the United States

Catron, John

On March 3, 1837, President Andrew Jackson's last day in office, Congress voted to expand the Supreme Court from seven to nine justices. Jackson lost no time in nominating John Catron (c. 1786–1865) of Nashville to fill one of the two new seats.

Details about Catron's early life are sketchy. It is believed that he was born about 1786 to a poor Pennsylvania family and was self-educated. He moved to Tennessee in 1812, fought under Jackson in the War of 1812, and joined the bar in 1815. In 1818 he moved to Nashville and pursued a specialty in land law.

When the Tennessee legislature added a seat to the state's highest court in 1824, Catron was elected to fill the position. He rose to become chief justice in 1831. Three years later he was forced to resign when a judicial reorganization abolished the court. Catron resumed his private legal practice after leaving the court and also became heavily involved in politics. In 1836 he served as Tennessee campaign manager for Martin Van Buren's presidential campaign.

After joining the Supreme Court in 1837, Catron supported states' rights and joined the majority in the Dred Scott decision. When the Civil War broke out, Catron threw his support to the Union and was forced to flee Nashville after Tennessee seceded. Catron returned home, where he was holding circuit court, when the war ended. His health was failing, however, and he died in May 1865, only a few weeks after returning to Nashville. Catron's seat was abolished after his death when Congress reduced the size of the Court.

Certiorari

A writ of certiorari is an order from a higher court directing a lower court to transmit the record of a case for review in the higher court. The vast majority of cases that reach the Supreme Court do so by this discretionary method of review.

The party filing a petition for a writ of certiorari in the Supreme Court is called the PETITIONER. The opposing party is called the RESPONDENT. Occasionally, both parties in a case may file petitions for certiorari asking the justices to review separate portions of a lower court's ruling.

The Court receives about 5,000 petitions for certiorari each year. However, the justices decide to hear only a small fraction of those cases—around 150 or so. Under the so-called rule of four, the votes of four justices are required to grant a petition of certiorari. In other words, a minority of justices can decide to hear a case, even though they may not have the votes to prevail.

The certiorari process involves both legal and political factors. By choosing which cases it will and will not review, the Court sets its own agenda. While some cases may be too important for the Court to ignore, the justices are generally free to decide whether or not to take on an issue.

For example, in recent years the justices appear to have deliberately ducked the issue of gay rights. This may have been because the justices most interested in the issue feared the Court would reject their views. When the Court finally agreed to hear one such case, it voted 5–4 in 1986 to uphold state criminal laws against homosexual behavior.

The Court's rules specify that it will grant certiorari only when there are "special and important reasons" for it to hear a case. The rules describe some of the circumstances the Court considers in deciding whether to accept a case for review:

– A conflict on an issue of federal law between different federal appeals courts, between different state courts, or between a federal appeals court and a state court.

– A ruling that "so far depart[s] from the accepted and usual course of judicial proceedings . . . as to call for an exercise of this Court's power of supervision."

– A ruling by a state court or a federal appeals court on "an important question of federal law which has not been, but should be, settled by this Court."

A petition for certiorari begins with a statement of the "question(s) presented" by the case. It includes a brief description of the case and a section listing the reasons why the Court should grant certiorari.

"A petition for certiorari should explain why it is vital that the question involved be decided finally by the Supreme Court," Chief Justice Fred M. Vinson once said. "If it only succeeds in demonstrating that the decision below may be erroneous, it has not fulfilled its purpose."

At the time of the filing, the petitioner pays a $200 fee for docketing the case. If the petition is granted, the petitioner pays an additional $100 fee. The U.S. government does not have to pay these fees. Someone who is too poor to afford the fees does not have to pay them either, but can file a petition *in forma pauperis* (in the character of a pauper).

Each justice, aided by his or her law clerks, is responsible for reviewing all the cases on the dockets. In recent years, some justices have used a "cert pool" system in which their clerks work together to examine cases and write a single memo for all the justices participating in the pool.

The decisions to grant or deny review of cases are made in CONFERENCES. A few days before a conference convenes, the chief justice compiles a "discuss list"—a list of cases deemed important enough for discussion and a vote. As many as three-fourths of the petitions for certiorari are denied a place on the list. This means that those petitions are rejected without further consideration. Any justice can ensure that a case is placed on the discuss list simply by requesting that it be listed.

The Court announces its decisions on petitions for certiorari in an orders list released in open court every

Monday the Court is in session. The Court has emphasized that its refusal to hear a case should not be taken as a decision on the merits of the case. Very occasionally, one or more justices may file a dissent from a denial of certiorari, explaining why they believe the case should have been accepted for review.

Recent research, including off-the-record interviews with several justices, has indicated some of the factors that influence the justices in deciding which cases the Court should hear. In addition to the importance of the legal issue, the justices may consider whether the issue needs to "percolate" more in lower courts and whether the case presents a "good vehicle" for deciding the issue. A justice sometimes may also consider whether the Court is likely to decide the case in line with his or her views.

Occasionally, after hearing oral argument in a case, the Court concludes for one reason or another that it should not have taken the case for review. For instance, a procedural problem may be discovered that would ordinarily preclude the Court from taking jurisdiction of the case. The Court then issues an order "dismissing the petition for certiorari as improvidently granted."

Source: Collection of the Supreme Court of the United States

Chase, Salmon P.

Chief Justice Salmon Portland Chase (1808–1873) is perhaps best known for presiding over the impeachment trial of President Andrew Johnson in 1868. Republican Radicals wanted a quick conviction, but Chase insisted that proper legal procedures be followed. His steadiness may have saved Johnson from impeachment.

Nine years after Chase's birth in Cornish, New Hampshire, his father died. Chase was then sent to Ohio to live with his uncle, Philander Chase, who soon became the Protestant Episcopal bishop of Ohio. Chase graduated from Dartmouth College in 1826, after which he moved to Washington, D.C., and opened a private school. He also studied law under Attorney General William Wirt. After being admitted to the bar in 1829, Chase moved to Cincinnati to practice law.

Chase strongly opposed slavery. In 1849 he was elected to the U.S. Senate, where he joined other leading abolitionists, such as William Seward and Benjamin Wade. After serving one term in the Senate, Chase was elected governor of Ohio in 1855 and reelected in 1857. He was elected to the Senate again in 1861, but resigned after only two days to become secretary of the treasury in Abraham Lincoln's cabinet. Friend and foe alike praised Chase's skill in running the Treasury Department during the Civil War. Chase disagreed with many of Lincoln's policies, however, and allowed an anti-Lincoln group within the Republican party to bandy about his name as a possible replacement for Lincoln on the Republican ticket in 1864. Nothing came of the effort, but Chase and Lincoln continued to quarrel. Chase resigned in the summer of 1864.

Chief Justice Roger Taney died only a few months later. Lincoln, who had great respect for Chase's abilities, nominated him despite their past differences. The Republicans also were eager to have a chief justice who would uphold the administration's extraordinary Civil War measures. In fact, Chase wrote a majority opinion in the *Legal Tender Cases* that declared unconstitutional his own work as secretary of the treasury in issuing paper currency.

Chase, who had harbored presidential ambitions for years, tried to get candidacies off the ground in both 1868 and 1872. The efforts were unsuccessful. Chase continued serving as chief justice until his death in 1873.

Chase, Samuel

Samuel Chase (1741–1811), a radical Federalist who openly pushed his political views while serving as a Supreme Court justice, survived an attempt to remove him through impeachment in 1804.

Chase was born in Somerset County, Maryland, and was admitted to the bar in 1761. Just three years later he became a member of the Maryland general assembly, where he developed a fiery reputation. A member of the "Sons of Liberty," Chase openly opposed the policies of the British-appointed governor of the colony and took part in rowdy demonstrations. His activities caused the Annapolis mayor and aldermen to call him a "busy, restless incendiary, a ringleader of mobs, a foul-mouthed and inflaming son of discord."

Chase served on thirty committees of the Continental Congress in 1778. In that same year, however, it was learned that he had attempted to corner the flour market through speculation. The revelation led to his dismissal from the Maryland delegation to the Continental Congress for two years. While Chase strongly supported the Declaration of Independence, he opposed the new Constitution. Chase contended that the Constitution would create an elitist government far removed from the people. Using the pen name Caution, he wrote a series of articles opposing ratification.

Source: National Portrait Gallery, Smithsonian Institution

Chase became a judge of the Baltimore criminal court in 1788. Only one year later, a string of business failures forced him to declare personal bankruptcy. In 1791 he became chief judge of the general court of Maryland, a post he held simultaneously with his position on the Baltimore criminal court. The Maryland assembly objected to Chase holding both posts, but a vote to strip him of all public offices failed. Chase was an unpopular judge. He was abusive and overbearing, although no one doubted his legal ability and integrity.

President George Washington appointed Chase to the Supreme Court in January 1796. His first opinion, in *Ware v. Hylton* (1796), held that treaties overruled state laws that contradicted them. The ruling struck down a Virginia law that violated the Treaty of Paris. In *Calder v. Bull* (1798), he wrote a definition of ex post facto laws that still stands today.

Chase became known for using his position to advance Federalist positions. He pushed for prosecution of Republican newspaper editors who opposed the Federalists, worked actively for passage of the Alien and Sedition Acts, and openly campaigned for President Adams's reelection in 1800.

The last straw for Chase's political opponents came when he denounced democratic "mobocracy" in a stormy speech to a grand jury in May 1803. Ten months later the House impeached him. At his Senate trial, Chase's attorney argued that the justice had not committed any indictable offense and thus could not be removed. The senators agreed and acquitted Chase of all eight charges. Chase withdrew from the public spotlight and thereafter was often too ill to attend Court sessions. He died in 1811.

Chief Justice

The office of chief justice of the United States is considered by many to be one of the most prestigious positions in the world. Its prestige has come in large part through the leadership and initiative of those who have held the job. So far, there have been sixteen chief justices, all of them men. (See BACKGROUND OF JUSTICES.)

In the very early years of the Supreme Court there was little indication that the title of chief justice would become so important. The Constitution mentions the position only once, in the article on impeachment of the president: "When the President of the United States is tried, the Chief Justice shall preside." The Judiciary Act of 1789, which established the Supreme Court, specified only "[t]hat the supreme court of the United States shall consist of a chief justice and five associate justices."

Yet because of tradition, popular perception of the office, and other intangible factors, the chief justice is widely perceived to be more than the first among equals.

Like the associate justices, the chief justice is appointed for life. Also like the associate justices, he casts

The mahogany bench of the Supreme Court was changed in 1972 from a straight-line design to a "winged" shape to improve sight lines and hearing. The chief justice occupies the center chair, with the associate justices seated to the left and right in order of seniority. The chairs vary according to each justice's height.   Source: Lee Troell Anderson

Chief Justices of the United States

Name	Years Served	Appointed by	Home State
John Jay	1789–1795	Washington	New York
John Rutledge	1795*	Washington	South Carolina
Oliver Ellsworth	1796–1800	Washington	Connecticut
John Marshall	1801–1835	Adams	Virginia
Roger B. Taney	1836–1864	Jackson	Maryland
Salmon P. Chase	1864–1873	Lincoln	Ohio
Morrison R. Waite	1874–1888	Grant	Ohio
Melville W. Fuller	1888–1910	Cleveland	Illinois
Edward D. White	1910–1921	Taft	Louisiana
William Howard Taft	1921–1930	Harding	Ohio
Charles Evans Hughes	1930–1941	Hoover	New York
Harlan Fiske Stone	1941–1946	Roosevelt	New York
Fred M. Vinson	1946–1953	Truman	Kentucky
Earl Warren	1953–1969**	Eisenhower	California
Warren E. Burger	1969–1986	Nixon	Minnesota
William H. Rehnquist	1986–	Reagan	Arizona

*Rutledge accepted a recess appointment and presided over the Court at its August 1795 term, at which two cases were decided. In December 1795, however, the Senate refused, 10–14, to confirm him.

**Warren accepted a recess appointment as chief justice in September 1953 and was confirmed by the Senate in March 1954.

only one vote in accepting and deciding cases. However, the chief justice presides over the Court at its public sessions and in its closed conferences. The chief justice also assigns the writing of opinions in cases in which he has voted with the majority. (See ASSIGNING OPINIONS.) One of his most important tasks is to decide which cases to put on the "discuss list" for each conference. Cases that are not put on the discuss list are automatically denied review by the Supreme Court. (Any associate justice may request that a petition for review be added to the list.)

Other Duties

In addition to his judicial duties on the Supreme Court, the chief justice has several other ceremonial and nonjudicial duties. One of these occurs every four years when he administers the oath of office to the president.

The chief justice also serves as chairman of the Judicial Conference of the United States and as chairman of the board of the FEDERAL JUDICIAL CENTER. (See JUDICIAL CONFERENCE, U.S.) In addition, he supervises the ADMINISTRATIVE OFFICE OF THE U.S. COURTS. Chief Justice Warren E. Burger estimated that he spent about a third of his time on administrative tasks that did not directly involve other justices. His successor, William H. Rehnquist, is less interested in administrative matters and does not spend quite so much time on them as Burger did.

Congress has given chief justices numerous extrajudicial tasks. For example, it has made the chief justice a member of the board of regents of the Smithsonian Institution and a member of the board of trustees of the National Gallery of Art and of the Joseph H. Hirshhorn Museum and Sculpture Garden.

In addition, some chief justices have voluntarily assumed nonjudicial roles that have engendered some controversy. (See EXTRAJUDICIAL ACTIVITIES.)

One reason why chief justices have taken on nonjudicial tasks may be that so many chief justices have been prominent in politics and retained an activist political temperament upon assuming command of the Supreme Court. John Marshall, Roger B. Taney, Salmon P. Chase, Charles Evans Hughes, Harlan Fiske Stone, and Fred M. Vinson had all been cabinet members. William Howard Taft had been president. Edward D. White had been a U.S. senator, and Earl Warren a governor. In fact, only four chief justices have come more or less directly from the bar: Morrison R. Waite, Melville W. Fuller, Warren E. Burger, and William H. Rehnquist.

First among Equals

The first three chief justices were not held in especially high esteem. The first, John Jay, came to the Court in 1789 and resigned six years later, in 1785, after having concluded a peace treaty with England and having been elected governor of New York.

His successor, John Rutledge, had been appointed an associate justice in 1790 but resigned the following year to become the chief justice of South Carolina. After Jay's resignation as chief justice, Rutledge volunteered for the post, and President George Washington accepted the offer. Rutledge was sworn in as a recess appointment on August 12, 1795.

While Congress was still in recess, reports of Rutledge's earlier criticism of the peace treaty Jay had negotiated provoked a storm of controversy. There were also persistent rumors that Rutledge was mentally unbalanced. When the Senate came back into session in December, it refused to confirm Rutledge, rejecting his nomination by a vote of 14 to 10.

Washington next offered the chief justiceship to Henry Clay, but Clay declined the offer, as did Justice William Cushing. Washington then nominated Oliver Ellsworth, who served from 1796 until he resigned in 1800.

President John Adams named Jay to succeed Ellsworth, but Jay refused to return to his old post, largely because of the onerous circuit duties imposed upon the justices. (See CIRCUIT RIDING.) Adams

then made a fateful choice and named his secretary of state, John Marshall.

John Marshall

Marshall's legal training was meager. He had little experience in the practice of law and none as a judge. Before his appointment as chief justice, however, Marshall had been a politician and diplomat. The skills he gained from these posts characterized his tenure on the Court. For three decades Marshall dominated the Court and the men who served with him as no other chief justice has ever done. Under his leadership the Court handed down dozens of rulings interpreting the Constitution that still stand today.

The most famous decision of the Marshall era was MARBURY V. MADISON, which established the Court's power to review and nullify acts of Congress. Later rulings also affirmed the Court's power to review state court decisions. With its decisions in MCCULLOCH V. MARYLAND and GIBBONS V. OGDEN, the Marshall Court moved boldly toward establishing national power and national supremacy over the individual states.

Perhaps Marshall's greatest achievement, however, was to increase public respect for the Supreme Court. When he became chief justice in 1801 the Court was held in low esteem. Its rulings, embodied in often unclear and confusing seriatim opinions (in which each justice commented on the case in series), did little to enhance the prestige of the third branch of government.

By his insistence on unanimity and the avoidance of dissenting and concurring opinions, Marshall gave the Court the authoritative voice it needed to deal effectively with many of the conflicts and controversies facing the country.

Two chief justices in the twentieth century, Charles Evans Hughes and Earl Warren, are frequently grouped with Marshall as the greatest chief justices the Court has had.

Charles Evans Hughes

Hughes served as an associate justice from 1910 to 1916 under the often indecisive chief justice Edward D. White. Hughes then resigned from the Court to run for the presidency in 1916, in an unsuccessful bid against Woodrow Wilson. In 1930 President Herbert Hoover named him to replace retiring chief justice William Howard Taft.

During his years as an associate justice, Hughes had become acutely aware of the need for leadership by a chief justice in conference discussions and in the assignment of opinions. He also had come to appreciate the value of harmony among the justices, who by now numbered nine.

As chief justice, Hughes became known for the conciseness and clarity with which he was able to summarize the essential points of a case and for the consideration he showed others. During oral arguments counsel who were nervous or long-winded were often saved by a simple question from Hughes that sought to clarify or rephrase arguments they had presented poorly.

In assigning opinions Hughes tried to avoid extreme points of view and let the centrist position prevail. If a conservative justice voted with the majority on the liberal side of an issue, Hughes would often assign the opinion to that justice. He would do the same if a liberal voted with a majority on the conservative side.

Hughes was extremely considerate of the other justices. The Court at that time held Saturday CONFERENCES, and Hughes ordinarily had the opinion-writing assignment delivered to the appropriate justice later that day. Knowing that Justice Benjamin N. Cardozo, who had had a heart attack before coming to the Court in 1932, would begin working on an assignment as soon as he received it, Hughes had Cardozo's assignments delivered on Sunday. So that Cardozo would not be aware of this special treatment, Hughes also delayed delivering assignments to Justice Willis Van Devanter, who lived in the same apartment house as Cardozo.

Earl Warren

Perhaps the most controversial of modern chief justices was former California governor Earl Warren. Good-natured and affable, Warren was not a particularly brilliant scholar or lawyer, but he was a hard worker. His sense of self-command and sensitivity to others, combined with a low-key persuasiveness, made him an exceptional leader.

Warren was named chief justice by President Dwight Eisenhower in October 1953 and was unanimously confirmed by the Senate in March 1954. Little more than two months later, a unanimous Court declared that school desegregation was unconstitutional. This decision in *BROWN V. BOARD OF EDUCATION OF TOPEKA* and many later rulings of the Warren era expanded the rights of blacks, criminals, and the underprivileged. They also aroused strong protest from those who feared the results of the social reforms to which these decisions led.

Despite his amiable relationships with his fellow justices, Warren could show a sterner side. On two occasions in early 1961, Warren publicly rebuked Justice Felix Frankfurter for expanding his written opinion as he announced it in open court and for lecturing the other justices when he delivered a dissenting opinion. Such rebukes were only the superficial signs of the deep differences between the two men concerning the proper posture for the Court. Warren espoused JUDICIAL ACTIVISM, while Frankfurter favored JUDICIAL RESTRAINT.

William Howard Taft

Although he is not usually ranked with Marshall, Hughes, and Warren, Chief Justice William Howard Taft is notable for his contributions to the Court as an administrator rather than as a judge or legal scholar.

The only chief justice to have served as president, Taft came to the Court in 1921 and immediately embarked on efforts to modernize the U.S. judicial system. A year after his appointment, Taft succeeded in persuading Congress to establish the Judicial Conference of the United States, the governing body for the administration of the federal judicial system.

More important to the Supreme Court was Taft's work in convincing Congress to enact the Judiciary Act of 1925. That law gave the Court—then laboring under a huge backlog of cases—almost unlimited discretion in deciding which cases to accept for review. As a result the caseload, at least for a time, became more manageable, and the Court was able to devote more time and energy to constitutional issues and important questions of federal law.

Child Labor

Until the twentieth century, children were often put to work at a young age. The abolition of child labor was a major goal of social reformers in the early decades of the twentieth century. Twice Congress passed laws aimed at keeping children out of mines and factories, only to see the laws struck down by a conservative Supreme Court. An effort to overturn the Court rulings by constitutional amendment failed. Then in 1941 the Court overruled its own precedent and upheld Congress's latest attempt to achieve the goal.

The first child labor act was passed in 1916. It prohibited the shipment in interstate commerce of any products made in factories or mines that employed children under age fourteen or that allowed children aged fourteen to sixteen to work more than a limited number of hours per week. The act was crafted to fall within an emerging Supreme Court doctrine that recognized a federal police power, tied to the commerce power, to bar harmful goods and services from interstate commerce.

The statute was contested by Roland Dagenhart, whose two teenage sons worked in a North Carolina cotton mill. Dagenhart sought an injunction against U.S. District Attorney W. C. Hammer to prevent him from enforcing the act.

By a 5–4 vote, the Court in *Hammer v. Dagenhart* (1918) declared the law unconstitutional. The majority opinion by Justice William R. Day distinguished the 1916 act from earlier police power statutes by noting that the earlier laws had prohibited goods that were inherently harmful, such as diseased cattle, lottery tickets, and impure food. Goods manufactured

Repeated attempts by Congress to curb child labor by taxing the products were rebuffed by the Supreme Court.   Source: Library of Congress

with child labor, Day said, "are of themselves harmless."

Day also renewed a distinction between commerce, which was subject to federal regulation, and production, which could be regulated only by the states. The act, he said, "exerts a power as to a purely local matter to which the federal authority does not extend."

In a dissenting opinion, Justice Oliver Wendell Holmes maintained that the act clearly lay within the federal commerce power and was no less constitutional because of its "indirect effects" of discouraging child labor. It did not matter, he added, that the evil that Congress sought to prevent was not the transportation of the goods, as long as Congress believed transportation "encourages the evil."

Holmes left little doubt that he believed the majority had been motivated by the five justices' personal opposition to the law. It was up to Congress, not the Court, to determine when effective regulation required prohibition, he said. In an often quoted line, Holmes added that "if there is any matter upon which civilized countries have agreed . . . it is the evil of premature and excessive child labor."

Congress in 1919 tried to circumvent the *Dagenhart* ruling by imposing a 10 percent tax on the net profits of any company that employed children under fourteen, or had children fourteen to sixteen work for more than specified time periods. Again the law was crafted to fall within Supreme Court precedents. But again the Court struck down the law.

Writing for the eight-justice majority in *Bailey v. Drexel Furniture Co.* (1922), Chief Justice William Howard Taft said the tax was a penalty intended to coerce employers to end their use of child labor. Taft said that just as use of the commerce power to regulate wholly internal matters of the states was invalid, so was use of the taxing power to achieve the same purpose. "To give such magic to the word 'tax' would be to break down all constitutional limitation of the powers of Congress," he said.

The Court did not adhere to the doctrines it used in striking down the two acts. Despite *Dagenhart,* the justices continued over the next two decades to sanction use of the commerce power as a police tool when

it was applied to universally recognized social evils. The Court followed the *Bailey* precedent in several cases striking down tax penalty schemes, including major New Deal acts to regulate agriculture and the coal industry. But in 1937 the Court abandoned this line of cases to uphold the National Firearms Act, which taxed certain firearms manufacturers and dealers in an effort to discourage sales of weapons likely to be used by criminals.

In 1924 Congress had approved a proposed constitutional amendment to give it the power to regulate child labor. Opposed by manufacturers and farm groups, the amendment won ratification from only twenty-eight of the thirty-six states needed for final approval.

In 1937, however, the Court signaled a shift in philosophy by approving a major New Deal labor enactment, the National Labor Relations Act. Congress quickly took advantage of the shift by passing the Fair Labor Standards Act (1938), which included wage and hours provisions and a child labor provision almost identical to the one struck down in *Dagenhart.*

Three years later, the Court unanimously upheld the law, including the child labor provision. Writing for the Court in *United States v. Darby Lumber Co.* (1941), Justice Harlan Fiske Stone called the *Dagenhart* ruling "a departure from the principles which have prevailed in the interpretation of the commerce clause both before and since. . . . It should be and now is overruled."

Circuit Riding

Almost from the beginning of the Supreme Court's history, justices have complained that the workload is too heavy. (See WORKLOAD OF COURT.) For the first hundred years, those complaints centered on the justices' circuit-riding duties.

In addition to establishing the size and jurisdiction of the Supreme Court, the Judiciary Act of 1789 required the justices to "ride circuit." This act provided no separate set of judges for the federal circuit courts. Instead, two justices sat with one district court judge

Rough roads, uncomfortable carriages, and poor accommodations made circuit riding one of the least pleasant parts of a justice's duties.
Source: Maryland Historical Society, Baltimore

at circuit courts in each of three circuits. In 1792 the six justices were required to attend a total of twenty-seven circuit courts a year and two sessions of the Supreme Court.

Riding circuit served an important function in the new nation: it helped to establish the notion of a national government in general and a federal judiciary in particular. But the distances the justices were required to travel were long, conditions were difficult, and questions were raised about the propriety of the justices participating at the circuit level in cases that were then reviewed by the Supreme Court.

As early as 1790 Chief Justice John Jay asked Congress to remove this burden. Congress responded with minor modifications in 1793. The Judiciary Act of 1801, passed by the Federalist Congress days before Thomas Jefferson was inaugurated president, abolished the duty, along with one seat on the Court. But Jefferson's Democratic-Republicans soon repealed the law, and circuit riding was reinstated.

As the country expanded westward, circuit-riding

duties grew more burdensome. One justice reported that he had traveled 10,000 miles in 1838 to fulfill these responsibilities. Congress increased the number of justices from six to nine during this period, largely because the circuit courts—and the justices—were overloaded.

But Congress refused to end the justices' circuit-riding duties. In a speech on the Senate floor on January 12, 1819, Sen. Abner Lacock of Pennsylvania summed up many of the congressional objections to the justices' pleas. If the justices were relieved of circuit duties, Lacock argued, they would become "completely cloistered within the City of Washington, and their decisions, instead of emanating from enlarged and liberalized minds, would assume a severe and local character." Lacock also expressed concern that the justices might fall under the sway of the president if they were to stay too long in Washington.

After the Civil War the workload of the justices grew even heavier. The ever expanding population and the industrialization that followed the Civil War increased the number of lawsuits that came to the Court. In addition, Congress expanded the Court's jurisdiction to include cases it had not been authorized to hear earlier. And Congress began to pass regulatory legislation, which led to additional lawsuits.

The long-sought demise of circuit-riding duties may have been hastened by the attempted murder of Justice Stephen J. Field by a litigant unhappy with one of his decisions as a circuit judge. In 1888 Field, sitting as a circuit judge in California, held invalid a marriage contract between Sarah Althea Hill and William Sharon, who had died by the time of the ruling. Hill, who had since married David Terry, one of Field's former colleagues on the California supreme court, was incensed at Field's ruling. As a result of their conduct in the courtroom when the ruling was announced, Hill and Terry were imprisoned for contempt of court.

A year later Field returned to California to hold circuit court. Because of concerns about his safety, he was accompanied by an armed federal marshal. The concerns were justified. As Field ate breakfast on a train to Los Angeles, he was accosted by Terry, who had boarded the train with his wife. The marshal, thinking that Terry was reaching for a knife to continue the attack on Field, shot and killed Terry. (State officials arrested the marshal and charged him with murder, but he argued that the state could not hold him for actions taken in the performance of his duties under federal law. The case came to the Court in 1890, which agreed with the marshal and ordered his release. Field did not participate in the case.)

Two years after the incident, Congress passed the Circuit Court of Appeals Act of 1891, at long last relieving justices of their circuit-riding duties.

The act created a new level of federal courts between the district and circuit courts on the one hand and the Supreme Court on the other. These new courts—called circuit courts of appeals—were to hear all appeals from decisions of the district and circuit courts. Their word was to be final in almost all diversity, admiralty, patent, revenue, and noncapital criminal cases. In 1911 Congress abolished the old circuit courts.

Each justice still has jurisdiction over one or more of the federal circuits, which now number thirteen, and may issue injunctions, grant bail, or stay an execution in these circuits. Requests for an injunction, bail, or stay of execution go first to the justice assigned to that circuit. If denied, the application may then be made to one of the other justices.

Citizenship

Citizenship was described by Chief Justice Earl Warren in 1958 as "man's basic right for it is nothing less than the right to have rights." Only after the Civil War did the United States establish a national definition of citizenship. The definition was part of the Fourteenth Amendment, which overruled the Supreme Court's infamous Dred Scott decision that barred blacks from citizenship.

The Court upheld legal barriers to citizenship for Asians, however, until Congress in 1952 eliminated race as a basis for denying citizenship. Since that time, the Court has focused on the grounds for revoking citizenship; it has generally limited congressional power to strip people of citizenship.

The Constitution refers to "citizens" in several places, but never defines who is a citizen or how one acquires citizenship. Two doctrines existed at the time the Constitution was written. In England, a citizen was a person who was born in that country and remained under its jurisdiction. In the rest of Europe, citizenship was determined by parental nationality. The English view was the prevailing assumption in America.

Slaves were not given the rights of citizens in the United States, and slaveholding states generally sought to bar freed blacks from citizenship as well. In the Dred Scott case (SCOTT V. SANDFORD [1857]), the Supreme Court barred blacks, including native-born free blacks, from citizenship. It also held that national citizenship depended on state citizenship. This ruling led ultimately to the Fourteenth Amendment, ratified in 1868. The first sentence of the amendment states that "[a]ll persons born or naturalized in the United States" and subject to its jurisdiction are citizens of the

Rosika Schwimmer, a Hungarian-born pacifist, was denied U.S. citizenship because she refused to swear to "take up arms" to defend the United States. In 1929 the Supreme Court upheld the decision.
Source: Library of Congress

United States and of the state where they reside. (See CIVIL WAR AMENDMENTS.)

Five years later the Court sharply restricted the amendment's impact by a narrow construction of the provision that states could not "abridge the privileges or immunities of citizens of the United States." In the *SLAUGHTERHOUSE CASES,* the Court ruled in 1873 that the privileges of national citizenship were limited. The Court held that the states had broad discretion to define the civil rights of people within their borders. Ever since, the Court has rejected virtually every claim for legal protection based on that clause.

Naturalization

The Constitution gives Congress the power "to establish an uniform Rule of Naturalization" (Article I, Section 8, Clause 4). After ratification of the Fourteenth Amendment, Congress limited naturalized citizenship to whites and to blacks of African descent. It specifically prohibited Chinese people from obtaining citizenship through naturalization. The Court has consistently sustained conditions on naturalization set by Congress. However, the Court ruled in *United States v. Wong Kim Ark* (1898) that under the Fourteenth Amendment, children born in the United States to resident alien parents are citizens even if their parents cannot become citizens.

Other conditions set by Congress have excluded from naturalization anarchists, members of the Communist party, and others who advocate the violent overthrow of the government. In addition, the government has interpreted the requirement of "good moral character" to exclude alcoholics, adulterers, polygamists, gamblers, convicted felons, and homosexuals. The Court has sustained these exclusions.

The Court did act in 1946 and 1950 to prevent conscientious objectors from being excluded from citizenship; it did so by means of a narrow construction of the congressional statute. In 1952 Congress took note of the rulings by allowing naturalization of conscientious objectors as long as they agreed to perform alternative service.

Loss of Citizenship

Naturalized citizens generally enjoy the same rights as those who are native-born. But naturalized citizens can lose their citizenship through denaturalization if they obtained it through fraud or bad faith. In 1943 the Court ruled that evidence of fraud had to be "clear, unequivocal, and convincing" to permit denaturalization. In 1964 the Court overturned a congressional provision that revoked the citizenship of any naturalized citizens who later resided in their native country for three continuous years.

In the Immigration and Nationality Act of 1952, Congress set out a long list of circumstances under which citizens could lose their citizenship. The Court in several cases has grappled with the issue of whether certain actions amount to a voluntary renunciation of citizenship and, if not, whether Congress has the power to revoke citizenship.

In *Perez v. Brownell* (1958) the Court upheld, by a 5–4 vote, the revocation of a person's citizenship for voting in a foreign election. The Court ruled that the provision was a valid exercise of congressional power over foreign affairs. It said that the Fourteenth Amendment did not nullify "the power otherwise possessed by Congress to withdraw citizenship." But *Perez* was overruled in 1967. In *Afroyim v. Rusk* (1967) the Court held, 5–4, that Congress has no power "to take away an American citizen's citizenship without his assent."

The Court struck down provisions of the 1952 act that permitted citizenship to be revoked if a person was convicted of desertion from the armed services or had left the country or remained abroad to evade military service. The Court threw out the provision affecting deserters in *Trop v. Dulles* (1958). Four justices found revocation of citizenship cruel and unusual punishment under the Eighth Amendment, while a fifth justice said the provision went beyond congressional power to regulate the armed forces. The Court invalidated the section affecting draft evaders in 1963 on grounds that it allowed punishment without the procedural safeguards of the Fifth and Sixth amendments.

In 1971 the Court muddied the issue of congressional control over citizenship. It sustained a provision—since repealed—that granted citizenship to someone born overseas to one American and one alien parent but revoked the citizenship unless the foreign-born child lived in the United States for five continuous years between the ages of fourteen and twenty-eight. In *Rogers v. Bellei* the Court ruled, 5–4, that Congress could impose conditions on citizenship for persons who do not meet the Fourteenth Amendment definition of a citizen. Justice Hugo L. Black complained in a bitter dissent that the decision overturned *Afroyim*. By 1992 the Court had not resolved the tension between the two rulings.

Civil Liberties

Civil liberties have been defined as claims of right that a citizen may assert against the government. For most of its history, the Supreme Court had little to say about the subject of individual freedom. In the twentieth century, however, the Court assumed a major role in protecting individual liberties. In the process it often found itself in political conflict with the other branches of the federal government, with the states, and with public opinion.

The original Constitution contains only a few provisions specifically protecting civil liberties. In Article I it prohibits ex post facto laws and bills of attainder and protects habeas corpus; in Article III it guarantees jury trials in criminal cases; and in Article VI it bans religious tests for officeholders.

Most of the civil liberties Americans enjoy today are embodied in the BILL OF RIGHTS. These include the freedoms of expression guaranteed by the First Amendment; the Fourth Amendment protection against unreasonable searches and seizures; and the rights in criminal and civil trials set out in the Fifth, Sixth, Seventh, and Eighth amendments.

Later constitutional amendments established liberties left unprotected by the Constitution. Slavery, specifically protected by the Constitution, was abolished by the Thirteenth Amendment. The right to vote, unmentioned in the Constitution, was extended to blacks in the Fifteenth Amendment, to women in the Nineteenth Amendment, and to eighteen-year-olds in the Twenty-sixth Amendment. Most important, the Fourteenth Amendment extended the guarantee of due process of law and equal protection of the laws to the states.

The framers of the Constitution intended for the separation of powers among the three branches of the national government and the limited powers of the federal government to be the most important protection of liberty under the new charter. They expected the Supreme Court to help secure liberty through the power of judicial review. Through the Civil War period, however, the Court's task of defining the powers of the federal and state governments had limited direct effect on individual liberties.

The Court's restrictive interpretation of the Fourteenth Amendment after the Civil War largely nullified its intended effect in expanding individual liberties. The modern era of civil liberties began only in 1925, when the Court first used the amendment to require states to comply with the Bill of Rights. (See INCORPORATION DOCTRINE.) It reached its peak with the criminal procedure revolution of the 1960s under the Warren Court. The Burger Court recognized some new liberties—most notably, the right to abortion.

Although the Burger and Rehnquist courts curbed some expansive rulings affecting criminal trials, the Supreme Court's role in securing civil liberties is now firmly established. Enforcement of the Bill of Rights against the states is universally accepted. And despite political criticism of specific rulings, the public appears to agree with and value the Court's role in checking on the other branches of government.

Civil Rights

Civil rights refers to the concept of being free from DISCRIMINATION when engaging in public activities, such as voting, or participating in other aspects of civic life; using public transportation or other PUBLIC AC-COMMODATIONS; buying or renting a home; or looking for or working in a job.

In the United States since the end of the Civil War, the term *civil rights* has referred in particular to the effort to eliminate racial discrimination against African Americans. But civil rights laws enacted since 1964 have also prohibited discrimination on the basis of national origin, religion, sex, age, and (since 1990) physical or mental disability.

In the nineteenth century the Supreme Court allowed racial discrimination to become legally entrenched. Before the Civil War the Court treated slavery as a political institution beyond its power to change. (See SLAVERY AND THE COURT.) After the war the Court largely blocked efforts by Congress to protect the legal rights of the former slaves. In *PLESSY V. FERGUSON* (1896) the Court gave its blessing to legally mandated racial SEGREGATION.

In the twentieth century the Court gradually began to undermine the "separate but equal" doctrine of *Plessy*. Meanwhile developments outside the Court—the birth of the modern civil rights movement, the migration of blacks to northern cities, and the growth of the federal government—were laying the groundwork for what became the civil rights revolution of the 1950s and 1960s. The Court played a critical role in this revolution, first with *BROWN V. BOARD OF EDUCATION OF TOPEKA* (1954) and its other rulings dismantling legal segregation, and then with its decisions giving broad effect to civil rights laws passed by Congress.

A backlash against civil rights began as early as the mid-1960s and grew as the efforts to eliminate racial discrimination and its legacy became more complex. Two remedies approved by the Supreme Court proved to be especially controversial: BUSING to help achieve SCHOOL DESEGREGATION, and AFFIRMATIVE ACTION plans to increase the enrollment of blacks in colleges and universities and to improve economic opportunities for blacks. The debate over remedies reflected the progress the nation had made in accepting the idea of civil rights. It also revealed the difficulty of translating equal legal rights into equal economic opportunities.

Reconstruction and Reaction

After the Civil War Congress took bold steps to try to guarantee equal rights for the freed slaves and other blacks. These steps were largely nullified by the Supreme Court.

The CIVIL WAR AMENDMENTS abolished slavery (Thirteenth), promised "EQUAL PROTECTION of the laws" (Fourteenth), and protected blacks' VOTING RIGHTS (Fifteenth). Congress also passed legislation to enforce the rights guaranteed by those amendments. The Civil Rights Act of 1866 purported to give blacks the same rights as whites to "make and enforce contracts" and "purchase, lease, [or] hold" property. The so-called Enforcement Acts passed in 1870 and 1871 were aimed at preventing intimidation of blacks trying to vote. The Civil Rights Act of 1875 prohibited discrimination in public accommodations.

The Court narrowly construed the Fourteenth Amendment. It invoked the amendment just once before 1900 to invalidate a law as impermissible racial discrimination. The 1880 case struck down a West Virginia law barring blacks from jury service. The Court also interpreted the Enforcement Acts to apply only to official deprivations of blacks' rights, not to the night-riders and Ku Klux Klan who terrorized blacks in much of the South. The Court ruled the 1875 act unconstitutional, saying Congress had no power to prohibit private discrimination; on the same ground it effectively made the 1866 act a dead letter.

Reconstruction lasted for only a decade. In 1876 the political deal that brought Rutherford B. Hayes to the presidency ended the national government's efforts to secure the rights of blacks in the South. The so-called Black Codes that denied rights to blacks stayed on the books in southern states, followed by the "Jim Crow" laws that segregated blacks from whites in hotels, theaters, and public transportation.

When the Court upheld segregation in *Plessy,* the legal fiction of "separate but equal" was quickly extended to other aspects of life. The lone dissent of Justice John Marshall Harlan proved prophetic: "The thin disguise of 'equal' accommodations . . . will not mislead any one, nor atone for the wrong this day done."

Transition Period

The chain of events that led to the demise of segregation began in the first half of the twentieth century. The Supreme Court during this period slowly moved to set itself against some of the legal injustices done to blacks.

The National Association for the Advancement of Colored People (NAACP), founded in 1909, began a legal attack on racial discrimination, which was later carried on by its spinoff organization, the NAACP Legal Defense and Educational Fund, Inc. Following World War I, blacks began to migrate to the North in search of improved opportunities. The Great Depression of the 1930s and the federal programs President Franklin D. Roosevelt created to help the nation recover from it made these northern blacks a powerful constituency within the dominant Democratic party.

By the 1940s militant groups were openly demanding an end to segregation. Their cause gained strength with the Allied victory in World War II—a victory over Nazi racism that black and white U.S. soldiers fighting together helped win, while the United States practiced racial segregation at home. In 1948 the Democratic party adopted a civil rights plank in the face of a walkout threat—later carried out—by its southern wing.

Civil rights forces had won a handful of victories from the Supreme Court by this time. The Court had struck down some devices used to disenfranchise blacks: Oklahoma's "grandfather clause" in 1915, and Texas's white Democratic primary in 1927, again in 1932, and yet again in 1944. Literacy tests and poll taxes, however, were upheld. The Court had struck down local residential segregation ordinances in 1917, but it had upheld private racial restrictive covenants in 1926. Twice, in 1914 and 1941, the Court had ruled that segregated railroads had failed to provide the "equal" facilities and services that *Plessy* required. Finally, the Court had begun to use the Fourteenth Amendment DUE PROCESS clause to review some of the miscarriages of justice visited on black defendants in the South—most dramatically in the *SCOTTSBORO CASES* of the 1930s.

The Court's "revolution of 1937"—its great ideological shift from property rights to individual rights—laid the groundwork for direct judicial intervention against racial discrimination. Four cases brought by the NAACP Legal Defense and Educational Fund undermined segregation in public higher education by strengthening the requirement that blacks be provided an education equal to that of whites. The Court in 1948 barred courts from enforcing racial covenants by expanding the definition of what kind of "state action" would trigger the Fourteenth Amendment equal protection clause. Then in 1952 the Court moved to take on the most explosive civil rights issue. It scheduled arguments for the end of the year on five companion cases testing the constitutionality of racial segregation in the nation's public elementary and secondary schools.

Civil Rights Revolution

The 1954 ruling in *Brown v. Board of Education of Topeka* has been described as the most socially and ideologically significant decision in the Court's history. It touched off the political opposition that Chief Justice Earl Warren had tried to avert. Several states enacted "interposition" statutes declaring the decision of no effect. The "Southern Manifesto"—signed by 101 of 128 southern members of Congress—urged states to "resist enforced integration by any means."

Over the next decade, those means included "freedom of choice" plans that kept schools segregated, repeal of compulsory attendance laws, public funding for private segregated schools, and even, in a handful of jurisdictions, the closing of public schools. By 1964 fewer than 2 percent of black pupils in the former Confederate states were attending desegregated schools.

The Supreme Court—and the federal judges in lower courts who were handing down school desegregation decrees—received little support in their efforts. President Dwight D. Eisenhower refused to endorse the *Brown* decision, promising only to carry out the law of the land. Congress passed two weak civil rights laws in 1957 and 1960, but deleted a provision to give the attorney general power to initiate actions on behalf of persons deprived of their civil rights.

The resistance to desegregation brought about its own destruction, however. The nation was shocked in 1957 when the army and the national guard had to be called out to protect black children being admitted to a Little Rock high school under court order. Nonviolent protests, such as "sit-ins" to desegregate lunch counters and "freedom rides" to desegregate bus lines, attracted violence that drew the nation's sympathy to the civil rights cause. In 1963 police loosed dogs and turned high-pressure hoses on demonstrators in Birmingham, Alabama. Later in the year a bomb thrown into a black church in Birmingham killed four little girls. Then on November 22, 1963, President John F. Kennedy, an unequivocal advocate of civil rights, was assassinated.

A nation sick of violence and now led by a southern president, Lyndon B. Johnson, finally used the political process to guarantee equal rights. Congress passed the Civil Rights Act of 1964, establishing broad prohibitions against discrimination in public accommodations (Title II), federally funded programs (Title VI), and employment (Title VII). (See JOB DISCRIMINATION.) The act also authorized court actions by the attorney general to challenge segregated public facilities and schools.

On December 1, 1955, Rosa Parks refused to relinquish her seat to a white person and move to the back of a Montgomery, Alabama, bus. Her arrest and trial sparked a bus boycott, one of the first organized protests against segregation in the South.
Source: Tommy Giles

A year later the Voting Rights Act of 1965 gave the federal government powerful legal weapons to guarantee the franchise for blacks. And in 1968—in the aftermath of the assassination of the civil rights leader, Rev. Martin Luther King, Jr.—Congress gave final approval to the Fair Housing Act, which prohibited racial discrimination in housing. (See OPEN HOUSING.)

The Court quickly and decisively rejected challenges to the new laws. Congress had linked the 1964 act to its commerce power; the Court stretched the definition of interstate commerce to give the law virtually unlimited reach. The Voting Rights Act intruded on an area traditionally reserved to the states, yet the Court found the act to be within Congress's power under the now fortified Civil War amendments. In 1968 the Court even revived the 1866 Civil Rights Act, deciding that Congress had, in fact, intended to prohibit private racial discrimination and had acted constitutionally in doing so.

Rev. Martin Luther King, Jr., and other civil rights leaders present a united front for their March on Washington, August 28, 1963.
Source: UPI Photo

Backlash and Consolidation

Violence of a different sort fed a civil rights backlash in the late 1960s: the inner city riots that flared between 1965 and 1968, and the more persistent menace of urban crime. Republican Richard Nixon used a law-and-order theme to win the presidency in 1968. He attacked the Warren Court's criminal law rulings and promised to appoint more conservative justices if elected. The justices Nixon appointed during his presidency shifted the Court to the right not just on criminal law but on civil rights issues as well.

In 1971 the Court's first major civil rights ruling under Chief Justice Warren E. Burger endorsed the use of busing to achieve desegregation and carried on the tradition of unanimous rulings in school desegregation cases. Three years later, however, the four Nixon appointees joined with one Warren Court holdover, Potter Stewart, in handing down a 5–4 decision that effectively prevented busing children between predominantly black inner city schools and mostly white suburbs. Court-ordered busing, in any event, aroused such deep political opposition that even many civil rights supporters questioned its use.

The Court in the late 1970s narrowly approved the limited use of affirmative action and minority preferences in university admissions, employment, and government contracting. In the 1980s the Reagan and Bush administrations urged the Court to change course. They won rulings that blocked preferential treatment for minorities in layoffs and limited set-aside programs for minority contractors by state and local governments. The issue remained divisive in the early 1990s.

A quarter-century after the 1964 act, the civil rights movement could count some successes and some disappointments. Discrimination in public accommodations had disappeared, and overt discrimination in employment had diminished. But economic statistics showed continuing disparities between the opportunities for blacks and those for whites. Residential segregation persisted—caused in part by economics and in part by continuing discrimination that open housing laws proved unable to stop. Residential segregation limited the extent of integration in schools: racially identifiable neighborhoods meant racially identifiable schools in much of the nation.

The Court's decisions in the 1970s and 1980s reflected concerns about how far the law could go in eliminating the vestiges of past discrimination. Beneath this emotional debate, however, lay a national consensus on the principle of equal rights. The Court had helped create this consensus, and it continued to hold up the goal of equal rights as an ideal for society to strive to achieve.

Civil War Amendments

After the Civil War, Congress approved and the states ratified three constitutional amendments that collectively appeared to guarantee blacks equal rights under the law. But over the next four decades the Supreme Court limited the impact of the amendments by narrowly construing their terms and limiting congressional power to enforce the provisions. In the twentieth century, however, the Court changed its course. It has used the amendments to outlaw most racial DISCRIMINATION and also to require states to comply with virtually all of the provisions of the BILL OF RIGHTS.

The Thirteenth Amendment was ratified in 1865 just eight months after the Civil War ended. It abolished "slavery or involuntary servitude" and authorized Congress to pass laws eliminating "all badges and incidents of slavery."

The Fourteenth Amendment, ratified in 1868, made blacks citizens. It also said that states could not abridge the "privileges and immunities" of U.S. citizens; deprive any person of life, liberty, or property without DUE PROCESS of law; or deny any person EQUAL PROTECTION of the laws.

The Fifteenth Amendment, ratified in 1870, prohibited federal and state governments from denying citizens the right to vote on the basis of race, color, or previous condition of servitude. (See VOTING RIGHTS.

Both the Fourteenth and Fifteenth amendments contained sections authorizing Congress to pass laws to enforce their provisions.

Restrictive Rulings

The Supreme Court's restrictive interpretation of the amendments had several causes. These included waning public enthusiasm for Reconstruction, concern for healing the wounds of war, and a limited sensitivity to issues of individual rights. The restrictions came in two lines of rulings. In the first, the Court narrowly defined the Fourteenth Amendment clauses concerning privileges and immunities, due process, and equal protection. In the second, the Court sharply restricted the enforcement power all three amendments granted to Congress.

During congressional consideration of the Fourteenth Amendment, supporters in both chambers made clear their belief that it would extend federal protection for a broad range of basic rights, including those guaranteed by the Bill of Rights, to people denied those rights by state action. But in the *SLAUGHTERHOUSE CASES* in 1873 the Court ruled, 5–4, that the Fourteenth Amendment protected only the limited privileges and immunities of U.S. citizenship. It did not protect "the entire domain of civil rights heretofore belonging exclusively to the States." The Court reinforced the decision in 1875 by specifically holding that the right to vote was not a privilege of U.S. citizenship.

Voting rights for blacks were further set back by a narrow reading of the Fifteenth Amendment in *United States v. Reese* (1876). The 8–1 decision struck down provisions of the Enforcement Act of 1870 that punished state officials who refused to accept or count black votes or who otherwise obstructed citizens from voting. The ruling invited states to circumvent the amendment by establishing qualifications for voting that were not formally based on race but still served to keep most blacks from voting. In 1898 the Court rejected challenges under the Fifteenth Amendment to two such devices: literacy tests and poll taxes.

In the most severe restriction of the amendments' effect, the Court ruled in the *Civil Rights Cases* (1883) that neither the Thirteenth nor Fourteenth Amendment gave Congress power to prohibit private racial discrimination. The 8–1 decision striking down the public accommodations provisions of the Civil Rights Act of 1875 held that the Fourteenth Amendment applied only to state action, not private conduct. The law could not be upheld under the Thirteenth Amendment, the Court said, because racial discrimination was not a "badge of slavery."

Thirteen years later, the Court went further and held that the Fourteenth Amendment did not even prohibit legally mandated racial segregation. The Court's ruling in *PLESSY V. FERGUSON* (1896) upheld state laws mandating racially segregated railway cars—and by implication those providing for racially segregated school systems. The Court based its decision on the ground that establishing "separate but equal" facilities for blacks and whites did not violate the Fourteenth Amendment's equal protection clause.

Ironically, one of the few occasions when the Court broadly construed the amendment's provisions benefited aliens rather than American blacks. In *Yick Wo v. Hopkins* (1886) the Court found an equal protection violation in San Francisco's discriminatory enforcement of a safety ordinance so as to prevent Chinese laundries from operating while granting permits to white-owned laundries.

Beginning in the late 1890s the Court also used the due process clause in several cases to protect business against state regulation. These rulings represented the doctrine of substantive due process—the view that the due process clause imposes substantive limits as well as procedural requirements on government actions. The most notable of these cases was *Lochner v. New York* (1905), striking down maximum hours legislation for bakers. But the Court repudiated the doctrine of substantive due process beginning in the late 1930s. (See PROPERTY RIGHTS.)

Protecting Individual Rights

The Court's willingness to use the Civil War amendments to protect individual rights came about gradually, case by case. In the issue of voting rights, the Court in 1915 used the Fifteenth Amendment to strike down so-called grandfather clauses that imposed voting qualifications on everyone except those whose father or grandfather had voted before adoption of the amendment. Again in 1944, the amendment was used to strike down the "white primary"—all-white Democratic nominating elections in one-party southern states.

Meanwhile, the Court in 1925 began to use the due process clause to apply provisions of the Bill of Rights to the states. (See INCORPORATION DOCTRINE.) These rulings had their greatest impact not in race-related cases but in criminal law and First Amendment cases.

The equal protection clause, on the other hand, was applied dramatically to vindicate the rights of blacks, beginning with the series of education cases that led up to the landmark SCHOOL DESEGREGATION case, *BROWN V. BOARD OF EDUCATION OF TOPEKA* (1954). In addition, the Court reinvigorated the Reconstruction-era civil rights statutes with a 1968 decision, *Jones v. Alfred H. Mayer Co.,* that upheld their use against private racial discrimination under the "badge of slavery" provision of the Thirteenth Amendment.

Clark, Tom C.

President Harry S. Truman was criticized in 1949 when he named Tom Campbell Clark (1899–1977), a Presbyterian, to replace Justice Frank Murphy, the only Roman Catholic on the Supreme Court at the time. Truman responded that religious affiliations should not matter when appointing justices. As a result of Clark's appointment, there was no Catholic on the Court for the first time in half a century .

Clark was born in Dallas, Texas, and received his undergraduate and law degrees from the University of Texas. He then practiced law in his father's firm and

Source: Collection of the Supreme Court of the United States

followed his father's lead in becoming actively involved in Democratic politics. Clark's political connections landed him an appointment as Dallas civil district attorney in 1927. After five years in that job, Clark returned to private practice.

A succession of jobs in the Justice Department followed. As a special assistant in the Justice Department starting in 1937, Campbell was the civilian coordinator for the program to move Japanese-Americans into camps during World War II. In 1943 Clark was promoted to assistant attorney general, and when Truman became president in 1945 he named Clark attorney general. In that job Clark pursued antitrust prosecutions, directed the Justice Department in prosecuting communists and other alleged subversives, and released the first attorney general's list of subversive political organizations.

Truman nominated Clark for the Supreme Court in 1949, and the Senate confirmed Clark by a 73–8 vote. Despite his pursuit of alleged subversives while serving in the Truman administration, Clark was relatively liberal on the Court. In 1952 he wrote the Court's opinion in *Wieman v. Updegraff,* striking down an Oklahoma law that required all state employees to sign loyalty oaths. The law also barred the hiring of persons who had belonged to certain organizations that were allegedly subversive, whether or not the person knew about the organization's goals. In the opinion for the Court, Clark wrote that the law violated due process because it did not differentiate between people who did and did not know about an organization's purpose.

In 1963 Clark wrote the Court's opinion striking down laws requiring Bible readings in schools. Such readings violated the separation of church and state, Clark wrote for the Court. "In the relationship between man and religion, the State is formally committed to a position of neutrality," he wrote.

After serving as a justice for nearly eighteen years, Clark resigned in 1967 when President Lyndon Johnson appointed his son, Ramsey Clark, attorney general. His resignation was intended to avoid any appearance of a conflict of interest. After leaving the Court, Clark served from 1968 to 1970 as director of the Federal Judicial Center, a judicial branch organization that works to improve court administration. Until his death in June 1977, Clark also sat on various U.S. courts of appeals by special arrangement.

Clarke, John H.

When President Woodrow Wilson appointed John Hessin Clarke (1857–1945) to the Supreme Court in 1916, Wilson hoped the liberal Clarke would help Justice Louis Brandeis pull the Court away from its reactionary course. Clarke greatly disappointed Wilson by resigning from the Court after only six years to promote U.S. participation in the League of Nations.

Clarke was born in Lisbon, Ohio, and received his undergraduate, master's, and law degrees from Western Reserve College. After passing the bar in 1878 and briefly joining his father's practice, Clarke moved to

Source: Collection of the Supreme Court of the United States

In his letter to Wilson in 1922 resigning from the Court, Clarke made it clear that he thought the Court was too wrapped up in constitutional minutiae. From 1922 to 1930 Clarke directed the League of Nations' Non-Partisan Association of the United States. He also promoted the League of Nations in speeches across the country.

In 1937 Clarke, who had retired from public life, emerged to endorse President Franklin D. Roosevelt's Court-packing plan over national radio. Clarke died in March 1945, only a month before the beginning of the San Francisco conference at which the United Nations was created.

Class Action

The class action—sometimes called a representative action—is a suit brought in a state or federal court by several individuals on behalf of a larger group of people who have the same legal interest. In recent decades, class actions have often served as the vehicle for bringing major civil rights and constitutional claims and important consumer and environmental litigation. Some recent Supreme Court decisions, however, have tightened the requirements for bringing such suits in federal court.

The class action benefits plaintiffs by making litigation more practicable, especially in consumer cases where a claim may be too small to pursue on an individual basis. Trying many of the claims in a single lawsuit is said to promote economy, efficiency, and uniformity, benefiting both defendants and courts. But some critics believe that class action rules encourage suits of dubious merit and sometimes all but force business defendants to settle.

To protect the due process rights of the members of the class, the Supreme Court has long held that the named plaintiffs must adequately represent the interests of the class. This rule requires an initial hearing to decide whether the suit should be certified as a class action. In addition, the active litigants typically must take some steps to make other members of the class aware of the suit and give them an opportunity to exclude themselves from the litigation.

Youngstown to embark on a career in corporate law. He owned the city's newspaper, the *Vindicator,* and used it to promote progressive reform. Clarke moved to Cleveland in 1897. Although he continued to represent corporate clients, Clarke maintained his liberal politics and backed antitrust legislation. He also supported suffrage for women, mandatory civil service, and public disclosure of campaign finances.

Clarke twice ran for the U.S. Senate, in 1894 and 1914, but lost the first time and withdrew the second in favor of another candidate. In 1914 Wilson appointed Clarke federal judge for the northern district of Ohio, a position Clarke held until Wilson nominated him for the Supreme Court in 1916. While on the Court, Clarke was a strong supporter of labor and an equally strong opponent of business monopolies.

The Court in the 1970s issued two decisions that tightened the rules for class actions. In *Zahn v. International Paper Co.* (1973), the Court held that to use federal diversity jurisdiction, each member of the class must have suffered an injury that meets the jurisdictional threshold of $50,000 for diversity suits. (Diversity jurisdiction permits cases involving residents of different states to be brought in federal court.) The next year, in *Eisen v. Carlisle & Jacqueline* (1974), the Court required plaintiffs in some class actions to individually notify members of the class at their own expense. The impact of the decisions has been to slightly reduce the number of large consumer and environmental class actions.

Clay, Henry

Henry Clay (1777–1852) of Kentucky earned his early reputation as a trial lawyer in capital cases. But his first love was politics, and he became one of the giants of Congress during the first half of the nineteenth century. Gifted with charm and eloquence, Clay was known as the "Great Compromiser" for his efforts to resolve sectional disputes over slavery. His initiatives included two plans to curb the expansion of slavery into the territories: the Missouri Compromise of 1820 and the Compromise of 1850.

Clay was also a spokesman for western expansion. He proposed an "American System" for economic development that featured a federally financed transportation network and high tariffs to protect U.S. industry.

Clay served two short stints in the Senate in 1806–1807 and 1809–1810. In 1810 he was elected to the House where he served, except for two brief periods, until 1825. He was elected Speaker of the House on the day he took office and remained Speaker as long as he was in the House. In 1830 Clay returned to the Senate, where he played a leading role in the debates over slavery that preceded the Civil War. He left the Senate in 1842 but returned in 1849 and served until his death in 1852.

Clay ran unsuccessfully for president as a Dem-ocratic Republican in 1824, as a National Republican in 1832, and as a Whig in 1844.

Like many other legislators of the day, Clay still found time to take legal cases. In 1807 he successfully defended Aaron Burr against charges of treason; the presiding judge in the circuit court was Chief Justice John Marshall.

Clay also argued several cases before the Supreme Court. It was said that the women of Washington turned out especially to see the popular and dashing Kentuckian present his case to the Court.

One of the most important of these cases was *Osborn v. Bank of the United States* (1824), in which the Court upheld the right of the Bank of the United States to sue state officials in federal court. Both in the courtroom and in political life, Clay was a strong advocate of the national bank. Indeed, Clay, Daniel WEBSTER, and their supporters in the Senate opposed Roger B. Taney's nomination to the Court in 1835 because Taney, as attorney general, had played a major role in President Andrew Jackson's war on the bank. Their opposition delayed Taney's confirma-

Source: Library of Congress

tion, but they were unable to kill the nomination outright.

Clay had more success in 1844, when his supporters in the Senate managed to kill four nominations to the Court submitted by President John Tyler. Clay's Whig followers, who controlled the Senate, thought Clay would win the presidency in that year's election, and they wanted to hold the seats open so that he could fill the vacancies.

Clay lost the election, however, and in 1849 returned to the Senate. His proposals to prevent the breakup of the Union prompted a debate that has often been called the greatest in the Senate's history. It marked the last appearance in the Senate chamber of the "great triumvirate"—Clay, Webster, an apostle of national unity, and John C. CALHOUN of South Carolina, the South's foremost defender of slavery and states' rights.

Clerk of the Court

The clerk of the Court helps keep the Supreme Court's judicial business running smoothly. The clerk and the clerk's staff manage all of the papers connected with the cases brought to the Court and advise attorneys and litigants of the Court's rules and procedures.

The importance of the clerk has long been recognized. The Court's first formal act upon convening in February 1790 was to establish the office, and the first clerk, John Tucker of Massachusetts, was appointed on February 3, 1790.

Tucker was charged with overseeing the courtroom, managing subordinate employees, collecting the salaries of the justices, and finding lodging for the justices when necessary. The modern clerk no longer has to find housing for the justices, but the other duties have increased enormously. The clerk administers the Court's dockets and argument calendars; receives and records all motions, petitions, jurisdictional statements, briefs, and other documents filed on the various dockets; distributes these papers to the justices; and collects the filing fees and assesses other court costs.

The clerk prepares and maintains the Court's order list and journal, in which are entered all the Court's formal judgments and mandates. In addition, the clerk notifies counsel and lower courts of all formal actions taken by the Court. The clerk requests the certified record of lower court action when the Court grants review of a case and supervises the printing of briefs after review has been granted in cases brought *in forma pauperis.*

Finally, the clerk's office supervises admissions to and occasional disbarments from the Supreme Court bar and gives procedural advice by telephone, by mail, and in person to counsel and litigants who have questions about the Court's rules and procedures.

The clerk is assisted in these duties by a twenty-five-member staff and a computerized information system that was installed in 1976.

By mid-1994 there had been only nineteen clerks of the Court, all of them men. Four of them each served for a quarter-century or more: Elias B. Caldwell, William T. Carroll, J. H. McKenney, and C. Elmore Cropley.

The 1790 rule that established the position prohib-

Clerks of the Supreme Court		
Name	**Term**	**State of Origin**
John Tucker	1790–1791	Massachusetts
Samuel Bayard	1791–1800	Pennsylvania
Elias B. Caldwell	1800–1825	New Jersey
William Griffith	1826–1827	New Jersey
William T. Carroll	1827–1863	Maryland
D. W. Middleton	1863–1880	D.C.
J. H. McKenney	1880–1913	Maryland
James D. Maher	1913–1921	New York
William R. Stansbury	1921–1927	D.C.
C. Elmore Cropley	1927–1952	D.C.
Harold B. Willey	1952–1956	Oregon
John T. Fey	1956–1958	Virginia
James R. Browning	1958–1961	Montana
John F. Davis	1961–1970	Maine
E. Robert Seaver	1970–1972	Missouri
Michael Rodak, Jr.	1972–1981	West Virginia
Alexander Stevas	1981–1985	Virginia
Joseph F. Spaniol, Jr.	1985–1991	Ohio
William K. Suter	1991–	Ohio

ited the clerk from practicing law before the Court. In the early years the clerk performed many of the duties later taken over by the REPORTER OF DECISIONS and the MARSHAL OF THE COURT. So varied were the responsibilities of the early clerks that they were described as a combination business manager-errand boy for the justices and the lawyers who appeared before the Court.

The Court did not provide for a salary for the clerk until nine years after it had created the position. Then it compensated the clerk at the rate of $10 a day for attendance in Court. For other services, the clerk was paid double the fees of the clerk of the highest court in the state where the Supreme Court was sitting.

But for almost one hundred years the office of the clerk was self-supporting. It paid salaries and other expenses of its operations out of filing fees. The hefty fees and other allowances gave some of the early clerks a handsome annual stipend. In 1881, for example, the clerk's net income was almost $30,000 a year—only slightly less than the president's and considerably more than the justices'.

Strict accountability for the Court's funds was not imposed until 1883. The filing fees now go to the U.S. Treasury, and Congress appropriates the money for the salaries and expenses of the clerk's office. In 1994 the clerk had an annual salary of $115,700.

Clerks

As the number of cases coming to the Supreme Court has increased, the justices have relied more on their law clerks. In 1994 thirty-five law clerks served the nine justices—almost twice as many as there were two decades earlier.

Each justice is allowed four clerks. The clerks are hired by the individual justices, usually for one year. Occasionally a clerk stays longer. In 1994 the salary for the law clerks was about $41,000.

The justices have complete discretion in hiring their clerks. The clerks are usually selected from candidates at the top of their classes in the country's most prestigious law schools. Some have previously clerked for a lower court judge.

Clerks sometimes later become justices themselves. In 1994 the Court included two justices who had once served as law clerks: John Paul Stevens clerked for Wiley B. Rutledge during his 1947–1948 term, and Rehnquist clerked for Robert H. Jackson during his 1952–1953 term. In addition, President Clinton's 1994 appointee to the Court, Stephen G. Breyer, clerked for Justice Arthur J. Goldberg during his 1964–1965 term.

The two major functions of the clerks are, first, to read, analyze, and often prepare memoranda for the justices on the thousands of cases that reach the Court each year and, second, to help a justice in preparing an opinion.

The nature and amount of a clerk's work depends on the work habits of the particular justice. Years ago, Justice Louis Brandeis once asked his clerk to check every page of every volume of *United States Reports* for information that he wanted. Justice Hugo L. Black insisted that some of his clerks play tennis with him. Chief Justice Harlan Fiske Stone liked his clerks to accompany him on his walks.

The role of the clerks in influencing the justices' votes and writing opinions has been a matter of speculation and occasional controversy. Rehnquist has written that he asks his law clerks to prepare first drafts of his opinions. Critics sometimes charge that law clerks have actually written opinions issued in the name of the justices or guided a justice's vote on a particular case. But the justices and clerks generally deny these suggestions.

"We couldn't get our work done without the clerks," Justice Byron R. White, who clerked for Chief Justice Fred M. Vinson during the 1946–1947 term, once said. "But I don't think they influence the results here all that much."

Whatever impact the clerks may have, they almost always remain in the shadows, inaccessible to the public and the press. The clerks talk among themselves about the views and personalities of their justices but rarely has a clerk discussed clashes among the justices or leaked news about an opinion before it was announced in Court. In 1973, however, news of the Court's historic abortion decision in *Roe v. Wade* was leaked more than a week before the ruling was announced. To guard against such leaks, Chief Justice

Warren E. Burger ordered all the law clerks not to speak to or be seen with reporters.

The first law clerk was hired by Justice Horace Gray in 1882. As early as 1850 the justices had sought congressional approval for the hiring of an "investigating clerk" to help each justice and to copy opinions. When that request was not granted, some of the justices used employees of the Court clerk's office to help them.

Gray's clerk, who had been the top graduate at Harvard Law School, served primarily as a servant and a barber, paid by the justice himself. It was not until 1886 that Congress provided $1,600 a year for a "stenographic clerk" for each justice. In the years that followed, clerks often served considerably longer than the one year that is typical now. Chief justices Charles Evans Hughes and William Howard Taft and Justice Frank Murphy all employed law clerks who stayed for five years or more.

Source: Collection of the Supreme Court of the United States

Clifford, Nathan

In 1880 Supreme Court justice Nathan Clifford (1803–1881) suffered a stroke that left him unable to participate in Court activities. Clifford, a staunch Democrat, refused to resign because the Republicans were in power and he wanted to live long enough that a Democratic president could appoint his successor. Clifford's plan was foiled; he died the following year while Republicans still held the White House.

Clifford was born in Rumney, New Hampshire, where he attended local academies before studying law in the office of Josiah Quincy, a prominent Rumney attorney. After being admitted to the bar in 1827, Clifford moved to Newfield, Maine, to practice law.

By the time Clifford was elected to the Maine legislature in 1830, at age twenty-seven, he was already a strong Jacksonian Democrat. He served four years in the house, the last two as Speaker. The legislature then elected him state attorney general, a post he held for four years. Clifford next set his sights on Washington, D.C. He won two terms in the U.S. House, but was defeated when he ran for a third term. Following that defeat in 1843, Clifford returned to Maine

to practice law. But he had made his mark in Washington.

Three years after Clifford left Washington, President James Polk named him attorney general. One of Clifford's chief jobs became mediating disagreements between Polk and James Buchanan, his secretary of state. In 1848 Polk sent Clifford to persuade Mexico to sign a treaty ending the war, and Clifford stayed in Mexico as U.S. minister from 1848 to 1849. When the Whigs gained power in 1849, Clifford once again returned to Maine to take up his law practice.

Buchanan nominated Clifford for the Supreme Court in late 1857. There was strong opposition to Clifford in the Senate. Some senators considered Clifford a party hack, while others thought he was a northerner with a southern soul. Nonetheless, he was confirmed in January 1858 by a 26–23 vote.

Nearly one in five of his opinions on the Court were dissents, as he supported limiting federal power when most of his colleagues favored expanding it. A firm believer in the Union, he agreed with the majority in *Ex parte Vallandigham* (1864), supporting the use of martial law during the Civil War. But he dissented in the *Prize Cases* (1863), disagreeing with the majority view that the Union blockade of the South was legal before Congress voted for war.

In 1877, near the end of Clifford's tenure on the Court, he served as chair of the electoral commission created to decide the disputed presidential election of 1876. The dispute centered on which presidential candidate had carried the southern states of South Carolina, Louisiana, and Florida. Clifford voted with the Democrats for Samuel Tilden, but Republican Rutherford B. Hayes won by one vote. Clifford refused to enter the White House while Hayes lived there because he considered Hayes an illegitimate president.

Comity

Comity refers to the deference that one court system gives to another in ruling on matters of overlapping JURISDICTION. It is intended to promote cooperation and avoid unnecessary collisions of authority.

In the U.S. legal system, comity underlies the requirement that states recognize judgments issued by courts from another state or by a federal court. Comity is also the basis of flexible rules that in some instances require federal courts to refrain from ruling on challenges to the actions of state officials or state courts.

Two constitutional clauses provide reasonably definite rules for state courts to follow in their relationships with the federal judiciary and with courts in other states. The SUPREMACY CLAUSE establishes the Constitution, federal laws, and treaties as binding on "the Judges in every State." In addition, each state is required to give "Full Faith and Credit . . . to the . . . judicial Proceedings of every other State" (Article IV, Section 1).

The demands of comity have led the Supreme Court to create and develop flexible rules for federal courts to follow when asked to block or overturn state actions that are challenged as improper or unconstitutional. The two most important rules are called the "exhaustion of remedies" requirement and the "abstention doctrine."

The first rule generally requires that individuals exhaust all possible state remedies for their complaint before challenging state action in federal courts. The second directs federal judges for the most part to abstain from acting on a matter within state hands until the state courts have had a full opportunity to correct the situation at issue.

Full Faith and Credit

The Supreme Court has interpreted the full faith and credit clause to prevent a court in one state from entertaining a legal dispute that has already been decided by a court in another state (provided that various procedural requirements were met). To fill in a gap in the language of the clause, the Supreme Court has held that judgments of federal courts are entitled to the same respect that is owed to state judgments.

Application of this requirement—for example, in divorce cases where spouses live in different states—is often complex and confusing, involving highly technical legal rules. Further, the clause requires a state court only to *recognize* the judgment of the other state's court. Each state is free to use its own laws and rules to determine the manner of *enforcing* a judgment from another state.

Exhaustion of Remedies

The exhaustion of remedies requirement applies most strongly in HABEAS CORPUS cases in which prisoners challenge state convictions as unlawful or unconstitutional. Since 1886 the Supreme Court has required that a prisoner exhaust available state remedies before seeking federal habeas corpus relief. Congress has also codified this requirement.

The same requirement does not apply, however, to many federal CIVIL RIGHTS cases. In a series of decisions beginning with *Monroe v. Pape* (1961), the Court held that an individual challenging a state action as a deprivation of civil rights "under color of law" need not exhaust available state judicial remedies. In 1982 the Court held that it was also unnecessary to exhaust state administrative remedies in such cases.

Some recent federal statutes—such as the employment discrimination provisions of Title VII of the Civil

Rights Act of 1964 and the open housing provisions of the Civil Rights Act of 1968—do require exhaustion of state remedies before bringing an action before a federal agency. On the other hand, the Voting Rights Act of 1965 expressly rejects any need to exhaust other remedies before initiating action in federal court.

Abstention Doctrine

The abstention doctrine generally prohibits a federal court from issuing an INJUNCTION to stay a proceeding in a state court, especially a criminal prosecution. The doctrine was developed by the Supreme Court with a series of cases in the 1940s. It also reflects a congressional policy in effect since adoption of the Anti-Injunction Act of 1793. That policy prohibits such federal court intervention unless authorized by Congress or necessary to protect the federal courts' own powers.

In 1965, however, the Court appeared to create a substantial exception to the abstention doctrine—permitting federal court injunctions to bar criminal prosecutions under a state law that was being challenged on First Amendment grounds.

In *Dombrowski v. Pfister* the Court ruled, 5–2, that abstention was inappropriate in cases in which state laws were "justifiably attacked on their face as abridging free expression or as applied for the purpose of discouraging protected activities." The decision barred Louisiana officials from threatening a civil rights leader with prosecution under state laws against subversive activities and communist propaganda.

Six years later, however, the Court returned to a stricter view of the abstention doctrine. The case, *Younger v. Harris* (1971), challenged an indictment under California's anti-syndicalism law. In an 8–1 decision the Court said that in the absence of evidence of bad faith, harassment, or the threat of irreparable injury, a federal court should not enjoin a state court action on the basis of a claimed violation of First Amendment rights.

Writing for the Court, Justice Hugo L. Black based the decision not on the Anti-Injunction Act, but on the broader notion of comity. Comity, he said, was designed to ensure that federal rights were protected "in ways that will not unduly interfere with the legitimate activities of the states."

In a series of rulings following *Younger,* the Court has extended the doctrine of nonintervention to limit federal injunctions halting a criminal proceeding begun after the injunction was requested and to curtail their use to intervene in some state civil proceedings. In one highly publicized decision, the Court in 1987 overturned a lower federal court's order that had shielded the Texaco oil company from posting a $10 billion bond in order to appeal a damage award won in state court by another oil company, Pennzoil, in a contract infringement action.

Commerce Power

The Constitution grants Congress the power to "regulate Commerce with foreign Nations, and among the several States" (Article I, Section 8, Clause 3).

The Supreme Court in 1824 interpreted broadly the federal government's power under the commerce clause. For more than a century afterward, however, conflicting Supreme Court rulings sometimes upheld and other times overturned congressional efforts to deal with social and economic problems by regulating interstate commerce.

Since 1937 the Court has swept aside almost all legal barriers to use of the commerce power. As a result, federal regulation extends to almost all economic matters that in any way affect interstate commerce.

Commerce and Navigation

The need for federal control over interstate and foreign commerce was one of the primary concerns of the Constitutional Convention in 1787. The states' control over commercial affairs under the Articles of Confederation had resulted in confusion for merchants and economic rivalries between the states. The condition was universally viewed as unacceptable. The inclusion of the commerce clause in the new Constitution did not arouse much discussion at the Philadelphia convention.

The first Supreme Court ruling on the commerce

power was *GIBBONS V. OGDEN* (1824). Chief Justice John Marshall gave the clause a sweeping interpretation in striking down a New York steamboat-monopoly law as an interference with a federal law on navigation. Marshall wrote that the commerce power "is complete in itself, may be exercised to its utmost extent, and acknowledges no limitations other than those prescribed by the Constitution."

Marshall rejected the view of a concurring justice, William Johnson, that the federal government's commerce power was exclusive and left "nothing for the states to act on." Instead, Marshall said, states were free to regulate "completely internal commerce." They could also pass laws similar to federal legislation as long as the laws did not impede or conflict with the federal law on the subject.

Congress did not begin to use the commerce power recognized in *Gibbons* until the late nineteenth century. Up to the 1880s the Court's rulings in this area focused on deciding when state actions unconstitutionally impinged on the federal commerce power. After several conflicting decisions, the Court settled on an approach to the issue in *Cooley v. Board of Wardens of the Port of Philadelphia* (1852). In upholding state regulation of city harbor pilots, the Court announced the so-called selective exclusiveness doctrine. This doctrine barred state regulation in areas where national uniformity was required but allowed local regulation if necessary to accommodate local circumstances and needs.

Still, federal power over navigation continued to grow with little resistance by the Court. Congress used control of the waterways as the basis for power-producing projects such as the Boulder Canyon dam and the Tennessee Valley Authority. The Court sustained the laws setting up both projects. In 1940 the Court upheld an expansive interpretation of the federal government's right to regulate dam construction on a portion of a nonnavigable river because it might be made navigable by the dam.

More recently, in 1978 the Court struck down a Washington state law that—much like the Pennsylvania law upheld in *Cooley* 126 years earlier—required state-licensed pilots on tankers entering and leaving Puget Sound. The Court said the law conflicted with federal power to regulate pilots on tankers licensed under federal law.

Congress and the Railroads

The extension of Congress's commerce power over the nation's railroads came less directly than it had in navigation, but ultimately it was just as complete.

Most early regulation of railways was by states. But the business panics of the 1870s and 1880s and the nation's westward expansion led to consolidation of vast interstate rail networks. As a result, state regulation became less effective just as the public was demanding tougher rules to prohibit discriminatory rebate and price-fixing practices.

The Court had upheld state regulation of intrastate rates as late as 1877. In 1886, however, it essentially ended state authority over interstate railroads by holding that states could not set intrastate freight rates for goods traveling between states. This decision made it necessary for Congress to step in. The result was the Interstate Commerce Act of 1887, which established the Interstate Commerce Commission (ICC). The act barred rebate and price-fixing practices and stipulated that rates should be reasonable and just but did not explicitly give the ICC power to set or adjust rates.

In 1894 the Supreme Court held that the ICC in fact had no rate-fixing power. Congress closed that legislative gap in 1906. The Court then upheld the ICC's power to adjust rates (1910) and to set rates (1914). In a pair of rulings in 1913 and 1914, the Court also upheld the ICC's power to regulate intrastate rates, saying that intrastate and interstate travel were "so related that the government of the one involves the control of the other."

The experience with the railroads provided the model for other federal regulatory systems that were also upheld by the Court over the next several decades. The Court in 1914 sustained Congress's decision to regulate oil pipelines under the Interstate Commerce Act. It later barred states from setting rates for electricity transmitted from one state to another and allowed the Federal Power Commission to set the price for natural gas found in one state and sold in another. In 1933 the Court upheld federal regulation of radio transmissions. "No state lines divided the radio waves, and national regulation is not only appropriate but essential to the efficient use of radio facilities," the Court said.

Trusts and Labor

In the late nineteenth and early twentieth centuries the Supreme Court was dominated by justices who believed in a laissez-faire economic philosophy. These justices opposed regulation that impinged on the free development of business and industry. That philosophy led the Court into controversial rulings that hindered or blocked Congress from dealing with the two major economic issues of the era: the rise of the great industrial "trusts" and the movement for workers' rights.

The Court during this era narrowly defined commerce to include the buying and selling of goods, but not manufacture or production, which were considered subject to state rather than federal regulation. Labor relations were also viewed as beyond the commerce power. In the area of labor relations, even state regulation was limited by the supposed rights of employers and employees to enter into contracts without government interference.

The distinction between commerce and manufacture led the Court initially to narrowly construe Congress's first effort to control the emerging industrial giants, the Sherman Antitrust Act of 1890. (See ANTITRUST.) The Court's sugar trust ruling, *United States v. E. C. Knight Co.* (1895), blocked the government from dismantling an industrial combination that controlled 90 percent of all the sugar processed in the United States. Writing for the Court, Chief Justice Melville W. Fuller reiterated that manufacturing was not commerce. He further held that the trust's indirect effects on commerce did not justify federal regulation.

In three rulings over the next ten years, however, the Court upheld government antitrust moves. The most important of these, *Swift & Co. v. United States* (1905), unanimously upheld an attack on the "beef trust." Justice Oliver Wendell Holmes declared that federal regulation of commercial activities within a single state was permitted if the activities were part of a "current of commerce among the states." This "stream of commerce" doctrine was a milestone in adapting the commerce clause to the realities of modern business growth.

The Court was slower to accept federal intervention to protect the rights of workers.

In 1908 the Court struck down two laws aimed at aiding railway workers, on the grounds that the laws went beyond the federal commerce power. In *Adair v. United States* the Court, by a vote of 6 to 2, overturned a law that prohibited "yellow-dog contracts" (contracts that required employees to agree not to join a union as a condition of employment). Justice John Marshall Harlan said there was not a sufficient "connection between interstate commerce and membership in a labor organization" to justify outlawing the contracts.

The Court split 5–4 in the second case in striking down the 1906 Employers' Liability Act, which made common carriers, such as railroads, liable for the on-the-job deaths or injuries of employees. Congress responded by passing a law limited to railway workers in interstate commerce. The Court upheld that law in 1912.

A longer confrontation with Congress came over the issue of CHILD LABOR. Twice the Court struck down laws aimed at outlawing child labor in manufacturing.

In *Hammer v. Dagenhart* (1918) the Court ruled, 5–4, that a 1916 law prohibiting interstate transportation of goods manufactured with child labor went beyond the federal commerce power. To reach that result, the Court had to distinguish a line of half a dozen cases dating from 1902 that had recognized a federal POLICE POWER—derived from the commerce power—to bar certain goods from interstate commerce.

Congress attempted to circumvent the *Dagenhart* ruling by imposing a 10 percent excise tax on goods made with child labor. In 1922 the Court struck down that act. The eight-justice majority said Congress could not use its taxing power to regulate wholly internal matters of the states.

By 1930 the Court had begun to recognize some federal power over labor relations. In that year it upheld the 1926 Railway Labor Act, which established procedures for settling railway labor disputes and barred railroads from interfering with workers' rights to join a union. But the Court remained opposed to broad intervention in labor affairs. It also resisted the expansion of the commerce power in other areas—a stance that led to a sharp confrontation with Congress and the president.

The New Deal

The centerpiece of President Franklin D. Roosevelt's economic recovery program was the National Industrial Recovery Act (NIRA) of 1933. The act indirectly extended federal power over economic affairs by authorizing the president to approve codes of fair competition drawn up by businesses in a given industry. The codes were to contain, among other things, hour and wage standards for workers.

On May 27, 1935, the Court unanimously held the act unconstitutional as an invalid delegation of legislative power by Congress and an improper effort to regulate intrastate commerce. The case, *Schechter Poultry Corp. v. United States,* involved a New York City poultry firm that the Court said was purely intrastate commerce. Writing for the Court, Chief Justice Charles Evans Hughes acknowledged that Congress could regulate intrastate commerce if it affected interstate commerce. But in this case, he said, any effects were too indirect to support federal regulation.

The Court's narrow view of the commerce power contributed to its invalidation of two other major New Deal programs in 1936: the Bituminous Coal Conservation Act and the Agricultural Adjustment Act (AAA). The Court's 6–3 decision in *Carter v. Carter Coal Co.* said Congress could not regulate the coal-mining industry because mining was production, not commerce, and the industry's effects on interstate commerce were "secondary and indirect." The farm-price stabilization scheme established by the AAA was

A unanimous decision May 27, 1935, declared unconstitutional the National Industrial Recovery Act, a major piece of New Deal legislation. The winners in Schechter Poultry Corporation v. United States *celebrate their victory: (left to right) Martin Schechter, Aaron Schechter, lawyer Joseph Heller, Joseph Schechter, and Alex Schechter.   Source: UPI/Bettmann*

thrown out as an improper use of the government's taxing and spending powers. The Court's view of agriculture as outside the commerce power was so entrenched that the administration did not even defend the act on that ground.

The dissenting justices in the *Carter Coal* case accused the majority of using an overly narrow distinction between direct and indirect effects to limit Congress's power to deal with pressing economic ills. "The power is as broad as the need that evokes it," Justice Benjamin N. Cardozo wrote. Within a year Cardozo's views gained a majority on the Court, thanks to an important switch by Justice Owen J. Roberts, previously a member of the conservative majority.

The Court announced its broadened view of the commerce power in a decision that upheld the National Labor Relations Act (NLRA). The case, *NLRB v. Jones & Laughlin Steel Corp.* (1937), arose after the steel company fired ten union employees from one of its factories. Writing for the new five-member majority, Chief Justice Hughes upheld an enforcement action by the National Labor Relations Board. The opinion emphasized the "immediate" and potentially "catastrophic" effect that a strike in a nationally organized industry would have on interstate commerce.

Hughes did not expressly overrule *Schechter Poultry* and *Carter Coal,* but the four dissenting justices said there was no way to reconcile the new ruling with those decisions. Encouraged by the new attitude on the Court, Congress broadened protection for workers in 1938 by passing the Fair Labor Standards Act. That act set a forty-hour work week and an eventual minimum wage of forty cents per hour for workers "engaged in commerce or in the production of goods for commerce." The act also barred from interstate commerce goods manufactured without compliance with the act's provisions and goods made with child labor.

A test of this statute reached the Court in 1941, and the Court unanimously upheld it. Writing for the Court in *United States v. Darby Lumber Co.,* Justice Harlan Fiske Stone said that shipment of manufactured goods was part of commerce and Congress "indisputably" had the power to prohibit such shipment as "a regulation of the commerce." The Court sustained the child labor provision by expressly overruling its

earlier *Dagenhart* ruling. It declared the Tenth Amendment no bar to the federal commerce power as long as the means Congress used were "appropriate and plainly adapted to the permitted end."

The Court allowed a further extension of federal commerce power in *Wickard v. Filburn* (1942). The ruling upheld a revised agricultural adjustment act that established marketing quotas for various commodities and penalized farmers who exceeded them. A farmer named Wickard was penalized for exceeding his wheat allotment. He contested the penalty by saying the wheat was to be used as feed grain for his own livestock. In upholding the penalty, the Court said Congress had the right to determine that use of home-grown wheat could have a "substantial economic effect" on interstate commerce since the wheat Wickard grew and used "competes with wheat in commerce."

Modern Commerce Power

Freed from earlier restrictions, the federal commerce power continued to expand almost without limit. Only twice—in 1976 and 1992—has the Court found that Congress overreached this power, and the Court later reversed one of those decisions.

The most important application of the broadened view of commerce power came in the area of CIVIL RIGHTS. In passing the Civil Rights Act of 1964, Congress prohibited racial discrimination in public accommodations if lodgings were provided to interstate travelers, if interstate travelers were served, or if a substantial portions of the goods sold or entertainment provided moved in interstate commerce.

In *Heart of Atlanta Motel v. United States* (1964), the Court unanimously upheld this portion of the act. The motel claimed that its business was purely local in character, but it did serve out-of-state travelers. The Court said Congress's power to regulate interstate commerce gave it the authority to regulate local enterprise that "might have a substantial and harmful effect" on that commerce. In a companion case decided the same day and in another decision five years later, the Court upheld application of the act to other businesses with a less direct connection to interstate commerce.

An expanded view of federal police power also allowed Congress to pass environmental protection laws that imposed a host of new regulations on business and industry. Despite continuous legal disputes over the laws, the Supreme Court has not been asked to throw out any of them on grounds that Congress exceeded its authority under the commerce clause. A 1968 congressional statute that prohibited loan-sharking activities was challenged as going beyond the federal commerce power. The Court in 1971 upheld the act on the ground that loan sharking was in a "class of activity" that affected interstate commerce and thus could be regulated under the commerce power.

The Court's two checks to expansive federal commerce power were based on grounds of state sovereignty under the Tenth Amendment. (See STATES AND THE COURT.)

In 1976 the Court in *National League of Cities v. Usery* struck down, 5–4, a federal law extending minimum wage and overtime requirements to state and local government employees. The majority said the law interfered with the essential functions of state and local governments. But the Court overruled the decision in 1985.

In 1992 the Court again cited state sovereignty in striking down a portion of a complex 1985 law regulating disposal of low-level radioactive wastes from nuclear power plants. The invalidated provision required states either to find places to store the nuclear wastes or to assume legal ownership of the wastes themselves. The 6–3 decision described the provision as improper coercion on the states.

Common Law

Common law refers to the collection of principles and rules—particularly those drawn from early, uncodified English law—that derive their authority from long usage and custom or from judicial recognition of custom. It is the historic basis of Anglo-American law and remains a vital concept in the development of CASE LAW in the states.

Two Supreme Court decisions more than a century apart have held that there is no federal common

law—either for the definition of criminal offenses or for the creation of rules for civil cases.

In *United States v. Coolidge* (1816) the Court held that federal courts had no criminal jurisdiction except that created by federal laws declaring certain offenses to be federal crimes. The ruling was a victory for the Jeffersonians, who contended that only the states could try common law crimes.

The issue was more complex in civil cases because of the federal courts' DIVERSITY JURISDICTION over suits involving citizens of different states. In those cases, according to the Judiciary Act of 1789, federal courts were to apply "the laws of the several states."

In *Swift v. Tyson* (1842) the Court held that federal courts in diversity cases were to apply only the written statutes of the states, not the common law or interpretation of the statutes set out in decisions of the state courts. The ruling may have been intended to create a national common law for states, but instead it led to conflicting interpretations of state law by state courts and federal courts within the same state.

In 1938 the Court, troubled by the lack of uniform interpretation of state law, took the opportunity presented by a diversity case and overruled *Swift v. Tyson*. In *Erie Railroad Co. v. Tompkins* the Court said that the Constitution required that the law in diversity cases be the law of the applicable state—both its written laws and the decisions of its courts. "There is no federal general common law," the Court stated.

Communism

World communism was seen as presenting a dual threat to the United States, both internal and external. The spread of communist regimes after World War II posed the most serious external challenge the West had ever faced. Domestically, communist ideology had political appeal for some critics of the existing economic order, especially during the Great Depression.

Fears for the survival of the American system led to the enactment of laws intended to curtail "subversive activities" and punish those who took part in them. The Supreme Court initially upheld the two

William Z. Foster and Benjamin Gitlow, Communist Workers' party candidates for president and vice president, at Madison Square Garden, New York, November 4, 1928.
Source: UPI/Bettmann

major antisubversive laws passed by Congress. Later, however, the Court struck down some parts of one of the laws and limited the enforcement of the other by interpreting it more strictly. (See also LOYALTY OATHS.)

The Smith Act (Title I of the Alien Registration Act of 1940) made it a crime, for citizens and aliens alike, to "advocate, abet, advise, or teach" the doctrine of overthrowing the government "by force or violence," or to be a member of an organization dedicated to the violent overthrow of the government. The McCarran Act (Internal Security Act of 1950) required organizations found to be communist-action or communist-front groups to register with the government and disclose their members and officers. Members of registered groups were barred from holding federal jobs or jobs in defense-related industries and from receiving passports.

Eleven leaders of the Communist party in the United States were indicted under the Smith Act in 1948 and convicted after a long and sensational trial.

In *Dennis v. United States* (1951) the Supreme Court, by a vote of 6 to 2, affirmed the convictions and upheld the constitutionality of the Smith Act.

The justices disagreed widely over how to measure the validity of the law against the restraints it placed on First Amendment freedoms of expression and association. Writing for a plurality of four justices, Chief Justice Fred M. Vinson paid lip service to the "clear and present danger" test. But he seemed in fact to apply a less stringent "sliding scale" rule that allowed the government to punish subversive advocacy—"even though doomed from the outset"—because of "the inflammable nature of world conditions." Justice Robert H. Jackson, concurring separately, explicitly disavowed the need to satisfy the clear and present danger test.

The other justices saw dangers to First Amendment freedoms. Justice Felix Frankfurter, concurring, said the act would inevitably lead to a "restriction on the interchange of ideas." But he deferred to Congress on the need for the law. Dissenting justices Hugo L.

Black and William O. Douglas said the act unconstitutionally infringed pure speech.

In the wake of the *Dennis* decision, new prosecutions under the Smith Act were brought against 121 second-rank Communist party officials and some rank-and-file party members. Convictions were obtained in every case brought to trial between 1951 and 1956. In 1957, however, the Court overturned, by a 6–1 vote, convictions obtained against fourteen persons in three cases. It thus sharply curtailed the use of the Smith Act to prosecute Communist party members.

The Court's decisions—known collectively by the name of one of the cases, *Yates v. United States*—imposed strict standards of proof in Smith Act prosecutions. Writing for the Court, Justice John Marshall Harlan said that the jury instructions in the cases had failed to distinguish between "advocacy of forcible overthrow as an abstract doctrine and advocacy of action to that end." Faced with the requirement to show a connection between advocacy and action, the government ended most Smith Act prosecutions. In 1961, however, the Court did uphold, by a 5–4 vote, convictions under the Smith Act's membership clause *(Scales v. United States).*

In the same year, the Court ruled on a challenge to the McCarran Act in a massive and prolonged case brought by the Subversive Activities Control Board to force the Communist party of the United States to register. The board twice ordered the party to register, and the party twice refused. In upholding the second order in *Communist Party v. Subversive Activities Control Board* (1961), the Court rejected the party's arguments that the registration provisions were unconstitutional as a bill of attainder or as an abridgment of First Amendment freedoms.

Writing for the Court, Frankfurter again deferred to Congress, saying that lawmakers had reasonably balanced private rights of free speech and association against the public interest in disclosure by a "foreign-dominated conspiracy" that had as its aim "to overthrow existing government in this country." In separate opinions, the four dissenting justices cited varied reasons for disagreeing with the majority. These reasons included one issue that Frankfurter found premature: a claim that the act's registration requirement violated the Fifth Amendment privilege against self-incrimination.

In later decisions, however, the Court barred enforcement of most of the law's implementing provisions. In *Aptheker v. Secretary of State* (1964) it invalidated the act's passport restrictions for members of registered organizations. The next year it barred enforcement of the registration requirement against individuals *(Albertson v. Subversive Activities Control Board* [1965]). And in *United States v. Robel* (1967) the Court declared unconstitutional the provision that barred members of registered organizations from jobs in defense-related facilities.

In the fall of 1967, Congress amended the McCarran Act to eliminate the registration requirement. Instead the Subversive Activities Control Board was authorized to place on a register the names of individuals and organizations it found to be communist. The board in 1968 did issue orders against three individuals thought to be members of the Communist party. But the U.S. Court of Appeals for the District of Columbia in 1969 set aside the board's order, holding that membership in the Communist party is protected by the First Amendment.

Concurring Opinions

A justice who agrees with the result of the majority opinion but who has reservations about the way it was written, the reasoning behind it, or specific points in it may decide to write a concurring opinion. (See OPINIONS.)

A justice may use a concurring opinion as a means of putting a particular interpretation, or "spin," on the majority opinion in the case or to try to influence how the Court's opinion is applied in future cases touching on the same issue. Occasionally, concurring opinions are little more than masked dissents. In some cases, a justice will concur in part and dissent in part.

Rulings in which there are many concurring opinions may do more to confuse than to clarify the direction of the Court's thinking. *United States v. United Mine*

Workers (1947) provides one example of the problems and vexations arising from the use of concurring opinions. Chief Justice Fred M. Vinson and justices Stanley F. Reed and Harold H. Burton upheld the civil and criminal contempt convictions against the United Mine Workers for two reasons. Justices Wiley B. Rutledge and Frank Murphy both dissented on the same grounds. Justices Felix Frankfurter and Robert H. Jackson agreed with Vinson, Reed, and Burton on one of the grounds but rejected the other. Justices Hugo L. Black and William O. Douglas concurred with Vinson for the reason that Frankfurter and Jackson had rejected but rejected the argument that Frankfurter had approved. The result was that in a 7–2 decision, only three justices agreed that the result the Court reached was the correct one.

In recent decades the number of concurring opinions has increased markedly. By one count there were ten times as many concurring opinions during the 1980s as in the 1940s. Critics complain that concurring opinions, like DISSENTING OPINIONS, undermine the authority of the Court and lead to uncertainty about the law. Some have even proposed that concurring opinions be eliminated or not reported. But these proposals have no significant support either among the justices or in the rest of the legal community.

Conferences

The Supreme Court justices grant or deny review and decide cases in meetings known as conferences. Conferences are scheduled for Wednesday afternoons and Fridays during weeks in which the Court hears oral ARGUMENTS. In May and June, when no oral arguments are scheduled, conferences are also held on Thursdays. The Court meets in conference the week before the new term begins in early October to grant or deny petitions for review that have accumulated over the summer.

Conferences are conducted in complete secrecy. No secretaries, clerks, stenographers, or messengers are allowed into the room. The practice began many years ago when the justices became convinced that a decision had been leaked, and suspicion focused on two pages who waited upon the justices in the conference room. The pages were later cleared when a member of the Supreme Court bar confessed that he had merely made an educated guess about the Court's decision in the case. Nonetheless, only justices have attended the conferences ever since.

In the Court's early years conferences were held in the Washington boardinghouses in which the justices lived. The justices now meet in an elegant oak-paneled, book-lined conference chamber adjacent to the chief justice's suite. Nine chairs are placed around a large rectangular table, each bearing the nameplate of the justice who sits there.

The chief justice sits at the east end of the table, and the senior associate justice at the west end. The other justices take their places in order of seniority, three on one side, four on the other. The junior justice is charged with sending for and receiving documents or other information the Court needs.

Justices are summoned to the conference room by a buzzer. Upon entering the room they shake hands with each other, a custom symbolic of harmony that began in the 1880s. The chief justice presides over the conference. He calls the first case to be decided, reviews the facts and the lower court decisions, sets out the applicable case law, and indicates his views and how he intends to vote. The discussion then passes to the senior associate justice, who is followed by the other justices in order of seniority. Seldom does one justice interrupt another.

The justices in principle can speak for as long as they wish. Chief Justice Charles Evans Hughes, however, grew impatient with long and occasionally irrelevant discourses during conferences and convinced his fellow justices to limit the time they spent on each case. As the number of cases considered during conference has grown, later Courts have tended to follow Hughes's example.

Justices also decide at their conferences whether to grant or deny review. Several days before a conference, the chief justice circulates the "discuss list," a list of those cases deemed important enough for discussion and a vote. Any justice may ask that a case be

The conference room during a break in the proceedings.   Source: U.S. Supreme Court

added to this list. Cases that are not deemed worthy to make the discuss list are placed on the "dead list" and rejected without further consideration.

Consideration in conference of the cases on the discuss list follows the same pattern as discussions of cases that have been argued before the Court. The chief justice notes the facts in the case and the opinion in the lower courts and indicates whether he believes review should be granted or denied. The other justices may then speak in order of seniority. An unwritten rule stipulates that four justices must agree that a case should be heard before it can be scheduled for oral argument.

Other than these procedural arrangements, little is known about what actually happens in conferences. Discussions are said to be polite and orderly for the most part, although occasionally they can be acrimonious. Chief Justice William H. Rehnquist has written that the "true purpose" of conferences is not impassioned debate to convince the other justices of the correctness of a particular view, but rather the determination of the view of the majority of the Court. Justices do sometimes change their position as a result of a conference discussion, he said, but such an event is the exception rather than the rule.

Confessions

The Supreme Court has said that confessions rank "among the most effectual proofs in the law." But because of the importance of confessions, there is a risk that police may sometimes use improper tactics in questioning suspects in order to elicit incriminating statements. To guard against this danger—and to enforce the Fifth Amendment privilege against SELF-IN-CRIMINATION—the Supreme Court as early as 1884 stated that a confession must be voluntary to be admissible as evidence in federal court. The requirement was extended to state trials in 1936.

The difficulty of applying the voluntariness test led the Warren Court in 1966 to establish more definite guidelines. The new rules required police to advise suspects of their rights to remain silent and to consult with a lawyer before or during any interrogation. The decision in *MIRANDA V. ARIZONA* generated a firestorm of criticism. Despite some restrictive interpretations, however, the core ruling has been reaffirmed by the Burger and Rehnquist courts. Contrary to critics' fears, the ruling has not substantially reduced the ability of police to obtain incriminating statements from suspects for later use at trial.

The Court in 1936 used the due process clause of the Fourteenth Amendment to bar coerced confessions in state courts, since it had not yet applied the Fifth Amendment to the states. In *Brown v. Mississippi* black suspects had been subjected to prolonged beatings before giving confessions, which were the only evidence against them and which they later repudiated. The Court unanimously overturned the defendants' convictions and death sentences. "The rack and torture chamber may not be substituted for the witness stand," wrote Chief Justice Charles Evans Hughes. Four years later, in *Chambers v. Florida* (1940), the Court recognized the danger of psychological coercion as it reversed the convictions of four black men who had confessed after several days of being held incommunicado and interrogated by police.

In the three decades after *Brown*, the Court decided thirty state confession cases, examining the "totality of the circumstances" surrounding the arrest and interrogation to determine whether the confession was voluntary. The cases changed the focus from the reliability of the confession to the tactics of the police in obtaining it. Seemingly, a confession was labeled "voluntary" if the Court approved of the police conduct and "involuntary" if it disapproved.

Meanwhile a rule had emerged in federal courts barring the use of confessions obtained after "unnec-essary delay" in a suspect's arraignment. In *McNabb v. United States* (1943) the Court overturned the convictions of several men who had confessed to killing a federal revenue agent after three days of questioning by federal officers. The questioning had taken place in the absence of any defense counsel and before the men had been formally charged with the crime. The Court reaffirmed the ruling in *Mallory v. United States* (1957), barring a confession obtained after an eighteen-hour delay between arrest and arraignment. The Court based its rulings on federal statutes requiring a prompt arraignment and on its supervisory power over lower federal courts.

The Court laid the groundwork for more definite rules for police in state cases by extending the right to legal counsel to the states *(Gideon v. Wainwright* [1963]). It then applied the Fifth Amendment right against self-incrimination to the states *(Malloy v. Hogan* [1964]). A week after *Malloy,* the Court barred the use of a confession because police had not adequately informed a murder suspect of his constitutional right to remain silent. The Court's 5–4 decision in *Escobedo v. Illinois* was designed to protect the suspect's Sixth Amendment right to counsel: police had denied Escobedo's repeated requests to see a lawyer. Two years later, in *Miranda,* the Court—again by a 5–4 vote—fashioned more detailed "procedural safeguards" for police interrogation as a way of protecting both the right to counsel and the privilege against self-incrimination.

The *Miranda* guidelines required police to advise suspects of their rights, but did not go so far as to require that a lawyer be present during questioning or that interrogation take place before a judicial officer. Still, the dissenting justices warned that the ruling would hamper law enforcement. Outside the Court, the ruling was denounced by many police and prosecutors and by a host of politicians, including the 1968 Republican party candidate for president, Richard M. Nixon. Nixon promised in his successful campaign to appoint justices more sympathetic to police.

Over the next decade, the Burger Court, with four Nixon-appointed justices, did narrow *Miranda* somewhat but stopped short of overturning it. At the same time the Court reaffirmed and extended a separate rule limiting police interrogation of suspects after they have been formally charged. In *Massiah v. United States* (1964) the Court found that police had violated a suspect's right to counsel by using an undercover agent to question him after he had been indicted and had retained a lawyer. The Burger Court extended this rule to bar use of a statement obtained from a suspect after arraignment *(Brewer v. Williams* [1977]). Three years later it extended the rule again to prevent the use of incriminating statements overheard by an undercover agent placed in a jail cell with the suspect *(United States v. Henry* [1980]).

In 1990, however, the Court made clear that the *Massiah* rule applies only after formal charging. In *Illinois v. Perkins* it upheld use of statements that a suspect made to an undercover agent while in jail on unrelated charges. The Court further held that the agent did not need to give *Miranda* warnings before questioning the inmate.

Voluntariness remains as a test for determining the admissibility of a confession, as indicated in a recent case *(Arizona v. Fulminante* [1991]). The Court barred as involuntary a confession obtained from a prison inmate by a government informant who offered to protect him from fellow inmates. But in a 5–4 vote, the Court overturned a 1967 decision to hold that the use of an involuntary confession does not necessarily require reversal of a conviction. Instead, Chief Justice William H. Rehnquist said, no new trial is needed if use of the involuntary confession is shown beyond a reasonable doubt to be "harmless error."

Confirmation Process

The televised Supreme Court confirmation hearings of the 1980s and 1990s represent a dramatic change from the days when the Senate barred reporters from confirmation debates to promote candor. Those days lasted until 1929. But the widely publicized, heavily lobbied confirmation process of the late twentieth century does have some parallels to earlier, frequently rough political battles over nomination to the Court.

Under Article II of the Constitution, the president nominates members of the Supreme Court, subject to the advice and consent of the Senate. (See NOMINATION TO THE COURT.) Once confirmed by the Senate, justices have life tenure on the Court.

Of 148 presidential nominations to the Court through May 1994, 28 failed to win the constitutionally required approval by the Senate.

All but six of the rejections for the Court came in the 1800s. Most of those were based on partisan political grounds. They included twelve nominations that failed primarily because the nominees were chosen by presidents who were lame ducks or in their final year in office, and senators wanted to "save the seat" for the next president to bestow. (See POLITICS AND THE COURT.) In the twentieth century, political and legal ideology have played a more important part in confirmation battles.

No nominee has been rejected solely on grounds of lack of professional qualifications. The withdrawal of George H. Williams, who was chosen by President Ulysses S. Grant to be chief justice in 1873, has been attributed to questions about his abilities, but it appears to have been due mainly to unanswered charges of personal corruption. G. Harrold Carswell, who was rejected by the Senate after being nominated by President Richard Nixon in 1970, was viewed as a mediocre judge, but he was also opposed because of his record as a segregationist.

The first Supreme Court nominee to testify before a Senate committee was Harlan Fiske Stone, who made an impressive appearance in 1925. He faced hostile questioning prompted in part by his role as attorney general in a criminal investigation of a member of the Senate. Felix Frankfurter was persuaded to appear in 1939; he faced questions about his membership in the American Civil Liberties Union and his acquaintance with a leading British socialist.

As recently as the 1960s, however, Senate hearings were typically perfunctory. Chief Justice William H. Rehnquist, who was simply a lawyer at the time, wrote a critical article about the Senate's limited inquiry in the nomination of Charles Whittaker in 1957. The hearings for Thurgood Marshall in 1967 and Abe Fortas in 1968 marked the beginning of longer and more confrontational hearings. Rehnquist himself faced some sharp questioning before he was confirmed, 68–26, as an associate justice in 1971 and, by a vote of 65 to 33, as chief justice in 1986.

The new style of hearings poses a delicate problem for senators and nominees. Questions about a nominee's views on legal issues can be viewed as an improper effort to find out how he or she will rule on a particular issue as a justice. Both of President George Bush's nominees to the Court—David H. Souter in 1990 and Clarence Thomas in 1991—faced persistent questions about their views on abortion rights, and their refusal to give direct answers left many senators dissatisfied.

The Nineteenth Century

The Senate first rejected a nominee for the Court in 1795 when it defeated George Washington's choice for chief justice, John Rutledge, because of Rutledge's criticism of the Jay Treaty with England. In 1811 it rejected James Madison's nomination of Alexander Wolcott because of his strict enforcement of the embargo laws as customs collector.

Politics continued to be the dominant factor in confirmation battles throughout the nineteenth century. Senate Whigs blocked Democrat Andrew Jackson's nomination of his secretary of the treasury, Roger B. Taney, as associate justice in 1835. They tried but failed to defeat him again when Jackson chose him as chief justice. John Tyler suffered five defeats in his nominations—the most of any president—all because of political disputes with the Senate.

James K. Polk's nomination of George Woodward in 1845 was rejected because Woodward had made slurs against Irish-Americans and other ethnic groups. On the eve of the Civil War, in 1861, the Senate rejected James Buchanan's lame-duck nomination of Jeremiah S. Black because his views on slavery were unacceptable to northern Republicans.

After the Civil War, in 1869, the Republican-controlled Senate rejected Grant's nomination of Ebenezer R. Hoar because Hoar had supported civil service reform and opposed the impeachment of President Andrew Johnson. Democrat Grover Cleveland suffered successive defeats in nominations in 1893 and 1894 because he chose two New Yorkers—William B. Hornblower and Wheeler H. Peckham—who were unacceptable to that state's Democratic senator.

Like the Republican presidents of the late nineteenth century, Cleveland selected nominees for the court who had conservative, probusiness views. Despite the stirrings of populist and progressive sentiment, however, legal ideology played little or no role in confirmation battles until the twentieth century.

The Twentieth Century

Woodrow Wilson's nomination of Louis D. Brandeis in 1916, however, touched off a sharp ideological fight in the Senate that was tinged with anti-Semitism. Brandeis, the first Jewish individual to be nominated for the Court, had a long record of political and legal advocacy on behalf of consumer and labor causes. Business and industry worked hard to defeat the nomination, but he was confirmed, 47–22.

In the next decade progressive-minded senators had their turn at opposing conservative nominees for the Court. Some Democrats criticized Warren G. Harding's 1922 nominee, Pierce Butler, for his work as a lawyer for railroad companies, but he was confirmed, 61–8. Stronger opposition developed to Herbert Hoover's nomination of Charles Evans Hughes as chief justice in 1930 because he was seen as too conservative. Hughes also was confirmed, however, by a vote of 52 to 26.

Three months later Democrats and progressive Republicans combined to defeat Hoover's next nominee, John J. Parker. The 39–41 vote followed a strong lobbying campaign by the American Federation of Labor and the National Association for the Advancement of Colored People. The groups accused Parker, a federal judge in North Carolina, of insensitivity to labor and racial problems.

All but one of Franklin D. Roosevelt's nine nominees to the Court had little difficulty in winning confirmation. His first nominee, Hugo L. Black, a senator from Alabama at the time, was criticized for supporting Roosevelt's controversial Court-packing bill and was also viewed as inexperienced. After he was confirmed in 1937, by a vote of 63 to 16, Black came under further criticism when it was disclosed that he had joined the Ku Klux Klan as a young man. The criticism died down after Black repudiated his earlier Klan involvement in a dramatic radio broadcast.

Since World War II party politics and legal ideology have combined to cause frequent confrontations between the president and the Senate over Court nominations.

Two of Harry S. Truman's nominees—Tom C. Clark and Sherman Minton—attracted scattered opposition on grounds of presidential cronyism. Dwight D. Eisenhower's two liberal appointees, Earl Warren and William J. Brennan, Jr., drew no significant opposition. But some conservative Republicans opposed John Marshall Harlan over what they regarded as his "internationalist" views. Civil rights issues led some southern Democrats to oppose Eisenhower's nominee Potter Stewart and Lyndon Johnson's nominee Thurgood Marshall (the Court's first black justice).

Five major confirmation fights have occurred since 1968.

Fortas. Johnson appointed Abe Fortas, a prominent lawyer and a close friend and adviser to the president, to the Court in 1965. In June 1968 Johnson nominated him to succeed Warren as chief justice. Johnson was a lame duck by this time, however, and Republicans wanted to hold the seat open until after the presidential election.

Fortas's role as an adviser to Johnson while on the Court, his acceptance of fees for a series of university seminars, and his liberal votes on criminal procedure issues gave Republican senators sufficient ammunition for a filibuster on the Senate floor. When a motion to end the filibuster failed, Fortas asked Johnson to withdraw his name from nomination. That action also killed the nomination of Homer Thornberry, a federal judge from Johnson's home state of Texas, to take Fortas's seat. Fortas resigned in 1969 because of new ethics charges.

Haynsworth, Carswell. Nixon had no difficulty in winning Senate confirmation of Warren E. Burger to succeed Warren in 1969. But he suffered two defeats in trying to fill Fortas's vacancy.

Nixon picked two federal appeals court judges from the South who had generally conservative views. The Democratic-controlled Senate rejected Clement F. Haynsworth in November 1969 by a vote of 45 to 55 because he had participated in cases in which, it was charged, he had a financial interest. Nixon's second choice, G. Harrold Carswell, had a less distinguished record than Haynsworth. He went down to a 45–51 defeat after opponents brought forward evidence of his record in opposing integration as a political candidate, lawyer, and judge.

Bork. Ronald Reagan's 1987 nomination of Robert Bork, a federal appeals court judge of pronounced conservative views, to succeed Lewis F. Powell, Jr., touched off an epic battle. Powell, a Nixon appointee, had been a swing vote on many issues. Bork's accession to the Court, liberals feared, would entrench a conservative majority.

In contentious hearings before the Senate Judiciary Committee, Bork reiterated his conservative views on some constitutional questions, such as the right to privacy, but softened others. Democrats described him as out of the mainstream and depicted his attempts to modify his earlier views as a "confirmation conversion." In the end, six Republicans joined all but two Democrats in rejecting Bork 42–58—the largest margin of defeat ever for a Supreme Court nominee.

Reagan turned next to another conservative from the federal appeals court in Washington, Douglas Ginsburg. But Ginsburg withdrew before being formally nominated after evidence surfaced that he had used marijuana while he was a law school professor. Reagan's third choice was a less doctrinaire conservative federal judge, Anthony M. Kennedy. Kennedy was unanimously confirmed in February 1988.

Thomas. When Bush selected Clarence Thomas, a prominent black conservative serving on the federal appeals court in Washington, to succeed Marshall in 1991, the choice touched a raw nerve in legal and racial politics. Established civil rights groups opposed Thomas on ideological grounds, but polls showed that most African Americans supported the nomination. Abortion rights groups viewed the confirmation fight as critical to preventing the Court from reversing *Roe v. Wade.* The same forces that had combined to defeat Bork slowly coalesced to fight Thomas with equal strength.

Thomas, however, showed himself more adept in

The Senate Judiciary Committee was thrust into the spotlight when, during Clarence Thomas's nationally televised confirmation hearings, Anita Hill, a former employee of Thomas's, alleged that he had sexually harassed her.   Source: R. Michael Jenkins

his confirmation hearing. He refused to answer all inquiries about his views on abortion, managed to divorce himself from some conservative views he had voiced before taking the bench, and won admiration for having risen from abject poverty as a child to a career in politics and the judiciary. Still, seven Democrats voted against him to produce a tie vote on the nomination in committee. The panel sent the nomination to the floor, however, and a vote was scheduled for October 8.

During the weekend before the scheduled vote, news reports disclosed that a former aide of Thomas's, Anita Hill, had charged that he had sexually harassed her while she worked for him. A public outcry forced the Judiciary Committee to reopen the hearing and call Hill, a law professor at the University of Oklahoma, to make her accusations under oath. Thomas

vehemently denied Hill's charges, and the hearings ended inconclusively. The Senate rescheduled the vote for October 15. With solid support from Republicans and scattered votes from Democrats, mostly from the South, Thomas won confirmation, 52–48.

Congress and the Court

Congress and the Supreme Court are separate but interdependent branches of the federal government. The Supreme Court defines the limits of congressional authority, while Congress confirms the Court's members, sets its JURISDICTION, and pays its bills. Just as the Court has used its power of JUDICIAL RE-

VIEW to influence the shape of federal legislation, so Congress has tried from time to time to use its powers over the Court to influence the Court's decisions.

In the first decade of the Court's existence, Congress took up the cause of the states by approving what became the Eleventh Amendment, barring federal courts from hearing suits brought against a state by a citizen of another state. Since then, Congress has approved three other successful constitutional amendments to overturn Court rulings. More frequently, Congress has passed new laws to circumvent Court decisions that invalidated or restricted previous legislation. (See REVERSALS OF RULINGS BY CONSTITUTIONAL AMENDMENT; REVERSALS OF RULINGS BY LEGISLATION.)

Congress has benefited from the Supreme Court's general willingness to support a broad construction of congressional powers under the Constitution. Chief Justice John Marshall's landmark opinion in *MCCULLOCH V. MARYLAND* (1819) gave Congress wide discretion in deciding how to carry out its "enumerated powers" set out in the Constitution (Article I, Section 8). Since then, the Court at various times has blocked congressional legislation in specific areas, but on balance the Court's rulings have supported the trend of increasing federal power.

The Court has been less helpful to Congress in its disputes with the president. Often the Court has tried to avoid refereeing conflicts between the other two branches of government. When the Court has ruled on questions of the SEPARATION OF POWERS, its decisions have sometimes favored Congress and other times supported the president. The Court's general willingness to permit broad exercise of presidential powers, however, has helped give the president the upper hand in many confrontations between the executive and legislative branches.

Powers of Congress

Article I of the Constitution begins by vesting in Congress "[a]ll legislative Powers herein granted." It goes on in Section 8 to enumerate specific powers granted to Congress, including the powers to tax and spend, regulate foreign and interstate commerce, declare war, and raise and maintain an army and navy. A final clause empowers Congress to "make all Laws which shall be necessary and proper" for carrying out the specifically enumerated powers.

Except during the period of laissez-faire constitutionalism in the late nineteenth and early twentieth centuries, the Court has generally upheld Congress's exercise of its major domestic powers. (See COMMERCE POWER; SPENDING POWERS; TAXING POWER.) The Court has claimed the right to declare acts of Congress unconstitutional since its landmark decision in *MARBURY V. MADISON* (1803). It has done so, however, only 128 times in two centuries—twice in the years before the Civil War and on average once each year since then. (See UNCONSTITUTIONAL STATUTES.)

In two areas of special importance to the operations of Congress, the Court has generally upheld its power to manage its internal affairs: disciplining its members and conducting investigations for legislative purposes. Although the Court has issued a few rulings setting limits on those powers, Congress conducts its day-to-day business largely free of interference from the Court. The Court's generally broad construction of the Constitution's "speech or debate clause" provides legal protection to members of Congress in exercising their purely legislative functions. (See CONGRESSIONAL IMMUNITY.)

Internal Affairs

The Court has never questioned the power that the Constitution gives each chamber of Congress to discipline its members and, by a two-thirds vote, to expel a member. The Court has also supported the power of each chamber to determine whether a member meets the qualifications of age, citizenship, and residency set out in the Constitution.

In 1969 the Court ruled that Congress cannot exclude a member-elect for any reason other than failure to meet one of the constitutionally specified qualifications. The 7–1 ruling in *Powell v. McCormack* held that the House had improperly excluded Rep. Adam Clayton Powell, Jr., D-N.Y., in 1967 because of allegations of misconduct and misuse of public funds. In essence, the Court said that the House could not punish Powell for any indiscretions until after it had seated him.

Investigations

The power to conduct investigations to determine the need for new laws and to evaluate the implementation of laws already on the books is central to the operation of Congress. The Court in 1927 endorsed a broad view of the investigative power. In *McGrain v. Daugherty* the Court upheld the Senate's power to subpoena former attorney general Harry M. Daugherty to explain his role in the Teapot Dome oil-lease scandal. The "power of inquiry—with process to enforce it—is an essential and appropriate auxiliary to the legislative function," the Court stated.

Thirty years later the Court underscored the requirement that congressional investigations must have a legislative purpose. Saying that there was "no congressional power to expose for the sake of expo-

In 1927 the Supreme Court took a broad view of the Senate's power to investigate by upholding its right to subpoena a former attorney general to explain his role in the Teapot Dome Scandal.
Source: Library of Congress

sure," the Court in *Watkins v. United States* (1957) reversed a conviction for contempt of Congress. The case involved a witness who had refused to answer questions from the House Un-American Activities Committee in 1954 about people he knew who had formerly been members of the Communist party. The 6–1 decision set two broad requirements. First, Congress had to set out the legislative purpose of an inquiry in sufficient detail for a witness to understand it. Second, a witness was entitled to ask for an explanation of the relevance of any particular question to the inquiry.

Watkins added to the controversy in Congress over the Warren Court's rulings on internal security matters, and four years later the Court narrowed the decision. In *Barenblatt v. United States* (1961) the Court upheld, by a vote of 5 to 4, a conviction for contempt of Congress. In this case, a witness had refused to answer questions about his own past or present membership in the Communist party. Over the next three years, the Court affirmed two other contempt convictions while reversing three on narrow grounds. The net effect of the rulings was to uphold Congress's investigative powers as long as a legislative purpose was made clear and procedural rules were followed.

Pressure from Congress

Congress has tried in various ways to influence the Supreme Court, but with limited success. It has succeeded occasionally in overturning specific decisions by the Court—by enacting a new statute when possible, or by proposing an amendment to the Constitution when necessary. Congress has been less successful in indirect methods of influencing the Court's behavior, although it has the power to determine the Court's membership and to adopt institutional and jurisdictional changes affecting the Court.

Through the CONFIRMATION PROCESS, the Senate has the final say on the membership of the Court. The president's power to nominate justices, however, gives the president a greater ability to shape the Court's political and ideological outlook, especially since Supreme Court justices are appointed for life. (See NOMINATION TO THE COURT.] Congress has the power to remove justices through impeachment, but it has never done so—and the one clear effort to use the power as political retaliation against the Court failed. (See IMPEACHMENT OF JUSTICES.)

Congress's attempts to exert institutional pressure on the Court have been sporadic and generally unsuccessful. It has most often considered plans either to change the Court's jurisdiction or to require extraordinary majorities for the Court to declare state or federal laws unconstitutional. The extraordinary majority proposals have all failed, however, and only once—in the early years of Reconstruction—has Congress repealed the Court's jurisdiction to stop it from issuing a particular decision.

Removal of Jurisdiction

The constitutional provision for Congress to make "exceptions" to the Court's appellate jurisdiction (Article III, Section 2) probably was not intended as a political weapon, but Congress has viewed it as such in several confrontations with the Court.

The first congressional attempts to repeal Supreme Court jurisdiction were occasioned by the Court's early decisions overturning state laws under the power granted by Section 25 of the Judiciary Act of 1789. Legislation to repeal the Court's Section 25 review power was introduced in 1822 but received little attention or support until the early 1830s. Two Court rulings against state sovereignty in 1830 and 1831, however, led to a major clash over the proper balance between the states and the federal government.

As part of that confrontation, the House ordered its Judiciary Committee to report a measure repealing Section 25. The committee made its report on January 24, 1831, but the bill was never fully debated in the House. Using parliamentary tactics, Court supporters were able to repulse the repeal movement by a wide margin. Moves to repeal the section were made in later years, but none came any closer to passage.

Congress prevailed in its second effort to limit the Court's power by changing its appellate jurisdiction. By repealing the Court's jurisdiction over appeals of HABEAS CORPUS cases, Congress in 1868 prevented the Court from ruling on—and probably sustaining—a constitutional challenge to Reconstruction policies.

In the Reconstruction Acts of 1867, Congress had substituted military rule for civilian governments in ten southern states that initially refused to rejoin the Union. In the same year Congress also moved to protect blacks and federal officials in the South from harassment by white southerners by expanding the Supreme Court's jurisdiction to review denials of writs of habeas corpus.

The first such case to reach the Court involved a Mississippi newspaper editor, William H. McCardle, who had been charged by military officials with disturbing the peace and other offenses because of his strong denunciations of Reconstruction. McCardle challenged his detention in a petition for a writ of habeas corpus, and the Court heard arguments in the case, *Ex parte McCardle,* between March 2 and 9, 1868.

After the arguments Radical Republicans in Congress became convinced that the Court would use the case to strike down the Reconstruction Acts. To avert such a ruling, they pushed through legislation to repeal the 1867 grant of appellate jurisdiction over habeas corpus cases and to prohibit the Court from acting on any appeals then pending. President Andrew Johnson vetoed the measure on March 25, but Congress enacted it over his veto two days later.

The Court on March 30 postponed any action on McCardle's case until a new round of arguments in December on the effects of the repeal measure. When the Court finally handed down its decision on April 12, 1869, it bowed to the congressional action, unanimously upholding the repeal measure and dismissing the case for lack of jurisdiction. Less than a month later, Chief Justice Salmon P. Chase wrote to a district judge that if the Court had ruled on McCardle's claim, it "would doubtless have held that his imprisonment for trial before a military commission was illegal."

Nearly a century later, congressional opposition to Court rulings restricting federal or state antisubversive legislation led to an unsuccessful effort to eliminate the Court's jurisdiction over many such cases.

The Court in the 1950s handed down several decisions limiting or overturning antisubversive laws even before its *Watkins* decision in June 1957, which limited the scope of congressional internal security investigations. The next month, Sen. William E. Jenner, R-Ind., introduced a bill that would have barred the Court from accepting appeals in five categories of cases. These categories included cases involving the

Rep. Adam Clayton Powell, D-N.Y., talks to reporters January 9, 1967. The Supreme Court decided that the House of Representatives had improperly prevented the flamboyant and powerful black legislator from taking his seat.   Source: Library of Congress

powers of congressional investigating committees and various kinds of state or federal antisubversive laws and regulations.

The bill attracted support from some conservatives and some southerners who were also dissatisfied with the Warren Court's rulings on school desegregation. But even some critics of the Court's decisions said the bill went too far. The next year, Jenner revised his bill at the suggestion of Sen. John Marshall Butler, R-Md. The new bill repealed the Court's jurisdiction in only one limited area; in the other areas, the bill sought to overturn the Court's rulings rather than changing its jurisdiction. The revised Jenner-Butler bill reached the Senate floor in August 1958 but was killed by a tabling motion, 49–41.

The Warren Court's school prayer decisions in 1962 and 1963 touched off congressional opposition that persisted into the 1980s. When constitutional amendments to overturn the rulings directly failed, some lawmakers offered bills instead to limit the federal courts' power to hear such cases. Court-stripping bills reached the Senate floor four times between 1976 and 1985 but won majority support only once, in 1979. The measure died that year. The 1985 proposal was defeated 62–36 after opponents contended it represented an unconstitutional exercise of congressional authority.

Extraordinary Majority

Members of Congress have occasionally sought to restrain the Court by requiring an extraordinary majority—typically two-thirds of the justices—for it to declare unconstitutional an act of Congress or a state law. One proposal that was introduced several times in the 1820s would have required a vote of five of seven justices to nullify a state law. But the Senate voted to recommit the one such bill that reached a floor vote. In January 1868—while the *McCardle* case was pending—the House passed a bill requiring the vote of two-thirds of the justices to nullify a federal law, but the Senate took no action on the measure. Similar proposals to require a two-thirds majority to invalidate an act of Congress were discussed in the 1930s and again in the 1950s but never strongly pushed.

Other proposals have called for giving Congress the final authority to determine the validity of its own legislation. One such proposal, offered in the 1920s by Sen. Robert M. La Follette, R-Wis., would have allowed Congress to reverse Supreme Court decisions holding federal legislation invalid, by repassing it with a two-thirds majority vote. Like similar proposals, it died in committee.

Size of Court

Congress changed the SIZE OF THE COURT seven times between 1801 and 1869. Several of the changes were aimed at influencing the Court's general outlook by either allowing or preventing appointment of new justices by the president.

Only one specific ruling can be said to have been affected by such a change, however. This was the Court's 5–4 reversal in 1871 of its previous position on the constitutionality of paper money. The decision resulted in part from the expansion of the Court that had been approved by the Republican-controlled Congress three years earlier. (See *LEGAL TENDER CASES*.)

The number of seats on the Court has remained at nine since then. Congress rejected the one proposal since that time to change the Court's size for political purposes. This was President Franklin D. Roosevelt's "Court-packing" plan of 1937.

Terms

Congress once used its power to set the terms of the Court to delay a particular decision by abolishing a term altogether.

In 1802 the Republican-dominated Congress postponed the Court's next meeting until February 1803 in order to delay a ruling on its law repealing the Judiciary Act of 1801. This act was an expansion of the federal judiciary that had been passed by the previous Federalist-controlled Congress. When the Court finally convened, it upheld the repeal measure. Congress has not used this method since to try to restrain the Court.

Salaries

Congress is barred by the Constitution from reducing the salaries of Supreme Court justices. On one occasion, in 1964, Congress showed its displeasure with some of the controversial decisions of the Warren Court by reducing a planned pay increase for the justices from $7,500 to $4,500. (See PAY AND PERQUISITES.) Congress has never tried to pressure the Court by withholding operational funds.

Several reasons can be given to explain why Congress has generally refrained from exercising the powers it has over the Court. First, the Court usually has supporters in Congress who will resist measures to reduce its powers. Second, the most drastic actions—impeachment or repeal of jurisdiction—now seem illegitimate, in part because they have gone unused for so long. Third, the Court's independence can sometimes serve Congress's political interests by shifting responsibility for unpopular decisions.

Finally, even without formal legislative action, Congress can sometimes pressure the Court into retreating from some of its decisions over time, espe-

cially as the Court's membership changes. Sometimes the Court's opinions acknowledge criticism from Congress or elsewhere. At other times the effects of political pressure can only be guessed at. Congress may respect the Court's independence, but its power over the Court also serves as a check on that independence.

Congressional Immunity

The concept of legislators having some immunity from legal actions was well established in England and the American colonies before the Revolution. To provide that protection, the Constitution states that members of Congress "shall in all Cases, except Treason, Felony and Breach of the Peace, be privileged from Arrest . . . ; and for any Speech or Debate in either House, they shall not be questioned in any other Place" (Article I, Section 6).

The privilege from arrest clause has become virtually obsolete, as various court decisions have limited its protections. The speech or debate clause, however, remains an important part of Congress's power of self-preservation, though its scope has been narrowed in recent years.

In its first interpretation of the speech or debate clause, the Supreme Court in 1881 extended the protection beyond actual floor debate to "things generally done . . . in relation to the business" before Congress. These included writing committee reports, offering resolutions, and voting.

In 1972 the Court refused to widen the protection beyond legislative business. In *Gravel v. United States* the Court held that Sen. Mike Gravel, D-Alaska, enjoyed immunity for his actions in releasing portions of the then-classified Pentagon Papers (a history of U.S. involvement in Vietnam). His immunity did not, however, cover his later arranging for their publication in a book. The ruling extended immunity to legislative aides, subject to the same limitations.

Two rulings in 1979 provided further openings for civil lawsuits against members of Congress.

In *Davis v. Passman* the Court held, 5–4, that federal employees, including members of Congress, are subject to civil suit for discrimination in employment under the equal protection provision that has been read into the due process clause of the Fifth Amendment. The ruling reinstated a suit by a woman who had been fired from her position as an aide to Rep. Otto E. Passman, D-La., simply because he preferred a man in the post. The ruling did not discuss the impact of the speech or debate clause, however, and the case was settled without a decision on that issue.

Also in 1979 the Court ruled that a lawmaker was not immune from libel suits for allegedly defamatory statements made in press releases or newsletters. The decision in *Hutchinson v. Proxmire* allowed a scientist to proceed with a suit against Sen. William Proxmire, D-Wis., for critical comments Proxmire had made about his federally funded research project.

The Court has grappled with the question of how to apply the speech or debate clause to criminal prosecutions of members of Congress. In *United States v. Johnson* (1966) the Court unanimously set aside a lawmaker's conviction for conspiracy to defraud the United States because the charge rested on an allegation that he had given a floor speech in return for a bribe.

The Court distinguished that ruling from a later one, however, when it upheld the bribery conviction of a former senator. Sen. Daniel B. Brewster, D-Md., had been convicted of taking $24,000 from a mail-order firm to influence his actions on postal rate legislation. Writing for the Court in *United States v. Brewster* (1972), Chief Justice Warren E. Burger explained that Brewster's acceptance of the bribe was "the illegal conduct." Thus there was "no need" to show Brewster's "performance of the illegal promise."

The ruling in Brewster's case appears to have clarified the issue. In the early 1980s, seven members of Congress were convicted on corruption charges in the so-called Abscam investigation. Although the lawmakers' appeals raised the speech or debate clause as barring or limiting the prosecutions, federal appeals courts upheld the convictions. The Supreme Court decided not to review the cases.

Constitutional Law

The U.S. Constitution was, at the time of its ratification in 1789, a unique document. Before that time the term *constitution* had been used in other countries to refer simply to the principles and assumptions underlying the existing governmental system. In the United States, the word gained added significance as a charter, a single document that established the structure of the government, defined and limited its powers, and could be amended only by a supermajority vote by both the national legislature and the states.

With the addition of the BILL OF RIGHTS in 1791, the Constitution also became a broad guarantee of individual rights, at least against actions by the new federal government.

Two centuries later, the U.S. Constitution is the longest-lived constitution in the world. It has been amended only twenty-seven times, and none of the amendments has fundamentally altered the governmental structure established in the Constitution.

Supreme Court's Role

The Supreme Court has played a critical role in the longevity of the Constitution. In fact, the Court has been described as a continuing constitutional convention. When it took on the power of JUDICIAL REVIEW—the power to declare acts of Congress unconstitutional—the Court became the ultimate arbiter of the meaning of the Constitution. In exercising that power it has defined, in greater detail than the Constitution provides, the powers of the federal government and the states, the respective authority of Congress and the president, and the scope of individual liberties. The Court's ability to adapt those definitions over time has reduced the pressure for constitutional amendments.

Despite the Court's lack of power to enforce its rulings, a tradition of compliance ensures that they will be obeyed, even by Congress and the president. As a result, constitutional law has a greater impact on the day-to-day lives of Americans than is the case in other countries, and the Supreme Court can accurately be described as the most powerful court the world has ever known.

The Constitution was written at Independence Hall, Philadelphia, during the summer of 1787.   Source: Library of Congress

The Supreme Court is not, however, exclusively or even primarily a constitutional court. Each year it issues 130 or so written decisions, which encompass a wide variety of constitutional, statutory, and common law issues. The diversity of its docket has been viewed as one source of the Court's strength. The Court does not reach out to decide sharply disputed constitutional issues in the abstract. Rather, it resolves them in the context of concrete disputes brought by individual litigants.

Often the Court can decide an individual case on some legal ground without touching the constitutional issue. By exercising JUDICIAL RESTRAINT, the Court can conserve its political strength for most effective use. Sometimes the Court can delay the consideration of a constitutional issue simply by refusing to accept cases for review. (See CERTIORARI.)

Methods of Interpretation

The Court has never adopted a single method of interpreting the Constitution. Its decisions sometimes reflect close reliance on the text of the Constitution, the intentions of the framers, and the historical context of the provision at issue. Other decisions place greater weight on later interpretations of the Constitution or on contemporary social, political, and moral values.

The different methods of interpretation often prompt sharp debate among the justices and among government officials, legal scholars, and the public at large. In recent years critics of some of the Court's decisions in the areas of criminal procedure and individual rights have advocated two overlapping theories for narrowing or overturning some expansions of constitutional rights by the Court.

One theory, called STRICT CONSTRUCTION, says the text of the Constitution should be "strictly construed" so as to limit expansions of individual rights in such areas as privacy and free speech. Another theory, called ORIGINAL INTENT, says the framers' intentions are the key to interpreting and applying any constitutional provision. Both theories have strong appeal among political conservatives, but both have been sharply criticized by many legal scholars.

The Supreme Court rejected the strict construction theory in its first landmark decision on the powers of the federal government, *MCCULLOCH V. MARYLAND* (1819). In what is sometimes called his most important opinion, Chief Justice John Marshall argued that the framers deliberately kept the Constitution brief with the intention that the powers of the new federal government would be broadly rather than narrowly construed.

"Its nature, therefore, requires that only its great outlines should be marked, its important objects designated, and the minor ingredients which compose those objects be deduced from the nature of the objects themselves," Marshall wrote. "[W]e must never forget that it is a constitution that we are expounding."

More than a century later, Justice Felix Frankfurter, a strong advocate of judicial restraint, argued that even though some constitutional provisions could be strictly construed, many others were written with deliberate "imprecision."

"Great concepts like 'Commerce among the several states,' 'due process of law,' 'liberty,' 'property,' were purposely left to gather meaning from experience," Frankfurter wrote in 1949. "[T]he statesmen who founded this nation knew too well that only a stagnant society remains unchanged."

On the contemporary Court, Chief Justice William H. Rehnquist and Justice Antonin Scalia have been the two strongest advocates for a narrower approach to interpreting the Constitution.

In a law review article written in 1976, while he was still an associate justice, Rehnquist argued that the Court should not endorse any legal right that is not "within the four corners" of the Constitution. He continued by saying that the Court should not use its authority "to make the Constitution relevant and useful in solving the problems of modern society."

Scalia's approach can be seen in his dissent in a 1992 abortion rights case. In explaining his view that the right to abortion is not protected under the Constitution, Scalia wrote: "I reach that conclusion . . . because of two simple facts: (1) the Constitution says absolutely nothing about it, and (2) the longstanding traditions of American society have permitted it to be legally proscribed."

Historical Watersheds

Constitutional development in the United States has not followed a tidy pattern. But some major historical watersheds can be marked.

Nation Building

In its first decades the Court helped lay the foundations for the national government. Marshall's opinion in *McCulloch v. Maryland* sustained a broad construction of congressional power, while his opinion in *GIBBONS V. OGDEN* (1824) established the supremacy of the federal COMMERCE POWER over the states.

The president and Congress made their own contributions to the expansion of national powers. President Thomas Jefferson, supposedly a strict constructionist, negotiated the Louisiana Purchase without explicit constitutional authority. Congress voted to create a fund for building roads, canals, and other in-

ternal improvements, even though presidents James Madison and James Monroe refused funding on constitutional grounds.

States' Rights

States' rights were not ignored during Marshall's era. States retained power over commerce if their laws did not conflict with federal policy. The Court in 1833 held that the Bill of Rights did not apply to the states.

Under Chief Justice Roger B. Taney, however, the Court accorded more deference to the states. The doctrine of "dual federalism" allowed states greater control over internal affairs, though the Court's rulings on the issues were frequently confused. *Charles River Bridge v. Warren Bridge* (1837) gave the states greater leeway in regulating corporations—thereby undermining one of Marshall's great opinions, *Dartmouth College v. Woodward* (1819).

The issue of slavery underlay some of the Taney Court's opinions narrowing federal powers, though the Court also had to insist on federal supremacy on the issue of returning fugitive slaves from northern states. The sectional rivalry led some to argue that states could annul federal laws, but the nullification theory was never tested before the Court.

In the Civil War the issue of secession was settled on the battlefield, but states' rights retained support on the Court even after the war. The Court's narrow construction of the privileges and immunities clause of the Fourteenth Amendment, in the *SLAUGHTER-HOUSE CASES* (1873) left most issues of individual rights to the states. The *Civil Rights Cases* (1883) found no constitutional authority for Congress to invade states' prerogatives by prohibiting racial discrimination in public accommodations. *PLESSY V. FERGUSON* (1896) found no constitutional bar to state-mandated racial segregation.

Laissez-Faire

The industrial revolution and the rise of the corporation created divisions and conflict in American society. A more activist Court came to be viewed as wielding the Constitution in favor of business and propertied interests in those disputes.

The Court narrowly defined commerce in its 1895

decision sharply restricting the impact of the new Sherman Antitrust Act. In the same year it threw out the federal income tax on constitutional grounds. Over the next decade the Court recognized a constitutional freedom of contract that was used in *Lochner v. New York* (1905) to strike down a state law concerning maximum working hours. In 1908 the Court used freedom of contract to invalidate a federal law against "yellow dog" contracts restricting workers' rights to join a union. In the same year the Court ruled in favor of a railroad contesting a state law concerning rate regulation. That decision established for the first time the power of federal courts to enjoin the operation of a state law challenged as unconstitutional.

During the same period, however, the Court's PO-LICE POWER decisions laid a constitutional basis for the modern regulatory state. The Court upheld state regulation of businesses and local zoning laws, despite the impact on property rights. The Court also recognized for the first time a national police power, derived from the federal commerce power. The police power provided a constitutional justification for the first of the modern regulatory statutes—the Pure Food and Drug Act of 1906.

Federal power also grew in the activist presidencies of Theodore Roosevelt, William Howard Taft, and Woodrow Wilson, and along with the national mobilization to fight World War I. The war and its aftermath brought the Court its first modern civil liberties issues—espionage and sedition cases challenged as violations of First Amendment rights. The Court found no constitutional bar to imprisoning people for advocating views opposed by the government.

The Court continued to strike down some state and federal economic measures in the 1920s and 1930s. This tendency culminated with the series of rulings striking down key portions of President Franklin D. Roosevelt's New Deal program in 1935 and 1936. The constitutional justifications for the rulings were narrow constructions of the federal powers of commerce, spending, and taxing. The decisions provoked a political confrontation that led to the demise of laissez-faire constitutionalism and wrought a permanent change in the Court's constitutional philosophy.

Revolution of 1937

Roosevelt devised his "Court-packing" plan of 1937 to remove the constitutional roadblocks to his programs. The defeat of the plan vindicated the Court's constitutional prerogatives. But two members of the Court, Chief Justice Charles Evans Hughes and Justice Owen J. Roberts, had already changed their views. While the plan was under debate, the Court handed down a series of decisions that upheld New Deal measures. These rulings amounted to a revolution in constitutional interpretation.

The Court sustained the National Labor Relations Act by abandoning the distinction between manufacturing and commerce that had been used to limit the federal commerce power. It upheld federal unemployment compensation and old age benefit programs by taking a broader view of the government's taxing and spending powers, even if they infringed on states' rights. The Court also dropped its theory of freedom of contract in order to uphold state minimum wage laws. Four years later, in 1941, the Court similarly found no constitutional bar to a federal wage and hours law and used that decision to sweep away states' rights limitations on the federal commerce power.

Roosevelt reinforced the change in constitutional philosophy in his selection of justices. He made nine appointments to the Court over a span of seven years. By 1941 all the justices opposed to his programs had retired. Constitutional roadblocks to the expansion of federal power in economic and welfare legislation all but disappeared.

Rights Revolution

Just as the Court was ceding its power to review social and economic legislation, it was laying the groundwork for a second revolution in support of individual rights. In a famous footnote, note four in *United States v. Carolene Products Co.* (1938)—the case dealt with the interstate shipment of skimmed milk—the Court suggested that it had a special role to play in defending freedoms guaranteed by the Bill of Rights and in protecting "discrete and insular minorities." The Court's solicitude for individual rights grew slowly in the 1940s and then ripened into the Warren

Justices of the 1993 Supreme Court pose with President Bill Clinton. Standing left to right: Antonin Scalia, Ruth Bader Ginsburg, Anthony M. Kennedy, John Paul Stevens, Chief Justice William H. Rehnquist, President Clinton, Harry A. Blackmun, Sandra Day O'Connor, David H. Souter, and Clarence Thomas.   Source: Ken Heinen for the Supreme Court of the United States

Court's revolution in civil rights in the 1950s and in criminal procedure in the 1960s.

The constitutional bases for the change were the DUE PROCESS and EQUAL PROTECTION clauses of the Fourteenth Amendment. During the laissez-faire era, due process had been the justification for protecting property rights. In the 1930s the Court invoked it instead to protect First Amendment rights: freedom of religion, freedom of speech, freedom of the press, the right of assembly. Due process, the Court said, meant that these "fundamental" rights were protected from abridgment by the states. In 1948 the Court ruled that the Fourth Amendment guarantees against unreasonable search and seizure were also applicable to the states as part of due process.

The Court gave new force to the equal protection clause in 1950 with two decisions striking down racial segregation in state higher education. Four years later the Warren Court's historic decision in *BROWN V. BOARD OF EDUCATION OF TOPEKA* (1954) forbade racial segregation in all public schools. Over the next decade the Court struck down state-mandated segregation in other contexts as well. In the 1970s the Court broadened the equal protection clause to limit sex discrimination.

Already under intense public criticism because of its civil rights rulings, the Warren Court in the 1960s undertook to guarantee the constitutional rights of criminal defendants in state justice systems. Under the INCORPORATION DOCTRINE the Court, step by step, required states to afford suspects and defendants almost all the rights guaranteed by the Fourth, Fifth, and Sixth amendments.

Three major rulings stand out. *Mapp v. Ohio* (1960) required states to apply the exclusionary rule to block the use of illegally seized evidence. *GIDEON V. WAINWRIGHT* (1963) required states to provide lawyers for indigent criminal defendants. *MIRANDA V. ARIZONA* (1966) laid down mandatory guidelines for police interrogation of suspects.

With these and other criminal procedure decisions, the Warren Court brought about a fundamental transformation in state courts throughout the country. But the controversies sparked by the decisions led to a political reaction that gradually lowered the Court's constitutional profile over the next two decades.

Retrenchment

Under chief justices Warren E. Burger and Rehnquist, the Court found less constitutional fault with police conduct and the operations of state court systems than it had previously. Capital punishment, which had been declared unconstitutional in 1972 by five Warren Court holdovers, was reinstated in 1976. The Court in 1973 refused to apply equal protection to eliminate unequal financing of public schools. It narrowed Warren Court precedents in First Amendment areas by setting out a less rigorous definition of obscenity and refusing to extend libel protections to suits brought by private figures.

Still, the Burger Court expanded the constitutional right to privacy in its abortion rights ruling *ROE V. WADE* (1973). And it extended freedom of speech to protect the right to spend money in political campaigns.

Rehnquist's elevation to chief justice in 1986 and further conservative appointments by presidents Reagan and Bush seemed to solidify a conservative majority. The new majority was less disposed to make expansive constitutional rulings on individual rights. The retrenchment, however, was not complete. The Court's major criminal procedure precedents were narrowed but left on the books. The Court continued to be protective of free speech rights in such rulings as its 1989 and 1990 decisions striking down laws

against desecration of the flag. Despite a concerted effort to overturn *Roe v. Wade,* the Court narrowly reaffirmed the decision in 1992, although it did give states somewhat greater leeway to regulate abortion procedures.

As in the past the Court's pronouncements on constitutional law defied neat generalizations. Justice Felix Frankfurter liked to tell the story of a property law professor who agreed to teach a constitutional law course, but then gave it up on the ground that the subject was "not law at all but politics." The Constitution began as a political document, a series of artful compromises designed to establish a new government empowered to deal with the social and economic problems of the day. Two hundred years later, it remains a political document—one that has endured precisely because of the Supreme Court's role in enforcing its essential dictates while adapting it to ever changing social and economic conditions.

Contempt of Court

To maintain decorum within the courtroom and to enforce obedience to its orders, courts possess the inherent power to punish people for contempt. A judge may punish individuals summarily for contempts committed in his or her presence. In recent years, however, the Supreme Court has used the DUE PROCESS guarantee to impose some procedural restraints on the exercise of this judicial power.

The Judiciary Act of 1789 reinforced the inherent power for the new federal judiciary by authorizing the courts "to punish by fine or imprisonment, at the[ir] discretion . . . all contempts of authority in any cause or hearing before the same." But a statute passed in 1831—after a federal judge was impeached for using the contempt power to punish an attorney for criticizing one of his opinions—limited the contempt power to three situations:

– misbehavior of any person in the court's presence "or so near . . . as to obstruct the administration of justice";

– misbehavior of an officer of the court in official transactions;

– disobedience or resistance to any lawful court order by an officer of the court or by "any party, juror, witness, or other person."

Contempt may be civil or criminal in nature. Civil contempt is the refusal to act as the court commands. It is punishable by imprisonment until the person obeys. Criminal contempt consists of doing something forbidden and is punishable by a definite term.

Little question has been raised about judicial power to use the contempt power to maintain order within the courtroom. As recently as 1970 the Supreme Court affirmed the power of a judge to keep peace in the courtroom, even at the cost of having a defendant bound and gagged or physically removed from the courtroom.

The Court has sanctioned use of the contempt power to punish witnesses before courts or grand juries for refusing to answer questions. The issue arises most often in the case of witnesses who have been granted immunity and thus have lost the privilege against SELF-INCRIMINATION. The Court in 1965 required a hearing before punishment of a grand jury witness for contempt in such cases. In 1975, however, it permitted use of the summary contempt power to punish an immunized trial witness.

The Court has restricted the summary contempt power by recommending, as early as 1925, that a judge turn a contempt matter over to a colleague if the judge was so personally involved as to be unable to be fair in imposing a sentence. It has since extended the right to a jury trial to many contempt cases.

In 1966 the Court used its power to supervise the conduct of lower federal courts to require a jury trial for anyone sentenced to more than six months in prison for criminal contempt. Then in *Bloom v. Illinois* (1968) the Court placed the requirement on a constitutional basis, ruling that state courts as well as federal courts must grant a jury trial to persons charged with serious criminal contempts. A 1974 decision extended the jury trial requirement to cases in which criminal contempt sentences, taken together, totaled more than six months.

Contract Clause

The Constitution prohibits the states—but not the federal government—from passing any law "impairing the obligation of contracts" (Article I, Section 10).

For nearly a century, the Supreme Court used this clause frequently to protect the PROPERTY RIGHTS of businesses and charitable corporations and generally to limit state power over economic affairs. In the late nineteenth century, the Court recognized a broader view of freedom of contract, derived from the DUE PROCESS clause of the Fourteenth Amendment. The Court used the new doctrine to further restrict state regulation of economic affairs. By the late 1930s, however, both doctrines had fallen into disfavor. Today contract rights are rarely used to bar state or federal action in economic matters.

Early Rulings

Three successive rulings by the Supreme Court under Chief Justice John Marshall construed the contract clause strictly. In *Fletcher v. Peck* (1810) the Court refused to allow the Georgia legislature to revoke a massive land grant of 35 million acres after the legislature had discovered that speculators had bribed many of the members of the previous legislature to approve the grant. Marshall said that the land grant was a valid contract despite the legislature's "impure motives" and that Georgia could not annul the titles granted under it. Two years later the Court similarly prevented the New Jersey legislature from changing or revoking a clear contractual grant of exemption from state taxes.

The most important of these early rulings was *Dartmouth College v. Woodward* (1819), which prevented the state of New Hampshire from changing Dartmouth College from a private college into a state university. Dartmouth had been established by royal charter and continued under the same charter after the formation of the Union. Marshall said that the charter was a contract with a private corporation and that the state had no power to change it. In a concurring opinion, however, Justice Joseph Story said that in future, states could reserve the power to make

Dartmouth College, 1803. When the New Hampshire legislature made radical changes in the status of the college, the result was the most famous contract clause case of the Marshall era.   Source: Dartmouth College

modifications in corporate charters without violating the Constitution.

Businesses were the major beneficiaries of the *Dartmouth College* ruling. The decision helped corporations raise capital by assuring investors that rights granted by state legislatures would be secure from later changes in political or popular opinion. Soon, however, the Court's rulings on the contract clause began to open loopholes in the protection it provided.

In *Ogden v. Saunders* (1827) the Court upheld a New York bankruptcy law after having struck down the state's first insolvency statute seven years earlier. In the first case, Marshall said New York's law improperly allowed debtors to use bankruptcy proceedings to cancel debts contracted before passage of the act. New York then revised the act to apply only prospectively, not retrospectively. The Court upheld the new law by a 4–3 vote, with Marshall casting the only dissenting vote of his thirty-four-year career. The ruling cleared the way for states to adopt bankruptcy laws, but the state laws became less important after Congress passed the first comprehensive federal bankruptcy act in 1898.

The Court justified its next two limitations on the contract clause by saying that certain state powers were inalienable—that is, they could not be contracted away even if the state wished to do so. These powers included eminent domain (the power to acquire private property for public use) and the POLICE POWER to protect public health, safety, and morals.

In *Charles River Bridge v. Warren Bridge* (1837) a company chartered by the Massachusetts legislature to operate a toll bridge across the Charles River into Boston invoked the contract clause to challenge construction of a second bridge nearby that was to be toll-free after six years. The Court rejected the plea by a 4–3 vote. Chief Justice Roger B. Taney said the company's charter contained no explicit grant of an exclusive franchise. He went on to say more broadly that "privileged corporations" should not be allowed to stand in the way of the government's "power of improvement and public accommodation."

In 1880 the Court unanimously upheld a constitutional amendment approved by the Mississippi legislature to ban lotteries that put out of business a lottery corporation chartered by a previous legislature. "All agree," the Court said, "that the Legislature cannot bargain away the police power of a state."

Together the eminent domain and police power exceptions reduced the restraining force of the contract clause. But at the turn of the twentieth century the Court found a broader protection for freedom of contract in the due process clause.

Lochner and After

In *Lochner v. New York* (1905) the Court used this new doctrine to strike down, by a vote of 5 to 4, a New York law limiting hours for bakery employees. Justice Rufus Peckham called such laws "meddlesome interferences with the rights of the individual." This infamous ruling had more symbolic than practical effect. Three years later, the Court upheld an Oregon law setting a ten-hour day for women working in laundries. And in 1917 the Court upheld another Oregon law setting a ten-hour day for all industrial workers.

The Court revived the *Lochner* doctrine in the 1920s and 1930s to strike down minimum wage laws and several other state laws regulating economic affairs. But in 1937 the Court laid the doctrine to rest in a 5–4 ruling, *West Coast Hotel Co. v. Parrish.* The decision upheld Washington state's minimum wage law for women and children. Chief Justice Charles Evans Hughes said that freedom of contract was not enshrined in the Constitution and that recent economic experiences required the Court to take a broader view of state power over economic matters.

The Court in 1934 upheld a Minnesota mortgage moratorium law that helped people unable to pay their mortgages to avoid foreclosure proceedings. But the Court emphasized that the law was temporary, and in two later decisions it struck down more sweeping laws from other states.

Over the next several decades, the contract clause seemed to have become a dead letter. In 1978, however, the Court sustained a challenge, based on the contract clause, to a New York pension law that retroactively increased employers' obligations. Interest in the contract clause was renewed as part of a property rights movement in the 1990s. But the Court in 1992 rejected an attack, based on the contract clause, brought by two major automobile manufacturers against a Michigan law expanding their workers' compensation liability. In *General Motors Corp. v. Romein* the Court said that liability for workers' injuries was governed by state law. It rejected the companies' argument that the old law was an implied term of their employment contracts.

Cost of Supreme Court

Compared to Congress and the president, the Supreme Court seems to operate on a shoestring. In fiscal year 1994, for example, Congress appropriated $25.9 million for the Court to pay the salaries of the nine justices and Court employees and to cover operating costs, including care of the Supreme Court building and grounds.

For the same fiscal year, the Executive Office of the President had a budget of $298 million, and Congress had an operating budget of $1.55 billion.

The Supreme Court budget for each fiscal year is drawn up by the MARSHAL OF THE COURT and the marshal's staff. It must be submitted by October 15—nearly a year in advance—to the Office of Management and Budget (OMB), the agency within the executive branch that prepares the president's budget. (The fiscal year begins the following October 1.)

OMB is prohibited by statute from making any changes in the proposed budget for the federal judiciary before submitting it to Congress in January.

Supreme Court requests in the president's budget are divided into two categories: salaries and expenses of the Supreme Court, and care of buildings and grounds. Before 1977 there were five categories: salaries, printing, miscellaneous expenses, car for the chief justice, and books for the Supreme Court.

In 1994 the salary of the chief justice was set at $171,500, while the associate justices had salaries of $164,100.

Congress considers the Supreme Court's budget together with the budget for the rest of the federal judiciary. Fiscal 1992 appropriations for the ninety-four district courts and thirteen circuit courts, not counting Supreme Court funds, were $2.2 billion. Another $45 million was set aside for the ADMINISTRATIVE OFFICE OF THE U.S. COURTS, the office that performs many of the support functions for the U.S. court system.

The preparation of the budget for the lower courts involves several steps before submission to Congress that do not apply to the Supreme Court. The budget of each lower court is sent to the Administrative Office by the court's chief judge. The Administrative Office consolidates these budgets into a national budget, which must then be approved by the JUDICIAL CONFERENCE of the United States. The Judicial Conference has no jurisdiction over the Supreme Court's budget.

The lower courts' budget requests must be submitted to the Administrative Office by May 1. There they are evaluated by specialists on the basis of program and project needs; the evaluation is carried out in May and June. The conclusions are reviewed by the director of the Administrative Office, then sent to committees of judges for review before they are delivered to the Judicial Conference for approval.

Committees of the Judicial Conference also review the requests and make recommendations to the budget committee, which also evaluates the requests and makes further recommendations. The Judicial Conference meets, usually in September, to consider the recommendations and prepare a final version of the requests, which is then forwarded to OMB.

Before the president sends the budget to Congress, the Administrative Office submits justifications for the funds requested to the two congressional subcommittees that will consider the requests first—the Senate and House appropriations subcommittees on commerce, justice, state, and the judiciary and related agencies. Formal subcommittee hearings generally begin in late January or early February.

The subcommittees hold public hearings. A justice of the Supreme Court and representatives of other parts of the federal judiciary are called upon to justify the requests. When the hearings on all departments and agencies covered by the appropriations bill have been completed, the subcommittees send their recommendations to the full Appropriations Committees, where the budget requests are again reviewed, perhaps modified, and sent on to the full House and Senate for consideration. Congress often reduces the judiciary's budget requests.

The funds Congress appropriates for the Supreme Court go directly to the Court, where they are controlled by the marshal, who disburses them for salaries and the other expenses of the Court. Before 1935 Congress channeled money for the Supreme Court through the Justice Department.

Counsel, Right to Legal

The Sixth Amendment provides that "[i]n all criminal prosecutions, the accused shall enjoy the right . . . to have the Assistance of Counsel for his defense." For most of U.S. history, this right depended on a defendant's ability to hire and pay his or her own lawyer. Beginning in the 1930s, however, the Supreme Court took steps to guarantee that almost all criminal defendants would actually have counsel. It did this by requiring the government to appoint and pay for a lawyer if a defendant cannot afford to do so.

The Court's initial step came in the first of the *SCOTTSBORO CASES* in 1932. The Court found a due process violation in an Alabama court's failure to provide adequate counsel to nine illiterate young black men charged with the capital offense of raping a young white woman. The Court based its decision in *Powell v. Alabama* on the specific circumstances of the case, though the ruling came to be viewed as requiring appointment of counsel for indigent defendants in all capital cases.

Six years later the Court established a broad rule requiring appointment of counsel in all federal criminal cases (*Johnson v. Zerbst* [1938]). In 1942 the Court decided not to impose the same rule on state courts. Writing for the 6–3 majority in *Betts v. Brady,* Justice

Clarence Earl Gideon's handwritten petition to the U.S. Supreme Court. The Court ruled unanimously that indigent defendants must be provided counsel in state trials.
Source: Supreme Court Historical Society

Owen J. Roberts said that the right to counsel was not "so fundamental and essential to a fair trial" that it was obligatory on the states, although due process might require appointment of counsel in "certain circumstances."

Far from settling the issue, the ruling brought uncertainty by inviting defendants who had not been provided a lawyer to try to fit their case into the "certain circumstance" exception. From 1950 to 1963, the Supreme Court did not uphold any state conviction against a claim of special circumstances. Among the factors that the Court said warranted reversal were the trial judge's conduct and the defendant's youth, ignorance, or lack of sophistication.

In 1963 the Court unanimously discarded this case-by-case approach, overruling *Betts v. Brady* in an opinion written by one of the dissenters in the earlier case, Justice Hugo L. Black. The ruling in *GIDEON V. WAINWRIGHT* mandated that states provide counsel for indigent defendants in all felony cases. "[A]ny person haled into court, who is too poor to hire a lawyer, cannot be assured a fair trial unless counsel is provided for him," Black wrote.

The Court's ruling brought about a revolution in state and federal criminal courts. Federal courts had implemented the 1938 decision largely by appointing unpaid counsel to represent indigent defendants. In 1964, one year after *Gideon,* Congress passed the Criminal Justice Act providing for paid appointed counsel in federal courts. State courts, with a far larger volume of criminal cases, had to move quickly to set up public defender offices or systems for appointing and paying private counsel.

The right to counsel also formed the basis for the beginning of the Court's rulings limiting police interrogation of suspects. In *Escobedo v. Illinois* (1964) the Court held that a suspect in custody had an absolute right to the aid of an attorney during police interrogation. Two years later, with its decision in *MIRANDA V. ARIZONA,* the Court ruled that suspects must be informed of their right to consult with a lawyer and to have a lawyer present during interrogation. (See CONFESSIONS.)

The Court in 1967 extended the *Gideon* ruling to juvenile delinquency proceedings *(In re Gault).* In 1972 the ruling was extended to misdemeanor cases if any imprisonment was imposed *(Argersinger v. Hamlin).* In 1979, however, the Court ruled, 5–4, that counsel need not be provided in misdemeanor cases if the defendant was not incarcerated, even if a jail or prison sentence could have been imposed *(Scott v. Illinois).*

The Court also extended the right to counsel outside the trial setting, but typically with limitations. In 1963 the Court ruled that indigent defendants had to be provided counsel to appeal their convictions. But in 1974 it limited the requirement to filing a single appeal rather than seeking discretionary review from a state supreme court or the U.S. Supreme Court. The Court ruled in 1967 that a defendant was entitled to have an attorney present at any pretrial lineup for identification, but five years later it undercut the decision by limiting the ruling to lineups conducted after indictment. The Court in 1973 also ruled that counsel need not be provided at hearings to revoke parole or probation except in unspecified special circumstances.

The Court's 1932 ruling in *Powell* had made clear that effective assistance of counsel meant more than merely having a lawyer present. In 1942 the Court overturned a conviction in a federal criminal case, finding that the judge had denied defendants effective aid of counsel by requiring a single attorney to represent them both. Apart from a clear conflict of interest, however, the competence of counsel has proved a difficult issue for defendants to raise in challenging their convictions.

The Court in the 1970s said in several cases that "ordinary error" would not be sufficient to reverse a conviction. In 1984 the Court for the first time set out an explicit standard for judging claims of ineffective assistance. Writing for the Court in *Strickland v. Washington,* Justice Sandra Day O'Connor stated that the test was "whether counsel's conduct so undermined the proper functioning of the adversarial process that the trial cannot be relied on as having produced a just result."

O'Connor added that courts "must indulge a strong presumption" in favor of the lawyer's competence. The strength of the presumption was shown in a second decision released the same day. The Court overturned an appeals court decision that a lawyer had provided ineffective assistance because he lacked criminal law experience and was given only a brief time to prepare for trial. Instead, the Court said, some evidence of serious prejudicial error was required to support that conclusion.

A year later the Court for the first time found a case where this standard worked to prove the defendant's claim. In *Evitts v. Lucey* (1985) the Court held that an attorney's failure to file a statement of appeal by the legal deadline did amount to evidence of ineffective assistance of counsel.

Court Packing

See SIZE OF THE COURT.

Courts, Lower

The Supreme Court is at the top of a three-tiered federal judicial system that also comprises ninety-four trial-level courts called *U.S. district courts* and thirteen intermediate appellate courts called *U.S. courts of appeals*. District courts and appeals courts constitute the lower courts of the federal judicial system. State court systems generally have a parallel structure, but with many variations. (See LEGAL SYSTEM IN AMERICA.)

The Supreme Court exerts broad power over the federal court system. It has the power to review decisions from the lower courts, and it also exercises general supervision over the courts. The Supreme Court can propose rules of procedure governing processes in the federal courts, although the proposed rules are subject to congressional veto. State courts operate as independent systems, but the Supreme Court can exercise final authority over them on issues of federal law.

The judges in the lower federal courts, like the nine Supreme Court justices, are appointed by the president subject to confirmation by the Senate and, under Article III of the Constitution, can serve for life. These courts are sometimes called *Article III courts.*

Congress has also created specialized tribunals—referred to as *legislative courts*—that have limited jurisdiction. Judges on these courts are appointed by the president subject to Senate confirmation, but they generally have fixed terms rather than life tenure. These tribunals include the Claims Court, which hears actions for money damages against the United States except personal injury (tort) suits, and the Tax Court, which hears some disputes over federal taxes.

Article III Courts

As of January 1, 1994, the federal judiciary included 546 district court judges, with 99 positions vacant, and 159 court of appeals judges, with 20 positions vacant.

District Courts

The federal judicial system is divided into ninety-four districts, with at least one district in each state and none of the districts crossing state lines. District courts try both civil and criminal cases. The courts range in size from two to as many as twenty or more active, full-time judges. In each district a chief judge, determined by seniority, handles administrative matters.

Two other kinds of judges handle cases at the district court level. Bankruptcy judges, appointed for fourteen-year terms by special panels of U.S. appeals court judges, decide bankruptcy cases subject to review by a district court judge. Magistrate judges (formerly called magistrates) are appointed by district court judges; they try some minor cases and may handle preliminary matters in other cases.

The losing party in a case may appeal to the U.S. court of appeals for the geographic area, or circuit, in which the district is located.

Courts of Appeals

There are thirteen intermediate appellate courts. Eleven of these are numbered circuit courts based around the country that cover circuits consisting of three to nine states. Two other appeals courts are based in Washington, D.C. The U.S. Court of Appeals for the District of Columbia hears appeals from the federal district courts for the District of Columbia and some appeals from federal regulatory agencies. The U.S. Court of Appeals for the Federal Circuit, established in 1982, hears appeals from specialized tribunals, including the Claims Court, and appeals in patent cases tried in the U.S. district courts.

A losing party in the court of appeals may petition the U.S. Supreme Court to review the decision by CERTIORARI. The Court has discretion over which cases it decides to hear.

Supervisory Power

The Supreme Court has exercised its supervisory power on a few occasions to establish important general rules for the federal courts. At other times, it has used the power simply to overturn a ruling in a particular case.

The Court's most controversial use of this power was to impose in 1943 a federal rule excluding any confessions obtained following an "unnecessary delay" in presenting a suspect for arraignment after arrest. In *Miranda v. Arizona* (1966) the Court imposed more detailed procedural requirements for police interrogation in state and federal cases.

The Court has used its supervisory power several times in cases for contempt of court. In 1954 it ordered a new hearing for a lawyer who had been found in contempt, on the grounds that the judge had shown personal animosity toward him in the dispute. In 1958 the Court shortened a contempt sentence after the lower court judge had ignored earlier suggestions that a reduction was necessary. In 1966 the Court issued a rule requiring a jury trial before anyone could be sentenced in federal court to more than six months in prison for contempt.

Rule-Making Power

The Judiciary Act of 1789 authorized all federal courts to make rules for the orderly conduct of their business. The Supreme Court in 1825 upheld Congress's power to delegate this responsibility to the courts.

Over the next century, the Supreme Court set out various rules applying to different types of lawsuits, but not until the 1930s was there a uniform set of rules governing procedure in all federal courts.

In 1933 Congress authorized the Supreme Court to propose rules governing postverdict proceedings in all criminal cases. The following year it granted similar authority to the Court to propose rules of civil procedure, subject to veto by Congress. In 1940 Congress gave the Court authority to propose rules governing criminal case procedures before a verdict.

Using advisory committees the Supreme Court proposed, and Congress approved, the Federal Rules of Civil Procedure, which took effect in 1938, and the Federal Rules of Criminal Procedure, which took effect in 1946. Both have since been revised through this same process of committee drafting, Supreme Court recommendation, and congressional examination and approval. (See TRIALS.)

Courts, Powers of

Judicial power was defined by Supreme Court justice Samuel F. Miller in the late nineteenth century as "the power of a court to decide and pronounce a judgment and carry it into effect."

This power is more tenuous than those granted to the legislative or executive branches under the U.S. system of SEPARATION OF POWERS. The Constitution gives Congress the power of the purse (the authority to approve all federal appropriations) and grants the executive branch the power of the sword (the authority to enforce laws).

The courts do not have those powers. The federal judiciary depends on Congress for funding and must look to the executive branch for assistance in enforcing its decisions if voluntary compliance is not forthcoming. Beyond the power of CONTEMPT OF COURT, courts have little equipment with which to enforce their rulings.

The limits on judicial power led Alexander Hamilton, writing in *The Federalist Papers,* No. 78, to call the federal judiciary "the least dangerous" and "the weakest" of the three branches of the proposed new government. Yet in the two centuries since the Constitution was written, the Supreme Court and the federal judiciary have evolved into an extraordinarily powerful institution of government.

The growth of this power can be attributed to the expansive use of court powers derived from English COMMON LAW, to the constitutional protections for judicial independence, and to the self-asserted power of JUDICIAL REVIEW (the power to decide whether the actions of other branches of government comply with the Constitution).

The Court has also acted to preserve this power through a doctrine of JUDICIAL RESTRAINT—rules that limit the authority of courts to act in a given case. Ultimately, the power of the judicial branch also depends on the Supreme Court's political strength: public confidence in its judgments and support for its place in the constitutional system. (See PUBLIC OPINION AND THE COURT.)

Origins

Although the Articles of Confederation did not provide for a system of national courts, the concept of a separate and relatively independent judiciary was generally accepted by the delegates to the Constitutional Convention. In contrast to the detailed provisions regarding the powers of Congress and the executive branch, however, the judicial article simply sketches the outline of a federal judiciary.

Article III of the Constitution begins by stating that "[t]he judicial power of the United States [not otherwise defined], shall be vested in one supreme Court, and in such inferior Courts as the Congress may from time to time ordain and establish." According to Section 2, the judicial power "shall extend" only to specified types of cases or controversies, including cases "arising under" the Constitution or federal laws and treaties and cases involving the states or citizens of different states.

To safeguard judicial independence, Section 1 provides that federal judges are to hold their posts during good behavior and that their salaries are not to be diminished during their terms in office. Judges may be removed from office only through the impeachment process described in Article II.

Hamilton viewed the national judiciary as essential to the powers of the new government. "The majesty of the national authority must be manifested through the medium of the courts of justice," Hamilton wrote in *The Federalist,* No. 16. Yet some delegates to the convention argued that state courts could handle all judicial business other than what the Supreme Court was to consider. As a compromise, Article III left it up to Congress to decide what lower federal courts to create.

Early Developments

In the Judiciary Act of 1789 Congress began filling in the details of the federal judicial system. Three provisions played key roles in the development of the powers of the federal judiciary.

First, the act established a system of lower federal courts: district courts in each of the states, and three circuit courts. Although the courts were not given the full measure of jurisdiction allowed under Article III,

In the early 1830s the Supreme Court rejected Georgia's efforts to assert its jurisdiction over Cherokees living on Indian land within its boundaries. The state refused to abide by the rulings and, supported by President Andrew Jackson, eventually forced the Cherokees out of the state. Jackson is alleged to have said: "Well, John Marshall has made his decision, now let him enforce it."   Source: Woolaroc Museum, Bartlesville, Oklahoma

their creation fulfilled Hamilton's goal of a national judiciary able to carry out the policies of the federal government. (See COURTS, LOWER.)

Second, Section 14—the so-called All Writs Act—authorized all federal courts to issue all writs "which may be necessary for the exercise of their respective jurisdictions, and agreeable to the principles and usages of the law." The section specifically authorized use of the powerful writ of HABEAS CORPUS to determine the legality of federal detentions. This general grant of power helped ensure that as the federal courts' jurisdiction grew, they would have at their disposal the customary judicial instruments for carrying out their decisions.

Third, the act's famous Section 25 gave the Supreme Court the power to review and reverse state court rulings that upheld a state law against a chal-

lenge that the law was in conflict with the Constitution, federal laws, or a federal treaty. This provision, viewed as an implementation of the Constitution's SUPREMACY CLAUSE, was critical to the expansion of national power over that of the states during the next half-century. (See STATES AND THE COURT.)

The act did not give the Supreme Court the power of judicial review over laws passed by Congress. But it appears that the delegates to the Constitutional Convention expected the Court to have this power. In any event the Court took the power for itself in the landmark decision *MARBURY V. MADISON* (1803). The power was used only twice before the Civil War, but this established the principle that the Court could enforce the Constitution even against one of the coordinate branches of the federal government.

In its early years the Supreme Court acted to establish its powers in another way—by refusing to assume powers outside its judicial functions. In 1792, after Congress had passed a law directing the justices to advise the secretary of war on veterans' pensions, five justices refused, saying the authority conferred was "not of a judicial nature." When President George Washington sought an advisory opinion on the neutrality issue in 1793, the justices declined.

The Supreme Court suffered an early rebuff to its power in its first decade. When the Court in 1793 upheld the right of a citizen of one state to sue another state in the Supreme Court, the states rose up in protest and quickly reversed the decision through the Eleventh Amendment. (See REVERSALS OF RULINGS BY CONSTITUTIONAL AMENDMENT.)

Expanding Powers

Federal judicial power grew in the nineteenth century. But the growth was gradual and was resisted at various times by the states, Congress, or the president.

The Federalist-dominated judiciary had been a political issue in the 1800 presidential campaign. (See ELECTIONS AND THE COURT.) After Thomas Jefferson was elected president, the lame-duck, Federalist-controlled Congress passed and President John Adams signed the Judiciary Act of 1801. The act expanded the lower federal courts and extended the jurisdiction of the federal courts to include virtually the entire power authorized by Article III. After Jefferson took office, the Republican-controlled Congress repealed the act in 1802. Federal courts remained courts of limited jurisdiction, subsidiary to the state courts, until after the Civil War.

Despite that setback, the Supreme Court under Chief Justice John Marshall, an ardent Federalist, solidified its power over the next three decades. Twice, in 1816 and 1821, it firmly rejected challenges to its power, under Section 25, to hold state laws unconstitutional. In 1824 it allowed a circumvention of the Eleventh Amendment by upholding a federal court suit against a state official, on the ground that the state itself was not being sued.

A prolonged confrontation with the state of Georgia over a dispute with the Cherokee Indians in the late 1820s and early 1830s provided the most critical test of the Court's power until the Civil War. The state asserted its control over Cherokee lands—with the support of President Andrew Jackson—even after the Court in 1832 rejected its claim. The Court was powerless to enforce its judgment. But the state ended its defiance when Jackson, to ensure federal supremacy on other issues, decided to take a strong stand against the states' power to nullify federal power.

Under Chief Justice Roger B. Taney, the Court showed more sympathy to states' rights, but without relinquishing any of the powers established under Marshall. The Court also approved some expansion of federal court powers. In 1838 it ruled that federal courts could issue a writ of MANDAMUS directing a federal official to perform "ministerial acts" (actions required by law and not involving exercise of policy discretion). In 1845 the Court made it easier for suits involving corporations to be brought in federal court. And in 1851 the Court extended federal admiralty jurisdiction to all inland waterways that carried interstate or foreign commerce.

On the eve of the Civil War, the Court decisively reaffirmed the federal courts' supremacy over state courts. The dispute involved an abolitionist newspaper editor in Wisconsin who had been convicted of violating the federal Fugitive Slave Act. A state court issued a writ of habeas corpus ordering him freed, but the Supreme Court in 1859 unanimously ruled that state courts had no power to thwart the rulings of federal courts (*Abelman v. Booth*).

Reconstruction and the Courts

Two major expansions of federal judicial power occurred in the Reconstruction era after the Civil War.

In 1867 Congress authorized federal courts to issue writs of habeas corpus in state cases where a person was being "restrained of his or her liberty in violation of the Constitution, or of any treaty or law of the United States." The aim was to prevent imprisonment of federal officials engaged in Reconstruction programs.

Congress the next year repealed the Supreme Court's appellate jurisdiction in such cases in order to prevent a ruling on the constitutionality of the Reconstruction Acts. The Court in *Ex parte McCardle* (1869) bowed to the repeal. (See CONGRESS AND THE COURT.) The basic expansion of federal power was left untouched, however, and Congress later acted to restore the Supreme Court's power as well. In the twentieth century, habeas corpus provided a basis for asserting federal control over state criminal courts.

Congress expanded the federal judiciary's power again with the Judiciary Act of 1875, which gave to the federal courts the jurisdiction permitted by Article III over all cases arising under the Constitution, federal law, or treaties involving more than $500.

Congress had two purposes in bestowing this jurisdiction over federal questions: to provide a federal forum for protecting the civil rights created in Reconstruction laws, and to protect the national railroads from inconsistent—and often unfriendly—state courts. The act also authorized removal of a case from state court to federal court when a federal question was involved. (See REMOVAL OF CASES.)

The 1875 act has been described as bringing about a revolution in the function of the federal courts. For the first time, all issues of federal law could be decided as an original matter in federal rather than state court.

The Twentieth Century

Federal courts have expanded their role enormously in the twentieth century by assuming powers they had not claimed in the 1800s. The two most important were the power to substantively review state criminal proceedings through habeas corpus and the power to issue injunctions against state and local officials. (See INJUNCTION.) In addition, the courts' federal question jurisdiction grew as Congress passed new laws extending federal power over the economy, enlarging federal criminal jurisdiction, and creating federally protected civil rights.

The Supreme Court had previously limited the use of habeas corpus to question the detention of state prisoners, by inquiring only whether the sentencing court had jurisdiction to impose the sentence. In *Frank v. Mangum* (1915) the Court adopted a broader rule. First, it held that a court could lose jurisdiction over a defendant by denying his or her federal rights. Second, it construed the 1867 Habeas Corpus Act to require a federal court to examine "the very truth and substance of causes of [the prisoner's] detention."

Although the Court developed various rules for deferring to state courts in habeas corpus cases, this new power meant that federal courts could order the release of a state prisoner based on constitutional issues that were not raised during his trial and appeal. The Court began tightening the rules for review beginning in the 1970s, but habeas corpus remained a powerful tool even under the restrictions.

The Court first approved the use of injunctions to block the enforcement of unconstitutional state laws in *Ex parte Young* (1908). The case involved an effort by a railroad to invalidate a state statute concerning rate regulation. Ostensibly, the Eleventh Amendment barred federal court suits against a state. But the decision got around the restriction by viewing such suits as being brought against a state official, who was to be enjoined as an individual rather than in an official capacity.

Although *Young* was a property rights case, the decision became important later as providing a remedy for state action infringing civil rights and civil liberties. In a pair of rulings in the 1970s, the Court extended the decision by upholding the power of lower federal courts to issue injunctions requiring states to pay the cost of future constitutional compliance.

In *Edelman v. Jordan* (1974) the Court found that the Eleventh Amendment barred a federal court from ordering states to pay for past constitutional violations. It suggested, however, that an order for prospective relief might be valid. Three years later the Court confirmed the suggestion in a follow-up ruling in a Detroit school desegregation case, *Milliken v. Bradley* (1977). In that case the Court unanimously upheld a lower court decree requiring the school district to establish—and pay for—remedial education programs.

In a more dramatic affirmation of judicial power, the Court in 1990 held, by a vote of 5 to 4, that a lower federal court can require a local government to raise taxes in order to correct a constitutional violation, such as school segregation. The ruling in *Missouri v. Jenkins* said that the judge in the case had erred by imposing the tax increase himself, but that an order to local officials was within a judge's power under the Fourteenth Amendment to remedy unlawful discrimination in the states. The dissenting justices said the ruling "disregard[ed] fundamental precepts for the democratic control of public institutions."

Children celebrating the beginning of summer vacation. All-white institutions such as this one came under scrutiny from courts, even if the school system did not resist integration.   Source: Congressional Quarterly

The courts' power has also been increased during the twentieth century by two new procedural devices: the declaratory judgment and the CLASS ACTION.

In a declaratory judgment, parties may seek a judicial declaration of rights at an earlier stage of a dispute. The Court in 1933 agreed to take jurisdiction of such a case, despite earlier doubts about the procedure; the next year, Congress passed legislation specifically authorizing courts to issue such rulings.

A class action, which allows multiple claims to be consolidated into a single lawsuit, has become the basis for high-impact civil rights and consumer litigation. The procedure has roots in common law. Its use increased after the Court in 1940 confirmed that a ruling in a class action could bind all individuals with the same interest even if they did not participate in the lawsuit.

One other basis for expanded judicial power in the twentieth century was the loosening of some of the doctrines of judicial restraint. One decision stands out: the Supreme Court's landmark reapportionment ruling, *BAKER V. CARR* (1962). That ruling held that the political question doctrine did not prevent a judicial ruling on a state legislature's failure to realign districts to account for shifts in population. The decision drew strong protests from the states, but the courts' role in supervising the drawing of legislative and congressional district lines has now become routine. (See REAPPORTIONMENT AND REDISTRICTING.)

Despite the enormous expansion of federal judicial power, some limits remain. The federal courts have no authority to overrule a state court's ruling on an issue of state law. They also have no power to enjoin a state court proceeding except under very limited circumstances. (See COMITY.) And the rules of judicial restraint are still honored, even if they are applied loosely or inconsistently at times.

The expansive use of federal judicial power has led in the twentieth century to several proposals to curb that power. Labor supporters succeeded in limiting the power of federal courts to issue injunctions in labor disputes. They failed, however, in a broader effort in the 1920s to give Congress the right to override a Supreme Court decision invalidating a federal law on constitutional grounds. Critics of more recent Supreme Court rulings on such issues as reapportionment, school prayer, and busing tried but failed to get Congress to pass laws or constitutional amendments stripping the federal courts of jurisdiction over those issues.

The critics of expanding judicial power contend that the courts often use their power to infringe on the rights of the political majority. Supporters of JUDICIAL ACTIVISM contend that the courts exercise that power to enforce legal rights as provided in the Constitution, which is the fundamental source of political authority in the United States. The political failure of proposals to curb the courts' authority suggests that the power of the courts is largely accepted, even if the decisions are sometimes unpopular. The Supreme Court's seeming attentiveness at times to public opinion suggests that the justices recognize the need to maintain a measure of public approval if the power of the courts is to be preserved.

Criminal Law and Procedure

Criminal law in the United States provides several protections for the rights of the accused that distinguish the American legal system from those of most other countries.

Substantive criminal law—the laws that define what constitutes a crime—must be interpreted strictly. The accused person, the Supreme Court has said, is entitled to fair notice that his or her conduct was criminal before the person can be punished for it.

The procedures used in bringing accusations, conducting TRIALS, imposing sentences, and reviewing convictions and sentences on APPEAL are visibly designed to protect the rights of the accused. The provisions in the BILL OF RIGHTS setting out rights for the defendant before, during, and after trial give a defendant important protections against the power of the government.

Supreme Court's Role

The Supreme Court's role in enforcing these rights has been intensely controversial since the 1960s, yet it began only a few decades earlier. Federal courts had limited criminal JURISDICTION until the early twentieth century, and the Supreme Court itself had no jurisdiction to hear appeals in criminal cases until 1889. The vast majority of criminal cases have always been handled in state courts, and the Supreme Court had consistently ruled in the nineteenth century that the Bill of Rights did not apply to the states.

In the 1920s the Court began to use the DUE PROCESS clause of the Fourteenth Amendment to define the rights of criminal defendants in state courts. Initially the Court had declined to construe the amendment, which had been ratified in 1868, to impose specific procedural requirements on the states. In the 1920s, however, it began establishing minimal safeguards for defendants in state courts. Then, in the 1960s, the Court required the states to comply with almost all the criminal procedure provisions of the Bill of Rights. (See INCORPORATION DOCTRINE.)

The due process revolution brought about by the Court under Chief Justice Earl Warren was strongly criticized by police, prosecutors, lawmakers, and the public. Critics claimed that the rulings elevated the rights of defendants over the rights of the public, hampered police and prosecutors, and allowed the guilty to go free because of technicalities. The Court's defenders maintained that the rights being safeguarded were not technicalities but fundamental protections of individual liberty. They further said that the rulings need not prevent police and prosecutors from carrying out their duties to apprehend and punish criminals.

Under two conservative chief justices—Warren E. Burger and William H. Rehnquist—the Court narrowed some of the most controversial of the criminal procedure rulings of the Warren Court but overruled only a few of the less important ones. The clearest change in doctrine involved defendants' remedies rather than their rights. The Burger and Rehnquist courts limited the ability of defendants to raise claims of constitutional violations in HABEAS CORPUS proceedings after their regular appeals had been completed. The primary responsibility for enforcing those rights was left in state courts rather than in the federal judiciary.

Substantive Law

The only crimes that Congress is expressly authorized to punish under the Constitution are piracies, felonies on the high seas, offenses against the laws of nations, counterfeiting, and treason. But its power to create, define, and punish crimes as needed to carry out the objects of the federal government has always been conceded.

Congress moved slowly to define new federal crimes. In an important victory for states' rights, the Supreme Court in 1812 declared that federal courts had no common law power to define and punish crimes. Federal courts could only consider offenses defined by Congress.

Congress created some new federal crimes in the Reconstruction era to protect the civil rights of blacks, but the Court invalidated some of the laws and narrowed others. In the late nineteenth and early twentieth centuries, Congress began expanding federal criminal jurisdiction under its COMMERCE POWER. The Court approved this so-called federal POLICE POWER in 1903 when it upheld, 5–4, a federal law prohibiting interstate transportation of lottery tickets (*Champion v. Ames*, also called the *Lottery Case*). A decade later the Court similarly upheld the antiprostitution Mann Act, which prohibited transportation of women across state lines for immoral purposes.

Federal criminal law continued to expand in the twentieth century through similar laws tied to Congress's commerce power or TAXING POWER. By 1972 the federal criminal code comprised more than 500 sections defining penal offenses against the United States. Despite its size, however, federal law did not amount to a comprehensive criminal code, nor did it displace the states in their primary responsibility for enforcing criminal law.

The Supreme Court has had only a minor role in defining criminal offenses. State law defines the most common crimes—murder, rape, robbery, burglary, and so forth—and the Court has seldom questioned those definitions. The Court has, however, struck down some criminal laws as unconstitutionally vague—for example, some vagrancy laws. Under the First Amendment the Court has limited state laws dealing with OBSCENITY and restricted the power of states to punish political speech. (See SEDITION LAWS; SPEECH, FREEDOM OF.)

The patchwork nature of the federal criminal code sometimes forces the Court to borrow definitions of offenses from state law or common law. Federal sentencing law, for example, provides for longer sentences based on prior convictions, but it contains no definition for one common crime: burglary. To fill in the gap, a unanimous Court in 1990 simply adopted the prevailing definition of burglary found in state law. In a more closely divided case in 1992, the Court, by a vote of 6 to 3, adopted a broad definition of extortion from common law in order to permit the use of the federal Hobbs Act against government officials accused of taking bribes to influence their official actions.

Procedural Rights

The original Constitution protects the rights of the accused by requiring jury trials in federal criminal cases. It also prohibits either the states or the federal government from passing laws that single out specific individuals for criminal punishment or impose retroactive punishment. (See ATTAINDER, BILL OF; EX POST FACTO.)

The more detailed protections contained in the Bill of Rights were largely drawn from English common law, with some additions. England recognized the privilege against SELF-INCRIMINATION found in the Fifth Amendment, for example. But the Fourth Amendment limits on SEARCH AND SEIZURE were a response to the British practice of general warrants that had so angered the American colonists. And in contrast to the Sixth Amendment guarantee of the right to legal counsel, England did not permit legal counsel in felony cases until the 1800s. (See COUNSEL, RIGHT TO LEGAL.)

Although these safeguards are known primarily for their importance to persons suspected or accused of crimes, they operate to shield all individuals against arbitrary or unduly intrusive government action. The various elements of the U.S. adversarial system of justice—the government's high burden of proof and the defendant's ability to confront witnesses and challenge evidence—have been viewed as making wrongful convictions less likely. As Justice Robert H. Jackson wrote in 1953, due process is "the best insurance for the Government itself against those blunders which leave lasting stains on a system of justice."

In defining due process, the Court at times has gone beyond the specific guarantees of the Bill of Rights. In 1935 the Court ruled that an accused person is denied due process of law if a prosecutor knowingly presents perjured testimony. In *Brady v. Maryland* (1963) it held that due process entitles a defendant to any "exculpatory" information (information favorable to the defendant) held by the prosecutor. In *Jackson v. Virginia* (1979) the Court said that a criminal conviction satisfies due process only if the judge or jury could reasonably have found that each essential element of the crime had been proved beyond a reasonable doubt.

The Court has left some procedural issues up to the states. In 1967, for example, the Court upheld Texas's habitual-criminal statute. That law provided for the trial jury to be informed of a defendant's prior criminal convictions at the same time that it considers the pending charge. Other states used a two-stage trial in such cases, but the Supreme Court found no constitutional requirement for such a procedure. The ruling went on to explain that the Court is not "a rule-making organ for the promulgation of state rules of procedure."

Due Process Revolution

The Warren Court's due process revolution consisted of a series of rulings from 1961 to 1969 that applied provisions of the Bill of Rights to the states. The rulings stirred up controversy in part because they went beyond regulating courtroom procedure to control the conduct of police in two major areas: searches and interrogation.

The Court had grappled with the issues of coerced CONFESSIONS and improper police searches before. In several cases since the 1930s it had barred the use of "involuntary" confessions based on a case-by-case review of police conduct. The Court had ruled in 1948 that state police were subject to the same Fourth Amendment limits on searches as federal law enforcement officers. It had declined, however, to require states to follow the EXCLUSIONARY RULE that barred the use of illegally seized evidence in criminal trials.

By the 1960s the Warren Court was prepared to say that stronger, more definite measures were needed to deter police misconduct. In *Mapp v. Ohio* (1961) the Court said the exclusionary rule was "a clear, specific, and constitutionally required . . . deterrent safeguard" to enforce the Fourth Amendment. Five years later, in *MIRANDA V. ARIZONA* (1966), the Court laid down detailed procedural rules for police to follow before questioning suspects.

Critics immediately denounced the *Mapp* decision as inevitably leading to the freeing of guilty defendants. In 1964 Burger, then a judge on the U.S. Court of Appeals for the District of Columbia, told a law school audience that the exclusionary rule "results in the escape of guilty persons" but had no certain deterrent effects on police. In *Miranda* Justice Byron R. White complained in dissent that "a good many criminal defendants . . . will now . . . either not be tried at all or will be acquitted if the State's evidence, minus the confession, is put to the test of litigation."

By the end of the 1960s police stations and criminal courtrooms across the country had moved to comply with the new rules. Police had *Miranda* warnings printed on cards to read to suspects and were receiving additional training on how to obtain and execute search warrants. In the courtroom, indigent defendants were being represented by public defenders or court-appointed lawyers as required by the 1963 decision concerning the right to counsel, *GIDEON V. WAINWRIGHT.*

At a time of rising public concern about crime, however, the new rules were strongly opposed in Washington and around the country. Congress tried to blunt the effect of *Miranda* in 1968 by saying that "voluntariness" was the sole test for using confessions in federal courts. In campaigning for the presidency,

Richard Nixon strongly criticized the Warren Court for "hamstringing the peace forces in our society and strengthening the criminal forces." Nixon promised, if elected, to appoint Supreme Court justices who would give greater weight to the needs of police in fighting crime.

Retrenchment

The Burger Court and later the Rehnquist Court fulfilled Nixon's promise to give greater attention to the needs of police and prosecutors. The Court did not overrule the Warren Court's major precedents, but it was receptive to pleas from prosecutors that the rulings were being extended too far or applied too strictly.

The change in attitude could be seen in the cases the Court decided to hear. In the mid-1960s, more than 90 percent of the Court's criminal docket consisted of cases brought by defendants who had lost in the lower courts. From the mid-1970s on, the proportions shifted; the bulk of the criminal docket consisted of cases brought by prosecutors seeking to reinstate convictions or sentences that had been thrown out in the lower courts.

The Court in the 1970s and 1980s narrowed *Miranda* by loosening the rule a bit and by allowing limited use of a suspect's statement even if police had not given proper warnings. The Court in 1984 created a "good faith exception" to the exclusionary rule. The exception permitted use of evidence obtained under a search warrant even if the warrant was later found to be invalid. Earlier, in 1976, the Court had limited the ability of state prisoners to raise claims about illegally obtained evidence in attacking their convictions in federal habeas corpus proceedings.

The Burger Court gave one final echo of the Warren Court's activism on criminal law: the 5–4 decision in 1972 throwing out CAPITAL PUNISHMENT as then administered. The five justices in the majority were all holdovers from the Warren Court; Nixon's four appointees dissented. Four years later the Court voted 7–2 to uphold revised death penalty laws if juries were given guidelines for imposing the death penalty. In later decisions the Court rejected broad challenges to capital punishment while occasionally tightening the procedures to be used in death penalty cases.

Those who disapproved of the expansion of protections for criminal defendants under Earl Warren expected the pendulum to swing the other way in Warren Burger's Court.   *Source: Supreme Court*

The Court's tilt toward the government under Burger became somewhat more pronounced after Rehnquist became chief justice in 1986. The three other justices named by President Ronald Reagan and the two appointed by George Bush solidified a conservative majority. The new majority was disinclined to create procedural rights for defendants; rather, it was interested in narrowing them, especially in the area of habeas corpus. The Rehnquist Court made it harder for prisoners to challenge convictions based on new constitutional rulings after their original trial and appeal or to file repeated habeas corpus petitions. The decisions reflected a desire for "finality" in criminal cases and an increased deference to state courts.

Like the Burger Court, however, the Rehnquist Court did not achieve a unified, consistent approach on criminal law issues. In 1987 it voted 5–4 to bar the use of so-called victim impact statements in sentencing hearings on the death penalty. (Victim impact statements consist of personal testimony by members of a murder victim's family.) Four years later, a five-justice majority led by Rehnquist reversed the decision, saying the previous ruling turned "the victim into a faceless stranger." In 1988 the Court refused to allow states to permit victims in child abuse cases to testify behind a screen to protect the children from additional trauma. Two years later the Court upheld, by a vote of 5 to 4, a modified procedure for the same purpose—presentation of the child's testimony by closed-circuit television.

The Rehnquist Court's final results on both of these issues reflected perhaps its most consistent underlying view: a desire to reduce the Court's role in supervising the administration of criminal law in the states. The Court's 1991–1992 term was noteworthy for the complete absence of any criminal cases involving day-to-day police work; there were no decisions on search and seizure or interrogation. In the same term, the Court sent a strong signal that it does not favor the use of due process to impose new procedural requirements on state courts.

In *Medina v. California* the Court ruled that states can impose on defendants the burden of proving they are too mentally ill to stand trial. Writing for the Court, Justice Anthony M. Kennedy said state courts are entitled to "substantial deference" on procedural matters. He emphasized what he termed the "limited operation" of the due process clause in requiring procedures beyond those specified in the Bill of Rights: "[T]he expansion of those constitutional guarantees under the open-ended rubric of the due process clause invites undue interference with both considered legislative judgments and the careful balance that the Constitution strikes between liberty and order."

Cruel and Unusual Punishment

The Eighth Amendment prohibits "cruel and unusual punishments" but does not specify what is cruel and unusual. The Supreme Court has said that punishments must be measured against "evolving standards of decency," but it has applied the amendment only rarely to overturn criminal sentences. The Court has also upheld limited use of the amendment to control abusive prison conditions.

Criminal Sentences

The Court's most controversial use of the Eighth Amendment was its 5–4 decision in 1972 invalidating CAPITAL PUNISHMENT as then administered. Two of the justices in the majority found the death penalty cruel and unusual punishment in all circumstances, while three others objected to the way capital punishment was being applied. Four years later, though, the Court voted 6–3 to uphold revised death penalty laws that allowed juries to impose a death sentence under guidelines designed to prevent arbitrary use of capital punishment.

The Court in 1910 used the Eighth Amendment to strike down a particularly severe sentence in the U.S.-occupied Philippines: a heavy fine, fifteen years of hard labor, and permanent deprivation of civil rights for the falsification of a public record *(Weems v. United States)*. In *Trop v. Dulles* (1958) the Court reversed a military court's decision to strip a convicted deserter of his U.S. citizenship.

In both decisions, the Court said the amendment must be interpreted expansively. In the main opinion in *Trop*, Chief Justice Earl Warren wrote, "The Amendment must draw its meaning from the evolving standards of decency that mark the progress of a maturing society."

The Court in 1892 had refused to apply the Eighth Amendment to state action. In 1947 it assumed that the amendment did apply to the states. Still, it rejected a plea by a Louisiana inmate to block the state from executing him following a botched electrocution attempt.

In 1962 the Court for the first time used the Eighth Amendment to invalidate a state law. In *Robinson v. California* the Court, by a 6–2 vote, held that it was cruel and unusual punishment to impose prison sentences upon persons whose only "crime" was that they were found to be drug addicts. The Court emphasized that the law did not punish the use, possession, or sale of drugs, but the " 'status' of narcotic addiction."

Six years later, however, the Court rejected, in a

Willie Francis survived Louisiana's first attempt to electrocute him when the chair malfunctioned. The Supreme Court in 1947 ruled that it was not cruel and unusual punishment for the state to carry out the execution.   Source: UPI/Bettmann

5–4 vote, a somewhat similar plea by a chronic alcoholic convicted of public drunkenness. Writing for the majority in *Powell v. Texas* (1968), Justice Thurgood Marshall said that the defendant had been convicted of "public behavior." The dissenting justices argued that the defendant could not avoid drinking and, once intoxicated, could not prevent himself from appearing in public.

In the 1980s, the Court was pressed to use the Eighth Amendment to limit the states' discretion to impose exceptionally long sentences for repeat offenders and in drug cases. But the Court issued such a ruling just once. In *Rummel v. Estelle* (1980) the Court, by a 5–4 vote, refused to hold that it was unconstitutionally cruel and unusual punishment for a state to impose a mandatory life sentence upon a "three-time

loser"—even though the defendant's three convictions were for petty, nonviolent offenses. Two years later, in a *per curiam* opinion, the Court upheld a forty-year sentence for possession of nine ounces of marijuana. Three justices dissented.

In 1983, however, the Court struck down a sentence of life imprisonment without possibility of parole for a South Dakota man previously convicted of seven nonviolent felonies *(Solem v. Helm)*. Justice Harry A. Blackmun switched to join the *Rummel* dissenters to form the majority in the case. One distinction between the two cases may have influenced the decision: in *Rummel* the defendant was eligible for early release on parole.

Eight years later a five-justice majority found no constitutional bar to a prison term of life without parole for a first-time drug offender. Writing for the Court in *Harmelin v. Michigan* (1991), Justice Antonin Scalia said that consideration of whether an individual deserves the particular statutory penalty is necessary only in capital punishment cases.

In a new area, the Court ruled in 1993 that the Eighth Amendment limits the government's power to seize property from convicted criminals or criminal suspects through civil or criminal forfeitures.

Prison Suits

The Court has been tentative in using the Eighth Amendment in suits over prison conditions. In 1976 the Court established some minimum requirements for the provision of health care in prisons. And in 1978 it upheld a lower court's decision to place a thirty-day limit on how long a prisoner could be held in isolation for discipline. But in 1981 the Court rejected a plea that "double bunking" prisoners in cells originally designed for one person constituted cruel and unusual punishment.

More recently, the Court has raised the burden of proof for inmates bringing Eighth Amendment claims, but also extended the prohibition into new areas. In *Wilson v. Seiter* (1991), the Court ruled, 5–4, that a prisoner who claims that the conditions of his confinement violate the Eighth Amendment must show "deliberate indifference" on the part of prison officials. The dissenting justices argued that proving inhumane conditions should be enough. In 1992, however, the

Court ruled that beating or other use of excessive force by a prison guard may violate the ban on cruel and unusual punishment even if it does not result in a serious injury to the prisoner. In 1993 it held that prisoners may have a right under the Eighth Amendment not to be involuntarily exposed to second-hand tobacco smoke. Both votes were 7–2, with Justices Antonin Scalia and Clarence Thomas dissenting.

Curator's Office

The office of the curator of the Supreme Court cares for the Court's historical papers and possessions, develops exhibits concerning the Court, offers educational programs for the public about the Court's history and its collections, and records events at the Court for future historians.

The Supreme Court's collections include antique furnishings; archives of documents, photographs, and cartoons; other memorabilia; and art.

More than 700,000 people visit the Supreme Court building each year—an average of about 3,000 a day. The curator's office provides courtroom lectures for an average of 600 visitors a day. The office is also responsible for the films and historical exhibits, which are open to the public on the ground floor.

The curator's office was established in 1974. The first curator was Catherine Hetos Skefos, who began her service in 1973, before the position was officially created. The second and current occupant of the post is Gail Galloway.

Currency Powers

The Constitution authorizes Congress to "coin Money, regulate the Value thereof, and of foreign Coin, and fix the Standard of Weights and Measures" (Article I, Section 8). This clause has been construed—with one significant but brief exception—to give Congress complete control over the nation's currency.

No national currency existed until the Civil War, when Congress authorized the printing of paper money, called "greenbacks," and made it legal tender for the payment of debts. In 1869 the Court upheld a federal tax that was intended to drive state banknotes out of circulation and leave a single uniform national currency.

That same year, however, the Court ruled that greenbacks could not be substituted as payment in cases where a contract specifically stipulated payment in gold (so-called gold clauses). At that time, gold was the preferred medium of exchange. In 1870, in the first of the *LEGAL TENDER CASES,* the Court ruled against the constitutionality of using paper money to pay debts contracted before passage of the greenback legislation in 1862. The ruling cast doubt on Congress's power to authorize paper money at all.

Amid great political controversy, the Court reversed itself on the issue just fifteen months later. But in 1872 the Court reaffirmed its earlier stance upholding the enforceability of gold clauses. As a result, more and more creditors insisted on gold clauses. Eventu-

An 1862 greenback.
Source: Library of Congress

ally almost every private and public bond contained a gold clause.

In 1933, during the Great Depression, Congress nullified all gold clauses. It had earlier devalued the dollar and required all holders to surrender their gold in exchange for paper money. The nullification statute was challenged on several grounds. The Court upheld it by 5–4 votes in a series of 1935 rulings collectively called the *Gold Clause Cases.*

Writing for the majority, Chief Justice Charles Evans Hughes backed Congress's power "to establish a uniform currency" and "to reject a dual system" of paper money and gold by voiding any private contracts that interfered with the decision. The ruling aided the efforts of President Franklin D. Roosevelt to achieve economic stabilization, but it was harshly criticized by four dissenters, led by Justice James C. McReynolds.

The ruling settled the issue of the government's power to control the nation's currency. Four decades later, when President Richard Nixon eliminated the gold standard, no serious constitutional questions were raised.

Source: Collection of the Supreme Court of the United States

Curtis, Benjamin R.

In the years leading up to the Civil War, tempers flared across the country as sectional differences drove the nation apart. This was true on the Supreme Court as well, where Justice Benjamin Robbins Curtis (1809–1874), an ardent abolitionist, angrily clashed with his colleagues in the Dred Scott case and other controversies. By 1857 Curtis's relations with the other justices, particularly Chief Justice Roger B. Taney, had become so hostile that he decided to resign after serving just under six years on the Court.

Curtis, the son of a Massachusetts ship captain, was born in Watertown, Massachusetts. While Curtis was still a child, his father died on a voyage abroad. His mother then raised Curtis with help from his half-uncle, George Ticknor, a Harvard professor. Curtis graduated from Harvard University in 1829 and Harvard Law School in 1832; he was the first Supreme Court justice to graduate from law school. Curtis first set up a law practice in Northfield, Massachusetts, but

in 1834 he moved to Boston to join the law practice of a distant cousin.

Following his election to the Massachusetts house in 1849, Curtis became a strong supporter of Daniel Webster. Webster grew unpopular with most Massachusetts abolitionists about this time when he sought a compromise on the slavery issue. Curtis, however, stood by him. Webster returned the favor in 1851 when President Millard Fillmore was seeking a replacement for the late Justice Levi Woodbury. Webster, who was then serving as Fillmore's secretary of state, suggested Curtis for the job. On the Court, Curtis specialized in admiralty law and commercial issues.

After serving on the Court from 1851 to 1857, Curtis returned to his successful law practice in Boston. He frequently appeared before the Supreme Court to argue on behalf of his clients. In 1868 he served as President Andrew Johnson's chief counsel during the impeachment proceedings. A grateful Johnson offered Curtis the job of attorney general, but he declined. Curtis died in 1874.

Cushing, William

Despite an undistinguished record as a lawyer, William Cushing (1732–1810) was one of the original justices nominated to the Supreme Court by President George Washington. He served longer than any other original justice.

Cushing was born March 1, 1732, to one of the oldest and most prominent families of colonial Massachusetts. Both his father and grandfather were government officials of the Massachusetts Bay province.

After graduating from Harvard in 1751, Cushing taught for a year in Roxbury, Massachusetts. He then began studying law under Jeremiah Gridley in Boston. In 1755 he established a private legal practice in his home town of Scituate. In 1760, Cushing became justice of the peace and judge of probates in Lincoln County, Massachusetts (now Maine). His legal skills were minimal, and he seemed to have trouble making decisions. His corporate clients quickly left him for other lawyers.

In 1772 his father, John Cushing, announced his retirement from the provincial superior court and insisted that his son succeed him. The colonial government preferred other candidates, but appointed Cushing to the post that year.

In 1774 the state legislature began impeachment proceedings against Cushing because of his perceived support of the British government. Faced with this pressure, he reluctantly refused to accept his salary through the British government. Cushing gained additional favor with revolutionary partisans when he was denied a seat on the governor's council because of his stand.

The next year, the new revolutionary government in Massachusetts retained Cushing as senior associate justice of the superior court when it reorganized the state's judicial system. In 1777 he became chief justice.

Cushing actively supported ratification of the Con-

Source: Library of Congress

stitution, although he was not a major figure at the state constitutional convention in 1779. Nine years later, he served as vice president of the state convention that ratified the Constitution.

In 1789 Washington nominated Cushing to the Supreme Court. Although Cushing served on the Court for twenty-one years, he wrote just nineteen opinions. He usually supported the Federalist position in his votes on the Court.

In 1794 Cushing was persuaded to launch an ill-fated campaign against Samuel Adams for the governorship of Massachusetts. He lost by a two-to-one margin but retained his seat on the Court. He remained a justice until his death in 1810.

D

Daniel, Peter V.

President Martin Van Buren was under great pressure when he nominated Peter Vivian Daniel (1784–1860) for the Supreme Court in early 1841. Justice Philip Barbour had died suddenly just a week before Van Buren, a Democrat, was to turn over the presidency to William Henry Harrison, a Whig. To keep the seat in Democratic hands, Van Buren quickly nominated Daniel, and the Democratic-controlled Senate confirmed him two days before Harrison took office.

Daniel was born at Crow's Nest, the estate owned by his wealthy family in Stafford County, Virginia. He attended Princeton University for one year, then moved to Richmond to study law under Edmund Randolph. Randolph was a powerful man who had served as attorney general and secretary of state under George Washington. Daniel's association with him helped him enter the state's top political circles. Daniel married Randolph's daughter Lucy.

In 1809 Daniel was elected to the Virginia house of delegates. He served there for three years until being elected to the Virginia privy council, an executive advisory and review body. In 1818 he was chosen lieutenant governor of Virginia and added that post to his privy council duties. He held both posts for the next seventeen years.

Daniel's loyalty as a Jacksonian Democrat did not go unnoticed in Washington. Jackson offered Daniel the post of attorney general, but Daniel rejected it because the salary was too low. In 1835 Daniel lost his two state jobs when he was defeated for reelection because of his support of Jackson. The next year, however, Jackson named him federal district judge for eastern Virginia.

After his elevation to the Supreme Court in 1841, Daniel favored states' rights and a weak federal government. His ideal society was a country of farmers, and he did not think that corporations should be able

Source: Collection of the Supreme Court of the United States

to file suit in federal courts. As a result, many of his opinions have become irrelevant to modern, industrialized America.

Daniel served on the Court for nineteen years until his death in 1860. His seat on the Court remained unfilled for two years after his death because the Republicans took office and restructured the court system.

Davis, David

Illinois attorney David Davis (1815–1886) served as Abraham Lincoln's campaign manager in 1860 and played a critical role in securing the Republican presidential nomination for him. Two years later Lincoln

Source: Library of Congress

lationship between Davis and Lincoln grew stronger in the 1850s, and the two men joined the Republican party when the Whig party began to collapse.

Lincoln appointed Davis to the Supreme Court in 1862. Probably his most important opinion is *Ex parte Milligan* (1866), in which he argued that even in wartime citizens still have constitutional rights.

Davis eventually grew tired of serving on the Court. In 1877 the Illinois legislature elected him to the U.S. Senate, and Davis resigned his Court seat to accept the new post. After his Senate term expired in 1883, Davis retired. He died in 1886.

Davis, John W.

John W. Davis (1873–1955) may be best known as the winner—after 17 days and 103 ballots—of the Democratic presidential nomination in 1924. But in legal circles he is considered one of the most influential attorneys ever to have appeared before the Supreme Court.

Davis was a member of the U.S. House of Representatives from West Virginia from 1911 to 1913. He then became solicitor general in Woodrow Wilson's administration. There he successfully argued *Wilson v. New* (1917) and the *Selective Draft Law Cases* (1918) before the Supreme Court. Both cases upheld expanded uses of federal powers, one regulating the maximum number of hours that interstate railway workers could work in a day, the other upholding the power of the federal government to draft young men into the military.

In 1918 Wilson named Davis ambassador to Great Britain. In that position he advised the U.S. delegation to the Paris Peace Conference in 1919. Upon his return to the United States in 1921, Davis renewed his legal practice. The following year he was elected president of the American Bar Association.

During the 1930s Davis argued against much of the New Deal legislation when it was challenged before the Supreme Court. One of his greatest victories came in 1952 when he argued successfully that President Harry S. Truman had overstepped his authority

rewarded his old friend by nominating him for the Supreme Court.

Davis was born in Cecil County, Maryland. He graduated from Kenyon College at age seventeen and from Yale Law School at age twenty. After obtaining his law degree, Davis set out for the West to seek his fortune. He eventually settled in Bloomington, Illinois, and won a state house seat there in 1844. During this period Davis began developing a relationship with Lincoln that grew over the years.

In 1847 Davis was chosen for the state constitutional convention. At the convention he advocated popular election of judges over the system, then current, of having legislators elect them. He won the fight, and the next year he was elected a judge of the state's eighth circuit. He was reelected twice and served in the position until 1862. Abraham Lincoln and Stephen Douglas were two of the prominent attorneys who argued cases before Judge Davis. The re-when he seized the nation's steel mills to avoid a strike during the Korean conflict.

Davis lost the last case he argued in the Supreme Court. In *Briggs v. Elliott* (1954), a companion case to *BROWN V. BOARD OF EDUCATION OF TOPEKA*, Davis was unable to persuade the Court that the doctrine of "separate but equal" should be continued. His chief opponent in that case was Thurgood Marshall, the future Supreme Court justice who is also considered one of the most influential attorneys to appear before the Court in the twentieth century.

When he died in 1955, Davis had argued 141 cases before the Supreme Court, more than any other attorney in the twentieth century.

Day, William R.

Justice William Rufus Day (1849–1923) is the author of the EXCLUSIONARY RULE, which bars the in-

Source: Library of Congress

troduction at criminal trials of evidence illegally seized by police.

Day set forth the rule in *Weeks v. United States* (1914). The case arose after federal agents arrested Freemont Weeks and searched his home without a warrant. A unanimous Court, in an opinion written by Day, overturned Weeks's conviction because it was based on evidence obtained in violation of his Fourth Amendment right against unreasonable search and seizure. The Court later expanded the rule to bar the use of evidence obtained in violation of other constitutional rights as well, and finally extended it to state courts.

Day was born in Ravenna, Ohio. He received his undergraduate degree at the University of Michigan, and attended Michigan's law school for one year before moving to Canton, Ohio, in 1872 to set up a law practice. His practice flourished, and he became good friends with William McKinley, another young attorney. Day's great popularity caused him to receive both the Democratic and Republican nominations for judge of the court of common pleas in 1886, and he was elected to that position. Three years later President Benjamin Harrison appointed him to the U.S. district court, but Day's poor health prevented him from accepting the appointment.

When his friend McKinley took office as president in 1897, Day joined the administration as first assistant secretary of state. He moved up to secretary of state for four months in 1898 before McKinley asked him to help represent the United States at the Paris Peace Conference, held to resolve the Spanish-American War. When Day returned home, McKinley appointed him to the U.S. Court of Appeals for the Sixth Circuit in Cincinnati.

Day was an appeals court judge for four years before President Theodore Roosevelt nominated him for the Supreme Court in 1903. Although he usually objected to federal regulation of commerce, he supported state regulation and argued, in a dissenting opinion in *United States v. United States Steel Corporation* (1920), that the company was violating the Sherman Antitrust Act.

After serving nearly two decades on the Court, Day resigned in November 1922. He died eight months later.

Death Penalty

See CAPITAL PUNISHMENT.

Decision Days

Decision days are the days on which Supreme Court decisions are publicly announced. During the 1991–1992 term opinions were released on Tuesdays and Wednesdays during the fourteen weeks that the court heard oral arguments. During other weeks they were released on Mondays. (See SCHEDULE OF ARGUMENTS AND CONFERENCES.)

In the Court's early years, decisions were announced whenever they were ready. There was no formal or informal schedule for the announcement of decisions or for conferences.

The tradition of announcing decisions on Monday—"Decision Monday"—began in 1857, apparently without any formal announcement or rule to that effect. This practice continued until April 1965, when the Court announced that decisions would henceforth be announced on days other than Monday.

Like the announcement of opinions, the day for release of the Court's order list—the summary of the Court's action granting or denying review—has changed over the years. During the nineteenth century, these summary orders were often released on Friday, called "Motion Friday." The practice of posting orders on Monday evolved gradually. Briefly in the 1971 term, orders were announced on Tuesday, but Monday was soon reinstated as the day for posting orders. A summary order on an urgent matter may, of course, be announced on a day other than Monday.

De Facto, De Jure

De facto and *de jure* are old legal terms meaning, respectively, "in fact" and "in law." In the United States, the terms have come to be used almost exclusively in the context of racial SEGREGATION in public schools.

De jure segregation refers to the separation of pupils by race as a result of official action. De facto segregation refers to the racial separation of pupils due to other causes, chiefly the racial character of residential neighborhoods on which school assignments are often based.

Although the distinction has been criticized as artificial, it has been central to the Supreme Court's handling of SCHOOL DESEGREGATION cases. The Court has required evidence of de jure segregation in order for lower courts to order desegregation remedies, including BUSING. It has also broadly defined the kinds of official actions by legislatures or local governing bodies or school boards that may constitute de jure segregation.

The Court has said, however, that remedies such as busing are inappropriate in cases of de facto segregation. In a 1991 decision, *Board of Education of Oklahoma City Public Schools v. Dowell,* the Court held that a lower federal court may lift a school desegregation decree if the school district has complied in good faith and eliminated the vestiges of past de jure discrimination to all "practicable" extent.

Defendant

A defendant is the party against whom a civil or criminal case is brought.

In criminal cases, the Constitution guarantees defendants an array of procedural rights. Supreme Court decisions have been critical in defining those rights in federal and state courts. The Constitution is less specific in defining the rights of defendants in civil cases. Still the Court has construed the due process clauses of the Fifth and Fourteenth amendments to require certain procedural protections for civil defendants.

The original Constitution contains several protections for criminal defendants, including the guarantee of jury trials in Article III and the prohibition against bills of attainder and EX POST FACTO laws in Article

I. (See ATTAINDER, BILL OF.) The Bill of Rights added broader protections. The Fifth Amendment established the privilege against self-incrimination and prohibited double jeopardy, while the Sixth Amendment guaranteed the right to counsel and several other rights designed to ensure a fair trial. (See TRIALS.)

The Warren Court in the 1960s applied these provisions of the Bill of Rights to the states under the INCORPORATION DOCTRINE. Those decisions touched off intense controversy. Since then the Court has relaxed a few of its more restrictive rulings in this area, but for the most part it has reaffirmed and in some cases extended the decisions.

In civil and criminal cases alike, the Court has emphasized the right to notice as one of the basic protections for defendants. The Sixth Amendment specifically requires that an accused be "informed of the nature and cause of the accusation." Besides the requirement of notice in an individual case, the Court has long held that due process requires criminal statutes to be sufficiently specific to place persons on notice as to what acts are proscribed. The Court has struck down some criminal laws under this "void for vagueness" doctrine.

The Court later extended the concept of notice to civil cases. In 1969 and 1972 it held that due process required that consumers be notified before their wages were garnisheed or property repossessed for nonpayment of debts.

One major issue affecting civil defendants has been the question of state court jurisdiction over out-of-state corporations. In the nineteenth century, the Court initially limited the ability to sue a corporation outside the state where it was chartered. Later, however, it upheld state laws requiring corporations to designate an agent for service of process (someone to accept legal papers in civil suits) in order to transact business within the state. Corporations continued to resist the jurisdiction of state courts in some instances, however, on grounds that they had only minimal contacts with a state.

In 1945 the Court made it significantly easier for state courts to assert jurisdiction over out-of-state corporations. The ruling in *International Shoe Co. v. Wash-ington* involved an effort by the state of Washington to levy unemployment compensation taxes against a shoe company that had no manufacturing plants or stores in Washington but had employed commissioned salespeople in the state for several years.

The Court rejected the company's plea that it could not be sued in Washington. The Court said a state could exercise jurisdiction over an out-of-state corporation whenever it had "sufficient contacts or ties with the state . . . to make it reasonable and just, according to our traditional conception of fair play and substantial justice." The ruling led to the enactment of state "long arm" statutes that defined in broad terms state jurisdiction over out-of-state businesses. The Court has construed these statutes liberally in favor of state court powers.

The Court has also ruled that states can generally define the defenses available to defendants in civil proceedings. In a pair of cases in 1917 and 1919 the Court ruled that states could limit the defenses employers could raise against claims arising from workplace injuries. In 1972 the Court upheld a state law that limited a tenant's defense in an eviction action to the issue of payment. The law required the tenant to raise other issues, such as failure to maintain the premises, in other proceedings.

Dicta

See OBITER DICTUM.

Discrimination

In the context of CIVIL RIGHTS, *discrimination* refers to laws, government policies, or private actions that deny or limit privileges, benefits, or opportunities to individuals based on prejudice against the group to which they belong.

Private and official discrimination on the basis of race has been pervasive in the United States from the era of slavery through the period of legally mandated SEGREGATION and into the present. Similar to racial

The pain and frustration of living with discrimination are clearly reflected on the marchers' faces and in their signs.
Source: Congressional Quarterly

discrimination is SEX DISCRIMINATION, to which women have been subject throughout the nation's history. Ethnic and religious minorities, the aged, and the disabled, among others, have also been victims of discrimination.

The Supreme Court used the EQUAL PROTEC-TION clause of the Fourteenth Amendment to strike down most forms of official racial discrimination and to limit some other forms of government discrimina-tion. Modern civil rights legislation began with the Civil Rights Act of 1964. This act and more recent laws prohibited racial and other forms of discrimina-tion by individuals and businesses in such areas as employment, housing, and PUBLIC ACCOMMODA-TIONS. (See OPEN HOUSING; JOB DISCRIMINA-TION.)

In interpreting the equal protection clause and the

civil rights acts, the Court created a complex body of law to define what kinds of legislative classifications or private decisions amount to illegal discrimination. Racial discrimination is all but completely prohibited. On the other hand, some laws treating men and women differently—for example, the exemption of women from the military draft—have been upheld.

Since the 1970s, so-called AFFIRMATIVE ACTION programs have been created by governments, colleges and universities, and private employers to help make up for past discrimination. These programs give spe-cial consideration to previously disadvantaged groups in such areas as government contracting, college ad-missions, and hiring and promotion. The creation of such programs has led to complaints—mostly from white men—that they amount to "reverse discrimi-nation." The Supreme Court, however, has ruled that affirmative action or minority preference programs and policies do not amount to illegal discrimination if they meet certain criteria.

Dissenting Opinions

If a justice does not agree with the result that a majority of the Court has reached in a particular case, he or she may issue a dissenting opinion. Unlike the author of the majority opinion, a dissenting justice is able to avoid the process of revising and compromising his opinion. As a result, many well-reasoned and well-written dissents are more memorable or more interesting to read than the majority opinion.

Dissents are often intended to accomplish more than a simple statement of dissatisfaction with the Court majority. A dissenting justice may hope that the dissent will convince a majority of the other justices to side with him or her. At the least, it may force the majority to take account of points in the dissent. A dissent may also be intended to undermine the majority opinion by pointing out different interpretations of the Constitution or suggesting points of attack for future litigation. A dissenting justice may also hope that a later Court will vindicate the views expressed in the dissent.

Dissent has been a long tradition on the Court. The first real dissent in a Supreme Court case was issued by Justice William Johnson in *Huidekoper's Lessee v. Douglass* (1805). But dissents did not become commonplace until well into the twentieth century. In 1989 dissents were filed in nearly two-thirds of all the cases in which the Court issued written opinions.

The growth in the number of dissents and CON-CURRING OPINIONS has been lamented by some who argue that they weaken the authority of the Court and make the law uncertain. Chief Justice Harlan Fiske Stone was one of those who believed that "dissents seldom aid in the right development of the law. They often do harm."

Others have defended dissenting opinions as a means for individual justices to maintain their independence. The most frequently quoted defense of dissent on the Court was given by Chief Justice Charles Evans Hughes. A "dissent in a court of last resort is an appeal to the brooding spirit of the law, to the intelligence of a future day, when a later decision may possibly correct the error into which the dissenting justice believes the court to have been betrayed," Hughes once wrote.

Dissents are more common during a time of ideological change in the Court's membership. The shift in ideology from the Warren Court to the Burger and Rehnquist courts may account for much of the increase in the number of dissents filed in the last three decades.

Because of either the sheer number or historical significance of their dissents, a few justices stand out as "great dissenters." Justice John Marshall Harlan delivered 380 dissents in his thirty-four years on the Court. He is most famous for his lone dissent against the "separate but equal" doctrine, which the Court upheld in *Plessy v. Ferguson* (1896).

Justice Oliver Wendell Holmes, Jr., did not write an extraordinarily large number of dissents—he averaged fewer than six for each year he sat on the Court—and few of his dissents were later adopted by the majority. But many of the dissents he did file were made memorable by his direct and pungent writing style. In his dissent opposing government wiretaps in *Olmstead v. United States* (1928), for example, Holmes wrote that he thought it "a less evil that some criminals should escape than that the government should play an ignoble part."

Other justices who almost certainly should be added to any list of great dissenters are Louis D. Brandeis, Benjamin N. Cardozo, Felix Frankfurter, William J. Brennan, and Thurgood Marshall.

District Courts

See COURTS, LOWER.

Diversity Jurisdiction

The Constitution gives federal courts JURISDICTION over cases "between citizens of different states."

In passing the Judiciary Act of 1789, Congress concurred with the need to ensure a neutral forum for the resolution of disputes between citizens of different states. The act gave the new circuit courts authority to hear such "diversity" cases.

Today, some federal judges and many legal experts question the need to safeguard citizens of one state from hostile treatment by courts in another state. However, Congress has refused to adopt recommendations to abolish diversity jurisdiction.

Congress has tried to keep trivial matters out of the federal courts by setting a minimum dollar figure that must be in controversy before most cases can enter the federal judicial system. This "jurisdictional amount" was set at $500 in 1789. It was raised to $2,000 in 1887, to $3,000 in 1911, and to $10,000 in 1958. In 1988 the jurisdictional amount was set at $50,000, the current level.

Since 1806 the Supreme Court has generally required "complete diversity" of residence to permit diversity jurisdiction. No party on one side of a case can be a citizen of the same state as any party on the other side if diversity is the basis for federal jurisdiction.

Another early ruling limited diversity jurisdiction in cases involving corporations. In 1810 the Court held that such a case could come into federal court only if all a corporation's stockholders were citizens of a state other than the plaintiff's state. The Court overruled that decision in 1844, however, and held that a corporation would be assumed to be a citizen of the state in which it was chartered. Later decisions further expanded diversity jurisdiction in corporate law cases by treating all of a corporation's stockholders as citizens of the state where the company was incorporated.

Federal courts hearing diversity cases must apply the substantive law of the state in which they are located. This requirement dates from 1789. It was strengthened by the Supreme Court's declaration, in the case of *Erie Railroad Co. v. Tompkins* (1938), that there is no general federal COMMON LAW for federal courts to apply in such cases. In cases where state law on a particular issue is unclear or has not been decided, the federal courts must try to decide the issue as the state's highest court would.

Docket

Each year the Supreme Court is asked to review several thousand cases but accepts only a small number. Of 6,300 new cases filed in the 1992–1993 term, the justices granted review in only ninety-seven.

Petitions that the CLERK OF THE COURT finds in proper form go on the "docket" with a number. A case the Court decides to hear is placed on the "calendar" and scheduled for oral argument.

Before 1970 the clerk maintained two dockets: an appellate docket for petitions for certiorari and appeals in cases where the docketing fee was paid, and a miscellaneous docket for *IN FORMA PAUPERIS* petitions and appeals and other requests not qualifying for the appellate docket. When a case on the miscellaneous docket was accepted for review, it was transferred to the appellate docket and renumbered.

Since 1970 all cases, except those falling within the Court's ORIGINAL JURISDICTION, are placed on a single docket. Only in the numbering is a distinction made between prepaid and *in forma pauperis* cases. Beginning with the 1971 term, prepaid cases were labeled with the year and a number. The first case filed in 1993, for example, would be designated 93-1. *In forma pauperis* cases contain the year but begin with the number 5000. Thus the second *in forma pauperis* case filed in 1993 would be numbered 93-5002.

Cases on the "original docket"—that is, the list of cases falling within the Court's original jurisdiction—were not affected by the 1970 change. Cases on the original docket that are carried over to the next term are no longer renumbered, however. Instead they retain the docket number assigned to them when they were first filed.

Double Jeopardy

The Fifth Amendment provides that no person "shall . . . be subject for the same offence to be twice put in jeopardy of life or limb." The Supreme Court has held that this guarantee protects an individual against multiple prosecutions for the same offense and against multiple punishments for the same crime.

The prohibition is not straightforward or absolute, however. The government may retry a defendant who successfully appeals a conviction. In some circumstances, the government may retry a defendant after an appeal by the prosecution itself. Also, under the "dual sovereignties" doctrine, a defendant may be prosecuted for the same crime by two different jurisdictions—for example, in both state and federal court.

The Supreme Court extended the double jeopardy clause to state as well as federal prosecutions in *Benton v. Maryland* (1969). (See INCORPORATION DOCTRINE.)

On the same day as the *Benton* decision, the Court ruled in *North Carolina v. Pearce* that a judge cannot impose a harsher sentence on a defendant in a retrial except on the basis of objective reasons related to the defendant's conduct after the imposition of the first sentence. But in 1973 the Court refused to apply this limitation to resentencing by a jury after retrial.

A defendant is placed in jeopardy beginning when the jury is sworn in. Thus, the government may revise, refile, or expand charges before trial without violating the double jeopardy clause. The double jeopardy clause does not prohibit a retrial if a jury fails to agree on a verdict or, in some circumstances, if a judge declares a mistrial for reasons unrelated to the government's conduct.

Since the mid-1970s, the Court has expanded the government's right to appeal a judge's decision to dismiss charges against the defendant after the beginning of trial. The Court ruled in 1975 that the government could appeal a trial judge's decision to dismiss charges after a jury verdict. Three years later the Court ruled, 5–4, that the government could also appeal a dismissal granted in midtrial. The Court's opinion explained that the defendant in the case had voluntarily risked retrial for the same offense by seeking dismissal of the charges based on legal grounds unrelated to his guilt or innocence.

The double jeopardy clause protects an individual who successfully appeals a conviction on a lesser charge from being retried on the original, more serious charge. In 1981 the Court, by a 5–4 vote, extended this rule to prevent a state from seeking the death penalty in a retrial after the jury in the defendant's first trial had sentenced him to life imprisonment rather than execution.

Since 1922 the Court has permitted dual prosecutions of a defendant for the same offense by different jurisdictions. "[A]n act denounced as a crime by both national and state sovereignties is an offense against the peace and dignity of both, and may be punished by each," Chief Justice William Howard Taft wrote for the Court in *United States v. Lanza*. The Court has reaffirmed the doctrine several times, permitting dual prosecutions by two different states or by a state and an Indian tribe. But because a state and a city are not separate sovereigns, the double jeopardy guarantee does protect an individual against prosecution by both city and state for one offense.

Douglas, William O.

William Orville Douglas (1898–1980) faced two impeachment threats while serving as a Supreme

Source: Library of Congress

Court justice. The first came in 1953 after he temporarily stayed the execution of convicted spies Julius and Ethel Rosenberg, but that attempt quickly fizzled. The second came in April 1970, just one week after the Senate rejected President Richard Nixon's nomination of G. Harrold Carswell to the Court. House minority leader Gerald R. Ford charged among other things that Douglas had violated federal law by practicing law, had not disqualified himself in cases where he had an interest, and advocated revolution in one of his books. However, a special House subcommittee that investigated the charges found no basis for impeachment.

Douglas was born in the town of Maine, Minnesota, but spent his early years in Yakima, Washington. He contracted polio as a child and developed a lifelong interest in the outdoors as he hiked in the mountains to restore strength in his legs. Douglas graduated from Whitman College in Walla Walla, Washington, and then graduated second in his class at Columbia University Law School in 1925. After working for two years as a Wall Street lawyer, Douglas abandoned the practice of corporate law in favor of teaching law at Columbia. In 1936 President Franklin Roosevelt appointed him to the newly created Securities and Exchange Commission (SEC), and the next year Douglas became chair. He continued serving on the SEC until Roosevelt nominated him for the Supreme Court in 1939.

Douglas was one of the most liberal and controversial individuals ever to serve on the Court. His outspoken character and his four marriages made him the target of repeated political attacks, including the two impeachment attempts. Douglas was a strong defender of the First Amendment rights of freedom of speech, religion, assembly, and the press. In 1971, when the government tried to stop newspapers from publishing the Pentagon Papers, Douglas wrote in a concurring opinion that freedom of the press was absolute and could never be restricted by the government. He also advocated a right to privacy, which, as he wrote in *Griswold v. Connecticut* (1965), was "older than the Bill of Rights." In an opinion written by Douglas, the Court in *Griswold* overturned a Connecticut law that barred married couples from using contraceptives. In 1973 the Court relied on the right to privacy to uphold a woman's right to have an abortion in *ROE V. WADE.*

In some of the other major decisions written by Douglas, the Court expanded the right to counsel to include state defendants charged with any offense serious enough to warrant a jail sentence, upheld the right to travel free of government interference, and struck down poll taxes in state and local elections.

After suffering a paralytic stroke in January 1975, Douglas tried to continue working. However, pain and disability caused by the stroke forced him to retire in November 1975. Douglas served on the Court for thirty-six years and seven months, longer than any other justice. He died in 1980.

Draft Law Cases

See SELECTIVE SERVICE RULINGS.

Dred Scott Decision

See SCOTT V. SANDFORD.

Due Process

Due process has been called the most important term in American constitutional law. It received an initial narrow interpretation by the Supreme Court in 1856. Since then due process has evolved into an expansive concept guaranteeing individuals procedural rights in criminal prosecutions, civil cases, and other government proceedings. The Court has also held that due process imposes substantive limits on government action. This finding was made first in some now discredited cases involving economic rights, and later in a line of cases supporting a right of privacy, including a qualified right to abortion. (See PRIVACY, RIGHT OF.)

Early Rulings

James Madison did not define the term when he wrote, in what became the Fifth Amendment, that "[n]o person shall be . . . deprived of life, liberty, or property, without due process of law." In its first decision interpreting due process, the Court in 1856 defined it as procedures that did not conflict with specific written provisions of the Constitution or with the established practice in England at the time of the settlement of the American colonies.

Earlier the Supreme Court had ruled that the BILL OF RIGHTS applied only to the federal government, not to the states. The post–Civil War Fourteenth Amendment gave individuals a due process guarantee against the states as well. In several decisions beginning in 1884, however, the Court held that due process did not require states to adopt the same criminal procedures used in the federal system.

In *Hurtado v. California* (1884) the Court held that a California procedure starting a criminal prosecution by use of a prosecutor's charge called an information, rather than by an INDICTMENT by a GRAND JURY, did not violate the due process clause. Justice Stanley Matthews said that due process permitted a procedure "newly devised in the discretion of legislative power" as long as it "preserves . . . principles of liberty and justice." Using the same flexible approach, the Court permitted six-person juries in state criminal cases *(Maxwell v. Dow* [1900]) and found no due process violation in a state judge's comment to a jury on a defendant's failure to testify *(Twining v. New Jersey* [1908]).

At about the same time the Court was expanding due process to protect PROPERTY RIGHTS. In 1897 the Court said that the liberty protected by the Fourteenth Amendment included an individual's right to earn a living and "to enter into all contracts which may be proper, necessary, and essential" for that purpose. The Court used this theory of freedom of contract in 1905 to strike down a state law setting maximum hours for bakers *(Lochner v. New York)* and in 1923 and 1936 to invalidate federal and state minimum wage laws.

In 1937, however, the Court all but repudiated the doctrine in upholding a state minimum wage law. "[R]egulation which is reasonable in relation to its subject and is adopted in the interests of the community is due process," the Court said in *West Coast Hotel Co. v. Parrish.*

Two other expansions of due process by the Court have proved to be more durable.

Criminal and Civil Applications

In criminal law, the Court began in the 1920s and 1930s to use due process as the basis for correcting miscarriages of justice in state criminal cases. In 1923 it upheld federal intervention to order the release of five black men who had been convicted of murder and sentenced to death after a trial so dominated by racial tensions that it was a travesty of justice. In 1927 the Court held unconstitutional a system that permitted the presiding judge to take a portion of every fine he assessed against persons convicted of violating a state prohibition law. Due process violations twice required new trials in the *Scottsboro Cases* in the 1930s. In 1936 the Court overturned a state conviction because it had been obtained by using a confession extracted by torture.

This ad hoc application of the due process clause was later replaced by the INCORPORATION DOCTRINE. This was the process by which the Warren Court in the 1960s required the states to comply with the specific criminal procedure provisions of the Bill of Rights.

The Burger Court in the 1970s continued to expand the concept of due process. In 1970 the Court held for the first time that due process required proof of guilt beyond a reasonable doubt in criminal cases. And in the 1976 capital punishment cases, the Court found that due process required states to use specific criteria to guide a judge or jury in imposing the death penalty.

The Court also applied due process restrictions in areas besides criminal law. In 1969 and 1972 the Court held that due process required that consumers be notified before their wages were garnisheed or property repossessed for nonpayment of debts. Other decisions in the 1970s required notice before termination of welfare benefits, dismissal of a teacher after ten years' service, and suspension of a student from public schools for misbehavior.

The procedures required to comply with due process are not always complicated and may in fact be quite simple. In 1990, for example, the Court said that the liberty of a mentally ill prison inmate to refuse antipsychotic drugs could be overcome after a hearing before prison staff rather than a judicial-style proceeding.

Privacy Rights

The Court's use of due process to protect privacy rights can be traced to two decisions in the 1920s. These rulings struck down a Nebraska law prohibiting teaching of any foreign language to children in the first eight grades and an Oregon law requiring all children to attend public schools. Both laws, the Court held, unreasonably interfered with personal liberty protected by the due process clause. Since then the Court has ruled that the "liberty interests" protected by due process include the right to marry, the right to use contraceptives, the right to an abortion, the right to travel, the right to refuse medical treatment, and some freedoms of expression and association not expressly named in the First Amendment.

In some of these cases, the Court's reliance on due process was obscured by use of other constitutional provisions. But in reaffirming the right to abortion in 1992, the Court stated explicitly that due process protects a "substantive sphere of liberty" that goes beyond the provisions of the Bill of Rights or the customs and practices that prevailed when the Fourteenth Amendment was adopted.

Source: Library of Congress

Duvall, Gabriel

Gabriel Duvall (1752–1844) served twenty-three years on the Supreme Court. Toward the end, his deafness and frequent absences from the Court became increasingly embarrassing. The eighty-two-year-old justice's retirement in 1835 helped solve what was becoming a major problem.

Duvall was born on the family plantation, Marietta, in Prince George's County, Maryland. He studied law and was appointed clerk to the Maryland convention in 1775. In 1777 he began a ten-year term as clerk of the Maryland house of delegates. During the revolutionary war, Duvall served as mustermaster and commissary of stores for the Maryland soldiers. He later became a private in the Maryland militia.

In 1787 Duvall moved up from clerk in the Mary-

land house of delegates to become a member himself. He was one of five men chosen to represent Maryland at the Constitutional Convention in Philadelphia, but the whole group decided not to attend. Duvall continued serving in the Maryland house until 1794, when he was elected to the Third Congress of the United States. He resigned after only one term to became chief justice of the general court of Maryland in 1796. When President Thomas Jefferson named him the first comptroller of the treasury in 1802, Duvall gave up his judicial post.

After Duvall had served as comptroller for nearly a decade, President James Madison nominated him for the Supreme Court in November 1811. Duvall usually voted with Chief Justice John Marshall during the near quarter-century he served on the Court. However, he dissented in *Mima Queen and Child v. Hepburn,* arguing that hearsay evidence should be admitted in a case about whether a slave's mother had been free. He also wrote a unanimous opinion, in *Le Grand v. Darnall,* supporting the claim that a slave had been freed when left property in the master's will.

Duvall resigned from the Court in 1835 and died nine years later at age ninety-one.

E

Education and the Court

Public education in the United States is primarily a local function. The federal government has no control over such areas as selection of curriculum, length of school year, qualifications of teachers, and so forth. Those policies are typically set by local school boards under general guidelines established by state law.

Despite this local control of most education policies, the Supreme Court has had a profound impact on public education. Its historic SCHOOL DESEGREGATION decision, *BROWN V. BOARD OF EDUCATION OF TOPEKA* (1954), thrust the Court into the difficult role of superintending the dismantling of racially segregated public school systems. A decade later the Court handed down a pair of controversial rulings that barred official prayer or Bible reading in public elementary and secondary schools. (See SCHOOL PRAYER.)

In many other rulings, however, the Court has avoided intruding too far into education policies. For example, in 1973 the Court declined to require states to provide equal financing for school districts despite evidence of wide disparities in the amount spent per pupil in different districts. The Court has generally deferred to school authorities on issues of students' rights.

No "Fundamental Interest"

The Court's first major pronouncement on public education came in 1925 when it ruled, on substantive due process grounds, that parents could not be required to send their children to public schools. (See PRIVACY, RIGHT OF.) That decision, *Pierce v. Society of Sisters,* struck down an Oregon law aimed at restricting parochial schools. The ruling was reaffirmed in a 1972 decision that upheld the right of Amish parents to choose a religious education for their children. (See RELIGION, FREEDOM OF.)

When the Warren Court in *Brown* outlawed racial segregation as a violation of the equal protection clause, it stressed the importance of education as the key to effective citizenship. Two decades later, however, the Burger Court cut off equal protection challenges to unequal school financing by refusing to declare education a "fundamental interest" *(San Antonio Independent School District v. Rodriguez* [1973]).

Schools have been funded primarily with money raised from taxing the real property within a district, a procedure that results in wide disparities in spending between poor districts and wealthier areas. In Texas, where the *San Antonio* case arose, the wealthiest district spent $594 for each schoolchild, while the poorest spent only $356.

A lower federal court, ruling on a suit brought by parents of Mexican-American pupils in San Antonio, held this unequal school financing to be unconstitutional. By a 5–4 vote, however, the Supreme Court disagreed.

"The undisputed importance of education will not alone cause this Court to depart from the usual standard for reviewing a State's societal and economic legislation," Justice Lewis F. Powell, Jr., wrote for the majority. Powell said the state's use of local property taxes to pay for schools was "not so irrational as to be invidiously discriminatory."

Despite the Court's ruling, litigation over school financing has continued in state courts. Some courts have imposed equal financing requirements on the basis of state constitutional provisions.

After the *San Antonio* ruling, the Supreme Court did place two new requirements on school districts. In 1974 the Court held that school districts receiving federal funds must make some effort to ensure that students who do not speak English are provided either a bilingual education or remedial English training. The unanimous ruling in *Lau v. Nichols* relied on the Civil Rights Act of 1964 rather than on the equal protection clause.

Eight years later, the Court ruled that school dis-

Mary Beth and John Tinker took part in a Vietnam War protest by wearing black armbands in school. That action got them suspended in 1965. In Tinker v. Des Moines Independent School District *(1969) the Supreme Court said that the suspensions violated the students' First Amendment rights.*   *Source: UPI/Bettmann*

tricts could not bar children of illegal immigrants from public schools. The 5–4 decision in *Plyler v. Doe* (1982), striking down a Texas law, found that imposing a severe penalty on children for their parents' misconduct was irrational because it served no "substantial goal of the State."

Students' Rights

The Court has recognized some constitutional limits on school authorities' power over students. In an important 1969 decision, the Court declared that students do not "shed their constitutional rights . . . at the schoolhouse gate." But the Court in the 1980s handed down a series of decisions taking a narrower view of students' rights.

The Court's ruling in *Tinker v. Des Moines Independen-*

dent Community School District (1969) upheld the right of a student to wear a black armband as a protest against the Vietnam War. The Court said school officials could limit expression only if the forbidden conduct would "materially and substantially interfere" with school discipline.

Six years later the Court ruled that schools may suspend students for misconduct only after providing some fair procedures for determining whether the misconduct actually occurred. For the ten-day suspension imposed in *Goss v. Lopez* (1975), the Court said the student had to be given notice of the charges and an opportunity to explain his version of the story.

Three decisions in the 1980s indicated the Court's shift toward even greater deference to school authorities.

In *New Jersey v. T.L.O.* (1985) the Court refused to require school authorities to obtain a warrant to search a student's locker. The Court said a search was constitutional when there were reasonable grounds for suspecting that it would turn up evidence and when the search itself was not "excessively intrusive."

One year later the Court upheld the right of school officials to suspend a student for a lewd speech given in a student assembly *(Bethel School District No. 43 v. Fraser* [1986]). In 1988 the Court held that school officials could censor student articles in a school newspaper if the paper was published as part of the school's curriculum *(Hazelwood School District v. Kuhlmeier).*

Eighth Amendment

See BAIL; CRUEL AND UNUSUAL PUNISHMENT.

Elections and the Court

The Supreme Court has been a recurring issue in presidential campaigns since 1800. Candidates of both major parties, and those of some third parties, have made the Court's rulings on a variety of issues targets for election-year rhetoric.

The Election of 1800

During the election of 1800, Jeffersonian Republicans charged that the federal judiciary was a Federalist bloc intent upon destroying republican liberties. The Jeffersonians also criticized the fact that both Chief Justice John Jay and his successor in that post, Oliver Ellsworth, had accepted diplomatic assignments from presidents George Washington and John Adams, respectively.

When Thomas Jefferson became president, he launched an attack on the judicial branch, encouraging Congress first to repeal the Judiciary Act of 1801 and then to impeach an associate justice, Samuel Chase, for making political speeches from the bench. The Jeffersonians succeeded in repealing the 1801 act

but failed in their efforts to remove Chase. (See IMPEACHMENT OF JUSTICES.)

The Election of 1860

The Court ruled in 1857 in the Dred Scott case *(SCOTT V. SANDFORD)* that Congress could not bar slavery from the territories. This ruling gave Abraham Lincoln an issue that carried him into the White House. Lincoln had criticized the ruling and argued for keeping the territories free during his unsuccessful campaign for the Senate in 1858.

The Republican platform of 1860 sharply criticized the Dred Scott decision, and Republicans hoped to overturn it through the appointment of loyal Republicans to the Court if Lincoln was elected. Lincoln won, but ultimately it took the Civil War to overrule *Scott.*

The Election of 1896

In 1895 the Court held the federal INCOME TAX unconstitutional. The decision in *Pollock v. Farmers' Loan & Trust Co.* angered progressives in Congress and other reformers. They felt that it protected private vested rights and frustrated Congress's attempts to make the wealthy pay their fair share of taxes. As a result the ruling became an issue in the 1896 presidential campaign.

The Democratic party favored the income tax and decried such judicial "usurpation" of legislative power. Its candidate, William Jennings Bryan, attacked the Court in his famous "cross of gold" speech at the Democratic national convention in Chicago in July. Bryan lost the election, but the effect of the Court's decision was eventually overturned with ratification of the Sixteenth Amendment in 1913. (See REVERSALS OF RULINGS BY CONSTITUTIONAL AMENDMENT.)

The Election of 1924

In the 1924 election the Progressive party made the Supreme Court's opposition to reform legislation a campaign issue. Sen. Robert M. La Follette, R-Wis., the party's presidential candidate, proposed a constitutional amendment giving Congress authority to overturn a Supreme Court decision declaring an act of Congress unconstitutional by reenacting the law.

Supreme Court decisions often become issues in political campaigns. In 1896 Democratic candidate William Jennings Bryan attacked the Court for its decision a year earlier in Pollock v. Farmers' Loan & Trust Co., *which invalidated the federal income tax.*
Source: Library of Congress

Republican President Calvin Coolidge, who was seeking reelection, defended the Court, saying it was the chief obstacle preventing "breakdown [of] the guarantees of our fundamental law." Coolidge won the election, and the Court continued to hand down conservative rulings on social and economic measures.

The Election of 1936

Franklin D. Roosevelt lashed out at the Court during his 1936 reelection campaign for its rulings striking down key measures of his New Deal program. Roosevelt accused the Court of using a "horse-and-buggy definition of interstate commerce" to cripple the federal government's ability to address the economic emergency posed by the Great Depression.

Behind the scenes, Roosevelt also discussed with his advisers ways to overcome the Court's opposition to his programs. The alternatives included possible constitutional amendments or expansion of the size of the Court so that Roosevelt could name justices sympathetic to his views. Despite his reelection by a landslide, Roosevelt's "Court-packing" plan drew strong opposition after it was unveiled in 1937. The plan failed, but Roosevelt's later appointments to the Court gave it a solid majority in support of an expanded federal role in economic affairs. (See SIZE OF THE COURT.)

The Election of 1968

During the 1960s the Warren Court revolutionized the criminal justice system by requiring states to adopt procedures guaranteeing suspects and defendants rights protected by the Bill of Rights. In the presidential campaign of 1968, Richard Nixon sharply criticized the Court's decisions, saying they were "seriously hamstringing the peace forces in our society and strengthening the criminal forces."

Nixon's law-and-order theme was an important factor in his election. In the White House he worked to fulfill his campaign pledge to change the Court's philosophy. He appointed Warren E. Burger, a hard-line judge of a federal appeals court, as chief justice in 1969. Burger and Nixon's three other successful nominees—Harry A. Blackmun, Lewis F. Powell, Jr., and William H. Rehnquist—helped establish a new majority that cut back on some of the Warren Court's expansive rulings on criminal procedure.

The Elections of 1980 and 1984

Ronald Reagan appealed to conservative voters in his 1980 and 1984 election campaigns by promising to seek the reversal of the Supreme Court's 1973 abortion rights decision, *ROE V. WADE*, and its rulings from the early 1960s forbidding officially prescribed prayers in public schools.

Reagan shifted the Court to the right by elevating Rehnquist to chief justice and naming three other generally conservative justices: Sandra Day O'Connor, Antonin Scalia, and Anthony M. Kennedy. The four helped form a 5–4 majority in 1989 upholding state restrictions on abortion procedures. But in 1992 O'Connor and Kennedy shifted positions in a ruling that gave states further discretion on abortion laws but also retained the main holding of *Roe v. Wade*.

Electronic Surveillance

The invention of the microphone, telephone, and audio recording devices gave law enforcement officers the ability to eavesdrop on private conversations as a way of gathering evidence in criminal cases.

When the Supreme Court first considered these practices in the 1920s, it ruled that electronic surveillance, or wiretapping, was not limited by either the Fourth or Fifth Amendment. Four decades later the Court reversed that position and ruled that electronic surveillance by state or federal officers was covered by the Fourth Amendment. The ruling led Congress to include procedures for judicially approved electronic surveillance in a 1968 anticrime bill.

The Court's decision in *Olmstead v. United States* (1928) reasoned that wiretapping was neither a search nor a seizure, since officers did not enter the suspect's house or take away any material items. Justices Oliver Wendell Holmes, Jr., and Louis D. Brandeis dissented. In his dissent, Brandeis argued that the ruling undermined the purpose of the Fourth Amendment to protect "the sanctities of a man's home and the privacies of his life."

The Federal Communications Act of 1934 included a provision against unauthorized disclosure of "intercepted" telephone communications. The Court in *Nardone v. United States* (1937) held that this provision forbade the use in federal courts of wiretap evidence obtained by federal agents.

The effect of the ruling was limited by two decisions in 1942. In one case the Court held that wiretap

A "bugged" telephone. Court opinions on the legality of eavesdropping changed as the devices became more sophisticated.
Copyright Washington Post; Reprinted by permission of the District of Columbia Public Library

evidence could be used against someone other than the person whose conversations had been overheard. In another case the Court ruled that the use of a "bug" (an electronic listening device, rather than a wiretap on telephone lines) did not violate the Federal Communications Act. In addition, before the Court extended the exclusionary rule to the states in 1961, it found no basis for prohibiting the use of wiretap evidence in state courts.

In 1961 the Court, on Fourth Amendment grounds, barred one form of electronic surveillance: use of a "spike mike" driven into a building wall to enable agents to overhear conversations within the building. The Court found that the penetration of the wall was sufficient to constitute physical intrusion in violation of the Fourth Amendment. Implicitly, the Court also repudiated part of the *Olmstead* doctrine by holding that under the Fourth Amendment the eavesdropping amounted to a "seizure" of the suspect's conversation.

Six years later the Court formally abandoned the *Olmstead* rule and turned instead to the privacy approach that Brandeis had advocated in dissenting from that opinion. "The Fourth Amendment protects people, not places," Justice Potter Stewart wrote for the Court in *Katz v. United States* (1967).

The 8–1 decision barred the use of evidence against a suspect in an illegal bookmaking case. The evidence had been obtained by use of a listening device on the outside of a public telephone booth. Stewart said the location of the device was irrelevant, reasoning that Katz had a legitimate expectation of privacy when he entered the booth. "[W]hat he sought to exclude when he entered the booth was not the intruding eye—it was the uninvited ear," Stewart said.

Following *Katz*, Congress in the 1968 Crime Control and Safe Streets Act provided statutory authorization for federal use of judicially approved electronic surveillance. Many states have since enacted similar legislation. The federal law provides that applications for warrants must be approved by either the attorney general or a specially designated assistant attorney general.

Twice in the 1970s the Court signaled its determination to strictly apply the warrant requirement for wiretaps. In 1972 the Court unanimously rejected the Nixon administration's position that no warrants were required for wiretaps or surveillance in national security cases. Two years later the Court effectively nullified hundreds of criminal prosecutions because Attorney General John N. Mitchell had allowed an aide other than the designated assistant attorney general to approve applications for wiretaps.

On the other hand, the Court in 1979 found no need in electronic surveillance cases for warrants to explicitly authorize covert entry. Congress must have known, the Court said, that most electronic bugs can only be installed by agents who enter the premises secretly. The same year the Court held that the use of "pen registers"—devices that record the numbers called from a telephone—was not covered by the 1968 wiretap law and did not amount to a search within the meaning of the Fourth Amendment.

Ellsworth, Oliver

Oliver Ellsworth (1745–1807) was the nation's second chief justice. He was President George Washington's third choice for the post. Washington initially turned to a former justice and then to a member of the Court. When John Jay resigned as chief justice in 1795, Washington first appointed John Rutledge to succeed him. The Senate rejected Rutledge, so Washington asked Associate Justice William Cushing to accept the job. Cushing declined, and Washington finally turned to Ellsworth.

Born in Windsor, Connecticut, Ellsworth graduated from Princeton in 1766. He was admitted to the bar in 1777, the same year he began a nine-year term as state's attorney for Hartford County. He was also named to be a delegate to the Continental Congress. In 1787, while serving as a member of the Connecticut delegation to the Constitutional Convention, Ellsworth coauthored the "Connecticut Compromise," which resolved an argument between large and small states over representation in the federal legislature.

Source: Independence National Historical Park Collection

As one of Connecticut's first two U.S. senators, Ellsworth helped write rules for the Senate and assisted in organizing the army, U.S. Post Office, and census. He also was instrumental in developing the conference report on the Bill of Rights. Ellsworth's most important action in the Senate was to head the committee that wrote the Judiciary Act of 1789, which established the federal judicial system.

As chief justice, Ellsworth lobbied his colleagues to agree on *per curiam* decisions, rather than each justice writing individual opinions for each case. John Marshall later took this same position and met with greater success.

Three years after Ellsworth's appointment to the Supreme Court in 1796, President John Adams sent him to France with two other negotiators to help resolve hostilities between the United States and France. The negotiations were only partially successful. The trip was arduous and sapped Ellsworth's health. In September 1800, while still in France, Ellsworth resigned as chief justice. He died in 1807.

Equal Protection

The Fourteenth Amendment to the Constitution forbids any state to "deny any person within its jurisdiction the equal protection of the laws." Along with the amendment's protections for the "privileges and immunities" of national citizenship and its guarantee of due process, the equal protection clause was intended to prevent official DISCRIMINATION against blacks.

In the decades after the Civil War the Supreme Court interpreted the equal protection clause in such a way that it was virtually useless. (See CIVIL WAR AMENDMENTS.) Only in the mid-twentieth century, with its historic school desegregation decision, *BROWN V. BOARD OF EDUCATION OF TOPEKA* (1954), did the Court begin to use the equal protection clause as a weapon against legally mandated racial SEGREGATION.

The Court has also held that the equal protection clause limits official discrimination against foreigners, or ALIENS, and requires heightened scrutiny of discrimination based on gender or illegitimacy. (See SEX DISCRIMINATION.)

In addition, the Court has used the equal protection clause to strike down some legislative classifications affecting certain "fundamental interests." These fundamental interests include voting rights, access to justice, and rights concerning marriage, procreation, and the family. The Court has not extended the fundamental interests doctrine since 1969.

Although the equal protection clause applies only to the states, the Court ruled in a companion case to *Brown* that the due process clause of the Fifth

The pediment of the U.S. Supreme Court building.
Source: Congressional Quarterly

Amendment contains an implicit equal protection requirement that applies to the federal government.

The equal protection clause does not apply to private discrimination. Before the enactment of modern civil rights laws, the Court defined "state action" broadly in order to bar some forms of private discrimination, such as restrictive covenants that forbade the sale of houses to blacks.

Traditional Standard

The first standard developed by the Supreme Court for measuring a particular classification against the equal protection guarantee grew largely out of its review of state tax and economic regulation. The Court struck down only a handful of such measures, most of them involving discrimination against out-of-state businesses. It declared that legislative classifications would be upheld unless they were "purely arbitrary."

The Court has reaffirmed this standard in modern times. "[I]n the local economic sphere, it is only the invidious discrimination, the wholly arbitrary act, which cannot stand consistently with the Fourteenth Amendment," the Court said in 1976.

Modern Standard

The Court's shift in focus from property rights to individual rights in the late 1930s led it to develop a more probing standard for examining charges of denial of equal protection. Under this standard, classifications that are "inherently suspect" or that affect fundamental rights or interests require "strict scrutiny" by the Court. A state must show more than "a rational basis" for the law. It must prove that it has a "compelling governmental interest" for making the challenged classification and that it can achieve that interest in no other way.

Race was declared to be a suspect category in *Korematsu v. United States* (1944), a decision that nonetheless upheld the government's wartime relocation of Japanese Americans on the West Coast. (See INTERNMENT CASES.) Ten years later the Court in *Brown* found that the equal protection clause barred racial segregation in public schools. The Court did not adopt a specific standard for reviewing racial classifications.

Only in 1967, in striking down a Virginia law banning interracial marriages, did the Court expressly state that all racial classifications are "inherently suspect" *(Loving v. Virginia)*. Since then, however, the Court has ruled that narrowly tailored AFFIRMATIVE ACTION plans that take race into account in university admissions, employment, or government contracting do not violate the equal protection clause.

In 1971, the Court held that laws treating aliens differently from citizens are also inherently suspect. But it has upheld a few such laws, especially those passed by the federal government.

The Court has wavered on what test to apply to cases challenging discrimination on the basis of sex. The Court has applied the traditional, rational basis test to most of them. More often than not it has sustained such laws under that approach. In other decisions, however, the Court has barred legislative classifications based on generalizations about differences in behavior or qualifications of men and women, calling such presumptions arbitrary or overly broad.

In 1976 a slim majority of the Court adopted a slightly higher test for sex discrimination cases. This test required the government to show that a gender-based classification was necessary to achieve some "important governmental objective." But this test has not been used in later cases.

The Court has refused to apply the compelling interest standard to test laws that discriminate against the poor or against illegitimate children. Some laws that distinguish illegitimate children from their legitimate siblings have been struck down, however, as arbitrary or archaic.

Fundamental Interests

The Court first articulated its fundamental interest test in the case of *Skinner v. Oklahoma* (1942). In invalidating a law authorizing compulsory sterilization of some criminals, the Court declared that marriage and procreation were "basic civil rights" and that equal protection required "strict scrutiny" of laws affecting those rights.

The fundamental interest doctrine next emerged in 1964 in one of the Court's "one-person, one vote" reapportionment decisions, *Reynolds v. Sims.* The Court later expanded the use of equal protection analysis to strike down overly long residency requirements for voting, poll taxes, and enforcement of candidate filing fees to prevent someone who is unable to pay the fee from being on the ballot.

The Court has also ruled that access to justice is a fundamental right. On that basis it has acted to protect the rights of indigents to appeals in criminal cases. In 1970 the Court barred imprisonment of indigents for failure to pay fines in criminal cases *(Williams v. Illinois).*

The Court in the early 1970s halted further expansion of the fundamental interest doctrine. In 1971 it ruled that access to housing was not a fundamental interest and upheld a state law restricting tenants' rights in landlord-tenant cases by applying a rational basis test.

Two years later the Court in *San Antonio School District v. Rodriguez* (1973) declared that education was not a fundamental interest. On that basis the Court upheld, 5–4, the prevailing pattern of financing public education through local property taxes despite the wide disparities that result in the amount spent per pupil in different districts.

Exclusionary Rule

The exclusionary rule prohibits evidence obtained by the government in violation of a person's constitutional rights from being used against that person in a criminal trial.

The rule was created by the Supreme Court in 1914 and extended to the states in 1961. It is most frequently applied to bar evidence obtained in violation of the Fourth Amendment SEARCH AND SEIZURE rules. But it also prevents the use of statements obtained in violation of a person's Fifth Amendment privilege against self-incrimination or Sixth Amendment right to counsel. (See CONFESSIONS.)

The exclusionary rule has been intensely controversial and has been cut back in recent years. Most notably, the Court in 1984 approved a "good faith" exception to the rule for evidence obtained under a search warrant later determined to have been improperly issued.

In its unanimous decision creating the exclusionary rule, *Weeks v. United States* (1914), the Court said that without a prohibition against use of evidence obtained from unlawful searches, the Fourth Amendment "might as well be stricken from the Constitution." At the same time, however, the Court created the "silver platter doctrine" allowing federal prosecutors to use evidence illegally obtained by state agents if the evidence was obtained without federal participation and then turned over to federal officials.

The Court based the silver platter doctrine on its view that the Fourth Amendment was not applicable to the states. When it did apply the Fourth Amendment to the states in 1949, the Court still did not impose the exclusionary rule, saying that the evidence ban was not required as part of due process.

The Court shifted its position in 1961, however, ruling 6–3 in *Mapp v. Ohio* that states must follow the exclusionary rule. Writing for the Court, Justice Tom C. Clark stated that the rule was needed to ensure that "the right to be secure against rude invasions of privacy by state officers" was not "an empty promise."

In the 1970s the Court limited the use of the ex-

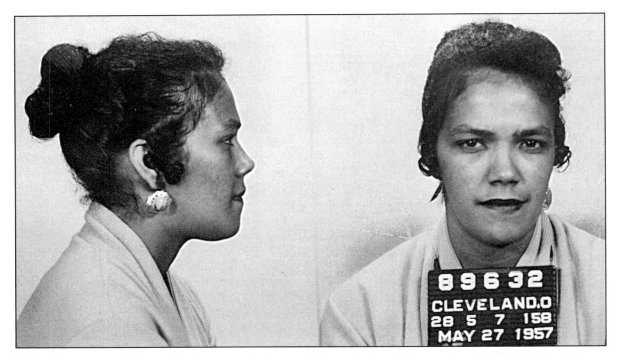

Dollree Mapp was arrested for possession of obscene materials seized during an illegal search. The American Civil Liberties Union, in an amicus curiae brief, raised the Fourth Amendment issue on which the Court decided her case.   Source: The Plain Dealer, *Cleveland, Ohio*

clusionary rule to overturn convictions, reflecting the lack of enthusiasm for the rule by some of the justices—especially Chief Justice Warren E. Burger and Justice William H. Rehnquist. It refused, for example, to forbid prosecutors to use illegally obtained evidence when questioning witnesses before grand juries or to require the release of prisoners in habeas corpus actions challenging convictions as having been obtained with illegally obtained evidence.

In 1984 the Court, by a vote of 6 to 3, limited the rule further. In *United States v. Leon* the Court "modified" the rule to permit the use of evidence "seized on a search warrant issued by a detached and neutral magistrate but ultimately found to be unsupported by probable cause." Writing for the Court, Justice Byron R. White stated that the rule had little deterrent effect in cases where police had first sought a search warrant. Dissenting justices, however, warned that the

good faith exception might eventually swallow the rule. The same year, the Court also approved an "inevitable discovery" exception. This permitted the use of illegally obtained evidence if prosecutors could show that it ultimately would have been discovered by lawful means.

Executive Privilege and Immunity

The Constitution makes no mention of executive privilege or executive immunity, yet they are important aspects of presidential power. Both concepts derive from the Constitution's system of SEPARATION OF POWERS.

Executive privilege is the president's prerogative to withhold information, documents, or testimony of aides from public or congressional scrutiny. Congress has never fully accepted this principle, but the Supreme Court recognized the existence of a qualified privilege in the Watergate tapes case, *United States v. Nixon* (1974).

Executive immunity is the established doctrine that shields the chief executive from judicial interference with presidential policy making. A court cannot order the president to take, or refrain from taking, any particular policy action, although the president or subordinates may be ordered to perform so-called ministerial duties—duties as to which there is little discretion.

History of Executive Immunity

The turmoil of Reconstruction and the troubled presidency of Andrew Johnson provided the backdrop for the leading Supreme Court decision on the president's immunity from judicial interference with the conduct of the presidency.

The state of Mississippi asked the Supreme Court to order the president to stop carrying out the congressional program of Reconstruction outlined in the Reconstruction Act of 1867. In *Mississippi v. Johnson* (1867), the Court refused.

Chief Justice Salmon P. Chase acknowledged that *MARBURY V. MADISON* (1803) had said that a court could issue a writ to order the president to perform a ministerial duty. But acts involving political discretion, Chase explained, were beyond judicial reach—either to require the president to take specific actions or to prevent him from acting.

In 1982 the Court strengthened the president's legal protections by granting absolute immunity from personal liability as a result of injuries or losses caused by the president's official actions. The 5–4 decision in *Nixon v. Fitzgerald* barred a suit against former president Richard Nixon by an Air Force whistleblower who claimed he had been fired for revealing cost overruns to Congress. The Court said the president needed absolute immunity from personal lawsuits because of "the singular importance" of the president's duties.

The question whether a president can be criminally prosecuted for actions taken while in office was left uncertain after President Gerald Ford granted Nixon a complete pardon, in advance of any criminal charges, for his actions during the Watergate affair.

Executive Privilege

Despite generally acknowledging a congressional right to inquire into executive branch matters, presidents from time to time have claimed an executive privilege to withhold information from Congress.

Some of the early precedents claimed for the practice are mixed. President George Washington refused to let the House see papers pertaining to the controversial Jay Treaty, but he acknowledged the Senate's right of access to the papers. President Thomas Jefferson partly complied when the House asked him for information about the Aaron Burr conspiracy.

In 1927 the Supreme Court held that executive privilege did not protect the executive branch from legitimate legislative investigation. But in 1948 the Court declared, in a private lawsuit, that there were areas of executive power—military and national security matters in particular—about which the president might properly refuse to disclose all facts relative to a decision.

The number of executive privilege claims has risen sharply since 1954. President Dwight D. Eisenhower invoked executive privilege to limit information provided during the much publicized army-McCarthy hearings (a security-related probe directed by Sen. Joseph R. McCarthy, R-Wis.). Presidents John F. Kennedy and Lyndon B. Johnson both defended executive privilege, but each assured Congress it would be asserted only with his personal approval.

President Nixon provided a similar assurance, though some officials in his administration did assert the privilege without presidential approval. Nixon vigorously defended the right to withhold information from Congress. The issue proved crucial to the outcome of the confrontation between Nixon, Congress, and the Watergate special prosecutor that ended in Nixon's resignation in August 1974.

In the face of a subpoena from Special Prosecutor Leon Jaworski for tapes of White House conversations between Nixon and his aides, Nixon claimed an ab-

The Supreme Court's decision in United States v. Nixon *(1974) cost President Richard Nixon his job.*   Source: Le Pelley, The Christian Science Monitor

solute privilege to reject judicial demands for information. On July 24, 1974, the Court unanimously rejected Nixon's plea to quash the subpoenas while for the first time explicitly recognizing a constitutional basis for executive privilege.

"Nowhere in the Constitution . . . is there any explicit reference to a privilege of confidentiality," Chief Justice Warren E. Burger wrote, "yet to the extent this interest relates to the effective discharge of a President's powers, it is constitutionally based."

After reviewing the prosecutor's need for evidence in the Watergate cover-up trial of Nixon aides, however, the Court concluded that Nixon's "generalized interest in confidentiality" had to yield "to the demonstrated, specific need for evidence in a pending criminal trial." Disclosure of the tapes, which contained damning evidence of Nixon's knowledge of the cover-up, led to Nixon's resignation on August 9, 1974.

Nixon lost a second executive privilege case in 1977 when the Court refused to restrict access to the records of his administration. The Court in *Nixon v. Administrator, General Services Administration* voted 7–2 to reject his plea to invalidate a 1974 act of Congress placing the records, tapes, and papers of his administration in federal custody.

Ex Parte

Ex parte is a Latin term meaning "on behalf of." A legal proceeding is said to be ex parte if it occurs on the application of one party without notice to the adverse party. A court can issue certain writs, including a writ of HABEAS CORPUS, or a TEMPORARY RESTRAINING ORDER on an ex parte basis if certain conditions are met. The name of the case appears as "Ex parte . . . " followed by the name of the party making the application.

Ex Post Facto

Ex post facto is a Latin phrase meaning "from a thing done afterward." An ex post facto law makes illegal an act that has already taken place or makes the punishment greater than it was at the time of the act. The Constitution prohibits either Congress or the states from passing ex post facto laws (Article I, Sections 9 and 10).

In its earliest ruling on the subject, the Supreme Court in 1798 held that the prohibition applied only to criminal laws, not to civil statutes. Generally, a criminal law found to be an ex post facto law can stay on the books but cannot be applied to offenses committed before enactment.

Only one congressional act has been invalidated as an ex post facto law. In striking down a loyalty oath for former Confederates, the Court in *Ex parte Garland* (1867) said the requirement punished actions that were not defined as illegal at the time they were committed. On the other hand, the Court has upheld the deportation of foreigners for criminal acts committed before enactment of the deportation law.

The Court has ruled some state changes in criminal sentencing to be ex post facto laws. In 1937, for example, it ruled against a Washington state law that required a judge to impose a maximum sentence for an offense rather than select a sentence from a range. But the Court has allowed states to provide higher penalties for new crimes committed afterwards by habitual criminals.

Extrajudicial Activities

Supreme Court justices may engage in extrajudicial activities if they so desire, but such activities have often sparked controversy both inside the Court and among its critics. The extrajudicial activities that cause most concern are those that appear political. Such activities can reflect adversely on the independence and impartiality not only of the individual justices but also of the Court.

Modern justices may be identified as sharing the general ideology of one or the other political party, but few of them are as openly political as many of the justices of the nineteenth century were. In that era, several justices actually ran for elective office while sitting on the bench. Others openly endorsed or opposed political candidates, while still others served as diplomats and special envoys.

At President George Washington's request, the first chief justice, John Jay, undertook a successful diplomatic mission to Great Britain in 1794 to try to patch up quarrels over British troops in the American Northwest and private debts to British creditors.

The Jay Treaty, which the chief justice negotiated during the visit, may have prevented another war between Britain and the United States, but Jay was sharply criticized in Congress for holding an appointment from the president at the same time as he served on the Court. He resigned from the Court upon his return from England, not because of the congressional criticism, but because he had been elected governor of New York while he was abroad.

Justices Samuel Chase and Bushrod Washington campaigned actively for presidential candidates John Adams and Charles Pinckney, respectively, in 1800. Other politically minded nineteenth-century justices included Smith Thompson, John McLean, Salmon P. Chase, David Davis, and Stephen J. Field.

Thompson, a Democrat, conducted an all-out but unsuccessful campaign to win the New York gubernatorial election in 1828. McLean sought but failed to win his party's presidential nomination in 1836, 1848, 1852, and 1856, all while he served on the Court.

Salmon Chase had been a U.S. senator, a governor, a cabinet member, and a presidential candidate before coming to the Court. Once on the Court, he presided over the Senate impeachment trial of President Andrew Johnson. In 1868 he sought unsuccessfully the presidential nomination of both parties.

Davis accepted nomination as a minor party candidate for president in 1872 before resigning from the Court in 1877 to serve in the Senate. Field periodically indicated his availability for the Democratic presidential nomination.

Far fewer justices have sought elective office in the twentieth century. In the middle years of the century Justice Robert H. Jackson was approached to run for governor of New York. Franklin D. Roosevelt and Harry S. Truman both considered Justice William O. Douglas as a running mate. After President Dwight Eisenhower suffered a heart attack, Chief Justice Earl Warren was widely considered as a possible Republican presidential nominee in 1956. Eisenhower recovered, ran again, and won.

1877 Electoral Commission

An ostensibly public-spirited activity on the part of five justices ended by involving the Court in one of its most serious political controversies. In 1877 justices Nathan Clifford, Samuel F. Miller, Stephen Field, William Strong, and Joseph P. Bradley were appointed to serve on the electoral commission to resolve the disputed presidential election between Democrat Samuel J. Tilden and Republican Rutherford B. Hayes the previous year.

The commission established by Congress consisted of fifteen members: three Republicans and two Democrats from the Senate, two Republicans and three Democrats from the House, and two Democrats and two Republicans from the Supreme Court. The Court itself was to choose the fifth member—Bradley, a Republican. Bradley is said to have initially favored Tilden but ultimately yielded to Republican pressure and supported Hayes. The commission vote favored Hayes, and, after a great deal of backroom bargaining, Congress declared him the winner. The partisan feelings generated by the dispute lowered the prestige of the Court in the eyes of much of the public.

Some twentieth-century justices have ignored the lesson of the Hayes-Tilden Commission and discovered for themselves that participation on supposedly nonpartisan commissions or investigative bodies can involve the Court in political controversy. Among these instances were the participation of Justice Joseph R. Lamar in international arbitration cases; Justice Owen J. Roberts's role on the German-American Mixed Claims Commission and the Pearl Harbor Review Commission, and Jackson's prosecution of Nazi war criminals at the Nuremberg trials following World War II. In addition to being concerned that Jackson's participation in the war trials would hurt the prestige of the Court, some justices complained that his year-long absence from the Court imposed extra work on them.

Perhaps the most controversial extrajudicial activity by a justice in the twentieth century was Warren's chairmanship of the commission that investigated the 1963 assassination of President John F. Kennedy. Before the commission released its findings on the facts and circumstances surrounding the shooting, critics of Warren's performance on the Court denounced the chief justice for neglecting his judicial duties and engaging in a "political" undertaking. After the commission concluded that Lee Harvey Oswald had acted alone in assassinating the president, those convinced that Oswald had been part of a conspiracy joined in the criticism of Warren.

White House Advisers

The Court has always refused to give the president advisory opinions, but since the time of John Jay, individual justices have given private advice to presidents. When made public, this informal relationship generally has resulted in criticism of the justice involved and the Court.

When Franklin Roosevelt indicated at a press conference in September 1939 that he had discussed the situation in Europe with justices Harlan Fiske Stone and Felix Frankfurter, there was a storm of protest over the involvement of justices in the foreign policy deliberations and decisions of the executive branch. Stone thereafter refused all invitations to confer with the president. Frankfurter, however, continued advising Roosevelt and his successors.

A more recent example is the advice that Justice Abe Fortas continued to give President Lyndon Johnson after Fortas's appointment to the Court in 1965. Fortas's role as an adviser to Johnson was a major factor in his failure to win Senate confirmation as chief justice in 1968.

F

Fair Trial

See TRIALS.

Federalism

The Constitution created a new form of government that the framers called "federal." It established a national government with direct power over citizens but preserved the states as sovereign units with power over their own affairs and their own citizens.

Two centuries later, federalism remains the organizing principle of government in the United States. The relationship between the national government and the states, however, has been dramatically changed. With the Supreme Court's approval, the federal government has taken on extremely broad powers, including powers that impinge on states' sovereignty. (See STATES AND THE COURT.)

The Constitution enumerated the powers of the new federal government in Article I, Section 8. Writing in *The Federalist* No. 45, James Madison described those powers as "few and definite," compared to the "numerous and indefinite" powers of the states. The Bill of Rights further protected states' rights in the Tenth Amendment: "The powers not delegated to the United States by the Constitution, nor prohibited by it to the States, are reserved to the States respectively, or to the people."

In *MCCULLOCH V. MARYLAND* (1819), however, the Supreme Court broadly construed federal powers—in part by reducing the significance of the Tenth Amendment. Chief Justice John Marshall emphasized that the amendment had modified the phrasing of the Articles of Confederation, which had reserved to the states all powers not "expressly delegated" to the central government.

During the tenure of Marshall's successor, Chief Justice Roger B. Taney, Tenth Amendment arguments received a friendlier hearing. The Court began to develop the concept of "dual federalism." In this view, the respective domains of state and federal government are neatly defined: each government is supreme and sovereign within its own sphere, and the central government's powers are limited by those reserved to the states.

During its laissez-faire period, which extended into the 1930s, the Court repeatedly used the Tenth Amendment to limit federal power. In 1937, however, the Court reversed itself and began sustaining key pieces of President Franklin D. Roosevelt's New Deal program expanding federal powers. When it upheld one of those laws, the Fair Labor Standards Act, in 1941 the Court described the Tenth Amendment as only "a truism" that did not "depriv[e] the national government of authority to resort to all means for the exercise of a granted power which are appropriate and plainly adapted to the permitted end."

In later years the Court upheld federal legislation that further encroached on states' powers—for example, by imposing conditions on federal aid. In addition, the Court broadened the PREEMPTION doctrine, which bars state legislation that conflicts with federal law or policies. States do retain substantial authority, however, in areas where the federal government has not acted.

Federal Judicial Center

Congress created the Federal Judicial Center in 1967 "to further the development and adoption of improved judicial administration in the courts of the United States." The center serves as the research, training, and development arm of the federal judiciary.

The center's seven-member board is headed by the

chief justice of the United States and includes two judges from the U.S. circuit courts, three judges from the U.S. district courts, and the director of the ADMINISTRATIVE OFFICE OF THE U.S. COURTS. The board meets four times a year, and the center's policy decisions are made at these meetings.

The center holds about 250 education and training seminars each year and undertakes research projects. One such project was the development of an electronic bulletin board for the dissemination of appellate court information.

The results of the center's research projects are often passed on to the U.S. JUDICIAL CONFERENCE, where they are used in making recommendations for improvements in the federal court system. The center, which is located in Washington, D.C., has about 160 employees. Its annual budget for fiscal 1994 was $18.5 million.

Felony

A felony is a criminal offense defined by state or federal law to be punishable by imprisonment for a minimum period—typically, a term exceeding one year. A crime with lesser punishment is considered a MISDEMEANOR.

The Constitution does not control the definition of felonies and misdemeanors, and the Supreme Court has relied on other distinctions as well in deciding when certain procedural rights do or do not apply.

In federal courts, a felony prosecution must be initiated by a grand jury indictment, as required by the Fifth Amendment. Federal statutes and the Federal Rules of Criminal Procedure permit a misdemeanor case to be brought by indictment or a prosecutor's charge called an information. The grand jury indictment requirement is one of the few provisions of the Bill of Rights that the Supreme Court has not extended to the states.

The Court has ruled that the Sixth Amendment rights to a jury trial and to appointment of legal counsel, both of which have been extended to the states, apply to all felony prosecutions. But "petty" offenses—defined in 1970 as those that may be punished by no more than six months in prison—do not require a jury trial in state or federal courts. Although the Court has required since 1938 that counsel be provided in all federal criminal cases, it ruled in 1979 that states need not provide counsel in misdemeanor cases if the defendant is not sentenced to jail or prison.

Field, Stephen J.

Stephen Johnson Field (1816–1899) is the only Supreme Court justice who was ever the target of an assassination attempt because of one of his decisions. The attacker was unhappy over Field's ruling in 1888, while he was sitting as a circuit judge in California, that a marriage contract was invalid. The case involved the man's wife and her deceased first husband.

Source: Collection of the Supreme Court of the United States

When Field returned to California the next year to hold circuit court, the man, David Terry, boarded a train Field was riding and struck him. An armed federal marshal traveling with Field shot and killed Terry who, ironically, was one of Field's former colleagues on the California supreme court.

Field was born in Haddam, Connecticut. He graduated as class valedictorian of Williams College in 1837. He then studied law with his brother and President Martin Van Buren's son, and was admitted to the bar in 1841. After practicing with his brother for seven years in New York, Field grew restless. He decided to go west and settled in Marysville, California, the heart of the gold fields. In 1850 he served as Marysville's chief local administrative official. Field's relationships with officers of the local court were not always cordial. He argued with a judge, was disbarred twice, and served a jail term for contempt of court.

Also in 1850 Field was elected to the California house. After an unsuccessful run for the state senate the next year, Field left public office and resumed his law practice. He was elected to the California supreme court in 1857 and served there until Abraham Lincoln appointed him to the Supreme Court in 1863. Field occupied the newly created tenth seat on the Court.

Although Field was a Democrat and Lincoln was a Republican, Field won the seat because of strong backing from the Oregon and California congressional delegations, his staunch backing of the Union cause, and his expertise in land and mineral issues. His opinions included an opposition to the income tax, and the view that companies not granted public subsidies should not be subject to public regulation.

Field's name came up as a possible Democratic presidential candidate in 1880 and 1884. However, his candidacies died quickly. He hoped to be named chief justice in 1888 when Morrison Waite died, but President Grover Cleveland chose Melville Fuller instead. By the 1890s Field's role on the Court was declining as his mental abilities faded. Finally, the other justices gently suggested to Field that he retire. He responded angrily to the suggestion but retired in December 1897 after serving thirty-four years and nine months. It was the longest service of a justice in the Court's history and a record that would stand for another seventy-five years. Field died in April 1899, sixteen months after retiring from the Court.

Fifteenth Amendment

See CIVIL WAR AMENDMENTS; VOTING RIGHTS.

Fifth Amendment

See DOUBLE JEOPARDY; GRAND JURY; SELF-INCRIMINATION.

First Amendment

See ASSEMBLY, FREEDOM OF; ASSOCIATION, FREEDOM OF; PETITION, RIGHT OF; PRESS, FREEDOM OF; RELIGION, FREEDOM OF; SPEECH, FREEDOM OF.

Flag Salute Cases

The Supreme Court issued one of its most eloquent rulings in behalf of freedom of religion and freedom of speech in a wartime decision that barred the government from requiring public school students to salute the United States flag in violation of their religious upbringing. The decision in *West Virginia Board of Education v. Barnette* (1943) reversed the position the Court had taken on the same issue just three years earlier. (See RELIGION, FREEDOM OF; SPEECH, FREEDOM OF.)

The earlier case involved two children, Lillian and William Gobitis, aged twelve and ten, who were expelled from a Minersville, Pennsylvania, school in 1936 for refusing to participate in daily flag salute ceremonies. The children were Jehovah's Witnesses, who are taught not to worship any graven image. Their parents asked for an exception to the requirement and, when it was refused, challenged the policy in federal court as a violation of their freedom of religion.

In Minersville School District v. Gobitis *(1940) the Court ruled against Jehovah's Witnesses Walter Gobitas and his children, who objected to saluting the flag on religious grounds. The Court records misspelled the family name. The Court later reversed its decision in* West Virginia Board of Education v. Barnette *(1943).   Source: UPI/Bettmann*

Two lower federal courts agreed with the parents, but the Supreme Court rejected their plea in an 8–1 decision in 1940. Writing for the Court in *Minersville School District v. Gobitis,* Justice Felix Frankfurter said religious liberty had to yield to political authority as long as that authority was not used directly to promote or restrict religion. "[T]he mere possession of religious convictions which contradict the relevant concerns of a political society does not relieve the citizen from the discharge of political responsibilities," Frankfurter said. Chief Justice Harlan Fiske Stone was the lone dissenter.

Two years later, three justices who had joined in the Gobitis decision—Hugo L. Black, Frank Murphy, and William O. Douglas—announced in a dissent in

an unrelated case that they had changed their minds on this issue. Their turnabout was followed the next year by the appointment of a strongly libertarian justice, Wiley B. Rutledge, which created a potential majority for overruling *Gobitis.*

The Court was given the opportunity in a challenge filed by several families of Jehovah's Witnesses to a flag salute requirement adopted by West Virginia schools after the earlier ruling. In a 6–3 decision announced on Flag Day, 1943, the Court reversed itself. The Court's opinion was written by Justice Robert H. Jackson, who had been appointed in 1941, the year after *Gobitis.*

Jackson rejected Frankfurter's argument in the earlier opinion that the Court should defer to legislative judgments on matters affecting fundamental freedoms. He denigrated the flag salute requirement as an effort to achieve "[c]ompulsory unification of opinion." And he closed with one of the most elegant passages in Supreme Court history.

"If there is any fixed star in our constitutional constellation," Jackson wrote, "it is that no official, high or petty, can prescribe what shall be orthodox in politics, nationalism, religion or other matters of opinion or force citizens to confess by word or act their faith therein. If there are any circumstances which permit an exception, they do not now occur to us."

Foreign Affairs

The Constitution specifically assigns some powers over foreign affairs to Congress and some to the president, but it makes no mention of many other powers of government that relate to foreign affairs. The Supreme Court has endorsed a broad view of presidential power in the field while generally limiting its own role in disputes involving foreign affairs.

Under the Constitution, Congress has the power to regulate commerce with other nations, to define offenses against the law of nations, and to declare war (Article I, Section 8). The president has the power to appoint and receive ambassadors, and to make treaties with "the Advice and Consent" of the Senate (Article II, Section 2). While it thus provides for a sharing of the WAR POWERS and TREATY POWER, the Constitution does not explicitly allocate governmental powers between Congress and the executive over day-to-day peacetime diplomacy.

Early Developments

Delegates to the Constitutional Convention debated the wisdom of lodging the foreign relations power almost exclusively in the hands of the chief executive. They did not write into the charter a broad grant of power over diplomacy comparable to the president's power over military affairs as commander in chief. Nonetheless, the president quickly gained primacy in foreign affairs in the early years of the Republic, though not without congressional resistance.

President George Washington in 1793 unilaterally proclaimed the neutrality of the United States in the war between England and France. Washington's action was defended by his secretary of the treasury, Alexander Hamilton. But Secretary of State Thomas Jefferson instigated James Madison, then a member of the House of Representatives, to defend the congressional initiative in foreign affairs. In 1794 Congress passed the first neutrality act, superseding the president's proclamation and establishing a congressional role in declarations of neutrality.

The Supreme Court's broad view of presidential power in foreign affairs was foreshadowed in 1800 by Rep. John Marshall's speech on the House floor defending President John Adams's unilateral decision to return a British fugitive to British authorities. "The President is the sole organ of the nation in its external relations, and its sole representative with foreign nations," Marshall declared.

As chief justice three decades later, Marshall defined a limited role for the courts in foreign affairs. In 1829 the Supreme Court refused to decide a dispute between the United States and Spain over title to part of the Louisiana territory. Explaining that decision, Marshall wrote: "The judiciary is not that department of the government to which the assertion of its interests against foreign powers is confided. . . . A question like this . . . is . . . more a political than a legal question."

Later rulings during the nineteenth and early twentieth centuries expanded the list of foreign policy issues that the Supreme Court treated as political questions. In such cases the Court either supported the decisions of the political branches of government or refused to judge them. These issues included recognition of foreign governments, presidential decisions about the status of belligerents under international law, and determination of the ratification of a treaty by another signatory nation.

States' Role

The Supreme Court has consistently acted to limit the states' role in foreign affairs. In 1796 the Court nullified a Virginia law that conflicted with a provision of the 1783 peace treaty with Britain. That provision guaranteed British citizens the right to sue in state courts to collect debts owed them before the Revolution. "A treaty cannot be the Supreme law of the land. . . ," Justice Samuel Chase wrote, "if any act of a State Legislature can stand in its way."

The Court has repeatedly reaffirmed this limitation on the states' ability to interfere with the national government in its conduct of foreign affairs. In 1920 the Court upheld the power of a treaty to remove from state jurisdiction a subject—in this case, migratory birds—normally left to its control. In 1968 the Court struck down an Oregon law that required state courts to deny an inheritance left to a foreigner unless the government of the alien's state of nationality would allow a U.S. citizen to inherit under the same circumstances. The states could not sit in judgment on the policies of foreign governments, the Court declared.

One small crack in the Court's opposition to state laws involving matters of foreign affairs appeared after World War I when the Court upheld state espionage laws. But in 1956 the Court overturned that ruling, deciding that the federal Smith Act of 1940 had preempted all state power over espionage and sedition.

Presidential Power

Foreign affairs were of secondary importance during most of the nineteenth century. They became more important as the United States emerged as a world power at the beginning of the twentieth century. Through most of the twentieth century, the president has played the main role in shaping and carrying out U.S. foreign policy. Congress has not played a major part in initiating policy, though it has influenced policy reactively through the process of appropriations, treaty ratification, and oversight.

The Supreme Court endorsed a sweeping view of presidential prerogatives in foreign affairs in *United States v. Curtiss-Wright Export Corp.* (1936). The case grew out of a war between Bolivia and Paraguay. U.S. arms manufacturers sold weapons to both sides. In 1934 Congress approved a resolution authorizing

President Franklin Roosevelt to impose an embargo on the arms shipments if, in his judgment, such a measure might contribute to ending the war. Roosevelt did so, and Curtiss-Wright Export Corp. and two other companies were convicted of selling arms to Bolivia in violation of that embargo.

The Court rejected, 7–1, Curtiss-Wright's claim that the resolution was an improper delegation of congressional power to the president. In an influential but controversial opinion, Justice George Sutherland said the president has "plenary and exclusive power. . . as the sole organ of the federal government in the field of international relations—a power which does not require as a basis for its exercise an act of Congress."

Commentators have criticized Sutherland's historical interpretation, but his conclusion formed the basis for Court decisions in 1937 and 1942 upholding the president's use of executive agreements that bypassed the need for Senate ratification of many international compacts. Advocates of broad presidential powers often cited the opinion in following decades to defend presidential actions in such areas as Cold War diplomacy and undeclared wars.

As presidential power grew, the Supreme Court refused to step in to decide foreign policy disputes between Congress and the president during the Vietnam War era and after enactment of the War Powers Resolution of 1973. The Court, in effect, left it to Congress to assert its powers to challenge presidential actions in foreign affairs—for example, by withholding appropriations.

The Court, however, stopped short of endorsing the broadest view of presidential power. In a 1981 decision the Court upheld President Jimmy Carter's executive agreement to end the Iranian hostage crisis. The agreement established an international tribunal to adjudicate claims by U.S. citizens against the Iranian government. In his opinion for the Court, Justice William H. Rehnquist said, "We do not decide that the President possesses plenary power to settle claims, even as against foreign governmental entities." Instead, Rehnquist concluded that the agreement was proper in part because of evidence that Congress had "acquiesced in the President's action."

Fortas, Abe

In May 1969, threatened with impeachment, Justice Abe Fortas (1910–1982) resigned from the Supreme Court. It was a mighty fall for the man who just eleven months before had been nominated for chief justice.

Fortas was born in Memphis, Tennessee. After obtaining his undergraduate degree from Southwestern College and his law degree from Yale Law School, Fortas briefly taught law at Yale. He soon left for Washington, D.C., to take part in Franklin Roosevelt's New Deal. In the mid-1930s and early 1940s Fortas held a succession of jobs in the Roosevelt administration. He worked for the Securities and Exchange Commission, the Public Works Administration, and the Department of the Interior. After World War II he helped found Arnold, Fortas, and Porter, which quickly became one of Washington's most prominent law firms. In 1948 Fortas successfully defended Lyndon Johnson against a challenge to Johnson's victory in the Democratic senatorial primary. The two men developed a close friendship, and Fortas became one of Johnson's key advisers.

In 1964 President Johnson wanted to name Fortas attorney general, but Fortas turned down the job. He much preferred remaining a confidential adviser to the president. The next year, however, Johnson nominated Fortas for the Supreme Court despite his opposition. Fortas was no stranger to the Court when he joined it in 1965. Only two years earlier he had been the winning counsel in *GIDEON V. WAINWRIGHT* (1963), the landmark case in which the Supreme Court required states to provide legal counsel to indigent defendants charged with felonies.

On the Warren Court Fortas consistently aligned himself with the liberal wing. One of Fortas's most important opinions for the Court came in *Tinker v. Des Moines Independent Community School District* (1969). In *Tinker* the Court overturned a school district's ban on students wearing black armbands to protest the Vietnam War.

In 1968 Chief Justice Earl Warren announced his intention to retire from the Court, and Johnson nom-

Source: Collection of the Supreme Court of the United States

inated Fortas to replace him. That was the beginning of the end for Fortas. The Senate investigation of Fortas's nomination revealed that after being appointed to the Court, Fortas had remained a close adviser to Johnson and had even lobbied on the president's behalf. Then Fortas admitted he had received $15,000 for leading a series of seminars at American University. That gave Senate Republicans all the ammunition they needed to block confirmation, and Johnson withdrew Fortas's name. Fortas remained an associate justice, however.

Then in May 1969 *Life* magazine reported that after becoming a justice Fortas had accepted a $20,000 fee for advising a foundation run by someone who was later indicted for stock manipulation. Two months after the indictment, Fortas had returned the fee. With threats of impeachment and calls for his resignation mounting, Fortas resigned from the Court on May 14, 1969, while proclaiming his innocence of any wrongdoing. He then returned to private law practice in Washington, D.C. Fortas died in 1982.

Fourteenth Amendment

See CIVIL WAR AMENDMENTS; DUE PROCESS; EQUAL PROTECTION; INCORPORATION DOCTRINE; REVERSALS OF RULINGS BY CONSTITUTIONAL AMENDMENT.

Fourth Amendment

See ARRESTS; EXCLUSIONARY RULE; PROBABLE CAUSE; SEARCH AND SEIZURE.

Frankfurter, Felix

In modern times, most Supreme Court justices have tried to remain removed from political issues—but not Felix Frankfurter (1882–1965). After his appointment to the Supreme Court in January 1939, Frankfurter remained a close adviser to President Franklin D. Roosevelt. During the spring and summer of 1939, for example, Frankfurter sent Roosevelt nearly 300 notes warning him about the rise of Hitler.

The close relationship led to problems later that year when Roosevelt revealed that he had discussed the European situation with Frankfurter and Justice Harlan Fiske Stone. Roosevelt's admission caused an uproar, with many observers claiming that justices should not be involved in the executive branch's foreign policy decisions. Although Stone stopped conferring with Roosevelt, Frankfurter ignored the hubbub and continued advising Roosevelt and later presidents.

Frankfurter was born in 1882 in Vienna, Austria, and moved to New York City with his parents in 1894. After receiving his degree from Harvard Law School in 1906, Frankfurter briefly worked for a New York law firm. He was soon recruited by Henry L. Stimson, the U.S. attorney for the southern district of New York. Stimson became Frankfurter's mentor. Frankfurter served as an assistant U.S. attorney from 1906 to 1909, went into private practice with Stimson for a short time, and then moved to Washington,

Source: Collection of the Supreme Court of the United States

D.C., when Stimson was named secretary of war. Frankfurter worked in the War Department for several years before returning to Harvard in 1914 to teach law. At Harvard Frankfurter's reputation as a legal scholar grew. He was offered a seat on the Massachusetts supreme court in 1932 but declined. He also turned down an offer from Roosevelt in 1933 to be solicitor general. In 1939, however, Frankfurter accepted his nomination by Roosevelt to the Supreme Court.

Before he joined the Court, Frankfurter was a founding member of the American Civil Liberties Union and worked with the National Association for the Advancement of Colored People. However, his opinions as a justice were frequently quite conservative. In *Wolf v. Colorado* (1949) Frankfurter wrote the majority opinion upholding the conviction of a man based on evidence seized by a deputy sheriff without a warrant. The Court overturned this decision in 1961 when it extended the EXCLUSIONARY RULE to actions by the states.

In *Minersville School District v. Gobitis* (1940) Frankfurter wrote the opinion for an 8–1 decision upholding a school board's requirement that children salute the flag each day even if doing so conflicted with their religion. Frankfurter wrote that the "mere possession of religious convictions which contradict the relevant concerns of a political society does not relieve the citizen from the discharge of political responsibilities." This decision was overturned just three years later, with Frankfurter strongly dissenting. Frankfurter retired in 1962 after serving twenty-three years on the Court. He died in 1965.

Freedom of Assembly

See ASSEMBLY, FREEDOM OF.

Freedom of Association

See ASSOCIATION, FREEDOM OF.

Freedom of Press

See PRESS, FREEDOM OF.

Freedom of Religion

See RELIGION, FREEDOM OF.

Freedom of Speech

See SPEECH, FREEDOM OF.

Fuller, Melville W.

When Chicago lawyer Melville Weston Fuller (1833–1910) was nominated for chief justice in 1888, the Philadelphia *Press* called him the most obscure individual ever named to the job. Obscure or not, his nomination by President Grover Cleveland aroused strong opposition in the Senate.

Many midwestern senators disliked Fuller because he represented several major railroads and had other ties to large corporations. Others critcized his failure to serve in the Civil War. The Senate finally confirmed Fuller, by a vote of 41 to 20, three months after Cleveland had nominated him.

Fuller was born in Augusta, Maine. He grew up in the house of his grandfather, a judge on the Maine

Source: Library of Congress

supreme court. After graduating from Bowdoin College in 1853, Fuller read law in Bangor. He spent just six months at Harvard Law School before passing the bar. He then established a practice in Augusta and became a writer for *The Age*, a local Democratic paper owned by his uncle. The West lured Fuller, and he moved to Chicago to practice real estate and commercial law.

In Chicago Fuller became active in politics. He managed Stephen Douglas's presidential campaign against Abraham Lincoln, attended the Illinois constitutional convention, and served in the Illinois house of representatives from 1863 to 1864. Fuller's legal practice also flourished, and his real estate investments on the North Shore helped make him a wealthy man.

When Cleveland began his first term as president in 1885, he offered Fuller the positions of civil service chair and solicitor general. Fuller declined both jobs. In April 1888, however, he accepted appointment as chief justice. Fuller had no judicial experience and had never held federal office, although he had argued cases before the Supreme Court.

Under Fuller's leadership the Court became known for its conservative leaning. In 1895 the Court ruled 8–1 that the Sherman Antitrust Act did not forbid manufacturing monopolies. Writing for the Court, Fuller said the states—not the federal government—had the authority to regulate such monopolies. This view ignored the reality that states lacked the ability to fight the gigantic trusts.

Also in 1895 the Court overturned an act of Congress that created the first general tax on personal income since the Civil War. The ruling resulted in the Sixteenth Amendment, which in 1913 empowered Congress to levy a federal INCOME TAX. In *PLESSY V. FERGUSON* (1896) the Court upheld the concept of "separate but equal" facilities for blacks and whites. (*Plessy* was overturned by the Court's ruling in *Brown v. Board of Education of Topeka* [1954] that separate facilities were inherently unequal.)

As chief justice, Fuller sought to keep the justices working toward a common goal even though they disagreed in individual cases. He instituted the practice of having justices shake hands at the beginning of their private conferences and before entering the courtroom, a practice that continues today. Fuller died in 1910 after serving as chief justice for nearly twenty-two years.

G

Garland, Augustus H.

Augustus H. Garland (1832–1899) of Arkansas was a preeminent lawyer and politician of his day who argued many cases with skill and success before the Supreme Court. He is remembered today primarily for his role in overturning the "test oath" Congress had enacted in the aftermath of the Civil War.

Under the 1865 law Congress barred attorneys from practicing law in federal courts unless they swore an oath that they had remained loyal to the Union throughout the Civil War. Those who swore the oath falsely were subject to perjury charges.

Garland had been admitted to the federal bar during the Supreme Court's 1860 term. When Arkansas seceded from the Union later that year, he went with the state. Eventually he served as a representative and then a senator in the Confederate Congress.

President Andrew Johnson gave Garland a full pardon in 1865. In 1867 Garland sought to practice law again in the federal courts, but he refused to swear the test oath. The case of *Ex parte Garland* came to the Supreme Court, which sided with Garland, 5–4, striking down the test oath law as unconstitutional.

The decision caused a furor in the North and led to legislative efforts to reform the Court. Congress also considered barring all former Confederates from the practice of law, but the bill was not approved.

Garland himself went on to become governor of Arkansas (1874–1876) and then a U.S. senator from Arkansas (1877–1885). He served as attorney general in Grover Cleveland's first term. At one point, Cleveland wanted to appoint Garland to fill a vacancy on the Supreme Court, but Garland refused. He reportedly told the president that he was unqualified because he thought a justice should serve for at least twenty years and he doubted he would live that long.

Garland did not live another twenty years, but after he left the Justice Department, he resumed his law practice and wrote a book on the Supreme Court, entitled *Experience in the Supreme Court of the United States with Some Reflections and Suggestions as to that Tribunal.* The book was published in 1898, the year before he died.

Gibbons v. Ogden

In a landmark opinion by Chief Justice John Marshall, the Supreme Court in *Gibbons v. Ogden* (1824) struck down a New York steamboat-monopoly law and gave a broad, but not unlimited, reading to Congress's power to regulate commerce.

Aaron Ogden operated a steam-driven ferry between Elizabethtown, New Jersey, and New York City in an uneasy partnership with Thomas Gibbons. Ogden had acquired a license from a firm that had been granted a monopoly by New York state law in 1798. Gibbons held a permit under the federal Coastal Licensing Act of 1793 for his two boats.

When Gibbons ran his boats to New York in defiance of the monopoly, Ogden sued for an injunction to block him. New York courts sided with Ogden, and Gibbons appealed to the Supreme Court.

For the Court, the case posed the legal question of whether the New York law interfered with Congress's power to "regulate Commerce . . . among the several States" (Article I, Section 8). (See COMMERCE POWER.) The dispute also pitted the nationalist beliefs of Federalists, including Marshall, against the states' rights views of Republicans, such as former president Thomas Jefferson.

Marshall's opinion for the Court declared that power over commerce, including navigation, "was one of the primary objects" in the formation of the federal government. Congress had "complete" power to regulate commerce between the states, he said, and any state law interfering with federal legislation in the area must fall. Marshall added, however, that the states retained the power to regulate "completely internal commerce" that "does not extend to or affect other states."

Marshall said that the New York law was invalid because it conflicted with the federal coastal licensing law. He added, however, that states could enact parallel regulations similar to those Congress adopted. The decision did not address the question of whether states could enact regulations in areas that Congress had not regulated.

The ruling was politically popular, since New York's steamboat monopoly had been under attack from several states. But Jefferson criticized the decision as "advancing towards the usurpation of all the rights reserved to the states." And slave owners feared Congress might exercise the commerce power to take control of the slavery issue from the states. (See SLAVERY AND THE COURT.)

Clarence Earl Gideon taught himself enough about the law to prepare his own petition to the Supreme Court.   Source: Flip Schulke, Life Magazine. 1964 Time Inc.

Gideon v. Wainwright

The Supreme Court's decision in *Gideon v. Wainwright* (1963) guaranteed the right to counsel to indigent criminal defendants. The ruling gave practical effect to a key provision of the Bill of Rights. It also showed that the Court can sometimes be moved to do justice by the efforts of a lone and ordinary individual.

Clarence Earl Gideon was a poor man who was tried and convicted of a felony in 1961 in a Florida state court. He was found guilty of breaking and entering a poolroom to commit a misdemeanor. He requested a court-appointed attorney, but the judge refused on the basis of a state law that provided for an appointed lawyer only in capital cases. The state law was in accordance with Supreme Court precedent. Gideon conducted his own defense and was convicted and sentenced to five years in prison.

Gideon then prepared his own petitions asking a federal court to declare his conviction invalid on the ground that his Sixth Amendment right to counsel had been violated. The Supreme Court seized on Gideon's case to reconsider its earlier decision, *Betts v. Brady* (1942), which had found no need to provide lawyers for indigent defendants in most criminal cases. To represent Gideon, the Court appointed a prominent Washington lawyer, Abe Fortas, who later served as a member of the Court himself.

The Court's decision sustaining Gideon's plea and overruling *Betts* was unanimous. "The right of one charged with crime to counsel may not be deemed fundamental and essential to fair trials in some countries," Justice Hugo L. Black declared, "but it is in ours." (See COUNSEL, RIGHT TO LEGAL.)

Gideon's case was remanded for a new trial—with a lawyer this time—and he was acquitted by the jury.

Ginsburg, Ruth Bader

Ruth Bader Ginsburg's path to the U.S. Supreme Court is a classic American story of overcoming obstacles and setbacks through intelligence, persistence, and quiet hard work. Her achievements as a student, law professor, advocate, and judge came against a background of personal adversity and institutional discrimination against women. Ginsburg surmounted those hurdles for herself and helped chart legal strategy in the 1970s to broaden opportunities for women by establishing constitutional principles limiting sex discrimination.

Born into a Jewish family of modest means in Brooklyn, Ruth Bader was greatly influenced by her mother, Celia, who imparted a love of learning and independence. Celia Bader died of cancer on the eve of her daughter's high school graduation in 1948.

Ruth Bader attended Cornell University, where she graduated first in her class and met her future husband, Martin Ginsburg, who became a tax lawyer and later a law professor at Georgetown University.

At Harvard Law School, Ruth Bader Ginsburg made law review, cared for an infant daughter, and then helped her husband complete his studies after he was diagnosed with cancer. He recovered, graduated, and took a job in New York, and she transferred to Columbia for her final year of law school.

Although tied for first place in her graduating class, Ginsburg was unable to obtain a Supreme Court clerkship or job with a top New York law firm. Instead, she got a two-year clerkship with a federal district court judge. She then studied civil procedure in Sweden and began to be stirred by feminist thought. Ginsburg taught at Rutgers University Law School from 1963 to 1972. She also worked with the New Jersey affiliate of the American Civil Liberties Union (ACLU) where her caseload included early sex discrimination complaints. In 1972 Ginsburg became the first woman given a tenured position on the Columbia law faculty. As director of the national ACLU's Women's Rights Project, she handled cases that led the Supreme Court to require heightened scrutiny of legal classifications based on sex.

President Jimmy Carter named Ginsburg to the U.S. Court of Appeals in the District of Columbia in 1980. There she earned a reputation as a judicial moderate on a sharply divided court.

Ginsburg was among several candidates President Bill Clinton considered in 1993 to replace Justice Byron R. White, who was retiring. White House aides later said Clinton was especially impressed with Ginsburg's life story. She was confirmed by the Senate 96–3 and sworn in August 10, 1993, as the court's second female justice and the first Jewish justice since 1969.

In her first weeks on the bench, Ginsburg startled observers with her unusually active questioning. She also pointedly used nonsexist language, for example substituting "letter carrier" for another justice's use of "postman" during one argument. As the term continued, Ginsburg's votes defied easy categorization. She displayed a close attention to legislative language that echoed the philosophy of judicial restraint she espoused during her confirmation hearings. But her votes and opinions also indicated liberal leanings on civil rights, labor law, and some criminal law issues.

Source: R. Michael Jenkins

Source: Library of Congress

Goldberg, Arthur J.

In 1965 President Lyndon Johnson became impatient to nominate Abe Fortas for the Supreme Court. He persuaded Justice Arthur Joseph Goldberg (1908–1989), who had joined the Court only three years earlier, to trade his seat for the post of ambassador to the United Nations. Goldberg accepted the switch in the hope that he would be able to work through the United Nations to end the war in Vietnam. However, he was sorely disappointed to leave the Court.

Goldberg was born in Chicago and received his undergraduate and law degrees from Northwestern University. After graduating from law school he entered private practice and specialized in labor law. During World War II Goldberg served as a special assistant in the Office of Strategic Services. Afterward he returned to practicing labor law; among his clients were the Congress of Industrial Organizations (CIO) and the United Steelworkers of America. In 1955 Goldberg played a prominent role in the merger between the CIO and the American Federation of Labor (AFL). He worked as a special counsel to the AFL-CIO until 1961, the year when President John F. Kennedy appointed him secretary of labor. The next year Kennedy named Goldberg to the Supreme Court.

During his nearly three years as a justice, Goldberg wrote two major opinions for the Court. Both were issued on June 22, 1964. In the first case, *Aptheker v. Secretary of State,* the Court voted 7–2 to declare unconstitutional a law denying passports to people belonging to organizations deemed subversive by the attorney general. In the second case, *Escobedo v. Illinois,* the Court ruled 5–4 that confessions obtained by police without informing suspects of their right to counsel could not be used in court. "We have . . . learned . . . that no system of criminal justice can, or should, survive if it comes to depend for its continued effectiveness on the citizens' abdication through unawareness of their constitutional rights," Goldberg wrote for the majority. "If the exercise of constitutional rights will thwart the effectiveness of a system of law enforcement, then there is something very wrong with that system."

After leaving the Court in 1965, Goldberg served as United Nations ambassador for three years before resigning in 1968. He ran an unsuccessful race for governor of New York in 1970 and then returned to Washington, D.C., to practice law privately. He died of heart disease in January 1989.

Grand Jury

A grand jury is a group of twelve to twenty-three people brought together to hear, in private, evidence presented by the state against persons accused of crimes. The grand jury issues an INDICTMENT if a majority of the jurors finds PROBABLE CAUSE to believe that the accused person has committed an offense. It is called a "grand" jury because it consists of a larger group of people than the "petit" jury that decides a defendant's guilt or innocence at trial.

The grand jury has changed drastically since adoption of the Fifth Amendment. The Fifth Amendment requires "a presentment or indictment of a grand jury" in a federal prosecution for "a capital, or otherwise infamous crime" (except in military courts martial). In England and colonial America, the grand jury was viewed as a safeguard against unjust prosecutions by the crown. In modern times, the grand jury has become an arm of the prosecutor's office, approving virtually all requests for indictments and exercising wide inquisitorial powers with few legal constraints.

The Supreme Court in 1884 declined to extend the grand jury requirement to the states *(Hurtado v. California)*. It has not changed that ruling even though most of the other provisions of the Bill of Rights have now been applied to the states. About half the states allow prosecutors to file charges directly without grand jury action. In cases where grand juries are used, however, the Supreme Court has barred racial discrimination in the selection process. (See JURIES.)

The Supreme Court has imposed few limits on the grand jury's investigative powers. Witnesses may be questioned without an attorney and need not be informed of the purpose of the investigation or even the possibility of their own indictment. A defendant who testifies falsely before a grand jury is subject to prosecution for perjury.

Under an 1892 ruling, a grand jury witness may claim the privilege against self-incrimination. Congress promptly moved to narrow that ruling with a statute allowing witnesses to be compelled to testify if they were given immunity from prosecution, or "transactional immunity." The Supreme Court upheld the new law in 1896.

The Court later broadened grand jury powers to compel testimony, by upholding a limited exemption from prosecution called "use immunity." The ruling in *Kastigar v. United States* (1972) bars the government from using a witness's compelled testimony or any evidence derived from it as the basis of a prosecution. It does, however, allow the government to bring charges with different, independently gathered evidence.

The Court in *United States v. Calandra* (1974) ruled, 6–3, that grand juries may use illegally obtained evidence as the basis for questioning witnesses. In 1976

and 1977 the Court allowed grand juries to require parties to provide voice samples and handwriting samples for identification. More recently, the Court ruled in 1991 that a grand jury may subpoena documents without showing that they are relevant to a criminal investigation or would be admissible at trial. In 1992 the Court held that prosecutors are not obligated to tell the grand jury about evidence favorable to the defendant.

Source: Collection of the Supreme Court of the United States

Gray, Horace

In 1882 Horace Gray (1828–1902) became the first Supreme Court justice to hire a law clerk. The clerk, whose salary came from Gray's own pocket, had been the top graduate of Harvard Law School. But instead of doing legal research, he primarily served as a servant and barber for Gray.

Gray was born into a wealthy Boston family. He graduated from Harvard College in 1845 and from Harvard Law School four years later. After passing the bar in 1851 Gray practiced in Boston for thirteen years. He added the job of reporter for the state supreme court to his legal duties in 1854 and continued in the post for the next decade. In 1864, at the age of thirty-six, he was appointed to the Massachusetts supreme court, becoming the youngest associate justice in the court's history. Gray rose to chief justice in 1873 and continued in that post until his appointment to the U.S. Supreme Court in 1881. During his seventeen years on the state court Gray was respected for his knowledge of legal precedent and his historical scholarship. He dissented only once, and none of his decisions was overturned during his lifetime.

When Justice Nathan Clifford died in July 1881, President James A. Garfield considered nominating Gray to replace him. Garfield died, however, before he could make the appointment. His successor, Chester A. Arthur, nominated Gray in December 1881. A firm believer in historical precedent, Gray in his opinions drew widely on historical sources.

In 1889 Gray, a sixty-one-year-old bachelor, married the daughter of Justice Stanley Matthews, his colleague on the Court.

After serving on the Court for twenty years, Gray sent a letter to President Theodore Roosevelt in July 1902 stating his intention to retire. Gray died in September before his retirement took effect.

Grier, Robert C.

Robert Cooper Grier (1794–1870) was the fifth choice for the Supreme Court seat made vacant when Justice Henry Baldwin died in April 1844. President John Tyler made two nominations, but he was forced to withdraw the first and the Senate refused to act on the second. The task of filling the seat then fell to the new president, James Polk. Polk nominated James Buchanan, the future president, who turned down the offer. Polk next nominated George Woodward, but the Senate rejected him. Polk finally turned to Grier, whom the Senate confirmed in August 1846, more than two years after Baldwin's death.

Born in Cumberland County, Pennsylvania, Grier was taught by his father, a Presbyterian minister. Grier graduated from Dickinson College in 1812. He taught school for a few years and then began to study the law privately. He passed the bar in 1817. Grier eventually established a very successful practice in Danville.

Democratic politicians in Harrisburg noticed Grier, who was a solid Jacksonian Democrat. He received a patronage appointment as president judge of the district court of Allegheny County in 1833. He served as president judge for thirteen years and developed a reputation for being thorough and knowledgeable.

In 1846 Polk nominated Grier for the Supreme Court, where he served for nearly twenty-five years. His major opinions included *Marshall v. Baltimore and Ohio Railroad Company* (1854), which decreed for matters of jurisdiction that corporate stockholders are legally considered citizens of the state where the company was incorporated; and the *Prize Cases* (1863), which said that the Union blockade of southern ports was legal, even before Congress voted for war.

Toward the end of his career on the Court, Grier's mental abilities and health deteriorated so far that he had trouble functioning. Grier made no move to step down, though, until a committee of his colleagues urged him to retire. He finally retired in January 1870 and died later that year.

Source: Collection of the Supreme Court of the United States

H

Habeas Corpus

The writ of habeas corpus (a Latin term meaning "you shall have the body") is a judicial instrument dating from seventeenth-century England, used to review the legality of a person's imprisonment by government authority. It is specifically protected by the U.S. Constitution. Habeas corpus saw only limited use in the nineteenth century. In the twentieth century it has become an important tool for federal courts to review the legality of criminal convictions in state courts. Since the mid-1970s, however, the Supreme Court has restricted habeas corpus by establishing new limitations on its use by inmates of state prisons.

The Constitution prohibits the suspension of "[t]he privilege of the Writ of Habeas Corpus . . . unless when in Cases of Rebellion or Invasion the public Safety may require it" (Article I, Section 9, Clause 2). Habeas corpus has been suspended only four times in U.S. history: during the Civil War, in South Carolina in 1871 to combat the Ku Klux Klan, in the Philippines in 1905, and in Hawaii during World War II. The Supreme Court has held that use of habeas corpus by the federal courts depends on congressional acts. Before the Civil War, Congress authorized federal use of habeas corpus only for federal prisoners or in other, limited circumstances—chiefly to protect federal officers from detention by state officials for enforcing federal laws.

In 1867 Congress extended federal habeas corpus power to state cases, intending to protect federal officials engaged in Reconstruction programs. The Habeas Corpus Act of 1867 expanded federal courts' power to "all cases where any person may be restrained of his or her liberty in violation of the Constitution, or of any treaty or law of the United States." The act also provided for Supreme Court review of lower court rulings denying habeas corpus relief to persons seeking it under this law.

Within a few months Congress repealed the

Arrested for treason and tried by a military tribunal during the Civil War, Lambdin P. Milligan was sentenced to be hanged. He filed for a writ of habeas corpus. The Court decided unanimously that the president did not have the power to authorize military trials in areas where the civil courts were functioning.
Source: Indiana Historical Society Library

Supreme Court's appellate jurisdiction over such cases in order to thwart an anticipated ruling on the constitutionality of the Reconstruction Acts. The basic expansion of the federal use of the writ, however, remained intact. Congress restored the Court's appellate jurisdiction over such cases in 1885.

There were few collisions between federal and state power for half a century after the 1867 act. One reason was that the Supreme Court had not yet applied the provisions of the Bill of Rights to the states. In addition, it historically had viewed habeas corpus relief as limited to cases where a sentencing court had no jurisdiction whatever.

Beginning in the 1880s the Court expanded the issues that could be reviewed in a habeas corpus proceeding. First, it said that someone imprisoned under an unconstitutional law is entitled to habeas corpus relief. Next, the Court reasoned that habeas corpus should also be available to review an unconstitutional conviction or punishment. Finally, in *Frank v. Mangum* (1915) the Court broadly declared that the 1867 act gave a state prisoner the right to "a judicial inquiry in a court of the United States into the very truth and substance of causes of his detention," even if that required the federal court "to look behind and beyond the record of his conviction."

The Court in *Frank* refused to order the release of a man who claimed that a mob atmosphere had tainted his trial, stating that the issue had been fully reviewed and rejected in the state courts. Eight years later, however, the Court in *Moore v. Dempsey* (1923) ordered the release of defendants who had been convicted in a similar mob atmosphere.

Over the next four decades, the Court continued to expand the basis for reviewing state court proceedings through habeas corpus. In *Brown v. Allen* (1953) the Court held that federal courts could rehear a prisoner's claims "on the merits, facts, or law." Ten years later, in *Townsend v. Sain* (1963), the Court indicated that a federal court should ordinarily conduct "a full and fair evidentiary hearing" on a prisoner's claim. In addition, it said that federal judges should not defer to a state judge's legal findings. Instead, federal judges have a "duty to apply the applicable federal law . . . independently."

In that same year the Court narrowed a doctrine that had minimized conflict between federal and state courts. Since 1885 the Court had ruled that state prisoners must exhaust their remedies in state courts before seeking habeas corpus relief in federal courts. But in *Fay v. Noia* (1963) the Court, by a vote of 6 to 3, allowed a state inmate who had failed to appeal his conviction to seek habeas corpus relief. The Court said the exhaustion requirement applied only if the defendant's failure to pursue state remedies amounted to "a deliberate by-passing of state procedures."

In the mid-1970s, the Court began cutting back on habeas corpus relief. In *Stone v. Powell* (1976) it barred the use of habeas corpus to relitigate claims about illegally obtained evidence. In 1977 it abandoned the "deliberate bypass" standard of *Fay v. Noia*. In an opinion written by Justice William H. Rehnquist, the Court ruled that an earlier failure to assert a federal claim bars habeas corpus relief unless inmates can show good reason for the omission and actual prejudice to their case as a result of the claimed violation of their rights *(Wainwright v. Sykes)*.

The Court has further restricted habeas corpus since Rehnquist became chief justice in 1986. It has barred inmates from using rulings issued after their convictions as a basis for habeas corpus relief, unless the principle of the new case is "fundamental to the integrity of the criminal proceeding." It has limited inmates to a single federal habeas corpus petition even where new evidence of possible rights violations was discovered later. It has thrown out habeas corpus petitions in cases where an inmate lost the chance for an appeal in state courts through procedural error—even one resulting from negligence on the part of the inmate's lawyer.

In 1992 the Court balked at one further proposed restriction. With Rehnquist in the minority, the Court rejected, 6–3, a plea by the Bush administration to require federal judges in many habeas corpus cases to accept the findings of state court judges without further evaluation. In 1993, however, Rehnquist led a 5–4 majority in a decision that made it harder for inmates to challenge trial-related errors in habeas corpus cases.

Hamilton, Alexander

Alexander Hamilton (1755–1804) was an outspoken advocate of a stronger national government during the period of the Articles of Confederation. He played a key role in the drafting and ratification of the Constitution. Hamilton was the principal author (with John Adams and James Madison) of the *Federalist Papers,* a collection of eighty-five essays that interpreted the Constitution and urged its ratification by state legislatures. In his essays Hamilton argued for a strong central government, a powerful presidency, and an independent federal judiciary with the power of JUDICIAL REVIEW over laws passed by Congress.

Source: Library of Congress

and proper" clause (Article I, Section 8). He also expressed a broad view of presidential power in foreign affairs in defending Washington's unilateral proclamation of neutrality in the dispute between England and France. Although Congress had power to declare war, Hamilton wrote, "it belongs to the 'executive power' to do whatever else the law of nations, co-operating with the treaties of the country, enjoin in the intercourse of the United States with foreign powers."

Hamilton's views also influenced the Supreme Court. By the time of his death in 1804, the Court had established the principle of judicial review in the landmark ruling *MARBURY V. MADISON* (1803). In *MCCULLOCH V. MARYLAND* (1819) the Court supported the doctrine of implied powers in a ruling that upheld creation of the second Bank of the United States.

Hamilton's defense of judicial review in *The Federalist Papers,* No. 78, was based on the need to enforce the limitations that the Constitution placed on the new government. The courts, he said, were intended as "an intermediate body between the people and the legislature in order, among other things, to keep the latter within the limits assigned to their authority."

In an oft-quoted passage Hamilton wrote, "The interpretation of the laws is the proper and peculiar province of the courts." Since a constitution is "a fundamental law," judges must "ascertain its meaning." In the event of a conflict with an act of Congress, "the Constitution ought to be preferred to the statute."

As secretary of the treasury under President George Washington, Hamilton put his stamp on presidential and congressional power in two major clashes with Washington's secretary of state, Thomas Jefferson. He defended the creation of the first Bank of the United States, arguing that Congress enjoyed broad implied powers under the Constitution's "necessary

Harlan, John Marshall

During his nearly thirty-four years as a justice, John Marshall Harlan (1833–1911) became known as the "great dissenter" on the Supreme Court. He dissented 380 times. Many of those were occasions when Harlan believed the Court read the Fourteenth Amendment too narrowly.

Harlan's most famous dissent occurred in *PLESSY V. FERGUSON* (1896), in which the Court, by an 8–1 vote, upheld the concept of "separate but equal" facilities for whites and blacks. The Court majority upheld a Louisiana law requiring railroads to provide separate cars for black and white passengers. In his dissent, Harlan charged that the law "is inconsistent with the personal liberty of citizens, white and black . . . and hostile to both the spirit and letter of the Constitution." Fifty-eight years later the Court overturned *Plessy* with its landmark decision in *Brown v. Board of Education of Topeka* (1954), in which it ruled that separate facilities are inherently unequal.

Harlan was born in 1833 in Boyle County, Kentucky, to a prominent family. His father served as U.S. representative from Kentucky and as state attorney general and secretary of state. Harlan studied law at Transylvania University before finishing his education

Source: Library of Congress

in his father's law office. He was admitted to the bar in 1853 and became Franklin County judge in 1858. The single year he spent as a judge was his only judicial experience before joining the Supreme Court.

Harlan initially favored a compromise to settle the sectional conflict that eventually exploded in the Civil War. When the war broke out, however, Harlan threw in his lot with the Union even though he was a slaveholder and a member of the southern aristocracy. He served as an officer with the Union forces until his father died in 1863. Harlan then resigned his commission and made a successful run for Kentucky attorney general. Despite his opposition to many policies of Abraham Lincoln's administration, Harlan gradually moved toward the Republican party.

In 1876 Harlan led Kentucky's delegation to the Republican national convention. The convention became deadlocked, and Harlan helped start a bandwagon toward Rutherford B. Hayes by swinging Kentucky's votes to the Ohio governor. Hayes never forgot Harlan's action in his behalf. Hayes considered

Harlan for the cabinet, but finally appointed him to the Supreme Court in 1877. Harlan served until his death in 1911, one of the longest tenures in Court history. In 1955 his grandson, also named John Marshall Harlan, became a Supreme Court justice.

Harlan, John Marshall

In 1955 President Dwight D. Eisenhower nominated John Marshall Harlan (1899–1971), grandson and namesake of the turn-of-the-century justice who was famous for his dissenting opinions, to the Supreme Court. The grandson was not shy about dissenting either.

Harlan was born in Chicago. He graduated from Princeton University in 1920, was a Rhodes Scholar at Oxford University, and graduated from New York Law School in 1925. He then embarked on a twenty-five-year career at a prominent Wall Street law firm,

Source: Collection of the Supreme Court of the United States

taking leaves of absence to serve in various public positions. From 1925 to 1927 he was assistant U.S. attorney for the southern district of New York, and from 1928 to 1930 he was special assistant attorney general of New York state. Twenty years later he took another leave from 1951 to 1953 to serve as chief counsel to the New York State Crime Commission, which investigated links between organized crime and state government. In 1954 Eisenhower named Harlan to the U.S. Court of Appeals for the Second Circuit. Later that same year Eisenhower promoted Harlan to the Supreme Court, and the Senate confirmed him in early 1955.

Harlan supported judicial restraint, a position that frequently put him at odds with his liberal colleagues on the Warren Court. In a dissent in *Reynolds v. Sims* (1964), Harlan expressed his frustration. "These decisions give support to a current mistaken view of the Constitution and the constitutional function of this Court," he wrote. "This view, in a nutshell, is that every major social ill in this country can find its cure in some constitutional 'principle,' and that this Court should 'take the lead' in promoting reform when other branches of government fail to act. The Constitution is not a panacea for every blot upon the public welfare, nor should this Court, ordained as a judicial body, be thought of as a general haven for reform movements."

Harlan retired in September 1971 after serving sixteen years on the Court. He died three months later.

Historical Society, Supreme Court

The Supreme Court Historical Society was founded in November 1974 to increase public interest in and knowledge about the Supreme Court and the federal court system. A nonprofit organization, the society collects and preserves memorabilia related to the Court's history. It supports historical research and publishes the results of that research in scholarly works and in publications for the general public.

The society, which has 2,600 members, is funded through membership contributions, gifts, and grants. It also sells Court-related books and memorabilia in a gift shop it operates on the ground floor of the Supreme Court Building.

The society has an active volunteer organization with committees on acquisitions, programs, special gifts, publications, and membership, among others. It publishes a quarterly newsletter and a yearbook. The society and the Court cosponsored the publication of *The Documentary History of the Supreme Court of the United States, 1789–1800,* a comprehensive documentary collection of material related to the first decade of the Court's history.

Historic Milestones

The U.S. Supreme Court has evolved over two centuries from what was expected to be the weakest branch of the new federal government into what has been called the most powerful court the world has ever known. Here are some of the major milestones in that development:

1787

Delegates to the Constitutional Convention agree on a plan calling for "one supreme Court" and for

The Royal Exchange, New York City, was the first home of the U.S. Supreme Court.   Source: Library of Congress

lower federal courts as established by Congress. Judges are to be appointed by the president subject to Senate confirmation. Judges' independence will be guaranteed by provisions for tenure "during good Behaviour" and protection against salary reductions.

1789

Congress passes the Judiciary Act of 1789, establishing the foundation of the federal judiciary. The act gives the Supreme Court certain powers, including the power to review state court rulings on issues of federal law. Lower federal courts are established but are given limited jurisdiction.

1790

The Supreme Court of the United States convenes for the first time. Only three of the six justices are present in New York for the opening day. With no cases to be heard, the term ends after only ten days.

1791

The BILL OF RIGHTS is ratified. The ten amendments to the Constitution include provisions to pro-

Old City Hall, Philadelphia, Pennsylvania, where the U.S. Supreme Court met from late 1791 to August 15, 1800.
Source: Library of Congress

tect freedom of speech and press, prohibit general search warrants, and guarantee jury TRIALS and other rights for the criminal DEFENDANT. (See PRESS, FREEDOM OF; SEARCH AND SEIZURE; SPEECH, FREEDOM OF.) Until the twentieth century, however, the Supreme Court rules that the amendments apply only to the federal government, not to the states.

1801

John Marshall, an ardent Federalist, is appointed chief justice by President John Adams. Marshall presides as the Court meets for the first time in the new capital city of Washington, D.C., using a small room in the basement of the Capitol. Marshall continues to lead the Court for thirty-four years, establishing the Court's authority and supporting the power of the new national government.

1803

The Court's decision in *MARBURY V. MADISON* establishes the Court's power to declare an act of Congress unconstitutional. (See JUDICIAL REVIEW.)

1805

The Senate acquits Justice Samuel Chase in a politically inspired IMPEACHMENT trial. The acquittal leads Republican president Thomas Jefferson to drop impeachment as a weapon in disputes with the judiciary.

1819

The Court's decision in *MCCULLOCH V. MARYLAND* upholds the establishment of a national bank and supports a broad construction of Congress's power under the "necessary and proper" clause of the Constitution.

1824

In *GIBBONS V. OGDEN* the Court strikes down a New York steamboat monopoly law on the grounds that it conflicts with Congress's power to regulate interstate commerce. The decision establishes the federal COMMERCE POWER as superior to that of the states, but allows states to regulate commerce within their borders if Congress has not acted.

The Supreme Court met in the U.S. Capitol from 1801 to 1935 except from August 24, 1814, when the building was burned by the British, to February 1817. Source: Library of Congress

1835

Chief Justice Marshall dies. President Andrew Jackson nominates his secretary of the treasury, Roger B. Taney, to succeed Marshall. The nomination is confirmed by the Senate in 1836. Taney serves until his death in 1864, leading the Court in a direction more favorable to states' rights.

1852

The Court's ruling in *Cooley v. Board of Wardens of Port of Philadelphia* settles on a doctrine of "dual FEDERALISM," giving the states greater power to regulate commerce where local interests outweigh national interests.

1857

The Court rules in *SCOTT V. SANDFORD* that Congress cannot bar slavery from the territories and that slaves are not citizens of the United States. The decision fuels sectional conflicts and hastens the onset of the Civil War.

1865–1870

The three CIVIL WAR AMENDMENTS abolish slavery, limit state action restricting individual rights, and guarantee VOTING RIGHTS for blacks. Subsequent Supreme Court rulings make the amendments virtually useless in protecting rights of blacks.

1873

The Court's ruling in the *SLAUGHTERHOUSE CASES* limits the scope of the Fourteenth Amendment by narrowly defining the "privileges and immunities" of U.S. CITIZENSHIP.

1883

The Court strikes down the Civil Rights Act of 1875, which prohibited racial DISCRIMINATION in PUBLIC ACCOMMODATIONS, as lying beyond Congress's power under the Thirteenth or Fourteenth Amendment.

1895

The Court rules, 5–4, that the federal INCOME TAX is unconstitutional. The decision feeds charges that the Court favors business and propertied interests. It is later reversed by the Sixteenth Amendment (1913).

1896

The decision in *PLESSY V. FERGUSON* upholds legally mandated racial SEGREGATION in public transportation. The "separate but equal" doctrine provides a legal basis for segregation in the South and elsewhere to continue for the next sixty years.

1905

The Court's ruling in *Lochner v. New York* adopts a broad "freedom of contract" theory to strike down a state law regulating working hours for bakers. The doctrine is subsequently used over the next three decades to strike down several other state and federal laws regulating economic activity. (See CONTRACT CLAUSE; PROPERTY RIGHTS.)

1916

Louis D. Brandeis, a prominent lawyer and social reformer, becomes the first Jewish justice. He is confirmed by the Senate, 47–22, after an unsuccessful

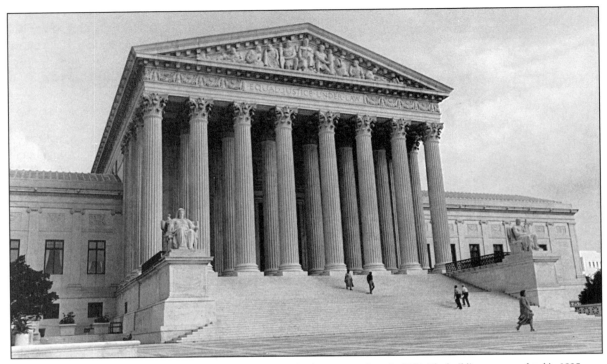

President William Howard Taft began advocating a separate home for the Supreme Court in 1912. The building was completed in 1935.
Source: R. Michael Jenkins

fight by business and industry groups to defeat the nomination.

1918

The Court strikes down a federal law designed to outlaw CHILD LABOR on the grounds that it lies beyond Congress's commerce power. Four years later, the Court invalidates a second law imposing a prohibitive tax on goods manufactured with child labor.

1935

The Supreme Court moves into its own building, across the street from the Capitol. Completed at a cost of more than $9 million, the building is variously described as a "marble palace" and a "marble mausoleum." (See SUPREME COURT BUILDING.)

1935–1936

The Court strikes down key parts of President Franklin D. Roosevelt's New Deal program. Roosevelt strongly criticizes the justices and privately considers ways to circumvent the Court.

1937

After being reelected in a landslide, Roosevelt proposes a "Court-packing" plan to give him power to appoint up to six justices. The plan is strongly criticized and rejected in Congress. In a major ideological shift, the Court discards the doctrine of freedom of contract in order to uphold state minimum wage laws. It approves expanded federal powers in upholding three major New Deal enactments. (See SIZE OF THE COURT.)

1943–1944

The Court unanimously approves a wartime curfew placed on Japanese-Americans. By a 6–3 vote, the Court also upholds relocation of Japanese-Americans from the West Coast to inland internment camps. (See *INTERNMENT CASES*.)

1952

The Court, by a vote of 6 to 3, nullifies President Harry S. Truman's seizure of steel mills to avert a wartime shutdown due to a strike. The decision in *YOUNGSTOWN SHEET AND TUBE CO. V. SAWYER* rejects the theory that the president has inherent power to act in an emergency without authority from Congress.

1953

Earl Warren, three-term progressive Republican governor of California, is chosen chief justice by President Dwight D. Eisenhower. Warren subsequently leads the Court for sixteen years in an era of unprecedented liberal JUDICIAL ACTIVISM.

1954

In *BROWN V. BOARD OF EDUCATION OF TOPEKA* the Court unanimously declares racial segregation in public elementary and secondary schools unconstitutional as a violation of the equal protection clause of the Fourteenth Amendment. One year later the Court says SCHOOL DESEGREGATION must be carried out "with all deliberate speed." Many school districts mount resistance or seek to circumvent the decision.

1961

The Court requires states to enforce the EXCLUSIONARY RULE, barring use of illegally seized evidence in criminal trials. Over the next eight years the Court issues a series of decisions requiring states to give criminal defendants other safeguards set out in the Bill of Rights. (See INCORPORATION DOCTRINE.)

1962

In *BAKER V. CARR* the Court permits federal court suits to require REAPPORTIONMENT AND REDISTRICTING by state legislatures. Later rulings establishing the principle of "one person, one vote" force reapportionment in every state but one during the 1960s.

1962–1963

The Court in two cases bars official prayer or Bible reading in public elementary and secondary schools. (See SCHOOL PRAYER.)

1963

In *GIDEON V. WAINWRIGHT* the Court holds that states must provide lawyers for indigent criminal defendants in felony cases. The Court extends the decision in 1972 to any case in which a jail sentence is imposed.

1964

Congress passes the Civil Rights Act of 1964, prohibiting racial and other forms of discrimination in employment, public accommodations, and federally funded programs. This is followed by the Voting Rights Act of 1965, which establishes strong safeguards for blacks wanting to vote, and by the Fair Housing Act of 1968, which bars discrimination in the sale or rental of housing. The Supreme Court upholds these laws and interprets them broadly.

1966

The decision in *MIRANDA V. ARIZONA* requires police to advise criminal suspects of their rights before questioning the suspects. The 5–4 decision is strongly denounced by police, prosecutors, and many public officials.

1967

Thurgood Marshall is named by President Lyndon B. Johnson as the first black justice to serve on the Supreme Court. For twenty years Marshall had directed the legal struggle against racial segregation on behalf of the Legal Defense and Educational Fund of the National Association for the Advancement of Colored People (NAACP).

1969

After making a campaign pledge to appoint more conservative justices, President Richard Nixon selects Warren E. Burger to succeed Earl Warren as chief justice. Burger and Nixon's three other appointees shift the Court to the right on criminal procedure issues but reject administration positions in other areas.

1971

The Burger Court's first major civil rights ruling upholds use of court-ordered BUSING to achieve school desegregation. In later rulings, the Court limits the power of lower courts to order busing between cities and suburbs.

1972

The Supreme Court rules, 5–4, that CAPITAL PUN-ISHMENT as then administered amounts to unconstitutional cruel and unusual punishment, invalidating all existing death sentences and touching off strong debate. The states then begin to reenact death penalty laws.

1973

In *ROE V. WADE* the Court guarantees a woman's right to an abortion during most of her pregnancy. Antiabortion groups then campaign to overturn the ruling by constitutional amendment or to enact new restrictions at the state and federal levels.

1974

The Court unanimously upholds the special prosecutor's subpoena to President Nixon for tapes of his conversations relating to the Watergate break-in and cover-up. Nixon, facing impeachment, releases the tapes, which show that he approved "hush money" to silence the burglars. He resigns.

1976

The Court, 7 to 2, upholds new state death penalty laws that allow juries to impose the death sentence under court guidelines. The Court, however, votes 5–4 to overturn mandatory death penalty statutes.

1978

The Court's ruling in the *Bakke* case says colleges and universities can consider an applicant's race as one factor in the admissions process but cannot set rigid quotas for minority students. Later decisions uphold careful use of AFFIRMATIVE ACTION in hiring and promotions and in government contracting.

1981

Sandra Day O'Connor, an Arizona appeals court judge, is appointed by President Ronald Reagan as the first woman justice to serve on the Supreme Court.

1983

The Supreme Court rules that Congress's use of the LEGISLATIVE VETO to override executive branch decisions without action by both chambers violates the principle of separation of powers.

1986

William H. Rehnquist, named to the Court by Nixon in 1971, is elevated by Reagan to chief justice after Burger retires. Reagan chooses another strong conservative, federal appeals court judge Antonin Scalia, to fill the seat vacated by Rehnquist.

1987

After a bitter ideological fight the Senate rejects nominee Robert Bork, 58–42, as too conservative. Reagan then picks a less doctrinaire conservative, Anthony M. Kennedy, his last Court appointee.

1991

Clarence Thomas, a black conservative, wins Senate confirmation for a Supreme Court seat, 52–48, after facing pointed questioning of his views and unresolved charges of sexual harassment.

1993

Ruth Bader Ginsburg, a federal appeals court judge, is appointed by President Bill Clinton as the second woman justice to serve on the Supreme Court.

Holmes, Oliver Wendell, Jr.

Oliver Wendell Holmes, Jr. (1841–1935), was one of the most brilliant legal thinkers ever to serve on the Supreme Court. At the suggestion of his colleagues, he finally retired in 1932 at age ninety after spending twenty-nine years on the bench.

Holmes was born in Boston; he graduated from

Source: Library of Congress

Harvard College in 1861. At the start of the Civil War, he was commissioned a second lieutenant in the Massachusetts Twentieth Volunteers. Holmes distinguished himself in the war, was wounded three times, and was mustered out a captain in recognition of his bravery. Holmes then returned to Harvard to study law and was admitted to the bar in 1867.

Holmes practiced law in Boston for fifteen years. He also taught constitutional law at Harvard, edited the *American Law Review,* and lectured on common law. His lectures were compiled into *The Common Law,* one of the most influential legal works of its time. In 1882 the governor of Massachusetts appointed Holmes to the Massachusetts supreme court. Holmes served on the court for twenty years, the last three as chief justice. Many of the more than 1,000 opinions Holmes wrote concerned labor disputes. His progressive labor views attracted the attention of President Theodore Roosevelt, who nominated Holmes for the Supreme Court in December 1902.

When Holmes joined the Court, it was becoming more activist. The Court began to wield its power of judicial review more frequently to overturn laws passed by Congress and state legislatures. Critics claimed the Court was making itself a "superlegislature" that was not accountable to the people. Holmes, who favored JUDICIAL RESTRAINT, joined in much of the criticism.

Holmes also was one of the great dissenters on the Court, often disagreeing with the Court's conservative rulings—and sometimes with more liberal decisions, such as the one that broke up the railroad trust in 1904. Above all, he was a pragmatist, looking at the facts of each case rather than trying to produce a result that would fit with a particular philosophy. In later years his dissenting opinions frequently became law when the Court adopted his views or a legislature wrote them into law.

Holmes wrote one of his most famous opinions in *Schenck v. United States* (1919). In that case the Court for the first time tried to determine when the government could curtail free speech rights guaranteed by the First Amendment. The case involved a man named Schenck who had been convicted under the

Espionage Act of mailing circulars to young men during World War I urging them to resist the draft. Schenck claimed he had a First Amendment right to distribute the circulars. In a unanimous opinion for the Court, Holmes said the circumstances of war warranted an abridgment of free speech rights. "The most stringent protection of free speech would not protect a man in falsely shouting fire in a theatre and causing a panic. . . ," he wrote. "The question in every case is whether the words used are used in such circumstances and are of such a nature as to create a clear and present danger." The "clear and present danger" test was used in numerous cases over succeeding decades, although it fell out of favor by the 1950s.

Housing the Court

Between February 1, 1790, when the Supreme Court first met in New York City, and October 7, 1935, when the justices convened in the first building built especially for the Court, the Court held its sessions in about a dozen different places.

Some of the earliest courtrooms were shared with other courts. After the Court moved to Washington in 1801, it held formal sessions in various rooms of the Capitol and, according to some sources, in two taverns as well. By the time the Court's own building was completed in 1935, justices were so used to working at home that many of them never actually moved into their new offices.

New York City

The Court first sat in New York City, which in 1790 was the nation's temporary capital. The Court held its sessions at the Royal Exchange Building at the intersection of Broad and Water Streets in what is now Manhattan's financial district. An open-air market occupied the first floor, and the courtroom on the second floor was a room sixty feet long with a vaulted ceiling.

The justices stayed in New York for two terms. The first lasted for ten days, February 1–10, 1790, and the second for only two days, August 2–3, 1790. There were no cases on the docket during these two terms, and the justices spent their time at such duties as appointing a Court crier—now called the CLERK OF THE COURT—and admitting lawyers to the BAR OF THE SUPREME COURT.

Philadelphia

Before the Court's second term, Congress had voted to move the capital from New York to Philadelphia. The Supreme Court joined the rest of the federal government there for its third term, which began on February 7, 1791, at Independence Hall, then known as the State House. Still having no cases to attend to, the Court adjourned the next day.

When the Court moved to Philadelphia, it was understood that the justices would sit in City Hall, but that building was not completed until the summer of 1791, in time for the Court's August 1791 term. The justices met in the east wing of the new City Hall, which also housed the state and municipal courts.

Those courts usually met at times different from the Supreme Court. In March 1796, however, the "Mayor's Court" was scheduled to hold a session in the same first-floor courtroom that the Supreme Court was using. As a result, the Supreme Court vacated the courtroom and held its session in the chambers of the Common Council on the second floor of the building.

The Court remained in City Hall until the end of the August 1800 term. City Hall also housed the U.S. Congress, which occupied the west wing, and the Pennsylvania legislature, which met in the central part of the building. The records indicate that while in City Hall the justices often kept late hours to hear oral arguments. Also, it was there that they began wearing robes for the first time.

Washington, D.C.

The act of July 16, 1790, that transferred the seat of the federal government from New York to Philadelphia also provided for a subsequent and permanent move to Washington, D.C. Congress and the president moved as scheduled in December 1800. But no provision had been made for housing for the Supreme Court. Less than two weeks before the Court was to convene, Congress on January 23, 1801, passed a resolution allowing the Court to use a room in the Capitol.

Since only the north wing of the Capitol was ready for occupancy at the time, Congress assigned the Court a small room—twenty-four by thirty feet—in the east basement, or first floor, entrance hall. There the Court held its first session in Washington on February 2, 1801. It was the first of a series of shared quarters assigned to the Court during its first 135 years in Washington.

By 1807 the north wing of the Capitol already needed renovation. In a letter to Chief Justice John Marshall on September 17, 1807, Benjamin Henry Latrobe, the architect of the Capitol and surveyor of public buildings, suggested that the Court move into the library formerly occupied by the House of Representatives.

The Court remained there for the February and summer 1808 terms. But as Latrobe himself noted in

a letter to James Monroe, the library was so cold and inconvenient that the Court decided to meet at Long's Tavern for the February 1809 session. Long's Tavern, where the first inaugural ball was held, was located on First Street, Southeast, where the Library of Congress now stands.

On February 5, 1810, the Court returned to the Capitol and met in the first courtroom designed especially for it. Located in the basement beneath the new Senate chamber, the courtroom was also used by the U.S. circuit court and probably by the Orphans' Court of the District of Columbia.

The Court remained in the new courtroom until August 24, 1814, when the British burned the Capitol during the War of 1812. It is said that the British used Supreme Court documents to start the fire. Congress moved first to the Brick Capitol, on the site of the present Supreme Court Building. Then, for the two years while the Capitol was being restored, Congress occu-

The Supreme Court occupied this chamber in the U.S. Capitol from 1860 until it moved to its permanent home in 1935.
Source: *Library of Congress*

pied a house rented from Daniel Carroll. The Court used the same house from February 6, 1815, until July 1, 1816; the house later became Bell Tavern.

The Court returned to the Capitol for its February 1817 term, occupying an undestroyed section in the north wing. It remained there until 1819, when it returned to its now repaired courtroom beneath the Senate chamber. The restoration was praised by some, but others found the room too small, too hard to find, and not befitting the highest court in the land.

Whatever its shortcomings, the courtroom at least lent a new aura of stability to the Court. The justices remained in their basement courtroom for forty-one years, surviving fires in 1851 and 1852. After the Court moved to new chambers in 1860, the basement courtroom became part of the law library of Congress.

In 1860 the Court moved from the basement to the old Senate chamber, located on the first floor of the Capitol on the east side of the main corridor between the rotunda and the current Senate chamber. The large room, with a dozen anterooms for office space and storage, was by far the most spacious and imposing quarters the Court had occupied. The galleries had been removed when the Senate moved to its new chambers, making the space even roomier.

The justices sat in chairs placed on a raised platform behind a balustrade. Behind the center chair was an arched doorway topped by a gilded American eagle and flanked by ten marble columns. The justices faced a semicircular colonnaded chamber. The area just in front of the bench was used for the presentation of arguments, and it was ringed by wooden benches for spectators. There were red drapes and carpets, and busts of former chief justices lined the walls.

Despite the dignity and spaciousness of the court-

A model of the Supreme Court building is inspected by Justices Louis D. Brandeis, Willis Van Devanter, Chief Justice William Howard Taft, Justices Oliver Wendell Holmes, Pierce Butler, George Sutherland, and Harlan Fiske Stone. Taft died in 1930 before his plan for a separate building for the Court was fulfilled.   Source: Library of Congress

room itself, the adjoining office space was cramped and inadequate. There was no dining hall, for example, so that the justices had to use the robing room for their meals. The conference room, where the justices met to discuss and decide cases, also served as the Court's library. Because some of the justices disliked having the conference room windows open, the room was frequently close and stuffy.

None of the justices had individual office space in the Capitol; each had to provide for his own and his staff's working quarters. This was inconvenient because spacious offices in Washington were difficult to find. Many of the justices solved the problem by working at home.

Nevertheless, the justices held sessions in these quarters for seventy-five years, with two exceptions. An explosion of illuminating gas on November 6, 1898, forced the Court to hold the November 7 and November 14 sessions in the Senate District of Columbia Committee room. During reconstruction of the courtroom from October to December 9, 1901, sessions were held in the Senate Judiciary Committee room.

New Court Building

President William Howard Taft began promoting the idea of a separate building for the Supreme Court around 1912. Taft continued to advocate the plan when he became chief justice in 1921. His persistence paid off in 1929, when Congress finally authorized some $10 million in funds for the construction of a permanent dwelling for the Court.

During construction of the new building, the Court continued to sit in the old Senate chamber. Its last major decision announced there, at the end of the 1934 term, was a ruling striking down President Franklin D. Roosevelt's National Industrial Recovery Act.

The new building was located at One First Street, Northeast. The Court held its first session there on October 7, 1935. Finally, 145 years after it first met in New York City, 134 years after it moved to Washington, and 6 years after Congress had appropriated funds for the building, the nation's highest tribunal had a home of its own. (See SUPREME COURT BUILDING.)

Source: Collection of the Supreme Court of the United States

Hughes, Charles Evans

Charles Evans Hughes (1862–1948) is the only justice to have served two separate terms on the Supreme Court. President William Howard Taft named him an associate justice in 1910, and Hughes served until 1916, when he resigned to become the Republican presidential candidate. He lost to Woodrow Wilson by only twenty-three electoral votes. Hughes rejoined the Court in 1930 when President Herbert Hoover nominated him as chief justice, and he then served until his retirement in 1941.

Hughes was born in Glens Falls, New York. He received his undergraduate and graduate degrees from Brown University, and graduated from Columbia Law School in 1884. At age twenty-two Hughes passed the bar. He then joined a Wall Street law firm, where he remained for twenty years except for a three-year break teaching law at Cornell University.

Investigations of fraudulent insurance practices, which Hughes conducted for the New York legislature, began to gain him a national reputation in 1905. The next year he was elected governor, helped along by an endorsement from President Theodore Roosevelt. Hughes served two terms before Taft tapped him for the Supreme Court in April 1910. Hughes accepted the appointment with the understanding that Taft would appoint him chief justice when the next opening occurred. When Chief Justice Melville Fuller died two months after Hughes joined the Court, however, Taft promoted Justice Edward White to replace him.

After leaving the Court in 1916 to run for president, Hughes returned to private law practice in New York. President Warren G. Harding appointed him secretary of state in 1921. Hughes faced strong opposition in the Senate when Hoover nominated him as chief justice in 1930. Many senators thought Hughes was too conservative and too closely tied to the nation's largest corporations. Nonetheless, the Senate confirmed his appointment by a 52–26 vote.

On the Court, Hughes championed free speech, freedom of assembly, and a free press. In 1937, as chief justice, Hughes wrote an opinion for the Court in *DeJonge v. Oregon* overturning the conviction of a man who had been charged with criminal syndicalism after he presided over a public meeting held by the Communist party. The man contended he was innocent because he had not advocated any unlawful acts, and the Court agreed. Hughes wrote that "peaceable assembly for lawful discussion cannot be made a crime."

In *Near v. Minnesota* (1931) Hughes wrote the majority opinion for the 5–4 Court overturning a Minnesota statute that barred malicious, scandalous, and defamatory publications. A scandal sheet had claimed that local officials were in collusion with gangsters, and a judge had ordered publication halted. The Supreme Court ruled that the judge's order was an unconstitutional prior restraint on the press. "The fact that the liberty of the press may be abused by miscreant purveyors of scandal does not make any the less necessary the immunity of the press from previous restraint in dealing with official misconduct," Hughes wrote. Hughes retired as chief justice in 1941.

Hunt, Ward

In January 1879, just seven years after coming to the Supreme Court, Justice Ward Hunt (1810–1886) suffered a paralytic stroke that prevented him from participating in any further Court activities. However, Hunt refused to resign because he wasn't yet eligible for a full pension. The Court began to drift toward stagnation because two other justices also were infirm. Three years after Hunt's stroke, Congress finally passed a law granting him a full pension if he would

Source: Library of Congress

retire from the Court within thirty days. Hunt retired the day the law took effect.

Hunt was born in Utica, New York. After graduating with honors from Union College at age eighteen, Hunt studied law. He formed a partnership with a local judge after being admitted to the bar in 1831. While building a successful practice, Hunt also became involved in politics.

Hunt was elected to the New York assembly as a Jacksonian Democrat in 1838, and in 1844 he served a year as Utica's mayor. During this period he gradually moved away from the Democratic party because he opposed the expansion of slavery and the annexation of Texas. By the mid-1850s Hunt had broken with the Democrats and helped found the Republican party in New York. Roscoe Conkling, who later was the boss of New York Republican politics, became one of Hunt's key allies. In 1865 Hunt was elected to the New York court of appeals, the state's highest court. He became commissioner of appeals in 1869 after a court reorganization.

When Justice Samuel Nelson retired in 1872, President Ulysses S. Grant considered several possible candidates to replace him. He finally settled on Hunt after a strong lobbying effort by Conkling, a close ally of the president. Hunt had an uneventful career on the Court. He wrote few major opinions before finally retiring in 1882, four years before his death.

I

Immunity

See CONGRESSIONAL IMMUNITY; EXECUTIVE PRIVILEGE AND IMMUNITY; OFFICIAL IMMUNITY.

Impeachment

The Constitution provides that the president, vice president, and "all civil Officers of the United States" can be removed from office "on Impeachment for, and Conviction of, Treason, Bribery, or other high Crimes and Misdemeanors" (Article II, Section 4). The House can impeach an official by majority vote. The Senate has the power to try an impeachment; conviction requires the votes of two-thirds of the senators present.

No Supreme Court justice has ever been removed from office by impeachment. Justice Samuel Chase was impeached in 1804 but acquitted by the Senate in 1805. (See IMPEACHMENT OF JUSTICES.)

Seven lower federal court judges have been impeached, convicted, and removed from office; another resigned after being impeached but before trial. Three other federal judges were impeached but acquitted.

The Constitution gives no definition of what "high crimes and misdemeanors" warrant impeachment. Some people argue that impeachment requires an indictable criminal offense, while others maintain that any serious official misconduct can be the basis for removal from office. Congress has never authoritatively resolved the issue.

Presidential Impeachments

Delegates to the Constitutional Convention discussed the impeachment provision almost exclusively as a means of controlling abuse by the president. The decision to include the vice president and other "civil officers" was made at the last minute.

The most dramatic impeachment trial was the unsuccessful attempt to remove President Andrew Johnson from office in 1868. Republicans in Congress initiated the move against Johnson, a former Democrat and a southerner, in large part because of opposition to his moderate policies on Reconstruction issues. The major accusation was that Johnson had violated the Tenure of Office Act by attempting to remove Secretary of War Edwin Stanton from office without the consent of the Senate. (See APPOINTMENT AND REMOVAL POWERS OF THE PRESIDENT.)

As required by the Constitution, Chief Justice Salmon P. Chase presided over the Senate trial. His fair handling of the case was considered an important factor in Johnson's acquittal.

The result in the Johnson impeachment came to be viewed as a vindication of presidential power and a negative precedent for use of impeachment against any future president. But in 1974 the House initiated impeachment proceedings against President Richard Nixon for his part in the cover-up of the 1972 Watergate break-in. The House Judiciary Committee in July 1974 approved articles of impeachment against Nixon, but he resigned before the matter could be brought to the House floor.

Judicial Impeachments

In *The Federalist Papers,* No. 79, Alexander Hamilton wrote that impeachment was "the only provision" for removal of judges found in the Constitution and was "consistent with the necessary independence of judges."

The political independence of the judiciary was tested by the Senate's first two impeachment trials, which involved charges initiated by Republican president Thomas Jefferson against Federalist members of the judiciary.

In 1803 Jefferson sent to the House evidence of drunken and profane behavior on the bench by U.S.

As required by the Constitution, Chief Justice Salmon P. Chase presided over the impeachment trial of President Andrew Johnson. Scholars applaud Chase's dignified handling of the proceedings, which some feel saved Johnson from conviction.   Source: Library of Congress

district court judge John Pickering of New Hampshire. The House responded immediately by passing a resolution impeaching Pickering on March 2, 1803. In May Jefferson similarly complained to a House member of partisan behavior by Justice Chase. Pickering was tried and convicted in the Senate in March 1804. Within hours of his conviction, the full House voted to impeach Chase.

Chase's acquittal eased the fears of Chief Justice John Marshall that he might be the next target of an impeachment. For his part, Jefferson said the acquittal showed that impeachment was "an impracticable thing—a mere scarecrow."

Nonetheless, impeachment has been used repeatedly since that time as a means of disciplining federal judges. Three U.S. district court judges were removed from office in the 1980s, all for charges arising from criminal prosecutions. Harry F. Claiborne of Nevada was impeached and convicted in 1986 for tax fraud.

Walter L. Nixon, Jr., of Mississippi was convicted in 1989 of lying under oath. And Alcee L. Hastings of Florida was convicted the same year for conspiracy to accept a bribe.

Claiborne and Nixon had both been previously convicted in criminal trials. Hastings had been acquitted in a criminal trial, but the Senate convicted him in the impeachment trial, in part because of evidence that the judge had perjured himself in the earlier trial.

Beginning with Claiborne's case, the Senate invoked a rule permitting evidence in impeachment trials to be heard by a fact-finding committee instead of by the full Senate. Nixon argued in a federal court suit that the shortcut violated the constitutional provision that the Senate has "the sole power" to try impeachments. But the Court in 1993 unanimously rejected the challenge.

Impeachment of Justices

A Supreme Court justice can be removed from office only through IMPEACHMENT in the House of Representatives and conviction by two-thirds of the Senate. Only one Supreme Court justice, Samuel Chase, has ever been impeached. He was tried in the Senate on charges of injudicious behavior. The trial ended in 1805 in an acquittal that protected the Supreme Court's independence at a time of deep partisan conflict.

Two other justices have faced serious attempts at impeachment, although neither was actually impeached. Abe Fortas resigned in 1969 after some House members laid plans for an inquiry into charges of financial misconduct. (See RESIGNATION.) On two separate occasions, the House investigated impeachment charges against William O. Douglas. The first investigation came in 1953 because of Douglas's temporary stay of execution of two convicted spies; the second was made in 1970 for political reasons and because of Douglas's conduct on and off the bench. In both cases, impeachment resolutions were rejected after subcommittee hearings.

There were scattered public calls for the impeachment of Chief Justice Earl Warren during the 1950s and 1960s in protest of the Court's rulings on such issues as SCHOOL DESEGREGATION and SCHOOL PRAYER, but no serious impeachment effort was ever initiated in the House.

Impeachment of Chase

Justice Chase was appointed to the Supreme Court in 1796. His impeachment and trial for partisan, harsh, and unfair judicial treatment while riding circuit had its roots in the Republican desire to rid the federal judiciary of Federalist influence. Chase had openly approved passage of the politically motivated Alien and Sedition Acts and had actively campaigned for the reelection of Federalist president John Adams in 1800. (See POLITICS AND THE COURT.)

Chase was severely criticized for his arbitrary handling of the sedition trial of Republican printer James T. Callender and the treason trial of John Fries, organizer of the Whiskey Rebellion of 1798. On another occasion Chase unsuccessfully pressured a Delaware grand jury to indict a Wilmington publisher for sedition. Finally, in May 1803 Chase delivered a political harangue to a Baltimore grand jury in which he denounced the Republican administration of President Thomas Jefferson.

Enraged, Jefferson wrote to a Republican House member on May 13, 1803, noting the Baltimore grand jury incident and asking, "Ought this seditious and official attack . . . go unpunished?" In January 1804, Rep. John Randolph of Virginia proposed an impeachment resolution against Chase. Of the eight charges, six dealt with the Callender and Fries trials and two pertained to the Delaware and Baltimore grand jury incidents. On March 12, the full House voted to impeach Chase by a party-line vote of 73 to 32.

Chase's trial in the Senate began January 2, 1805. He read a statement saying that he had "committed no crime or misdemeanor . . . for which I am subject to impeachment" and denying any "improper intentions" in any of the episodes cited in the charges. After a month's delay for Chase to prepare his defense, the proceedings resumed in February. Fifty-two witnesses testified, including Chief Justice John Marshall, whose testimony was viewed as unfavorable to Chase's cause.

After the testimony, the major debate focused on whether a justice must have committed an indictable crime to be impeached and convicted. On March 1, 1805, the Senate was ready to vote. Of the thirty-four members present, twenty-five were Republicans—more than the twenty-three needed for conviction—and nine were Federalists. At least six Republicans sided with the Federalists on each vote, however, and Chase was acquitted of all charges. The closest vote was on the charge involving the Baltimore grand jury: there were eighteen votes for conviction, sixteen for acquittal.

Attempts to Impeach Douglas

Douglas, appointed to the Court in 1939, was a controversial justice because of his liberal views and outspoken opinions—and because of his several marriages, two to women considerably younger than he.

The first attempt to impeach him began after Douglas, on June 17, 1953, temporarily stayed the executions of convicted spies Julius and Ethel Rosenberg. Rep. W. M. (Don) Wheeler, D-Ga., introduced a resolution of impeachment the next day. On June 19, the full Court overturned Douglas's stay. When a special subcommittee of the House Judiciary Committee considered the impeachment resolution, Wheeler was the only witness. The full committee tabled the resolution on July 7.

The second attempt to impeach Douglas followed the Senate's rejection in 1969 and 1970 of two of President Richard Nixon's nominees for the Court, Clement Haynsworth, Jr., and G. Harrold Carswell. (See NOMINATION TO THE COURT.)

On April 15, 1970, House minority leader Gerald R. Ford, R-Mich., made five major charges against Douglas in a floor speech. The most serious accusation was that Douglas had violated federal law by practicing law in his association with the Albert Parvin Foundation. The foundation was established by a wealthy industrialist to promote international cooperation through education.

Douglas maintained that he had acted only as an adviser to the foundation, for which he received $12,000 a year plus travel expenses. Douglas had ended his association with the foundation in May 1969.

Ford also said that Douglas should have disqualified himself from obscenity cases involving Ralph Ginzburg, the publisher of a magazine that had paid Douglas $350 for an article he had written. He also charged that a book written by Douglas, *Points of Rebellion,* could be construed to advocate violent overthrow of the existing political order.

The charges were referred to the House Judiciary Committee, which established a five-member subcommittee to investigate. After months of hearings and deliberations, the subcommittee on December 3 voted 3–1 with 1 abstention that it found no grounds for impeachment of Douglas. In its formal report, the subcommittee stated that Douglas had not violated federal law or judicial ethics by failing to disqualify himself from Ginzburg's cases and that he had never acted as an attorney for the Parvin Foundation.

Income Tax

The Constitution provides that the federal government can impose a "direct" tax only if it is in proportion to the population of each state (Article I, Section 9, Clause 4). In 1895 the Supreme Court interpreted this clause to strike down the nation's first peacetime general income tax. The decision, which was extremely controversial, was overturned by the Sixteenth Amendment in 1913 and implicitly repudiated by the Court itself in 1916. (See REVERSALS OF RULINGS BY CONSTITUTIONAL AMENDMENT.)

The Constitution does not define "direct" taxes. As early as 1796, however, the Court in sustaining a levy on carriages said that only head taxes and taxes on land were direct taxes required to be apportioned by population.

A federal tax on personal income was first imposed during the Civil War and stayed on the books until 1872. In *Springer v. United States* (1881) the Court unanimously upheld that tax as applied to attorneys' income on the ground that it was an indirect tax.

In the 1890s there was renewed support for a federal income tax. This was partly a result of industrialization, which brought an increase in wealth based on earnings as opposed to wealth based on land. It also resulted from a loss of revenue due to the depression of 1893. Congress yielded and in 1894 levied a tax of 2 percent on personal income in excess of $4,000. Only about 2 percent of the population earned more than this amount. The tax was immediately challenged.

The issue reached the Supreme Court in a case brought by a stockholder in a New York bank to enjoin the bank from paying the new tax. The case, *Pollock v. Farmers' Loan & Trust Co.* (1895), was evidently arranged between parties with the same interest, but the Court agreed to hear the case anyway.

Attorneys for Pollock argued two basic points that later historians have regarded as weak. First, they said that a tax on the income from land was the same as a tax on the land itself. It was therefore an unconstitutional direct tax since it had not been apportioned. Second, they claimed that the tax also failed to meet the Constitution's uniformity test (Article I, Section 8,

In his famous Cross of Gold speech to the Democratic National Convention in July 1896, William Jennings Bryan denounced the Supreme Court's overturning of the income tax law. He said those who are unwilling to share of the burdens of government are unworthy of the blessings of government.
Source: Library of Congress

and a full Court rendered its second decision just six weeks after the first on May 20, 1895. By a 5–4 vote, the Court reaffirmed its decision to strike down the tax on income from land, similarly invalidated the tax on income from personal property, and then threw out the entire law on the ground that Congress would not have approved a tax on wages and salaries alone.

In writing both of the Court's opinions in the case, Chief Justice Melville W. Fuller glossed over precedent. He dismissed the pronouncements in the carriage tax case as mere dicta and distinguished the Civil War tax as a levy on earned income rather than on income from land or personal property. The four dissenters submitted separate opinions, reproving the majority for disregarding a century of precedent and sharply criticizing it for the political implications of its ruling.

The Court's decision was widely denounced as protecting propertied interests and usurping legislative power. Democratic presidential nominee William Jennings Bryan bitterly criticized the ruling in his "Cross of Gold" speech at the party's national convention in 1896. Many Democrats and progressive Republicans gained election to Congress on pledges to help reenact an income tax.

Sensitive to the outcry, the Fuller Court did not apply the *Pollock* precedent to succeeding tax cases. Instead it upheld as excise or indirect taxes levies on commodity exchange sales, inheritances, tobacco, and stock sales. In 1911 the Court upheld a tax on corporate income passed two years earlier, on the ground that it was an excise tax "measured by income" on the privilege of doing business.

Ratification of the Sixteenth Amendment in 1913 gave Congress power to impose taxes on income "from whatever source derived, without apportionment among the several States, and without regard to any census or enumerations." Congress later that year enacted an income tax law that was upheld by the Court in 1916. Implicitly criticizing its 1895 position, the Court in *Stanton v. Baltic Mining Co.* said that the Sixteenth Amendment gave Congress no new powers of taxation but simply guaranteed that the income tax would never again be "taken out of the category of indirect taxation to which it inherently belonged."

In the meantime the Court had answered the

Clause 1) because it applied only to income over a certain amount. More broadly, Pollock's attorneys called the tax a "communistic" assault on the rights of private property—an argument calculated to appeal to economically conservative justices on the bench.

Only eight justices heard the arguments (Justice Howell E. Jackson was ill with tuberculosis). The Court handed down its decision on April 8, 1895. Six of the eight agreed that the tax on the income from land was identical to a tax on the land and thus unconstitutional. But the eight divided evenly on the issues of whether income from personal property was also a direct tax and whether the law failed to meet the uniformity test.

Pollock's attorneys asked for reargument since the tie vote left in place the circuit court's decision sustaining most of the tax provisions. The Court agreed,

question—left undecided in the income tax cases—of whether the tax rate had to be uniform. During the Spanish-American War Congress had imposed an inheritance tax on legacies of more than $10,000; the tax rate varied with the amount of the bequest and the relationship of the heir to the deceased. The Court in *Knowlton v. Moore* (1900) ruled that the tax was a permissible indirect tax and was also uniform within the meaning of the Constitution as long as it applied in the same manner to the same class throughout the United States.

Incorporation Doctrine

The Supreme Court developed the incorporation doctrine between 1925 and 1969 to require the states to abide by almost all of the major provisions of the BILL OF RIGHTS. These decisions have stood even though the justices displayed great uncertainty and disagreement about the rationale for the doctrine as it

was established, case by case, over more than four decades.

Before the Civil War, the Court had consistently held that the Bill of Rights applied only to the federal government, not to the states. After the Civil War, the Court recognized the DUE PROCESS clause of the Fourteenth Amendment as a limitation on state action. But it ruled in several cases that the clause did not require the same procedures in state criminal trials that the Bill of Rights required in federal cases.

Dissenting from those rulings, Justice John Marshall Harlan argued that the due process clause "incorporated" many of the specific guarantees of the Bill of Rights regarding criminal procedure. In another dissent in 1907, he similarly argued that freedom of speech and freedom of the press were "essential parts of every man's liberty" and that the states, under the due process clause, could not infringe on those rights.

The first crack in the Court's refusal to apply the Bill of Rights against state action came quietly in a case dealing with the First Amendment. In *Gitlow v. New York* (1925) the Court upheld New York's crimi-

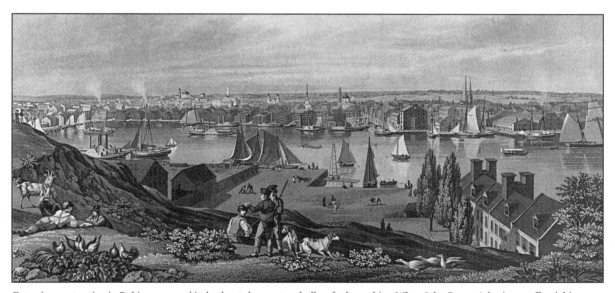

Extensive construction in Baltimore caused its harbor to become too shallow for large ships. When John Barron's business suffered, his lawyer argued that Fifth Amendment protections against the taking of private property without compensation should apply to states. The U.S. Supreme Court, in Barron v. Baltimore *(1833), disagreed and started an argument that lasted well into the twentieth century.*
Source: *Maryland Historical Society, Baltimore*

nal anarchy law, but only after declaring: "For present purposes, we may and do assume that freedom of speech and of the press . . . are among the fundamental personal rights and 'liberties' protected by the due process clause of the Fourteenth Amendment from impairment by the states."

Over the next two decades the Court continued to declare that states could not violate major provisions of the First Amendment, including freedom of the press (1931), the free exercise of religion (1933), freedom of assembly (1937), and the establishment clause (1947).

The Court proceeded more tentatively in the area of criminal law. It found due process violations in five state criminal cases between 1923 and 1936, including the pair of decisions handed down in the SCOTTS-BORO CASES. Each ruling was based, however, on the particular facts of the case rather than on a literal application of the pertinent provisions of the Bill of Rights. In *Palko v. Connecticut* (1937) the Court held that the due process guarantee did not require states to comply with the Fifth Amendment prohibition against double jeopardy.

Writing for the Court in *Palko,* Justice Benjamin N. Cardozo said that some of the Bill of Rights provisions had been applied to the states by "a process of absorption," but that the doctrine applied only to protections that were "of the very essence of a scheme of ordered liberty." Five years later the Court again rejected the broader incorporation doctrine, ruling in *Betts v. Brady* (1942) that the due process guarantee did not encompass the right to legal counsel established by the Sixth Amendment.

The justices debated the issue most extensively in a 1947 decision, *Adamson v. California.* The Court reaffirmed by a 5–4 vote its 1908 decision not to apply the privilege against self-incrimination to the states. Four dissenters, led by Justice Hugo L. Black, argued that the Fourteenth Amendment was intended "to extend to all of the people of the nation the complete protection of the Bill of Rights." Two of the four—justices Frank Murphy and Wiley Rutledge—went further and argued that the Fourteenth Amendment protected additional rights not listed in the Bill of Rights.

In a concurring opinion responding to the dissent, Justice Felix Frankfurter argued that total incorpora-

tion was impractical, pointing in particular to the Seventh Amendment right to a jury trial in civil cases involving more than twenty dollars. On the other hand, he maintained that selective incorporation was necessarily subjective. He argued instead that the due process clause encompassed those procedures required by "civilized decency." Black, in turn, criticized that test as too subjective.

A series of seemingly unpredictable criminal procedure rulings during the 1950s led to dissatisfaction with the Court's approach. For that reason, the Court resumed the process of selective incorporation beginning with *Mapp v. Ohio* (1961). That decision, based on the Fourth Amendment, extended the exclusionary rule to the states. During the rest of the decade, the Warren Court used the incorporation doctrine to apply the key provisions of the Fifth and Sixth amendments to the states. The decisions included:

GIDEON V. WAINWRIGHT (1963), requiring states to provide legal counsel to indigent defendants in serious criminal cases.

Malloy v. Hogan (1964), applying the Fifth Amendment privilege against self-incrimination to the states. (Together with *Gideon,* the decision formed the basis of the limits on police interrogation established by MIRANDA V. ARIZONA [1966].)

Duncan v. Louisiana (1968), requiring jury trials under the Sixth Amendment in serious state criminal cases.

Benton v. Maryland (1969), applying the ban on double jeopardy to the states.

The Court in 1962 had held that the Eighth Amendment ban on CRUEL AND UNUSUAL PUNISHMENT applied to the states. On that basis, the Court in 1972 declared that CAPITAL PUNISHMENT, as administered by the states at the time, was unconstitutional.

The incorporation doctrine was not all-encompassing. The Court still has not imposed on states the Fifth Amendment requirement of indictment by a grand jury in all criminal cases or the Seventh Amendment requirement of jury trial in civil cases. It has never expressly held that the Eighth Amendment ban on excessive bail or excessive fines applies to the states. Outside the criminal law area, it has left standing its

1875 ruling that the Second Amendment applies only to the federal government, not to the states. (See ARMS, RIGHT TO BEAR.)

Indictment

An indictment is a formal written accusation by a GRAND JURY, based on evidence presented by a prosecutor, charging one or more persons with specified criminal offenses. An alternative method of initiating a criminal case is a written accusation by a prosecutor, which is called an *information*.

The Fifth Amendment provides that "no person shall be held to answer for a capital, or otherwise infamous crime, unless on a presentment or indictment of a Grand Jury," except in cases involving the military. The Supreme Court has not required indictments for "petty offenses" in federal courts and has not made the grand jury indictment provision mandatory for the states. About half the states permit prosecutors to bring charges by an information, although prosecutors in those states often use the grand jury indictment procedure for more serious cases.

Grand juries need not be unanimous to indict; typically they can return an indictment by majority vote. The federal grand jury, for example, consists of sixteen to twenty-three persons, with twelve votes required to indict. The grand jury determines only whether there is PROBABLE CAUSE to believe that the accused has committed a crime. At trial the prosecution must prove the defendant guilty beyond a reasonable doubt in order to obtain a conviction.

The historic purpose of indictment by grand jury—to protect against unjustified prosecutions—diminished as the grand jury evolved into an arm of the prosecutor's office. The indictment continues to serve the function of informing defendants of some details of the charges against them so that they can prepare their defense. If evidence at trial varies from the indictment, the defendant may be entitled to have the charges dismissed.

A defendant may also seek dismissal of an indictment before trial by attacking the grand jury selection process or the legal sufficiency of the charges. (See JURIES.) But a defendant may not contest an indictment on the ground that the grand jury considered inadequate or incompetent evidence, including evidence that was illegally obtained.

In Forma Pauperis

More than half of the 5,000 cases the Supreme Court is asked to review each year are filed *in forma pauperis* (a Latin term meaning "in the manner of a pauper"). In such cases the $300 filing fee is waived, and the required number of copies of briefs and other materials is reduced. Most of these paupers' cases are filed by prisoners.

Criminal defendants who have been represented by appointed counsel in the lower federal courts are entitled to file paupers' cases. Others must petition the court for permission to file *in forma pauperis*. Traditionally, the Court accepted these petitions without question. But as the requests to proceed *in forma pauperis* have grown in number, the Court has given them more scrutiny. In a few cases it has denied the requests, holding that the petitioner was not really a pauper. In *In re McDonald* (1989) the justices issued a general denial of pauper status to a litigant who had made seventy-four filings to the Court concerning his criminal conviction. In 1991 the Court issued a new rule that allowed it to deny pauper's status when it considered the case to be malicious or frivolous.

Very few of the cases filed *in forma pauperis* are accepted for review. But a substantial portion of the Court's rulings on criminal procedure arise from the paupers' cases it does accept.

Injunction

An injunction is an order directing someone to halt a course of action that will cause irreparable injury to someone else, for which no adequate compensation can be made by a later lawsuit. The term (or its variant, injunctive relief) can also be used for a judicial order directing someone to perform an action or course of actions.

Injunctions are powerful remedies—effective, flexible, and open-ended. For that reason, they have been an important tool for courts in modern constitutional and civil rights cases. (See COURTS, POWERS OF.)

Injunctions may be temporary, simply preserving the status quo pending final resolution of the issues in a dispute. They may also be permanent bans on a certain course of action. An injunction must be obeyed until it is reversed or lifted.

The Supreme Court has traditionally held that Congress must authorize the federal courts to issue injunctions. Congress has done so since 1789, but it has also exercised its power to limit the circumstances in which federal courts may issue injunctions.

The Judiciary Act of 1789 made clear that injunctions were permitted only when no legal remedy existed to resolve a dispute. More specific limitations followed. The Anti-Injunction Act of 1793 forbade the courts to use injunctions to stay state court proceedings. In 1867 Congress forbade federal courts to use injunctions to interfere with the assessment or collection of federal taxes. Both provisions remain on the books today, though the Court has recognized a limited exception permitting an injunction against state criminal prosecutions to prevent denial of First Amendment rights. (See COMITY.)

Early in the century, injunctions were extensively used by federal courts sympathetic to the efforts of property owners and employers to curtail the activities of organized labor. This brought the enactment of laws in 1914 and 1932 limiting use of injunctions in labor disputes. (See ANTITRUST.)

Congress in 1910 and 1937 required that injunctions halting enforcement of state laws or acts of Congress that had been challenged as unconstitutional be granted only by panels of three federal judges, not by a single federal judge. These provisions were repealed in 1976. (See THREE-JUDGE COURT.)

The recent use of the injunction in public law cases stems from the Supreme Court's decision in *Ex parte Young* (1908). In that case the Court ruled that the sovereign immunity doctrine might bar a damage action against a state but does not bar injunctive relief against a state official acting unconstitutionally. On

that basis, federal courts since the 1950s have fashioned increasingly detailed decrees directed at state and local officials concerning their actions in such areas as school desegregation and institutional litigation involving prisoners' rights and the rights of mental patients.

Internment Cases

Twice during wartime the federal government partly suspended civil liberties to permit the detention without trial of thousands of civilians. Both times the Supreme Court looked the other way.

In the first instance, President Abraham Lincoln suspended HABEAS CORPUS during the Civil War, allowing military authorities to detain civilians suspected of disloyalty. Then, during World War II, President Franklin D. Roosevelt authorized the relocation of Japanese-Americans on the West Coast to internment camps, ostensibly to protect the nation against sabotage.

Although the Court failed to block the actions, it later found the Civil War use of military tribunals unlawful. The Court's rulings permitting the World War II relocation and internment programs are now widely viewed as mistakes. This can be seen in Congress's decision in 1988 to authorize compensation for surviving residents of the camps.

Civil War

Lincoln's unilateral suspension of habeas corpus in April 1861 was immediately tested. John Merryman, arrested by Union soldiers in Maryland on charges of aiding secessionists, obtained a writ of habeas corpus challenging his detention. Prison officials refused to comply with the writ, citing Lincoln's proclamation. Sitting as a circuit justice, Chief Justice Roger B. Taney ruled Lincoln's action unconstitutional. He stated that the president had usurped legislative power by suspending habeas corpus and had usurped judicial power by arresting and imprisoning someone without due process of law.

Although Merryman was later turned over to civil authorities and indicted for treason, Lincoln refused to bow to Taney's opinion, citing the need for emergency measures to preserve the Union. During the next two years hundreds of people were arrested without being told why and were detained without sufficient evidence or legal action until the emergency that led to the arrest had passed. Military officers disregarded judicial orders for the release of prisoners. After 1862 Lincoln widened the military's powers to permit the arrest of anyone resisting the draft or discouraging military enlistments. Thousands of citizens in the North who were suspected of disloyalty were arrested, imprisoned, and then released without trial after the emergency passed.

Although Congress sanctioned the suspension of habeas corpus in 1863, the military tribunals' power over civilians outside the war zone remained doubtful. But the Court in 1864 refused to address the issue, saying that it had no power to review the proceedings of a military commission. In 1866, however, the Court ruled in *Ex parte Milligan* that martial law must be confined to "the theater of active military operations." The Court was unanimous in finding Lincoln's actions unlawful, though four justices argued that the extension of military authority could have been authorized by Congress.

World War II

In February 1941, ten months before the Japanese attacked Pearl Harbor, President Roosevelt issued an executive order under his authority as commander in chief to place Japanese-Americans living on the West Coast under rigid curfew laws. A congressional resolution in March 1942 supported the president's action. Roosevelt later ordered the removal of all persons of Japanese ancestry from the coastal region for the duration of the war. By the spring of 1942, about 112,000 people—two-thirds of them U.S. citizens, the rest aliens—had been relocated to internment camps. The constitutionality of the curfew, exclusion, and relocation programs came before the Supreme Court in three cases decided in 1943 and 1944.

In *Hirabayashi v. United States* the Court in June 1943 unanimously upheld the curfew order as "within the boundaries of the war power" as jointly exercised by Congress and the president. Eighteen months later, in *Korematsu v. United States,* the Court upheld, by a 6–3 vote, the exclusion of Japanese-Americans from their West Coast homes. In his opinion for the Court, Justice Hugo L. Black opened by saying that racial distinctions were "immediately suspect" and must be subjected to "the most rigid scrutiny." Nonetheless, Black accepted the claimed

During World War II President Franklin D. Roosevelt ordered more than 100,000 Japanese- Americans living on the West Coast to relocate to camps in the interior. The Supreme Court upheld the president's action in Korematsu v. United States. *Source: AP/Wide World Photos*

military necessity for barring the U.S. citizens from their homes—views that dissenting justice Frank Murphy depicted as racist generalizations.

In a third case decided the same day as *Korematsu*, the Court skirted a direct ruling on the constitutionality of the relocation program, but ordered the release of a Japanese-American girl from one of the internment camps after military officials had verified her loyalty.

Evidence discovered decades later showed that government officials had deliberately misled the Court about the military need for the evacuations. In response, federal district courts in the mid-1980s set aside the convictions of Gordon Hirabayashi, Fred Korematsu, and Minoru Yasui, whose conviction had been affirmed along with Hirabayashi's.

Interstate Commerce

See COMMERCE POWER.

Source: North Carolina Division of Archives and History

Iredell, James

James Iredell (1751–1799) was ahead of his time. As a Supreme Court justice in 1793, he wrote a dissenting opinion in *Chisholm v. Georgia* arguing that a state could not be sued in federal court by a citizen from another state. His view was adopted five years later when the Eleventh Amendment was added to the Constitution. In 1798 he established a precedent for the landmark case of *Marbury v. Madison* (1803) when he argued in *Calder v. Bull* that courts should have the right to declare laws unconstitutional.

Iredell was born in Lewes, England. He used family connections to get a job in America in 1768 as comptroller of the customs in Edenton, North Carolina. He read law while serving as comptroller, and in 1770 he started practicing law. Although he was British by birth, Iredell allied himself with the revolutionary cause. In 1776 he resigned from his position as collector for the crown at Edenton.

Iredell reluctantly accepted a post as a superior court judge in North Carolina's new judicial system in 1778. He disliked the hardships of riding circuit and resigned after only a few months to resume private law practice. The next year he began a three-year term as North Carolina attorney general, and in 1787 the legislature appointed him to revise the state's legal code.

Iredell drew George Washington's eye in 1788 at the state ratification convention, where he served as floor leader for the Federalists. When Robert Harrison declined an appointment to the Supreme Court in 1790, Washington turned to Iredell. In his diary, Washington wrote that he chose Iredell because "in addition to the reputation he sustains for abilities, legal knowledge and respectability of character, he is of a State of some importance in the Union that has given no character to a federal office." Responsible for the large southern circuit, Iredell rode nearly 2,000 miles to attend local courts in the South, making the trip five times from 1790 to 1794. Iredell served on the Court for nine years until his death at age forty-eight.

J

Jackson, Andrew

President Andrew Jackson (1767–1845) transformed the Supreme Court from a bastion of national supremacy into a pro–states' rights tribunal. He was able to accomplish this through the appointment of six justices during his two terms in the White House (1829–1837). He challenged the Court's authority to bind either Congress or the president with its interpretations of the Constitution. In the confrontation between the Court and the state of Georgia over the Cherokee Indian cases, Jackson refused to help enforce the Court's decisions until his own political needs led him to protect the power of the federal government. (See STATES AND THE COURT.)

Jackson's views set him at odds with Chief Justice John Marshall. Marshall wrote the Court's decision in 1819 upholding the creation of the second Bank of the United States; Jackson opposed the bank and killed it by vetoing a bill to recharter it in 1832. In his veto message Jackson said Congress and the president could interpret the Constitution independently of the Court. "The opinion of the judges has no more authority over Congress than the opinion of Congress has over the judges, and on that point the President is independent of both," Jackson wrote.

Jackson gave the Court no help when Georgia refused to comply with its ruling in 1832 overturning the convictions of two missionaries. The missionaries had been convicted of violating a state law against going onto Indian territory. Jackson is alleged to have responded, "Well, John Marshall has made his decision, now let him enforce it." Although Jackson probably never uttered those words, they did reflect his sentiments.

When South Carolina set forth the theory of nullification in challenging the federal tariff, Jackson found himself obliged to defend federal power. He proposed what became the Force Act of 1833, allowing the president to use armed force to execute federal court rulings. Georgia officials, realizing that Jackson would no longer back them in defying the Court, released the missionaries eight months after the ruling.

On Marshall's death in 1835, Jackson selected his former secretary of the treasury, Roger B. Taney, to be chief justice. Taney and three of Jackson's other five appointees served on the Court through the beginning of the Civil War.

Jackson, Howell E.

A year after being appointed to the Supreme Court in 1893, Howell Edmunds Jackson (1832–1895) de-

Source: Collection of the Supreme Court of the United States

veloped a severe case of tuberculosis. Jackson, who didn't want to resign, took a leave from the Court to recuperate in the West. In May 1895, however, a full Court was needed to rehear a case on the constitutionality of income taxes. Jackson was still sick, but he traveled back to Washington to hear the case and dissent from the Court's ruling that income taxes were unconstitutional. Three months later he died of his illness.

Jackson was born in Paris, Tennessee. He graduated from West Tennessee College in 1849 and then studied at the University of Virginia and Cumberland University before passing the bar and starting a law practice in his hometown. In 1859 Jackson moved to Memphis to form a legal partnership that specialized in corporate, railroad, and banking law. Although he opposed secession, Jackson joined the Confederate government in 1861 as custodian of confiscated property, a post he held for the entire Civil War. After the war Jackson resumed his private practice and served as a judge in the court of arbitration for western Tennessee.

Jackson served one year in the Tennessee house of representatives and in 1882 was elected to the U.S. Senate. In the Senate, Jackson's seat was next to that of Benjamin Harrison, a Republican senator from Indiana who later became president and appointed Jackson to the Supreme Court. In 1886 Jackson reluctantly resigned from the Senate at the request of President Grover Cleveland to fill a vacancy on the Sixth Federal Circuit Court. When the circuit court of appeals was created in 1891, Jackson was named its first presiding judge.

Harrison nominated Jackson for the Supreme Court in February 1893, but Jackson served little because of his illness. He died in August 1895, slightly more than two years after joining the Court.

Jackson, Robert H.

When Chief Justice Harlan Fiske Stone died in 1946, it was widely assumed that President Harry Truman would promote Justice Robert Houghwout Jackson (1892–1954) to chief justice. It was rumored,

however, that two other justices threatened to resign if Jackson was elevated to chief. Truman decided not to take the risk and instead appointed Secretary of the Treasury Fred Vinson to head the Court.

Jackson blamed Justice Hugo Black for his failure to obtain the chief justiceship. At the time Jackson was on a year-long leave of absence to serve as U.S. prosecutor at the post–World War II war crimes trials in Nuremberg, Germany. When he learned that Truman had passed him over for chief justice, Jackson released a vitriolic letter in which he charged that Black had improperly heard a case in which he had an interest. The charge was unfounded, but it cemented the two justices' mutual hatred.

Jackson was born in Spring Creek, Pennsylvania. He apprenticed in a local law firm at age eighteen, completed a two-year course at Albany Law School in one year, and then started what became a lucrative law practice. In 1934 he was appointed general counsel for the Internal Revenue Bureau. Jackson quickly moved up in the administration of Franklin Roosevelt. He was named assistant attorney general in

Source: Collection of the Supreme Court of the United States

1936, solicitor general in 1938, and attorney general in 1940. Jackson became one of Roosevelt's strongest supporters in Washington, and he backed the president's Court-packing plan. Roosevelt rewarded his friend by naming him to the Supreme Court in 1941.

On the Court, Jackson was a strong supporter of First Amendment rights. He believed that where a law interfered with free speech or assembly, the Court needed to examine the statute with special care. One of Jackson's most important opinions for the Court came in *West Virginia Board of Education v. Barnette* (1943). In the decision, written by Jackson, the Court struck down a state law requiring schoolchildren to salute the flag even if doing so conflicted with their religious beliefs. "If there is any fixed star in our constitutional constellation, it is that no official . . . can prescribe what shall be orthodox in politics, nationalism, religion or other matters," Jackson wrote for the Court. Jackson served on the Court for thirteen years until his death in October 1954.

Jay, John

John Jay (1745–1829), the first chief justice of the United States, helped set the groundwork for a strong and independent judicial branch of government.

He was born in New York City, and graduated from King's College (later Columbia University) at age nineteen. Four years later he was admitted to the bar. His long career of public service began in 1773, when he served as secretary of the Royal Boundary Commission. He represented New York at both the first and second continental congresses, and in December 1778 was elected president of the Continental Congress. His diplomatic career began the next year, when he was sent to Spain to seek diplomatic recognition and economic aid. In 1783 he helped negotiate the Treaty of Paris, which formally concluded the revolutionary war, and from 1784 to 1789 he served as secretary of foreign affairs.

In an effort to capitalize on Jay's foreign policy experience, President George Washington offered him the position of secretary of state. Jay declined, and Washington appointed him chief justice of the new

Source: National Portrait Gallery, Smithsonian Institution

Supreme Court in 1789. During his tenure, Jay championed the gradual freeing of slaves, the welfare of prisoners, and a reduction in the number of crimes carrying the death penalty. Although he privately offered advice to President Washington on behalf of the Court, Jay formally refused to rule in advance whether certain proposed government actions were legal—thus reinforcing the Constitution's limits on judicial power.

In 1794, when he was still chief justice, Jay was sent to England to negotiate a treaty designed to ease hostilities between England and the United States. When he returned, Jay learned that he had been elected governor of New York. He resigned from the

Supreme Court to accept the governorship, which he held for two terms, from 1795 to 1801.

In December 1800, President John Adams nominated Jay to serve as chief justice again, and the Senate quickly confirmed him. However, Jay rejected the job. He cited health reasons and his belief that the Court lacked "the energy, weight, and dignity which are essential to its affording due support to the national government." Jay retired from public service in 1801, and for the next twenty-eight years lived on his 800-acre estate in Westchester County, New York, where he died in 1829.

Jefferson, Thomas

Thomas Jefferson (1743–1826) was the author of the Declaration of Independence and a key advocate of adding the BILL OF RIGHTS to the Constitution. His views of popular sovereignty led him to oppose the strengthening of the new national government and to become a staunch defender of states' rights. As president (1801–1809), Jefferson clashed repeatedly with Chief Justice John Marshall and the federal judiciary, which he and his fellow Republicans saw as a Federalist bastion.

As secretary of state under President George Washington, Jefferson argued against creation of the first Bank of the United States. He contended that Congress could enact laws only if they were "indispensable" to carrying out the enumerated powers in the Constitution. Later, in opposing the Alien and Sedition Acts, Jefferson wrote the Kentucky Resolutions, describing any federal acts outside the powers delegated by the states to be "unauthoritative, void and of no force."

As president, Jefferson won the repeal of the Judiciary Act of 1801, which the lame-duck Federalist Congress had passed to expand the size and power of the federal judiciary. Jefferson refused to deliver commissions to four Federalist-appointed judges. His refusal led to the Supreme Court's landmark ruling in *MARBURY V. MADISON* (1803). Jefferson viewed the ruling as an intrusion on presidential prerogatives

even though the Court stopped short of ordering him to deliver the commissions.

Jefferson initiated a successful impeachment proceeding against a federal judge in New Hampshire in 1803 by sending the House of Representatives evidence of the judge's drunken and profane behavior on the bench. A few months later, Jefferson similarly complained to the House about the behavior of Supreme Court justice Samuel Chase. Although Jefferson took no further part in the impeachment proceedings against Chase, the Senate's refusal in 1805 to convict the justice was a political embarrassment for Jefferson. (See IMPEACHMENT OF JUSTICES.)

Jefferson made three appointments to the Supreme Court, two of whom proved to be steadfast supporters of his archenemy, Marshall. Marshall's rulings upholding the second Bank of the United States (*MCCULLOCH V. MARYLAND* [1819]) and striking down a New York steamboat monopoly law (*GIBBONS V. OGDEN* [1824]) angered Jefferson, who warned a friend of the "usurpation of all rights reserved to the states." By the time of Jefferson's death in 1826, it was clear that Marshall's views about the powers of the new government, and not Jefferson's, had prevailed.

Job Discrimination

Employment discrimination—that is, hiring practices that exclude members of certain groups—has been widespread in the United States throughout much of the nation's history. Groups that have been affected by job discrimination include blacks; women; religious minorities, such as Catholics and Jews; ethnic minorities, such as Asian-Americans and Hispanics; persons of middle age or older; and the disabled.

Until the mid-twentieth century, someone who had been denied a job or had been fired from a job on the basis of factors such as race, gender, religion, ethnic origin, age, or disability had little, if any, legal recourse. Beginning in 1964, however, Congress enacted an array of CIVIL RIGHTS statutes that prohibit discrimination in employment on the basis of race or color, sex, religion, national origin, age, or disability.

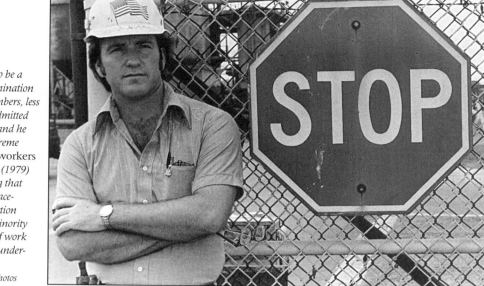

Brian Weber claimed to be a victim of reverse discrimination when black union members, less senior than he, were admitted to a training program and he was excluded. The Supreme Court in United Steelworkers of America v. Weber *(1979) denied his claim, saying that employers may adopt race-conscious affirmative action programs to increase minority participation in areas of work where they have been under-represented.*
Source: AP/Wide World Photos

The Supreme Court has upheld these statutes and for the most part has construed them broadly. When the Court in 1989 issued several restrictive rulings on technical aspects of the laws, Congress responded by passing laws countering the decisions. (See REVERSALS OF RULINGS BY LEGISLATION.)

Early Rulings

Civil war and emancipation did little to free blacks from job discrimination. Most of the southern states enacted so-called Black Codes restricting the kinds of jobs blacks could hold. Women were also barred by law from some jobs and professions, and by custom from many others. (See SEX DISCRIMINATION.) Many private employers had discriminatory hiring practices; some labor unions limited membership to whites.

The Supreme Court's first modern rulings on employment discrimination came in cases brought by blacks under federal labor laws. In 1944 the Court interpreted federal labor law to require unions to represent all employees fairly "without hostile discrimination" against any of them. The case, *Steele v. Louisville and Nashville Railroad Co.,* involved an all-white union

that had agreed with the railroad to end employment of blacks as firemen.

In 1945, in another case involving discrimination by labor unions, the Court upheld the validity of New York state's fair employment law, one of the first such laws to be enacted. A union that limited its membership to whites and Native Americans claimed that the law violated its constitutional rights, but the Court rejected the argument.

Ruling on another state law concerning fair employment—this one from Colorado—the Court in 1963 rejected a state trial court's conclusion that such laws unduly burdened interstate commerce.

Civil Rights Laws

The following year, Congress approved the first federal law prohibiting job discrimination. Title VII of the Civil Rights Act of 1964 prohibited employers of more than twenty-five workers and unions representing more than that number, union hiring halls, and employment agencies from discriminating on the grounds of race, color, religion, sex, or national origin in their hiring, classification, training, or promotion. In 1972 Congress extended coverage to employers and unions with fifteen or more employees or members, state and local governments, and educational institutions.

In its first full discussion of the scope of Title VII, the Court gave a broad reading to the act. *Griggs v. Duke Power Co.* (1971) involved a complaint by blacks that the North Carolina power company had unfairly discriminated when it required them to have a high school diploma or pass a general intelligence test as a condition for employment or promotion. They claimed that neither requirement was related to successful job performance and that the requirements disqualified a substantially higher number of blacks than whites.

By an 8–0 vote the Court agreed. Writing for the Court, Chief Justice Warren E. Burger said the law required "the removal of artificial, arbitrary, and unnecessary barriers to employment when the barriers operate invidiously to discriminate on the basis of racial or other impermissible classification." Four years later the Court reaffirmed its view that tests were discriminatory if they excluded more blacks than whites and were not proven to be job-related.

Also in 1975 the Court handed down the first of several rulings that upheld the broad authority of lower federal courts under Title VII to award back wages, retirement benefits, or retroactive seniority to victims of illegal job discrimination. In *Albemarle Paper Co. v. Moody* the Court ruled, 7–1, that back pay was a proper, and preferred, remedy for past job discrimination even if the discriminatory practices had ended. Without the threat of back pay awards, the Court said, employers "would have little incentive to shun practices of dubious legality."

The next year the Court upheld, 5–3, the authority of federal courts to award retroactive seniority rights to persons denied employment or promotion by biased policies. Such awards fulfill the "make-whole" purposes of Title VII, the Court said in *Franks v. Bowman Transportation Co.* (1976). Also in 1976 the Court upheld the award of retroactive retirement benefits to male employees of the state of Connecticut who had been required to work longer than women employees before they could retire.

In 1979 the Court ruled that Title VII did not bar an employer from voluntarily establishing an AFFIR-MATIVE ACTION training program that preferred blacks over whites.

In the 1980s the Court began to shift away from its liberal reading of job discrimination laws. That shift led to a series of restrictive decisions in 1989. In the most important of the cases, the Court backed away from *Griggs* by ruling, 5–4, that plaintiffs in an employment discrimination suit must show more than statistical disparities to make out a case. The decision in *Wards Cove Packing Co. v. Atonio* became a major focus of debate. In October 1991 Congress passed and President George Bush signed a law that overturned the ruling and eight other decisions between 1986 and 1991 that had made it harder for plaintiffs to win employment discrimination cases.

Johnson, Thomas

When President George Washington in November 1791 nominated Thomas Johnson (1732–1819) to be

Source: Collection of the Supreme Court of the United States

a Supreme Court justice, Johnson was hesitant to accept the position because of the hardships of CIRCUIT RIDING. Chief Justice John Jay assured him that efforts would be made to lessen the burden. Johnson accepted the appointment, only to be assigned to the large southern circuit, which included all the territory south of the Potomac River. He appealed to Jay for relief, but the chief justice declined to rotate assignments. Johnson endured the rigors of riding circuit for a little more than a year before resigning from the Court, citing health problems. He wrote only one opinion as a justice.

Before his appointment to the Court, Johnson was a military commander and Maryland statesman. Born in Calvert County, Maryland, Johnson was educated at home. He studied law in the office of an Annapolis attorney and was admitted to the bar in 1760. During the first Continental Congress in Philadelphia, Johnson served on the committee that wrote a petition of grievances to present to King George III.

Johnson developed his military skills during the Revolution, serving as first brigadier-general of the Maryland militia. In 1777 Johnson led nearly 2,000 soldiers from Frederick County, Maryland, to General Washington's headquarters in New Jersey. That same year, Johnson became Maryland's first governor. In that post Johnson worked hard to keep Washington's army supplied with men and equipment.

After serving as a Supreme Court justice from November 1791 to February 1793, Johnson was appointed by President Washington to serve on the commission that planned the city that became Washington, D.C. Washington tried to appoint Johnson secretary of state in 1795, but Johnson declined the offer. He retired from public life and died in 1819 at age eighty-six.

Source: Collection of the Supreme Court of the United States

Johnson, William

During his first twenty-five years as an associate justice, William Johnson (1771–1834) was the most independent member of the Marshall Court. Johnson has been called "the first great Court dissenter"; he is credited with creating a tradition of dissenting opinions.

Johnson was born in Charleston, South Carolina. During his childhood, his family was forced to leave its home when the British captured Charleston and his father, a revolutionary patriot, was imprisoned in Florida. The family was reunited after several months and returned to South Carolina.

After graduating at the top of his Princeton class in 1790, Johnson returned to Charleston to begin reading law. He was admitted to the bar in 1793. A year later, he began serving in the South Carolina house of representatives, rising to the position of Speaker by 1798. In 1799 Johnson was selected as one of three judges to sit on South Carolina's court of common pleas, the state's highest court.

In 1804 President Thomas Jefferson tapped Johnson to be his first Republican nominee to the Supreme Court. Johnson wasn't thrilled with the job. He once wrote Jefferson that the Court was no "bed of roses," and in his early days on the bench he tried to get himself appointed to another job. Nonetheless, he served on the Court for thirty years until his death in 1834.

Johnson wrote nearly half of the seventy dissenting opinions issued during his tenure on the Court. His tradition of dissenting did not win him friends among his fellow justices. In a letter to Jefferson dated December 10, 1822, Johnson wrote: "Some Case soon occurred in which I differed from my Brethren, and I felt it a thing of Course to deliver my Opinion. But, during the rest of the Session, I heard nothing but lectures on the Indecency of Judges cutting at each other."

Judgment of the Court

The judgment of the court is the official decision of a court based on the rights and claims of the parties to a case that was submitted for determination.

In rendering its judgment, the Supreme Court may uphold the decision made in the lower court. It may modify that decision, or it may reverse the decision altogether. Finally, it may vacate, or void, the lower court decision. If the Court modifies, reverses, or vacates the decision, it may remand, or send back, the case to the lower court for reconsideration. The Court's opinion gives guidance to the lower court on the principles of law it should consider. (See OPINIONS.)

Judicial Activism

Judicial activism is a judicial philosophy characterized by expansive use of the powers of a court to lower the procedural requirements for deciding a case or to broadly construe a court's substantive authority to impose a decision on other branches of government.

Unlike its opposite, JUDICIAL RESTRAINT, judicial activism is rarely defended as such by those who are said to practice it. Instead, the term is used primarily by critics. Judges who are viewed as judicial activists usually say they are strictly enforcing legal or constitutional rights through a proper use of the power of JUDICIAL REVIEW.

Judicial activism is not tied to a particular political or legal philosophy or ideology.

During the late nineteenth and early twentieth centuries, the Supreme Court vigorously used its powers—overturning precedent, declaring laws unconstitutional, and narrowing barriers to judicial decision making—to protect property rights. Under Chief Justice Earl Warren, the Court in the 1950s and 1960s was equally vigorous in using its powers to expand individual rights.

Under Warren's successor, Warren E. Burger, the Court in the 1970s and 1980s was described by its critics as practicing "rootless activism." It continued to overturn prior rulings and throw out legislation, but the decisions sometimes expanded and sometimes restricted individual rights. Chief Justice William H. Rehnquist, who succeeded Burger in 1986, has advocated judicial restraint in terms of deferring to the political branches of government, but he has also called for a greater willingness to overturn precedent—a viewpoint usually associated with judicial activism.

Procedural Activism

Procedurally, judicial activism means disregarding the doctrines of judicial restraint that call for courts to refrain from deciding cases if they do not meet certain requirements and to avoid ruling on constitutional issues unless absolutely necessary to a decision in the case.

The Court's landmark ruling in *MARBURY V. MADISON* (1803) has been described as an extreme example of procedural activism. The act of Congress that the Court declared unconstitutional in that case could have been construed narrowly to avoid the constitutional issue, and the rest of Chief Justice John Marshall's opinion amounts to dicta—that is, comments unnecessary to the decision. Similarly, the Court could have decided the Dred Scott case (*Scott v. Sandford* [1857]) by dismissing the suit on narrow grounds without ruling on Congress's power to bar slavery in the territories or on the issue of citizenship for blacks.

In other examples of procedural activism, the Court has often set aside the rule against deciding "collusive suits"—most famously, in the 1895 decision striking down the federal INCOME TAX. (See TEST CASE.) It has also overridden concerns about MOOTNESS to rule on cases, such as the 1973 abortion rights decision, *Roe v. Wade*. In the 1960s the Court substantially narrowed the POLITICAL QUESTION doctrine, which considered certain types of political disputes to be beyond the courts' power to decide.

Substantive Activism

In substantive terms, judicial activism is seen in a court's willingness to rule acts of Congress or state laws unconstitutional and to strictly enforce constitutional rights, particularly the provisions of the BILL OF RIGHTS and the DUE PROCESS and EQUAL PROTECTION clauses of the Fourteenth Amendment.

The Supreme Court's record does not suggest reckless activism in striking down federal laws. In two centuries it has ruled 128 acts of Congress unconstitutional. In the same time the Court has struck down more than 1,200 state laws and local ordinances—a much larger number that reflects its role in establishing the supremacy of federal law and the federal Constitution.

The pace of such rulings, however, has increased sharply since the Civil War. Just two acts of Congress and fewer than forty state and local laws were ruled unconstitutional before 1861. Beginning in the mid-1880s, the Court used the due process clause and a narrow conception of Congress's commerce power to strike down federal and state laws regulating economic conduct.

Since 1937 the Court has engaged in judicial activism more frequently in support of individual rights. The Court signaled this change of philosophy in a famous footnote—"Footnote Four"—in *United States v. Carolene Products Co.* (1938). The Court announced in the body of the decision that it would uphold economic regulation as long as the regulation had a rational basis, but in the footnote Justice Harlan Fiske Stone suggested the need for stricter review of laws that abridged constitutional rights, interfered with access to the political process, or adversely affected "discrete and insular minorities."

Although tentatively phrased, the footnote has been cited by the Court innumerable times since then in support of active intervention in defense of individual rights. Justice Lewis F. Powell, Jr., once called it "perhaps the most far-sighted dictum in our modern judicial heritage."

Federal courts' enforcement of these rights since the 1960s, especially in CIVIL RIGHTS cases, has brought stronger accusations of improper judicial activism. Courts have imposed more detailed requirements on state and local officials in such areas as school desegregation, prisoners' rights, and conditions in state mental hospitals. Despite the criticisms, the Supreme Court has generally upheld the courts' powers in such cases. (See COURTS, POWERS OF.)

Judicial Conference, U.S.

The Judicial Conference of the United States is the body that makes policy for administering the federal judicial system. In effect, it serves as the system's board of trustees or board of directors.

By law, the Conference is charged with conducting "a continuous study of . . . the general rules of [judicial] practice and procedure" and recommending "such changes in and addition to those rules as the Conference may deem desirable to promote simplicity in procedure, fairness in administration, the just determination of litigation, and the elimination of unjustifiable expense and delay."

To carry out that mandate, the Conference has committees on the ADMINISTRATIVE OFFICE OF THE U.S. COURTS, budget, codes of conduct, court security, criminal law and probation, defender services, federal-state jurisdiction, ethics, judicial improvements, judicial resources, rules of practice and procedure, and space and facilities, among others. It also approves the budget requests for the federal district and circuit courts that are submitted to Congress each year. (See COURTS, LOWER.)

Congress created the Judicial Conference in 1922 at the urging of Chief Justice William Howard Taft. It was then called the Judicial Conference of Senior Circuit Judges and was composed of the chief justice of the Supreme Court, the chief judges of the nine circuit courts of appeal, and the attorney general, who was then responsible for the administrative affairs of the courts.

Until 1940 the reports of the Conference were included in the annual reports of the attorney general. When the Administrative Office of the U.S. Courts was created in 1939, administrative responsibility for the courts was transferred to it. The Administrative Office has operated under the supervision and direction of the Judicial Conference ever since.

The chief justice is the presiding officer of the Conference. The number of members has more than doubled since 1922. In the 1950s a district court judge representing each regional circuit joined the Judicial Conference. In late 1986 the chief judge of the U.S. Court of International Trade was added.

The conference has no separate budget of its own. Whatever staff assistance is needed is provided by the Administrative Office of the U.S. Courts.

Judicial Power

See COURTS, POWERS OF.

Judicial Restraint

Judicial restraint is a judicial philosophy of refraining from exercising the potential powers of a court either by strictly defining the procedural requirements for judicial action or by narrowly defining the substantive basis for JUDICIAL REVIEW of the conduct of other branches of government. It stands in contrast to the philosophy of JUDICIAL ACTIVISM.

The Supreme Court has emphasized the need for judicial restraint throughout its history, even on some occasions when its actions appeared to amount to judicial activism instead. It has made this philosophy concrete through a host of legal doctrines, derived both from constitutional limitations on JURISDICTION and from self-imposed constraints. (See CASE OR CONTROVERSY RULE; COMITY; JUSTICIABILITY; MOOTNESS; POLITICAL QUESTION; PRECEDENT; RIPENESS; STANDING TO SUE; TEST CASE.)

In addition, the Court has developed discretionary rules that limit the use of its power to declare unconstitutional laws passed by Congress or by the states. Justice Louis D. Brandeis summarized some of these rules in an influential concurring opinion in *Ashwander v. Tennessee Valley Authority* (1936). Brandeis said the Court avoided deciding many constitutional questions by adhering to certain rules:

It would not consider the constitutionality of legislation in friendly, nonadversary cases.

It would not decide any constitutional question unless a decision on the matter was "absolutely necessary."

It would not set out a constitutional rule broader than warranted by the facts in the specific case before it.

It would resolve a dispute on a nonconstitutional basis rather than on a constitutional basis, if possible.

It would not consider a challenge to a law's validity except by someone who could show that he or she was actually injured by the operation of the law. This rule bars a constitutional challenge by a public official "interested only in the performance of his official duty."

It would not consider a challenge to the constitutionality of a law by someone who had benefited from the law.

It would construe a congressional statute so as to avoid a ruling of unconstitutionality if at all possible, "even if a serious doubt of constitutionality is raised."

These rules reflect a blend of constitutional elements, policy considerations, and political reality. Their application varies from case to case and time to time, depending on the vote of the majority of the justices. Even if an individual justice has a consistent philosophy toward the use of judicial power, the changing composition of the Court means that the rules may be followed strictly at times and less so at others. Thus, there have been major decisions of the Court that count as exceptions to each one of Brandeis's rules—as well as to other rules that he did not mention.

The distinction between procedural and substantive restraint may explain some apparent inconsistencies in the attitudes of individual justices. An "activist" justice, for example, may take a broad view of the Court's responsibility to enforce constitutional provisions, but the same justice may follow the rules for procedural restraint quite strictly. An advocate of judicial restraint may on occasion set aside some of the doctrines of procedural restraint, but that same justice may take a narrower view of the Court's substantive power with regard to the other branches of government.

An example of this distinction is the Supreme Court's decision in *Payne v. Tennessee* (1991), overturning a four-year-old precedent barring the use of so-called victim impact statements in capital punishment cases. The decision was announced by Chief Justice William H. Rehnquist, who is viewed as an advocate of judicial restraint. The ruling reflected a narrow view of the substantive constitutional requirements for a fair trial in death penalty cases. But Rehnquist used the case to set forth a less restrictive test for overturning prior decisions, especially in cases affecting individual rights.

In an especially sharp dissent, Justice Thurgood Marshall, who is considered an activist justice, denounced what he called "this radical new exception to the doctrine of stare decisis." (See STARE DECISIS.) Four decades earlier, Marshall had persuaded the Court that a one hundred-year-old precedent—the "separate but equal" doctrine—was unconstitutional. The result was the landmark decision in *Brown v. Board of Education of Topeka* (1954).

Judicial Review

Judicial review is the power of courts to measure the acts of Congress, the actions of the executive, and the laws and practices of the states against the Constitution and to invalidate those that conflict with its provisions. This power, especially as applied to overturning an act of Congress, is recognized as the most distinctive contribution of the United States to constitutional government. But it is also often criticized as an interference with majority rule and with the authority of the legislative and executive branches.

The Constitution does not mention judicial review,

but two sections give some textual basis for the power. Article III, Section 2 states, "The judicial Power shall extend to all Cases . . . arising under this Constitution." And the SUPREMACY CLAUSE provides that the Constitution "and the Laws of the United States which shall be made in pursuance thereof . . . shall be the supreme Law of the Land" (Article VI, Section 2).

Judicial review is firmly established as one of the major self-control mechanisms of the American system of government. Use of this power by the Supreme Court and lower federal courts has often had enormous impact on American law, politics, and society.

Like the other powers in the Constitution, judicial review is a limited power. Judicial review does not permit the courts to second-guess the wisdom of legislative or executive branch decisions; the courts can only decide on the legality of the decisions. The federal judiciary does not review a state court's interpretation of its own state law. In addition, the Supreme Court has developed doctrines of JUDICIAL RESTRAINT that limit the exercise of its review power. By deciding which cases it will and will not review, the Court for the most part can set its own agenda, choosing the best time and best case to decide an issue and sometimes deliberately leaving important issues undecided for legal or political reasons.

Early Development

The Constitutional Convention apparently did not discuss judicial review. The convention did, however, consider and reject a proposal by James Madison that would have lodged the veto power in a council composed of members of the executive and judicial branches. In the debate on this proposal, some delegates expressed their belief that "the Judges in their proper official character . . . have a negative on the laws" and so should not be given the chance to impose "a double negative."

Alexander Hamilton set forth the argument for judicial review during the debate on ratification of the Constitution. In *The Federalist Papers*, No. 78, Hamilton rejected the idea that the legislative body could be "the constitutional judge of their own powers." Instead, he said, it was "far more rational to suppose that the courts were designed to be an intermediate

Hylton v. United States *(1796) was the first case that challenged the validity of an act of Congress, a tax on carriages. Neither side questioned the Supreme Court's authority to review the statute, which it upheld.*   Source: Library of Congress

body between the people and the legislature in order, among other things, to keep the latter within the limits assigned to their authority."

When the First Congress passed the Judiciary Act of 1789 establishing the federal judiciary, it specifically gave the Supreme Court the power to review state laws and court rulings. Section 25 of the act granted the Court the power to review and reverse or affirm the final rulings of a state court upholding a state law against a challenge that it was in conflict with the U.S. Constitution, federal laws, or a federal treaty. (See COURTS, POWERS OF.)

The act made no mention of the Supreme Court's power to review acts of Congress. But when the first case challenging the validity of an act of Congress came to the Supreme Court in 1796, both sides in the matter simply assumed that the Court had the power to strike down the act. The Court upheld the statute, which involved a tax on carriages.

Seven years later, in the landmark case of *MARBURY V. MADISON* (1803), the Court for the first time

did declare unconstitutional a provision of an act of Congress. The case arose from a political battle over federal judgeships and pitted President Thomas Jefferson, a Republican, against a committed Federalist, Chief Justice John Marshall. The case was filed in the Supreme Court under Section 13 of the Judiciary Act of 1789, which authorized the Court to issue a judicial order called a "writ of MANDAMUS" to "any courts or persons holding office, under the authority of the United States."

Marshall's opinion in the case established the principle of judicial review over actions of the executive branch and over acts of Congress. He determined that Jefferson's secretary of state, James Madison, had wrongfully withheld judicial commissions from four Federalist-appointed justices of the peace for the District of Columbia. But Marshall did not order Madison to deliver the commissions, on the ground that Congress had enlarged the Court's power beyond the provisions of Article III of the Constitution. With two exceptions, that article limited the Court's jurisdiction to handling appeals rather than cases brought before it directly. (See ORIGINAL JURISDICTION.)

Marshall's reasoning was less than clear, but his language was forceful and his final conclusion unmistakable. "It is emphatically the province and duty of the judicial department to say what the law is," Marshall wrote. Unless the courts had the power to "disregard" a law contrary to the Constitution, he continued, Congress would be given "a practical and real omnipotence" and the Constitution would be "reduced to nothing."

States' Rights

With *Marbury v. Madison* the Supreme Court became the effective instrument for enforcing the supremacy of the U.S. Constitution. During Marshall's thirty-four years as chief justice, the Court used this power not to thwart Congress but to enhance national power by striking down state laws and upholding acts of Congress challenged as infringing upon states' rights. (See STATES AND THE COURT.)

The Court first struck down a state law in 1796; the case involved a Virginia statute that limited the ability of British creditors to collect money owed by Virginia debtors. The Court's decision in *Ware v. Hyl-ton* invalidated the state law because it conflicted with the peace treaty with Britain after the Revolutionary War, which prohibited either country from establishing legal obstacles to the recovery of debts owed by its citizens to those of the other nation.

In 1816 and 1821 the Supreme Court struck down state laws in two more cases from Virginia that rejected challenges to the Court's authority to review state court rulings. The disputes involved seemingly minor issues: title to a piece of property confiscated during the Revolutionary War from a British landowner, and a conflict between a federally authorized lottery and the state's antilottery statute. But the Supreme Court decisions were important because they upheld the Court's power, under Section 25 of the Judiciary Act of 1789, to review state court rulings. The Court said such review was consistent with the Constitution and necessary to ensure the supremacy and uniformity of federal law.

The power of judicial review was most forcefully reaffirmed in the landmark case of *MCCULLOCH V. MARYLAND* (1819). The issue was Congress's chartering of the second national bank, which many states opposed. Maryland imposed a hefty tax on the bank, and the bank's Baltimore cashier, James McCulloch,

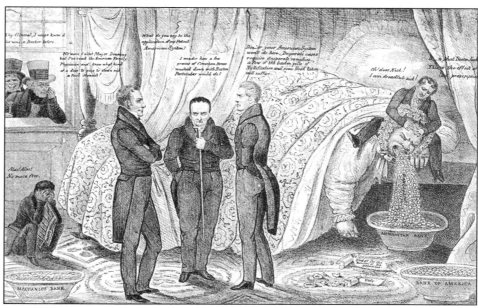

In September 1833 President Andrew Jackson ordered federal funds withdrawn from the United States Bank and distributed among state banks. Although in McCulloch v. Maryland *(1819) the Supreme Court had upheld Congress's power to establish a national bank, Jackson carried on a relentless campaign to undermine it, as shown in this cartoon of "Mother Bank."*
Source: *Library of Congress*

challenged the tax in court as an unconstitutional infringement on the bank's operations. The Supreme Court upheld Congress's power to establish the bank and then struck down the Maryland tax as an interference with the supremacy of federal law. Marshall's opinion in the case established that the Supreme Court, not the states, would determine the scope of the national government's power.

Reaction and Resistance

The Supreme Court's use of its power of judicial review stirred controversy and opposition. Critics offered several proposals to limit the Court's power, but none was enacted by Congress before the Civil War. Immediately after the Civil War, however, Congress did act to limit the Court's power of judicial review by exercising its own power under the Constitution to make "exceptions" to the Court's appellate jurisdiction (Article III, Section 2). The Court bowed to Congress in the dispute, but over the next several decades it became more assertive in challenging Congress.

By 1825 the Supreme Court had nullified as unconstitutional at least one law from each of ten states. In response, critics considered repealing Section 25 of the Judiciary Act of 1789, amending the Constitution to have the Senate rather than the Court review all cases involving a state, or passing a law to require that five—or all seven—justices concur before a state law was held invalid.

Jefferson, who had criticized several of the Court's decisions while serving as president and after leaving the White House, proposed the impeachment of justices to limit the Court's power. He urged that Congress require each justice to write an individual opinion in each case, denounce the views of those with whom it disagreed, and then impeach any justice who did not change his views.

None of these proposals was approved by both chambers of Congress. By the time of Marshall's death in 1835, the Court's power, while still controversial, seemed firmly established.

Under Marshall's successor, Chief Justice Roger B. Taney, the Court seemed more supportive of states' rights. That philosophy was reflected in the Taney Court's most famous decision, the ruling in the Dred Scott case *(Scott v. Sandford* [1857]) that Congress had

no power to prohibit slavery in the states or territories. But the Taney Court also preserved the federal courts' power against that of the states. In 1842 the Court held that federal courts were not bound by state judges' interpretations of state laws. And in 1859 it ruled that state judges had no power to interfere with federal judicial proceedings.

The aftermath of the Civil War resulted in the first successful challenge to the Court's power of judicial review. The issue was the constitutionality of the Reconstruction Act of 1867, which established military rule in the ten southern states that initially refused to rejoin the Union. A Mississippi newspaper editor, William McCardle, forced the issue before the Court when he challenged his detention by a military tribunal for editorials he had written that were harshly critical of the Reconstruction. McCardle sought a writ of HABEAS CORPUS ordering his release and, when a federal circuit court denied the writ, appealed the case to the Supreme Court.

Ironically, Congress had given the Supreme Court authority to hear appeals in habeas corpus cases in February 1867 in order to protect blacks and federal officials in the South from harassment by white southerners. McCardle's appeal generated rumors that the Court would use the case to declare the Reconstruction Act unconstitutional. Congress responded with a law—passed over President Andrew Johnson's veto and after argument in McCardle's case before the Court—stripping the Court of the power to hear habeas corpus cases, including any pending cases.

After postponing a final decision in the case to consider the effect of the repeal statute, the Court in April 1869 issued a unanimous decision upholding the law and dismissing the case for lack of jurisdiction. "We are not at liberty to inquire into the motive of the legislature," Chief Justice Salmon P. Chase wrote in *Ex parte McCardle*. "We can only examine into its power under the Constitution, and the power to make exceptions to the appellate jurisdiction of this Court is given by express words."

The Court confronted the issue again in 1869 when another Mississippi newspaper editor, Edward M. Yerger, applied directly to the Supreme Court for a writ of habeas corpus. The Court agreed to hear the

In Lochner v. New York *(1905) the Court struck down a law setting maximum work hours for bakers as a violation of the contract clause. This decision was the first of many that overturned legislation that aimed to control the nation's economy and improve living standards for workers.*
Source: Dante Tranquille

case, holding that Section 14 of the Judiciary Act of 1789 gave it original jurisdiction in habeas corpus cases. Bills were promptly introduced in Congress to bar any Supreme Court jurisdiction over habeas corpus matters until Reconstruction was completed. But the bills died after Yerger's lawyers and the attorney general agreed on a compromise. In 1885, with Reconstruction over, Congress repealed the limitation on the Supreme Court's habeas corpus jurisdiction.

The Court's Second Century

In its second century the Supreme Court began to use its power of judicial review more often to overturn acts of Congress and decisions of state legislatures. Critics, both on and off the bench, charged that the Court was acting as a superlegislature. The Court's judicial review power remained intact, but its use of the power changed in response to political circumstances—in particular, the changing composition of the Court itself.

From the 1890s to the mid-1930s, the Court often used its power to overturn social and economic legislation. The period is sometimes called the *Lochner* era after the decision (*Lochner v. New York* [1905]) that struck down a New York law setting maximum hours for bakers, on the grounds that it was an unconstitu-

tional infringement of freedom of contract. During the 1920s the Court struck down some twenty federal laws—more than in the previous half century. In the 1930s the Court issued a dozen decisions within a three-year period striking down parts of President Franklin D. Roosevelt's New Deal program.

Justices in the minority in these decisions criticized them in dissenting opinions. Writing in the *Lochner* case, for example, Justice John Marshall Harlan said the Court had gone beyond its legitimate power. "Under our system of government," Harlan wrote, "the courts are not concerned with the wisdom or policy of legislation." Three decades later Justice Harlan Fiske Stone similarly criticized the Court's decision to strike down the Agricultural Adjustment Act. "For the removal of unwise laws from the statute books," Stone wrote, "appeal lies not to the courts but to the ballot and to the processes of democratic government."

In his infamous "Court-packing" plan of 1937, Roosevelt sought to restore his legislative agenda not by curbing the Court's formal power but by enlarging the Court so that he could make new appointments to change its ideological composition. The defeat of Roosevelt's plan resulted from a vigorous defense of the Court's independence in Congress and across the nation. (See SIZE OF THE COURT.) Over the next four years, however, Roosevelt was able to make seven appointments to the Court as individual justices retired. The reconstituted Court sustained New Deal programs and began to exercise the power of judicial review more often in the area of CIVIL LIBERTIES and CIVIL RIGHTS.

That trend accelerated under Chief Justice Earl Warren in the 1950s and 1960s, and resulted in challenges to the Court's power in Congress and in the states. The Court's historic school desegregation decision, *BROWN V. BOARD OF EDUCATION OF TOPEKA* (1954), was met by massive resistance in the South. Southern members of Congress encouraged defiance of the ruling, and several states enacted "interposition" statutes declaring the *Brown* decision of no effect. In response, the Court in 1958 issued an opinion—personally signed by each of the nine justices—describing the *Brown* decision as "the supreme law of the land" and "binding" on every state legislator, executive official, and judge.

During the same period the Court issued several rulings restricting antisubversive legislation passed by Congress or the states and limiting congressional internal security investigations. Legislation introduced in the Senate in 1957 sought to bar the Court from accepting appeals in these areas. Even many critics of the Court's rulings thought that removing the Court's jurisdiction was too drastic, so the bill was changed to leave the Court's power essentially intact while attempting to overturn the specific decisions. The revised bill was killed by a 49–41 vote in August 1958.

A pair of Warren Court rulings in 1962 and 1963 that prohibited organized prayer or Bible reading in public schools also provoked efforts in Congress to overturn the decisions by constitutional amendment or, as an alternative, to limit the federal courts' power to hear school prayer cases. Court-stripping bills reached the Senate floor four times between 1976 and 1985 but won majority support only once, in 1979. The measure died that year. The 1985 proposal was defeated, 62–36, after opponents claimed that it represented an unconstitutional exercise of congressional authority.

An Enduring Power

Although controversies have surrounded the Court's use of judicial review, the underlying power endures. In fact, the power of judicial review has not been seriously endangered at any time in the nation's history.

The Court dramatically reaffirmed the power with its 1974 decision in the case involving the Watergate tapes. By ordering President Richard Nixon to turn over tapes of presidential conversations concerning the Watergate break-in and cover-up, the Court demonstrated that the power of judicial review extends even into the Oval Office. Nixon's decision to accept the Court's ruling and turn over the tapes that forced him to resign his office showed that even the president could not set himself against the Court's power.

Congress too has been unwilling—with one exception after the Civil War—to directly challenge the Court's power of judicial review. The failure of Court-limiting proposals actually serves not to weaken the Court's power but to strengthen it. Each time Congress tries to curb the Court and fails, the failure strengthens the public perception that the Court is an unassailable institution and that its decisions, except in extreme circumstances, are final.

Juries

Trial by jury has been a central part of the Anglo-American system of justice as far back as the thirteenth century. The Constitution requires jury TRIALS for "all Crimes except in Cases of Impeachment" (Article III, Section 2). The Bill of Rights includes additional guarantees. The Fifth Amendment requires INDICTMENT by a GRAND JURY for any capital or "infamous" crime. The Sixth Amendment requires trial "in all criminal prosecutions" by "an impartial jury" chosen from the state or district where the offense is alleged to have occurred. The Seventh Amendment requires jury trials in common-law civil suits involving more than twenty dollars.

Most states included similar jury trial protections in their own constitutions, but they varied in details and in judicial interpretations. Only in 1968 did the Supreme Court apply the Sixth Amendment to the states and require jury trials for serious criminal cases. The Court has not required the states to guarantee indictment by grand jury or to provide jury trials in civil cases or in juvenile delinquency proceedings. In criminal cases, the Court has allowed the states to use six-person juries in noncapital cases and to permit nonunanimous verdicts by twelve-person juries.

In federal cases, the jury trial requirement has never extended to petty offenses. Federal law now specifies that no jury is required for offenses punishable by six months' imprisonment or less and fines of $500 or less. The Court has assumed the necessity of twelve-member juries and unanimous verdicts in federal criminal cases, though it has permitted six-person juries in civil cases. The scope of the jury trial requirement in civil cases has posed difficulties for the Court as Congress has created new statutory causes of action. Jury trials have been required in cases that are considered analogous to suits recognized in COMMON LAW, but not for other causes of action.

Criminal Cases

Since the Court originally held that the Bill of Rights did not apply to the states, the question of requiring the states to provide jury trials first arose under the post–Civil War Fourteenth Amendment. In 1876 the Court held that the Seventh Amendment right to jury trial in civil cases was not a privilege or immunity of federal citizenship protected against state action. Then, in *Maxwell v. Dow* (1900), the Court held that neither the privileges or immunities clause nor the due process clause of the Fourteenth Amendment required state juries to consist of twelve persons. "Trial by jury has never been affirmed to be a necessary requisite of due process of law," the Court said as it upheld Utah's use of an eight-person jury.

The Court reversed itself in 1968, near the end of the Warren Court's process of applying the provisions of the Bill of Rights to the states. (See INCORPORATION DOCTRINE.) In *Duncan v. Louisiana* the Court held, 7–2, that a Louisiana man had been denied due process of law when he was convicted of battery and sentenced to two years in prison without a jury trial. Calling trial by jury "fundamental to the American scheme of justice," the Court required states to provide jury trials "in all criminal cases which—were they to be tried in a federal court—would come within the Sixth Amendment's guarantee." Ten years later the Court specified that the right to a jury trial extended to any charges punishable by more than six months in prison.

The twelve-person jury and unanimous verdict had been features of the jury system since fourteenth-century England. But in applying the Sixth Amendment to the states, the Court decided that neither of those features was constitutionally mandated in state courts.

In *Williams v. Florida* (1970) the Court upheld the use of six-person juries in noncapital cases, saying that the twelve-person requirement was "not an indispensable component of the Sixth Amendment." Justice Thurgood Marshall was the sole dissenter on the point.

Eight years later, however, the Court unanimously rejected Georgia's use of a five-person jury in misdemeanor cases. The justices offered various rationales, but Justice Lewis F. Powell, Jr., explained the decision most succinctly. "A line has to be drawn somewhere if the substance of jury trial is to be preserved," he wrote.

The Court followed a similar path on the issue of jury unanimity. In 1972 it upheld the use of nonunanimous verdicts in two cases: 11–1 and 10–2 verdicts in *Apodaca v. Oregon*, and 9–3 verdicts in *Johnson v. Louisiana*. Justice Byron R. White was the Court's spokesperson on the issue, concluding that verdicts by "substantial majorities" did not violate due process or the standard of reasonable doubt.

The vote in both *Apodaca* and *Johnson* was 5–4. In *Apodaca* White would also have held nonunanimous verdicts permissible under the Sixth Amendment—opening the way for their possible use in federal courts. But Powell joined the four dissenters on that point to preserve unanimous verdicts in federal cases.

Seven years later the Court dealt with what it called the "intersection" of the two modifications it had allowed, by prohibiting the use of nonunanimous verdicts by a jury of fewer than twelve persons. "Lines must be drawn somewhere," the Court said in *Burch v. Louisiana* (1979).

Civil Cases

The Seventh Amendment provides that the right to jury trial in "Suits at common law" involving more than twenty dollars "shall be preserved." The Court has tried to adhere to the distinction between actions in law (suits for money damages) and actions in equity (suits seeking injunctive relief) in deciding whether jury trials are required in federal courts. But the distinction is sometimes difficult to draw. The Court in 1916 refused to apply the Seventh Amendment to the states and has made no move to reconsider that decision.

In creating new statutory causes of action, Congress sometimes has provided for monetary awards to be determined by administrative agencies or by judges rather than by juries. In 1937 the Court upheld the National Labor Relations Board's power to award back pay despite the similarity to a contract action in common law. In 1977 the Court extended this ruling to permit a government agency to recover a civil penalty in a court proceeding with no right to a jury trial *(Atlas Roofing Co. v. Occupational Safety and Health Administration)*.

On the other hand, in two cases in 1974 the Court held that a jury trial was required in a statutory action for eviction and an action under the federal Fair Housing Act of 1968. Both actions, the Court said, resembled suits recognized in common law.

The use of six-person juries in civil cases reached the Court in 1973 after some federal courts had adopted local rules permitting the smaller panels. In *Colgrove v. Battin* the Court upheld the practice by a 5–4 vote. The majority said that the Seventh Amendment did not incorporate "the various incidents of trial by jury." Two justices dissented on constitutional and statutory grounds, two others solely on statutory grounds.

Civil litigation—and the role of the jury in civil cases in particular—emerged as a major legal issue from the 1970s into the 1990s. Critics blamed excessive jury awards for encouraging an explosion of litigation. They sought to control the jury's discretion in awarding damages in various ways, including constitutional attacks on punitive damage awards.

The Court in 1989 rejected one line of argument, holding that the excessive fines clause of the Eighth Amendment did not apply to a punitive damage award in a civil case between private parties. Two years later the Court agreed that the due process clause of the Fourteenth Amendment did set some limits on punitive damage awards. But the 7–1 decision in *Pacific Mutual Life Insurance Co. v. Haslip* (1991) held that juries have broad discretion in awarding punitive damages as long as the awards "are not grossly out of proportion to the severity of the offense and have some understandable relationship to compensatory damages."

An Impartial Jury

Even before the Supreme Court required the states to provide jury trials in criminal cases, it laid down rules that juries must be selected from a representative cross-section of the community. The Court has prohibited the systematic exclusion of racial or ethnic groups from jury pools and overturned laws automatically exempting women from jury duty. Most recently, the Court has forbidden the prosecution or the defense in criminal cases, and both sides in civil trials, to make so-called peremptory challenges of potential jurors on grounds of race.

The Court has also sought ways to ensure an impartial jury in highly publicized criminal cases. But it has ruled that some efforts to control pretrial publicity, such as gag orders or trial closures, violate the right of the press and public to attend and report on trials. (See PRESS, FREEDOM OF.)

In 1880 the Court struck down a West Virginia law that excluded blacks from jury service, on the grounds that it violated the equal protection clause of the Fourteenth Amendment *(Strauder v. West Virginia)*. On the same day, however, the Court rejected an equal protection claim in a Virginia case where blacks had never been called for service on either a grand jury or petit jury. The effect was to allow officials to keep blacks off juries as long as the policies were not officially acknowledged.

This superficial approach prevailed until the

Court's ruling in *Norris v. Alabama* (1935), the second of the *SCOTTSBORO CASES*. Again presented with evidence that no blacks had ever been called for jury service, the Court declared that its responsibility was to ascertain "not merely whether [the equal protection guarantee] was denied in express terms but also whether it was denied in substance and effect." The Court later extended the decision to forbid the systematic exclusion of any substantial racial or ethnic group from jury service *(Hernandez v. Texas* [1954]).

The early West Virginia case had also upheld a state law excluding women from jury duty, and the Court reaffirmed that holding some eighty years later. In *Hoyt v. Florida* (1961) the Court rejected a plea by a Florida woman that the practice of permitting women to claim an automatic exemption from jury service violated the equal protection rights of women defendants. Fourteen years later the Court reversed itself on the issue by an 8–1 vote. "If it ever was the case that women were unqualified to sit on juries or were so situated that none of them could be required to perform jury service, that time has long since passed," the Court declared in *Taylor v. Louisiana* (1975).

The Court has not gone so far as to require that an individual jury reflect any specific racial mix. But in a series of decisions beginning in 1986, the Court has forbidden the parties in criminal or civil trials to use peremptory challenges to exclude potential jurors solely because of their race.

The Court's decision in *Batson v. Kentucky* (1986) held that a prosecutor's use of race-based peremptory challenges was state action that violated the equal protection rights of both the defendant and potential jurors. In 1991 the Court extended the rule to civil cases by a 6–3 vote, reasoning that the statutory provision for peremptory challenges and the judge's role in actually excusing jurors also amounted to state action subject to the equal protection requirement *(Edmonson v. Leesville Concrete Co.)*. That decision opened the way for the Court to rule that a criminal defendant also could not excuse potential jurors solely on the basis of race. The vote in *Georgia v. McCollum* (1992) was 7–2, but Chief Justice William H. Rehnquist and Justice Clarence Thomas said they concurred only because of the 1991 precedent.

In 1994, the Court also ruled, 6–3, that lawyers cannot exclude potential jurors because of their gender *(J.E.B. v. Alabama ex rel. T.E.B.)*. The decision ordered a new trial for a Tennessee man in a paternity suit because the Alabama district attorney had used peremptory challenges to select an all-female jury.

Jurisdiction

Jurisdiction is the power of a court to hear and decide a case based on its authority over the subject matter of the case and the presence of the proper parties in the case.

All federal courts are courts of limited jurisdiction, in contrast to the general jurisdiction held by state court systems. The scope of the federal "judicial power" is defined in Article III, Section 2 of the Constitution. (See LEGAL SYSTEM IN AMERICA.)

Basically, the federal courts' jurisdiction falls into two categories. The first consists of cases that warrant federal consideration because of the subject matter: a claim or question arising under the Constitution, federal statutes or treaties, or admiralty or maritime law. The second category includes cases that warrant federal attention because of the parties involved: the United States, a state, citizens of different states, or representatives of foreign countries.

Article III gives the Supreme Court ORIGINAL JURISDICTION over two types of cases in the second category: cases involving foreign diplomats, and cases involving states. With those exceptions, the Constitution grants Congress the power to determine how much of the broad area outlined in Article III actually comes within the federal courts' jurisdiction.

Initially, in the Judiciary Act of 1789, Congress gave the federal courts limited jurisdiction. Only after passage of the Judiciary Act of 1875 did the federal courts exercise broad "federal question" jurisdiction.

Congress has tried to keep trivial matters out of the federal courts by setting a minimum dollar figure that must be in controversy before most cases can enter the federal judicial system. This "jurisdictional amount" was set at $500 in 1789. It was raised in 1887 ($2,000), 1911 ($3,000), 1958 ($10,000), and 1988 ($50,000, the current level). The requirement affects mostly DIVERSITY JURISDICTION cases (those involving residents of different states) and some federal question cases. Many recent federal statutes specify federal jurisdiction over cases without regard to the amount of money involved.

A Matter of Subject

The Constitution envisioned that federal courts would have the final word on cases raising claims under the Constitution, federal laws, and treaties. But the Judiciary Act of 1789 created a system in which most federal questions were resolved in state courts, subject to review by the Supreme Court if the federal claim was denied. Only after the Reconstruction-era Judiciary Act of 1875 could virtually all cases arising under the Constitution, federal laws, or treaties be initiated in federal courts.

The 1789 act did specify federal jurisdiction over admiralty or maritime matters—an area in which uniformity was seen as vital to trade and commerce. Initially, the Supreme Court narrowly defined the waters covered by this jurisdiction, but it eventually expanded its view to include virtually all navigable and potentially navigable waterways in the nation.

A Question of Party

To preserve national sovereignty, provide a neutral forum, and ensure federal control of foreign relations, the Constitution gave federal courts jurisdiction over cases in which the United States itself was a party, cases between states and between citizens of different states, and cases involving representatives of foreign governments.

In 1793 the Supreme Court followed the literal language of Article III and upheld the right of citizens of one state to sue another state in federal court over the state's objection. The decision in *Chisholm v. Georgia* sparked a firestorm of protest, however, and was overturned by the Eleventh Amendment five years later. (See REVERSALS OF RULINGS BY CONSTITUTIONAL AMENDMENT.)

The federal courts' diversity jurisdiction has also been controversial, but it has proved more durable. Since 1890 efforts have been made to abolish diversity jurisdiction as an anachronism, but Congress has refused.

Supreme Court Jurisdiction

Congress may not expand or curtail the Supreme Court's original jurisdiction, but these cases make up a tiny portion of the caseload of the modern Court. The Court's appellate jurisdiction, however, is subject to "such exceptions and . . . regulations as the Congress shall make."

In the 1789 act, Congress gave the Supreme Court jurisdiction over appeals from the circuit courts in civil cases involving more than $2,000. Not until 1889 did the Court have jurisdiction to hear appeals in criminal cases.

In addition, the 1789 act granted the Supreme Court authority to take appeals from rulings of state high courts that upheld state laws or state actions against challenges that they were in conflict with the U.S. Constitution, federal laws, or treaties. In 1914 this power was expanded to cover state court rulings upholding or denying a federal right or challenge.

Two federal acts—the Circuit Court of Appeals Act of 1891 and the Judiciary Act of 1925—established the jurisdictional rules that currently shape the Supreme Court's workload. The 1891 act created the circuit courts of appeals as intermediate appellate courts between federal district courts and the Supreme Court. (See COURTS, LOWER.) The 1891 law and, most notably, the 1925 act reduced the types of cases that the Court was obliged to hear and expanded its authority to select cases for review under a writ of CERTIORARI.

The Court's MANDATORY JURISDICTION was further curtailed in 1988, giving the justices virtually complete control over the selection of cases on the Court's docket.

Justiciability

Justiciability is the characteristic that makes a case appropriate for judicial decision. The term embraces several doctrines—including MOOTNESS, POLITICAL QUESTION, RIPENESS, and STANDING TO SUE—that the Supreme Court has fashioned out of constitutional limits on the power of the federal courts and self-imposed rules of JUDICIAL RESTRAINT.

Writing in 1937, Chief Justice Charles Evans Hughes said that a justiciable controversy "must be definite and concrete, touching the legal relations of parties having adverse legal interests," and "admitting of specific relief through a decree of a conclusive character." Three decades later Chief Justice Earl Warren gave a similar definition but added that justiciability was "a concept of uncertain meaning and scope."

The Court's decisions show that it has invoked the doctrine inconsistently. For example, in *Poe v. Ullman* (1961) the Court refused to rule on the constitutionality of Connecticut's ban on contraception, describing the case as nonjusticiable because the ban was not being enforced. But in *Epperson v. Arkansas* (1968) the Court did rule on a similarly unenforced state law, this one prohibiting the teaching of evolution in Arkansas schools.

K

Kennedy, Anthony M.

Anthony McLeod Kennedy (1936–) was President Ronald Reagan's third choice for the Supreme Court seat vacated by the retirement of Justice Lewis Powell in 1987.

Reagan first nominated Robert H. Bork, a judge on the Court of Appeals for the District of Columbia Circuit. Known for both his strong conservatism and keen intellect, Bork was severely attacked during his confirmation hearings in the Senate. It did not help Bork that as solicitor general in 1974, he had fired Special Prosecutor Archibald Cox during the Watergate scandal. The Senate rejected Bork's nomination by a 42–58 vote. He thus became the first Supreme Court nominee rejected by the Senate since G. Harrold Carswell in 1970.

Reagan next nominated Douglas H. Ginsburg, one of Bork's colleagues on the court of appeals. The nomination was withdrawn, however, after Ginsburg admitted he had smoked marijuana when he had been a student and professor at Harvard Law School. Reagan finally turned to Kennedy, a judge on the U.S. Court of Appeals for the Ninth Circuit. The Senate confirmed Kennedy 97–0.

Kennedy was born in Sacramento, California. He graduated from Stanford University in 1958, studied at the London School of Economics, and graduated from Harvard Law School in 1961. He then spent a year practicing law with a San Francisco firm before returning to Sacramento upon his father's death. Kennedy took over his father's practice, which included both law and lobbying activities. He also taught part time at the McGeorge School of Law. President Gerald Ford appointed Kennedy to the Ninth Circuit Court of Appeals in 1975. Kennedy remained on the appeals court for a dozen years until the Sen-

Source: National Geographic Society

ate confirmed him for the Supreme Court in early 1988.

With Kennedy's appointment, the Court's transition from liberalism to conservatism was nearly completed. In 1989 Kennedy joined conservative majorities to limit the use of affirmative action, allow states to execute people who were sixteen or seventeen when they committed a capital crime, and uphold Missouri's law barring the use of public facilities to perform abortions.

L

Lamar, Joseph R.

Joseph Rucker Lamar (1857–1916) was greatly surprised when President William Howard Taft nominated him for the Supreme Court in 1910. He was little known outside the South, and he expected the Senate to reject him because he was a Democrat. However, the Senate confirmed him by voice vote only five days after the nomination.

Born into a socially prominent Georgia family, Lamar had several notable relatives. They included Mirabeau Buonaparte Lamar, president of the Republic of Texas from 1838 to 1841, and Lucius Quintus Cincinnatus Lamar, associate justice of the Supreme Court from 1888 to 1893.

After his mother died when he was eight, Lamar moved with his father, James, to Augusta, Georgia. There, James Lamar gave up his legal career to become a minister in the Disciples of Christ church. He was greatly influenced in the move by Alexander Campbell, founder of the new Protestant denomination and president of Bethany College when James Lamar attended the institution. In Augusta, Joseph became good friends with Woodrow Wilson, whose father was minister of the city's leading Presbyterian church.

Lamar graduated from Bethany College in 1877, and then read law at Washington and Lee University and clerked for Henry Clay Foster, a prominent Augusta attorney. He passed the Georgia bar, married the daughter of the president of Bethany College, and taught Latin at the college for a year.

Lamar began practicing law in 1880 in partnership with Foster. While in practice, he served two terms in the Georgia legislature. He also helped rewrite the state's legal codes.

In 1903 Lamar was appointed to the Georgia supreme court, where he served until 1905. Citing overwork and homesickness, he resigned to return to private practice.

Source: Collection of the Supreme Court of the United States

Taft nominated Lamar to the Supreme Court in 1910, and Lamar once again began to overwork himself. His most important opinions were *United States v. Midwest Oil Company* (1915), in which he supported the government's decision to keep control of public land rich in oil for military purposes, and *Gompers v. Buck's Stove and Range Co.* (1911), in which he upheld the use of injunctions to end labor boycotts.

Lamar suffered a stroke in September 1916 and died three months later after having served as a justice for only five years. "The whole country has reason to mourn," President Wilson telegraphed Lamar's widow. "It has lost an able and noble servant. I have lost in him one of my most loved friends."

Lamar, Lucius Q. C.

In 1888 Lucius Quintus Cincinnatus Lamar (1825–1893), a Confederate veteran, became the first native-born southerner appointed to the Supreme Court following the Civil War. There was strong opposition to his nomination among Senate Republicans, but senators Stanford of California and Stewart of Nevada argued that rejecting Lamar would be seen as a ban on all Confederate veterans. Lamar was narrowly confirmed by a 32–28 vote.

Nine years after Lamar was born in Eatonton, Georgia, his father committed suicide. In 1845 Lamar graduated from Emory College, and two years later he married the daughter of its president, Rev. Augustus B. Longstreet. Lamar then began reading law, passed the bar in 1847, and moved his family to Oxford, Mississippi, where his father-in-law became president of the University of Mississippi. In Oxford Lamar practiced law and taught mathematics.

In 1852 Lamar moved back to Georgia to establish

Source: Library of Congress

a legal practice with a friend in Covington, and the next year he was elected to the Georgia house. Lamar's law practice soon dissolved, and he failed to obtain the hoped-for Democratic nomination for Congress, prompting him to move back to Mississippi. There he lived on a plantation, practiced law, and adopted an extreme viewpoint favoring states' rights. He was elected to Congress in 1857 but resigned before the end of his term. After returning to Mississippi, Lamar wrote the state's ordinance of secession at the Mississippi Secession Convention of 1861.

During the Civil War, Lamar served as colonel of the Eighteenth Mississippi Regiment until illness forced him to leave active service in May 1862. He served during the remainder of the conflict as a judge advocate for the Army of Northern Virginia.

When the war ended, Lamar, who had been a strong advocate of the southern cause before and during the war, publicly advocated reconciliation of North and South. He was reelected to the U.S. House in 1872 and to the Senate in 1877. In the midst of his second Senate term he resigned to become secretary of the interior under President Grover Cleveland. Cleveland nominated him for the Supreme Court in 1887. Lamar consistently supported the rights of business, drawing a distinction in *Kidd v. Pearson* (1888) between manufacturing and commerce that made it more difficult for Congress to regulate manufacturing.

Seventeen years after Lamar's death, his cousin, Joseph R. Lamar, became a Supreme Court justice.

Law Clerks

See CLERKS.

Legal Office of the Court

The Supreme Court's own legal office was established in 1973 to serve two primary functions. First, the legal office acts as "house counsel" on questions directly concerning the Court and the SUPREME

COURT BUILDING. Second, the office provides permanent and specialized help to the justices in addition to the assistance they receive from their law CLERKS.

Legal System in America

The United States has fifty-two separate court systems: the federal judicial system, and an independent court system in each of the fifty states and the District of Columbia. (See COURTS, LOWER.) The overlapping court systems reflect the continuing vitality of the principles of FEDERALISM, but they also give rise to much confusion, complexity, and uncertainty.

Differences and Similarities

Collectively, the state courts are far larger than the federal judiciary, and they handle the vast bulk of the nation's judicial caseload. Federal judges make up less than 3 percent of the total number of judges in the nation. In 1990 more than 100 million new cases were filed in the state court systems, compared to about 1.4 million in the federal courts.

State courts differ greatly in size, organization, and resources. But some general comparisons can be made between state courts overall and the federal judiciary. By and large, federal courts are better funded, better staffed, and better equipped than state courts. Federal judges have higher salaries and smaller average caseloads than state court judges.

State courts are courts of general JURISDICTION. With some exceptions, they have authority to try any kind of case, including cases involving issues of federal law. Federal courts, by contrast, are courts of limited jurisdiction. They try those cases that are within the "judicial power of the United States" as defined in Article III of the Constitution and as authorized by Congress. Chiefly, federal jurisdiction extends to cases arising under the Constitution, federal law, or treaties; and cases involving the United States, a state, or citizens of different states. (See DIVERSITY JURISDICTION.)

Despite their differences, the federal and state court systems also have some similarities. Federal and state caseloads alike consist primarily of relatively minor matters. More than two-thirds of the state court caseloads consist of traffic cases or other local ordinance violations. More than half of the federal court cases are bankruptcies—some involving major corpo-

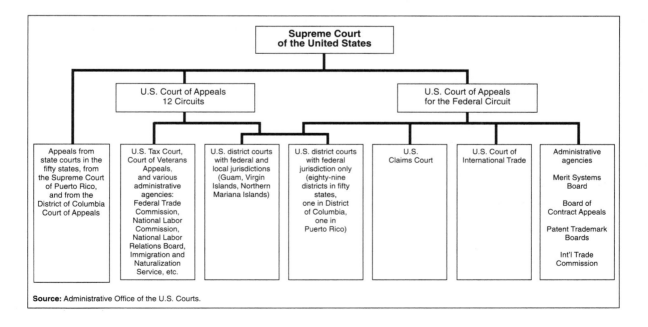

Source: Administrative Office of the U.S. Courts.

rate reorganizations, but most of them filed by individuals.

The vast majority of cases in both state and federal courts are never brought to trial. Most criminal cases are concluded through a process called PLEA BARGAINING, in which the defendant pleads guilty, typically in exchange for some assurances about the likely sentence. Most civil cases, including personal injury or "tort" suits, also are settled without trial or else dropped.

The overlapping jurisdiction of state and federal courts is a source of confusion and gives an opportunity for legal manipulation. State and federal prosecutors sometimes cooperate, and sometimes compete, in bringing criminal cases that can be prosecuted under either state or federal law. Many civil cases can be brought in either state or federal court, and some cases can be brought in any one of several states. Sorting out which state's law applies to each particular issue in such a case can be difficult. For the plaintiff in such a suit, choosing the court in which to file a case permits "forum shopping"— selecting the court where the law is most favorable or the judges viewed as most sympathetic to the particular type of case.

State and federal courts alike have felt increasing pressure since the 1970s. Caseloads have been rising faster than the growth in population for much of the period. Judicial salaries have lagged, making it harder to recruit and retain judges. Criminal caseloads in particular have increased, crowding out civil cases and causing long delays in some jurisdictions before private suits can be scheduled for trial. A massive case—such as a CLASS ACTION arising from a mass disaster, environmental hazard, or allegedly unsafe product—may sorely test judges' ability to manage complex litigation.

Federal Courts' Role

The federal judiciary evolved from a small, subsidiary court system with limited impact on the life of the nation into a still small but extraordinarily powerful institution with enormous impact on Americans' daily lives.

Under the Articles of Confederation, the United States had neither a Supreme Court nor any federal system of courts. The Constitution established the Supreme Court but left it to Congress to establish lower federal courts. Congress also had authority to determine the jurisdiction of the lower courts within the limits set in Article III.

The Judiciary Act of 1789 created a structure that lasted for more than a century. It established federal trial-level courts, called district courts, in each of the thirteen states to handle maritime and minor civil cases. In addition, it established three circuit courts, composed of two Supreme Court justices and a district court judge, to hear criminal cases and civil suits involving more than $500 and to exercise some appellate jurisdiction over the district courts. (See CIRCUIT RIDING.)

For most of the nineteenth century the federal courts had very limited jurisdiction. Not until 1875 did Congress grant them "general federal question jurisdiction"—jurisdiction over all issues arising under the Constitution, federal law, or treaties. That jurisdiction is now regarded as indispensable to their powers. (See COURTS, POWERS OF.)

In 1891 Congress established the court structure that, with modifications, still exists today. The Circuit Courts Act created the circuit courts of appeals as intermediate appellate courts between the trial-level district courts and the Supreme Court. These courts were intended primarily to relieve pressure on the Supreme Court's docket. (See APPEAL.) The act also introduced the principle of discretionary Supreme Court review by the writ of CERTIORARI. Three decades later Congress passed the Judiciary Act of 1925 to give the Supreme Court greater control over the selection of its docket.

From the beginning federal courts have provided a national forum on matters concerning national interests. For example, maritime jurisdiction was vital in the nation's early days when ships were a dominant mode of transportation. The jurisdiction of the federal courts was expanded in 1875 to provide a similarly uniform body of law for the national railroads. In the twentieth century federal courts have had the primary role in enforcing new federal CIVIL RIGHTS laws.

The federal courts had little criminal jurisdiction until the twentieth century. Even today they handle few cases involving "street crime," such as murders, rapes, robberies, or burglaries. But the federal courts do play a major role in white-collar crime through laws, such as the mail fraud and wire fraud statutes, that rely on Congress's commerce power to convert state offenses into federal crimes. Since the 1980s the number of federal prosecutions for drug-related offenses has also risen sharply. In 1990 such cases made up about one-fourth of the federal courts' criminal caseload.

Much of the federal courts' civil caseload consists of suits involving citizens of different states brought under the diversity jurisdiction. These suits, which made up about one-fourth of the civil caseload in 1990, range from routine automobile accident cases to major financial disputes. Federal courts apply state law, not federal law, in deciding such cases. The rest of the civil caseload covers the extent of federal constitutional and statutory law—from securities and labor law to environmental and civil rights litigation and civil enforcement actions brought by the federal government.

Federal judges are selected by the president, subject to Senate confirmation. Federal judgeships are lifetime appointments. By their selection of judges, presidents can try to shape the federal courts' legal philosophy. President Jimmy Carter increased the number of women, blacks, and Hispanics appointed to the federal bench, and many of his appointees held liberal views on many legal issues. Presidents Ronald Reagan and George Bush, on the other hand, have appointed fewer blacks and members of other minorities, and many of their appointees hold conservative views. Since federal judges have life tenure, their decisions cannot be controlled and often cannot be accurately predicted.

State Courts' Role

State courts were established before the federal courts, and they have handled most court cases throughout the nation's history. State court systems vary widely in structure and quality.

Structurally, state courts have many variations on the three-tiered model of the federal courts: trial-level courts, intermediate appellate courts, and a supreme court.

Many states have two levels of trial courts. The lowest courts may be called county, municipal, or justice courts; they typically handle local ordinance violations, minor civil cases, and misdemeanors (crimes punishable by up to one year in jail). The higher trial court, often called a superior, circuit, or district court, handles larger civil suits and felony cases (crimes punishable by one or more years in prison).

Some states divide civil and criminal courts, while other states combine them in trial courts that have what is called "unified jurisdiction." In addition, many states have specialized trial-level courts for some types of cases, such as family courts that handle divorces, child custody matters, and delinquency cases.

Most states have a single intermediate appellate court whose judges sit in panels of three to decide appeals in civil or criminal cases. Some states, however, have separate appeals courts for civil and criminal cases. In some states, most appeals go to the appeals courts, subject only to discretionary review by the state supreme court. In other states, many kinds of cases may be appealed to the highest court.

A major contrast between the federal and state judiciary is the use of popular elections in the selection or retention of state court judges, as opposed to the lifetime appointment of federal judges.

The excitement about self-government in the nation's early days led to the idea that judges, like governors and legislators, should be elected and not appointed. In 1812 Georgia became the first state to provide for election of lower court judges. By the second half of the nineteenth century, most judges across the country were being selected through popular elections.

Many critics viewed popular election as subject to political influence and corruption. Some states decided to shift to an appointive system; others adopted a nonpartisan judicial ballot to try to dilute the influence of political parties. Then, in the 1930s, a system emerged that combined appointments with a form of popular election. The system called for judges to be initially appointed and then to be subject to a yes-or-no vote on whether they would be kept in office. Missouri in 1940 became the first state to adopt the system, which has since been called the Missouri plan.

Although several states have adopted the Missouri plan for some or all courts, popular election survives

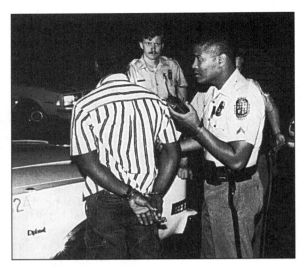

If they are going to come into contact with the U.S. legal system at all, most people will do so at the state level, probably beginning with an arrest. Here Prince Georges County, Maryland, police take a man into custody.   Source: R. Michael Jenkins

in many other states. Even the retention elections involve some political activity that federal judges, once in office, need not engage in. As a result, state courts have often been considered more subject to influence by popular opinion than federal courts. In the nineteenth century courts in many states were viewed as hostile to railroads, utilities, and other big corporations. Through the first half of the twentieth century, courts in many southern states were guilty of racial discrimination in their operations and their decisions.

Since the early twentieth century, however, state courts have become more professional. Reform efforts pushed by lawyers, businesses, and civic groups have played a major part in this development. Some state courts now rival the federal judiciary in quality and stature.

State laws vary widely. Criminal laws in the states are broadly similar but differ on legal details and, most notably, on sentences. For example, about two-thirds of the states permit capital punishment; the rest do not. Laws governing civil matters—contracts, personal injury suits, landlord-tenant law, and so forth—have wider variations. For example, some states have relatively liberal rules for recovering damages in per-

sonal injury suits, while others have more restrictive rules.

State CONSTITUTIONAL LAW can also vary from state to state. The state supreme court in each state can interpret its own constitution independently of the U.S. Supreme Court, even if the provisions of the state constitution are similar or identical to those of the U.S. Constitution. The state must afford individuals the rights protected by the U.S. Constitution, as interpreted by the U.S. Supreme Court, but it can also go further under its own constitution.

Several state supreme courts have been particularly willing to develop independent doctrines of constitutional law. The California and New Jersey supreme courts, for example, interpreted their constitutions to require equalization of public school financing within a few years of the U.S. Supreme Court decision rejecting that argument under the federal Constitution. The California supreme court also recognized a right to abortion before the U.S. Supreme Court's ruling in *Roe v. Wade* (1973).

The U.S. Supreme Court's shift away from expansive constitutional rulings in the 1970s led to increased interest in state constitutional law. Justice William J. Brennan, Jr., delivered a widely noticed speech in 1977 encouraging the trend. But the development led to a backlash in some states. For example, some state supreme court rulings outlawing capital punishment have been overturned by constitutional amendments. And California voters approved a constitutional amendment requiring state courts to follow the U.S. Supreme Court's interpretations of the Fourth Amendment on search and seizure.

Supreme Court's Role

The Supreme Court establishes constitutional standards governing the operations of the state and federal courts. It also exercises a broad supervisory and rule-making power over the federal court system. In some ways, however, the Court's influence over the day-to-day operations of state or federal courts is limited.

For the most part, state legislatures and Congress, not the Supreme Court, determine the nature of the courts' business. It is Congress that has been responsible for expanding the jurisdiction of the federal courts.

Enacting criminal laws and setting the range of criminal sentences are legislative, not judicial, functions. State courts play a greater role in shaping the rules governing some types of civil litigation, such as personal injury suits. But legislatures can, within limits, define the legal remedies and procedural rules to be used in these cases too.

Members of the Supreme Court do not directly lobby Congress on legal issues, apart from an annual appearance by one or two justices to testify before congressional committees in support of the federal judiciary's budget. Chief Justice Warren E. Burger used his annual report on the judiciary and other public presentations to speak out regularly on issues of judicial administration. His successor, Chief Justice William H. Rehnquist, has spoken out less often, although in 1991 he endorsed a judicial pay raise and opposed legislation to establish federal jurisdiction over any crime committed with a gun.

Through its rulings, the Supreme Court can have some effect on the patterns of litigation in the lower courts. Favorable or unfavorable decisions in particular types of suits may encourage or discourage parties from bringing such suits. Many controversial legal issues affecting the operations of the courts, however, have been debated—and will continue to be debated—in forums other than the Supreme Court.

Legal Tender Cases

During the Civil War a constitutional challenge to the Union government's use of paper money to finance the war effort led to an embarrassing pair of Supreme Court decisions that first rejected and then upheld Congress's power to authorize currency as legal tender for public and private debts. (See REVERSALS OF EARLIER RULINGS.)

In 1863 the Supreme Court had refused to hear a case contesting Congress's decision to authorize the printing of paper money, or "greenbacks." Two years later it agreed to hear a case raising the issue, *Hepburn v. Griswold*. The case was argued in 1867, reargued in 1868, and decided amid intense political controversy on February 7, 1870.

In a 4–3 decision announced by Chief Justice Salmon P. Chase, the Court ruled against the constitutionality of using paper money to pay debts contracted before passage of the greenback legislation in 1862. Chase said the use of paper money rather than gold would result in "a long train of evils," including "the losses of property, the derangement of business, the fluctuations of currency and values, and the increase of prices to the people and government."

For that reason, he concluded, paper money was not "an appropriate and plainly adapted means" for Congress to use to pay for the war. Ironically, Chase had backed the government's wartime greenback program as secretary of the treasury, although he was privately hostile to the paper-money plan.

Chase announced the decision on the same day that President Ulysses Grant announced two nominations to fill vacancies on the Court: Joseph Bradley and William Strong. After Grant's nominees were confirmed by the Senate, the Court on April 1, 1870,

President Ulysses S. Grant was accused of packing the Court when his first two appointees, William Strong and Joseph Bradley, voted to overturn the ruling in the first Legal Tender Case.   Source: Library of Congress

announced that it would hear two more pending legal tender cases: *Knox v. Lee* and *Parker v. Davis* (1871).

In light of subsequent events, Grant was charged with "packing" the Court with these appointments. Strong had previously defended the legal tender legislation, and Bradley had been a railroad lawyer whose clients supported paper money. On the other hand, Chase had rushed the Court's decision on a highly partisan issue. He had joined with the Court's three Democratic-appointed justices to form a precarious majority while he was courting the Democrats in hopes of winning the party's presidential nomination.

The Court reversed itself, 5–4, on May 1, 1871—just fifteen months after its first ruling on the issue. Writing for the majority, Strong rebutted Chase's arguments point by point. With regard to Congress's power to authorize a national currency, Strong said that "the degree of the necessity for any congressional enactment, or the relative degree of its appropriateness, . . . is for consideration in Congress, not here."

The Court's quick reversal was almost universally deplored. A later chief justice, Charles Evans Hughes, called the turnabout one of the Court's "self-inflicted wounds," though he disputed the suggestion that Grant had tried to pack the Court. Later evidence does show that Grant had learned of the Court's decision in the first case before appointing Bradley and Strong. But every prominent Republican lawyer supported the constitutionality of the greenback law, so it would have been difficult for Grant to pick someone who did not agree with him on the issue.

Legislative Veto

The legislative veto was a device that enabled Congress to retain a measure of control over the implementation or execution of a law. It permitted one or both chambers—or in some cases one or more committees in Congress—to veto an executive branch action without passing a new law. The device was popular with Congress but unpopular with presidents of both parties, who viewed it as a violation of the principle of SEPARATION OF POWERS.

In *Immigration and Naturalization Service v. Chadha* (1983) the Supreme Court agreed with that view, holding that the legislative veto violated the Constitution's requirements that all laws be passed by both houses of Congress and presented to the president for approval or disapproval.

The legislative veto had originated in the Hoover administration as part of a 1932 law allowing the president to reorganize executive branch departments subject to a veto by either house of Congress. Over the next fifty years, legislative veto provisions were included in more than two hundred laws governing such important subjects as budget impoundments, campaign laws, energy, federal salaries, foreign trade, and war powers. The device grew in popularity in the 1970s when a more assertive Congress included legislative vetoes in a host of regulatory statutes as a way to check new regulatory initiatives.

Presidents from Herbert Hoover on protested the legislative veto. Lower courts upheld some of the provisions and struck down others. One ruling invalidating a legislative veto provision came from the federal appeals court in San Francisco. The case involved an immigration law amendment that allowed either chamber of Congress to veto a decision by the Immigration and Naturalization Service (INS) to suspend the deportation of an alien.

The INS in 1974 had suspended the deportation of Jagdish Rai Chadha, a citizen of Kenya who had overstayed his student visa. In December 1975 the House exercised its power to veto Chadha's stay of deportation. Chadha challenged the law and won a ruling from the appeals court in 1980. The Supreme Court heard the appeal in the case in February 1982. It asked for a second round of arguments, which were held on the opening day of the October 1982 term.

It took the Court all term to reach a decision. On June 23, 1983, Chief Justice Warren E. Burger announced the Court's 7–2 decision holding the legislative veto unconstitutional. Burger's opinion said that with limited exceptions, Congress could act with force of law only by passing a bill in both chambers and presenting it to the president for approval or disapproval. Burger said legislative vetoes might be useful and convenient, but "convenience and efficiency are not the primary objectives—or the hallmarks—of democratic government."

In a lengthy dissent, Justice Byron R. White called the legislative veto "an important if not indispensable political invention that allows the president and Congress to resolve major constitutional and policy differences, assures the accountability of independent regulatory agencies, and preserves Congress' control over lawmaking." He called the ruling destructive and listed many of the two hundred laws that he said had been struck down "in one fell swoop."

The effects of the ruling proved to be less sweeping. The Court itself in 1987 held unanimously that in most of the laws, only the legislative veto provision was nullified by the ruling, not the whole statute. More important, Congress did not rush to repeal legislative veto provisions. In fact, it continued to add such provisions to new laws. Despite the unconstitutionality of such laws, agencies have generally refrained from challenging them to avoid alienating Congress.

Libel

A libel is a printed or broadcast statement about an individual that defames the person's character or reputation and can be the basis for a recovery of damages in a civil lawsuit. Until 1964 the Supreme Court viewed libel as outside the protection of the First Amendment and left it to the states to set the standards for plaintiffs to meet in order to win damage awards. The Court's landmark decision in *NEW YORK TIMES CO. V. SULLIVAN* (1964), however, began a process of bringing civil libel law under constitutional protection. Public officials and public figures now face high legal barriers to recovering damages in libel cases. Suits by private individuals are also subject to special rules established by the Court in order to prevent self-censorship by the news media.

The *New York Times* standard of "actual malice" required high-ranking public officials seeking damages in a civil libel suit to prove that a news organization had published a defamatory falsehood "with knowl-

edge that it was false or with reckless disregard whether it was false or not." A fragmented Court in 1966 extended the rule to lower ranking public officials, and a more unified Court extended the rule in 1971 to political candidates.

The Court has had great difficulty in deciding what requirements to impose on plaintiffs who are in the public eye but who are not in government or politics. In 1967 the Court was fragmented in ruling that such "public figures" must also meet the actual malice standard in libel cases. A public figure was defined as someone who commanded public attention "by position alone" or had "thrust his personality into the 'vortex' of an important public controversy." The plaintiffs in the cases were a state university football coach who had been implicated in a gambling scandal and a retired general who led a riot to protest the desegregation of the University of Mississippi.

In 1971—once again without a majority opinion— the Court applied the actual malice rule in a libel suit brought by a distributor of nudist magazines in connection with a false report about his arrest for obscenity. A plurality of three justices said that the actual malice rule applied to any discussion of public issues, even if it included defamatory statements about private individuals. The other two justices in the majority concurred on different grounds, while three justices argued that private individuals should not be subject to the actual malice rule.

In 1974 a bare majority formed behind a new rule giving greater, but not unlimited, protection to plaintiffs who were private figures. In *Gertz v. Robert Welch, Inc.* the Court held that the actual malice rule did not apply to private figures. Instead, states could set the standard of proof for plaintiffs in such cases subject to two restrictions. First, plaintiffs must show some fault, or at least negligence, on the part of the defendant. Second, the judge or jury could base damages only on the plaintiff's proven "actual losses"—including the flexible concept of "pain and suffering"—and punitive damages could not be awarded unless the *New York Times* standard was met.

Gertz was a mixed ruling for plaintiffs and the press on the burden of proof and damage issues, but it was a clear victory for plaintiffs on the definition of private

> " *The growing movement of peaceful mass demonstrations by Negroes is something new in the South, something understandable. . . . Let Congress heed their rising voices, for they will be heard.* "
>
> —*New York Times editorial*
> *Saturday, March 19, 1960*

Heed Their Rising Voices

As the whole world knows by now, thousands of Southern Negro students are engaged in widespread non-violent demonstrations in positive affirmation of the right to live in human dignity as guaranteed by the U. S. Constitution and the Bill of Rights. In their efforts to uphold these guarantees, they are being met by an unprecedented wave of terror by those who would deny and negate that document which the whole world looks upon as setting the pattern for modern freedom...

In Orangeburg, South Carolina, when 400 students peacefully sought to buy doughnuts and coffee at lunch counters in the business district, they were forcibly ejected, tear-gassed, soaked to the skin in freezing weather with fire hoses, arrested en masse and herded into an open barbed-wire stockade to stand for hours in the bitter cold.

In Montgomery, Alabama, after students sang "My Country, 'Tis of Thee" on the State Capitol steps, their leaders were expelled from school, and truckloads of police armed with shotguns and tear-gas ringed the Alabama State College Campus. When the entire student body protested to state authorities by refusing to re-register, their dining hall was padlocked in an attempt to starve them into submission.

In Tallahassee, Atlanta, Nashville, Savannah, Greensboro, Memphis, Richmond, Charlotte, and a host of other cities in the South, young American teenagers, in face of the entire weight of official state apparatus and police power, have boldly stepped forth as protagonists of democracy. Their courage and amazing restraint have inspired millions and given a new dignity to the cause of freedom.

Small wonder that the Southern violators of the Constitution fear this new, non-violent brand of freedom fighter... even as they fear the upswelling right-to-vote movement. Small wonder that they are determined to destroy the one man who, more than any other, symbolizes the new spirit now sweeping the South—the Rev. Dr. Martin Luther King, Jr., world-famous leader of the Montgomery Bus Protest. For it is his doctrine of non-violence which has inspired and guided the students in their widening wave of sit-ins; and it is this same Dr. King who founded and is president of the Southern Christian Leadership Conference—the organization which is spearheading the surging right-to-vote movement. Under Dr. King's direction the Leadership Conference conducts Student Workshops and Seminars in the philosophy and techniques of non-violent resistance.

Again and again the Southern violators have answered Dr. King's peaceful protests with intimidation and violence. They have bombed his home almost killing his wife and child. They have assaulted his person. They have arrested him seven times—for "speeding," "loitering" and similar "offenses." And now they have charged him with "perjury"—a *felony* under which they could imprison him for *ten years.* Obviously, their real purpose is to remove him physically as the leader to whom the students and millions

of others—look for guidance and support, and thereby to intimidate *all* leaders who may rise in the South. Their strategy is to behead this affirmative movement, and thus to demoralize Negro Americans and weaken their will to struggle. The defense of Martin Luther King, spiritual leader of the student sit-in movement, clearly, therefore, is an integral part of the total struggle for freedom in the South.

Decent-minded Americans cannot help but applaud the creative daring of the students and the quiet heroism of Dr. King. But this is one of those moments in the stormy history of Freedom when men and women of good will must do more than applaud the rising-to-glory of others. The America whose good name hangs in the balance before a watchful world, the America whose heritage of Liberty these Southern Upholders of the Constitution are defending, is *our* America as well as theirs...

We must heed their rising voices—yes—but we must add our own.

We must extend ourselves above and beyond moral support and render the material help so urgently needed by those who are taking the risks, facing jail, and even death in a glorious re-affirmation of our Constitution and its Bill of Rights.

We urge you to join hands with our fellow Americans in the South by supporting, with your dollars, this combined appeal for all three needs—the defense of Martin Luther King—the support of the embattled students—and the struggle for the right-to-vote.

Your Help Is Urgently Needed . . . NOW!!

Stella Adler	Dr. Alan Knight Chalmers	Anthony Franciosa	John Killens	L. Joseph Overton	Maureen Stapleton
Raymond Pace Alexander	Richard Coe	Lorraine Hansbury	Eartha Kitt	Clarence Pickett	Frank Silvera
Harry Van Arsdale	Nat King Cole	Rev. Donald Harrington	Rabbi Edward Klein	Shad Polier	Hope Stevens
Harry Belafonte	Cheryl Crawford	Nat Hentoff	Hope Lange	Sidney Poitier	George Tabor
Julie Belafonte	Dorothy Dandridge	James Hicks	John Lewis	A. Philip Randolph	Rev. Gardner C.
Dr. Algernon Black	Ossie Davis	Mary Hinkson	Viveca Lindfors	John Raitt	Taylor
Marc Blitzstein	Sammy Davis, Jr.	Van Heflin	Carl Murphy	Elmer Rice	Norman Thomas
William Branch	Ruby Dee	Langston Hughes	Don Murray	Jackie Robinson	Kenneth Tynan
Marlon Brando	Dr. Philip Elliott	Morris Iushewitz	John Murray	Mrs. Eleanor Roosevelt	Charles White
Mrs. Ralph Bunche	Dr. Harry Emerson	Mahalia Jackson	A. J. Muste	Bayard Rustin	Shelley Winters
Diahann Carroll	Fosdick	Mordecai Johnson	Frederick O'Neal	Robert Ryan	Max Youngstein

We in the south who are struggling daily for dignity and freedom warmly endorse this appeal

Rev. Ralph D. Abernathy *(Montgomery, Ala.)*	Rev. Matthew D. McCollom *(Orangeburg, S.C.)*	Rev. Walter L. Hamilton *(Norfolk, Va.)*	Rev. A. L. Davis *(New Orleans, La.)*
Rev. Fred L. Shuttlesworth *(Birmingham, Ala.)*	Rev. William Holmes Borders *(Atlanta, Ga.)*	I. S. Levy *(Columbia, S.C.)* Rev. Martin Luther King, Sr. *(Atlanta, Ga.)*	Mrs. Katie E. Whickham *(New Orleans, La.)*
Rev. Kelley Miller Smith *(Nashville, Tenn.)*	Rev. Douglas Moore *(Durham, N.C.)*	Rev. Henry C. Bunton *(Memphis, Tenn.)*	Rev. W. H. Hall *(Hattiesburg, Miss.)*
Rev. W. A. Dennis *(Chattanooga, Tenn.)*	Rev. Wyatt Tee Walker *(Petersburg, Va.)*	Rev. S.S. Seay, Sr. *(Montgomery, Ala.)*	Rev. J. E. Lowery *(Mobile, Ala.)*
Rev. C. K. Steele *(Tallahassee, Fla.)*		Rev. Samuel W. Williams *(Atlanta, Ga.)*	Rev. T. J. Jemison *(Baton Rouge, La.)*

COMMITTEE TO DEFEND MARTIN LUTHER KING AND THE STRUGGLE FOR FREEDOM IN THE SOUTH

312 West 125th Street, New York 27, N.Y. UNiversity 6-1700

Chairmen: A. Philip Randolph, Dr. Gardner C. Taylor; *Chairmen of Cultural Division:* Harry Belafonte, Sidney Poitier; *Treasurer:* Nat King Cole; *Executive Director:* Bayard Rustin; *Chairmen of Church Division:* Father George B. Ford, Rev. Harry Emerson Fosdick, Rev. Thomas Kilgore, Jr., Rabbi Edward E. Klein; *Chairman of Labor Division:* Morris Iushewitz

Please mail this coupon TODAY!

Committee To Defend Martin Luther King
and
The Struggle For Freedom in The South
312 West 125th Street, New York 27, N.Y.
UNiversity 6-1700

I am enclosing my contribution of $_____
for the work of the Committee.

Name_____

Address_____

City_____ Zone_____ State_____

☐ I want to help   ☐ Please send further information

Please make checks payable to:
Committee to Defend Martin Luther King

figures. Gertz himself had been a lawyer in a widely publicized police brutality suit, maliciously defamed by an extreme right-wing publication. The ruling in his favor loosened the definition of private figure and repudiated the "public issue" test from the 1971 case.

Later libel rulings further relaxed the definition of private figures to include an heiress involved in a widely publicized divorce case, a man convicted of contempt for refusing to appear before a grand jury investigating Soviet espionage, and a university scientist criticized by a U.S. senator for an allegedly wasteful use of federal research money. As Justice William H. Rehnquist wrote in one of the rulings, "A libel defendant must show more than mere newsworthiness [on the part of the plaintiff] to justify application of the demanding burden of *New York Times."*

The Court dealt media defendants a blow in 1979 by rejecting the claim of a privilege to refuse to answer questions about the editorial process leading to publication of an allegedly libelous story. The 6–3 decision in *Herbert v. Lando* said that nothing in the First Amendment prevented plaintiffs from obtaining the information they needed to prove actual malice under the *New York Times* rule.

Several other procedural rulings in the 1980s favored the news media. In the most important, the Court in 1986 held that plaintiffs who were private figures had the burden of proof of showing that an allegedly defamatory statement was false.

Over the years many public officials and others had criticized the *New York Times* rule for imposing too great a burden in libel suits and for inviting irresponsible reporting and commentary by the news media. During the 1970s Chief Justice Warren E. Burger and Justice Byron R. White had suggested reconsidering the rule. In 1988, however, the Court strongly reaffirmed the rule and extended it to a different context: satire.

In *Hustler Magazine v. Falwell* the Court unanimously reversed a damage award for emotional distress won by the television evangelist, Rev. Jerry Falwell, for a parody advertisement about him in a nationally distributed sex magazine. Writing for the Court, Rehnquist, now chief justice, said that satire—just like other forms of political debate—needed constitutional protection from civil damage awards. On that basis, he said, a plaintiff could not recover damages for emotional distress resulting from a parody or satire unless the plaintiff could show that it contained "a false statement of fact which was made with 'actual malice,' i.e., with knowledge that it was false or with reckless disregard as to whether or not it was true."

Library of the Court

The Supreme Court library contains about 300,000 volumes and is located on the third floor of the SUPREME COURT BUILDING. Its use is limited to Court personnel, members of the BAR OF THE SUPREME COURT, members of Congress and their legal staffs, and government attorneys. The library is usually willing to grant access to its books to members

---

Facing page:
The purpose of this ad was to publicize and raise money for the cause of civil rights. Commissioner L.B. Sullivan of Montgomery, Alabama, claimed the ad libeled him. In deciding against Sullivan, the Supreme Court established a new standard for libel suits.
Source: New York Times

Librarians of the Court	
Henry Deforest Clarke	1887–1900
Frank Key Green	1900–1915
Oscar Deforest Clarke	1915–1947
Helen C. Newman	1947–1965
Henry Charles Hallam, Jr.	1965–1972
Edward G. Hudon	1972–1976
Betty H. Clowers, acting librarian	1976–1978
Roger F. Jacobs	1978–1985
Stephen G. Margeton	1985–1988
Shelley L. Dowling	1989–

Source: Collection of the Supreme Court of the United States

of the public or press who specify a particular research interest.

In the early years of the Court, the justices had no library of their own. It was not until 1812 that Congress allowed the justices to use the Library of Congress.

After repeated refusals to give the Court its own library, Congress in 1832 gave the justices the 2,011 law books in the Library of Congress but retained the right of members of Congress to use them. Because the Court had no librarian at the time, the CLERK OF THE COURT was put in charge of the books. By 1863 the number of law books had increased to almost 16,000.

In 1884 responsibility for the Court's collection of books was shifted from the clerk to the MARSHAL OF THE COURT. The post of librarian was created in 1887. The office of the librarian remained in the marshal's department until 1948, when Congress made it a separate office.

The Court library has the most complete set available of the printed briefs, records, and appendices of Court cases. It also contains all federal, state, and regional reports; federal and state statutory codes; legal periodicals; legal treatises; digests; and legislative and administrative source material. There are also special collections in international law, military law, British law, patent and trademark law, and Supreme Court history.

In order to protect this collection, books and other materials may not be removed from the building. Members of the Supreme Court bar, however, may request that material be sent to them when they are arguing a case.

Lincoln, Abraham

Abraham Lincoln (1809–1865) owed his election as president in part to the Supreme Court's decision in the Dred Scott case (*SCOTT V. SANDFORD* [1857]). In that case the Court ruled that Congress could not keep slavery out of the territories. As the Republican presidential candidate in 1860, Lincoln strongly criticized the controversial decision, which also split the Democratic party into northern and southern wings. In the White House, Lincoln skirted the Constitution and tested the Supreme Court as he expanded presidential powers to fight the Civil War and preserve the Union. (See WAR POWERS.) Lincoln freed the slaves by presidential fiat during the war, but after his death his five appointees to the Supreme Court had a mixed record on issues of civil liberties and racial equality.

Lincoln opposed the extension of slavery into the territories. His criticism of the Court's ruling in *Scott* brought him to national prominence. As a candidate he vowed to work to overturn the ruling if elected president. In his first inaugural address, he questioned the Court's authority to issue final rulings on "vital questions affecting the whole people" in private litigation, such as the Dred Scott case. (See ELECTIONS AND THE COURT.)

Against this backdrop, Lincoln and Chief Justice Roger B. Taney, author of the Dred Scott decision, immediately clashed over the president's unilateral suspension of the privilege of the writ of HABEAS COR-PUS at the outset of the Civil War. In 1861 Taney, sitting as a circuit justice, held the action unconstitutional. Lincoln responded that constitutional niceties had to yield to wartime emergency measures. The issue was partly mooted in 1863 when Congress autho-

Abraham Lincoln reading the Emancipation Proclamation to his cabinet, July 22, 1862. Seated, left to right, Secretary of War Edwin M. Stanton, the president, Secretary of the Navy Gideon Welles, Secretary of State William H. Seward, and Attorney General Edward Bates. Standing, left to right, Secretary of the Treasury Salmon P. Chase (who would be appointed chief justice in 1864), Secretary of the Interior Caleb B. Smith, and Postmaster General Montgomery Blair.   Source: Library of Congress

rized Lincoln to suspend habeas corpus at his discretion. After the war, however, the full Court vindicated Taney's position by ruling that Lincoln's use of military tribunals outside the war zone was unconstitutional. (See INTERNMENT CASES.)

Lincoln's unilateral decision in 1861 to declare a blockade on southern ports was also tested in the Supreme Court, which narrowly upheld his action. Lincoln had acted with Congress out of session in April 1861. Congress ratified the blockade in July after Lincoln informed the lawmakers that the actions had been necessary to preserve the Union "whether strictly legal or not." In the *Prize Cases* (1863) the Court ruled, 5–4, that Lincoln had acted within his authority as president in moving to "suppress the insurrection." Lincoln had named three members of the Court by this time; all voted to sustain his position.

The Court ruled on challenges to other wartime measures only after the war had ended. During the war the Court sidestepped a challenge to the use of paper money, or "greenbacks," to pay for the war. After the war, the Court first limited and then upheld the use of the new currency. (See *LEGAL TENDER CASES*.) Years later, in 1881, the Court sustained the federal income tax statute that was enacted in 1862 and stayed on the books until 1872.

Lincoln issued the Emancipation Proclamation, freeing the slaves in the secessionist states, under his authority as commander in chief. His plan for Reconstruction called for abolishing slavery but not for establishing black suffrage. After Lincoln was assassinated in 1865, President Andrew Johnson followed his conciliatory approach to the former Confederate states, although the Republican-controlled Congress favored a more stringent approach.

Lincoln's five appointees to the Supreme Court were largely political choices. One was Salmon P. Chase, Lincoln's secretary of the treasury, who served as chief justice from 1864 to 1873. Lincoln also appointed two dominant figures of the post–Civil War period, Samuel Miller and Stephen J. Field. Miller, an Iowan, and Field, a Californian, were strongly pushed by lawmakers from western states. Lincoln also nominated to the Court David Davis, who had been his campaign manager, and Noah H. Swayne, a leading Ohio Republican.

On the bench, Lincoln's appointees generally were in accord with the nationalist, probusiness stance the Court adopted for the rest of the century. They divided on the critical *SLAUGHTERHOUSE CASES* (1873) that limited the impact of the Fourteenth Amendment on the states. Miller and Davis voted with the majority, while Chase, Field, and Swayne dissented. Ten years later, in the *Civil Rights Cases* (1883), the four remaining Lincoln appointees all joined in the 8–1 decision to overturn the 1875 Civil Rights Act prohibiting racial discrimination in public accommodations.

Livingston, Henry B.

Eight years before President Thomas Jefferson nominated him to be an associate justice in 1806, Henry Brockholst Livingston (1757–1823) killed a man in a duel. He is believed to have fought several other duels as well.

Source: Library of Congress

Livingston was born into a powerful New York family that was part of the colonial aristocracy. His father, William Livingston, was governor of New Jersey and helped lead resistance to British colonial policies in New York. Henry graduated from Princeton in 1774 and was commissioned a major in the Continental Army when the revolutionary war began. He served under generals Schuyler and St. Clair, participated in the siege of Ticonderoga, and was an aide to Benedict Arnold during the Saratoga campaign. By the time the war ended, Livingston had attained the rank of lieutenant colonel.

After leaving the army, Livingston served in Spain as private secretary to his brother-in-law, John Jay, who was the American minister there. Livingston's dislike of Jay, which eventually grew to include bitter public attacks on his brother-in-law, began in Spain.

Although he had a reputation as a genial man, Livingston also had a violent streak. He fought several duels, killing one opponent. In 1785 an attempt was made on his life. A year after the attack, Livingston was elected to the first of three terms in the New York assembly. He also began practicing law. At about this same time, Livingston and other members of his family began to move away from Federalism to anti-Federalism.

In 1802 Livingston was appointed to the New York supreme court, where two of his relatives by marriage already served. Jefferson nominated him for the U.S. Supreme Court four years later. Livingston served on the High Court for sixteen years until his death in 1823.

During his tenure on the Court, Chief Justice John Marshall wrote most of the opinions. Livingston, who returned to Federalism, probably because of Marshall's influence, was particularly expert in cases dealing with foreign ships captured in wartime; he wrote eight opinions on this subject.

Loyalty Oaths

Loyalty oath statutes are laws that require individuals to prove their allegiance to the United States before they can hold certain public positions. Such laws were common at two critical periods of American history—the Civil War era and the onset of the Cold War. Constitutional challenges led to Supreme Court rulings overturning the most stringent of these statutes. But the Court has permitted states to require public employees to take loyalty oaths as long as the oaths are narrowly drawn and carefully applied.

Civil War Era

In the Civil War era, loyalty oath laws were aimed at individuals who had supported the Confederacy. A federal law required individuals to take an oath that they had not served the Confederacy in order to hold federal office or to practice law in the federal courts. A broad provision in Missouri's state constitution required all officeholders, voters, jurors, lawyers, teachers, and clergy to take an oath that they had not served, supported, or sympathized with the Confederacy.

The Supreme Court struck down both laws in 1867 in a pair of decisions called the *Test Oath Cases* (individually, *Ex parte Garland* and *Cummings v. Missouri*). The Court's 5–4 decisions held that the loyalty oath laws violated the constitutional ban on ex post facto laws because they imposed punishment for past actions that were not defined as illegal when they occurred. The Court also held the provisions to be unconstitutional bills of attainder—that is, legislative acts imposing punishment without judicial trial.

Cold War

Eighty years later, in the early stages of the Cold War, loyalty controls were aimed at Communists and Communist sympathizers. (See COMMUNISM.) Presidents Harry S. Truman and Dwight Eisenhower instituted controversial programs aimed at ensuring that only "loyal" persons held federal jobs. Congress imposed a loyalty oath requirement to hold office in labor unions. Many states required loyalty oaths by public employees, especially teachers.

The Supreme Court generally upheld these laws in the 1950s, but it shifted course in the 1960s and overturned many such measures.

The labor provision, contained in the Taft-Hartley Act of 1947, required union officers to sign affidavits that they were not members of the Communist party or of any organization that taught or believed in the overthrow of the federal government by forcible, illegal, or unconstitutional means. The Supreme Court upheld the law, ruling that Congress had the authority to try to prevent "political strikes" that could disrupt interstate commerce *(American Communications Association v. Douds* [1950]).

State loyalty oath requirements were upheld in a series of divided rulings in the 1950s. The Court in 1951 affirmed a Los Angeles ordinance requiring city employees to attest their loyalty through affidavit and oath. The next year the Court upheld a New York City law permitting the dismissal of any teacher found to be a member of an organization listed by the state as subversive.

The justices who dissented from these rulings eventually gained a narrow majority during the later years of the Warren Court. A Florida law requiring teachers to swear that they had never lent "aid, support, advice, or counsel" to the Communist party was struck down in 1961 as too vague. In 1964 the Court overturned a Washington state law on similar grounds. In 1965 it struck down a revamped labor provision barring current or former Communist party members from union office as an unconstitutional bill of attainder.

In 1966 the Court voted 5–4 to overturn an Arizona law that interpreted Communist party membership as a violation of the state's loyalty oath. Writing for the Court, Justice William O. Douglas said the law infringed on the First Amendment freedom of association by punishing people without determining whether they shared the party's illegal purposes. The next year, in *Keyishian v. Board of Regents* (1967), the Court struck down on grounds of vagueness the same New York statute concerning subversive membership that it had upheld fifteen years earlier.

Under Chief Justice Warren E. Burger, the Court reaffirmed these rulings in a series of decisions in 1971 and 1972. But the Court did permit states to require employees to take affirmatively worded oaths, declaring their support for the existing system of constitutional government. Separately, the Court allowed states to require applicants for admission to the bar to take oaths of loyalty to the state and federal constitutions.

Lurton, Horace H.

During the Civil War, Horace Harmon Lurton (1844–1914) had an illustrious career in the Confederate Army. He was captured during the siege of Fort Donelson but escaped from Camp Chase in Columbus, Ohio. He then joined General John Hunt Morgan's band of raiders, which was famous for its surprise attacks on Union railroads, bridges, and other installations. Lurton was captured again in July 1863. During his imprisonment he contracted tuberculosis. His mother, fearing for Lurton's health, traveled to

Source: Collection of the Supreme Court of the United States

Washington and persuaded President Lincoln to release her son and let him return to the South with her.

Lurton was born in 1844 in Newport, Kentucky. He went to Chicago at age sixteen to attend the University of Chicago, but returned to the South when the Civil War began. After recuperating at home following his release from prison, Lurton enrolled at Cumberland University Law School and graduated in 1867. He then established a private practice with James A. Bailey, who eventually moved on to the U.S. Senate. In 1875 Lurton was appointed by the governor to the sixth chancery division of Tennessee, making him at age thirty-one the youngest chancellor in state history.

Lurton resumed his private law practice in 1878. In 1886 he was elected to the Tennessee supreme court, where he served for seven years. President Grover Cleveland then appointed him to the U.S. Court of Appeals for the Sixth Circuit. On the court Lurton became friends with William Howard Taft, the presiding judge. In 1909 Lurton became Taft's first nominee for the Supreme Court. During his brief tenure on the Court, Lurton's originally conservative views became more progressive. He agreed frequently with Oliver Wendell Holmes, Jr., and was a strong supporter of the Sherman Antitrust Act. He served only four and a half years before dying of a heart attack in 1914.

M

McCulloch v. Maryland

A states' rights challenge to the chartering of the second Bank of the United States led in 1819 to a landmark Supreme Court decision supporting expansive congressional power.

Congress chartered the private bank in 1816 to try to restore financial stability following the War of 1812. The bank was unpopular in many states, especially after the nation sank into a depression that many blamed on the bank's tight credit policies. Two states passed laws prohibiting the bank from operating within their borders, while six others, including Maryland, tried to tax the bank's branches out of existence.

James McCulloch, the manager of the bank's Balti-more branch, refused to pay the tax, claiming it was an unconstitutional infringement on the federally chartered bank. Maryland contended that Congress had exceeded its powers when it chartered the bank and that in any event the state had the power to tax the bank within its borders.

The case, *McCulloch v. Maryland,* was argued before the Supreme Court for nine days in late February and early March 1819 by six of the nation's greatest lawyers. Among them was Daniel Webster, who defended the constitutionality of the bank even though he had voted against its creation as a young Federalist congressman from Massachusetts. Chief Justice John Marshall announced the Court's decision just three days later, upholding the creation of the bank and barring states from taxing it.

Despite the Supreme Court's decision in McCulloch v. Maryland *(1819) the Bank of the United States remained under attack. This cartoon depicts President Andrew Jackson attacking the bank with his veto stick. Vice President Martin Van Buren, center, helps kill the monster, whose heads represent Nicholas Biddle, bank president, and directors of the state banks.*
Source: Library of Congress

Marshall's opinion solidified the "implied powers" doctrine, which held that Congress's powers were not strictly limited to the "enumerated powers" listed in the Constitution (Article I, Section 8). Marshall said that creation of the bank was valid under the Constitution's "necessary and proper" clause, which authorized Congress to enact "all Laws which shall be necessary and proper for carrying into Execution" the powers specifically provided.

"Let the end be legitimate, let it be within the scope of the Constitution," Marshall wrote, "and all means which are appropriate . . . which are not prohibited . . . are constitutional." Maryland's tax, he continued, could not stand because the states had no power to levy a tax on "an instrument employed by the government of the Union to carry its powers into execution."

The ruling provided a basis for expanding the power of Congress as it considered such issues as a national tariff and road and canal construction. It was unpopular in some states. The debate over the ruling prompted Marshall to write a series of anonymous newspaper articles defending it. The bank also continued to be controversial. President Andrew Jackson vetoed a bill to recharter the bank in 1832, and it went out of existence in 1836.

Source: Collection of the Supreme Court of the United States

McKenna, Joseph

Realizing he needed further legal training when he was nominated to the Supreme Court in 1897, Joseph McKenna (1843–1926) studied for a few months at Columbia University Law School before joining the Court. Nonetheless, his poor education and writing ability severely handicapped him during his first years on the bench.

Shortly after McKenna's birth in Philadelphia, his family moved to California. McKenna attended public schools there, graduated from the law department of the Benicia Collegiate Institute in 1865, and was admitted to the bar in 1866. In that same year he was elected district attorney for Solano County. McKenna also plunged into Republican party politics and be-came acquainted with Leland Stanford, a railroad magnate and California's first Republican governor.

Political defeats plagued McKenna after his election to the state legislature in 1875. He was an unsuccessful candidate for Speaker of the California assembly and left the legislature in 1876. He then suffered defeats during two runs for the U.S. Congress before finally being elected in his third attempt in 1885. During his four terms in the House, McKenna worked for bills to extend railroad land grants and restrict the freedoms of Chinese workers. In the House McKenna became friends with William McKinley, then chair of the Ways and Means Committee. It was President McKinley who later appointed him to the Supreme Court.

On the recommendation of Stanford, who was then a senator, President Benjamin Harrison appointed McKenna to the Ninth Judicial Circuit in 1892. After five years as a circuit judge, McKenna was promoted to attorney general in 1897. He served only one year in that post before McKinley chose him for the Supreme Court. The Senate confirmed the nomination by voice vote despite objections by many senators to McKenna's close ties to Stanford and western railroad interests.

McKenna wrote one of his most important opinions for the Court in 1920, two years after World War I ended. The case, *Schaefer v. United States,* arose when five officers of a German-language newspaper in Philadelphia were convicted of publishing false news articles designed to hurt recruiting efforts and help Germany win the war. The articles were all reprinted from other publications, but in each case the officers had deleted or added to parts of the articles. In his opinion for the Court, McKenna said it was unnecessary to prove that the articles presented an immediate danger to the nation, but only that they had a bad effect. Justices Holmes and Brandeis strongly dissented from McKenna's opinion. "Convictions such as these, besides abridging freedom of speech, threaten freedom of thought and of belief," Brandeis wrote.

McKenna served on the Court for nearly twenty-seven years, writing over 600 opinions. Usually in the majority, he generally supported the growth of federal power and deferred to legislative decisions.

In 1915 he had a stroke, and his mental powers failed noticeably in the 1920s. Chief Justice Taft and other members of the Court finally persuaded him to retire in 1925, when he was eighty-one years old.

Source: Library of Congress

McKinley, John

Like many other early Supreme Court justices, John McKinley (1780–1852) was nominated after someone else turned down the nomination. On his last day in office, President Andrew Jackson nominated William Smith of Alabama to fill one of two newly created seats on the Court. When Smith declined the nomination, the new president, Martin Van Buren, chose McKinley for the Court.

Born in Culpeper County, Virginia, McKinley spent most of his youth in Kentucky. He was admitted to the bar at age twenty after teaching himself law. He practiced in Frankfort and Louisville before moving to Alabama, a prosperous territory that was about to become a state. McKinley settled in Huntsville and quickly became a leading social and political figure. In 1820 he was elected to the Alabama legislature. Two years later he sought election to the U.S. Senate by the state legislature, but lost by one vote. When the incumbent died four years later and the seat opened up, McKinley ran again and won by three votes.

As a senator, McKinley supported strict construction of the Constitution and a reform of federal land policies to give small landholders some protection against speculators. He was defeated for reelection in 1831 by Alabama governor Gabriel Moore. The next year he won election to the U.S. House, where he strongly backed President Andrew Jackson. He also supported Martin Van Buren, who became vice president under Jackson in 1832 and was elected president himself in 1836.

McKinley was elected to the U.S. Senate again in

1837, but never began his term because Van Buren named him to the Court before Congress met. During his fifteen years as a justice, McKinley championed states' rights and slavery. In *Bank of Augusta v. Earle* (1839), his dissenting opinion argued that states should be able to regulate banking in their own territory. In another dissent he pointed out that federal law had no role in a lawsuit about property in one state.

McLean, John

In 1829 President Andrew Jackson struck a deal with John McLean (1785–1861). Jackson agreed to appoint McLean to the Supreme Court if McLean would give up his presidential ambitions. Jackson kept his part of the bargain, but McLean did not. During his thirty-two years as an associate justice, McLean ran for president four times, changing parties with each race. He lost all four times.

Source: Collection of the Supreme Court of the United States

Following McLean's birth in Morris County, New Jersey, his family moved to Virginia and then Kentucky. The family finally settled on a farm near Lebanon, Ohio, when McLean was twelve years old. McLean attended the county school and also worked as a farmhand to earn enough money to hire two Presbyterian ministers as tutors. In 1804 he began a two-year apprenticeship to the clerk of the Hamilton County Court of Common Pleas in Cincinnati, and he also started studying law.

The year 1807 was momentous for McLean. He was admitted to the bar, married, and returned to Lebanon to open a printing office. He began publishing the *Western Star,* a weekly newspaper that was strongly Jeffersonian. He gave up the printing business in 1810, however, to turn his full attention to practicing law. The next year he experienced a profound religious conversion that made him a devout Methodist for the remainder of his life.

After serving four years in Congress, beginning in 1813, McLean was elected to a judgeship on the Ohio supreme court in 1816. In that same year, he actively supported James Monroe for president. Monroe rewarded the favor in 1822 by appointing McLean commissioner of the General Land Office and, a year later, postmaster general. By all accounts McLean was a skilled administrator. Within a few years under his direction, the postal service became the largest agency in the executive branch.

Jackson nominated McLean for the Supreme Court in January 1829. During his thirty-two years on the Court, McLean's most famous opinion was his dissent in the Dred Scott case *(SCOTT V. SANDFORD* [1857]). The Court's majority held that slaves were not citizens, that the Missouri Compromise was unconstitutional, and that Congress had no authority to stop the spread of slavery. McLean and Justice Benjamin Curtis, both ardent abolitionists, wrote dissenting opinions upholding the Missouri Compromise and Congress's power to ban slavery in the territories.

McLean also wrote an important opinion about other Court opinions. In *Wheaton v. Peters* (1834) he held that the opinions were in the public domain and could be published without violating copyright laws.

McLean became senior associate justice in 1845

and thereafter often presided over the Court when Chief Justice Roger B. Taney was ill.

McReynolds, James C.

James Clark McReynolds (1862–1946) may have been the nastiest person ever to serve on the Supreme Court. Much to the surprise of President Woodrow Wilson, who appointed him, McReynolds also turned out to be one of the most conservative justices to serve during the twentieth century.

McReynolds was anti-Semitic and openly shunned the Court's two Jewish justices, Louis Brandeis and Benjamin Cardozo. For three years after Brandeis joined the Court, McReynolds refused to speak to him. At one point McReynolds refused to sit next to Brandeis when a group photograph was taken. McReynolds also wouldn't speak to Justice John H. Clarke, whom he considered dim-witted.

McReynolds was born in Elkton, Kentucky. He was named class valedictorian when he graduated from Vanderbilt University in 1882, and he received

Source: Library of Congress

his law degree from the University of Virginia in 1884. McReynolds practiced law in Nashville, Tennessee, for most of the next two decades. He ran for Congress in 1896, but his arrogant personality alienated voters, and he lost the election.

In 1903 McReynolds was appointed an assistant U.S. attorney. During his four years at the Justice Department, McReynolds prosecuted several antitrust cases. He resigned in 1907 to practice law in New York City. Wilson named him attorney general in 1913. McReynolds's bad temper and arrogance quickly earned him many enemies among members of Congress and executive branch officials. Wilson tried to deal with the problem by appointing McReynolds to the Supreme Court in 1914.

Wilson believed that McReynolds held liberal opinions, an assumption based on McReynolds's eagerness in battling the trusts when he was at the Justice Department. However, McReynolds turned out to have extremely conservative views that were almost always the opposite of Wilson's. McReynolds was one of the four conservative justices who consistently voted to strike down President Franklin Roosevelt's New Deal programs. McReynolds retired in 1941 after serving twenty-six years on the Court, and died five years later.

Mandamus

A writ of mandamus (a Latin term meaning "we command") is a court order to a lower court or government department or official requiring the performance of some nondiscretionary governmental action. Its companion is the writ of prohibition, which bars a government official or lower court from taking certain action.

Both writs are viewed as extraordinary legal remedies and are rarely used today. Customarily, if the Supreme Court rules that a party is entitled to the writ, it does not actually issue the writ, on the assumption that the court or official will comply with its ruling without the order.

Congress authorized the Supreme Court to issue writs of mandamus to federal officials in the Judiciary

Act of 1789. In *MARBURY V. MADISON* (1803), however, the Court ruled the provision unconstitutional as an improper expansion of its limited ORIGINAL JURISDICTION under Article III of the Constitution. As federal JURISDICTION has expanded, however, the types of cases in which the writ can be issued have also increased.

Mandatory Jurisdiction

Mandatory jurisdiction, as distinguished from discretionary jurisdiction, denotes the cases that a court is obligated to hear and decide. When Congress establishes a right of APPEAL in certain cases, the Supreme Court is required to decide such cases even if the justices, for administrative reasons, might prefer not to.

Over the past hundred years, an increasing number of cases coming to the Court along the appeals route have been transferred to the discretionary CERTIORARI route, so that the Court now enjoys virtually complete control over its caseload.

This process began in 1891 with creation by Congress of the circuit courts of appeals. The Circuit Court of Appeals Act provided for Supreme Court review in several types of cases only if the new intermediate appeals courts certified the case to the Supreme Court or if the Supreme Court itself decided to grant review by issuing a writ of certiorari. A right of appeal remained to parties in several other types of cases, including constitutional questions, matters of treaty law, and capital crimes.

The Judiciary Act of 1925 eliminated the right of appeal from appeals court rulings except in cases in which the appeals court held a state law invalid under the Constitution, federal law, or treaties. A right of appeal from district court decisions remained, however, in cases under antitrust or interstate commerce laws, appeals by the government in criminal cases, suits to halt enforcement of state laws or other official state actions, and suits designed to halt enforcement of Interstate Commerce Commission orders.

During the 1970s these direct appeal routes from district courts were all redirected by Congress through the courts of appeals. After 1976 direct appeal remained only in a few kinds of cases. These included cases in which district courts held an act of Congress invalid and in which the United States or its employees were a party. Direct appeal could also be made from decisions of three-judge district courts involving reapportionment, some civil rights matters, and some federal campaign-spending cases.

From state courts, only two types of cases retained a right of direct appeal under the 1925 act. These were cases in which a state law was upheld against a federally based challenge and cases in which a federal law or treaty was held invalid.

In 1988 Congress all but eliminated the Court's mandatory jurisdiction by repealing the obligatory review of decisions striking down acts of Congress, appeals court decisions striking down state laws as unconstitutional, and final judgments of state supreme courts questioning the validity of a federal law or treaty.

The 1988 act meant that the only remaining major category of cases that have a mandatory right of appeal to the Supreme Court consists of cases heard by a THREE-JUDGE COURT involving congressional or statewide legislative reapportionment.

Marbury v. Madison

Sometimes called the single most important ruling in the history of the Supreme Court, *Marbury v. Madison* (1803) established the principle of JUDICIAL REVIEW and the Court's power to declare an act of Congress unconstitutional. Chief Justice John Marshall's opinion in the case contains a ringing and oft-quoted assertion of judicial power: "It is, emphatically, the province and duty of the judicial department to say what the law is."

This constitutional landmark arose from a political dispute in the aftermath of the bitter presidential election of 1800. Republican Thomas Jefferson defeated incumbent Federalist John Adams for the presidency. Adams, in his final days in office, attempted to entrench Federalists in the judiciary by appointing sixteen new circuit court judges and forty-two new justices of the peace for the District of Columbia. But commissions for four of the new justices of the peace, including William Marbury, were not delivered before Adams's last day in office.

When President Jefferson's secretary of state, James Madison, refused to give the four men their commissions, Marbury asked the Supreme Court to issue a writ of MANDAMUS ordering him to do so. The case presented a dilemma for Marshall, a committed Federalist whom Adams had named chief justice immediately after his electoral defeat. If the Court issued the order, Madison might refuse, and the Court had no means to enforce compliance. If the Court did not issue the writ, it risked surrendering judicial power to Jefferson and the Republicans.

Marshall's solution has been called a "masterwork of indirection." He wrote that the judicial appointments were complete despite the failure to deliver the commissions—thus rebuking Madison's position. But he concluded that the Court had no power to issue the writ of mandamus as Marbury requested. Marshall said that Congress had added unconstitutionally to the Court's ORIGINAL JURISDICTION by authorizing the Court, in the Judiciary Act of 1789, to issue such writs to officers of the federal government.

Contemporaries did not regard Marshall's claim of authority as having the importance that it has now gained. Jefferson continued to believe that the legislature was the only branch capable of determining the validity of its actions. The Court did not again declare an act of Congress unconstitutional until the so-called Dred Scott case (*SCOTT V. SANDFORD* [1857]). (See UNCONSTITUTIONAL STATUTES.)

Marshall himself later expressed a willingness to sacrifice the Court's role as the final authority on the constitutional validity of federal statutes in the face of continuing Republican attacks on the Court.

When the Republican-controlled Congress impeached and tried Justice Samuel Chase in 1805, Marshall wrote to his embattled colleague: "I think the modern doctrine of impeachment should yield to an appellate jurisdiction in the legislature." Chase's acquittal in the Senate, however, made Marshall's plan for congressional review of the Court's decisions unnecessary.

Marshall, John

John Marshall (1755–1835) was the nation's third chief justice. He effectively established the American system of constitutional law and its doctrine that courts have the power to review legislative actions.

Marshall was born in a log cabin near Germantown, Virginia. His father, who served as assistant surveyor to George Washington and as a member of the Virginia house of burgesses, was his primary teacher. Marshall was largely self-taught in the law.

Marshall participated in several major battles in the revolutionary war, including the siege of Norfolk, Brandywine, Monmouth, Stony Point, and Valley Forge. He attended a course of law lectures at the College of William and Mary in 1780 and was admitted to the bar that same year. He quickly built a lucrative

Source: Library of Congress

practice with his specialty of defending Virginians against their British creditors.

He served three separate terms in the Virginia house of delegates (1782–1785, 1787–1790, and 1795–1796). During his 1787 term, Marshall was a key figure in persuading Virginia to ratify the U.S. Constitution. He quickly became one of Virginia's leading Federalists. From 1796 to about 1806, financial troubles related to a land investment in the northern neck of Virginia consumed much of Marshall's attention. It may have been his need to make money that drove Marshall to write *The Life of George Washington*, a five-volume biography published from 1804 to 1807. The book was poorly written, and Jefferson guaranteed it would not have large sales when he ordered federal postmasters not to take orders for it.

While struggling to repay his debts, Marshall rejected many appointments offered him by presidents George Washington and John Adams. The offers included U.S. attorney general in 1795, minister to France in 1796, associate justice of the Supreme Court in 1798, and secretary of war in 1800. In 1797 Marshall did accept an appointment as one of three envoys sent to France to lessen hostilities between the United States and France. When the envoys arrived, agents of the French foreign minister demanded a $250,000 bribe for him and a $12 million loan for France before anyone would talk to the Americans. The U.S. emissaries refused to pay and were praised by Congress for their resistance in what became known as the XYZ Affair.

George Washington persuaded Marshall to run for the U.S. House of Representatives in 1799, and he won. The next year President John Adams appointed him secretary of state. Marshall became the effective head of the U.S government later that year when Adams retired to his home in Massachusetts for a few months.

Adams's first choice for chief justice when Oliver Ellsworth resigned in 1800 was John Jay, the Court's first chief justice. Jay declined the offer, and Federalists urged Adams to elevate Associate Justice William Paterson. Adams nominated Marshall instead. The Senate confirmed Marshall as chief justice in January 1801, and he served until his death in July 1835. During that period, Marshall heard more than 1,000 cases, and wrote more than 500 opinions. Some of his opinions, like the landmark ruling in *MARBURY V. MADISON* (1803) that established the judiciary's right to review legislative actions, helped define the shape of the new federal government and the Court's role in that government.

The Court received little respect before Marshall became chief justice. Largely through the force of his personality and the quality of his mind, the Court gained prestige. Marshall eliminated the often confusing series of opinions issued in each case, striving instead for unanimous opinions that clearly set forth the Court's view. He also worked to make the Court a truly coequal branch of government.

At age seventy-six, Marshall underwent surgery for the removal of kidney stones. The surgery was successful, but Marshall's health deteriorated rapidly three years later when he developed an enlarged liver. He died in Philadelphia on July 6, 1835, just three months shy of his eightieth birthday. As the Liberty Bell tolled to mark his death, it cracked.

Marshall, Thurgood

In 1954 Thurgood Marshall (1908–1993) was the winning attorney when the Supreme Court declared in *BROWN V. BOARD OF EDUCATION OF TOPEKA* that separate schools for blacks and whites were inherently unequal. Eleven years later President Lyndon Johnson named him solicitor general, making him the government's chief advocate before the Supreme Court. In 1967 Marshall was named to the Supreme Court, becoming the first black justice in the nation's history.

Marshall was born in Baltimore. He graduated with honors from Lincoln University in 1930 and first in his class from Howard University Law School in 1933. While at Howard, Marshall developed an interest in CIVIL RIGHTS. He became involved with the National Association for the Advancement of Colored People (NAACP) and in 1940 was named director of the NAACP Legal Defense and Educational Fund. In that position, which Marshall held for more than two decades, he directed NAACP legal efforts aimed at

Source: Library of Congress

ending DISCRIMINATION in voting, housing, public accommodations, and education.

In 1961 President John F. Kennedy nominated Marshall for the Second Circuit Court of Appeals. Southern Democratic senators strongly opposed the nomination and managed to block confirmation for a year. When Marshall was nominated to the Supreme Court by Kennedy's successor, southern members of the Senate Judiciary Committee subjected Marshall to intense questioning, but the Senate confirmed him by a 69–11 vote.

Marshall was one of the most consistently liberal voices in the Court's history. During the years of the Warren Court, Marshall's liberal views usually placed him in the majority. But as the Court turned conservative under chief justices Warren Burger and William Rehnquist, Marshall increasingly found himself dis-

senting. He dissented from Court decisions that required reporters to reveal the names of confidential sources to grand juries; declared that the right to an education is not guaranteed by the Constitution; held that in most cases children cannot be bused across school district lines to achieve racial integration; and ruled that the death penalty does not constitute cruel and unusual punishment. He also dissented from decisions upholding congressionally imposed limits on funding for abortion, striking down limits on independent spending in presidential campaigns, and upholding Georgia's law making sodomy a crime.

As the Court became dominated by conservative justices, Marshall grew increasingly frustrated by his role. Citing his age, he retired in 1991. Marshall died of heart failure January 24, 1993.

Marshal of the Court

The marshal of the Court is easily recognized as the officer who calls the Supreme Court to order by crying "Oyez, Oyez, Oyez" (an Old French word meaning "hear ye"). The marshal is the court's general manager, paymaster, and chief security officer. The marshal attends all the Court's sessions, manages approximately 200 employees, supervises the SUPREME COURT BUILDING and its grounds, pays the justices and other employees, orders supplies, and pays the Court's bills.

Marshals of the Court	
Richard C. Parsons	1867–1872
John C. Nicolay	1872–1887
John Montgomery Wright	1888–1915
Frank Key Green	1915–1938
Thomas E. Waggaman	1938–1952
T. Perry Lippitt	1952–1972
Frank M. Hepler	1972–1976
Alfred Wong	1976–1994
Dale E. Bosley	1994–

The marshal, whose original duties were to keep order in the courtroom, also oversees the Supreme Court Police Force. A chief of police and seventy-five officers patrol the building, grounds, and adjacent streets. The marshal and aides also receive visiting dignitaries and escort the justices to formal functions outside the Court.

During the Court's public sessions, the marshal (or the marshal's deputy) and the CLERK OF THE COURT, both dressed in traditional cutaway suits, station themselves at either end of the bench. At exactly 10 a.m. the marshal pounds the gavel and announces: "The Honorable, the Chief Justice and the Associate Justices of the Supreme Court of the United States." As the justices take their seats, he calls for silence by crying "Oyez" three times and announces: "All persons having business before the Honorable, the Supreme Court of the United States, are admonished to draw near and give their attention, for the Court is now sitting. God save the United States and this honorable Court."

During oral argument the marshal or the marshal's assistant flashes the white and red lights that warn counsel that the time for presenting arguments is about to expire. In addition, the marshal is responsible for serving process and orders issued by the Court. Today, the job of actually serving papers—usually disbarment orders—is delegated to U.S. marshals.

The position of marshal was created by the Judiciary Act of 1867, which gave the Court authority to appoint a marshal, remove him, and set his compensation. In 1994 the marshal's salary was set at $115,700. Before 1867 the marshal's duties were performed by either the clerk or the marshal of the district in which the Court was located. Between 1801 and 1867, for example, the twelve men who served as marshal of the District of Columbia also served informally as marshal of the Court.

Source: Collection of the Supreme Court of the United States

Matthews, Stanley

It took nominations from two different presidents before the Senate finally confirmed Stanley Matthews (1824–1889) for the Supreme Court. Even then, the Senate approved the nomination by the narrowest possible margin, 24–23.

Matthews was born in Cincinnati and graduated from Kenyon College in 1840. After reading law for two years, he moved to Maury County, Tennessee, where he was admitted to the bar at age eighteen. He established a legal practice there and also became editor of the *Tennessee Democrat,* a weekly newspaper that backed James K. Polk for president. Matthews remained in Tennessee for only two years before moving back to Cincinnati.

Within a year after returning home Matthews was appointed assistant prosecuting attorney for Hamilton County and became editor of another newspaper, the *Cincinnati Morning Herald.* In 1848 he was elected clerk of the Ohio house, at least partly because of his strong opposition to slavery. He next served as judge on the Hamilton County Court of Common Pleas (1851–1853), member of the Ohio senate (1855–1858), and U.S. attorney for southern Ohio (1858–1861). Despite his personal opposition to slavery, as U.S. attorney Matthews used the Fugitive Slave Act to prosecute W. B. Connelly, a reporter who had helped two slaves escape.

Matthews left his legal career behind to serve as an officer in the Union Army during the Civil War. One of the units Matthews served with was the Twenty-third Ohio Regiment, which also included an officer named Rutherford B. Hayes. Years later President Hayes nominated Matthews to the Supreme Court, but the nomination was unsuccessful.

In 1863 Matthews resigned his army command when he was elected to the Cincinnati superior court. He returned to private practice in 1865 but remained extremely active in politics. In 1876 he campaigned for presidential candidate Hayes and was one of Hayes's chief advocates at the 1877 electoral commission. When Hayes chose Ohio senator John Sherman as his secretary of the treasury, the Ohio legislature elected Matthews to fill Sherman's seat.

Hayes nominated Matthews for the Supreme Court in January 1881, but the nomination aroused strong opposition in the Senate. Some senators viewed the appointment as a reward for having helped Hayes in his disputed victory over Tilden, while others saw Hayes and Matthews simply as old cronies. The Senate refused to act on the nomination. After President James A. Garfield took office, he nominated Matthews in March 1881, and the Senate confirmed him in May.

Matthews wrote the majority opinions in *Hurtado v. California* (1884), which upheld a murder conviction even though there had been no indictment from a grand jury, and in *Yick Wo v. Hopkins* (1886), which found that a California law had been unfairly applied to discriminate against Chinese laundry owners. He served on the Court until his death in March 1889.

Merits, On the

In its legal sense, this phrase refers to the legal rights of the parties involved in a case. To make a decision on the merits means to decide in favor of one of the parties in a case based on the substantive facts and law involved, rather than on matters of procedure or jurisdiction.

Miller, Samuel F.

When a new court circuit was created west of the Mississippi, members of Congress and politicians from the western states urged President Abraham Lincoln to appoint Samuel Freeman Miller (1816–1890) of Iowa to the seat. Lincoln complied, and Miller became

Source: Library of Congress

the first Supreme Court justice from west of the Mississippi. He had no judicial experience.

Miller, born in Richmond, Kentucky, took up medicine as his first career. He received his medical degree from Transylvania University in 1838 and set up a practice in Barboursville, Kentucky. However, he soon developed a strong interest in law and politics. After studying law on the side, he passed the bar exam in 1847. He eventually decided he could not remain in Kentucky, particularly after the Kentucky constitutional convention of 1849 entrenched the position of slavery in the state. He freed his own slaves and moved to Iowa, a free state.

In Iowa Miller took up a legal career, establishing a successful practice in Keokuk, and jumped into politics. He helped organize the Republican party in Iowa and by 1860 was one of the state's top Republican figures. He also was a strong supporter of Lincoln for the Republican presidential nomination. In 1861 Miller sought the Republican gubernatorial nomination, but lost to incumbent governor Samuel J. Kirkwood.

After his appointment to the Supreme Court in 1862, Miller was twice considered for chief justice. He did not receive the nomination either time. His name also came up as a possible presidential candidate in 1880 and 1884, but his candidacies never got off the ground.

Miller wrote over 600 majority opinions while on the Court. Among these were the *SLAUGHTERHOUSE CASES* (1873), which supported a Louisiana law granting a monopoly to certain butchers, and *Wabash, St. Louis and Pacific Railway Co. v. Illinois* (1886), which upheld federal control over interstate commerce.

Miller remained on the Court until his death in 1890.

Source: Collection of the Supreme Court of the United States

Minton, Sherman

President Harry S. Truman nominated Sherman Minton (1890–1965) to the Supreme Court in 1949 based in large part on Minton's reputation as a liberal senator. Once on the Court, however, Minton turned out to be quite conservative.

Minton was born in Georgetown, Indiana. After graduating at the top of his class from Indiana University's law school in 1915, he received a scholarship to spend a year studying at Yale Law School. In 1933 Minton was appointed Indiana public counselor and was then elected to the U.S. Senate, where he served from 1935 to 1941. In the Senate, where he was known as a New Dealer, Minton befriended fellow senator Truman and endorsed President Franklin Roosevelt's Court-packing plan. Minton lost his bid for a second term in the Senate. In 1941 Roosevelt asked Minton to be his administrative assistant and later that year nominated him to the U.S. Court of Appeals for the Seventh Circuit. Minton served as an appeals court judge for the next eight years until his nomination to the Supreme Court.

Minton is one of a handful of justices who have surprised presidents by seeming to change their political views after being appointed to the Court. In 1952

Minton wrote an opinion in *Adler v. Board of Education, City of New York,* upholding a state law requiring the dismissal of any public employee who belonged to a subversive organization. The law was specifically aimed at public school teachers. Minton wrote for the 6–3 majority that the law did not deny anyone the rights of free speech and assembly. "His freedom of choice between membership in the organization and employment in the school system might be limited, but not his freedom of speech or assembly," Minton wrote.

Minton served on the Court for seven years before becoming ill with pernicious anemia. He resigned due to ill health on October 15, 1956, and died nine years later.

> PD 47   METROPOLITAN POLICE DEPARTMENT
> Rev. 8/73   **WARNING AS TO YOUR RIGHTS**
>
> You are under arrest. Before we ask you any questions, you must understand what your rights are.
>
> You have the right to remain silent. You are not required to say anything to us at any time or to answer any questions. Anything you say can be used against you in court.
>
> You have the right to talk to a lawyer for advice before we question you and to have him with you during questioning.
>
> If you cannot afford a lawyer and want one, a lawyer will be provided for you.
>
> If you want to answer questions now without a lawyer present you will still have the right to stop answering at any time. You also have the right to stop answering at any time until you talk to a lawyer.

As a result of the ruling in Miranda v. Arizona *(1966) a police officer must advise a person placed under arrest of his or her right to remain silent and to be represented by an attorney.*

Miranda v. Arizona

Miranda v. Arizona (1966) is the Warren Court's best known and perhaps most controversial decision extending constitutional protections to criminal defendants and suspects. The ruling requires police to give certain warnings to suspects. Police must tell suspects that they have the right to remain silent, the right to consult with a lawyer, and the right to have a lawyer appointed for them if they cannot afford one; and that the government can use any statement they do make against them at trial.

By 1966 the Supreme Court had been grappling with the issue of CONFESSIONS for three decades. In the four cases decided in *Miranda,* suspects had been questioned incommunicado in what Chief Justice Earl Warren called a "police-dominated" atmosphere. The warnings were needed, the five-justice majority said, to counteract the inherently coercive nature of stationhouse questioning. A suspect could waive those rights and give a statement without consulting a lawyer, the Court held, but the prosecution had to show that the waiver was made voluntarily, knowingly, and intelligently.

The dissenting justices criticized the ruling on constitutional and practical grounds. Justice Byron R. White said the rule was "a deliberate calculus to prevent interrogation, to reduce the incidence of confessions and to increase the number of trials." *Miranda* was criticized by police, prosecutors, and public officials at all levels of government. Republican Richard Nixon made law and order a major theme of his successful 1968 campaign for the presidency and promised to appoint justices more sympathetic to police and less concerned with defendants' rights. (See ELECTIONS AND THE COURT.)

With four Nixon-appointed justices, the Burger Court began narrowing *Miranda.* In *Harris v. New York* (1971) the Court voted 5–4 to allow the use of statements obtained in violation of *Miranda* to impeach the defendant's credibility if he or she testified. In 1974 the Court allowed a prosecutor to use a statement made by a suspect who had not been fully warned of his rights as a lead to finding a government witness. In 1975 the Court ruled that police could resume questioning suspects who asserted their right to remain silent if the police waited for an interval and advised the suspects again of their rights.

Later rulings by the Burger and Rehnquist courts have been mixed; significantly, they have accepted *Miranda* as settled law. In 1981, for example, the Court ruled that once an accused requested counsel, questioning had to cease until a lawyer was present or the accused initiated some new contact with police. The opinion was written by Justice White, one of the *Miranda* dissenters.

Three years later the Court created a limited "public safety" exception to *Miranda* in a case in which a police officer asked a suspect, "Where's the gun?" and then advised him of his rights. Justice Sandra Day O'Connor, a conservative and President Ronald Reagan's first appointee to the Court, dissented. "Were the Court writing from a clean slate, I could agree," O'Connor wrote. "But *Miranda* is now the law . . . and the Court has not provided sufficient justification for blurring its now clear strictures."

Misdemeanor

A misdemeanor, as distinguished from a felony, is a less serious criminal offense defined by federal or state law as punishable by a fine or imprisonment for a limited period of time—typically up to one year—and usually in a facility other than a penitentiary.

The Supreme Court has allowed some procedural rights guaranteed by the Bill of Rights to be omitted in some misdemeanor cases, although the Court has sometimes used other distinctions in making its decisions. For example, the right to legal counsel first guaranteed to indigent defendants in state felony cases in 1962 was extended in 1972 to state misdemeanor prosecutions if they actually resulted in a prison sentence *(Argersinger v. Hamlin)*. But in *Scott v. Illinois* (1979) the Court ruled, 5–4, that states need not provide counsel if a defendant received no jail or prison sentence, even though the offense could have resulted in incarceration.

On the other hand, the Court ruled in 1938 that in federal courts counsel must be provided in all criminal prosecutions.

The Court has also narrowed the Sixth Amendment right to a jury trial, which by its terms applies to "all criminal prosecutions." The Court, however, has always excluded "petty" offenses from the requirement in federal courts. After extending the jury trial provision to the states, the Court specified that states must provide trial by jury for all persons charged with

offenses that can be punished by more than six months in prison *(Baldwin v. New York* [1970]). The Court has not specified how to distinguish between "serious" and "petty" offenses where the crime is punishable by less than six months' imprisonment.

In federal courts a felony prosecution must be initiated by a grand jury indictment, as required by the Fifth Amendment. But federal statutes and the Federal Rules of Criminal Procedure permit a misdemeanor prosecution to be brought by indictment or by a prosecutor's charge called an information. The Court has not extended the requirement of grand jury indictment to the states. As a result, state prosecutors may bring criminal charges in felony or misdemeanor cases by means of an information rather than an indictment.

The Constitution also specifies that IMPEACHMENT may be used to remove the president, vice president, or other civil officers of government upon conviction of "Treason, Bribery, or other high Crimes and Misdemeanors." The all-encompassing phrasing has eliminated any necessity to define the terms as they apply to the impeachment process.

Moody, William H.

William Henry Moody (1853–1917) achieved national fame in 1892 as the prosecutor of Lizzie Borden, the Massachusetts woman charged with killing her parents with an ax. Borden's acquittal by a sympathetic jury did not tarnish Moody's reputation.

Moody was born in Newbury, Massachusetts, and graduated with honors from Harvard in 1876. He then attended Harvard Law School, but left after a few months to study law privately. After being admitted to the bar in 1878, Moody moved to Haverhill, Massachusetts, to establish a practice. His clients soon included most of the region's industries and manufacturers. As his practice and reputation grew, Moody became involved in Republican politics. In 1888 he began his public career as city solicitor for Haverhill.

Two years later Moody became district attorney for the eastern district of Massachusetts, and in 1895 he

Source: Library of Congress

gerous radical. Nonetheless, the Senate confirmed the nomination by a voice vote.

A strong believer in JUDICIAL RESTRAINT, Moody supported Congress's use of the commerce clause to address social problems. But he also argued, in the majority opinion in *Twining v. New Jersey* (1908), that states should be able to set their own rules for criminal procedure. Moody served on the Court for just under four years before acute rheumatism crippled him and forced him to retire in 1910.

Moore, Alfred

In 1782 Alfred Moore (1755–1810) replaced James Iredell as North Carolina attorney general. Seventeen years later, he replaced Iredell as a justice on the Supreme Court after Iredell died.

Moore, born in New Hanover County, North Car-

won a special election to the U.S. House of Representatives. Moody was respected in the House for his mastery of the details and facts involved in legislation. Also in 1895, he met Theodore Roosevelt and the two men formed a close friendship.

In 1901 Roosevelt became president upon the assassination of President William McKinley. Moody joined Roosevelt's cabinet the next year as secretary of the navy, a position in which he excelled. In 1904 Roosevelt named Moody attorney general, giving him responsibility for prosecuting the trusts. Moody, a progressive Republican, happily complied with the president's directive.

When Roosevelt nominated Moody for the Supreme Court in 1906, some senators opposed the nomination on the grounds that Moody was a dan-

Source: Collection of the Supreme Court of the United States

olina, was a descendant of Roger Moore, a leader of the 1641 Irish Rebellion, and James Moore, who served as governor of South Carolina in the early eighteenth century. He attended school in Boston and then returned home to read law under his father, a colonial judge. He received his law license at age twenty.

Moore served as captain of a Continental regiment during the Revolution and fought in several successful battles. He left the army in 1777 to return home when his father died. He continued his military activities by joining the local militia and taking part in raids on British troops in Wilmington. The British responded by plundering his property.

Moore began a ten-year stint as North Carolina attorney general in 1782 and became a state superior court judge in 1799. In December 1799 President John Adams nominated him to replace Iredell on the Supreme Court. Moore was apparently Adams's second choice. Adams had wanted William R. Davie for the job, but Davie had just been appointed a diplomatic agent to France.

Moore had an undistinguished career on the Court, writing only one opinion during the five years he served. Citing ill health, he resigned in 1804 and returned home once again to help establish the University of North Carolina. He died six years later.

Mootness

A court will not decide a case when it is moot—that is, when circumstances are sufficiently altered by time or events to remove the dispute or conflict of interests. The Supreme Court has linked the mootness doctrine to the Constitution's CASE OR CONTROVERSY RULE, but it has also recognized several exceptions that permit courts to decide cases that seem to be moot.

Criminal cases formerly had been deemed moot if the defendant had served his or her prison sentence. However, the Court now will find such a case viable if the defendant might continue to suffer adverse legal consequences as a result of the challenged conviction.

A similar rule applies in civil cases if the challenged judgment or situation may continue to have an adverse effect on the plaintiff.

The Court also has created an exception for conduct or situations that are necessarily of short duration—"capable of repetition, yet evading review" if the mootness rule is strictly applied. An example is the landmark abortion rights ruling, *ROE V. WADE* (1973), in which the Court ruled on the issues even though the plaintiff was no longer pregnant by the time the case reached the Supreme Court.

The Court sometimes applies the mootness doctrine strictly. In *DeFunis v. Odegaard* (1974) the Court sidestepped a challenge to a state law school's affirmative action admissions program. The Court based its decision on the ground that the plaintiff—who had obtained a court order admitting him to the school while the litigation was pending—was to graduate regardless of the Court's decision. In *City of Los Angeles v. Lyons* (1983) the Court overturned a court order restricting Los Angeles police from using choke holds by saying that the plaintiff in the case had not shown that the choke hold would be used against him in the future.

Murphy, Francis W.

Francis William Murphy (1890–1949) was nominated to the Supreme Court in 1940 by President Franklin Roosevelt. But Murphy didn't want to be a justice. What he really wanted was to be secretary of war in Roosevelt's cabinet, but he didn't get the appointment. Murphy was so anxious to become involved in World War II that during Court recesses he served as an infantry officer at Fort Benning, Georgia, an activity that earned him the displeasure of Chief Justice Harlan Fiske Stone.

Murphy was born in Harbor Beach, Michigan. After receiving his undergraduate and law degrees from the University of Michigan, he clerked for a Detroit law firm for three years. He served in France and Germany during World War I and stayed in Europe to take graduate courses in London and Dublin after the

Source: Library of Congress

war ended. He then returned to the United States and held a succession of public positions. These included chief assistant attorney general for the eastern district of Michigan (1919–1920), judge on the Detroit Recorders Court (1923–1930), mayor of Detroit (1930–1933), governor general of the Philippines (1933–1935), U.S. high commissioner to the Philippines (1935–1936), governor of Michigan (1937–1939), and U.S. attorney general (1939–1940).

On the Court Murphy staunchly defended civil liberties. One of his most notable opinions came in *Thornhill v. Alabama* (1940). In that case the Court voted 8–1 to overturn the conviction of a man charged with violating an Alabama law that barred picketing. The justices ruled that picketing was protected by the First Amendment. "In the circumstances of our times the dissemination of information concerning the facts of a labor dispute must be regarded as within that area of free discussion that is guaranteed by the Constitution," Murphy wrote for the Court. Murphy served on the Court for nine years until his death in July 1949.

N

Nelson, Samuel

Samuel Nelson (1792–1873) was President John Tyler's third choice as a Supreme Court nominee. Tyler's relations with Congress were so bad that impeachment proceedings were introduced against him in the House in 1842. This enmity did not bode well for Tyler's Supreme Court nominees. When Justice Smith Thompson died in 1843, Tyler first nominated Secretary of the Treasury John Spencer to fill the seat. The Senate rejected Spencer in January 1844. Tyler then nominated Reuben Walworth, New York state chancellor, but the Senate tabled the nomination. In

Source: Collection of the Supreme Court of the United States

February 1845 Tyler nominated Nelson, a respected New Yorker with extensive judicial experience, and the Senate finally confirmed him on a voice vote.

Nelson, born in Hebron, New York, grew up on farms in upstate New York. After initially leaning toward a career in the ministry, Nelson chose the law instead following graduation from Middlebury College in 1813. He clerked in a law office, became a member of the bar in 1817, and established a thriving law practice in Cortland, New York. In 1820, the same year he voted for President James Monroe as a presidential elector, Nelson was appointed postmaster of Cortland. The next year he was a delegate to the state constitutional convention. At the convention, Nelson advocated abolishing property qualifications for voting.

Nelson's judicial career, which lasted nearly fifty years, began in 1823 when he became a judge of the Sixth Circuit of New York. After moving up to associate justice of the New York supreme court in 1831, Nelson became chief justice in 1837. He continued serving on the New York court until he was nominated to the Supreme Court.

Most of Nelson's twenty-seven years on the Court were relatively quiet. One of his most notable opinions was a dissent in the *Prize Cases* (1863). The case arose out of actions by President Abraham Lincoln after hostilities broke out at Fort Sumter in April 1861. As part of his effort to prepare the Union to fight the Civil War, Lincoln ordered a blockade of southern ports without receiving approval from Congress. In the *Prize Cases,* by a 5–4 vote, the Court upheld Lincoln's right to act until Congress convened in special session in July. Nelson sharply dissented, arguing that only Congress could declare war and that Lincoln's blockade proclamation was illegal until Congress approved it in July.

With his health failing, Nelson resigned from the Court in 1872 and died the next year.

New York Times Co. v. Sullivan

The Supreme Court's landmark decision in *New York Times Co. v. Sullivan* (1964) set constitutional limits on LIBEL law. It substantially expanded the protections for the press as well as for individuals to criticize government officials. The ruling helped bring about an increase in bold investigative reporting by the news media. The case began, however, not as a free press issue but as a civil rights dispute.

Civil rights leader Martin Luther King, Jr., was arrested in Alabama in 1960 on a charge of perjury. To raise money for his legal defense, leaders of King's Southern Christian Leadership Conference placed a full-page advertisement in the *New York Times.* The advertisement included two paragraphs describing King's previous arrests and civil rights demonstrations by students of a black state college in Montgomery, Alabama.

Although he was not named in the advertisement, L. B. Sullivan, an elected Montgomery city commissioner responsible for the police department, claimed that the passages libeled him by falsely depicting the conduct of the police. The advertisement did contain several errors. King had been arrested four times, not seven as the ad had stated. The ad incorrectly characterized the student demonstrations and exaggerated the police response. It said, for example, that police had "ringed" the campus when they had only been deployed near it.

Sullivan sued the four clergymen who placed the ad and the *New York Times,* which had not checked the ad for accuracy. A jury awarded Sullivan $500,000. The *Times* and the civil rights leaders appealed to the U.S. Supreme Court, which unanimously threw out the award.

In an opinion for six justices, Justice William J. Brennan, Jr., dismissed the Court's earlier dicta viewing all libel as outside the protection of the First Amendment. "None of . . . [those] cases sustained the use of libel laws to impose sanctions upon expression critical of the official conduct of public officials," Brennan said.

The suit, Brennan stated, must be considered "against the background of a profound national commitment to the principle that debate on public issues should be uninhibited, robust, and wide-open." Forcing critics of official conduct to guarantee the accuracy of their remarks to avoid liability would lead to self-censorship, he said.

Instead, Brennan concluded, the Constitution requires that a public official be barred from recovering damages in libel suits unless the official proves the defamatory statement was made with " 'actual malice'—that is, with knowledge that it was false or with reckless disregard of whether it was false or not." Applying that rule, the Court found that there was no evidence to sustain a libel award against the *Times* or the civil rights leaders.

Three justices said they would have gone further and barred public officials from ever recovering libel damages for false statements about their public conduct. The Court later extended the "actual malice" requirement to libel suits brought by "public figures," but allowed private individuals to recover damages under a lower standard.

New York Times Co. v. United States

See PENTAGON PAPERS CASE.

Nixon, Richard

President Richard Nixon (1913–1994) attempted to reshape the Supreme Court to reflect his conservative views on issues of law and order during his presidency (1969–1974). The Court, however, did not support Nixon on certain other issues, including some of his expansive claims for presidential power. Eighteen months into his second term, the Court unanimously ruled against his position in the Watergate tapes case and set in motion the final events that forced him to resign from office on August 9, 1974. (See PRESIDENT AND THE COURT.)

In his 1968 presidential campaign, Nixon strongly criticized the Warren Court's decisions on criminal procedure and promised to select justices who would be more sympathetic to police and less protective of defendants' rights. (See ELECTIONS AND THE COURT.) As president, Nixon appointed four justices, including Chief Justice Warren E. Burger, who had a reputation as a hard-line judge on the U.S. Circuit Court of Appeals for the District of Columbia. Burger was confirmed easily by the Democratic-controlled Senate in June 1969.

Nixon's effort to name a second conservative after the resignation of Justice Abe Fortas ran into trouble. The Senate rejected his first two choices for the post. Charges of conflict of interest sank the nomination of federal appeals court judge Clement Haynsworth, Jr.; another federal appeals court judge, G. Harrold Carswell, was rejected because of his record as a segregationist and his lack of intellectual qualifications. (See NOMINATION TO THE COURT.)

Nixon's third choice for the seat, federal appeals court judge Harry A. Blackmun, was unanimously confirmed in May 1970. Nixon's other two appointees—Lewis F. Powell, Jr., a Richmond, Virginia, attorney, and William H. Rehnquist, an assistant attorney general—both were easily confirmed in December 1971.

Source: The White House

The four Nixon appointees helped form a new majority that generally refused to extend the Warren Court's criminal procedure rulings but stopped short of overruling them. (See CRIMINAL LAW AND PROCEDURE.) Some of his appointees voted against Nixon's positions on other issues, including ABORTION, aid to parochial schools, and SCHOOL DESEGREGATION.

Nixon made several very broad assertions of presidential power. He claimed the right to exercise the pocket veto during brief congressional recesses. Two federal appeals courts rejected that position. He claimed the power to "impound" funds appropriated by Congress. The Supreme Court rejected that position after Nixon left office (*Train v. City of New York* [1975]). (See SEPARATION OF POWERS.) He also claimed an inherent power to engage in domestic ELECTRONIC SURVEILLANCE without a judicial warrant in national security investigations. The Court rejected that claim by a 6–2 vote (*United States v. U.S. District Court* [1972]).

Nixon continued the war in Vietnam that he had inherited from his predecessor, President Lyndon B.

Johnson. Acting under his powers as commander in chief, he expanded the war by authorizing air raids and then a land invasion into Cambodia. Some members of Congress and others claimed Nixon's actions were illegal, but the war ended without an authoritative ruling by the Supreme Court on the issues. Nonetheless, Congress passed, over Nixon's veto, the War Powers Act of 1973, requiring the president to notify Congress within forty-eight hours of committing U.S. armed forces overseas. (See WAR POWERS.)

During Nixon's 1972 reelection campaign, burglars broke into the Democratic National Committee headquarters at the Watergate complex in Washington. Investigations showed that the burglars had been employed by Nixon's campaign committee and that some of his top White House aides had helped cover up the connection. The scandal led to a criminal investigation by a special prosecutor and to IMPEACHMENT proceedings against Nixon in the House of Representatives.

In April 1974 the special prosecutor, Leon Jaworski, obtained a subpoena ordering Nixon to turn over tapes of his conversations with his aides relating to the Watergate break-in and cover-up. Nixon's lawyers moved to quash the subpoena. Judge John J. Sirica of the U.S. District Court for the District of Columbia denied the motion. Late in the Supreme Court term, the case moved onto its docket, and the Court decided to hold a special summer session to hear the case on July 8, 1974.

The Court ruled July 24. By a vote of 8 to 0 in *United States v. Nixon*, it rejected Nixon's claim of an absolute executive privilege to withhold the evidence sought by the special prosecutor. (See EXECUTIVE PRIVILEGE AND IMMUNITY.) Chief Justice Burger wrote the opinion; Rehnquist, who had served in the Justice Department under one of the Watergate defendants, former attorney general John Mitchell, did not participate.

For a few hours after the ruling, there was no word of Nixon's reaction. Then came a statement that the president accepted the decision. Within the week the House Judiciary Committee had voted three articles of impeachment against Nixon.

Facing a House debate on impeachment, Nixon decided to release the tapes on his own. Contrary to Nixon's previous statements, the tapes showed that he had participated in the decisions to pay "hush money" to the original Watergate defendants. Even many of his supporters conceded that the evidence amounted to a "smoking gun" that was all but certain to result in impeachment by the House and conviction by the Senate.

Nixon decided instead to resign. He left office on August 9, 1974. On September 8, 1974, his successor, President Gerald R. Ford, issued Nixon a "full, free, and absolute pardon" for any offenses he "committed or may have committed" during his years in office.

Nomination to the Court

Under Article II of the Constitution the president has the power to nominate members of the Supreme Court, subject to the advice and consent of the Senate. This is the principal way the president can exert influence over the Court's work. Since Supreme Court justices are appointed for life, presidents may have long-lasting influence over the direction of the Court by careful selection of nominees. All presidents have attempted to place on the Court justices whose views coincided with their own. Most presidents have had some success in this effort, though there are notable exceptions.

The framers of the Constitution expected the Senate to play a role in the initial selection of nominees for the Court. Presidents from George Washington to George Bush, however, have usually not consulted widely with senators before making their choices. Still, the Senate has scrutinized Supreme Court nominees more carefully than nominees for other positions. Out of 148 nominations for the Court, 28 have failed to win approval. (See CONFIRMATION PROCESS.)

Selection Process

The appointment of a justice involves a mix of personal and political factors.

Presidents have typically appointed justices from their own political party; only thirteen times has a president picked a member of the opposition party for the Court. Republican presidents have appointed nine Democratic justices; Democratic presidents have named three Republicans to the Court; and President John Tyler, a Democrat turned Whig, appointed Democrat Samuel Nelson. (See POLITICS AND THE COURT.)

Judicial experience has been an important factor, but less so than might be expected. Of the Court's 108 justices, 67 served previously on a state or federal court. Franklin D. Roosevelt appointed six justices who had no prior judicial experience. Both Ronald Reagan and George Bush, on the other hand, listed judicial experience as a prerequisite for their nominees to the Court.

Presidents have often turned to members of their own cabinet in nominating justices. John Adams, Andrew Jackson, and Abraham Lincoln each chose a member of his cabinet as chief justice: John Marshall, Roger B. Taney, and Salmon P. Chase, respectively. More recently, Franklin Roosevelt appointed two of his attorneys general, Frank Murphy and Robert H. Jackson, to the Court. Harry S. Truman named his attorney general, Tom C. Clark. John Kennedy and

President Richard Nixon nominated both Lewis F. Powell, Jr., (left) a Democrat, and William H. Rehnquist, (right) a Republican, to the Supreme Court on October 21, 1971.   Source: UPI/Bettmann

Richard Nixon both picked high-ranking Justice Department officials: Byron R. White and William H. Rehnquist, respectively.

Personal friendship has occasionally been the reason for a president's selection. Examples include William Howard Taft's nomination of Horace H. Lurton, Woodrow Wilson's selection of Louis D. Brandeis, Truman's choice of Fred M. Vinson as chief justice, Kennedy's choice of White, and Lyndon B. Johnson's unsuccessful nomination of Abe Fortas for chief justice.

Geographical representation was once a key factor. Before the Civil War seats on the Court were traditionally designated for New England, New York,

Pennsylvania, and Virginia. But this factor has become less important.

Efforts to provide a measure of religious balance were reflected in the traditions of a "Catholic seat"—first held by Taney in 1836—and a "Jewish seat," first held by Brandeis in 1916. These traditions too have faded. Nixon broke the tradition of a "Jewish seat" by nominating three Protestants in succession to succeed Fortas in 1969. Reagan named two Catholics to the Court—Antonin Scalia and Anthony M. Kennedy—while William J. Brennan, Jr., served in what had been called the "Catholic seat."

On the other hand, race and sex seem now to be important factors in the selection process. Thurgood

Marshall, appointed by Lyndon Johnson in 1967 as the Court's first black justice, was succeeded by another African American, Clarence Thomas. Bush discounted the importance of race in the selection, but stressed Thomas's rise from a poor background in explaining his choice. Reagan fulfilled a campaign pledge to put a woman on the Court when he nominated Sandra Day O'Connor in 1981. President Clinton named Ruth Bader Ginsburg in 1993 as the Court's second female justice.

In making appointments, presidents rely on the advice of the attorney general as well as personal and political advisers. Members of Congress sometimes recommend nominees. Justices themselves have sometimes advised presidents on filing vacancies, although that once-common practice might provoke controversy today.

Taft, the only person to serve as both president and chief justice, was able to put his conservative stamp on the Court's decisions for a decade by his influence on President Warren G. Harding. Taft first lobbied for his own appointment as chief justice in 1921 and then selected or approved Harding's three other appointees. In lobbying for the appointment of Pierce Butler in 1922, Taft sharply criticized two other prominent judges considered as potential nominees: Benjamin N. Cardozo and Learned Hand.

Cardozo did win appointment to the Court in 1932, in part on the recommendations of then chief justice Charles Evans Hughes and another member of the Court, Harlan Fiske Stone. Hughes also successfully urged Franklin Roosevelt to name Stone as his successor in 1941 and counseled Truman in 1946 on his choice of a chief justice after Stone's death.

Appointments and Disappointments

Several presidents, including Jackson, Lincoln, Franklin Roosevelt, Nixon, and Reagan, have been notably successful in influencing the Court's conduct through judicial appointments. Roosevelt's nine appointments made the Court more supportive of federal power and more receptive to claims involving racial justice and civil liberties. Appointments of conservative justices by Nixon and Reagan shifted the Court's decisions in such areas as civil rights and criminal procedure.

Several other presidents have had cause for disappointment in the views of some of the justices they named to the Court.

Two of President Thomas Jefferson's appointees, H. Brockholst Livingston and Thomas Todd, became consistent supporters of Jefferson's adversary, Chief Justice Marshall. Later, Jefferson warned his successor, James Madison, against appointing Joseph Story to the Court. Jefferson was proved correct when Story showed himself to be an even stronger proponent of a powerful Court than Marshall.

Theodore Roosevelt, a vigorous "trustbuster," appointed Justice Oliver Wendell Holmes, Jr., who initially voted against the administration's antitrust efforts. Woodrow Wilson appointed James C. McReynolds, who repeatedly voted against the administration's position and continued as a staunch conservative on the Court through the New Deal era.

Republican president Dwight D. Eisenhower named two of the key figures of the Court's liberal activist era—Brennan and Chief Justice Earl Warren. Once when asked if he had made any mistakes as president, Eisenhower quipped, "Yes, two, and they are both sitting on the Supreme Court."

Even for those presidents who have been largely successful in influencing the Court through their appointments, some exceptions can be noted. Some of Lincoln's appointees were less supportive of civil rights for blacks than he might have been if he had lived to complete his second term. Some of Nixon's appointees opposed administration positions on some issues, including school desegregation. Two of Reagan's appointees, O'Connor and Kennedy, voted in 1992 to reaffirm the abortion rights ruling *Roe v. Wade* (1973), which the Reagan and Bush administrations had urged the Court to overrule.

Oaths of Office

Justices of the Supreme Court must take two oaths of office before they can officially discharge their duties as jurists on the highest court of the land. The first is the "constitutional" oath, which all federal employees must take. The second is the "judicial" oath, required for all federal judges.

The constitutional oath, which is required by Article VI, Section 3 of the Constitution, reads:

"I, ..., do solemnly swear that I will support and defend the Constitution of the United States against all enemies, foreign and domestic, that I will bear true faith and allegiance to the same, that I take this obligation freely, without any mental reservation or purpose of evasion, and that I will well and faith-fully discharge the duties of the office on which I am about to enter. So help me God."

The judicial oath was included in the Judiciary Act of 1789 and has been modified over the years. In 1992 its text read as follows:

"I, ..., do solemnly swear or affirm, that I will administer justice without respect to persons, and do equal right to the poor and to the rich, and that I will faithfully and impartially discharge and perform all the duties incumbent on me as [a justice of the Supreme Court], under the Constitution and laws of the United States. So help me God."

Like other traditions of the Supreme Court, the investiture ceremonies have changed over the years. In the last twenty years or so, the constitutional oath has been administered to the new justice in a private cer-

William Howard Taft signing the oath of office as the tenth chief justice of the United States, July 11, 1921.   *Source: UPI/Bettmann*

emony, usually in the justices' robing room. The judicial oath is then taken in a special session of the Court before the justice's family and friends. In recent years, however, several justices have taken the constitutional oath in a ceremony at the White House. Justice David H. Souter, for example, took his constitutional oath in the White House East Room. Justice Clarence Thomas took his in a ceremony on the South Lawn.

The chief justice generally administers the oath of office, but another justice or any other federal judge or magistrate may do the honors. Outgoing chief justice Warren E. Burger administered the oaths to incoming chief justice William H. Rehnquist, for example. Justice Byron R. White administered the judicial oath to Thomas because Chief Justice Rehnquist was absent from the office due to the death of his wife.

Obiter Dictum

Obiter dictum (a Latin term meaning "said in passing"; plural, "obiter dicta") is a statement by a justice expressing an opinion that is included with, but is not essential to, an opinion resolving a case before the Court. Dicta are not construed as precedent and are not binding in future cases. But on occasion the opinion expressed in these asides does become the basis for future rulings on similar issues.

For example, a famous footnote in a 1938 decision, *United States v. Carolene Products Co.*, laid out a rationale for heightened judicial scrutiny of laws that adversely affected "discrete and insular minorities." The footnote was not needed to decide the case, but it became the most important part of the ruling. It provided the basis for many later decisions on issues involving racial DISCRIMINATION and other EQUAL PROTECTION issues.

On the other hand, the Court sometimes retreats from the broad implications of its decisions by, in effect, downgrading part of a holding to the status of dictum. For example, in the well-known police interrogation case, *MIRANDA V. ARIZONA* (1966), the Court declared that the prosecution "may not use" a suspect's statement to police unless the suspect was given detailed warnings of his or her rights. Five years

later, however, the Court upheld the right of a prosecutor to use a statement obtained in violation of the *Miranda* rules to cross-examine a defendant once he took the stand. The Court in the later case described the broader prohibition on using such statements announced in *Miranda* as dictum.

Obscenity

Although the Supreme Court has never considered obscenity to be protected by the First Amendment, it did not provide a definition for lower courts to use in determining whether material is obscene until 1957. After much confusion, the Court sixteen years later established a somewhat looser definition that is still in effect. Sexually explicit material that does not meet the definition of obscenity may nonetheless be subject to some government regulations that could not be enforced against other forms of expression.

Obscenity was listed as one of several categories of unprotected expression in *Chaplinsky v. New Hampshire* (1942). The Court dealt with the issue in detail only in 1957 when it affirmed obscenity convictions obtained under a federal statute and a California law. "Sex and obscenity are not synonymous," Justice William J. Brennan, Jr., explained in his opinion for the Court in *Roth v. United States*. Material could be found obscene only if it met this test: "whether to the average person, applying contemporary standards, the dominant theme of the material taken as a whole appeals to the prurient interest." Justices Hugo L. Black and William O. Douglas, who were First Amendment absolutists, dissented.

After *Roth* the Court grew increasingly fragmented on the obscenity issue. A majority seldom agreed on applying a single standard. Nonetheless, two additions to the definition gained a measure of acceptance: to be considered obscene, material had to be "patently offensive to current community standards of decency" and "utterly without redeeming social importance." By 1967 the justices' views were so divergent that they adopted the practice of simply reversing obscenity convictions by a *PER CURIAM* OPINION whenever five justices found material not obscene under their separate standards. In *Stanley v. Georgia* (1969) the Court ruled that private possession of obscene material could not be punished.

In 1973 a five-member majority formed behind a new definition of obscenity. In *Miller v. California* Chief Justice Warren E. Burger said states could enact laws regulating obscenity if the definition was limited to materials "which, taken as a whole, appeal to the prurient interest in sex; which portray sexual conduct in a patently offensive way; and which, taken as a whole, do not have serious literary, artistic, political, or scientific value."

Burger's opinion in a companion case, *Paris Adult Theatre I v. Slaton,* explicitly rejected the 1970 recommendation of a presidential commission on obscenity and pornography that restrictions on sale or display of pornographic books or films to consenting adults should be lifted. In a dissent in that case, Brennan said that it was impossible to write a clear test for obscenity and urged that anti-obscenity laws be limited to prohibiting distribution to juveniles or "obtrusive exposure to unconsenting adults."

In *Miller,* Burger said that local standards rather than a national standard were to be used to determine offensiveness. The test, he insisted, would adequately protect First Amendment interests since appellate courts would independently review the constitutional issues. A year later, the Court did just that in overturning a Georgia jury's finding that the movie *Carnal Knowledge* was obscene. In *Pope v. Illinois* (1987) the Court tightened the definition of obscenity by ruling that the literary, scientific, or artistic value of challenged material was to be determined based on national rather than local community standards.

The Court has also been fragmented in its decisions concerning the government's power to regulate material that is indecent but not obscene. In 1976, in a 5–4 decision without a majority opinion, the Court upheld a local zoning ordinance requiring that adult bookstores and movie theaters be dispersed rather than concentrated in a single area of a city. Two years later the Court again divided 5–4 in upholding the Federal Communications Commission's authority to punish radio or television stations for broadcasting indecent material—at least during hours when children

"THAT'S TO TAKE CARE OF OBSCENITY CASES"

Herblock on All Fronts (New American Library, 1980)

Denying First Amendment protection to obscene materials has always been the easy part of the problem; the difficult part is determining what is obscene. Herblock's 1977 cartoon illustrates the Court's dilemma.   Source: Herblock on All Fronts, New American Library, 1980

were listening. In 1982 the Court yet again divided 5–4 in ruling that the First Amendment limits the power of public school officials to remove "objectionable" books from library shelves, but without specifying what standards apply. In 1986, however, the Court did permit school officials to suspend a student for a lewd speech at a school assembly.

In its most recent indecency ruling, the Court again split 5–4, without a majority opinion, in upholding a ban on nude dancing. Writing for a plurality of three justices in *Barnes v. Glen Theatre, Inc.* (1991), Chief Justice William H. Rehnquist said an Indiana law furthered a substantial governmental interest by protecting societal order and morality—sufficient justification for overriding the First Amendment protections accorded to symbolic speech. Justice David H. Souter found a narrower justification in control of the secondary effects of adult entertainment establishments, such as prostitution and sexual assaults. Justice Antonin Scalia saw no First Amendment interests implicated by the law. The four dissenting justices said there was no compelling interest to override First Amendment concerns.

The Court has been more decisive in dealing with child pornography. In 1982 it upheld state laws prohibiting the promotion of sexual performances by children. In *Osborne v. Ohio* (1990) it upheld a ban on the private possession of child pornography. The Court said that the government's compelling interest in protecting the physical and psychological well-being of minors justified an exception to its earlier ruling protecting the personal possession of obscene materials.

Source: Collection of the Supreme Court of the United States

O'Connor, Sandra Day

President Ronald Reagan made history in August 1981 when he nominated Sandra Day O'Connor (1930–   ) as the first woman justice in the nation's history. The Senate confirmed O'Connor, a judge on the Arizona Court of Appeals, by a 99–0 vote.

O'Connor was born in El Paso, Texas. She graduated from high school at age sixteen and earned both undergraduate and law degrees at Stanford University. Although she was one of the outstanding students in her law school class, O'Connor had trouble finding a job when she graduated in 1952 because women were still not often employed in the legal profession. When she applied to one law firm for a job as an attorney, she was offered a position as a secretary instead.

O'Connor became deputy county attorney for San Mateo County, California, in 1952. She and her husband then moved to Germany, where she worked as a civilian attorney for the U.S. Army. They next settled in Phoenix, Arizona, where O'Connor split her time between practicing law, raising children, and performing volunteer work. In 1965 she was appointed assistant attorney general in Arizona, the first

woman to hold that job. After four years in that post, O'Connor served for six years in the Arizona state senate. She was majority leader from 1973 to 1974. She was elected to the Maricopa County Superior Court in 1975 and in 1979 was appointed to the Arizona Court of Appeals, where she served for two years until her nomination to the Supreme Court.

O'Connor joined a Court that was becoming increasingly conservative. She usually, though not always, helped push the Court further to the right. On most cases, O'Connor aligned herself with Chief Justice Warren Burger and Justice William Rehnquist, the Court's two most conservative members. In 1985 the three dissented when the Court ruled that police may not shoot a fleeing suspect unless they believe the person might kill or seriously injure someone nearby. The three, joined by Justice Byron White, also dissented in 1986 when the Court voted 5–4 to strike down a Pennsylvania law designed to discourage women from having abortions. In 1989, after Burger had left the Court, O'Connor, Chief Justice Rehnquist, White, and Justice John Paul Stevens dissented when the Court ruled that burning the flag was a form of expression protected by the First Amendment.

Official Immunity

English COMMON LAW established limits on the right to bring legal actions against the government or its officers. This concept of official immunity has been carried over into American law, but over time the protections have been restricted to allow some legal recourse for persons who claim injury as a result of wrongful actions by the government.

The Constitution establishes a broad CONGRESSIONAL IMMUNITY in the "speech or debate" clause, and the Supreme Court has held that the president is entitled to absolute immunity from personal liability because of his constitutional duties. (See EXECUTIVE PRIVILEGE AND IMMUNITY.) Other forms of immunity—for executive branch officials, legislators, judges, and the government itself—depend on extensions of common law concepts.

Sovereign Immunity

The United States cannot be sued in federal court unless Congress expressly authorizes such lawsuits. The Federal Tort Claims Act of 1946 does waive the government's immunity for certain personal injury claims against government employees or contractors.

The Supreme Court recognized sovereign immunity as early as 1834. It relaxed the doctrine somewhat in *United States v. Lee* (1882), which allowed a son of the Confederate general Robert E. Lee to recover the family home, Arlington, after claiming that it had been illegally seized by federal officials. The Court, by a vote of 5 to 4, reasoned that the United States did not have title to the estate and that sovereign immunity did not prevent a suit to enforce an established property right if the United States is not a necessary party to the suit.

Five years later, in 1887, Congress passed the Tucker Act, specifically granting the Court of Claims (now the U.S. Claims Court) and federal district courts jurisdiction over such property rights cases. Cases under the Federal Tort Claims Act are also brought in the Claims Court.

Sovereign immunity continues to bar suits against federal officials that seek a share of government property or seek to compel the exercise of government authority. But a suit by an individual claiming he or she is threatened or injured by an official's action taken under an allegedly unconstitutional law or in excess of legal authority is usually allowed to proceed.

Executive Immunity

Executive immunity protects subordinate federal officials for reasonable actions taken in good faith in the performance of their duties. But they may be held personally liable for damage caused by acts in excess of their authority.

State and local executive officials are subject to suit under federal CIVIL RIGHTS law (Section 1983 of Title 42 of the U.S. Code) for depriving a citizen of constitutional rights "under color of state law." A key Supreme Court ruling, *Monroe v. Pape* (1961), encouraged the growth of such suits, but later decisions have read an array of immunities into Section 1983.

In *Butz v. Economou* (1978) the Court held that federal officials enjoy only a qualified immunity for so-called constitutional torts (personal injury suits based on a claim of a violation of an individual's constitutional rights). In those cases, the Court said, federal officials are subject to liability according to the same standards developed under federal civil rights laws for state and local officials.

When it extended absolute immunity to the president in 1982, the Court refused to accord the same protection to presidential aides. It did, however, broaden the standards for executive immunity for such aides, other federal officials, and state and local officials as well. In *Harlow v. Fitzgerald* the Court said the aides were subject to liability if their actions violated "clearly established" statutory or constitutional rights—a difficult test to meet in many such cases.

Legislative Immunity

The Court in 1951 recognized an absolute immunity for state legislators from federal civil suit based on a common law immunity and the Constitution's "speech or debate" clause. The ruling in *Tenney v. Brandhove* dismissed a suit against members of a California legislative committee investigating un-American activities for allegedly violating the plaintiff's freedom of speech.

In 1979 the Court extended legislative immunity to members of a bistate regional planning agency. The ruling may open the way to extending the same immunity to many public bodies or officials that promulgate rules of general applicability.

Judicial Immunity

The Supreme Court first recognized the principle of judicial immunity in 1869. It has continued to accord judges absolute protection from personal liability for all judicial acts except "acts where no jurisdiction whatever" exists.

In *Stump v. Sparkman* (1978) the Court reaffirmed the doctrine of judicial immunity, rejecting a federal civil rights suit based on extreme facts. The judge in the case had granted a mother's petition to have her daughter sterilized without a hearing or any notice to the daughter. The Court said the judge was immune from suit because granting the petition was a judicial act and no state law or decision specifically denied the judge the authority to grant the petition.

Open Housing

Congress enacted the first federal CIVIL RIGHTS law prohibiting racial DISCRIMINATION in the sale or rental of real property in 1866, but the law went all but ignored for more than a century. The Supreme Court revived the law in 1968, just two months after Congress had passed the Fair Housing Act of 1968. The two laws now provide overlapping protections against discrimination in housing.

State Discrimination

Passed to enforce the newly ratified Thirteenth Amendment prohibiting slavery, the Civil Rights Act of 1866 provided that "citizens, of every race and color" were to enjoy the same rights to "purchase, lease, sell, hold, and convey real and personal property . . . as is enjoyed by white citizens." When the Supreme Court in 1883 struck down the PUBLIC ACCOMMODATIONS provisions of a later civil rights law, it nonetheless implicitly upheld the 1866 act by acknowledging Congress's power under the Thirteenth Amendment to erase "the necessary incidents of slavery."

The 1866 act became a dead letter, however, as cities and states moved to adopt "Jim Crow" SEGREGATION laws, including laws to maintain racially separated neighborhoods. One such law, in Louisville, Kentucky, forbade members of one race to buy, reside on, or sell property on streets where a majority of the residents were of the other race.

The Louisville ordinance was struck down by the Supreme Court in 1917. The Court based its decision in *Buchanan v. Warley* on the Fourteenth Amendment due process protection for PROPERTY RIGHTS, rather than on the equal protection clause of the amendment or on the 1866 act.

Officially imposed housing segregation was quickly replaced in many localities by private agreements, called restrictive covenants. Under such covenants, the white residents of a particular block or neighborhood agreed to refuse to sell or lease their homes to blacks. The Court in 1926 upheld these covenants, adhering to its earlier rulings that Congress had no authority to protect individuals from private discrimination.

Twenty-two years later, however, the Court in *Shelley v. Kraemer* (1948) effectively nullified restrictive covenants by forbidding the states to enforce them. Writing for a unanimous Court—with three justices not participating—Chief Justice Fred M. Vinson said that the Fourteenth Amendment did not prevent "voluntary adherence" to such covenants, but that judicial enforcement of the agreements constituted state action in violation of the equal protection clause.

In two companion cases from the District of Columbia, the Court could not rely on the Fourteenth Amendment, which applied only to the states. Instead, it relied on the 1866 act to bar enforcement.

Individual Discrimination

Despite the Court's rulings on state enforcement of restrictive covenants, blacks and other minorities still had little protection from housing discrimination by individual home and apartment owners. Then Congress moved toward adoption of a broad open housing law just as a case trying to breathe new life into the 1866 Civil Rights Act was reaching the Supreme Court.

Joseph Lee Jones claimed that the Alfred H. Mayer Company had violated the 1866 act by refusing to sell him a home in a suburban section of St. Louis County, Missouri, because he was black. A federal district court dismissed the case, and the court of appeals affirmed the dismissal on the grounds that the 1866 act (in modern form, Section 1982 of Title 42 of the U.S. Code) applied only to state discrimination.

In a 7–2 decision, the Supreme Court in June 1968 reversed the court of appeals, holding that the 1866 law barred individual as well as state-backed discrimination in the sale and rental of housing.

Writing for the Court in *Jones v. Alfred H. Mayer Co.*, Justice Potter Stewart said the act "was designed to do just what its terms suggest: to prohibit all racial discrimination." He found the law within Congress's powers under the antislavery amendment: "At the very least, the freedom that Congress is empowered to secure under the Thirteenth Amendment includes the freedom to buy whatever a white man can buy, the right to live wherever a white man can live."

Meanwhile, Congress in April had completed action on the Fair Housing Act of 1968. The act banned discrimination on the basis of race, color, religion, or national origin in the sale, lease, and financing of housing, and in the furnishing of real estate brokerage services. Single-family houses sold or rented by owners and small, owner-occupied boardinghouses were exempted. A 1974 amendment extended the ban to discrimination on the basis of sex.

In its ruling in *Jones* the Court stressed that the 1866 act was not a "comprehensive open housing law" like the new Fair Housing Act. Together the two laws, along with the equal protection clause if state action is involved, now provide several legal options to use in housing discrimination cases.

The Court in 1969 ruled that the 1866 law permitted actions for damages or injunctive relief. The Fair Housing Act provides for conciliation procedures under the Department of Housing and Urban Development (HUD) or state fair-housing agencies. Only in 1979 did the Court hold that it also allowed a direct civil action without prior resort to HUD or state authorities. The 1968 act also authorizes the attorney general to go to court to enjoin "a pattern or practice of housing discrimination."

The importance of overlapping legal protections was seen in a case involving the refusal by a Chicago suburb to rezone property to permit the construction of low- and moderate-income housing. (See ZONING.) In *Village of Arlington Heights v. Metropolitan Housing Development Corporation* (1977) the Court ruled that without a showing of discriminatory motive, the refusal to rezone did not amount to a violation of the equal protection clause. On remand, however, the court of appeals found that the village's action would violate the Fair Housing Act if it had a discriminatory effect, even though there was no evidence of a discriminatory intent.

Operations of the Court

The Supreme Court is a small part of the federal judiciary and the one most bound by tradition and custom. The nine justices work in a single, if palatial, building in the nation's capital with a support staff numbering in the hundreds, not thousands.

Court proceedings are clothed in tradition that lends continuity not only to the Court itself but to the laws of the land. These traditions help the Court to project an image of wise, just, and serene jurists calmly deliberating over and deciding legal questions that are crucial to the conduct of national life.

The Court's insistence on the secrecy of its deliberations protects the justices from disclosure of any of the bickering or ineptitude that surely occurs from time to time. The elaborate courtesy and adherence to seniority on the Court also serve its image as an august deliberative body above everyday squabbles. The imposing SUPREME COURT BUILDING, called by some the "marble palace," has erased the memory of the many years during which the justices were shunted from one makeshift courtroom to another. (See HOUSING THE COURT.)

To a great degree this image of calm deliberation is accurate. The high standards necessary to effective judicial performance and public trust have been consistently maintained by a succession of mostly able jurists. There have been few personal scandals involving the justices, and any embarrassments the Court has suffered have been resolved fairly quickly. With some notable exceptions, the justices have not displayed their political sympathies openly.

The Court is hardly immune to the problems of management, procedure, maintenance, and personnel faced by any other institution. The Court must be administered, budgeted, staffed, and locked up after work each day. Moreover, it is at the apex of a substantial federal judicial system that includes ninety-four district courts, thirteen courts of appeal, and two special courts, along with their judges and attendant staff. (See COURTS, LOWER.)

In addition to everyday administrative problems, the Court in recent decades has had to contend with an increasing caseload. Since 1960 the number of cases filed in federal district courts has more than tripled, to about 300,000. During the same period the number of cases appealed to the Supreme Court has more than doubled, reaching more than 7,200 in the 1992–1993 term. From this mountain of work the Supreme Court culls the legal issues it considers most worthy of its judgment. (See WORKLOAD OF THE COURT.)

The Court at Work

A justice once described the Court as nine individual law firms. Each justice works largely in isolation from the other justices, aided by up to four law CLERKS and perhaps as many secretaries. Justices may confer privately with each other on particular cases, but more often such communication takes place through memos. All the justices usually come together only at their regularly scheduled CONFERENCES.

The Court organizes its work by one-year terms that begin on the first Monday in October. These formal annual sessions now last nine months, concluding in late June or early July, when the Court has taken action on the last case argued before it in that session.

Throughout the term certain times are set aside for oral ARGUMENTS and conferences, for WRITING OPINIONS and announcing decisions. In the 1992–1993 term, the court heard 116 cases argued and issued 107 signed opinions.

During both the formal session and the summer recess, the justices spend a great deal of time considering petitions asking the Court to review a case. Petitions range from elegantly printed and bound documents to single sheets of prison stationery, scribbled in pencil and filled with grammatical and spelling errors. (See PETITION, RIGHT OF.)

During the 1992–1993 term, the Court was asked to review about 6,300 cases, in addition to about 900 that were carried over from the previous term. The vast majority of these cases are denied review, dismissed, or withdrawn. Others are decided summarily, that is, without hearing argument and without issuing a full opinion. (See SUMMARY JUDGMENT.)

Altogether, the Court granted review in 97 cases in the 1992–1993 term. In addition, 66 cases had been set for review in earlier terms and were carried over into the 1992–1993 term.

Many of the Court's procedures have been modified since the Court first convened in 1790. The length and timing of the term have changed, for example. So too have the days set aside for argument, conferences, and announcing decisions. (See DECISION DAYS.) Still, the procedures for reviewing, arguing, and deciding cases have remained largely unchanged. The following paragraphs describe the procedures in effect in the early 1990s.

Reviewing Cases

Cases may come to the Supreme Court through petitions for writs of certiorari, appeals, or requests for certification. The main difference between the CERTIORARI and APPEAL routes is that the Court has

The bench of the U.S. Supreme Court with attorneys' table in the foreground. The chief justice occupies the center chair, and the associate justices are seated according to their seniority.   Source: Congressional Quarterly

complete discretion to grant a request for a writ of certiorari, but may be obligated to accept and decide a case that comes to it on appeal.

Most cases reach the Court by means of a writ of certiorari. In the relatively few cases to reach the Court by means of appeal, the appellant must file a jurisdictional statement explaining why the case qualifies for review and why the Court should grant it a hearing. More and more often the justices have disposed of these cases by deciding them summarily, without oral argument or formal opinion.

Those who file petitions for certiorari must pay the Court's standard fee of $200 for putting the case on the DOCKET. Prepared by the CLERK OF THE COURT, the docket is the list of cases pending before the Court. If the petition is granted, an additional fee of $100 is assessed. The U.S. government does not have to pay these fees, nor do persons too poor to afford them. The latter may file IN FORMA PAUPERIS petitions instead.

The third method of appeal, certification, is seldom used. Certification is a request by a lower court—usually a court of appeals—for a final answer to questions of law in a particular case. After examining the certificate, the Supreme Court may order the case argued before it.

Each justice, aided by his or her law clerks, is responsible for reviewing all cases on the dockets. In recent years several justices have used a "cert pool" system for this review. Their clerks work together to examine cases, writing a pool memo on several petitions. The memo is then given to the justices, who determine if more research is needed. Other justices prefer that either they or their own clerks review each petition themselves.

Justice William O. Douglas thought the review of the cases on the docket was in many ways the most interesting and important aspect of the justices' work. Others, apparently, have found it time-consuming and tedious; they advocate the cert pool as a means to reduce the burden on the justices and their staffs. Justice John Paul Stevens withdrew from the cert pool, saying it did not save him or his clerks any time.

Decisions to grant review are made in regularly scheduled conferences held in the conference room adjacent to the chief justice's chambers. A buzzer summons the justices to the conference room, where they shake hands with each other, take their appointed seats, and begin the discussion.

A few days before the conference convenes, the chief justice compiles a "discuss list"—a list of cases deemed important enough for discussion and a vote on whether they should be given a full review. Appeals are placed on the discuss list almost automatically, but as many as three-quarters of the petitions for certiorari are denied a place on the list and are thus rejected without further consideration. Any justice can have a case placed on the discuss list simply by making the request.

At the start of the conference, which is held in complete secrecy, the chief justice briefly outlines the facts of each case on the discuss list. Then each justice, beginning with the senior associate justice, comments, usually indicating whether he or she favors full review or not. A traditional but unwritten rule specifies that four affirmative votes are needed for a case to be scheduled for oral argument.

Petitions for certiorari, appeal, and *in forma pauperis* status that have been disposed of during conference are placed on a certified orders list. This list is released the following Monday in open Court.

Arguments

Once the Court announces it will hear a case, the clerk of the Court puts the case on the calendar for oral arguments. Generally, cases are argued roughly in the order in which they are granted review. At least three months usually elapses between the time when review is granted and the time when argument takes place. Under special circumstances, the date scheduled for oral argument may be advanced or postponed.

Well before oral argument, the justices receive briefs and records from the attorneys in the case. The amount of attention they give the briefs—from a cur-

sory glance to a thorough study—depends on the nature of the case and the work habits of the individual justices.

Arguments are heard on Monday, Tuesday, and Wednesday for seven two-week periods beginning in the first week of October and ending in the last week of April or the first week of May. Arguments take place from 10 a.m. to noon and from 1 to 3 p.m. Because most cases are limited to one hour of argument, the Court can hear four cases a day.

Attorneys who argue cases before the Supreme Court must be members of the BAR OF THE SUPREME COURT. Each side has thirty minutes in which to argue its case. A white light flashes to indicate that only five minutes are left. A red light indicates that the time has expired; the attorney may continue talking only to complete a sentence.

An exception to the time limitation is sometimes made for an AMICUS CURIAE—a person who volunteers or is invited to take part in the case before the court but who is not a party to it. Counsel for an amicus may take part in oral argument if the party supported by the amicus permits it and if the Court approves.

Typically only one attorney on a side may present argument. Attorneys are strongly advised not to read from prepared texts, but most attorneys do use an outline or notes to make sure they cover the important points.

During oral argument the justices may interrupt with questions or remarks as often as they wish. On average, questions consume about ten minutes of the allotted half-hour. Although questioning may upset and unnerve attorneys, it has several advantages. It serves to alert counsel about what aspects of the case need further elaboration or more information. For the Court, questions can bring out weak points in an argument, or sometimes strengthen it.

Conferences

Once oral argument has taken place, the case is considered in closed conference. The four cases that were argued on Monday are discussed and decided at a Wednesday afternoon conference. The cases argued on Tuesday and Wednesday are discussed and decided at Friday conferences that last all day. These conferences are the same ones at which the justices consider new motions, appeals, and petitions.

The chief justice is the first to speak, indicating his view of the case and how he plans to vote. The other justices follow in order of SENIORITY. The justices can speak for as long as they wish, although in the interests of efficiency long discourses are discouraged. Justices are not supposed to interrupt one another.

Other than these procedural arrangements, little is known about what actually goes on in these secret conferences. Discussions are said to be mostly polite and orderly, though sometimes bitter. Consideration of the issues in a particular case may be full and probing or else short and perfunctory, leaving the real debate to occur during the drafting of the written opinions.

Opinions

The next step is the writing of OPINIONS. An opinion is a reasoned argument explaining the legal issues in the case and the precedents on which the opinion is based.

Soon after the case is decided in conference, the task of writing the majority opinion is assigned. The chief justice makes the assignment when he has voted with the majority. If he is in the minority, the justice with the most seniority in the majority makes the assignment. (See ASSIGNING OPINIONS.)

Any justice may decide to write a separate opinion. Justices who are in agreement with the Court's ruling but disagree with some of the reasoning in the majority opinion, may write CONCURRING OPINIONS. Justices who disagree with the decision may write DISSENTING OPINIONS or go on record as dissenters without an opinion. More than one justice can sign a concurring or dissenting opinion. Justices may concur with or dissent from only a portion of the majority opinion.

Writing opinions can be a long and tedious process. Draft copies are circulated secretly among the justices, and new drafts are then written and rewritten to accommodate their comments. Occasionally justices who voted with the majority in conference may change their vote because they find the majority

opinion unpersuasive or a dissenting opinion particularly convincing.

The amount of time that passes between the vote on a case and the announcement of the decision varies from case to case. In simple cases where few points of law are at issue, the opinion can sometimes be written and cleared by the other justices in a week or less. In more complex cases, especially those with several dissenting or concurring opinions, it can take six months or more. Some cases may have to be reargued or the initial decision reversed after the drafts of the opinions have been circulated.

Formerly draft opinions were printed in a print shop in the basement of the Supreme Court Building. Strict security precautions were taken, and each copy was numbered to prevent extra copies from being removed from the building. In 1980 the Court began to use word processors to prepare draft opinions. Today the Court has replaced its old typesetting machines with a computerized word-processing system.

Issuing Opinions

When the drafts of an opinion, including dissents and concurring views, have been written, circulated, discussed, and revised, if necessary, the final versions are printed. Before the opinion is produced, the REPORTER OF DECISIONS adds a "headnote," or syllabus, summarizing the decision and a "lineup" at the end showing how each justice voted.

Under current procedures, opinions are released only on Tuesdays and Wednesdays during the weeks when the Court is hearing oral arguments. In other weeks, opinions are released on Mondays, along with orders issued by the Court.

Two hundred copies of the "bench opinion" are printed. As the decision is announced in Court, the bench opinions are distributed to journalists and others in the public information office. Another copy, with any necessary corrections, is sent to the U.S. Government Printing Office, which prints "slip" opinions. About 3,400 of these slip opinions are distributed to federal and state courts and agencies. The Court receives 400 of these, which it makes available free to the public through the public information office as long as supplies last. The Government Printing

Office also prints the opinion for inclusion in *United States Reports,* the official record of Supreme Court opinions.

The public announcement of opinions in Court is probably the Court's most dramatic moment. Those who are present to hear the announcement are participating in a very old tradition—though one that may not last. Depending on who delivers the opinion and how, announcements can take a considerable amount of the Court's valuable time.

Supreme Court justices do not elaborate on their written opinions. The Court has long felt that its opinions must speak for themselves and that efforts by the justices or by the public information office to explain or interpret the opinions are unnecessary.

Nevertheless, the Court has taken steps to make it easier for the news media to report the written opinions accurately. These include announcing decisions on more than one day a week and handing down no more than seven decisions in a single day. The latter arrangement, however, is sometimes ignored toward the end of a term.

Supporting Personnel

Although most of the justices' work cannot be delegated to others, support personnel perform many jobs that ensure the smooth functioning of the Court and allow the justices to concentrate on matters of law rather than on administration. The clerk handles all the judicial paperwork involved in reviewing cases. The reporter of decisions is in charge of editing and printing the written opinions. The MARSHAL OF THE COURT is responsible for maintaining the building and its security, and the librarian maintains the large LIBRARY OF THE COURT.

The Court also has a PUBLIC INFORMATION OF-FICE, a CURATOR'S OFFICE, and a LEGAL OFFICE OF THE COURT. The justices each select their own law clerks and other personal staff.

In addition, several other groups work with the Court but are not employees of it. These include the FEDERAL JUDICIAL CENTER, ADMINISTRATIVE OFFICE OF THE U.S. COURTS, the U.S. Judicial Conference, and the Supreme Court Historical Society.

(See HISTORICAL SOCIETY, SUPREME COURT; JU-DICIAL CONFERENCE, U.S.)

Opinions

In every case it decides, the Supreme Court issues a ruling in favor of one or the other party. Almost always it also issues an opinion, known as the Court opinion or the majority opinion, explaining the legal grounds and reasoning behind the ruling. Justices who disagree with the majority ruling or reasoning may issue separate opinions that explain their views of how the case should have been decided.

Court opinions set out principles of law that lower courts are expected to follow when deciding cases involving similar issues. These principles may be narrowly drawn, applying primarily to the parties involved in the case. Or they may be quite broad, affecting entire segments of the population.

The impact of any one opinion depends on several factors, including the number of people affected by it, how controversial the subject matter is, and the extent of support of or dissent from the opinion by the other justices.

In many cases, the Court issues a single opinion with which all of the justices agree. Until the 1940s, the Court typically decided the vast majority—80 percent or more—of its cases each term with unanimous opinions. Since the 1943–1944 term, however, the Court has been unanimous in fewer than half of its cases each term. At times, fewer than one-fourth of the decisions in a term have been unanimous. In the Rehnquist Court's terms in the early 1990s, the number of unanimous decisions increased. In the 1992–1993 term, the Court was unanimous in 46 (43 percent) of its 107 signed opinions.

Any justice may file a separate opinion in a case, and other justices may join his or her opinion. There are three kinds of separate opinions.

A justice who agrees with the result in a case and with the majority's reasoning may also write a separate CONCURRING OPINION. The justice may want to stress one point or to put a particular interpretation on the Court's opinion.

If a justice agrees with the result in a case but not the legal rationale, he or she may file an opinion "concurring in the judgment." The justice may disagree with some aspect of the majority's approach or may have a completely different basis for deciding the case.

Finally, a justice who disagrees with both the ruling and the reasoning of the majority may file a DISSENTING OPINION. Sometimes, a justice may file an opinion concurring with part of a decision and dissenting from another part.

The number of separate opinions has increased as the number of unanimous decisions has fallen. In the 1991–1992 term, there were sixty-five dissenting opinions and forty-seven concurring opinions.

Occasionally no opinion will be endorsed by a majority of the justices. In those cases, the opinion that is signed by the largest number of justices is known as a PLURALITY OPINION. A plurality opinion does not establish a binding precedent for future cases, as does a *PER CURIAM* OPINION. Typically a *per curiam* opinion is used when the Court is applying settled law to a case.

Very rarely do the justices all file separate opinions. This occurred in *Furman v. Georgia* (1972) when, by a 5–4 vote, the Court nullified all death penalty statutes in the United States. Each justice wrote a separate opinion stating his reasons for either agreeing with or dissenting from the ruling. In a very few cases the Court's opinion is unsigned.

Unanimous Opinions

It was not until John Marshall took his seat as chief justice in 1801 that unanimity became the norm on the Court. Before Marshall's tenure each justice would announce his own opinion and the reason for it. During Marshall's thirty-five years on the Court, the practice of such separate, or *seriatim*, opinions was largely abandoned. But Marshall could not prevent all dissent. The first real dissent, by Justice William Johnson, came during Marshall's tenure, and Marshall himself filed nine dissents and one special concurrence.

Under Marshall's successor, Chief Justice Roger B.

Taney, dissent became more frequent. Unlike Marshall, Taney did not insist on delivering the sole opinion of the Court, and the use of *seriatim* opinions was even resumed.

Nonetheless, a tradition of unity prevailed for most of the nineteenth century. The Court generally gave single opinions with only an occasional concurrence or dissent. Concurring or dissenting opinions were issued in only about a tenth of the cases decided in the mid- and late nineteenth century.

By the late twentieth century, concurring and dissenting opinions were appearing in about three-quarters of all Supreme Court cases. There are many reasons for this increase, but an important one is the ideological complexion of the Court.

A unanimous opinion is especially desirable in cases of crucial importance to the nation. One such case was *BROWN V. BOARD OF EDUCATION OF TOPEKA* (1954), which declared school segregation inherently discriminatory and thus a denial of equal protection under the Fourteenth Amendment. Another was *United States v. Nixon* (1974), in which the Court voted unanimously that President Richard Nixon must turn over White House tapes that were sought as evidence in the Watergate cover-up.

The *Brown* Decision

Brown was a catalyst for the civil rights revolution of the late 1950s and 1960s. The opinion would doubtless have been far less effective and far-reaching if it had not been unanimous. The existence of dissenting or even concurring opinions would have given opponents of desegregation an opening to challenge the decision.

Chief Justice Earl Warren drafted an opinion that quickly won the endorsement of five of the justices. But Warren feared that two, Felix Frankfurter and Robert H. Jackson, might write concurring opinions and that one, Stanley F. Reed, might dissent. Warren met individually with Frankfurter and Jackson to discuss his draft with them. Both found it acceptable and agreed to join in the opinion. Warren then met repeatedly with Reed who, according to later accounts by his clerk, strongly believed that a Supreme Court decision declaring school segregation unconstitutional would halt the progress being made in improving race relations.

Reed apparently listened closely to Warren's argument that a unanimous opinion was critically important on such a sensitive ruling. Ultimately he agreed to put aside his own misgivings for the national good. Even with a unanimous opinion, however, *Brown* met resistance throughout the South. It took many years and more Supreme Court cases before mandated school segregation was abolished.

The Nixon Tapes

In *United States v. Nixon* the Court rejected Nixon's argument invoking "executive privilege" to withhold the Watergate tapes from the federal trial court. The case set the executive branch and the Supreme Court on a collision course. A unanimous opinion was necessary to minimize any risk that Nixon might defy the Court's order to turn over the tapes.

Chief Justice Warren E. Burger had assigned himself the job of writing the opinion. To save time he circulated the draft opinion piece by piece. Other justices were not satisfied with what they were seeing and began drafting their own versions of the opinion. Burger was annoyed but was forced to compromise to ensure continued support. The final result was a rather unusual joint product, with several justices writing various parts of the final opinion. However, the final opinion was issued in Burger's name and was signed by every member of the court (except William H. Rehnquist, who did not participate in the case).

Forming an Opinion

Although individual justices may have made a tentative decision about a case even before the oral argument, opinions are not assigned and written until after the case has been argued in open court and tentatively decided in the justices' closed conference.

Soon after the conference, a justice is assigned to write the majority opinion. If the chief justice is in the majority, he makes the assignment; if he is in the minority, the assignment task falls to the senior associate in the majority. (See ASSIGNING OPINIONS.)

Each justice approaches the task of WRITING OPINIONS in his or her own way. Some involve their CLERKS heavily in the process. Chief Justice William H. Rehnquist has written that his law clerks prepare the first draft of his opinions after extensive consultation with him. Rehnquist reviews the draft, making any changes he deems necessary and sometimes rewriting it entirely. He then returns the draft to the clerk, who prepares a clean draft and perhaps suggests further revisions before the opinion is ready to circulate to the other justices.

Some justices, such as William O. Douglas, give their clerks little to do in drafting opinions. Some justices are able to write drafts quickly. Others spend days and weeks drafting and redrafting before they are satisfied with the product.

Once completed, the draft opinion is circulated and the comments of the other justices solicited. Minor comments are likely to be included without much fuss. Whether substantive comments are incorporated may depend on how far apart the author of the draft and the commenting justice are in their views and on the tentative vote. If the commenting justice's vote is needed to maintain a majority, the author may rewrite the draft until both parties are satisfied. If there is a large majority, the author of the majority opinion may be less willing to change the draft to incorporate a viewpoint that is significantly different from that of the majority.

In these cases a dissatisfied justice may elect to write a concurring, or even a dissenting, opinion. Drafts of dissenting and concurring opinions are usually not written until the draft of the majority opinion has been circulated. Occasionally a justice in the majority finds a concurring or dissenting opinion more convincing than the majority opinion and changes his or her vote. If enough justices change their vote, the concurring or dissenting opinion may become the majority position.

When the drafts of all the opinions, including dissents and concurring views, have been discussed and revised, if necessary, the REPORTER OF DECISIONS adds a "headnote" summarizing the decision and a "lineup" at the end showing how each justice voted. The final opinions are then printed by the Court's computer system under close security. They are then ready to be announced in open court. (See DECISION DAYS.)

Original Intent

Original intent is a method of interpreting the Constitution that determines the meaning of a passage mainly by looking at the intentions of its framers. The Supreme Court has often relied in part on historical evidence in interpreting the Constitution, but political conservatives in the 1980s argued for more scrupulous attention to original intent as a way of narrowing or overturning some expansive rulings on individual rights.

President Ronald Reagan's attorney general, Edwin Meese III, touched off the contemporary debate over original intent with a speech to the American Bar Association in July 1985. After criticizing several recent Supreme Court decisions, Meese called for the Court to adopt a "Jurisprudence of Original Intention" that he said would prevent decisions from being "tainted by ideological predilection." Among those who voiced similar views was federal appeals court judge Robert Bork, who in 1987 was an unsuccessful nominee for the Supreme Court.

The Court itself has debated the issue throughout its history. Chief Justice Roger B. Taney advocated an original intent approach in his opinion in the Dred Scott case, *SCOTT V. SANDFORD* (1857). Taney said the Constitution "speaks not only in the same words, but with the same meaning and intent with which it spoke when it came from the hands of its framers." Writing in 1920, however, Justice Oliver Wendell Holmes, Jr., argued that the Constitution must be interpreted "in the light of our whole experience and not merely in the light of what was said a hundred years ago."

One difficulty with original intent is that historical evidence is often either ambiguous or disputed. In the landmark school desegregation case, *BROWN V. BOARD OF EDUCATION OF TOPEKA* (1954), for example, the Court asked attorneys before reargument to address the issue of whether the authors of the Fourteenth Amendment intended to permit racially segregated schools. In its decision, however, the Court said that the history was "inconclusive" and that the changed role of public education required it to decide the issue in a different context anyway.

Critics of original intent also maintain that sometimes the text of the Constitution conflicts with the intentions of its authors. The First Amendment, for example, was probably not intended to provide protection of sexually explicit materials, but the free press clause contains no exceptions. Similarly, the Fourteenth Amendment equal protection clause was written to protect the legal rights of blacks, but its language can be used in the same way to protect those of women.

Despite criticism of original intent among legal scholars, by 1992 three members of the Court—Chief Justice William H. Rehnquist and associate justices Antonin Scalia and Clarence Thomas—were frequently emphasizing historical arguments in their rulings on constitutional issues. Since they lacked a majority for this approach, however, the impact of original intent on the Court's rulings remained limited. (See also CONSTITUTIONAL LAW; STRICT CONSTRUCTION.)

Original Jurisdiction

The original jurisdiction of a court is its power to hear and decide cases from the beginning. It is distinguished from appellate jurisdiction, which is the power to hear and decide an APPEAL from a lower court. The Supreme Court's original jurisdiction is set out in the Constitution, but these cases make up a tiny fraction of the Court's workload.

Under Article III the Supreme Court has original jurisdiction over two types of cases: those involving representatives of a foreign nation, and those in which a state is a party. In its landmark decision *MARBURY V. MADISON* (1803), the Court held that Congress cannot expand or reduce the Court's original jurisdiction.

Congress has asserted the power to decide whether the Court's original jurisdiction over certain matters is exclusive or concurrent—that is, whether it is shared with other federal courts or state courts. The Judiciary Act of 1789 gave the Court exclusive jurisdiction over all civil suits between a state and the United States or between two states, while suits between a state and an individual might be heard first in other courts. The act also allowed foreign diplomats to initiate suits in other courts.

In 1887 the Court decided that it would not exercise its original jurisdiction over criminal cases between states and citizens of other states. The ruling rejected a plea by Wisconsin for assistance in enforcing penalties against an out-of-state corporation.

The Court hears only a handful of cases under its original jurisdiction, almost all of them based on the state-as-party jurisdiction. Foreign ambassadors enjoy diplomatic immunity from being sued and, understandably, have not filed original actions before the Court.

When the Court does hear an original action—for example, a boundary dispute between two states—it typically appoints a "special master" to consider the factual issues before ruling on the case.

P

Packing the Court

See SIZE OF THE COURT.

Pardons

Except in cases of impeachment, the Constitution gives the president the unlimited power "to grant reprieves and pardons for offenses against the United States" (Article II, Section 2). The Supreme Court has supported the president's discretion to exercise the pardon power against all challenges. The president may attach conditions, the Court has held, as long as they are not contrary to the Constitution or federal laws.

Presidents have issued pardons and granted amnesty (a general pardon to groups or communities) since George Washington's amnesty to the western Pennsylvania "whiskey rebels" in 1795. The most famous pardon in U.S. history was that granted by President Gerald R. Ford on September 8, 1974, to former president Richard Nixon after Nixon's resignation from the presidency.

Two post-Civil War rulings confirmed the extent of the president's pardoning power in the face of conflicting congressional action. In the Supreme Court's 1867 decision striking down a loyalty oath for former Confederates, *Ex parte Garland*, the Court ruled also that the pardon issued to southerner Augustus Garland prevented enforcement of the oath requirement against him in any event. In 1872 the Court upheld President Abraham Lincoln's wartime pardon offer to Confederates to restore property taken from them if they swore allegiance to the Union. Congress had tried to block the property restoration effect of the pardon.

The Court's most recent ruling reaffirmed the independence of the pardoning power from legislative acts. In *Schick v. Reed* (1974), President Dwight D. Eisenhower had commuted the death sentence of a child murderer to life in prison without possibility of parole, a sentence not at that time authorized by law for the crime of murder. Schick, the prisoner, sought to be released from prison after serving twenty years. He contended that he had served the equivalent of a "life" sentence and that in the meantime the Supreme Court had invalidated existing death penalties in its 1972 capital punishment ruling.

In a 6–3 decision the Court upheld the conditional commutation of Schick's sentence. The pardoning power, Chief Justice Warren E. Burger wrote, "flows from the Constitution alone, and not from any legislative enactments, and it cannot be modified, abridged, or diminished by the Congress."

Parochial Schools, Aid to

The Supreme Court has ruled that government aid to church-related elementary and secondary schools sometimes violates the First Amendment prohibition against the establishment of religion. It has struggled, however, to define a consistent approach to the issue.

In its first ruling on the issue, the Court in 1930 upheld a Louisiana policy of lending textbooks to pupils in public and parochial schools alike. The Court adopted the "child benefit" theory, holding that the policy furthered the education of all children in the state and did not benefit only church-related schools. In 1947 the Court extended this rationale to uphold, by a vote of 5 to 4, a New Jersey law that permitted local boards of education to reimburse parents for the costs of sending their children to school on public transportation (*Everson v. Board of Education*).

The Court again applied the child benefit theory in 1968 to uphold, by a 6–3 vote, New York's textbook loan program for parochial schools. Encouraged by this ruling, parochial schools persuaded some states to pass laws authorizing more direct assistance, such as teacher salary subsidies, tuition reimbursements, and tuition tax credits. The Court ruled, however, that those programs went too far.

In *Lemon v. Kurtzman* (1971) the Court struck down a Rhode Island law authorizing a salary supplement for some teachers in nonpublic schools and a Pennsylvania law authorizing reimbursement to nonpublic schools for teachers' salaries, textbooks, and instructional materials. The ruling held that assistance to parochial schools was constitutional only if it was secular in its purpose and effect and did not entangle the government in its administration.

In applying this test, the Court has made some very fine distinctions. It has barred maintenance and repair grants to nonpublic schools and tuition reimbursements to parents of students in those schools, but upheld a state income tax deduction for tuition costs available to parents of students in public or private schools. It struck down a law reimbursing nonpublic schools for the costs of testing, but then upheld a similar program strictly limited to the costs of administering state-mandated standardized tests. Textbook loans and diagnostic services for speech and hearing were permitted, but not reimbursement for the cost of field trips.

Despite criticism of these distinctions, the Court in 1985 reaffirmed its basic approach by striking down two more aid programs. In *Grand Rapids School District v. Ball* the Court barred a Grand Rapids, Michigan, program of providing remedial and enrichment classes to students at nonpublic schools either during regular school hours (by a 7–2 vote) or after the school day (by a 5–4 vote). On the same day, the Court struck down, by a vote of 5 to 4, New York's system of providing remedial and counseling services to disadvantaged children in nonpublic schools *(Aguilar v. Felton)*.

In contrast to its rulings on aid to elementary and secondary schools, the Court had little difficulty in the 1970s in upholding direct government aid to church-affiliated colleges and universities. Beginning with *Tilton v. Richardson* (1971), the Court in three cases approved state and federal programs aiding sectarian institutions of higher education through construction grants, state-issued revenue bonds, or general annual grants.

Paterson, William

While a member of the judiciary committee in the new U.S. Senate, William Paterson (1745–1806) helped draft the Judiciary Act of 1789. The act created the structure of the federal judiciary, including the system of circuit and district courts. (See COURTS, LOWER.)

Two years after Paterson's birth in County Antrim, Ireland, his family emigrated to America. They eventually settled in Princeton, New Jersey. Paterson re-

Source: Collection of the Supreme Court of the United States

ceived his undergraduate degree from the College of New Jersey (Princeton) in 1763 and his master's degree in 1766. He read law in the office of Richard Stockton and opened his own law practice in 1769.

In 1775 Paterson was elected a delegate to the provincial congress of New Jersey, the first of several important positions he held in the state and federal governments. He served as New Jersey attorney general (1776–1783), U.S. senator (1789–1790), and governor of New Jersey (1790–1793). In 1787, while serving as a delegate to the Constitutional Convention in Philadelphia, Paterson introduced the New Jersey Plan. It called for a unicameral legislature where each state would have an equal vote. Later he joined with Alexander Hamilton in developing plans for the city that became Paterson, New Jersey.

Paterson was appointed to the Supreme Court in 1793 by President George Washington. As a justice he rode circuit and tried several cases related to the Whiskey Rebellion in western Pennsylvania. In several sedition trials, he took a Federalist position. Paterson was in line to become chief justice when Oliver Ellsworth resigned in 1800. President John Adams refused to elevate Paterson because of his close ties to Hamilton. In 1804 failing health caused Paterson to miss a Court session, and he died two years later.

Pay and Perquisites

In 1993 the chief justice of the United States earned $171,500 and the associate justices, $164,100 each. In 1789 Congress stipulated that the chief justice was to be paid $4,000 a year and the associate justices, $3,500. Those salaries were not raised until 1819.

The Court depends on Congress to adjust salaries, and, like most working people, the justices have not always been satisfied with the level of their compensation. In 1816 Justice Joseph Story complained that the cost of living had doubled and that the expenses of the justices had quadrupled since their pay had been set in 1789. Congress took little heed. Although he was offered a lucrative law practice in Baltimore

Justices' Salaries

Years	Chief justice	Associate justices
1789–1819	$4,000	$3,500
1819–1855	5,000	4,500
1855–1871	6,500	6,000
1871–1873	8,500	8,000
1873–1903	10,500	10,000
1903–1911	13,000	12,500
1911–1926	15,000	14,500
1926–1946	20,500	20,000
1946–1955	25,500	25,000
1955–1964	35,500	35,000
1964–1969	40,000	39,500
1969–1975	62,500	60,000
1975	65,625	63,000
1976[a]	68,800	66,000
1977	75,000	72,000
1978[a]	79,100	76,000
1979[a]	84,700	81,300
1980[a]	92,400	88,700
1981[a]	96,800	93,000
1982–1983[a]	100,700	96,700
1984	104,700	100,600
1985–1986	108,400	104,100
1987–1989	115,000	110,000
1990	124,000	118,600
1991	155,000	148,300
1992[a]	166,200	159,000
1993[a]	171,500	164,100

[a] Cost-of-living adjustment.

that would have more than doubled his income, Story decided not to leave the Court.

At least one justice did resign from the Court in part because of the low pay. In a letter to a friend, Justice Benjamin R. Curtis said he was considering leaving the Court because he could not maintain his family in the style that he desired on his Court salary. As an associate justice, Curtis was making $4,500 a year. "I have no right to blame the public for not being willing to pay a larger salary," he wrote, "but they have no right to blame me for declining it on account of its inadequacy."

Curtis, who resigned in September 1857 at the age of forty-eight, had also been greatly disturbed by the Court's decision in the Dred Scott case.

In 1866 Chief Justice Salmon P. Chase urged that the number of justices be reduced by three so that the salaries of the remaining justices might be raised. Congress did reduce the number of seats, but it did not raise the justices' salaries. Chief Justice Chase continued to earn $6,500 a year, the associate justices $6,000. (See SIZE OF THE COURT.)

More than a century later, the failure of Congress in early 1989 to approve a recommended raise for federal judges and other high-level federal officeholders moved Chief Justice William H. Rehnquist to break with tradition and do some serious lobbying as head of the judicial system. He appeared before a congressional committee, met privately with congressional leaders, and held a press conference to urge Congress to increase the salaries of federal judges. His appearance before the House Post Office and Civil Service Committee on May 3, 1989, was the first time a sitting chief justice had testified before Congress.

Later in that year Congress did enact a substantial pay raise for federal judges, including the Supreme Court justices. Salaries were raised 7.9 percent in 1990 and another 25 percent in 1991. After that they were to be adjusted each year for increases in the cost of living.

1964 Controversy

Article III, Section I of the Constitution bars Congress from reducing the salaries of Supreme Court justices. The legislature, however, has absolute control over increases in wages and over appropriations for the operation of the Court itself. (See COST OF SUPREME COURT.) Only once, in 1964, has Congress deliberately exercised this power of the purse to show its displeasure with Court rulings.

In that year Congress considered the first increases in pay for top-level federal employees since 1955. The House approved a $7,500 raise for members of Congress and all federal judges, including the justices. The Senate, however, limited the increase for the justices to $2,500. The final version of the bill set the pay raise for Supreme Court justices at $4,500, $3,000 less than the increase for members of Congress.

The amendment's chief sponsor in the Senate insisted that the differential would establish a "semblance of equity" between the justices and members of Congress. But there was little doubt that the amendment was approved to punish the Court for several recent controversial decisions it had handed down on such issues as obscenity, school prayer, and civil rights.

Although the American Bar Association and others sharply criticized Congress, the legislature refused to budge. In 1965 the House voted down a bill that would have given the justices the same increase that members of Congress had received. Congress did not approve another pay raise until 1969.

Retirement

For its first eighty years, the Court had no RETIREMENT plan for its justices. Until 1869 justices who were unable to carry out their duties because of age or disability often hesitated to submit their resignations, knowing they would receive no retirement benefits. Because justices are appointed for life, they cannot be forcibly retired when they reach a certain age.

It was in large measure the incapacity of justices Robert C. Grier and Samuel Nelson that prompted Congress to set up a retirement system for the Court. The system, enacted in 1869, stipulated that any justice who reached the age of seventy and had served on the Court for ten years could resign and continue to receive full salary. Congress has since modified that law to ensure that justices who retire at age seventy with at least ten years of service or at age sixty-five with at least fifteen years of service will receive their full salary. Justices with fewer than ten years of service who retire because of disability may receive one-half of their annual salary.

Perquisites

In addition to the prestige of the office, Supreme Court justices have several perquisites. Each justice is entitled to four law clerks, two secretaries (the chief justice has three), and a messenger. Justices may also use the Court dining room, exercise room, and library, as well as the services of a Court barber (for which they pay). The chief justice is provided with a car, paid for by the government, and the Court maintains a small fleet of cars for the official use of the other justices. But most of the justices drive themselves to and from work.

Peckham, Rufus W.

Three months after political infighting caused the Senate to reject his brother Wheeler's nomination to the Supreme Court, Rufus Wheeler Peckham (1838–1909) was nominated by President Grover Cleveland and confirmed by the Senate.

Peckham was born in Albany, New York. After reading law at his father's law firm, he was admitted to the bar and joined his father's firm. Then he set out on a career in public life that mirrored his father's. Like his father, Peckham served as district attorney for Albany County. In 1881 he became corporation counsel for the City of Albany. He also plunged into politics and befriended then governor Grover Cleveland, who later appointed him to the Supreme Court.

Peckham's sound reputation as a lawyer, along with his connections and family name, helped him be elected to the New York supreme court in 1883 and to the New York court of appeals three years later. His father had previously served on both courts.

Peckham finally eclipsed his father in 1895 when Cleveland nominated him to the Supreme Court.

During his nearly fourteen years on the Court, Peckham consistently supported property rights and the individual's right to make contracts. In 1898 he dissented when the Court upheld a Utah law that limited the working day in mines. The Court ruled that the law was a proper use of the state's power to protect workers' health.

Source: Collection of the Supreme Court of the United States

Peckham delivered one of his most important opinions in *Lochner v. New York* (1905). In that case the Court, by a vote of 5 to 4, overturned a New York law that limited the hours that bakery employees could work. The majority held that the law denied due process and infringed upon the freedom of contract. In the majority opinion, Peckham wrote: "Statutes of the nature of that under review, limiting the hours in which grown and intelligent men may labor to earn their living, are mere meddlesome interferences with the rights of the individual." Peckham served on the Court until his death.

Pentagon Papers Case

In an unprecedented clash between national security and freedom of the press, the Supreme Court in 1971 refused to block newspapers from publishing ac-

Signaling a victory for the Washington Post *and* New York Times, *the chief of the presses at the* Post *holds the first edition of the paper announcing the Court's decision in the Pentagon Papers case June 30, 1971. Newspapers all over the country immediately resumed publication of the papers.   Source: UPI/Bettmann*

counts of a classified government study of U.S. involvement in Vietnam. But the justices stopped short of saying that the government could never prevent the press from publishing material on national security grounds. (See PRESS, FREEDOM OF.)

The case involved articles published in the *New York Times* and *Washington Post* that were based on a 7,000-page history of the U.S. role in Vietnam. The study, which became known as the Pentagon Papers, indicated that the United States was more heavily involved in the Vietnamese civil war than officials had publicly admitted. Copies of the papers were leaked to the press by Daniel Ellsberg, an analyst who had helped prepare the report and had then become an antiwar activist.

The *Times* published its first article on the report on June 13, 1971. On June 15 the government obtained a temporary restraining order in U.S. district court against publication of any further articles. The district

court judge refused on June 19 to grant a permanent injunction, but an appeals court judge immediately reinstated the restraining order pending further proceedings.

Meanwhile, the *Post* had obtained the papers and had published its first article about the report on June 18. The government then tried to block the *Post* from further publication. Despite rebuffs by the district and appeals courts, the government won a temporary restraining order pending review of both cases by the Supreme Court. The Court scheduled arguments for June 26.

Just four days later the Court announced its decision. By a 6–3 vote, the Court in *New York Times Co. v. United States* ruled that the government had failed to meet "the heavy burden of showing justification" for restraining further publication of the Pentagon Papers.

Each of the nine justices wrote a separate opinion. Only two, Hugo L. Black and William O. Douglas, said the government could never impose a prior restraint against the press. Justice William J. Brennan, Jr., said the government might properly restrain the press in a clear emergency. Justices Potter Stewart and Byron R. White stated that a prior restraint could be imposed under less stringent conditions. Justice Thurgood Marshall emphasized that Congress had refused to give the president the authority to prohibit publications disclosing matters of national security or to make such disclosures criminal.

In their dissents, Chief Justice Warren E. Burger and justices John Marshall Harlan and Harry A. Blackmun all criticized the haste with which the cases had been handled. They suggested that evidence to support the injunction against further publication might have been fleshed out if lower court proceedings had been conducted without what Burger called "unwarranted deadlines and frenetic pressures."

Per Curiam **Opinion**

Per curiam is a Latin term meaning "by the court." A *per curiam* opinion is an unsigned opinion of the Supreme Court, or an opinion written by the whole

Court. *Per curiam* opinions are usually issued in decisions that apply settled law to the case at hand. These opinions are usually quite short. On rare occasions a justice files a dissent to a *per curiam* opinion.

Petition, Right of

The First Amendment right "to petition the Government for redress of grievances" had its origins in the Magna Carta and the development of the English parliamentary system. The Supreme Court's few rulings on the clause have made clear that, like other First Amendment freedoms, the right of petition is not absolute.

Congress in the 1830s received so many antislavery petitions that in 1840 the House adopted a standing rule, which remained in effect for five years, prohibiting the receipt of any petitions seeking abolition of slavery. During World War I, petitions seeking repeal of the espionage or SEDITION LAWS sometimes resulted in imprisonment.

In a major decision on the right of petition, the Supreme Court in 1954 upheld the authority of Congress to require registration by certain lobbyists. The 5–3 ruling in *United States v. Harriss* narrowed the law to apply only to lobbyists or organizations who solicited, collected, or received contributions in order to conduct their lobbying, and then only to those lobbyists and organizations whose main purpose was to influence legislation. The decision thus exempted so-called grass-roots lobbying by general advocacy groups using their own members and their own funds.

In 1980 the Court upheld military regulations requiring the approval of the base commander before military personnel may send a petition to members of Congress. In 1984 the Court ruled that an individual may be sued for LIBEL for defamatory statements included in a petition. And in 1985 it upheld a statutory limit of ten dollars on the amount a veteran can pay an attorney for representing him or her in pursuing claims with the Veterans Administration.

Petitioner

When the Supreme Court agrees to review a decision of a lower court, the parties to the case are called the petitioner and the respondent. In an appeal, the parties are called the appellant and appellee.

The term *petitioner* is used in other contexts as well.

In general, a petitioner is one who files a petition with a court seeking action or relief. A petitioner may be a plaintiff—a party who brings a civil action in trial court or who sues to obtain a remedy for injury to his or her rights—or an appellant.

Petitioner is also the name given to a person who files for other court action where charges are not necessarily made. For example, a party may petition the court for an order requiring another person or party to produce documents. The party against whom the action is brought is called the respondent.

Pitney, Mahlon

Mahlon Pitney (1858–1924), an associate justice of the New Jersey supreme court, met President William Howard Taft at a dinner party on February 12, 1912, in Newark. The two men discussed one of Pitney's colleagues, Francis J. Swayze, whom Taft was considering for the bench. To Pitney's great surprise, seven days after the meeting Taft nominated Pitney to be an associate justice of the Supreme Court.

Some liberal senators and union leaders opposed Pitney's appointment, citing his antilabor record as a New Jersey judge. The Senate, however, confirmed his appointment on a 50–26 vote. Following the vote Woodrow Wilson, governor of New Jersey and Pitney's former classmate at Princeton, sent him a telegram saying that "a better choice could not have been made."

Pitney was born in Morristown, New Jersey. After graduating from the College of New Jersey (now Princeton) in 1879, he learned the law from his father and passed the New Jersey bar in 1882. He then practiced law in the industrial town of Dover for seven years. His father was appointed vice chancellor

Source: Collection of the Supreme Court of the United States

of New Jersey in 1889 and Pitney moved back to Morristown to run his legal practice.

Pitney was elected to Congress as a Republican in 1894. He served there until 1899, when he resigned because he had been elected to the New Jersey senate. As Pitney bided his time before a planned race for the governorship, he became senate president.

Pitney abandoned his gubernatorial ambitions when Governor Foster M. Voorhees appointed him to the New Jersey supreme court in 1901. He was appointed chancellor of New Jersey in 1908, one step up from the position his father had held nineteen years earlier. He held that post for four years until his nomination to the Supreme Court.

As a justice, Pitney consistently opposed expanding the rights of workers, but he supported workers' compensation laws and laws concerning minimum wages and hours. A hard worker, Pitney suffered mental and physical stress while on the Court. He had a stroke in August 1922 and retired four months later. His death in 1924, at age sixty-six, has been blamed on overwork while he was a justice.

Plaintiff

A plaintiff is a person who brings a civil lawsuit—that is, a complaint against another individual, against a business or other incorporated or unincorporated association, or against government officials, in which the plaintiff seeks damages for the violation of a legal right or enforcement of a legal right.

The most common types of civil suits involve contracts, property claims, or torts. Such suits can be traced to English COMMON LAW. The Supreme Court has only a limited role in these areas, which are governed mostly by state statutes or case law. (See LEGAL SYSTEM IN AMERICA.)

Occasionally, the Court has recognized constitutional requirements in these areas—for example, the rules limiting recovery by plaintiffs in LIBEL cases. But the Court has had little to say about plaintiffs' rights in personal injury lawsuits despite the many controversies about such suits since the 1960s.

The Court has not acted to guarantee indigent plaintiffs access to the courts in the same way that it has tried to protect the rights of indigent criminal defendants. (See DEFENDANT.) In *Boddie v. Connecticut* (1971) the Court held, 8–1, that a state could not constitutionally bar an indigent plaintiff from its divorce court for failure to pay a sixty-dollar filing fee. In two cases later the same year, however, the Court upheld the application of filing fees to prevent indigents from filing for bankruptcy or seeking judicial review of a denial of welfare benefits.

The Court's role has been more important in defining plaintiffs' remedies in CIVIL RIGHTS and constitutional cases. In one significant line of cases, the Court created a new basis for recovering legal damages: the so-called constitutional tort.

The Court's decision in *Bivens v. Six Unknown Agents*

of Federal Bureau of Narcotics (1971) allowed a plaintiff to sue for monetary damages for a violation of his Fourth Amendment rights during a search and arrest by federal narcotics agents. Even though there was no statutory authorization for the suit in federal court, the Court said it was recognizing the right of action to provide a parallel remedy to federal suits against state or local officials for depriving a person of civil rights under color of state law.

Eight years later the Court allowed a second suit for a constitutional tort. The plaintiff in *Davis v. Passman* (1979) brought a SEX DISCRIMINATION complaint against a member of Congress, alleging that the lawmaker's refusal to hire her because she was a woman violated her Fifth Amendment rights to due process and equal protection of the laws.

In 1982, however, the Court made it harder for plaintiffs to recover damages in such cases by broadening the standards for executive immunity from such suits. (See OFFICIAL IMMUNITY.)

Plea Bargaining

A plea bargain is an agreement by which a defendant pleads guilty in exchange for a prosecutor's promise of less severe punishment than could be expected after trial. The plea bargain has become a fixture of the U.S. criminal justice system. The overwhelming majority of criminal cases in both state and federal courts are resolved through guilty pleas, and the Supreme Court has imposed few restraints on the process.

Plea bargaining has no formal constitutional or statutory basis. Instead, it developed and spread for practical reasons. As the Supreme Court said in its first decision formally upholding the practice, plea bargaining provides a "mutuality of advantage" for the state and the defendant.

The ruling in that case, *Brady v. United States* (1970), sustained a plea bargain by a defendant charged under a portion of the federal kidnapping law that allowed a death sentence only after trial. In a different case two years earlier, the Court had struck down that portion of the law on the ground that it had the "inevitable effect" of penalizing the defendant's Fifth Amendment right not to plead guilty and Sixth Amendment right to trial by jury.

Despite the earlier ruling, the Court unanimously refused to strike down the defendant Brady's plea as coerced. "We cannot hold that it is unconstitutional for the State to extend a benefit to a defendant who in turn extends a substantial benefit to the State and who demonstrates by his plea that he is ready and willing to admit his crime," Justice Byron R. White wrote for the Court.

The Court in the 1960s had imposed procedural requirements to ensure that defendants pleading guilty were waiving their rights voluntarily and knowingly. Judges typically ask defendants to acknowledge that they understand what they are doing, that they have been adequately counseled, and that they are entering the plea voluntarily. Unlike the practice in some European countries, however, judges in the United States typically make no inquiry into the circumstances of the crime itself.

The Supreme Court has ruled that the state must keep any promises made during the plea-bargaining process. In *Santobello v. New York* (1971) the Court ruled that the state's failure to keep its commitment to recommend a reduced sentence in exchange for a guilty plea required that a defendant be given the opportunity for a trial.

On the other hand, the Court in 1973 ruled that a defendant who had pleaded guilty gave up his right to challenge his conviction later by arguing that the grand jury that had indicted him had been unfairly selected. In 1978 the Court found no due process violation in a prosecutor's threat to bring an additional indictment if the defendant did not accept a plea bargain. In 1987 the Court held that a state could reinstate a charge against a defendant who broke a plea bargain by refusing to testify against others as promised—even though the defendant had already pleaded guilty to a lesser offense and had begun serving time.

Plessy v. Ferguson

A century ago Homer Plessy, who was one-eighth black and appeared white, challenged a Louisiana law segregating blacks from whites on railway trains. The Supreme Court's 8–1 decision in *Plessy v. Ferguson* (1896) upheld the law and allowed southern states to establish legally mandated racial SEGREGATION in almost every aspect of daily life. The Court finally repudiated the "separate but equal" doctrine in 1954 in the landmark SCHOOL DESEGREGATION decision, *BROWN V. BOARD OF EDUCATION OF TOPEKA.*

The Court had handed down two decisions regarding segregation in public transportation before *Plessy.* In 1878 the Court had unanimously struck down an earlier Louisiana law forbidding segregation on public carriers, saying the law was an impermissible burden on interstate commerce. But in 1890 the Court had upheld a Mississippi law requiring segregation on public transportation on the ground that it dealt only with intrastate traffic. (See PUBLIC ACCOMMODATIONS.)

Plessy was arrested for attempting to take a seat in the coach reserved for whites on a trip from New Orleans to Covington, Louisiana. The state courts upheld the law, and Plessy appealed to the Supreme Court.

In his opinion for the Court, Justice Henry B. Brown said that the law did not violate the federal government's commerce power, the antislavery Thirteenth Amendment, or the equal protection clause of the Fourteenth Amendment.

Brown acknowledged that the Fourteenth Amendment was designed "to enforce the absolute equality of the two races before the law," but said it "could not have been intended . . . to enforce social, as distinguished from political equality." He then rejected as "a fallacy" Plessy's argument that the segregation law "stamps the colored race with a badge of inferiority."

"If this be so," Brown wrote, "it is not by reason of anything found in the act, but solely because the colored race chooses to put this construction on it."

Although the ruling dealt directly with public transportation, Brown added that the law did not appear to be "more obnoxious" than the congressional act segregating schools in the District of Columbia, "the constitutionality of which does not seem to have been questioned."

In an eloquent and prophetic dissent, Justice John Marshall Harlan predicted that the decision would prove "quite as pernicious" as the Court's 1857 ruling in the Dred Scott case (*SCOTT V. SANDFORD*). "Our Constitution is colorblind and neither knows nor tolerates classes among citizens," Harlan wrote. "The thin disguise of 'equal' accommodations for passengers in railroad coaches will not mislead any one, nor atone for the wrong this day done."

In 1946 the Supreme Court struck down, on the grounds of the commerce power, state segregation laws affecting interstate carriers. Eight years later, in *Brown,* the Court expressly repudiated the separate-but-equal doctrine of *Plessy,* saying that racial segregation in schools inherently denied black children equal educational opportunities in violation of the equal protection clause.

Plurality Opinion

Occasionally no opinion in a case elicits the support of a majority of the Supreme Court justices. In such instances, the opinion supported by the largest number of justices, called a plurality opinion, prevails. Plurality opinions are not regarded as establishing precedent.

Plurality opinions are more likely to occur when there is a vacancy on the Court or when a justice does not participate in a case for some reason. That happened, for example, in the case of *Colegrove v. Green* (1946). With Justice Robert H. Jackson absent and a vacancy on the Court due to the death of Chief Justice Harlan Fiske Stone, the Court declined, 4–3, to compel a state legislature to redraw congressional district boundaries that had not been reconfigured for nearly fifty years. The matter was a political question beyond judicial power to resolve, Justice Felix Frankfurter wrote in the Court opinion, which was joined only by justices Stanley F. Reed and Harold H. Burton. The critical fourth vote deciding the case was cast by Justice Wiley B. Rutledge, who disagreed with Frankfurter's analysis but agreed that the case should be dismissed.

If the issue is pressing enough, plurality opinions almost always signal that another case involving the same point will eventually find its way to the Court in search of a definitive opinion. Such was the case with *Colegrove*. In *Baker v. Carr* (1962) the Court ruled, 6–2, that federal courts could properly consider constitutional challenges to legislative malapportionment. One of the two dissenters was Frankfurter, the only one of the three supporters of the Court's plurality opinion in *Colegrove* still to sit on the Court.

Police Power

Police power is the general authority of the state to govern its citizens, its land, and its resources. Although the phrase does not appear in the Constitution, the Supreme Court has used the concept in determining the permissible extent of governmental power and the boundaries between state and federal authority, especially in economic matters.

The Court has usually given state and local governments broad latitude to use the police power to protect public health, safety, and morals, and to control economic and business matters for the public good. The Court cited the police power, for example, when it upheld Louisiana's slaughterhouse monopoly in the *SLAUGHTERHOUSE CASES* (1873), Massachusetts's compulsory vaccination law (1905), and pre-Prohibition state laws banning the manufacture or sale of alcoholic beverages. Police power was the key concept in the landmark ruling, *Euclid v. Ambler Realty Co.* (1926), that validated local ZONING laws.

For nearly a century, there were only two significant limits on the states' police power, both drawn from the Constitution. These were the federal government's COMMERCE POWER to regulate interstate commerce and the ban in the CONTRACT CLAUSE on state laws "impairing the obligation of contracts." Today the restraints against economic regulation are weaker, but claims of individual rights, including freedom of expression and the right to privacy, are often

recognized as a limitation on the government's use of its powers.

The Court gave an expansive interpretation to the police power in its first extended treatment of the subject, *Mayor of New York v. Miln* (1837). The decision upheld a New York law that sought to control the entry of undesirable people by requiring the master of any ship arriving in New York harbor from outside the state to report to the mayor the name, birthplace, age, and occupation of every passenger. The Court found no conflict with federal power and upheld the law on the basis of the state's "undeniable and unlimited jurisdiction over all persons and things within its territorial limits . . . where the jurisdiction is not surrendered or restrained by the Constitution of the United States."

In later decisions the Court did hold that the federal government's commerce power limited the states' authority to control entry by individuals or to restrict out-of-state corporations. But the broad view of police power survived, and it allowed states to begin dealing with social and economic problems that the national government did not face until the end of the nineteenth century or later.

Many regulations were upheld even during the period when the justices had a largely laissez-faire economic philosophy. For example, at the turn of the century the Court cited the states' power to protect the health of workers in upholding maximum-hours laws for miners in Utah and women laundry workers in Oregon, even though it struck down a similar New York law for bakery workers in a controversial decision, *Lochner v. New York* (1905).

A key decision was the Court's ruling in *Munn v. Illinois* (1877; sometimes called the *Granger Cases)* upholding state regulation of grain warehouse and elevator rates. Despite a strong dissent calling the laws an invasion of property rights, the Court said that states had the power to regulate businesses that were "clothed with a public interest." This "public interest" doctrine proved difficult to apply, but it survived until 1934 when the Court in *Nebbia v. New York* ruled that states could regulate any business for the public good as long as the regulation was reasonable and was effected through appropriate means.

During this period the Court also recognized for

Among the thousands of people coming to the United States in the nineteenth century were paupers, carriers of contagious diseases, and escaped criminals. In The Mayor of New York v. Miln *(1837) the Supreme Court ruled that a state could use its police power to require the captain of an arriving ship to provide it a list of passengers.*   Source: Chicago Historical Society

the first time what amounted to a federal police power derived from the federal government's authority to regulate interstate commerce. In *Champion v. Ames* (1903; called *The Lottery Case*), the Court voted 5–4 to uphold a federal law against transporting lottery tickets from a state or foreign country into another state. Justice John Marshall Harlan explained that Congress's power to regulate commerce included the power to prohibit "a species of interstate commerce which . . . has become offensive to the entire people of the nation."

Congress used this newfound power to enact regulatory statutes such as the Pure Food and Drug Act of 1906 and a host of criminal laws, beginning with the antiprostitution Mann Act of 1910, tied to interstate trafficking or transportation.

For several decades, however, the Court resisted use of state or federal police power over some economic matters, especially labor conditions. It struck down a federal child labor law in 1918, a federal minimum wage law for the District of Columbia in 1923, and a state minimum wage law in 1936. The Court's resistance ended in the late 1930s under pressure from President Franklin D. Roosevelt.

Since that time the Court has given greater weight to individual rights in determining the validity of police power enactments by the states or the federal government. It has upheld laws against OBSCENITY, but only under guidelines designed to protect First Amendment rights. It has permitted broad use of zoning powers, but struck down one local ordinance that prevented a grandmother from living in the same house with her grandsons. It has affirmed broad public health measures, but curtailed the states' right to control abortion. In these and other areas, the police power remains a concept that—as the Court said in one of its early cases—remains incapable of precise definition.

Political Question

The political question doctrine calls for the federal courts to refrain from ruling on governmental questions that lie entirely within the discretion of the "political" branches of the national government—Congress and the president.

As with other rules of JUDICIAL RESTRAINT, the Supreme Court's application of the doctrine has varied. Two major rulings in the 1960s narrowed the doctrine, but it remained sufficiently strong to keep the Court from ruling on challenges to the legality of U.S. actions during the Vietnam War. (See WAR POWERS.)

The Court's inaction in the Vietnam War cases reflects a long-standing policy of leaving questions of FOREIGN AFFAIRS largely to the political branches. In several rulings the Court has stressed that the nation should speak with one voice on matters of foreign policy.

In similar fashion, the Court has also refused to intervene in questions of legislative process or procedure, including issues concerning constitutional amendments. It has left their resolution to Congress. (See AMENDING PROCESS.) The Court has repeatedly held that contested elections are matters for decision by the relevant legislative body rather than the federal judiciary.

The political question doctrine has also been cited to sidestep disputes arising under the constitutional guarantee of "a Republican Form of Government" for the states (Article IV, Section 4). The Court set forth the political question doctrine in 1849 in explaining its decision to stay out of a dispute between two competing groups, each of which claimed to be the legitimate government of the state of Rhode Island. It was up to Congress, not the Court, to enforce the constitutional guarantee, Chief Justice Roger B. Taney wrote in *Luther v. Borden*. (See STATES AND THE COURT.)

On the other hand, the Court has been willing to rule in matters such as the *Pocket Veto Case* (1929) where the political branches reach an impasse on an issue. (See VETO POWER.) In two more recent cases the Court set aside the doctrine to rule on matters that Congress or the president asserted were entirely within their respective prerogatives.

In *Powell v. McCormack* (1969) the Court held that neither chamber of Congress has the power to exclude a member who meets the constitutional qualifications and has been duly elected. (See CONGRESS AND THE COURT.) In the Watergate tapes case (*United States v. Nixon* [1974]) the Court said the political question doctrine did not prevent it from ruling on the validity of a claim of executive privilege by President Richard Nixon. Nixon invoked the claim to bar enforcement of a subpoena for tapes of his conversations regarding the Watergate break-in and cover-up. (See PRESIDENT AND THE COURT; SEPARATION OF POWERS.)

The Supreme Court's key ruling narrowing the political question doctrine was the landmark reapportionment decision, *BAKER V. CARR* (1962). In his opinion for the Court, Justice William J. Brennan, Jr., defined the doctrine so as to reduce its scope. Brennan also appeared to say that the doctrine pertains only to purely federal issues and not to the federal courts' relationship to the states.

Brennan listed six criteria that he said were found in the Court's previous cases involving the political question doctrine. The first and most clearcut was "a textually demonstrable constitutional commitment of the issue to a coordinate political department." The next two criteria were based on the difficulty that courts would have in finding standards for deciding the question, while the final three all dealt with the political risks of judicial intervention.

In the *Powell* case, however, Chief Justice Earl Warren essentially discarded all of Brennan's criteria except the first. Warren reasoned that unless the Constitution explicitly committed a matter to Congress or the president, the Court had both the capacity and obligation to rule on it, even at the risk of an "embarrassing confrontation" with another branch of the federal government.

Four years later, the Court revived the political question doctrine when it overturned a lower court's ruling that subjected the training and discipline of national guard troops to judicial review and supervision

(Gilligan v. Morgan [1973]). The Court said the Article I clause giving Congress responsibility for "organizing, arming and disciplining" state militias was the type of wording that precluded judicial review. In an admonition to lower courts, the justices added that the narrowing of the political question doctrine "is no reason for the federal courts to assume its demise."

Politics and the Court

The Supreme Court in its decisions sometimes refers to Congress and the executive as the "political branches" of government, but the Court itself has always been a political institution too.

Politics has been a primary motivation in a president's selection of nominees to the Court and has of-

ten played a role in the senatorial CONFIRMATION PROCESS as well. (See NOMINATION TO THE COURT.) Many justices had political careers before their appointments, and a few—mostly in the 1800s—took part in political activities after joining the bench. (See EXTRAJUDICIAL ACTIVITIES.)

In modern times, the political element has become less openly partisan as the Court has evolved into a more equal and autonomous component of the federal system. Justices generally refrain from political activities and maintain a distance from both the president and Congress.

Presidential Politics

George Washington chose six supporters of the new federal government to constitute the original Supreme Court in 1790 and named five more justices with similar views as vacancies arose during his eight

President Dwight D. Eisenhower (front row, third from right) stands with members of the Supreme Court and two Court clerks (back row, left). During his eight years in office Eisenhower had the opportunity to appoint five new justices, including a replacement for Chief Justice Fred Vinson, standing to his left.   Source: Collection of the Supreme Court of the United States

years in office. With the birth of political parties, Washington's successor, John Adams, near the end of his term attempted to ensure Federalist control of the Court by choosing a loyal Federalist, John Marshall, as chief justice.

Since then, presidents have appointed members of the opposition party to positions on the Court just thirteen times—and political considerations lay behind almost all of those exceptions.

Republican president Abraham Lincoln, for example, picked Democrat Stephen Field, a distinguished justice from the California supreme court, to help cement the state's loyalty during the Civil War. Democrat Franklin D. Roosevelt elevated Republican Harlan Fiske Stone to chief justice in the hope of promoting bipartisanship on the eve of World War II.

Dwight Eisenhower had an eye on northern Catholic voters when he selected William J. Brennan, Jr., a Democrat and a Catholic, one month before the 1956 presidential election. Richard Nixon was pursuing his "southern strategy" in 1971 when he chose Lewis F. Powell, Jr., a Richmond, Virginia, lawyer and a nominal Democrat.

In some cases, political affiliation was a misleading indication of the nominee's views on legal issues. Justice Louis D. Brandeis called himself a Republican, but held social and economic views in line with those of Democratic president Woodrow Wilson. Wilson's predecessor, Republican William Howard Taft, chose two conservative Democrats for the Court, Horace H. Lurton and Joseph R. Lamar, and elevated another, Edward D. White, to chief justice. Later, as chief justice himself, Taft recommended another conservative Democrat, Pierce Butler, for appointment by Warren G. Harding.

Other presidents who have named justices of the opposite party were Republicans Benjamin Harrison (Howell E. Jackson) and Herbert Hoover (Benjamin N. Cardozo); Democrat Harry S. Truman (Harold H. Burton); and Whig John Tyler (Samuel Nelson, a Democrat).

Presidents have occasionally nominated someone as a justice in order to get him out of another position. Andrew Jackson appointed John McLean, who had served as postmaster general for six years, because McLean refused to permit political removals from post

office positions. Wilson named his attorney general, James C. McReynolds, to the Court after McReynolds came into conflict with the administration and some powerful members of Congress. Calvin Coolidge is said to have appointed Stone to the Court because of problems he was creating as attorney general.

On other occasions, appointment to the Court has been a president's reward to a supporter for political loyalty and service. Lincoln named his former campaign manager, David Davis, to the Court. John F. Kennedy appointed Byron R. White, who had led Kennedy's drive for independent voters in the 1960 election. Eisenhower's selection of Earl Warren as chief justice in 1953 came after Warren had delivered the California delegation's votes to Eisenhower at the 1952 Republican nominating convention and had campaigned for Eisenhower in the general election campaign.

Congressional Politics

John Adams's selection of the Federalist Marshall as chief justice, ironically, did not please the Federalist-controlled Senate, whose members preferred to elevate Associate Justice William Paterson. The Senate yielded after Adams remained firm. But during the rest of the nineteenth century, the Senate succeeded in blocking many other nominees, frequently for purely partisan reasons.

In particular, the Senate often denied confirmation to nominees late in a president's term simply to save the seat for an incoming president to fill. In 1829, for example, the Senate refused to confirm John Quincy Adams's nomination of John Crittenden, saving the seat for Andrew Jackson to fill.

Tyler, a former Democrat turned Whig, had no personal political base in the Senate when he succeeded to the presidency after the death of William Henry Harrison in 1841. Estranged from Whigs and Democrats alike, Tyler suffered three successive defeats on nominations to the Court in 1844 and two more in 1845 as the Democrats awaited the inauguration of James K. Polk.

Millard Fillmore, who became president after the death of Zachary Taylor, similarly failed in three tries to fill a vacancy on the Court in his last seven months in office. And on the eve of the Civil War in 1861, Republicans blocked a lame-duck appointment by Democratic president James Buchanan.

The Senate has defeated just one lame-duck nominee to the Court in the twentieth century: Abe Fortas, chosen by Lyndon Johnson to succeed Warren as chief justice in 1968. Warren submitted his resignation in June to take effect on the confirmation of a successor. Republicans, with an eye on the November election, wanted to save the seat. After argumentative hearings with Fortas over his liberal views and his role as an adviser to Johnson, the Republicans staged a filibuster on the Senate floor.

Democrats fell short, 45–43, of the two-thirds majority they needed to cut off debate on October 1. Fortas asked that his nomination be withdrawn the next day. Johnson then asked Warren to stay in his post. Warren agreed and remained on the Court through the 1968–1969 term.

Politics on the Court

In the Court's first century, several justices engaged in political activities while on the bench, including three—McLean, Salmon P. Chase, and Field—who either sought or expressed interest in nomination as president. Justice Charles Evans Hughes also had presidential ambitions, but he chose to resign from the bench in 1916 in order to run, unsuccessfully, as the Republican presidential nominee.

Justices in that era did not maintain the distance from other branches of government that is now expected of them. For example, word of the Court's ruling in the Dred Scott case and the first of the *Legal Tender Cases* was passed to presidents Buchanan and Grant respectively before the decisions were announced.

Several nineteenth-century justices lobbied effectively with presidents to urge appointment of certain candidates for vacancies on the Court. That practice continued in the twentieth century. As chief justice, William Howard Taft lobbied both the president and Congress. He either selected or approved three of the four justices Warren G. Harding appointed to the Court: Butler, George Sutherland, and Edward T. Sanford. In addition, Taft helped push through Congress the Judiciary Act of 1925, giving the Court greater control over its selection of cases to hear.

President Ronald Reagan escorts his nominee, Sandra Day O'Connor, through the White House garden. Reagan fulfilled a campaign promise by naming the first woman to the Supreme Court.   Source: George Tames/New York Times

Franklin Roosevelt and Truman both relied on advice from justices in selecting a new chief justice—and in both cases the choices proved to be disappointing. When Chief Justice Hughes, who had been renamed to the Court in 1930, announced his retirement in 1941, Roosevelt asked him and Justice Felix Frankfurter for help in choosing between elevating Harlan Fiske Stone or appointing Attorney General Robert H. Jackson. Both justices recommended Stone. Roosevelt chose Stone and then named Jackson to Stone's seat. Stone, however, was not regarded as an able leader. He failed to control some bitter feuds on the Court during his five years as chief justice—in particular one between Jackson and Hugo L. Black.

When Stone died in 1946, Truman sought advice

from the now retired Hughes and another retired justice, Owen J. Roberts. Jackson was viewed by many, including himself, as the leading contender, but both Hughes and Roberts urged Truman to pick someone who could restore peace among the members of the Court. Truman turned to his secretary of the treasury, Fred M. Vinson, who had a reputation as an able administrator. Vinson succeeded in muting the clashes between members of the Court but failed to restore harmony.

To this day justices still occasionally confer with presidents on nominations to the Court. In 1962 Kennedy discussed his intention to appoint Arthur J. Goldberg with Chief Justice Warren and with Frankfurter, whose retirement was creating the vacancy. In 1981 William H. Rehnquist recommended his former law school classmate, Sandra Day O'Connor, to President Ronald Reagan for a Supreme Court seat.

Pornography

See OBSCENITY.

Powell, Lewis F., Jr.

In his sixteen years on the Supreme Court, politically moderate Lewis Franklin Powell, Jr. (1907–), increasingly found himself in the middle between evenly split liberal and conservative factions. In this role, he cast the decisive fifth vote on a wide range of issues, making him the single most important member of the Court.

Powell was born in Suffolk, Virginia. He received both his undergraduate and law degrees from Washington and Lee University in Lexington, Virginia. In 1932 he earned a master's degree at Harvard Law School.

After graduating from Harvard, Powell specialized in corporate law and litigation at a Richmond law firm that was one of Virginia's oldest and most prestigious. Powell served as attorney for some national corporations. He eventually became a senior partner and re-

mained associated with the firm until his nomination to the Supreme Court.

Powell gained a national reputation as a moderate in the 1950s and 1960s. During that period he served as president of the Richmond school board (1952–1961) and as a member and president of the Virginia state board of education (1961–1969). Faced with intense pressure to close schools to fight desegregation, Powell consistently worked to keep the schools open.

His moderate views gained a national platform when he served a one-year term from 1964 to 1965 as president of the American Bar Association. His liberal side came to the fore when he criticized inadequate legal services for the poor and pushed to create the legal services program of the Office of Economic Opportunity. He expressed more conservative views on social ills and sternly denounced the use of civil disobedience. His conservative side also came through when he served in 1966 as a member of President Lyndon B. Johnson's Crime Commission. While a member of the commission, Powell joined in a minority statement criticizing Supreme Court decisions upholding the right of criminal suspects to remain silent.

Source: Library of Congress

President Richard Nixon nominated Powell to the Supreme Court on October 21, 1971, to replace retiring justice Hugo Black. The Senate confirmed the nomination by a vote of 89 to 1.

Powell cast the pivotal vote in a number of important 5–4 decisions. In 1978, he provided the fifth vote to permit state universities to adopt affirmative action admissions policies as long as they did not set rigid racial quotas. In 1986, he joined a five-justice majority in upholding state antisodomy laws. He later said he regretted that vote. Powell retired on the last day of the Court's October 1986 term.

Precedent

One reason for the continuity that is characteristic of U.S. law is the Supreme Court's reliance on precedent in arriving at decisions. Except in rare cases where there is no judicial opinion to be cited, any decision is based primarily on earlier relevant opinions of the Supreme Court or lower courts as interpreted in light of the case under consideration.

This adherence to the decisions of an earlier day is called the doctrine of *STARE DECISIS* (a Latin phrase meaning "let the decision stand"). This rule of precedent has a very practical basis: the need for stability in law. As Justice Louis D. Brandeis wrote in *Burnet v. Coronado Oil and Gas Company* (1932), "in most matters it is more important that the applicable rule of law be settled than that it be settled right."

The Court follows this rule to a varying degree. Most of the time it upholds or modifies the precedent. Less often the Court overturns an earlier decision altogether; such rulings may be dramatic and far-reaching, particularly when basic constitutional issues are involved.

The count varies on how often the Court has overturned its earlier rulings. One estimate puts the number at about two hundred. (See REVERSALS OF EARLIER RULINGS.)

In 1810 the Court in *Hudson and Smith v. Guestier* overruled an 1808 decision concerning the jurisdiction of a foreign power over vessels offshore. The Court overruled only eight more decisions in the next sixty years.

After the Civil War, changing conditions and changes in the composition of the Court placed increasing strain on the reverence for precedent. In 1870 the Court held the Legal Tender Acts unconstitutional. A year later, with two new members, the Court reversed itself and upheld the same laws.

Twenty-five years later, the Court found the statute authorizing a peacetime income tax unconstitutional. That ruling revised a century-old definition of "direct taxes" and ignored previous rulings that seemed to dictate that the Court should uphold the tax laws. This ruling was itself eventually reversed by adoption of the Sixteenth Amendment in 1913.

The Supreme Court in the twentieth century clearly has felt free to overrule its previous decisions. The court's reversals on child labor, minimum wage, and maximum hour laws; New Deal legislation; and state flag-salute laws are among the major chapters of Supreme Court history in the first half of the twentieth century. In the thirty years from 1961 to 1991, the Court overruled as many previous decisions as it had in its entire history before 1961.

As its actions have made clear, the modern Court views *stare decisis* as "a principle of policy and not a mechanical formula of adherence to the latest decision, however recent and questionable, when such adherence involves collision with a prior doctrine more embracing in its scope, intrinsically sounder, and verified by expression." The Court made that declaration in the case of *Helvering v. Hallock* (1940).

The Court tends to apply the doctrine of *stare decisis* more faithfully to questions of statutory law than to constitutional issues. One reason for this is that Congress can overturn a decision on a statutory issue by revising the law in question but a decision on a constitutional question can be reversed only by the Court itself or by a constitutional amendment. (See REVERSALS OF RULINGS BY CONSTITUTIONAL AMENDMENT; REVERSALS OF RULINGS BY LEGISLATION.)

The rule of precedent is also made more flexible by the Court's practice of "distinguishing" a new case from a precedent that might seem to be controlling, by pointing out factors that make the two situations different and therefore warrant different results. A precedent may eventually be distinguished into uniqueness and uselessness.

That process took place during the late 1930s and 1940s with regard to the Court's 1896 decision in *PLESSY V. FERGUSON*, allowing "separate but equal" facilities for blacks and whites. By the time the Court in 1954 officially overruled *Plessy*, the decision's value as a precedent had long been destroyed.

Supporters of the right of women to have an abortion feared that a similar process was taking place for *ROE V. WADE* (1973). Following that landmark decision overturning state laws barring abortions, the Court upheld several state laws restricting the circumstances under which women may have abortions. In one 1989 decision, four justices explicitly called for overturning *Roe v. Wade*. In 1992, however, the Court reaffirmed what it called the "essential holding" of *Roe v. Wade*. The Court's main opinion, jointly written by Justices Sandra Day O'Connor, Anthony M. Kennedy, and David H. Souter, stressed the importance of *stare decisis* in preserving respect for the Court. A decision to overrule *Roe*, the justices wrote, would result in "both profound and unnecessary damage to the Court's legitimacy, and to the Nation's commitment to the rule of law."

Preemption

The preemption doctrine invalidates state laws, under the SUPREMACY CLAUSE of the Constitution, because they conflict with federal law. The Supreme Court first established the doctrine in 1824 and has applied it more often since the 1930s as the federal government expanded its regulation of economic affairs under the COMMERCE POWER.

Chief Justice John Marshall set forth the preemption doctrine in his landmark opinion in *GIBBONS V. OGDEN* (1824) striking down a New York steamboat monopoly law as conflicting with a federal navigation act. Marshall said that states could not enact laws in conflict with federal law, but they could pass laws covering the same subject if they did not impede the operation of the federal statute.

Some preemption cases involve laws in which Congress has specifically stated an intention either to override state law or to allow parallel state regulation. Although some of these cases present no great difficulty, others require the Court to closely examine the laws to determine how broadly to apply the express preemption and what state laws may coexist with overlapping federal regulation.

Generally Congress does not include an explicit statement on preemption. In those cases the Court must try to discern congressional intent on the question and must also examine the interrelationship between the state and federal laws.

In an often cited decision, the Court in 1947 described three circumstances in which it would find that a state law was preempted by federal law:

The federal regulatory scheme may be "so pervasive as to make reasonable the inference that Congress left no room for the States to supplement it."

The federal interest in the subject may be "so dominant that the federal system will be assumed to preclude enforcement of state laws on the same subject."

The state policy "may produce a result inconsistent with the objective of the federal statute."

The Court's decisions do not appear to adopt a consistent approach in applying these tests. In general the Court has tended to allow state laws designed to protect public health or safety or to prevent fraud. It has been less deferential to strictly economic regulation by the states. But a sampling of the decisions shows that there are many exceptions to this pattern.

For example, the Court in 1963 allowed California to enact stricter standards for avocadoes than were required under federal law, but in 1977 it struck down a state's requirement for labeling package weight for flour that differed from federal regulation. The Court in 1978 upheld a state's oil-spill liability law that went beyond a federal law imposing liability for clean-up costs only. Ten years later, however, the Court used preemption to limit the states' ability to impose liability on government defense contractors. In two decisions overturning laws in areas traditionally reserved to the states or local governments, the Court in 1954 limited the power to penalize truckers for violating weight limitations and in 1973 barred some antinoise restrictions on airports and airlines.

Most preemption cases have involved commerce power cases. In 1956, however, the Court invoked the doctrine to overturn state antisedition laws as superseded by the federal law on the subject. (See SEDITION LAWS.) The decision in *Pennsylvania v. Nelson* created a storm of controversy. Two years later the House passed a bill to bar courts from finding preemption unless federal law contained an "express provision" to that effect or there was "a direct and positive conflict" between state and federal law. The measure died in the Senate, however.

The Court's difficulties in deciding preemption cases can be seen in three closely divided decisions issued in 1992, two of which were so fractured that there was no majority opinion for the Court.

In one case the Court, by a 5–3 vote, broadly construed a preemption provision in the 1978 airline deregulation act to prevent the states from enacting laws to require airlines to include specific disclosures about fares in their advertising *(Morales v. Trans World Airlines, Inc.)*. In another case the Court ruled, 5–4, that the federal Occupational Safety and Health Act preempted a state law that imposed special training requirements for some employees in the hazardous materials disposal industry *(Gade v. National Solid Wastes Management Association)*.

In a third decision the Court ruled that the federal cigarette-labeling act preempted some but not all liability suits against tobacco companies. The justices divided three ways in *Cipollone v. Liggett Group.* Two said that the act preempted all civil damage suits, while three said the law had no preemptive effect. The four justices in the middle said that the labeling requirement barred state court suits based on allegations that the companies had failed to warn consumers of the health hazards of smoking. But they voted to allow suits based on claims that the companies had deliberately concealed evidence of the health risks or had fraudulently claimed that smoking was not hazardous.

President and the Court

Over two centuries, the powers of the president have grown far beyond what the framers of the Constitution envisioned. The gradual shift in power from the states to the federal government broadened the scope and range of executive authority. The great crises of the twentieth century—two world wars, the Great Depression, and the Cold War—also fostered the expansion of presidential power.

For the most part, the Supreme Court has either supported or accepted the growth of presidential power. The Court has handed down only a few rulings setting limits on presidential authority, most of them in the twentieth century.

Two factors help explain why the Court has so rarely curbed the powers of the chief executive. First, the Constitution uses broad language to describe the powers of the president. Article II vests the president with "the executive Power," makes the president commander in chief, and directs the president to "take Care that the Laws be faithfully executed." This very

President Franklin D. Roosevelt and Congress cooperated to bring the country out of the Great Depression, but the Supreme Court declared many of the New Deal statutes unconstitutional. A frustrated president retaliated by coming up with a plan to increase the Court's size.   Source: Library of Congress

general phrasing provides an uncertain basis for constitutional challenges to presidential action.

Second, the respect in which the presidency is held helps insulate presidential power from challenges in the courts. The president has advantages over the legislative and judicial branches of government in capturing the public eye and attracting political support. The result, as Justice Robert H. Jackson wrote in 1952, is that the president "exerts a leverage upon those who are supposed to check and balance his power which often cancels their effectiveness."

Nonetheless, on a few occasions the Court has drawn the line against extensions of presidential power. In 1935 it blocked President Franklin D. Roosevelt from implementing a key part of his economic recovery program and, in a more lasting decision, protected members of independent regulatory agencies from dismissal by the president. In 1952, during the Korean War, the Court prevented President Harry S. Truman from seizing steel mills to keep them operating in the face of a threatened strike. (See *YOUNGSTOWN SHEET AND TUBE CO. V. SAWYER.*)

In 1972 the Court rejected President Richard Nixon's assertion of the power to conduct ELECTRONIC SURVEILLANCE without a warrant in domestic intelligence investigations. Two years later the Court rejected Nixon's claim of executive privilege and ordered him to turn over tapes of his conversations concerning the Watergate cover-up. The contents of those tapes forced him to resign from office just two weeks later. (See EXECUTIVE PRIVILEGE AND IMMUNITY.)

Specific Powers

The list of specific powers granted to the president in Article II of the Constitution is shorter than the enumeration of Congress's powers in Article I. In addition to his role as commander in chief, the president is empowered to:

Make treaties, but only with the advice and consent of the Senate. (See TREATY POWER.)

Appoint ambassadors, "other public Ministers," and judges—including the members of the Supreme Court—but again only with the Senate's approval. (See APPOINTMENT AND REMOVAL POWERS OF THE PRESIDENT; CONFIRMATION PROCESS; NOMINATION TO THE COURT.)

Require heads of executive departments to furnish written opinions "upon any Subject relating to the Duties of their Respective Offices."

Issue reprieves and PARDONS, except in cases of impeachment.

Recommend legislative measures deemed "necessary and expedient."

Veto any bill passed by Congress, subject to being overridden by two-thirds votes in both the House and Senate. (See VETO POWER.)

These specific powers have been construed very broadly. As early as 1789 the president's appointment power was interpreted as including the power to remove executive branch officials. Thus department heads became dependent on the president rather than remaining more or less independent officials, as the Constitution appears to have viewed them.

In legislative affairs, presidents have used the veto power more frequently since the Civil War than they did before. Also, the president's role in recommending legislation gradually became more important. By the mid-twentieth century, most bills that became law were either proposed by the president or shaped during the legislative process to gain presidential approval.

The constitutional command contained in the "take care" clause gives the president additional powers. The responsibility to see that the laws are "faithfully executed" makes the president subordinate to the law. But the clause also includes affirmative powers that range from the administrative interpretation of acts of Congress to the declaration of martial law in times of civil disorder or national emergency.

The Issue of Inherent Authority

Before setting out the specific powers, Article II declares in its opening sentence: "The executive Power shall be vested in a President of the United States of America." Presidents, justices, and constitutional scholars have disagreed about the exact meaning of this language.

Some have argued that the provision is simply a

designation of office and does not add anything in substantive power. William Howard Taft took this position in a book written after he had served as president and before he became chief justice. "The president can exercise no power," Taft wrote, "which cannot be fairly and reasonably traced to some specific grant of power or justly implied and included within such grant as proper and necessary."

Others have maintained that the executive power provision is a broad grant of inherent authority, adding to the enumerated powers. Theodore Roosevelt, for example, viewed the president as a "steward of the people" with a broad mandate to act in the public welfare as he saw it. "My belief was that it was not only his right but his duty to do anything that the needs of the nation demanded unless such action was forbidden by the Constitution or by the laws," the former president wrote in his autobiography.

Taft's view prevailed during much of the nineteenth century. Twentieth-century presidents, however, including Taft himself, have acted on the basis of broader conceptions of presidential power. Franklin Roosevelt stretched executive authority to combat the Depression and to fight World War II—usually with congressional authorization, but sometimes without. Truman claimed inherent authority in his effort to take over the steel mills. Nixon repeatedly made broad assertions of presidential power in waging war in Southeast Asia and in seeking to nullify congressional decisions on budgetary matters.

These more expansive claims of inherent authority led to a handful of Supreme Court rulings that tended to curb presidential power. Although it has rejected presidential claims of extraconstitutional authority, however, the Court has shown no inclination to narrow the broad construction of presidential powers established by two centuries of precedent and practice.

The Foreign Role

The Supreme Court has almost without exception supported presidential authority in FOREIGN AFFAIRS and on WAR POWERS issues.

It is Congress's role to declare war, but even without express congressional authorization to send U.S. armed forces abroad, the Court has never ordered U.S. troops returned from overseas. The Court in 1863 gave President Abraham Lincoln after-the-fact support for his decision to blockade southern ports in 1861 without waiting for Congress to authorize the action (*Prize Cases*). During the 1960s and 1970s, it refused to rule on challenges to U.S. military actions in Vietnam and Cambodia, leaving presidential policies in effect unless Congress chose to block them.

The Court in 1936 endorsed a sweeping view of presidential power in foreign affairs. Writing for the Court in *United States v. Curtiss-Wright Export Corp.*, Justice George Sutherland said that the foreign affairs powers did not depend on the Constitution but rather flowed directly to the federal government as an element of national sovereignty. On that basis, Sutherland concluded that the president could act alone in foreign relations matters.

Sutherland's historical and legal analysis has been widely criticized. Furthermore, the reasoning was not essential to the decision, which upheld a presidential arms embargo imposed under a congressional statute. Nonetheless, the Court has not modified the broad grant of executive power sanctioned by the ruling.

Domestic Power

The Court has generally supported the president's executive powers in domestic matters.

As early as 1839 the Court affirmed the president's overall responsibility for the executive branch, declaring that the chief executive "speaks and acts through the heads of the several departments." In 1842 the Court said that rules and regulations issued by the executive branch have binding effect—a decision that underlies the great expansion of administrative rule making in the twentieth century.

Since 1792 presidents have had statutory authority to use troops to quell disorder. Ever since 1827 the Court has steadily backed the president's authority to decide when and if an emergency exists that requires the use of troops. In the most dramatic of these rulings, the Court in 1895 upheld the conviction for contempt of court of union leader Eugene V. Debs, who had violated a court order obtained by the government to suspend a strike that was blocking all rail traffic west of Chicago. "If the emergency arises," the Court wrote in *In re Debs*, "the army of the nation, and all of its militia, are at the service of the nation to compel obedience to its laws."

The Court has also supported executive discretion in the absence of a statute or sometimes in apparent disregard of a statute. In 1890 it upheld the power of the president to assign federal marshals to protect a Supreme Court justice whose life had been threatened, even though no law specifically authorized those duties. In 1915 the Court backed President Taft's decision in 1909 to withdraw some public lands from public use even though Congress had provided that all public lands containing minerals were to be open to exploration and purchase. "The President was in a position to know when the public interest required particular portions of the people's lands to be withdrawn from entry or relocation," the Court declared.

Two world wars led presidents to claim greater powers over the national economy. Woodrow Wilson and Franklin Roosevelt both seized industrial plants to prevent interruption of production during wartime. While Wilson acted under broadly phrased congressional statutes, Roosevelt had no specific statutory authority for his actions until the enactment of the War Labor Disputes Act in 1943.

In one instance Roosevelt dispatched troops to seize and operate a struck aircraft plant for about a month in June and July of 1941. In a legal opinion, Attorney General Robert Jackson—who was later appointed to the Court—justified the action by saying that the president had the inherent constitutional duty "to exert his civil and military as well as his moral authority to keep the defense effort of the United States as a going concern." Roosevelt's actions stirred controversy, but the single wartime court test of the seizure power proved inconclusive. In *Montgomery Ward & Co. v. United States* (1944) the Supreme Court dismissed a challenge to a seizure of the company's property as being moot when the army returned the property to company control.

Eight years later, however, the Court rejected Truman's claim of inherent power to seize steel mills to avert a wartime labor strike. The decision in *YOUNGSTOWN SHEET AND TUBE CO. V. SAWYER* (1952) was based in part on Congress's refusal several years earlier to grant the president such power. In a concurring opinion Robert Jackson, now a justice, said that the president needed congressional authorization to justify such actions. "Congress, not the Executive, should control utilization of the war power as an instrument of domestic policy," Jackson wrote.

Confrontations

The steel seizure case was one of several pivotal confrontations in U.S. history between the president and the Supreme Court. In some of these episodes, the president emerged as the victor; in others, the Court prevailed in the constitutional battle.

Jefferson

The first of these clashes pitted Thomas Jefferson against the Federalist-dominated Court led by Chief Justice John Marshall. Jefferson regarded his election as president in 1800 as a revolution, but one that was incomplete because of Federalist control of the federal judiciary. A dispute ensued over John Adams's lame-duck appointments of four Federalist judges. That dispute led to Marshall's landmark opinion in *MARBURY V. MADISON* (1803), asserting the Court's power to declare acts of Congress unconstitutional. To counter Marshall's influence, Jefferson turned to the only means provided by the Constitution to remove judges: impeachment. But the impeachment proceedings that Jefferson initiated against Justice Samuel Chase failed, and Jefferson then dropped the idea—establishing a precedent that has since served to protect the Court from political retaliation. (See IMPEACHMENT OF JUSTICES.)

Jackson

Andrew Jackson clashed with Marshall as well, most notably in refusing to enforce the Court's 1832 ruling in a running dispute between the state of Georgia and the Cherokee Indians. However, Jackson's tacit support for Georgia's defiance of the Court ended when he realized the dispute could encourage other states to defy federal authority on broader issues. The temporary stalemate showed that the Court lacked the power to enforce its own orders and ultimately had to rely on the executive branch to carry out its decisions if challenged.

Lincoln

The Court's inability to enforce its orders allowed President Lincoln to prevail in his confrontation with Chief Justice Roger B. Taney at the outset of the Civil War. Lincoln and Taney locked horns over the president's decision to suspend the writ of HABEAS CORPUS. Sitting as a circuit justice, Taney ruled the action unconstitutional and sternly rebuked Lincoln for usurping legislative and judicial power. Lincoln refused to comply with Taney's order and defended his actions as justified by wartime emergencies. Only after the war had ended did the full Court rule that Lincoln's use of military tribunals outside the war zone had been unconstitutional. By then, the issue was largely moot.

Franklin Roosevelt

Roosevelt's clash with the Court came after a series of rulings in 1935 and 1936 that invalidated key parts of his New Deal program. After winning reelection by a landslide, he announced in February 1937 a plan to

President Harry S. Truman lost in his bid to seize steel mills that were threatening to strike during the Korean War.
Source: Jim Berryman/Washington Post

pack the Court with justices who would support his programs. (See SIZE OF THE COURT.) The cool reception for the plan in Congress and the public backlash against it demonstrated the broad support for the Court's role in the constitutional system of checks and balances. But Roosevelt eventually won, as vacancies over the next four years allowed him to appoint justices whose views were in line with his own.

Nixon

Nixon campaigned for the presidency in 1968 on a pledge to remake the Supreme Court. He then had several setbacks from a Court that included four of his own appointees. First, in 1972 the Court refused to recognize an inherent presidential power to use wiretapping without obtaining a warrant, in order to investigate domestic groups suspected of subversive activities. That 6–2 decision was written by one of Nixon's appointees, Justice Lewis F. Powell, Jr.

In a more dramatic confrontation two years later, the Court voted 8–0 to reject Nixon's plea of executive privilege in the Watergate tapes case. The Court's opinion in *United States v. Nixon* (1974) was written by the man Nixon had appointed as chief justice in his first year in office, Warren E. Burger. Burger was joined by two other Nixon appointees, justices Powell and Harry A. Blackmun. (Nixon's fourth appointee, William H. Rehnquist, recused himself.) By submitting to the decision Nixon sealed the fate of his presidency: he resigned two weeks later.

A year after Nixon left office, the Court rejected one more of his broad claims of presidential authority: the power to impound funds appropriated by Congress. Presidents since Jefferson had occasionally refused to spend money as Congress had provided. In most of the previous instances presidents had found authority for the impoundment in the language of the authorizing statute. Nixon used the impoundment power more often than earlier presidents and claimed a constitutional basis for it independent of statutory provisions.

The Court in 1975 ruled on one of Nixon's impoundment decisions, his refusal to distribute $18 billion in state aid under the Water Pollution Control Act of 1972. In *Train v. City of New York* the Court unanimously ruled that Nixon had exceeded his authority.

Although the decision was based on the language of the act, it implied that Nixon's claim of such a power was shaky.

Nixon's presidency saw more legal battles over presidential powers than any other. Presidents Ronald Reagan and George Bush both took expansive views of presidential authority but generally avoided direct confrontations. In one final echo of the Nixon era, however, the Court in 1988 upheld the constitutionality of the provisions of the post-Watergate Ethics in Government Act. That act authorized appointment of an "independent counsel" to investigate and prosecute cases of alleged wrongdoing by high officials of the executive branch. Reagan's solicitor general had argued that the law intruded on presidential authority, but the Court in *Morrison v. Olson* upheld the statute by a 7–1 vote.

Press, Freedom of

The First Amendment of the Constitution prohibits Congress from passing any law abridging the freedom of the press. The framers, however, provided few details of what that clause meant. They probably intended to prohibit any system of government censorship, or prior restraint, in the United States. But it is unclear whether they also intended to protect the press from being punished for criticizing the government under the doctrine of seditious libel (scandalous or malicious criticism of the government or its officials).

Before World War I the Supreme Court had few occasions to rule on free press issues. Several editors were among those tried and convicted under the controversial Sedition Act of 1798, but no challenge to the law reached the Court before the act expired in 1801. Press censorship was imposed under martial law during the Civil War, but again the Court never ruled on the constitutionality of the actions. Some of the convictions after World War I under state and federal SEDITION LAWS involved newspaper editors, but the Court rejected free speech and free press claims alike in sustaining the convictions. In one of the cases, *Gitlow v. New York* (1925), the Court held for the first

time that the First Amendment applies to the states as well as to the federal government.

Since then the Court has struck down some laws as unconstitutional prior restraints on the press. It has also restricted subsequent punishment by limiting the civil liability of the press for claims of LIBEL or invasions of privacy. But the Court has rejected efforts to establish a broad constitutional right of access to government institutions or information. It has also refused to recognize a constitutional privilege limiting government inquiries into the news-gathering process.

Prior Restraints

The Court's first review of a case of prior restraint of the press arose from a Minnesota law that prohibited as a public nuisance the publication of malicious, scandalous, or defamatory newspapers and magazines. Even if the defamatory allegations were true, the law permitted that fact to be used as a defense only if the allegations were made with good motive and for justifiable ends.

In *Near v. Minnesota* (1931) the Court by a 5–4 vote

Gov. Huey Long of Louisiana used a newspaper tax in an attempt to silence certain papers that were critical of him. In Grosjean v. American Press Company *(1936) the Supreme Court unanimously decided that such a tax is a "prior restraint" on the press that violates the First Amendment.*   Source: UPI/Bettmann

lifted an injunction issued under the law against the publisher of a weekly periodical. The publisher had printed anti-Semitic attacks against a Jewish gangster in Minneapolis and had criticized local authorities for allegedly being in collusion with the gangster. Writing for the majority, Chief Justice Charles Evans Hughes acknowledged that the law did not operate as a prior restraint in the same sense as a licensing system. But he said that the power to suppress a newspaper as a public nuisance unless certain defenses could be shown was "the essence of censorship."

Hughes did not rule out all prior restraints. He suggested four situations in which government censorship might be permitted: publication of crucial war information, such as the number and location of troops; obscene publications; publications inciting acts of violence against the community or violent overthrow of the government; and publications that invade "private rights."

Later in the 1930s the Court extended the prior restraint doctrine to protect the distribution of leaflets, pamphlets, and handbills in the face of local ordinances that either prohibited distribution altogether or required a permit for it. In 1960 the Court struck down a local ordinance against distribution of unsigned handbills.

Meanwhile, the Court had adopted one of the exceptions to the prior restraint doctrine that Hughes had suggested: obscenity. In *Kingsley Books v. Brown* (1957) the Court by a 5–4 vote upheld a New York statute that allowed public officials to seek injunctions against the sale of obscene publications. A 1961 decision upheld similar injunctions against public showings of obscene films. But in *Freedman v. Maryland* (1965) the Court limited the impact of those decisions by establishing procedural safeguards for such injunctions, including a requirement for "a prompt final judicial decision."

Six years later the Court refused to apply another of Hughes's exceptions, in the most dramatic confrontation between the press and the government in the nation's history: the PENTAGON PAPERS CASE (1971). By a 6–3 vote, the Court refused to grant the government's request to block newspapers from publishing articles based on a classified study of U.S. involvement in Vietnam. But the various justices' opinions in *New York Times Co. v. United States* left open the possibility that national security considerations might sometimes permit prior restraint against the press.

Subsequent Punishment

English common law recognized the government's right to impose criminal punishment on those who maliciously criticized the government. Legal scholars disagree on whether the First Amendment was intended to prohibit that doctrine, called the seditious libel doctrine, in the United States. But—as the Supreme Court stated in a 1964 decision—the political repudiation of the Sedition Act of 1798 effectively settled the issue.

Unlike libel against the government, however, the issue of civil or criminal liability for libeling private individuals went largely unchallenged on constitutional grounds until the Court's landmark ruling in *NEW YORK TIMES CO. V. SULLIVAN* (1964). That decision protected news organizations by requiring that public officials must demonstrate "actual malice" to recover damages for libel. The ruling was later extended to civil suits brought by public figures, and a lesser measure of protection was afforded to defendants sued by people who were not public figures. The Court also struck down two state criminal libel statutes in 1966. Similar laws have gone all but unused since then, but the Court has not conclusively ruled on their validity.

The Court has also imposed limits on private damage suits against the news media for invasion of privacy, but its rulings in this area have been more tentative.

In 1975 the Court struck down a Georgia statute concerning the privacy right of rape victims. Under that law the father of a murder-rape victim had recovered civil damages from a television station that had obtained the girl's name from public records and had then included her name in a news account about the case. The ruling in *Cox Broadcasting Corp. v. Cohn* left open the possibility that the states could pass laws that kept such information out of public records altogether.

But in 1989 the Court, by a vote of 6 to 3, overturned a civil damage award in another suit involving the privacy of rape victims, even though state law prohibited disclosure of a rape victim's name. The newspaper in the case *(The Florida Star v. B.J.F.)* had obtained the name from an arrest report mistakenly released by the local sheriff's office.

News Gathering

News organizations have argued that their news-gathering function requires access to government proceedings and institutions. Nonetheless the Supreme Court has refused to create a general constitutional right of access except in one context: criminal trials. The Court has also refused to recognize a journalist's privilege to withhold information from the government to protect a news source or to block a newsroom search to protect confidential information.

The Court dealt with the issue of confidential sources in 1972 in three cases in which reporters challenged subpoenas to testify before grand juries. Two had been reporting on a radical group, the Black Panthers, while the other had been researching drug users. All three said they could not have gained access to the groups without promising them confidentiality.

In a 5–4 ruling in *Branzburg v. Hayes* (1972), the Court said that the First Amendment does not give journalists "a testimonial privilege that other citizens do not enjoy." Writing for the majority, Justice Byron R. White stated that "the public interest in law enforcement" was not outweighed by whatever burden might result from requiring the reporters to testify.

In *Zurcher v. The Stanford Daily* (1978) the Court similarly rejected, by a vote of 5 to 3, a claim that police had to use a subpoena rather than a search warrant to obtain evidence from news organizations. The newspaper contesting the search had argued that use of a subpoena would have avoided an intrusive search of its newsroom and given it an opportunity to challenge the investigation. The Court found no constitutional basis for such a requirement. Two years later, however, Congress passed a law prohibiting newsroom searches by federal, state, or local government officials except in special circumstances.

The issue of access to government proceedings and institutions reached the Court in 1974, in two cases

In 1816 Thomas Jefferson remarked, "When the press is free, and every man is able to read, all is safe." In writing the First Amendment, the nation's founders acknowledged that democratic government could not survive without the free and open exchange of ideas.

Source: Government Printing Office

challenging federal and state policies that limited press access to prison inmates. By 5–4 votes in *Pell v. Procunier* and *Saxbe v. Washington Post,* the Court sustained rules that barred reporters from designating inmates they wished to interview. Reporters could, however, communicate with specific inmates by mail and also visit prisons and talk with inmates they met during such visits.

In both cases the Court rejected the press's claims of right to access. As Justice Potter Stewart wrote in the *Pell* case, nothing in the First Amendment requires "government to afford the press special access to information not shared by members of the public generally." The Court reaffirmed that position in another prison access case in 1978.

Meanwhile, a broader access issue was working its way toward the Court: the question of access to criminal trials.

Beginning in the 1960s, the Court was concerned with the question of how to prevent pretrial publicity or news coverage of a trial from interfering with a criminal defendant's right to a fair trial. One approach to the problem consisted of so-called gag orders, which barred the press from publishing articles containing certain types of information about pending court cases.

In *Nebraska Press Association v. Stuart* (1976) the Court overturned an order issued by a Nebraska judge prohibiting any news accounts of a preliminary hearing in a highly publicized mass murder case. Writing for the unanimous Court, Chief Justice Warren E. Burger noted that the judge could have used less drastic means to ensure that publicity did not prevent the defendant from receiving a fair trial. Several justices indicated that they believed a gag order was unconstitutional in any circumstances.

The *Nebraska Press Association* decision encouraged some judges to try closing preliminary hearings altogether to minimize pretrial publicity. The ruling in *Gannett Co. v. DePasquale* (1979) appeared to endorse this approach. By a vote of 5 to 4 the Court in that case ruled that the closure of a preliminary hearing with the agreement of the prosecution and the defense did not violate the Sixth Amendment guarantee of a public trial. A year later, however, the Court reversed direction and held that the First Amendment

prevents a judge from closing a criminal trial to the press or public except in very limited circumstances.

The vote in that case, *Richmond Newspapers v. Commonwealth of Virginia* (1980), was 7–1, but there was no majority opinion. In a plurality opinion for himself and two other justices, Burger relied mainly on the historical tradition of open court proceedings. Justice William J. Brennan, Jr., wrote an opinion for himself and Justice Thurgood Marshall that emphasized a "structural" view of the First Amendment as protecting informed public debate by guaranteeing "the indispensable conditions of meaningful communication."

In a footnote, Burger suggested that the ruling might also apply to civil trials, but the Court has not ruled on that issue directly. In two decisions in the 1980s, though, the Court did guarantee press and public access to jury selection proceedings in criminal trials and to preliminary hearings—thus implicitly reversing the *Gannett* decision.

Electronic Media

The Supreme Court has made clear that the First Amendment extends to electronic media, such as broadcasting and cable services, as well as to newspapers. But because of the government's role in licensing or franchising the electronic media, the Court has upheld regulations that could not be applied to print media.

Citing the limitation on the number of broadcast frequencies, the Court in 1943 sustained the power of the Federal Communications Commission (FCC) to determine who receives broadcast licenses. It emphasized, however, that the FCC must award licenses on the basis of neutral principles that do not favor one applicant over another because of an applicant's particular views.

Beginning in the late 1940s the FCC developed a policy that required broadcasters to devote a reasonable percentage of time to coverage of public issues and to provide an opportunity for presentation of contrasting points of view on those issues. Broadcasters challenged this "fairness doctrine" as a violation of their right to determine the content of broadcasts free from governmental interference.

In 1969 the Court in *Red Lion Broadcasting Co. v. Fed-*

eral Communications Commission unanimously rejected the broadcasters' argument. Again citing the scarcity of broadcast frequencies, the Court said that a broadcaster "has no constitutional right to be the one who holds the license or to monopolize a radio frequency to the exclusion of his fellow citizens." In 1987, however, broadcasters finally won their battle against the fairness doctrine when the FCC voted 4–0 to discard it.

The Court ruled in 1973 that broadcasters could refuse to sell commercial time for issue-related advertising. In 1981 it upheld a law that required broadcasters to provide candidates for federal office with "reasonable access" to buy commercial time. The Court earlier had decisively rejected any such right of access to print media. In *Miami Herald Publishing Co. v. Tornillo* (1974) the Court unanimously struck down a Florida law that required newspapers to grant political candidates equal space to reply to criticism of their public records.

The FCC began regulating cable television in the 1960s in part to protect broadcasters from unfair competition and in part to require cable companies to serve local community needs. The Court in 1972, by a 5–4 vote, upheld an FCC regulation requiring cable operators to provide a certain amount of original programming in addition to retransmission of broadcast signals. Two years later the FCC scrapped that rule and adopted broader regulations that required new cable systems to allocate channels for public, educational, local government, and leased use. The Court in 1979 said that those rules went beyond the Communications Act of 1934 by imposing common carrier obligations on cable systems. The decision hinted that such rules might be unconstitutional as well.

In 1986 the Court for the first time held that the First Amendment applies to the cable-franchising process. The ruling in *City of Los Angeles v. Preferred Communications, Inc.* allowed an unsuccessful applicant for a cable franchise in a part of Los Angeles to pursue a claim that the city's decision to grant only one franchise in the area violated its rights under federal antitrust law and under the First Amendment. The brief, unanimous ruling gave no details on how to resolve the claims.

Prima Facie

Prima facie (a Latin term meaning "at first sight") denotes the quantity of evidence sufficient to establish a claim or defense unless contradicted by the other side and to justify submitting the issue to the jury, or to the judge in a nonjury trial.

A party that fails to establish a prima facie case may have the case dismissed, or a verdict may be directed against the party at the close of the evidence.

Privacy, Right of

The Constitution does not mention privacy, but the Supreme Court has recognized privacy as a constitutional right that limits the government's power to interfere with personal conduct in areas such as child rearing, marriage, contraception, and ABORTION.

A right of privacy has also been asserted as a basis for tort lawsuits for publication of some types of private information. The Court's rulings in this area have established First Amendment limits on such suits. (See PRESS, FREEDOM OF.)

The Supreme Court first recognized this category of personal rights in *Meyer v. Nebraska* (1923), which struck down a state law against teaching modern foreign languages in public schools in the first eight grades. It ruled that the law deprived teachers, parents, and children of a measure of personal liberty, which the Court said included the right to "engage in any of the common occupations of life, to acquire useful knowledge, to marry, establish a home and bring up children, . . . and generally to enjoy those privileges long recognized at common law as essential to the orderly pursuit of happiness by free men."

Two years later the Court in *Pierce v. Society of Sisters* (1925) similarly struck down an Oregon law requiring all children to attend public schools. It stated that the law "unreasonably interferes with the liberty of parents . . . to direct the upbringing and education of [their] children."

In 1942 the Court invoked the equal protection

Estelle Griswold (left), who opened a birth control clinic in New Haven in violation of an 1879 Connecticut law prohibiting the use of contraceptives, and Mrs. Ernest Jahncke, president of the Planned Parenthood League of Connecticut, celebrate their 1965 victory in the Supreme Court. In Griswold v. Connecticut *the Court struck down the law and recognized a constitutional right to privacy. Source: UPI/Bettmann*

clause to protect personal privacy. Striking down an Oklahoma law providing for sterilization of some convicted felons, the Court said that marriage and procreation were "fundamental" rights. Laws affecting those rights, it said, were subject to strict scrutiny and could be justified only by a pressing governmental objective. Twenty-five years later the Court gave a similar analysis when it struck down state laws against interracial marriages as a violation of equal protection and due process. "The Fourteenth Amendment requires that the freedom of choice to marry not be restricted by invidious racial discrimination," the Court declared in *Loving v. Virginia* (1967).

The Court's first extended discussion of the right of privacy, in those terms, had come two years earlier. The ruling in *Griswold v. Connecticut* (1965) struck down, by a 7–2 vote, a state law that prohibited married couples from using contraceptives.

Justice William O. Douglas's opinion, written for a five-justice majority, based the right of privacy on what he called the "penumbras" of several provisions of the Bill of Rights, including the First, Third, Fourth, Fifth, and Ninth amendments. In a concurring opinion, three of the justices more specifically relied on the Ninth Amendment, which provides that the "enumeration in the Constitution of certain rights shall not be construed to deny or disparage others retained by the people."

Justice John Marshall Harlan did not join Douglas's opinion, but called the law an "invasion of privacy" that violated "the concept of ordered liberty" protected by the Fourteenth Amendment. In his concurring opinion, Justice Byron R. White spurned the "right of privacy" label, but found that the law violated the Fourteenth Amendment by infringing "the freedoms of married persons" without justification. The dissenting justices, Hugo L. Black and Potter Stewart, criticized the law but found no constitutional right of privacy to justify striking it down.

The doctrinal divisions were more evident in 1972 when the Court struck down a Massachusetts law that permitted the distribution of contraceptives to unmarried individuals to prevent the spread of disease but not to prevent conception. The law imposed no such limitation on distribution to married persons. The 6–1 decision in *Eisenstadt v. Baird* held that the law denied equal protection by treating married and unmarried persons differently. The Court avoided ruling on the state's authority to ban distribution of contraceptives altogether.

The next year the Court explicitly recognized a right to privacy in its abortion rights ruling, *ROE V. WADE* (1973). But the Court was again uncertain on the origin of the privacy right, refusing to decide firmly whether the right to abortion was based on "the Fourteenth Amendment's concept of personal liberty . . . as we feel it is" or on the Ninth Amendment protection of unenumerated rights.

Over the next decade the Court seemed to settle on the Fourteenth Amendment rationale. But the Court refused to give abortion rights the strength of equal protection principles when it upheld state and federal laws banning the use of public funds to pay for abortions for poor women. In two pivotal abortion rulings in 1989 and 1992 the Court's principal opinions scrupulously avoided the word *privacy* altogether.

The limit to the Court's support for the right of privacy was seen in a 1986 decision that upheld, by a 5–4 vote, state laws providing criminal punishment for private, consensual homosexual conduct. Writing for the majority in *Bowers v. Hardwick,* Justice White doubted the existence of the right but said that in any event it did not protect the right to engage in homosexual activity.

Nonetheless, the Court in 1990 tentatively extended the principles of its earlier rulings into a new and uncharted area: "right to die" cases. In *Cruzan v. Director, Missouri Dep't of Health,* all of the justices recognized an individual's right to refuse life-sustaining medical treatment in some cases. They said the right was grounded in the liberty interest protected by the due process clause.

The case involved a comatose automobile accident victim. Chief Justice William H. Rehnquist's opinion for the five-justice majority limited the right by ruling that a state could require "clear and convincing" evidence that the patient had previously indicated her wish to reject extraordinary medical procedures in such circumstances. The four dissenting justices found the evidentiary requirement too strict.

Probable Cause

Probable cause is the standard of proof required under the Fourth Amendment to justify arresting a criminal suspect or conducting a search for evidence or contraband. It is also the standard of proof required for a GRAND JURY to issue an indictment. This requirement applies to federal courts under the Fifth Amendment and has also been adopted in state courts by constitution or statute.

The Fourth Amendment prohibits "unreasonable searches and seizures" and states that "no Warrants shall issue, but upon probable cause." When police seek an arrest or search warrant, a judge or other judicial officer determines whether probable cause has been shown. When police do not obtain a warrant beforehand, they must be able to show that they had probable cause to justify an arrest or, with certain exceptions, to justify a search. (See SEARCH AND SEIZURE.)

A defendant who challenges an arrest or search after the fact may be able to prevent the use at trial of any evidence obtained if police did not have probable cause at the time. (See EXCLUSIONARY RULE.)

The Court has given different meanings to probable cause in different contexts. For an arrest, police must have "reasonably trustworthy information" at the time of the arrest concerning facts and circumstances that would lead a "reasonably prudent" person to believe that the suspect had committed or was committing an offense. For a search, police must have information to support a reasonable belief that the law was being violated or that evidence of a crime would be found.

The information or evidence needed to show probable cause can include evidence that would not be admissible at trial—for example, hearsay. But because of the judicial preference for warrants, the Court has said that probable cause may be examined less critically when police obtain a search warrant than when they act without a warrant.

The Court has also given a special meaning to probable cause in its decisions holding that administrative regulatory inspections are subject to the Fourth Amendment. In *Camara v. Municipal Court* (1967) the Court ruled that inspectors may search a place of business without any specific information of a regulatory violation if the inspection followed "reasonable legislative or administrative standards."

Property Rights

The Supreme Court's attitude toward property rights has changed drastically from era to era. It was protective of property rights in the early nineteenth century and again from the 1890s through the mid-1930s. Since 1937, however, the Court has given federal and state governments wide discretion to take property for public use or to limit the use of private property through economic regulation or land use controls.

The original Constitution contained only one explicit protection for property rights: the CONTRACT CLAUSE prohibiting the states from passing any law "impairing the obligation of contracts." The Bill of Rights added broader protections, specifically, the Fifth Amendment provisions that no one be deprived of property without DUE PROCESS of law and that private property not be taken without "just compensation." But until after the Civil War these provisions applied only to the federal government, not the states.

The Supreme Court showed concern for property rights in some of its earliest cases. In 1796 it upheld the rights of British creditors to be paid for property confiscated during the revolutionary war. In 1813 it upheld the right of noncitizens to inherit land in Virginia despite a state law to the contrary. And in the famous *Dartmouth College* case in 1819 Chief Justice John Marshall used the contract clause to protect private corporations from state laws impairing rights granted in their charters.

Under Chief Justice Roger B. Taney the Court gave greater weight to community rights than to property rights in some cases. In *West River Bridge Co. v. Dix* (1848) it emphatically declared that the power of eminent domain—the government's right to take property for public use—was "paramount to all private rights vested under the government." The Court continued to use the contract clause, however, to protect banks and other corporations from state laws abridging their rights.

Both legal doctrines continued for several decades after the Civil War. Use of the contract clause to strike down state laws increased sharply during the period 1865–1873. But later in the 1870s the Court strongly reaffirmed the power of eminent domain and refused to extend the just compensation requirement of the Fifth Amendment to the states under the Fourteenth Amendment. In one case, *Mugler v. Kansas* (1877), the Court found no need to compensate the owner of a brewery closed as a public nuisance under a state law banning the sale or manufacture of alcoholic beverages.

In the late 1890s a probusiness Court began to view government limits on property rights much more skeptically. Under a broader theory of freedom of contract the Court overturned an array of social and economic regulations into the 1930s. The Court in the 1890s also narrowed the new federal ANTITRUST law, struck down the federal INCOME TAX, and upheld the power of federal judges to enjoin strikes.

The Court ruled in 1897 that the just compensation clause did apply to state governments. On that basis, it held in *Smyth v. Ames* (1898) that state-regulated rates for railroads must be high enough to ensure a "fair return" on investment—and the courts would decide what return was fair. Over the next four decades the Court applied this standard to benefit corporations.

The Court changed course in 1937. It discarded freedom of contract and property rights as a basis for second-guessing legislative judgments on economic issues. Among many decisions reflecting this new attitude were rulings in 1942 and 1944 that reduced the Court's role in reviewing state rate regulation. Since then the Court has consistently upheld economic

Rev. Eleazar Wheelock (above left), with the charter of Dartmouth College behind his left hand, was the institution's founder and first president. He designated his son, John Wheelock, to succeed him.
Source: Dartmouth College

John Wheelock (above right), ill-suited to succeed his father, was constantly at odds with Dartmouth's board of trustees. To shore up his position, he persuaded the state legislature to change the school from a private to a public institution.
Source: Dartmouth College

Dartmouth's trustees, who had lost control of the renamed Dartmouth University, sued William H. Woodward (right), the college secretary. The Supreme Court decided that the school's original charter was the same as a contract, which the state legislature could not arbitrarily change. *Source: Dartmouth College*

measures if they were rationally related to a legitimate state purpose; "minimum rationality" and almost any purpose would suffice.

Regulatory Taking Doctrine

In the 1980s the Court began to be more critical of government land-use and ZONING regulations that severely limited use of private property. Two doctrines competed with each other. The "harmful or noxious use" doctrine—traced back to the *Mugler v. Kansas* ruling—allowed local or state governments to go so far as to effectively close down an existing business if the use of the property harmed the community or surrounding property. But the "regulatory taking" doctrine—first recognized in *Pennsylvania Coal Co. v. Mahon* (1922)—held that regulations that went "too far" could constitute a taking of property and could be struck down.

Under the harmful use doctrine, the Court had allowed regulations to close down an urban brickyard (1915), to destroy a diseased cedar tree grove to protect a nearby apple orchard (1928), and to effectively shut down a gravel quarry in a developing suburb (1962)—all without compensation to the owners. In the *Pennsylvania Coal* case, however, the Court struck down a state law that barred underground coal mining if the excavation posed structural dangers to surface buildings, houses, or streets.

The increase in land-use and environmental restrictions in the 1970s and 1980s led to more conflicts between property owners and developers on one side and government regulators and environmentalists on the other. Property rights advocates won two rulings in 1987. In *First English Evangelical Lutheran Church v. County of Los Angeles* the Court held that an owner may be entitled to compensation for a "temporary taking" even if the government later changes a regulation to permit use of the property. And in *Nollan v. California Coastal Commission* the Court indicated that it would be more critical in deciding whether land-use regulations met the test of previous cases that they "substantially advance a legitimate state interest."

Property rights advocates won two more victories in the 1990s. In *Lucas v. South Carolina Coastal Council* (1992), the Court backed a beachfront property owner's claim to compensation because a coastal protection scheme destroyed all economically viable use of the site. And in *Dolan v. City of Tigard* (1994), the Court ruled that a landowner or developer can be required to set aside part of a property to offset the impact of new construction only if the government shows a "rough proportionality" between the conditions and the harm from the project.

Public Accommodations

The Supreme Court in the late 1800s overturned a congressional act prohibiting racial DISCRIMINATION in public accommodations and upheld legally mandated SEGREGATION on public carriers, such as railroads. In the 1950s the Court began to strike down state-mandated segregation in public accommodations. Then, in 1964, the Court upheld Congress's decision to include a broad prohibition against private discrimination in public accommodations in the Civil Rights Act of 1964.

Segregation Protected

In the 1870s there was little state-imposed segregation in transportation or public accommodations, but many proprietors, especially in the rural South, refused to serve blacks. In the Civil Rights Act of 1875, Congress sought to prohibit such exclusions by barring discrimination on the basis of race or color in public accommodations, including "inns, public conveyances on land or water, theaters, and other places of public amusement."

Five cases under the law—collectively called the *Civil Rights Cases*—reached the Supreme Court. By an 8–1 vote, the Court in 1883 declared the law unconstitutional, saying it went beyond Congress's power under the Thirteenth or Fourteenth Amendment. The decision left open the possibility that Congress might bar private discrimination on public carriers through its COMMERCE POWER, but Congress did not do so.

Instead, some states moved to require segregation on public transportation, encouraged by a pair of Supreme Court rulings on the issue. In 1878 the Court overturned a Louisiana law forbidding segregation of public carriers, saying it amounted to an unconstitutional burden on interstate commerce. Then, in 1890, the Court upheld a Mississippi law requiring segregated transportation by construing it to apply only to intrastate travel and not to travel between states.

Those rulings set the stage for the Court's decision in *PLESSY V. FERGUSON* (1896) to uphold a new Louisiana law requiring separate but equal railroad accommodations for the races. That holding protected segregation from direct legal attack for the next sixty years. But the Court in two cases, in 1914 and 1941, did rule that public carriers had infringed black travelers' rights by failing to provide them facilities or service equal to what was available to whites.

The Court took a more significant step toward overturning segregation in public interstate transportation in 1946. In *Morgan v. Virginia* the Court held that Virginia's law imposing segregation on interstate bus travel amounted to an unconstitutional burden on interstate commerce. The opinion cited conflicting state laws that either required or prohibited segregation in interstate bus travel. Two years later the Court upheld a Michigan law prohibiting segregation in public transportation, saying that it did not interfere with Congress's power to regulate interstate commerce.

Discrimination Outlawed

In 1954 the Supreme Court in *BROWN V. BOARD OF EDUCATION OF TOPEKA* renounced the separate but equal doctrine as it applied to public schools. Beginning with *Muir v. Louisville Park Theatrical Assn.* (1954), the Court summarily declared that state-imposed segregation in public accommodations and transportation was unconstitutional as well. Relying on *Brown,* the Court ordered an end to state-imposed segregation on public beaches, municipal golf courses, and vehicles of interstate transportation; in public parks, municipal auditoriums, and athletic contests; in seating in traffic court; and in prisons and jails.

In a pair of cases the Court in 1960 and 1961 also prohibited racial discrimination by privately owned businesses operated on public property. Those cases served as precedent for a series of cases decided in 1962—commonly known as the "Sit-In Cases"—that prevented state or local officials from using trespass laws to help enforce laws that required segregation in eating places.

Still, most private owners of hotels, stores, restaurants, theaters, and other public accommodations remained free to discriminate until the passage in 1964 of the most comprehensive civil rights act since 1875. Title II of the Civil Rights Act of 1964 prohibited discrimination on grounds of race, color, religion, or national origin in public accommodations if the discrimination was supported by state law or other official action, if lodgings or other service were provided to interstate travelers, or if a substantial portion of the goods sold or entertainment provided moved in interstate commerce.

The power of Congress to use the commerce clause as authority for barring private discrimination was uncertain. But the Court acted quickly to resolve the issue, upholding the act six months after it was passed.

In *Heart of Atlanta Motel v. United States* (1964) the Court unanimously rejected a claim that the act exceeded Congress's commerce power, pointing to "the overwhelming evidence of the disruptive effect that racial discrimination has on commercial intercourse." The Court said that it found the 1883 decision in the *Civil Rights Cases* "without precedential value" since Congress in 1875 had not limited prohibition of discrimination to those businesses that impinged on interstate commerce.

The Court had no difficulty in establishing the Atlanta motel's connection to interstate travel. In a companion case, it also upheld application of the act to a private business with a less direct connection to interstate commerce. In *Katzenbach v. McClung* the Court enforced the act against Ollie's Barbecue in Birmingham, Alabama, which served a primarily local clientele but obtained 46 percent of its food from interstate commerce. Five years later the Court similarly permitted enforcement of the act against a small recreational area near Little Rock, Arkansas, on the ground that the food it sold was composed of ingredients purchased in other states.

Public Information Office

The Supreme Court justices believe that their opinions and orders must speak for themselves. Thus, the public information office is the Court's outlet on matters other than the interpretation of its opinions and orders.

Created in 1935, the public information office is responsible for answering questions from the public, facilitating coverage of the Court by the news media, and distributing information about the Court and the justices. It is the only really "open" office of the Court.

The public information office releases the opinions and orders of the Court to the press as soon as they are announced in open court. It also releases special announcements about the Court or the justices. The Court's informal orders, its schedule of sessions and conferences, and changes in Court procedures are usually posted on a bulletin board in the public information office.

In 1982 the press room adjoining the public information office was modernized and expanded. It houses carrels for several major news organizations that cover the Court on a regular basis and has facilities for other journalists as well. In addition, the major television and radio networks have separate broadcast booths on the ground floor where reporters tape-record their news stories and then transmit them directly to their offices.

The public information office also maintains petitions, motions, briefs, responses, and jurisdictional statements on all current cases for the use of Court staff and the press. It supervises the assignment of Court press credentials and admission to the press section of the courtroom, and serves as liaison between the press and all other offices of the Court, including the chambers of the justices.

The public information office also serves as a source of news and information within the Court itself, circulating news items and publishing the regular employee newsletter, *The Docket Sheet*.

The current public information officer, Toni House, is the fourth person to hold the post. Her predecessors were Ned Potter, Banning E. Whittington, and Barrett McGurn. House has held the post since 1982.

Public Opinion and the Court

The Supreme Court was intended as an independent check on the political branches of the federal government. To that end, the framers of the Constitution insulated the Court from public opinion by providing for the justices to be appointed rather than elected and to be given lifetime tenure rather than fixed terms. Yet the Court is not expected to completely ignore the popular will or the legitimate roles of the other branches of government.

First published as a serial in an antislavery weekly, Harriet Beecher Stowe's novel, Uncle Tom's Cabin, *appeared as a book in 1852; some 300,000 copies were sold that year. The book and numerous stage adaptations helped to popularize the abolitionist cause.*   Source: *The New York Historical Society, New York City*

As a result, the Court at times seems to reflect public opinion and at other times to flout it. The Court mirrored prevailing attitudes, for example, when it upheld convictions under state and federal sedition laws in the 1920s, but went against public sentiment when it struck down several economic regulatory measures. Over time, however, the justices' views are inevitably influenced by changing trends and values in the nation at large.

The public's attitude toward the Court varies as well. Often, large segments of the public have strongly disapproved of certain decisions. But the public also tends to view the Court with a kind of reverence—trusting the Court to be above politics and relying on it to protect individual freedom and to prevent abuses by Congress, the president, or the states.

When the Court does come under public criticism, its detachment from the political process limits its ability to defend itself. Justices make few public appearances and rarely respond directly to public criticism. Sometimes, public disapproval of a decision by the Court results in reversal of the ruling by constitutional amendment or by congressional legislation. On rare occasions, public criticism even leads the Court to reconsider its own rulings. One example occurred when the Court reversed itself in the span of three years in the FLAG SALUTE CASES of 1940 and 1943. In many other instances, however, controversial decisions by the Court have eventually won approval or at least acceptance by the public.

Marshall and Taney Courts

The Supreme Court ran up against popular opinion in its first decade after it ruled that a state could be sued in federal court by an individual of another state. The decision in *Chisholm v. Georgia* (1793) aroused protest from the states; within five years it was overturned by the Eleventh Amendment. (See REVERSALS OF RULINGS BY CONSTITUTIONAL AMENDMENT.)

The episode provided a valuable lesson for the justices by impressing on them the risks of direct confrontation with a popular viewpoint that was widely shared and deeply felt. Respect for public opinion was evident in later decisions by the early Court, especially during the long tenure of Chief Justice John Marshall.

Marshall was a master at combining restraint and boldness. He nursed public opinion toward respect for the federal government, particularly for the federal judiciary. The Marshall Court laid down the great legal precedents for national supremacy without taking a doctrinaire stand against states' rights. By the time of Marshall's death in 1835, public opinion had grown more accustomed to the sense of nationhood and had come to respect the Court as a symbol of the principles that bound the nation together while preserving local autonomy.

Under Chief Justice Roger B. Taney the Court faced—and ultimately failed—a more treacherous test of its ability to satisfy public opinion: the slavery issue. Like Marshall, Taney attempted to build public respect for the Court, but slavery forced the justices to choose between the proslavery sentiment in the South and the growing antislavery feelings in the North.

Taney led the Court in giving greater leeway to the states on a variety of issues, partly in the hope of avoiding entanglement with the slavery issue. But abolitionists came to view the Court as an accomplice of slaveholders and slave states. Then, in 1857, the Court's ruling in the Dred Scott case *(SCOTT V. SANDFORD)* provoked a storm of abuse. By ruling that Congress could not bar slavery from new territories, Taney had hoped to settle the issue. Instead, the ruling aroused contempt and loathing in the North without turning the South from moving toward secession.

During the Civil War, the Supreme Court was reduced to near impotence. When Taney ordered a Maryland secessionist to be brought before him on a writ of HABEAS CORPUS, the order was defied. The northern press then denounced Taney for supporting traitors. By 1863, one year before his death, Taney wrote that he saw no hope that the Court would "ever again be restored to the authority and rank which the Constitution intended to confer upon it."

From Civil War to New Deal

From the end of the Civil War to the New Deal era under President Franklin D. Roosevelt, the Supreme Court faced two major issues: race relations and economic regulation. Its decisions upholding racial SEGREGATION and supporting business and propertied interests reflected in part the public sentiment of the late nineteenth century. By the turn of the century, however, the Court was falling out of step with public opinion on economic issues. In the late 1930s the Court reversed itself and began sustaining economic regulations much like those it had been striking down as recently as a few years earlier. (See CIVIL RIGHTS; PROPERTY RIGHTS.)

After the Civil War, northern members of Congress had been intent on creating greater racial equality in the South through constitutional amendment and legislation. As the ardor of Reconstruction abated, however, the Court narrowly construed the new amendments and weakened the civil rights laws with only scattered northern protests. When the Court upheld racial segregation in *PLESSY V. FERGUSON* (1896), the ruling went largely unnoticed.

The Court drew more controversy with its rulings on economic issues. It sided with business by narrowing federal ANTITRUST laws, upholding use of federal court injunctions against strikes, and overturning laws aimed at protecting workers. It sided with railroads by restricting state authority to regulate their rates and practices. In 1895 it struck down a federal INCOME TAX.

The effect of the decisions was to give the Court a reputation as a tool of special privilege. Organized labor, farmers, and progressives kept working for their economic agenda. The income tax ruling was overturned by the Sixteenth Amendment in 1913. The Court's antitrust rulings became an issue in the 1912 presidential campaign and led to the passage of a new, broader antitrust act in 1914. And labor eventually won enactment of federal legislation curtailing the use of injunctions against strikers.

Despite popular rebuffs, the Court in the 1920s and early 1930s continued to strike down economic regulatory measures. Its decisions in the CHILD LABOR cases prompted an unsuccessful drive for a constitutional amendment to overturn the rulings. More dramatically, its decisions striking down several key pieces of Franklin Roosevelt's New Deal program in 1935 and 1936 led the president, after reelection to a second term, to propose his notorious "Court-packing" plan in 1937.

Roosevelt badly misjudged public opinion toward the Court. Despite the president's personal popularity, Congress received a deluge of mail protesting his plan to enlarge the Court. In June, the Senate Judiciary Committee rejected the plan, calling it an attempt to make the Court "subservient to the pressures of public opinion of the hour." (See SIZE OF THE COURT.)

Nonetheless, the Court had already begun to change its stance, apparently in direct response to the pressure of public opinion. In March and April 1937 it voted 5–4 to uphold state minimum wage laws and the National Labor Relations Act. In May the Court upheld the federal unemployment compensation and Social Security acts.

Retirements from the Court gave Roosevelt the chance to name six new justices over the next four years. The appointments allowed him to create a solid majority on the Court to sustain his economic programs.

The Modern Era

Under Chief Justice Earl Warren, the Supreme Court entered an unprecedented era of liberal JUDICIAL ACTIVISM. In contrast to the probusiness activism of earlier eras, the Warren Court exercised its judicial powers in behalf of underprivileged and underrepresented elements of society. Blacks and other racial minorities were the immediate beneficiaries of its civil rights rulings, beginning with *BROWN V. BOARD OF EDUCATION OF TOPEKA* (1954). Underrepresented urban and suburban dwellers gained an equal voice in state legislatures from reapportionment cases beginning with *BAKER V. CARR* (1962). The Court moved to protect the constitutional rights of criminal defendants with decisions in the 1960s applying the Bill of Rights to the states. (See INCORPORATION DOCTRINE.)

Warren sought to minimize public criticism of these decisions. He wrote a deliberately understated opinion in *Brown* and lobbied the other justices to make the decision unanimous. *Baker v. Carr* put off detailed questions about the redistricting and reapportionment issues. The Court brought about a revolution in criminal procedure step by step rather than in one broad stroke.

Nonetheless, the Court came under sustained attack. Its SCHOOL DESEGREGATION decisions provoked massive resistance in the South and spawned billboards that read, "Impeach Earl Warren." The Court's rulings in the early 1960s that barred organized prayer in the public schools drew strong criticism from religious elements in the South and elsewhere. (See SCHOOL PRAYER.) Then, with its criminal procedure decisions, the Court became the target of fierce criticism that it was handcuffing the police and letting criminals go free.

As a result, the Supreme Court became a major issue in the 1968 presidential campaign. Richard Nixon campaigned on a "law and order" platform and promised to select justices reflecting his views. (See ELECTIONS AND THE COURT.) As president, Nixon appointed four justices, including Chief Justice Warren E. Burger. Nixon's appointees helped form a more conservative majority that halted further expansion of the Warren Court's rulings on the exclusionary rule and police interrogation.

In 1973 the Burger Court produced an activist decision of its own: the abortion rights ruling, *ROE V. WADE.* Over the next two decades, the decision became the focal point of an increasingly polarized debate. Efforts to overturn the ruling by constitutional amendment failed, but Congress and many state legislatures did pass laws limiting the use of public funds to pay for abortion or attempting to regulate abortion procedures. ABORTION became a major issue in several Supreme Court confirmation battles, including the Senate's rejection of Robert Bork in 1987 and narrow approval of Clarence Thomas in 1991. (See CONFIRMATION PROCESS.) When the Court reaffirmed *Roe v. Wade* in 1992, it justified the decision in part by saying that public respect for the Court might be lowered if it appeared to be reversing itself because of popular pressure.

Like many other controversial decisions, however, the abortion rights ruling has come to enjoy a measure of popular support. Public opinion polls have shown majority support for women's right to choose an abortion. Similarly, *Brown v. Board of Education of*

A message on a T-shirt communicates a point of view with speed and directness.   Source: R. Michael Jenkins

Topeka has become a universally honored landmark for equal rights, although the Court's rulings on other civil rights issues, such as BUSING and AFFIRMATIVE ACTION, remain controversial. Even some of the most controversial criminal procedure decisions of the Warren Court have won a measure of acceptance. The rights warnings that police are required to give suspects under *MIRANDA V. ARIZONA,* for example, are now accepted as routine, and the decision has been reaffirmed by both the Burger and Rehnquist courts.

The broad public approval of the Court's role was perhaps best dramatized by its 1974 decision in the Watergate tapes case. Just two years after President Nixon's landslide reelection, the Court unanimously ordered him to turn over tapes of his conversations with aides relating to the Watergate break-in and cover-up. Despite the strong political feelings in the country, there was no doubt that Nixon had to comply with the ruling, which led directly to his resignation from office. Contrary to Taney's pessimistic prediction a century earlier, the Court was exercising its full authority at a time of constitutional crisis—and receiving broad public support in doing so.

R

Ratings of Justices

When the president nominates someone to be a justice of the Supreme Court, the American Bar Association (ABA) evaluates the candidate's legal and intellectual qualifications for the job. These evaluations, which have been made since 1956, have often aroused controversy and have become an issue in the confirmation process. Sometimes the ABA has "rated" potential nominees even before someone was nominated.

The ABA is a national membership organization of attorneys. In 1946 it established a standing committee on the federal judiciary to give the organization a voice in the selection process by evaluating candidates for federal judgeships. The first Supreme Court nominee to be evaluated was William J. Brennan, Jr., in 1956.

Under current rules, the ABA committee may determine that a nominee is "well qualified," "qualified," or "not qualified." To be considered qualified or well qualified, the candidates "must be at the top of

Serving on the 1932 Court were four justices whom scholars have rated as "greats" and three considered "failures." Among the greats: Louis D. Brandeis (seated, left), Chief Justice Charles Evans Hughes (seated, center), Harlan Fiske Stone (standing, second from right), and Benjamin Cardozo (standing, right). Among the failures: Willis Van Devanter (seated, second from left), James C. McReynolds (seated, second from right), and Pierce Butler (standing, second from left). Source: Library of Congress

the legal profession, have outstanding legal ability and wide experience, and meet the highest judicial standards of integrity, professional competence, and judicial temperament."

The committee reserves its appellation of "well qualified" for those Supreme Court nominees "found to merit the committee's strongest affirmative endorsement."

Both the procedures and the rankings have changed since 1956. Presidents Dwight Eisenhower and Gerald Ford submitted lists of prospective nominees to the ABA panel to evaluate before settling on a nominee. President Richard Nixon also agreed to prescreening but withdrew his consent after the names of prospective candidates reached the press. The Nixon administration blamed the committee for the leaks.

Since Nixon's nominations of Lewis F. Powell, Jr., and William H. Rehnquist in 1971, the ABA standing committee has made its evaluations after the nomination has been made. Presidents Ronald Reagan and George Bush never agreed to prescreenings for Supreme Court nominees. President Jimmy Carter never had an opportunity to name a justice to the Court.

The ABA approved Powell as "one of the best lawyers available." Rehnquist was rated "highly qualified" by nine members of the committee, but three said that they were "not opposed" to the appointment, a rating category that is no longer used.

Generally, the ABA committee is unanimous in rating Supreme Court nominees as well qualified. Anthony M. Kennedy and David H. Souter, for example, both received unanimous endorsements from the committee.

Split votes on the nominations of Robert H. Bork and Clarence Thomas led to charges that the ABA panel is biased. In 1987 ten members of the panel found Bork highly qualified, four found him unqualified, and one voted not opposed. In 1991 the ABA panel rated Thomas qualified, with two members finding him unqualified. In both cases the nominees' supporters charged that the unfavorable ratings gave senators ammunition to oppose the nominations. The Senate rejected Bork's nomination, and it narrowly confirmed Thomas, 52–48.

Greats and Failures

In 1970 sixty-five law school deans and other judicial experts evaluated the Court's first 100 justices. Based on their ratings, the "greats" were Chief Justice John Marshall, Joseph Story, Chief Justice Roger B. Taney, the first John Marshall Harlan, Oliver Wendell Holmes, Jr., Chief Justice Charles Evans Hughes, Louis D. Brandeis, Harlan Fiske Stone, Benjamin N. Cardozo, Hugo L. Black, Felix Frankfurter, and Chief Justice Earl Warren.

Rated as "failures" were Willis Van Devanter, James C. McReynolds, Pierce Butler, James F. Byrnes, Harold H. Burton, Chief Justice Fred M. Vinson, Sherman Minton, and Charles E. Whittaker.

Reagan, Ronald

In winning election as president in 1980 and re-election in 1984, Ronald Reagan (1911–) championed a conservative platform. That platform promised to undo many of the Supreme Court's most controversial rulings of the 1960s and 1970s. (See ELECTIONS AND THE COURT.) Reagan's four appointments to the Court did shift it to the right but failed to bring about the outright reversal of the decisions that he had most strongly criticized.

Reagan had opposed the Warren Court's rulings on criminal procedure and school prayer in the 1960s when he was a national conservative spokesperson and governor of California. In the 1970s he had criticized the abortion rights ruling, *Roe v. Wade* (1973), and the Court's affirmative action decisions.

President Reagan made his first appointment to the Court in 1981, just seven months after taking office. Fulfilling a campaign pledge, he nominated Sandra Day O'Connor to be the Court's first woman justice; the Senate unanimously confirmed her appointment.

When Chief Justice Warren E. Burger retired in 1986, Reagan nominated the Court's most conservative member, William H. Rehnquist, to succeed him. He chose a conservative federal appeals court judge,

Although President Ronald Reagan's four conservative appointees to the Supreme Court shifted it philosophically to the right, the president failed in his attempt to reverse the liberal decisions against which he had campaigned.   Source: AP/Wide World

sustain initiatives to cut back government regulation of business.

In the October 1983 Court term, the administration won favorable rulings on affirmative action, the exclusionary rule, and deregulation. But in its next two terms the Court—in some cases with O'Connor's help—rejected the administration's position on school prayer, aid to parochial schools, and affirmative action. The addition of Scalia and Kennedy to the Court contributed to some further administration successes in the October 1988 term. These included decisions that limited affirmative action and, for the first time, upheld a state law imposing significant restrictions on abortion procedures.

Four years after Reagan left office, however, two of his appointees—O'Connor and Kennedy—disappointed conservatives by joining in a decision that retained *Roe v. Wade* in a modified form (*Planned Parenthood v. Casey* [1992]). In the same term the two joined with Justice David H. Souter, an appointee of President George Bush, to reinforce the school prayer ruling and to reject some efforts to restrict federal habeas corpus.

Antonin Scalia, to fill Rehnquist's seat. Rehnquist was confirmed 65–33; Scalia was approved unanimously.

In 1987 Reagan picked a prominent conservative, Robert Bork, to succeed Justice Lewis F. Powell, Jr. The nomination aroused strong opposition, and a major confirmation battle took place. After contentious hearings and vigorous lobbying on both sides, the fight ended with Bork's rejection by the Senate, 42–58. (See CONFIRMATION PROCESS.) Reagan went on to choose another conservative, federal appeals court judge Anthony M. Kennedy, for the seat; the Senate confirmed him unanimously.

Reagan's two solicitors general—Rex E. Lee and Charles Fried—tried to persuade the Court to carry out the administration's legal agenda. They urged the Court to overturn *Roe v. Wade*, permit prayer in schools, allow aid to parochial schools, narrow the use of affirmative action, ease restrictions on police, and

Reapportionment and Redistricting

Legislative bodies in the United States—the House of Representatives, state legislatures, and most city or county councils—are composed of members who are elected from designated districts. This system of choosing members requires two processes: *apportionment*, to allocate the seats; and *districting*, to draw the specific lines for each district.

In the 1960s the Supreme Court brought about a revolution in state government by imposing a constitutional requirement that individual voters have substantially equal representation in legislative bodies: one person, one vote. Equal representation was to be achieved through reapportionment and redistricting. The Court's rulings—beginning with a Tennessee case, *BAKER V. CARR* (1962)—came in response to the nearly universal failure of rural-dominated state legislatures to reapportion themselves to take account of the shift in population from rural areas to cities and suburbs. Many legislatures also left old congressional district lines in place, which once again gave rural areas an advantage.

Under the Constitution, House seats are apportioned among the states by population at least every ten years (Article I, Section 2), but districting is left to the states. Most state constitutions specified equal population districts for legislative seats, and Congress in 1872 required that House districts be of approximately equal population. In 1901 and 1991, Congress specified that House districts also be "contiguous and compact." In 1929, however, a reapportionment law dropped all those requirements. In 1932 the Supreme Court upheld a Mississippi redistricting law that failed to provide districts of equal population.

The "Political Thicket"

The issue returned to the Court in 1946 in a case from Illinois. The suit, *Colegrove v. Green*, claimed that the population inequality of the state's congressional districts denied voters in the more populous, urban districts EQUAL PROTECTION of the law as guaranteed by the Fourteenth Amendment. The Court dismissed the case. It could have done so on the basis of the 1932 ruling, but instead Justice Felix Frankfurter crafted an opinion—joined by only two other justices—that blocked reapportionment and redistricting cases in federal courts for the next sixteen years.

Frankfurter said that Congress had full authority under the Constitution to override state laws and procedures for electing members of Congress (Article I, Section 4). On that basis, he said that the remedy for the unequal districting lay with either the state legislature or Congress, but not the courts. "Courts ought not to enter this political thicket," he said.

The vote in the case was 4 to 3. Justice Robert H. Jackson did not take part in the decision, and Chief Justice Harlan Fiske Stone died two months before the decision was announced. The critical fourth vote to dismiss the suit came from Justice Wiley B. Rutledge, who dissociated himself from Frankfurter's broad position but agreed with the dismissal of this case to avoid collision with the political departments of the government. The three dissenting justices, led by Justice Hugo L. Black, argued that districting issues

were well within the power of federal courts to redress constitutional grievances caused by state action.

Federal and state courts repeatedly relied on *Colegrove* over the next sixteen years to throw out reapportionment and redistricting cases. In *Gomillion v. Lightfoot* (1960) the Supreme Court created a narrow exception to the rule by holding that a claim of racial discrimination in drawing city boundaries could be heard in federal court as a violation of the Fifteenth Amendment. In writing the Court's opinion Frankfurter was careful to distinguish *Colegrove* and to reaffirm the general bar against reapportionment or redistricting suits.

One Person, One Vote

The Court's 6–2 decision in *Baker v. Carr* (1962) rejected Frankfurter's view that reapportionment and redistricting was a POLITICAL QUESTION that federal courts could not resolve. But the ruling left other issues to be decided later. Within the next two years the Court formulated a standard that came to be known as "one man, one vote" or "one person, one vote."

The phrase appeared first in *Gray v. Sanders* (1963). In that decision the Court struck down an unusual county-unit system used in Georgia in statewide primary elections. The county-unit system gave an advantage to the numerous rural counties at the expense of urban areas. In his opinion for the Court, Justice William O. Douglas declared that the equal protection clause required that all voters in a statewide election must have an equal vote. Political equality, Douglas concluded, "can mean only thing—one person, one vote." Justice John Marshall Harlan was the lone dissenter.

The next year the Court applied the same principle to congressional districts in another case from Georgia, *Wesberry v. Sanders* (1964). The 6–3 decision did not rely on the equal protection clause; rather, it was based on the constitutional provision that representatives be chosen "by the People of the several States" (Article I). Writing for the Court, Justice Black said that the phrase "construed in its historical context . . . means that as nearly as is practicable, one man's vote in a congressional election is to be worth as much as another's." Harlan led three dissenters in criticizing

The Court's decision in Gray v. Sanders *(1963) introduced the concept that political equality must be based on "one person, one vote." Reprinted by permission of United Feature Syndicate, Inc.*

the majority's position as "manufactured out of whole cloth."

Later in 1964 the Court also required equal-population districts for both houses of bicameral state legislatures. This time the requirement was based on the equal protection clause. "Legislators represent people, not trees or acres," Chief Justice Earl Warren declared in *Reynolds v. Sims*. He rejected the argument that states could follow the model of the U.S. Senate and apportion seats in one legislative chamber on some basis other than population. Harlan, dissenting alone, called the series of decisions "profoundly ill advised and constitutionally impermissible."

There was strong opposition to the rulings from rural organizations and state legislators who faced a loss of power as a result. But the states failed in efforts to get Congress to approve legislation or a constitutional amendment to negate the effects of the deci-

sion. Opponents also tried to force Congress to call a constitutional convention on the issue and gathered support from thirty-three states—one short of the number needed. After that vocal opposition faded, in part because so many states had already taken steps to comply with the decisions.

Applying the Test

In applying the "one person, one vote" standard, the Court has required strict mathematical equality for congressional districts. It has allowed some leeway in state legislative districts. In 1968 the Court extended the equal population rule to local legislative bodies, though it created a narrow exception in 1973. The exception permitted weighted voting in special-purpose electoral districts, such as those devised to regulate water supplies in the West.

The Court laid down the rule for congressional districting in *Kirkpatrick v. Preisler* (1969). That decision struck down a plan that allowed a variance of 3.1 percent from the average district population. Writing for the Court, Justice William J. Brennan, Jr., said that even minor variations would not be permitted unless the state could show that they were unavoidable.

The Court reaffirmed the *Kirkpatrick* holding in striking down a Texas plan with a 5 percent variation in 1973 and a New Jersey plan with less than a 1 percent variation in 1983. But three justices who joined the Court after *Kirkpatrick*—Chief Justice Warren E. Burger and justices Lewis F. Powell, Jr., and William H. Rehnquist—questioned the rule of strict mathematical equality in the Texas case. Along with Justice Byron R. White, they dissented in the New Jersey case.

Regarding state legislative apportionment, the Court's pivotal ruling came in *Mahan v. Howell* (1973). In that case the Court voted 5–3 to uphold a Virginia reapportionment allowing a deviation of up to 16.4 percent from equal population districts for seats in the state house. Writing for the Court, Justice Rehnquist said that the variations were justified by "the rational state policy of respecting the boundaries of political subdivisions." Later that year the Court upheld state legislative redistricting plans that permitted populations to differ by 7.8 percent and 9.9 percent. In 1983 it voted 5–4 to uphold a Wyoming law that guaranteed each county at least one vote in the state's lower house—even though the variation among the counties was enormous.

Other Issues

The Court has also been drawn into disputes over redistricting plans challenged because of the use of racial or political factors in drawing district lines. Political gerrymandering—the drawing of district lines so as to give an advantage to a particular party—has occurred throughout the nation's history. In 1986 the Court opened the door slightly to federal court review of the practice. The case, *Davis v. Bandemer,* involved a challenge by Indiana Democrats to a state legislative reapportionment drawn by the state's Republican-controlled legislature. Echoing *Baker v. Carr,* the Court voted 6–3 to permit such challenges in federal courts. "The issue is one of representation," Justice White wrote, "and we decline to hold that such claims are never justiciable." The three dissenting justices, led by Justice Sandra Day O'Connor, warned that the ruling would invite the losing party in every reapportionment "to fight the battle anew in federal court."

By a 7–2 majority, however, the Court went on to uphold the challenged apportionment plan. White said that the Indiana Democrats needed to show both a discriminatory intent and a discriminatory effect over more than one election. The test, White said, was whether the evidence showed "continued frustration of the will of a majority of the voters or effective denial to a minority of voters of a fair chance to influence the political process."

In 1993 the Court also held that voters could challenge so-called racial gerrymandering. The ruling threatened to undo redistricting plans in a number of states that had contributed to the election of a record number of blacks and Hispanics to Congress in 1992.

The case, *Shaw v. Reno,* involved a North Carolina congressional redistricting plan drawn to create two districts with majority black populations. One of the districts, the 12th, wound around the state in a snake-like fashion for more than 160 miles in order to pick up black neighborhoods in four metropolitan areas.

In an earlier decision, *United Jewish Organizations of Williamsburgh v. Carey* (1974), the Court had upheld some use of racial criteria in state legislative districting and apportionment. The 7–1 ruling rejected a challenge by Jewish groups to a New York plan that concentrated nonwhite majorities in two Brooklyn districts while dispersing the Hasidic Jewish community.

In the new case, however, the Court ruled, 5–4, that white voters can use the equal protection clause to challenge a district that is "highly irregular" in shape and drawn to "segregate voters by race." Writing for the Court, Justice O'Connor said the practice "bears an uncomfortable resemblance to political apartheid" and risks perpetuating "the very patterns of racial bloc voting that majority-minority districting is sometimes said to counteract." The dissenting justices complained that the majority had failed to identify the harm that the white voters had suffered. Justice White noted that whites constituted about 79 percent of the voting age population in the state but still had a majority in ten (or 83 percent) of the twelve congressional districts. "Though they might be dissatisfied at the prospect of casting a vote for a losing candidate," White said, "surely they cannot complain of discriminatory treatment."

Reed, Stanley F.

Historians report that when the Supreme Court took its first vote in conference in 1954 on whether to overturn school segregation, Justice Stanley Forman Reed (1884–1980) cast the lone vote to uphold segregation. Reed, a southerner, apparently thought that the progress made in improving race relations could be impeded or halted if the Court outlawed separate schools for blacks and whites. However, Chief Justice Earl Warren lobbied hard with Reed, arguing that the Court must speak with a unanimous voice on such a critical issue. Reed finally agreed, and the Court issued a unanimous opinion in the landmark case of *Brown v. Board of Education of Topeka.* In *Brown* the Court declared that separate schools for blacks and whites were inherently unequal and violated the equal protection clause of the Fourteenth Amendment. The Court's unanimous opinion in *Brown* set the stage for the civil rights revolution of the late 1950s and 1960s.

Source: Library of Congress

Reed was born in Minerva, Kentucky, and received undergraduate degrees from Kentucky Wesleyan and Yale universities. He then studied law at the University of Virginia and Columbia University without obtaining a degree. After studying civil and international law at the Sorbonne in Paris, Reed began practicing law in Maysville, Kentucky. While continuing his law practice, Reed also served four years in the Kentucky general assembly.

In 1929 Republican president Herbert Hoover appointed Reed general counsel for the Federal Farm Board. Two years later Reed was appointed general counsel for the Reconstruction Finance Corporation, a Depression-era agency that loaned money to banks, businesses, and farmers. Reed's next appointment, as special assistant to the attorney general, came in 1935 in the Democratic administration of Franklin D. Roosevelt. Later that year, Roosevelt named Reed solicitor general, a post he held until Roosevelt nominated him to the Supreme Court in 1938.

Reed served on the Court for nineteen years before retiring in 1957. A firm believer in big govern-

ment, he agreed with Chief Justice Fred M. Vinson's dissent in the *Steel Seizure Cases*. After leaving the Court, Reed briefly served as chair of the U.S. Civil Rights Commission. He also argued a total of sixty cases before the Court of Claims and the Court of Appeals in the District of Columbia. Reed died in 1980 at age ninety-five.

Rehnquist, William H.

When William Hubbs Rehnquist (1924–   ) joined the Supreme Court in 1971, the Court was still quite liberal. By the time he was elevated to chief justice in 1986, however, the Court had become increasingly conservative.

Rehnquist was born in Milwaukee. After serving in the air force during World War II, Rehnquist received undergraduate and graduate degrees from Stanford University. He then received a second master's degree from Harvard University before returning to Stanford to enroll in law school. Rehnquist graduated first in his law school class in 1952. Immediately after graduation Rehnquist became a law clerk to Supreme Court justice Robert H. Jackson. After clerking for a year Rehnquist moved to Phoenix, Arizona, to practice law. Republican party politics also attracted him, and he was heavily involved in the 1964 presidential campaign of Republican candidate Barry Goldwater.

In 1969 Rehnquist joined the Nixon administration as assistant U.S. attorney general in the Office of Legal Counsel. In that post Rehnquist reviewed all constitutional law issues affecting the executive branch. Two years later Nixon nominated him to the Supreme Court.

The nomination was controversial, especially with civil rights groups. During Rehnquist's confirmation hearing, a memorandum favoring separate but equal schools for blacks and whites came to light. Rehnquist, who had written the memo while clerking for Justice Jackson, maintained that the views expressed in it were Jackson's and not his own. The Senate confirmed Rehnquist by a 68–26 vote.

After joining the Court, Rehnquist quickly developed a reputation for being its most conservative member. He dissented from Court decisions overturning all death penalty laws in the United States, upholding a woman's right to abortion, and forcing racially segregated private schools to admit black students. He also dissented when the Court struck down a state law allowing death sentences in rape cases, upheld systemwide busing orders to desegregate schools in two Ohio cities, ruled that citizens and reporters have a First Amendment right to attend criminal trials, and overturned a Louisiana law requiring schools that taught evolution to teach "creation science" as well.

In 1986 President Ronald Reagan elevated Rehnquist to chief justice. The nomination was roundly attacked, especially by civil rights groups, who claimed that Rehnquist had harassed black voters in Phoenix during the 1950s and early 1960s. Nonetheless, the Senate confirmed Rehnquist 65–33.

Under Rehnquist's direction the Court moved even further to the right than it had under Chief Justice Burger. By 1989 the Court was solidly conservative. In that year it overturned a minority set-aside program in Virginia and made it harder for workers to prove that employers had engaged in racial discrimination. It also allowed states to impose the death penalty on people who were sixteen or seventeen when they committed a capital crime and upheld a Missouri law barring the use of public facilities to perform abortions.

Source: Collection of the Supreme Court of the United States

Religion, Freedom of

Freedom of religion is basic to the American concept of liberty. The First Amendment protects religious freedom with two distinct clauses: "Congress shall make no law respecting an establishment of religion, or prohibiting the free exercise thereof." The Supreme Court applied the free exercise clause to the states in 1940 and the establishment clause in 1947.

Although these commands appear to be absolute, the Court has found them difficult to apply in cases where general laws affect religious practices or where government actions benefit or accommodate religious groups or institutions.

Under the free exercise clause, the Court said the government could not infringe on religious liberty except to protect a "compelling state interest." In 1990, however, the Court dropped that test and held that the free exercise clause does not impose any barrier to the enforcement of "a valid and neutral law of general applicability."

Under the establishment clause the Court has adopted a three-part test for government actions that are challenged as violating the principle of separation of church and state. The actions must be secular in both purpose and effect, and they must not result in excessive government entanglement with religion. Several justices have criticized the test, but the Court rejected a plea by the Bush administration in a 1992 SCHOOL PRAYER case to modify it.

Free Exercise Clause

The Supreme Court's two earliest cases construing the free exercise clause came in the late nineteenth century. They upheld federal laws aimed at the belief in polygamy held at that time by the Mormons (the Church of Jesus Christ of Latter-Day Saints). The laws barred plural marriages in Utah Territory and denied the vote in the Idaho Territory to bigamists, polygamists, or anyone who advocated multiple marriages. In both cases—*Reynolds v. United States* (1879) and *Davis v. Beason* (1890)—the Court distinguished between protected religious beliefs and conduct that could be subject to secular regulation. "However free the exercise of religion may be," the Court said in the Idaho case, "it must be subordinate to the criminal laws of the country."

In 1905 the Court once again elevated state law over religious practices. In *Jacobson v. Massachusetts* the Court rejected a challenge to a compulsory vaccination law brought by Seventh-Day Adventists who were opposed to it on religious grounds. Since the Court had not yet applied the First Amendment to the states, the case was framed as a challenge under the due process clause of the Fourteenth Amendment. But the Court found the law a valid exercise of the state's police power.

Two decades later the Court took a broader view of due process protections. In *Pierce v. Society of Sisters* (1925) it overturned an Oregon law requiring all school-age children to attend public schools. The ruling was based on parents' right to control the upbringing of their children, but it has since been cited as a free exercise ruling.

As the Court began enforcing the provisions of the First Amendment against the states in the 1930s, freedom of religion issues were sometimes intertwined with free speech and free press claims. For example, in 1938 the Court overturned a local ordinance banning distribution of handbills that had been enforced against a Jehovah's Witness, on the grounds that it was an unconstitutional prior restraint on the press.

In 1940 the Court expressly extended the free exercise clause to the states and also made clear that it protected some conduct as well as religious beliefs. In *Cantwell v. Connecticut* the Court struck down a state law that forbade solicitation for religious causes without a license certifying the religion as bona fide. The Court held that the law placed "a forbidden burden upon the exercise of [religious] liberty," but added that legitimate regulation of religiously based conduct would be upheld.

On that basis, the Court in 1942 sustained the enforcement of a requirement for a peddler's license fee against Jehovah's Witnesses. The five-justice majority reasoned that the door-to-door sale of religious literature by the Jehovah's Witnesses was more commercial than religious. Just one year later, though, the Court reversed itself. In *Murdock v. Pennsylvania* (1943) newly appointed justice Wiley Rutledge joined the four dissenters in the earlier case to hold that a similar license fee amounted to a tax on the free exercise of religion.

Also in 1943 the Court reversed itself on another freedom of religion dispute. In the second of the FLAG SALUTE CASES, the Court held that states cannot require schoolchildren to salute the flag as part of daily classroom exercises—overturning its 1940 decision on the issue. With *Murdock* the flag salute ruling moved the Court away from the "secular regulation" rule that had dominated its free exercise doctrine.

In the 1960s the Court tried to craft a more general rule for determining when a state could compel obedience to a secular law that conflicted with religious beliefs.

In *Braunfeld v. Brown* (1961) the Court refused to grant an exemption from a state Sunday-closing law to a store owner who was an Orthodox Jew. The store owner said that he closed his store in observance of the Sabbath on Saturday and needed to stay open on Sunday to make up the lost revenue. The Court found no violation of free exercise, because the closing law made the plaintiff's religious practice only more expensive, not illegal. There was no majority opinion, but a plurality of four justices said that a general law that advanced the state's secular goals but resulted in an "indirect burden on religious observance" was valid "unless the State may accomplish its purpose by means which do not impose such a burden."

Two years later the Court adopted a stricter test,

The constitutional ban on the establishment of an official state religion has encouraged diversity in religious practices and tolerance of others' beliefs. Here are symbols of some of the many religions in America: Bahaism, Buddhism, Christianity, Hinduism (top); Islam, Jainism, Judaism, Sikhism (bottom). Source: Imagefinders

declaring that only a compelling state interest could justify limitations on religious liberty. The 7–2 decision in *Sherbert v. Verner* (1963) reinstated unemployment compensation benefits to a Seventh-Day Adventist who had been fired from her job because she refused to work on Saturday, her Sabbath. The Court did not expressly overrule *Braunfeld*, but the dissenting justices said the ruling had that effect.

During the 1960s the Court broadened the protection of religious beliefs in another context: conscientious objection to military service. By broadly construing a congressional statute, the Court in 1965 said that conscientious objector status could be claimed by someone who did not believe in a Supreme Being in the orthodox sense. Five years later the Court construed the exemption to include persons who objected to all war on moral or ethical grounds, rather than for strictly religious reasons. In 1971, however, the Court found no constitutional requirement to grant conscientious objector status to persons who opposed a particular war as unjust.

The Court's general expansion of religious liberty continued in *Wisconsin v. Yoder* (1972). That decision blocked the enforcement of compulsory school attendance laws for Amish children. Amish parents claimed that high school education taught values contrary to Amish religious beliefs. Chief Justice Warren E. Burger applied the *Sherbert* rule and found no compelling interest for enforcing the law against the Amish.

After citing the *Sherbert* decision as the controlling case on free exercise issues during the 1970s and 1980s, the Court unexpectedly discarded it in favor of a less stringent standard. The ruling in *Employment Division, Department of Human Resources of Oregon v. Smith* (1990) held that states could bar the sacramental use of peyote without infringing on the free exercise of religion.

In his opinion for the Court, Justice Antonin Scalia said that the free exercise clause does not exempt an individual from obeying "a valid and neutral law of general applicability" that happens to infringe on religious practices. The vote in the case was 6 to 3. Justice Sandra Day O'Connor, in a separate concurrence, and the three dissenters all criticized the majority's decision to drop the "compelling state interest" test of previous cases.

Establishment Clause

The establishment clause has been interpreted to mean not only that Congress cannot establish a national church but also that it cannot act to give any direct support to religious groups or institutions. Historians and legal scholars disagree about the meaning that the framers intended for the provision. For example, did the framers intend to prohibit any governmental acknowledgment of religion, such as a Thanksgiving Day proclamation?

The Supreme Court has never taken such an absolutist position on the issue. In its first decision on the clause in 1899, it upheld a federal construction grant to a Roman Catholic hospital, reasoning that the aid benefited the church only indirectly. When it applied the establishment clause to the states in 1947, the Court said the First Amendment requires the government to be "a neutral" but "not [an] adversary" toward religion. The decision in *Everson v. Board of Education* upheld a policy of reimbursing parents for the cost of transporting their children to parochial schools. (See PAROCHIAL SCHOOLS, AID TO.)

Since that time the Court has sustained tax exemptions for churches, Sunday-closing laws, and legislative chaplaincies. On the other hand, the Court has cited the establishment clause in barring government-sponsored school prayer and limiting government assistance to parochial schools. The Court in the 1980s

This fanciful 1857 drawing depicts Mormon leader Brigham Young, seated at right, with his wives and some children. Mormons who practiced polygamy found themselves in conflict with state laws that prohibited multiple marriages. The Court in Reynolds v. United States *(1879) said religious practices may not take precedence over a state's criminal laws.*
Source: Library of Congress

also prohibited government-sponsored religious holiday displays in public buildings, though it found no establishment clause violation in displays that mixed religious and secular elements.

In *Walz v. Tax Commission* (1970) the Court, by a vote of 8 to 1, sustained the universal practice of exempting churches from paying property or income taxes. Writing for the Court, Chief Justice Burger noted that churches were one of several types of nonprofit institution that enjoy tax exemptions. On that basis, he concluded that the New York law being challenged was secular in purpose and effect—the two tests required under existing establishment clause doctrine. Burger then added a third test: whether the exemption resulted in excessive involvement with religion. He said that taxation of churches posed a risk of entanglement, while the tax exemption created "only a minimal and remote involvement between church and state."

The Court sustained Sunday-closing laws in four companion cases decided in 1961. The laws were challenged as violating both the establishment and free exercise clauses. On the establishment clause issue, the Court reasoned that despite the laws' religious origins, they served a valid secular purpose by providing a uniform day of rest. In 1985, however, the Court found an establishment clause violation in a Connecticut law that gave all employees the right to refuse with impunity to work on their Sabbath. By giving workers that right, the state gave religious concerns priority over all others in setting work schedules and thereby advanced religion, the Court said.

In 1983 the Court rejected, by a vote of 6 to 3, an establishment clause challenge to tax-supported legislative chaplaincies. In *Marsh v. Chambers* Chief Justice Burger justified the practice on historical grounds rather than applying the three-part test of purpose, effect, and entanglement.

The next year the Court used both historical practice and the traditional doctrine of the establishment clause to sanction an official display of the nativity scene as part of a city's Christmas exhibit in a main shopping district. Writing for the five-justice majority in *Lynch v. Donnelly* (1984), Chief Justice Burger stated that the display had a secular purpose, since it included such elements as a Santa Claus and reindeer as well as a crèche. In a dissent, Justice William J. Brennan, Jr., said the ruling left open the question of a public display on public property of a crèche alone, without secular elements.

That issue reached the Court just a few years later. The case, *County of Allegheny v. American Civil Liberties Union* (1989), challenged the display of a crèche in the center of a county courthouse and a separate holiday display, outside a government building, that included both a menorah and a Christmas tree. By different majorities, the Court barred the display of the crèche alone (5–4) but permitted the other (6–3). Writing for the majority, Justice Harry A. Blackmun said the prominent display of the crèche by itself "sends an unmistakable message that [the county] supports and promotes . . . the crèche's message." But the menorah's message, Blackmun said, "is not exclusively religious."

Remand

A remand is an action by an appeals court to send a case back to the court from which it came for further proceedings. A remand is usually unnecessary when an appellate court affirms the lower court's judgment. When the Supreme Court reverses or vacates a lower court judgment, it typically remands the case for proceedings "consistent with" or "not inconsistent with" the Court's opinion. In some cases, the lower court's action on remand may be clear. In other cases, however, significant issues may remain for the lower court to decide.

Removal of Cases

In creating the federal judiciary, Congress in 1789 provided a limited right to persons initially charged in state courts to "remove," or transfer, the case to a federal court if the federal court also had JURISDICTION over the case. With the growth of federal jurisdiction, Congress has expanded this right of removal. The right has been used only rarely, however, and the Supreme Court has defined it rather restrictively.

The Judiciary Act of 1789 provided for removal of cases in civil suits involving foreigners residing in the United States, diversity of residence or land grant sources, or amounts more than $500. Statutes enacted in 1815 and 1833 expanded the right to include cases involving federal customs officials and revenue officials.

In the Civil War Congress extended the removal right to all persons sued in state courts for actions under federal authority during the war. The Civil Rights Act of 1866 provided for a broad right of removal of cases to safeguard federal constitutional rights.

Under current law, a case may be removed to federal court by (1) defendants in any civil case that could have been initiated in federal court; (2) federal officials sued or prosecuted in state court for official acts; or (3) defendants in any case, civil or criminal, who can show that they are denied, or are unable to enforce, their constitutional civil rights in a state court.

The removal provision involving civil rights has been strictly construed by the Supreme Court, as is shown by two rulings in 1966. In one case, *Georgia v. Rachel*, the Court upheld the removal of state trespassing charges against civil rights demonstrators who had been arrested for trying to exercise their right of equal access to public accommodations under the Civil Rights Act of 1964. In the other, *City of Greenwood, Miss. v. Peacock*, the Court refused to allow removal of a case in which civil rights demonstrators were charged with obstructing the streets and disturbing the peace. The Court said that the difference between the two cases was that the Georgia demonstrators were clearly exercising a right guaranteed by federal law, but that no federal law gave the Mississippi demonstrators the right to obstruct the streets or disturb the peace.

Reporter of Decisions

The reporter of decisions is responsible for editing the opinions of the Supreme Court. The reporter and a staff of nine people check all citations after the justices have delivered their opinions, correct typographical and other errors, and add the headnotes, the voting lineup of the justices, and the names of counsel that appear in the published version of the opinions.

Reporters of Decisions	
Alexander J. Dallas	1790-1800
William Cranch	1801-1815
Henry Wheaton	1816-1827
Richard Peters, Jr.	1828-1843
Benjamin C. Howard	1843-1861
Jeremiah S. Black	1861-1862
John W. Wallace	1863-1875
William T. Otto	1875-1883
J. C. Bancroft Davis	1883-1902
Charles Henry Butler	1902-1916
Ernest Knaebel	1916-1946
Walter Wyatt	1946-1963
Henry Putzel, Jr.	1964-1979
Henry C. Lind	1979-1987
Frank D. Wagner	1987-

The reporter also supervises the printing of the opinions and their publication in the official *United States Reports*.

The Court's orders and decisions are first circulated as "Preliminary Prints." Users of these prints are asked to "notify the reporter of decisions . . . of any typographical or other formal errors, in order that corrections may be made before the bound volume goes to press." The orders and decisions are printed by the U.S. Government Printing Office and sold by the superintendent of documents.

The post of reporter of decisions began informally. The first reporter, Alexander J. Dallas, who served from 1790 to 1800, was self-appointed. He had published a volume of Pennsylvania court decisions before the Supreme Court moved to Philadelphia in 1791 and thereafter simply added the Court's decisions to those of the state court. He published four volumes of decisions covering the Supreme Court's first decade. Dallas was also a journalist, editor, patron of the arts, and secretary of the treasury (1814–1816). Most accounts of the early Supreme Court indicate

that Dallas, a lawyer, undertook the first reports as a labor of love and a public service.

Dallas was succeeded unofficially in 1801 by William Cranch, who continued to sit as a judge and later chief justice of the circuit court in Washington, D.C., where the court had moved in 1801. Cranch's reports were noted for their accuracy and clarity.

In his preface to the first volume, Cranch wrote of his belief that a permanent record of Court decisions would keep the justices from making arbitrary decisions. "Every case decided is a check upon the judge," Cranch wrote. "He cannot decide a similar case differently, without strong reasons, which, for his own justification, he will wish to make public." Indeed, during Cranch's service, the justices began supplementing their oral opinions with written texts in important cases.

Cranch's successor, Henry Wheaton, was the first reporter formally appointed by the Court. In 1816 Congress provided for publication of Court decisions and, a year later, set the reporter's salary at $1,000 a year. Wheaton, like other early reporters, still felt the need to supplement his income. An attorney, he argued several cases before the Court and then reported them. Over the years, the reporter's salary gradually increased. In 1994 the reporter was paid a salary of $115,700.

Justices have not always been pleased with the work of the reporters. In 1843 Richard Peters was fired by four of the justices acting in the absence of the chief justice and their other colleagues. Peters had fallen out of favor with several justices as a result of differences over inclusion of their opinions in the reports.

Peters's successor, Benjamin C. Howard, was criticized in 1855 by Justice Peter V. Daniel, who complained that his name had not been inserted at the beginning of his dissenting opinion and said that he was uncertain whether he would allow his dissents to be published in the reports. Justices Noah H. Swayne and Nathan Clifford complained that reporter John W. Wallace, who served from 1867 to 1875, failed to publish their opinions or else butchered them.

Wallace was the last reporter whose name appeared on the cover of the Court's published reports. The first ninety-six volumes of the reports were titled

Dall. 1–4, Cranch 1–15, Wheat. 1–12, Pet. 1–16, How. 1–24, Black 1–2, and Wall. 1–23. After 1874 the name of the reporter of decisions appeared only on the title page of the reports.

Resignation

Seventeen justices have resigned from the Supreme Court for reasons other than RETIREMENT.

Some justices left the Court to run for elective office or to take other work. The first chief justice, John Jay, resigned in 1795 to become governor of New York. Five years later, he declined reappointment as chief justice for reasons of health and because he felt that the Court lacked sufficient stature within the national government.

Justice Charles Evans Hughes resigned in 1916 to run unsuccessfully for the presidency. Fourteen years later he returned to the Court as chief justice. Justice Arthur J. Goldberg resigned in 1965 when President Lyndon Johnson asked him to become U.S. ambassador to the United Nations.

Justice James F. Byrnes resigned in 1942, after serving only sixteen months, to take a more active part in the war effort. He served first as director of the Office of Economic Stabilization and then as director of the Office of War Mobilization. In 1945 Byrnes accompanied President Franklin Roosevelt to the meeting in Yalta with Stalin and Churchill. As secretary of state in the Truman administration, he attended the Potsdam Conference. In 1950 he was elected governor of South Carolina.

At least three justices have resigned for reasons of conscience. Justice John A. Campbell resigned in 1861, soon after the outbreak of the Civil War, to return to his native Alabama despite the fact that he had opposed secession and had freed all his own slaves.

Justice Benjamin R. Curtis resigned in 1857, after disagreeing with Chief Justice Roger B. Taney over the Dred Scott decision (*Scott v. Sandford* [1857]), which held that Congress did not have the authority to prohibit slavery in the territories. Justice Curtis, a strong advocate of freedom for slaves once they were on free territory, also felt that justices were not paid enough.

Justice Tom C. Clark retired in 1967 to avoid any possible charges of conflict of interest after his son, Ramsey Clark, was appointed attorney general.

Abe Fortas, the only justice ever to resign amid charges of judicial misconduct, submitted his resignation on May 14, 1969, a few weeks after *Life* magazine published reports that Fortas, during his first year on the Court, had received the first of what were to be annual fees of $20,000 from the family foundation of Louis Wolfson. Wolfson was later convicted of violating federal securities laws. In submitting his resignation, Fortas denied any wrongdoing, saying that the fee in question had been returned and the relationship terminated. He was resigning nevertheless, he said, to quiet the controversy and enable the Court to proceed with its work without disruption.

Respondent

A respondent is someone who is compelled to answer the claims or questions posed in court by a petitioner. Both a defendant and an appellee may be called respondents. The term also includes those parties who answer in court during actions in which charges are not necessarily brought or in which the Supreme Court has agreed to review the decision of a lower court.

Restraint, Judicial

See JUDICIAL RESTRAINT.

Retirement

Neither the Constitution nor the law states when or under what circumstances a justice should retire from service on the Supreme Court. Justices are appointed for life and "shall hold their Offices during good Behavior," according to Article III, Section 1 of the Constitution.

For the first eighty years of the Court's existence, Congress made no pension provisions for justices who wished to retire. As a result, several of them stayed on

Justice Stephen J. Field in his library on his eightieth birthday in 1896. Field managed to avoid the issue of his retirement when his fellow justice, John Marshall Harlan, attempted to raise the subject. Field finally retired in 1897 after thirty-four years of service on the Court.
Source: Supreme Court Collection

the Court until their deaths, even after they were no longer physically or mentally capable of performing their duties.

That situation was improved by passage of the Judiciary Act of 1869, in which Congress provided that any judge who had served on any federal court for at least ten years, and who was seventy or older, could resign and receive a pension equal to his salary at the time of resignation.

The law now provides that a justice, if he or she wishes, may retire at age seventy after having served ten years or at age sixty-five after fifteen years of service, with compensation commensurate with his or her salary. That law was enacted in 1937 in response

to President Franklin D. Roosevelt's Court-packing proposal, which Congress opposed.

Roosevelt had proposed his plan in 1936 to undermine the influence of aged conservatives on the Court who were blocking implementation of most of his economic recovery programs. At the time all members of the federal judiciary except Supreme Court justices were allowed to retire from regular service rather than resign. Judges who retired were still entitled to the salary of the office, plus any increases.

Supreme Court justices, however, had to resign, and their pensions were subject to the same fluctuations as those of other retired government officials. When Justice Oliver Wendell Holmes, Jr., was prevailed upon to resign in 1932, his pension was $10,000 a year—half his annual pay as a justice—because the Hoover administration, attempting to economize, had set that amount as the maximum pension for former government employees.

Chief Justice Charles Evans Hughes later said that he thought two of the more conservative members of the Court would have joined Holmes and resigned if the pension benefits had been more generous. As it was, justices Willis Van Devanter and George Sutherland remained on the Court, forming the nucleus of the conservative majority that struck down one New Deal law after another.

The Supreme Court Retirement Act of 1937 quickly proved effective. Roosevelt signed it into law on March 1, 1937, and on May 18 Justice Van Devanter announced his retirement.

Unwilling Retirees

Pension issues aside, some aging justices in ill health have left their seats only after considerable pressure from their colleagues on the Court.

After the election of President Andrew Jackson in 1832, Chief Justice John Marshall and Justice Gabriel Duvall, both in failing health, were reluctant to resign because they feared that the "radical" new president would choose equally radical new justices to take their places. Chief Justice Marshall remained on the Court until his death in 1835. Justice Duvall submitted his resignation that same year after learning that Jackson intended to nominate Roger B. Taney, a man of whom Duvall approved, to his seat. (As it happened, Taney did not take Duvall's seat. After Marshall's death, Jackson named Taney chief justice, and Philip Barbour of Virginia took Duvall's chair.)

In 1869 it was apparent that Justice Robert C. Grier was both physically and mentally unable to carry out his duties. Early the next year the other justices formed a committee to tell Grier that they all thought he should resign. Soon after meeting with the committee, Grier retired.

One of the members of that committee was Justice Stephen J. Field, who himself stayed too long on the Court. The other justices thought that a reminder to Field of the Grier incident might induce him to consider resigning. Chief Justice Charles Evans Hughes

later recounted how Justice John Marshall Harlan, who was selected to talk to Field, asked Field if he remembered what had been said to Grier that day. "Yes!" Field is said to have responded. "And a dirtier day's work I never did in my life." That ended any further effort of the justices to try to convince Field to resign, but he did retire not long after.

Life after Retirement

Some justices largely disappeared from public view upon their retirement; others continued to lead active public lives. Justice Stanley F. Reed, for example, left the Court in 1957 at the age of seventy-two. For a brief period he served as chairman of President Dwight Eisenhower's U.S. Civil Rights Commission. Reed soon left the commission, however, because he felt his continued involvement with the federal judiciary disqualified him. Reed argued thirty-five cases before the Court of Claims and twenty-five cases before the Court of Appeals in the District of Columbia during his retirement. He died twenty-three years after leaving the Court.

Other retired justices were equally active. Justice Owen J. Roberts resigned from the court in 1945 at age seventy and returned to his alma mater, the University of Pennsylvania, where he served as dean of the law school from 1948 to 1951. Justice Charles Evans Whittaker helped devise a code of ethics for the Senate Ethics Committee after his retirement in 1962. Justice Louis D. Brandeis, who was eighty-two when he retired from the Court in 1939, devoted the remaining two years of his life to the Zionist movement and to a boycott of German products.

Altogether, thirty-five justices have retired from the court. Seventeen have resigned. One, Justice Charles Evans Hughes, is counted twice because he resigned, served a second time, and then retired. Forty-eight justices have died while on the Court.

Reversals of Earlier Rulings

The doctrine of STARE DECISIS, or respect for PRECEDENT, requires the Supreme Court to follow its previous decisions. Still, the Court has reversed its own rulings at least 207 times from its founding through the end of the 1992–1993 Court term. This calculation is necessarily imprecise, because the Court does not always state explicitly that it is overruling a precedent. By counting decisions that amount to a repudiation of a previous ruling, some experts reach a much higher number. Whatever the exact number, the practice has occurred throughout the Court's history.

The Supreme Court first reversed one of its rulings in 1810, upholding the French seizure of a U.S. merchant ship and discarding a precedent from two years before. There were only eight more reversals in the next sixty years.

The Court's first major turnaround came in 1871 when it upheld the use of paper money in the second of the *LEGAL TENDER CASES*. The 5–4 decision reversed a 4–3 ruling handed down the year before. Two justices appointed after the earlier ruling helped form the new majority, leading to charges that the Court had been "packed."

Laissez-Faire Era

For a half-century beginning in the mid-1880s, the Court adopted a conservative laissez-faire philosophy that led it to strike down measures for economic regulation. Several of those decisions required the Court to reverse earlier rulings.

The most dramatic was the 5–4 ruling in 1895 that struck down the federal INCOME TAX. That decision repudiated the Court's initial ruling on the federal taxing power in 1796. The 1895 ruling was overturned by the Sixteenth Amendment in 1913.(See REVERSALS OF RULINGS BY CONSTITUTIONAL AMENDMENT.)

In another important decision, the Court in 1886 prohibited state regulation of railroad rates, thereby overruling a precedent established in 1877. Congress responded a year later by creating the Interstate Commerce Commission (ICC), first of the federal regulatory agencies. Several other Court decisions discarded precedents in order to limit the taxing power of the states. A decision in 1890 barred states from prohibiting the sale of liquor, overturning a precedent dating from 1847.

Revolution of 1937

In 1937 the Supreme Court made a dramatic shift away from property rights and toward individual rights. Over the next sixteen years the Court overturned forty-five of its precedents, many of them economic rulings from the laissez-faire era.

The Court signaled the shift with a decision in March 1937 to uphold state laws concerning minimum wage. Justice Owen J. Roberts provided the key vote in the 5–4 ruling, switching his position from a case decided the year before. The Court was under pressure at the time because of President Franklin D. Roosevelt's controversial Court-packing plan, and some viewed Roberts's vote as a capitulation to the White House. Later it became known, however, that Roberts had voted in conference to uphold the challenged law in December 1936—two months before Roosevelt unveiled his plan.

In another major ruling four years later the Court upheld a federal minimum wage law that included a prohibition on child labor virtually identical to a measure the Court had struck down in 1918. In several other rulings the Court threw out previous limits on state regulation of businesses and on state and federal taxation. A 1944 decision gave state utility commissions greater discretion in setting rates.

The Court also reversed several precedents to give greater protections to CIVIL LIBERTIES and CIVIL RIGHTS. In 1942 the Court upheld a local licensing fee applied to Jehovah's Witnesses—only to reverse itself the next year after granting reargument in the case. Six weeks later the Court reversed itself on another religious freedom case. By a vote of 6 to 3 the Court barred school districts from requiring children to salute the flag as part of daily classroom exercises—reversing its 1940 ruling on the issue. (See FLAG SALUTE CASES; RELIGION, FREEDOM OF.)

In 1944 the Court barred Texas's all-white Democratic party primary, setting aside a 1935 precedent. (See VOTING RIGHTS.) The new ruling relied on a 1941 decision, which had overturned a 1921 precedent in order to uphold federal regulation of party primaries. (See CAMPAIGNS AND ELECTIONS.)

Warren Court

The Supreme Court under Chief Justice Earl Warren once again swept aside forty-five precedents in sixteen years. The Warren Court brought about a DUE PROCESS revolution in criminal law, struck down racial SEGREGATION, and required state legislative REAPPORTIONMENT AND REDISTRICTING.

In *BROWN V. BOARD OF EDUCATION OF TOPEKA* (1954) the Court unanimously struck down the "separate but equal" doctrine established in *PLESSY V. FERGUSON* (1896) to uphold racial segregation. *Brown* began the process of court-ordered SCHOOL DESEGREGATION. Two years later the Court formally overruled *Plessy* as it applied to segregated public transportation.

Fifteen decisions in the 1960s overturned precedents in order to apply the provisions of the Bill of Rights to state criminal trials. Many of the rejected precedents dated from the 1940s and early 1950s. (See INCORPORATION DOCTRINE.)

Two landmark decisions were *Mapp v. Ohio* (1960), requiring states to follow the EXCLUSIONARY RULE and bar use of illegally seized evidence in criminal trials; and *GIDEON V. WAINWRIGHT* (1963), requiring appointment of lawyers for indigent criminal defendants. (See COUNSEL, RIGHT TO LEGAL.)

Later in 1963 the Court broadened state prisoners' rights to challenge their convictions through federal HABEAS CORPUS proceedings. In 1964 it applied the Fifth Amendment privilege against SELF-INCRIMINATION to the states and also required states to determine whether CONFESSIONS were voluntary before allowing them to be introduced into evidence.

In 1967 the Court reversed a 1928 ruling to hold that the Fourth Amendment limits on SEARCH AND SEIZURE apply to wiretapping and other types of ELECTRONIC SURVEILLANCE. Congress acted the next year to establish procedures for judicial warrants to authorize wiretaps.

The Court's reapportionment decisions began with *BAKER V. CARR* (1962). The decisions overturned a pair of rulings from the 1940s that held such disputes to be political questions—that is, questions not for the courts to decide. The new rulings required state legislatures across the country to redraw district lines to reflect changes in population distribution.

In 1968 the Court overruled a 1906 precedent in order to revive a Reconstruction-era civil rights law by applying it to private racial DISCRIMINATION. The next year the Court overturned a 1927 decision and narrowed the permissible scope of state SEDITION LAWS.

Burger Court

The Court under Chief Justice Warren E. Burger overturned fifty-three precedents in seventeen years—a record comparable to that of the Warren Court but less consistent.

The states first won and then lost on the question of whether Congress could extend federal protection for minimum wage and overtime to state employees. The Court in 1976 voted 5–4 to bar such regulation under the Tenth Amendment. In 1985 Justice Harry A. Blackmun changed sides to produce a new 5–4 decision upholding federal coverage for state workers. (See STATES AND THE COURT.)

In two rulings in 1979 and 1982 the Court discarded precedents in order to invalidate state laws designed to conserve natural resources, such as natural gas and water, by limiting their shipment out of state. In an important ruling for local governments, the Court in 1978 permitted federal civil rights suits against municipalities—overturning a Warren Court precedent from 1961.

In 1984 the Court held, 5–4, that federal courts could not order state officials to comply with their own state law. The decision, which was a setback for civil rights advocates, overturned precedents dating to 1887.

The Court established two new precedents in First Amendment areas. A 5–4 decision in 1973 loosened the standards for determining OBSCENITY, giving state and federal governments greater power to regulate such materials. In 1976, however, the Court extended First Amendment protection to commercial speech—discarding a 1942 decision. (See SPEECH, COMMERCIAL.)

Two new rulings on jury selection struck down laws that automatically exempted women from jury

A 1991 decision held that the use of an involuntary confession does not necessarily require reversal of a criminal conviction. Another 1991 ruling eased the rules on searches of automobiles. Two rulings in 1991 and 1992 made it harder for state prisoners to win new trials through federal habeas corpus. In 1991, by a vote of 5 to 4, the Court reversed a four-year-old decision in order to permit the use of "victim impact statements" in sentencing hearings for the death penalty.

In an important tax decision, the Court in 1988 discarded part of an 1895 ruling to hold that the federal government can tax the interest on state and local government bonds.

The Court ended the 1991–1992 term with a decision that narrowly reaffirmed one controversial precedent—the 1973 abortion rights ruling, *ROE V. WADE*. But the decision overturned two later extensions of *Roe* that had barred states from imposing waiting periods before a woman could obtain an abortion or from specifying information to be given to a woman before an abortion could be performed.

duty and barred prosecutors from using race as a basis for disqualifying potential jurors in criminal cases. Both overturned Warren Court precedents. (See JURIES.)

After reaching a decision in 1972 prohibiting CAPITAL PUNISHMENT as it was then administered, the Court in 1976 upheld new death penalty laws as long as juries were given guidelines on the use of the penalty. The Court had rejected such a requirement in 1971. Several later reversals in the early 1980s made it harder for criminal defendants to challenge police searches.

Rehnquist Court

Under Chief Justice William H. Rehnquist the Court, through the end of the 1992–1993 term, reversed earlier decisions twenty-two times in seven years. Many of the turnarounds favored the government in criminal cases.

Reversals of Rulings by Constitutional Amendment

A Supreme Court ruling based on the Constitution can be reversed only by adoption of a constitutional amendment. On four occasions Congress and the states have formed alliances to overturn Supreme Court decisions in this way. In several other cases, amendments to nullify unpopular rulings have been proposed but have failed.

States' Rights

The Eleventh Amendment was ratified in 1795, after states protested the Supreme Court's literal interpretation of the constitutional provision giving it jurisdiction over cases arising between a state and citizens of another state or of a foreign country (Article III, Section 2).

During the writing of the Constitution, supporters said the provision would permit suits only when the state was the plaintiff. But in *Chisholm v. Georgia* (1793) the Supreme Court held that the provision permitted suits in federal court by citizens of one state against another state.

The decision shocked the country. Anti-Federalists argued that it compromised the sovereignty of the states, and they worried that citizen suits could further jeopardize the states' financial plight. A year later the House and Senate overwhelmingly approved a constitutional amendment to bar citizen suits against states. Three-fourths of the states approved the amendment in less than a year.

The Supreme Court acquiesced in the amendment in February 1798. Later interpretations of the amendment, however, have allowed suits against state officials for violating individuals' constitutional or civil rights.

Citizenship and Civil Rights

The Fourteenth Amendment, ratified in 1868, began as an effort by Congress to eliminate doubts about the constitutionality of the Civil Rights Act of 1866, aimed at protecting the legal rights of freed slaves.

As originally drafted, the first section of the amendment gave Congress power to make laws to secure to the citizens of each state "all privileges and immunities" of citizenship and to guarantee "all persons . . . equal protection in the rights of life, liberty and property." The provision was intended to undo the effect of the Supreme Court's earlier ruling in *Barron v. Baltimore* (1833) that the Bill of Rights did not apply to the states.

The amended version passed by Congress and ratified by the states did not give Congress a positive grant of power. Instead, it prohibited the states from making any law that abridged the privileges and immunities of citizens of the United States; deprived any person of life, liberty, or property without due process of the law; or denied anyone equal protection of the laws.

The Supreme Court in the 1870s and 1880s narrowly construed that section of the Fourteenth Amendment. Only in the twentieth century did the Court use the amendment to apply the Bill of Rights to state action and to extend equal protection of the laws to blacks.

The first section of the amendment also overturned the Supreme Court's ruling in the Dred Scott case (*SCOTT V. SANDFORD* [1857]), which held that blacks could never become U.S. citizens. A sentence added by the Senate declared that all persons born or naturalized in the United States and subject to its jurisdiction are citizens of the United States. (See CITIZENSHIP.)

Income Taxes

The Sixteenth Amendment, ratified in 1913, overturned the Supreme Court's decision in *Pollock v. Farmers' Loan & Trust Co.* (1895), which struck down a federal INCOME TAX law. In that case the Court held that a tax on income from real estate was a direct tax, which under the Constitution had to be apportioned by population (Article I, Section 9, Clause 4).

In Pollock v. Farmers' Loan & Trust Co. *(1895) the Court ruled the income tax unconstitutional. Public opinion may have sided with the Court at that time, but by 1913 the nation had ratified the Sixteenth Amendment, which exempted income taxes from the Constitution's apportionment requirement.*
Source: Library of Congress

The decision was highly unpopular with both laborers and farmers. In elections in following years the voters returned to Congress more and more Democrats and progressive Republicans who favored enactment of an income tax. In the midst of a depression in 1909, Democrats attached an income tax proposal to a Republican tariff reform measure. Conservative Republicans opposed the tax and countered with a proposal for a constitutional amendment, thinking that it would not be approved by enough state legislatures for ratification. Contrary to expectations, however, the required number of state legislatures ratified the amendment in less than four years.

The Right to Vote

In 1970 Congress enacted a provision lowering the voting age for federal, state, and local elections to eighteen years. President Richard Nixon signed the measure into law in June 1970, even though he believed that the change required a constitutional amendment. The Nixon administration brought suit to test the validity of the measure. By a 5–4 vote, the Court ruled in December 1970 that Congress had the authority to lower the voting age for federal elections but not for state and local elections *(Oregon v. Mitchell)*.

The decision created administrative difficulties for the forty-seven states that did not allow eighteen-year-olds to vote. State election officials said that the task of producing dual registration books, ballots, and voting machines could not be completed in time for the 1972 elections.

To help the states, the Senate and House gave overwhelming approval in March 1971 to a constitutional amendment to lower the voting age to eighteen years in all elections. The states ratified the Twenty-Sixth Amendment on July 1, 1971, just three months and seven days after it was submitted.

Unsuccessful Amendments

Congress or the states have tried but failed to pass constitutional amendments to overturn several Supreme Court rulings.

After two rulings overturning federal CHILD LABOR laws, Congress in June 1924 approved a constitutional amendment to authorize federal legislation on the subject. By 1938 twenty-eight states had ratified the amendment—eight short of the required number. The amendment became unnecessary in 1941, however, when the Court itself overturned its previous ruling.

Other proposed amendments on reapportionment, school prayer, busing, and abortion have failed to win approval in Congress.

Reversals of Rulings by Legislation

Congress can reverse the effect of a Supreme Court decision that restricts or invalidates a federal law, by reenacting the statute in modified form. The Court generally acquiesces in such legislative overrides. Sometimes it goes so far as to suggest how a law might be changed to eliminate constitutional or statutory flaws.

Occasionally the Court does not go along with congressional efforts to void Court decisions by legislation. An example occurred over the issue of CHILD LABOR. After the Court declared unconstitutional the 1916 child labor law, which barred shipment in interstate commerce of goods made by children, Congress passed a second measure placing a prohibitively high tax on profits of such goods. The Court declared this law invalid, too. Congress then approved a constitutional amendment forbidding child labor, which fell short of ratification. Finally, in 1941 the Court itself reversed its earlier holdings.

Early Examples

Congress first reversed the Supreme Court by legislation in 1852. In that year the Court ruled that a bridge built across the Ohio River obstructed interstate commerce and must either be raised so that ships could pass under it or be taken down. Congress immediately passed a law declaring that the bridge did not obstruct interstate commerce and requiring instead that ships be refitted so that they could pass under the bridge. In 1856 the Court sustained the law.

Another legislative reversal occurred after the Court held in 1890 that in the absence of congressional authorization, liquor in its original container imported into a state through interstate commerce was not subject to state prohibition laws. Accepting the Court's implicit invitation, Congress later in the year permitted the states to prohibit such shipments of liquor, and the Court upheld that statute in 1891.

At the turn of the century the Court accepted congressional efforts to modify its rulings limiting the powers of the Interstate Commerce Commission (ICC). In a series of cases in the late 1890s the Court stripped the new agency of all its essential regulatory powers, including its rate-making powers. Congress responded in 1906 with a law specifically authorizing the commission to adjust unreasonable and unfair rates. The Court in 1910 upheld that grant of power. Encouraged, Congress then gave the ICC authority to set original rates. The Court in 1914 upheld that power as well—thus completely reversing its earlier decisions.

Civil Rights

The Court in 1883 ruled unconstitutional the CIVIL RIGHTS Act of 1875, on the ground that Congress, in attempting to prohibit racial discrimination in public accommodations, had exceeded its authority under the Thirteenth and Fourteenth amendments. Eighty years later Congress sought to reverse the ruling, this time justifying the Civil Rights Act of 1964 under its power to regulate interstate commerce. Six months after this statute was signed into law, the Court unanimously sustained its constitutionality.

Unions and Antitrust

Congress and the Court had a prolonged confrontation about whether labor unions were exempt from federal ANTITRUST law. The Court in 1908 ruled that some union practices, including the boycott, were illegal restraints of trade. Congress attempted to reverse the effect of the decision in the Clayton Act of 1914 by providing for an antitrust exemption for labor unions pursuing lawful objectives. Nonetheless, the Court in 1921 held that some union practices still ran afoul of antitrust law. In 1932 Congress sought to reverse that decision with the Norris-LaGuardia Act, and in 1938 the Court went along with the legislative override.

New Deal Legislation

During the New Deal period Congress overturned more of the Court's decisions on important measures than in any other period in the nation's history. Between 1934 and 1936, the Court struck down six major acts passed by Congress as part of President Franklin D. Roosevelt's program to lift the country out of the Great Depression. The Court became more liberal on economic issues beginning in 1937. Congress then revised five of the six laws the Court had declared invalid and enacted a new law—the National Labor Relations Act—to substitute for the other measure, the National Industrial Recovery Act. Between 1937 and 1940 the Court sustained all the new acts.

Tidelands Oil

Congress in one instance successfully overruled both the Court and a president. In 1947 the Court ruled that the federal government, not the states, owned the three-mile strip of oil-rich submerged land adjacent to the ocean shores. After several attempts Congress in 1951 finally approved a law to give the states ownership of these tidelands, but President Harry S. Truman vetoed it. After the Republicans gained control of the White House and Congress in 1952, a similar bill was passed, and this time it was signed into law in 1953. The Supreme Court upheld the measure the next year.

Confessions

As part of a broad anticrime measure, Congress in 1968 sought to undo the effects of three Supreme Court decisions dealing with CONFESSIONS and identification testimony. The law provided that confessions were admissible in evidence if given voluntarily (thus reversing *MIRANDA V. ARIZONA* [1966]) and without regard to any delay in arraigning the defendant (overruling *Mallory v. United States* [1957]). In addition, the law sought to overturn the ruling in *United States v. Wade* (1967) requiring attorneys to be present at some police lineups, by declaring that an eyewitness identification of a criminal was always admissible in a federal criminal trial.

The effect of the law has been largely symbolic. The provisions did not apply to state courts, where most criminal prosecutions occur, and they have been largely ignored in federal court.

Civil Rights in the 1980s

The Court in the 1980s began to restrict some civil rights laws, just when congressional support for civil rights policies was increasing. Twice during the decade Congress reversed individual decisions of the Court. Then in 1991 Congress passed, and President George Bush signed into law, a measure intended to reverse five decisions handed down in 1989 that made it harder to win JOB DISCRIMINATION suits.

In 1980 the Court tightened the Voting Rights Act of 1965 by ruling that it applied only to intentionally discriminatory practices. In amending the law in 1982, Congress eliminated the intent requirement. In 1986 the Court applied the amended law as Congress provided.

The Court in 1984 narrowed a 1972 law prohibiting SEX DISCRIMINATION at schools receiving federal aid to education by ruling that the ban applied only to a specific program or department that was receiving assistance rather than to the whole school. Four years later, in 1988, Congress passed legislation over President Ronald Reagan's veto to reverse the decision.

The Court's employment discrimination cases in 1989 led to another lengthy showdown between Congress and the president. Civil rights supporters promptly tried to reverse the decisions. President Bush said he favored corrective legislation but argued that the Democratic-sponsored measures in Congress would require employers to adopt quota systems. Citing the quota issue, Bush vetoed a bill Congress sent to him in late 1990. Congressional Democrats tried again in 1991 and, after long maneuvering and compromising with the White House, passed a bill that Bush agreed to sign.

Review, Judicial

See JUDICIAL REVIEW.

Right to Bear Arms

See ARMS, RIGHT TO BEAR.

Ripeness

Just as the MOOTNESS doctrine prevents a court from deciding a case after it is too late, the ripeness doctrine may prevent it from deciding a case too soon. As with other rules of JUDICIAL RESTRAINT, however, the Supreme Court has not applied the ripeness doctrine with complete consistency.

A case may be considered not ripe if the injury complained of has not occurred, if a threatened injury is not fairly certain to occur, or if the facts needed for an intelligent resolution of the dispute are not available.

Thus, for example, the Court in *United Public Workers v. Mitchell* (1947) refused to rule on a case brought by federal civil workers challenging the Hatch Act's restrictions on political activities. The Court declared that the plaintiffs were not threatened with "actual interference" with their interests. On the other hand, the Court in 1952 passed on the merits, without ever discussing ripeness, a state law requiring dismissal of teachers who advocated violent overthrow of the government.

In a later loyalty oath case, *Cramp v. Board of Public Instruction* (1961), the Court crafted a reconciliation of the two rulings. The ruling stated that the vagueness of the oath subjected the plaintiff and other government employees to "the risk of unfair prosecution and the potential deterrence of constitutionally protected conduct."

The Court may also be willing to overlook ripeness problems if a delay in ruling could frustrate government policy. For example, in *Buckley v. Valeo* (1976) the Court issued an early ruling on the constitutionality of the Federal Election Campaign Act, since a challenge to the law appeared inevitable and the decision called for resolution of strictly legal rather than fact-dependent questions.

Roberts, Owen J.

Owen Josephus Roberts (1875–1955) came to the Supreme Court as a president's second choice. In 1930 the American Federation of Labor and the National Association for the Advancement of Colored People lobbied hard to block Herbert Hoover's nomination of federal judge John J. Parker to the Supreme Court. Parker's opponents claimed that he was insensitive to labor and racial issues. The Senate rejected Parker 39–41, the first time in the twentieth century that it rejected a Supreme Court nominee. The victory, however, turned out not to be very sweet for the NAACP. Parker continued to serve on the Fourth Circuit Court of Appeals and wrote some influential opinions favor-

Source: Office of the Curator, Supreme Court

ing black rights. Roberts, Hoover's second choice for the Court, was less supportive of civil rights claims.

Roberts was born in Germantown, Pennsylvania. He graduated Phi Beta Kappa from the University of Pennsylvania in 1895 and with honors from the University of Pennsylvania Law School in 1898. He then entered private practice in Philadelphia and taught part time at the university. In 1901 Roberts was named assistant district attorney in Philadelphia, but he returned to private practice in 1905.

After being appointed a special deputy attorney general in 1918, Roberts prosecuted several cases under the Espionage Act. Six years later, President Calvin Coolidge named him and former senator Atlee Pomerene as government prosecutors in the Teapot Dome scandal. Hoover considered Roberts a liberal, but still nominated him to the Supreme Court in 1930.

On the Court Roberts turned out to be less liberal than some people had expected. In *Betts v. Brady* (1942) Roberts declared for the majority that the Fourteenth Amendment due process guarantee did not require states to appoint counsel in every criminal case where defendants couldn't afford their own attorney. In 1963 the Court overturned this decision, ruling that states must provide attorneys to defendants charged with serious crimes who request them.

As the Court began to consider numerous laws passed as part of President Franklin D. Roosevelt's New Deal program, Roberts usually cast the swing fifth vote. Initially he voted against most of Roosevelt's program. However, as Roosevelt and others attacked the Court for allegedly imposing its own will on the nation, Roberts apparently had a change of heart and began to vote in favor of the New Deal. Roberts's switch was one of the key factors that helped kill Roosevelt's Court-packing plan.

While serving as a justice, Roberts also oversaw the investigation into the bombing of Pearl Harbor. He resigned from the Court in 1945 after having served for fifteen years. Roberts was dean of the University of Pennsylvania Law School from 1948 to 1951, and died in 1955.

Roe v. Wade

The Supreme Court in *Roe v. Wade* (1973) gave women a qualified constitutional right to ABORTION. The decision touched off an intense legal and political controversy that continued into the 1990s. Efforts to overturn the ruling by constitutional amendment failed. But the Court itself narrowed the impact of the ruling by refusing to require public financing of abortions for poor women and by upholding some state regulations that made abortions more difficult to obtain.

The highly emotional issue reached the Court in two cases brought by women under assumed names. *Roe v. Wade* challenged a Texas law forbidding abortions except to save the pregnant woman's life; *Doe v. Bolton* challenged four provisions of Georgia law requiring that an abortion be performed only in an accredited hospital and only after review by a hospital staff committee and examination of the woman by two doctors other than her own physician.

The Court's 7–2 decision to strike down the laws extended earlier decisions that recognized a constitutional right to privacy. (See PRIVACY, RIGHT OF.) That right, Justice Harry A. Blackmun said in his opinion for the Court, probably came from the "liberty" protected by the due process clause of the Fourteenth Amendment. But whatever its source, Blackmun said, "this right is . . . broad enough to encompass a woman's decision whether or not to terminate her pregnancy."

The Court said that the right was a qualified one. The state's "important interests in safeguarding

Norma McCorvey, surrounded by reporters in 1989, was the real "Jane Roe" of Roe v. Wade. *McCorvey's challenge to the constitutionality of Texas's statute forbidding abortion led to the Supreme Court's 1973 opinion declaring that the right to privacy protects a woman's right to terminate a pregnancy.*   Source: UPI/Bettmann Newsphotos

health, maintaining medical standards, and protecting potential life" were "sufficiently compelling" to justify government regulation "at some point in pregnancy," Blackmun wrote.

Blackmun went on to establish a controversial "trimester analysis" that barred any regulation of abortion during the first three months of pregnancy; allowed limited regulation to protect the woman's health and safety during the second three months; and allowed the government to ban abortion only during the final trimester of pregnancy—when the fetus was thought capable of living on its own.

Chief Justice Warren E. Burger concurred in the opinion, but wrote separately to say that the decision did not permit "abortion on demand." In dissent, however, Justice Byron R. White said the ruling allowed for abortion to satisfy "the convenience, whim or caprice of the putative mother." And in a separate dissent, Justice William H. Rehnquist said the decision "partakes more of judicial legislation than it does of a determination of the intent of the drafters of the Fourteenth Amendment."

By 1992 Rehnquist, now chief justice, and White were joined by justices Antonin Scalia and Clarence Thomas in voting to overturn *Roe*. But in a fragmented decision, the Court in *Planned Parenthood v. Casey* (1992) reaffirmed the core holding of *Roe* while permitting states to regulate procedures as long as they did not impose an "undue burden" on a woman's right to abortion.

Source: *Franklin D. Roosevelt Library*

Roosevelt, Franklin D.

President Franklin D. Roosevelt (1882–1945) led the nation during the Great Depression and World War II. As president from 1933 to 1945, he determined to use the powers of his office as needed to bring the country through these two great crises. During his first term, however, the Supreme Court threw out key parts of his New Deal program. Roosevelt responded in 1937 with a controversial "Court-packing" plan aimed at changing the Court's constitutional philosophy on economic issues. The plan failed, but Roosevelt still succeeded in transforming the Court by

making nine appointments to it as vacancies arose during the rest of his presidency. (See PRESIDENT AND THE COURT.)

Working with large Democratic majorities in Congress, Roosevelt pushed through an extraordinary economic relief and recovery program. Two of its centerpieces were the Agricultural Adjustment Act (AAA) and the National Industrial Recovery Act (NIRA). The AAA was designed to lift farm income by raising prices through reduced production, and the NIRA was intended to restore industrial production by prescribing "codes of fair competition" for wages, prices, and trade practices. The constitutional basis for the program was the congressional power to regulate interstate commerce and to provide for the general welfare, combined with Roosevelt's claimed emergency executive powers. (See COMMERCE POWER.)

The Supreme Court was not receptive to such broad uses of federal power. Between January 1935 and June 1936 the Court ruled against the administration in eight out of ten major cases involving New Deal statutes. In the most devastating single day—May 27, 1935, called "Black Monday"—the Court unanimously struck down the NIRA as an unconstitutional delegation of legislative power to the president, and a federal farm mortgage relief act as unfair to creditors. (See UNCONSTITUTIONAL STATUTES.) On the same day the Court also rejected Roosevelt's attempt to unilaterally remove a member of the Federal Trade Commission. (See APPOINTMENT AND REMOVAL POWERS OF THE PRESIDENT.)

In January 1936 the Court, by a vote of 6 to 3, threw out the AAA as an improper use of the TAXING POWER to regulate agriculture, an area reserved to the states. In May the Court, again by a 6–3 vote, cited similar grounds in invalidating an act designed to stabilize the coal industry.

Roosevelt considered several plans to circumvent the Court, including constitutional amendments either to broaden congressional power or to limit the Court's power to invalidate acts of Congress. He decided instead on a plan to pack the Court by appointing new judges. After winning a landslide reelection, Roosevelt sent Congress a message on February 5, 1937, proposing a judicial "reorganization." Roosevelt proposed to increase the number of Supreme Court justices to as many as fifteen, creating one new seat for each justice who, upon reaching the age of seventy, declined to retire. Roosevelt said the bill would relieve the justices' workload, but its purpose was really to give the president six new Court appointments.

The plan met vigorous opposition from the public. Newspapers strongly criticized it. In Congress, Democrats divided over the proposal, with Sen. Burton K. Wheeler, D-Mont., a staunch New Dealer, leading the fight against it. Wheeler helped seal the fate of the proposal during Senate Judiciary Committee hearings by presenting a letter signed by Chief Justice Charles Evans Hughes questioning the asserted premise for the plan. Hughes said that the Court was "fully abreast of its work" and that additional justices would actually delay the Court's work by prolonging deliberation on each case.

The Court itself killed the Court-packing plan, however, with a series of decisions announced between late March and late May 1937 upholding New Deal measures. Hughes and Justice Owen J. Roberts now joined the three dissenters from the earlier cases to form 5–4 majorities for upholding state minimum wage laws and three federal acts: the National Labor Relations Act, a federal unemployment compensation law, and the Social Security Act for old age benefits.

In addition, a new retirement act signed by Roosevelt in March permitted justices to retire at age seventy without losing pension benefits. On May 18 Justice Willis Van Devanter, a New Deal foe, announced he would retire at the end of his term, giving Roosevelt his first opportunity to appoint someone to the Court. Roosevelt picked Hugo L. Black, an Alabama senator who had been a strong supporter of the New Deal. By 1941 retirements and deaths had allowed Roosevelt to name six other justices and to elevate a New Deal supporter, Harlan Fiske Stone, to chief justice.

All the justices appointed by Roosevelt had no constitutional objections to the march of federal power. Some, such as Felix Frankfurter and Robert H. Jackson, were advocates of JUDICIAL RESTRAINT. Others—notably, Black, William O. Douglas, Frank Murphy, and Wiley B. Rutledge—held strong civil libertarian views that began to be reflected in the Court's rulings during the 1940s.

In addition to the justices he appointed, Roosevelt left a second constitutional legacy: a vast expansion of presidential power. He dominated the legislative process with presidential initiatives and a record use of the VETO POWER. He increased the use of executive agreements in foreign policy, bypassing the Senate's role in ratifying treaties. (See TREATY POWER.) He stretched presidential authority in the events leading up to World War II and then presided over an extensive, congressionally authorized wartime system of wage, price, and production controls. (See WAR POWERS.)

The Court sustained the wartime economic measures. Earlier in Roosevelt's tenure it had upheld broad presidential authority in foreign affairs. The Court also sustained Roosevelt's orders in the Japanese-American *INTERNMENT CASES*. Later presidents cited Roosevelt's actions to justify even broader claims of inherent power in foreign policy and national security, creating conflicts between Congress and the White House that the Court was reluctant to try to resolve.

Rutledge, John

In August 1795 President George Washington made a recess appointment of John Rutledge (1739–1800) to succeed John Jay as chief justice. Rutledge presided unofficially during the Court's August term, but in December 1795 the Senate rejected his nomination by a 10–14 vote. Upon learning of the action, Rutledge tried to drown himself. He suffered periods of insanity until his death.

The Senate rejected Rutledge, a conservative who had opposed independence from England, because of his strong opposition to the Jay Treaty with England.

Source: Library of Congress

The Jay Treaty was designed to ease tensions between the United States and England, but many felt that the United States gave away far more than it received in return.

Rutledge's mother, Sarah Hext Rutledge, was only fifteen years old when he was born in 1739 in Charleston, South Carolina. The wealthy Rutledge family was a major force in South Carolina politics near the end of the eighteenth century. John Rutledge first studied law in the office of Andrew Rutledge, Speaker of the South Carolina commons house of assembly, and later studied at the Inns of Court in London.

Rutledge had been home from England for only three months before he was elected to the provincial legislature in 1761. A succession of other public positions followed. The most important of these included delegate to the Stamp Act Congress (1765), member of the Continental Congress (1774–1776 and 1782–1783), president of the South Carolina general assembly (1776–1778), governor of South Carolina (1779–1782), and chief of the South Carolina delegation to the Constitutional Convention (1787).

In 1789, President Washington nominated Rutledge to be an associate justice of the Supreme Court. Rutledge was confirmed and participated in circuit court activities, although he never sat as a justice because of his illness and the Court's inactivity. He resigned in February 1791 to accept what he believed was a more important position: chief justice of the South Carolina supreme court. The importance of the U.S. Supreme Court continued to grow after his resignation, however, and in 1795 Rutledge asked Washington to appoint him chief justice. Washington complied, but the Senate rejected the nomination. Rutledge lived for several years after his failed suicide attempt and died in July 1800.

Rutledge, Wiley B.

Wiley Blount Rutledge (1894–1949) was determined to become a lawyer and let nothing stop him. After he graduated from the University of Wisconsin in 1914, Rutledge couldn't afford to attend law school

Source: Library of Congress

there. He moved to Indiana, where he attended Indiana University Law School part time and taught school in Bloomington to support himself.

His health weakened by overwork, Rutledge contracted a serious case of tuberculosis. After spending several years recuperating and teaching high school, he began attending law school at the University of Colorado full time and graduated in 1922.

Rutledge was born in Cloverport, Kentucky. After receiving his law degree, he practiced law for two years before returning to the academic world as a professor of law and a law school dean for more than fifteen years. It was as dean of the University of Iowa College of Law that Rutledge first came to the attention of President Franklin Roosevelt. As dean, Rutledge was outspoken in his support of Roosevelt's Court-packing plan. In fact, Rutledge's statements so outraged some Iowa state legislators that they threatened to withhold university salary increases in protest. Roosevelt appointed Rutledge to the U.S. Court of Appeals for the District of Columbia in 1939, a post he held until Roosevelt promoted him to the Supreme Court in 1943.

Rutledge, like many of the justices appointed by Roosevelt, was a strong defender of the First Amendment. He believed that First Amendment rights should have a preferred position when they came into conflict with other rights guaranteed by the Constitution. Rutledge served on the Court for six years until his death in 1949.

S

Sanford, Edward T.

When Edward Terry Sanford (1865–1930) was named to the Supreme Court in 1923, he joined his friend, Chief Justice William Howard Taft. The two men were so close that some observers claimed that Taft in effect had two votes at the Court. Their closeness continued to the end of their lives; both men died on the same day, March 8, 1930.

Sanford was born in Knoxville, Tennessee. He was educated at the University of Tennessee and Harvard, and received his law degree from Harvard Law School in 1889. He then studied in France and Germany for a year before returning to Knoxville and beginning to practice law.

Source: Library of Congress

In 1905 Sanford was named special assistant to U.S. attorney general William H. Moody. As one of President Theodore Roosevelt's "trustbusters," Sanford had the task of prosecuting the fertilizer trust under the Sherman Antitrust Act of 1890. Two years after his initial appointment, Sanford moved up to the post of assistant attorney general. In 1908 Roosevelt nominated him federal district court judge for the middle and eastern districts of Tennessee. Sanford held that post until President Warren G. Harding nominated him to the Supreme Court in 1923.

One of Sanford's most notable opinions for the Court came in *Whitney v. California* (1927). In *Whitney* the Court upheld the conviction of a woman for violating California's criminal syndicalism law by working with the Communist Labor party. The party urged the overthrow of capitalism by a revolutionary class struggle. In his opinion for the Court, Sanford wrote that the California law was not "an unreasonable or arbitrary exercise of the police power of the State, unwarrantedly infringing any right of free speech, assembly or association." Sanford served on the Court for seven years until his death in March 1930.

Scalia, Antonin

Upon joining the Supreme Court in 1986, Antonin Scalia (1936–) quickly became known as one of its most conservative members. He regularly voted with Chief Justice William H. Rehnquist and challenged Rehnquist for the title of most conservative justice.

Scalia was born in Trenton, New Jersey. He graduated from Georgetown University in 1957 and Harvard Law School in 1960, after which he practiced law for seven years in Cleveland. In the late 1960s he left private practice to teach law at the University of Virginia law school. In the 1970s Scalia held a series of positions in the administrations of Richard Nixon

Source: Collection of the Supreme Court of the United States

and Gerald Ford. He was general counsel for the White House Office of Telecommunications Policy, chair of the Administrative Conference of the United States, and assistant attorney general.

In 1977 Scalia left the government to teach for five years at the University of Chicago Law School. President Ronald Reagan appointed him to the U.S. Court of Appeals for the District of Columbia Circuit in 1982. In 1986 Reagan nominated Scalia to the Supreme Court seat left vacant by Rehnquist's promotion to chief justice.

In three significant cases in which the Court took a conservative position by a 5–4 vote, Scalia voted with the majority. In those cases the Court upheld a Missouri law barring the use of public facilities for abortions, allowed states to execute persons who were sixteen or seventeen when they committed a capital crime, and made it harder for workers to prove that

their employers had committed racial discrimination. In 1987 Scalia joined Rehnquist in dissenting when the Court voted 7–2 to overturn a Louisiana law requiring public schools that taught the theory of evolution to teach "creation science" as well.

Scandals

See IMPEACHMENT OF JUSTICES; RESIGNATION.

Schedule of Arguments and Conferences

During its formal annual session, the Supreme Court sets aside certain times for oral ARGUMENTS, for CONFERENCES, for the writing of opinions, and for the announcement of decisions. (See DECISION DAYS; WRITING OPINIONS.)

Until 1955 the Court often heard oral arguments five days a week. Friday arguments were abandoned when the Court's conference was moved to that day. Arguments are now heard on Monday, Tuesday, and Wednesday for seven two-week sessions beginning in the first week of October and ending in the last week of April or first week of May. Each of these periods is followed by a recess of two weeks or longer in which the justices consider the cases and deal with other Court business.

Since the early 1800s, when justices heard arguments from 11 a.m. until 4 or 5 p.m., the schedule for hearing arguments has been changed several times. The current schedule calls for oral arguments to take place from 10 a.m. to noon and from 1 to 3 p.m. The current schedule was adopted in the 1969 term.

Argument in most cases is limited to one hour, which means the Court can hear twelve cases a week. Exceptions to the limit of one hour per case must be sought and granted before arguments begin.

In the early years the private conferences—in which the justices discuss which cases to review and, after oral argument, their opinions about how each case should be decided—were often held in the evenings or on weekends. Sometimes they were held in the common boardinghouse the justices shared. The number of cases for which review was sought and the cases awaiting a final decision determined when and how often conferences were held.

Later Saturday was set aside as the regular conference day. Since 1955, when the Court issued an order stopping oral arguments on Friday, the Court has used Friday as its conference day.

Between 1955 and 1975 the Court held its first conference of each term during opening week, following its formal call to order on the first Monday in October. To streamline the procedure, the justices began meeting in the last week in September, before the session formally convened. At this initial conference the Court attempts to resolve leftover matters—appeals, petitions for certiorari, and so forth—from the previous session. The September conference allows the Court to announce its orders on these matters by opening day rather than a week after the session begins.

During its term the Court holds conferences each Friday during the weeks when arguments are heard, and one on the Friday just before the beginning of each two-week argument period. To reduce the workload of its Friday sessions, the Court also holds Wednesday conferences during the weeks when oral arguments are scheduled.

Although the last oral arguments are heard by late April or early May of each year, the conferences continue until the end of the term to consider cases remaining on the Court's agenda.

In the Court's early years, decisions were announced whenever the justices were ready. Today, opinions are released only on Tuesdays and Wednesdays during weeks when the Court is hearing oral arguments. In other weeks, they are released on Mondays.

The Court's order list (the summary of the Court's action granting or denying review) is also released on Mondays. The order list is not announced in open court, as decisions are, but is posted at the beginning of the Monday session. The list can be obtained from the clerk and the public information officer.

School Desegregation

Beginning in 1896 the Supreme Court first condoned racial SEGREGATION in public schools, then began to undermine it. Finally, in *BROWN V. BOARD OF EDUCATION OF TOPEKA* (1954), the Court declared the practice unconstitutional as a violation of the EQUAL PROTECTION clause of the Fourteenth Amendment.

The next year, in *Brown (II)*, the Court ruled that schools must desegregate "with all deliberate speed." The ruling did not, however, yield quick or consistent results. Over the next four decades, desegregation was hampered by several factors, including resistance from government officials and parts of the public, the difficulty of devising new systems for pupil assignment, and persistent racial separation in residential neighborhoods.

Separate But Unequal

The Supreme Court in *PLESSY V. FERGUSON* (1896) ruled that separate public facilities for blacks and whites did not violate the equal protection clause. In that ruling the Court pointed approvingly to the system of separate schools for blacks and white as "the most common instance" of segregation. The Court decided three cases involving segregated schools over the next three decades, but it never directly ruled on the question of whether state-required segregation denied black children equal protection of the laws.

In the 1930s the National Association for the Advancement of Colored People (NAACP) decided to try to overturn school segregation by demonstrating inequalities between schools for blacks and those for whites that contradicted the Court's stated "separate but equal" doctrine. The strategy succeeded in four cases decided by the Court between 1938 and 1950.

In *Missouri ex rel. Gaines v. Canada* (1938) the Court required the admission of a qualified black undergraduate to Missouri's single, all-white law school. It found that the state's offer to pay his tuition to a school in another state was inadequate. In 1948 the Court issued a similar ruling in a case from Oklahoma.

Texas had responded to a similar case by creating a separate law school for blacks. But in *Sweatt v. Painter* (1950) the Court found that the new school was inferior to the all-white school. On that basis the Court ruled unanimously that the state was not providing "substantial equality in . . . educational opportunities" to whites and blacks.

On the same day the Court ruled unanimously that a black graduate student at the University of Oklahoma had been denied equal protection when he was separated from the rest of the student body by being assigned a special seat in the classroom and special tables in the library and cafeteria *(McLaurin v. Oklahoma State Regents for Higher Education)*. The decision foreshadowed the Court's conclusion four years later in *Brown* that separate educational facilities were "inherently unequal."

Reaction and Resistance

The Court tried to minimize opposition to its decision to outlaw racial segregation in public elementary and secondary schools. Despite the low-key opinion written by Chief Justice Earl Warren in *Brown (I)* and the Court's acceptance of gradual compliance in *Brown (II)*, however, fierce opposition arose in the South. Beginning in late 1955, government officials and citizen groups in many states engaged in a campaign of "massive resistance" to the decision.

The Court first addressed the problem of massive resistance in *Cooper v. Aaron* (1958). The Court refused the plea by the Little Rock, Arkansas, school board to postpone further desegregation in the face of the official and public hostility that had accompanied the integration of the city's Central High.

"Constitutional rights . . . are not to be sacrificed or yielded to the violence and disorder which have followed upon the actions of the Governor and the Legislature," the Court declared. The decision did not end the official defiance, however. Governor Orval Faubus closed the city's high schools for a year rather than comply.

In other states school officials devised a variety of "freedom of choice" plans for pupil assignment to avoid desegregation. In 1963 the Court rejected one of these: a Knoxville, Tennessee, plan that allowed

students assigned to schools where they were in the minority to transfer to schools where their race was in the majority.

Over the next five years the Court expressed greater impatience with the resistance to desegregation. Then, in May 1968, the Court unanimously declared that still segregated school systems must devise desegregation plans that promised to be effective. Rejecting a freedom of choice plan that had resulted in just 15 percent of a county's black pupils attending integrated schools, the Court said that school boards must "come forward with a plan that promises realistically to work, and promises realistically to work now."

Fashioning the Remedy

The Court's insistence on desegregation plans that produced demonstrable results brought two questions to the fore: Must individual schools reflect the overall racial balance in the community rather than the population mix in their immediate neighborhood? If so, must pupils be transported—that is, bused—beyond their normal geographic zones to achieve some sort of racial balance?

In 1971 the Court held that school officials could adopt—and federal courts could order—plans that included BUSING, racial balance quotas, and gerrymandered districts as interim methods of eliminating school segregation. The Court's decision in *Swann v. Charlotte-Mecklenburg County Board of Education* was unanimous, and the opinion was written by the new chief justice, Warren E. Burger.

Over the next few years the Court's unanimity in school desegregation cases broke down as it ruled on cases involving so-called de facto segregation in northern and western cities and busing between cities and suburbs in different school districts. (See DE FACTO, DE JURE.) The two most important decisions were setbacks for those who favored strong measures to achieve school integration.

In *Milliken v. Bradley* (1974) the Court overturned, 5–4, a district court plan to desegregate schools in Detroit by busing students between school districts in three counties. In *Pasadena City Board of Education v. Spangler* (1976) the Court ruled, 6–2, that school districts were not required to maintain a specific racial balance if shifting residential patterns resulted in "re-segregation" once a desegregation plan had been implemented.

The Court did approve one new legal weapon against segregated schools. In *Runyon v. McCrary* (1976) the Court barred racially discriminatory admissions policies in private schools. The 7–2 decision was based on the 1866 Civil Rights Act, which gave "all persons . . . the same right . . . to make and enforce contracts . . . as is enjoyed by white citizens."

The Role of the Lower Courts

The Supreme Court largely avoided school desegregation issues in the 1980s, leaving it to lower courts to supervise and monitor the continuing litigation within its guidelines. Then, between 1990 and 1992, it handed down three decisions that defined the courts' role in school desegregation cases.

In *Missouri v. Jenkins* (1990) the Court ruled that federal district courts can order local officials to raise taxes to correct constitutional violations, such as school segregation. The 5–4 decision essentially upheld a judge's ruling to double the local property tax in Kansas City, Missouri. The tax increase was intended to pay for an ambitious school desegregation plan based largely on compensatory and remedial education programs in inner-city schools. (See COURTS, POWERS OF.)

The Court in its next two decisions more narrowly defined the role of the lower courts. In *Board of Education of Oklahoma City Public Schools v. Dowell* (1991) the Court ruled, 5–3, that formerly segregated school districts may be freed of school busing orders if they can prove that any elements of past discrimination have been removed to all "practicable extent." In *Freeman v. Pitts* (1992) the Court said that lower courts had discretion to withdraw supervision of some aspects of a desegregation plan—including pupil assignments—even if desegregation had not been achieved in other areas, such as faculty assignments or school spending.

Later in 1992 the Court returned to the issue of segregation in higher education for the first time since *Brown*. In *United States v. Fordice* the Court said the state of Mississippi had to take more active steps to

integrate its state university system. In a concurring opinion—his first in a school desegregation case—Justice Clarence Thomas said that the ruling should not be construed to mean that states cannot maintain "historically black institutions—open to all on a race-neutral basis, but with established traditions and programs that might disproportionately appeal to one race or another."

School Prayer

Before the 1960s it was a common practice to conduct prayer or Bible readings as devotional exercises in public schools. In the early 1960s the Supreme Court ruled that such activities violated the First Amendment principle of separation of church and state. The rulings were very controversial, and prolonged efforts were made to pass constitutional amendments to overrule them. Despite the controversy the Court has reaffirmed the rulings—most recently, with its 1992 decision barring prayers at high school graduation ceremonies. (See RELIGION, FREEDOM OF.)

The first two Supreme Court rulings concerning religious exercises in public schools involved "released time" programs—programs that released students from regular classwork, usually once a week, to receive religious instruction. The Court in 1948 struck down, by an 8–1 vote, a program in which religion teachers came into the public schools to provide religious instruction to volunteer participants. But four years later it voted 6–3 to uphold a released time program in which the instruction was provided to students during class hours but outside the school.

The school prayer issue reached the Court a decade later. The New York Board of Regents recommended to school districts that they adopt a twenty-two-word, nondenominational prayer to be repeated voluntarily by students at the beginning of each school day. Parents of ten pupils in the New Hyde Park school district challenged the use of the prayer as contrary to their religious beliefs and a violation of the establishment clause.

In *Engel v. Vitale* (1962) the Supreme Court agreed, 6–1, that the prayer violated the establishment clause. "It is no part of the business of government to compose official prayers for any group of the American people to recite as a part of a religious program carried on by government," Justice Hugo L. Black wrote. The option for students to remain silent or leave the room was immaterial, Black said, because the government's support for the prayer necessarily produced an "indirect coercive effect upon religious minorities."

A year later the Court ruled, by a vote of 8 to 1, that prescribed daily Bible reading in the public schools violated the establishment clause. The ruling came in companion cases in which Unitarian parents challenged a Pennsylvania law requiring the reading of ten Bible verses a day *(Abington School District v. Schempp)* and a Baltimore woman challenged a city rule requiring Bible readings or recitation of the Lord's Prayer *(Murray v. Curlett)*.

In his opinion for the Court, Justice Tom C. Clark crafted a more precise test for establishment clause cases than had been laid down in earlier rulings. State programs touching upon religion or religious institutions, he wrote, must have "a secular legislative purpose and a primary effect that neither advances nor inhibits religion." In *Lemon v. Kurtzman* (1971) the Court added a third element to this test: the program must not result in excessive government entanglement with religion.

Justice Potter Stewart was the lone dissenter in the school prayer and Bible-reading cases. In the New York case he argued that the Board of Regents' prayer could not be viewed as an effort to establish a government religion. In the Bible-reading cases, he argued that pupils were not forced to participate. He also contended that banning the exercises infringed on the rights of the majority under the other religion clause of the First Amendment, which guarantees the free exercise of religion.

Despite the Court's near unanimity, there was strong public opposition to both decisions. Constitutional amendments to permit voluntary prayer in the schools were introduced in Congress repeatedly over the next two decades. In three floor votes—in the Senate in 1966 and 1984 and the House in 1971—amendments gained majorities but fell short of the two-thirds vote needed to submit the proposals to the states for ratification.

Meanwhile, advocates of school prayer had come up with an alternative plan: so-called "moment of silence" laws. Twenty-three states passed such laws, which generally directed teachers to set aside a moment during each school day for students to engage in quiet meditative activity.

The issue reached the Court in a challenge to Alabama's law, which specifically provided that the moment of silence was for "meditation or voluntary prayer." In *Wallace v. Jaffree* (1985) the Court ruled, 6–3, that the law was in fact meant to promote religion and therefore violated the establishment clause of the Constitution.

Two concurring justices, Lewis F. Powell, Jr., and Sandra Day O'Connor, suggested that some moment of silence laws might be valid, but not one that was so clearly a subterfuge for returning prescribed prayer to the public schools. When the Court heard a challenge to a more neutrally framed New Jersey law two years later, it resolved the case on a different issue, leaving the matter unsettled.

The Reagan administration had urged the Court to uphold the moment-of-silence law. The Bush administration followed suit by urging the Court to soften the *Lemon* test. The plea came in a case in which two lower federal courts had found prayers at public high school graduation ceremonies to be violations of the establishment clause.

In *Lee v. Weisman* (1992) the Court voted 5–4 to reaffirm its previous rulings. "The Constitution forbids the State to exact religious conformity from a student as the price of attending her own high school graduation," Justice Anthony M. Kennedy wrote for the majority. In a bitter dissent Justice Antonin Scalia said that the ruling "lays waste a tradition that is as old as public-school graduation ceremonies themselves."

The Court has upheld another approach to the issue of religion in schools: an act of Congress requiring that student religious groups be allowed to meet in public high schools on the same basis as other extracurricular clubs. In *Board of Education of the Westside Community Schools (Dist. 66) v. Mergens* (1990) the Court ruled, 8–1, that the "equal access" statute did not breach the Constitution's required separation of church and state.

Scottsboro Cases

Nine young illiterate black men, aged thirteen to twenty-one, were charged in 1931 with the rape of two white women on a freight train passing through Tennessee and Alabama. Eight of them were convicted and sentenced to death after a one-day trial held in Scottsboro, Alabama. Two Supreme Court rulings in 1932 and 1935, called the *Scottsboro Cases*, resulted from challenges growing out of the case. The rulings were the first step in the creation of a constitutional right to counsel in state criminal cases and a constitutional rule against racial discrimination in the selection of juries. (See COUNSEL, RIGHT TO LEGAL; JURIES.)

Community hostility to the defendants was intense. The trial judge had appointed all the members of the local bar to serve as defense counsel, but the local lawyer who finally agreed to represent them undertook the task with reluctance and conducted only a pro forma defense. The defendants challenged their convictions, claiming that they had effectively been denied the assistance of counsel because they did not have the chance to consult with their lawyer or prepare a defense.

The Supreme Court agreed in a 7–2 decision, *Powell v. Alabama* (1932). Writing for the Court, Chief Justice Charles Evans Hughes cited all the adverse circumstances of the defendants: their youth, illiteracy, presence in a hostile community, and distance from their homes. He concluded that the judge's refusal to give them "reasonable time and opportunity to secure counsel" constituted a violation of the DUE PROCESS clause of the Fourteenth Amendment.

Hughes limited the ruling to capital cases, saying it was unnecessary to decide whether denial of counsel in other criminal prosecutions would also be a due process violation.

The nine "Scottsboro boys" confer with their lawyer, Samuel Leibowitz, who represented them after eight were convicted of rape and sentenced to death. Source: Brown Brothers, Sterling, Pa.

On retrial one of the defendants, Clarence Norris, moved to quash the INDICTMENT and the pool of potential trial jurors, on the ground that qualified blacks had been systematically excluded. The judge denied the motion. Norris was convicted again and then challenged the second conviction as a violation of his right to EQUAL PROTECTION of the laws under the Fourteenth Amendment.

In *Norris v. Alabama* (1935) the Court unanimously agreed. Once again, Chief Justice Hughes wrote the opinion. The Court's duty, he said, was "to inquire not merely whether [the equal protection guarantee] was denied in express terms but also whether it was denied in substance and effect." Pointing out that no black had served on a jury in that county within the memory of any person living, Hughes found the evidence sufficient basis for reversing Norris's conviction.

In further proceedings between 1935 and 1937,

four of the defendants were convicted again and given prison sentences. Charges were dropped against the other five.

Scott v. Sandford

Dred Scott was a Missouri slave whose effort to secure his freedom led to a Supreme Court decision, *Scott v. Sandford* (1857), which denied Congress the power to ban slavery in the territories and barred blacks from citizenship. The ruling hastened the onset of the Civil War. It was overturned by the Fourteenth Amendment after the war's end. (See REVERSALS OF RULINGS BY CONSTITUTIONAL AMENDMENT; SLAVERY AND THE COURT.)

Scott was owned by an army surgeon, Dr. John Emerson of St. Louis. He accompanied Emerson on postings to Illinois and the Wisconsin Territory between 1834 and 1838. Illinois was a free state, and slavery was prohibited in the Wisconsin Territory under the Missouri Compromise of 1820.

Some time after returning to St. Louis in 1838, Emerson died. In the mid-1840s, Emerson's widow moved to New York and left Scott in the care of Henry Blow, a member of the family that had originally owned Scott. Blow opposed the extension of slavery and lent financial support to Scott to test whether his residence on free soil in Illinois and the Wisconsin Territory made him a free man.

A lower state court found in Scott's favor, but in 1852 the Missouri supreme court reversed the decision and held that under Missouri law Scott remained a slave. Mrs. Emerson then aided Scott in a new bid for freedom by arranging for his sale to her brother, John A. Sanford.

Scott filed a new suit in federal circuit court in Missouri against Sanford (whose name was misspelled in court records). But the circuit court ruled that Scott was not a citizen and had no right to bring suit in federal court. Scott appealed to the Supreme Court.

The Court delayed its decision until after the 1856 election. When it did rule, the decision went against Scott. In the opinion considered as presenting the formal view of the Court, Chief Justice Roger B. Taney

Dred Scott.   *Source: Library of Congress*

Harriet Scott.   *Source: Library of Congress*

agreed that Scott could not bring suit because slaves and their descendants "are not included, and were not intended to be included, under the word 'citizens' in the Constitution."

Chief Justice Taney went on to declare that Congress had no power to prohibit slavery in territories added after the adoption of the Constitution. So Scott had not become a free man by his residence in the Wisconsin Territory. Nor was Scott free because of his residence in Illinois. Scott was a slave in Illinois, Taney said, and his status in Missouri depended on its laws rather than those of Illinois.

The opinion was strongly criticized in the North on legal and political grounds. It fueled sectional animosity, aggravated the split between northern and southern Democrats, and contributed to the election of Republican Abraham Lincoln as president in 1860. (See ELECTIONS AND THE COURT.)

The post-Civil War Fourteenth Amendment expressly provided that "all persons born or naturalized in the United States . . . are citizens of the United States and of the State wherein they reside."

Scott himself gained his freedom following Sanford's death later in 1857. But he lived as a free man only sixteen months before dying of tuberculosis.

Seal of the Court

The seal of the Supreme Court, like the seals of the president, vice president, and Department of State, derives from the Great Seal of the United States. Designed by Charles Thomson and adopted by Congress in June 1782, the Great Seal features a bald eagle holding a striped shield and clutching an olive branch and arrows in its talons. A banner reading "E Pluribus Unum" (Out of Many, One) is unfurled above its wings.

The first seal of the Supreme Court was commissioned February 3, 1790, with the command that it "shall be the Arms of the United States, engraved on a circular piece of Steel the Size of a Dollar, with these words in the margin—'The Seal of the Supreme Court of the United States'." This seal was last used in

The first seal of the Court.
Source: Collection of the Supreme Court of the United States

The Court's current seal.
Source: Collection of the Supreme Court of the United States

August 1831 in the papers for *Saml. Worcester v. The State of Georgia.* After four successive alterations, the seal has evolved into a larger, less ornate version, designed in 1905 and used today. The clerk of the Court stamps this seal on all official Court documents.

Search and Seizure

The Fourth Amendment provides that the "right of the people to be secure in their persons, houses, papers, and effects, against unreasonable searches and seizures shall not be violated." It strengthens this protection by stating that "no Warrants shall issue, but upon probable cause, supported by Oath or affirmation, and particularly describing the place to be searched, and the persons or things to be seized."

The Supreme Court's earliest interpretations of the Fourth Amendment came in the late nineteenth and early twentieth centuries. The rulings restricted law enforcement practices in federal cases, and they aroused little controversy. An example is the 1914 decision establishing the EXCLUSIONARY RULE to bar the use of illegally obtained evidence in federal trials.

The Warren Court's decision in 1961 to enforce the exclusionary rule on the states, however, began a period of severe criticism of the Court's rulings on search and seizure from police, prosecutors, and others. The Burger and Rehnquist courts have eased the restrictions on police by limiting the application of the exclusionary rule outside criminal trials and adopting a more tolerant view of police conduct in individual cases.

The Warrant Requirement

The Supreme Court has always viewed the warrant requirement as central to fulfilling the Fourth Amendment. As the Court said in 1967, a search of private property is deemed unreasonable without a valid search warrant except in cases of consent or in certain limited circumstances.

The "particularity" requirement means that a warrant must be sufficiently specific to remove the element of discretion from whoever executes it. The PROBABLE CAUSE requirement means that police must have more than suspicion to justify the search. And the warrant must be issued by what the Court described in 1948 as "a neutral and detached magistrate."

Construing that last requirement, the Court in 1971 forbade the use of evidence obtained in a police search based on a warrant issued by a state official who was also the chief investigator and prosecutor in the case. In 1972, however, the Court upheld the authority of a municipal court clerk to issue search warrants in cases involving municipal laws.

In the 1960s the Warren Court sought to ensure that magistrates had something other than a police officer's tip from an unnamed informant before issuing a search warrant. In *Aguilar v. Texas* (1964) and *Spinelli v. United States* (1969) the Court required that police give the magistrate specific information and an independent basis for judging the reliability of the information. In *Illinois v. Gates* (1983), however, the Court dropped that test and returned to what it called "the totality of circumstances analysis that traditionally had informed probable cause determinations."

A warrant is unnecessary if the individual who owns or occupies the place to be searched consents to the search. The consent must be voluntary, but the Court in 1973 held, by a vote of 6 to 3, that individuals who are asked to consent need not be informed of their right to refuse *(Schneckloth v. Bustamonte)*. The Court has upheld police searches even when someone other than the target of the search consented. In 1990, for example, the Court found no Fourth Amendment violation when police searched a house with the consent of someone who appeared to live in the house but who in fact had moved out.

Searching for Evidence

In two of its earliest rulings on the Fourth Amendment, the Court limited what investigators could seize in a search. One of the rulings has since been explicitly overturned, the other substantially weakened.

In *Boyd v. United States* (1886) the Court held that the Fourth Amendment forbade searches or subpoenas for private business papers if the search or subpoena forced a person to produce self-incriminating evidence. In *Gouled v. United States* (1921) the Court set out the rule that government officials, even with a search warrant, could not seize "mere evidence" but only "instrumentalities" of crime or fruits of crime. Both cases reflected the Court's sensitivity to property rights during that era.

The Court abandoned the "mere evidence" rule in 1967, while it was expanding Fourth Amendment protection in other contexts. Writing for the Court in *Warden v. Hayden,* Justice William J. Brennan, Jr., said that the rule had proved to be confusing since the distinction between evidence and instrumentalities of crime was hard to draw. More broadly, Brennan said that the Fourth Amendment protected privacy, not property, and nothing in the amendment indicated that items seized as evidence were "more private than property seized . . . as an instrumentality."

The abolition of the "mere evidence" rule curtailed Fourth Amendment protection for private papers, as can be seen in two later decisions. In *United States v. Miller* (1976) the Court ruled that a depositor's bank records were not private papers protected by the amendment. And in *Andresen v. Maryland* (1976) the Court undercut *Boyd* to allow use of an attorney's business records as evidence against him.

The Court has also found no Fourth Amendment bar to the use of such evidence as voice samples and handwriting examples obtained from suspects. Before the Fourth Amendment was extended to the states, the Court did find a due process violation in the use of a stomach pump to obtain evidence of narcotics possession. But lesser intrusions have been upheld. In *Schmerber v. California* (1966) the Court upheld the

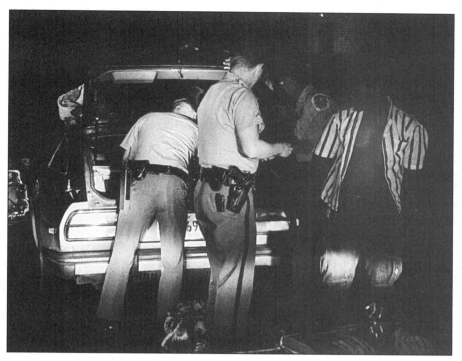

Since 1925 the Court has made numerous decisions dealing with searches of automobiles, their occupants, and even closed packages found in a car. In general, the Court has decided that people and their paraphernalia are entitled to less privacy in cars than in their homes or places of business.
Source: R. Michael Jenkins

taking of blood samples from a suspect to obtain evidence. In two other cases, *Skinner v. Railway Labor Executives' Association* and *National Treasury Employees Union v. Von Raab* (both 1989), the Court upheld mandatory drug testing for transportation workers and federal law enforcement officers. The Court agreed that the collection of urine samples was a "search" under the Fourth Amendment, but it found the practice reasonable because of the government's interests in protecting passenger safety and ensuring the integrity of officers involved in drug enforcement.

Arrests and Searches

The Supreme Court has recognized two main exceptions to the warrant requirement: searches incident to a lawful arrest and searches of a moving vehicle. The Court's rulings in both areas have often been confusing.

Searches Incident to Arrest

As early as 1914 the Court recognized the right of police during a lawful arrest to conduct a warrantless search of the suspect and the place where the suspect was arrested, searching for weapons as well as contraband or instruments of crime. In 1947 the Court construed this authority broadly in permitting use of evidence found during a warrantless five-hour search of a suspect's apartment after his arrest.

In two cases in 1948 the Court described the search incident to an arrest as "a limited right" and appeared to say that officers must obtain a search warrant if "practicable" except in cases of "exigent circumstances." In 1950 the Court backed away from that requirement, instead holding that the reasonableness of a search incident to arrest depended on "the total atmosphere of the case."

In *Chimel v. California* (1969) the Court tried to craft a clearer rule. The Court stated that searches incident to arrest were reasonable only if limited to the person arrested and the area immediately under his or her control. Under that doctrine the Court in 1970 and 1971 found that police had exceeded their authority in conducting a warrantless search of a suspect's house after his arrest on the street and in searching a suspect's car after arresting him in his house. In 1978 the Court refused a plea to create a "homicide scene" exception to uphold a warrantless search of an entire apartment that took place over several days.

In 1973 the Court upheld police authority to search motorists who had been stopped for automobile or traffic violations—even if the offenses would ordinarily have resulted in citations rather than arrests. In 1977 it broadened the authority to search for weapons as part of a "stop and frisk" detention. (See ARRESTS.) A ruling in 1983 upheld police authority to inventory a suspect's possessions once he or she is brought into custody. And in 1990 the Court said that without a search warrant police may still make a "protective sweep" of a house after making an in-home arrest, if they have a "reasonable, articulable suspicion" that someone dangerous is in the house.

Automobile Searches

The Supreme Court since 1925 has allowed some warrantless searches of moving vehicles, especially automobiles. Generally, such searches are permissible if police have probable cause to believe the cars are involved in illegal activity or if police are inventorying the contents of the car after a valid arrest.

The rationale the Court gave for the automobile exception in its landmark case, *Carroll v. United States* (1925), was the vehicle's mobility. Half a century later the Court in *United States v. Chadwick* (1977) gave a different reason: "a diminished expectation of privacy." This second rationale helps explain decisions earlier in the 1970s that allowed police to search an automobile that had been towed to a police garage after an arrest or refused to exclude evidence that had been found in routine "inventory" searches of impounded cars.

Since *Chadwick* the Court has steadily enlarged the automobile exception. In 1978 it ruled that passengers in a car could not object to the warrantless search of the vehicle they were riding in. In 1982 the Court found that police who had probable cause to search a car could also search closed containers or packages, such as a briefcase, found within the car—reversing a decision handed down just one year earlier. In *California v. Avecedo* (1991) the Court supported police discretion in the opposite situation, upholding a search of an entire car when police had probable cause only to search a container found in the vehicle.

Second Amendment

See ARMS, RIGHT TO BEAR.

Sedition Laws

Sedition consists of offenses against the authority of the government that do not amount to treason. In the early twentieth century the federal government and thirty-three states passed laws prohibiting sedition or two related political offenses: criminal anarchy (the teaching that government should be overthrown by force or violence) and criminal syndicalism (the doctrine of bringing about political change or a change in industrial ownership through the commission of a crime, sabotage, or other unlawful act). The Supreme Court upheld these laws in several early First Amendment challenges. In 1969, however, the Court ruled that political advocacy could be punished only if it amounted to actual incitement to use force. (See SPEECH, FREEDOM OF.)

Federal Law

The first sedition act was passed by the Federalist-dominated Congress in 1798. The act set stiff penalties for false, scandalous, or malicious writings about the president, Congress, or the government. Republicans charged that the law abridged freedom of speech and the press. Despite twenty-five arrests and ten convictions under the law, no challenge to the act reached the Supreme Court before the Republicans gained power and allowed it to expire.

During World War I, Congress passed two laws, the Espionage Act of 1917 and the Sedition Act of 1918, making it a crime to engage in various activities that would hamper the war effort: to make a false statement with the intent to interfere with the armed forces or obstruct recruiting, to obstruct the sale of war bonds, or to say or write anything to cause con-

Socialist leader Eugene V. Debs was convicted for inciting insubordination, disloyalty, and mutiny in the armed forces, and for obstructing military recruitment when he told his listeners, "You need to know that you are fit for something better than slavery and cannon fodder." The Supreme Court upheld his conviction in Debs v. United States *(1919).*   Source: New York University, Tamiment Institute Library

1918. The other two cases involved articles published in German-language newspapers, which the government viewed as encouraging disloyalty in the armed forces or obstructing recruitment.

The Court's decisions affirming the convictions created the "clear and present danger" doctrine. The doctrine allowed the government to restrict free speech if the words in question raised a clear and present danger of bringing about evils that Congress had the authority to prevent.

The Sedition Act was repealed in 1921. The Espionage Act stayed on the books, but the Court's only wartime decision reviewing a conviction under the law, in 1944, applied the clear and present danger test to find the evidence in the case insufficient to sustain the conviction.

State Laws

State laws punishing sedition, criminal anarchy, or criminal syndicalism dated from the assassination of President William McKinley in 1901 by a professed anarchist. They increased in number during the conflict between industry and labor in the early decades of the twentieth century. The Court initially sustained these laws, but in two cases in 1937 it found such measures overly broad and reversed convictions obtained under them.

The first of the state cases to reach the Court, *Gitlow v. United States* (1925), involved a Socialist party member. The person had been convicted under New York's criminal anarchy law for distributing a pamphlet calling for the overthrow of the government through "class action of the proletariat in any form." The Court applied a less stringent test than the clear and present danger doctrine: the so-called bad tendency test. Convictions for political advocacy could be upheld, the Court said, if the activities tended to have the effect of inciting the overthrow of the government, even if they did not actually produce a clear danger of such overthrow.

Two years later, in *Whitney v. California* (1927), the Court sustained the conviction of a member of the California branch of the Communist Labor party based on a resolution urging revolutionary class struggle to overthrow capitalism. Although the defendant

tempt or scorn for the United States, the flag, or the uniform of the armed forces. In 1919 and 1920 the Court in six cases affirmed convictions under the laws for various antiwar activities.

The first of the cases, *Schenck v. United States* (1919), involved the distribution by members of the Socialist party of a pamphlet opposing the recently passed selective service law. *Debs v. United States* (1919) involved an antirecruitment speech given by Socialist leader Eugene V. Debs. *Pierce v. United States* (1920) arose from an antirecruitment pamphlet distributed by Socialist party members. *Abrams v. United States* (1919) involved five Russian-born immigrants who criticized the U.S. government for sending troops into Russia in

had advocated a resolution urging political change through the ballot, he had remained in the party after the class struggle resolution was adopted.

Two justices, Oliver Wendell Holmes, Jr., and Louis D. Brandeis, dissented in several of the cases, including *Abrams* and *Gitlow*. They concurred in *Whitney* only on procedural grounds. In eloquent opinions in these cases, Holmes and Brandeis unsuccessfully urged broader protection for political advocacy by strictly applying the clear and present danger doctrine that Holmes had authored in *Schenck*.

The Court in 1937 handed down two decisions narrowing state sedition laws. In *DeJonge v. Oregon* the Court unanimously reversed a conviction under an Oregon law that had been construed to prohibit holding a public meeting under Communist party auspices. (See ASSEMBLY, FREEDOM OF.) In *Herndon v. Lowry* the Court abandoned the bad tendency test in favor of something like the clear and present danger test. The 5–4 decision reversed the conviction of a Communist party organizer under a Georgia law prohibiting any attempt to persuade someone to participate in an insurrection against the government.

State criminal syndicalism laws reemerged in the 1960s as states tried to restrain activists in the civil rights and antiwar causes. In 1969 the Court cast doubt on the continuing validity of such laws. *Brandenburg v. Ohio* involved a Ku Klux Klan leader who warned a rally that "there might have to be some revengance [*sic*] taken" if the government "continued to suppress the white race." In reversing the conviction, the Court set out what has come to be known as the "incitement" test. This standard distinguishes between advocacy of the use of force as an abstract doctrine, which is protected by the First Amendment, and actual incitement to use force, which is not protected.

Segregation

Segregation is the practice of racial separation. It was established by law or custom in much of the United States, most extensively in the South, from the era of slavery through the mid-twentieth century.

The Supreme Court, in the decades after the Civil War, helped create the climate that allowed segregation to flourish. Then, beginning in the 1950s, it played the lead role in dismantling the system of legally mandated segregation. Despite the Court's rulings and the enactment of federal, state, and local CIVIL RIGHTS laws, however, racial separation has persisted in the United States, particularly in residential neighborhoods and public elementary and secondary schools.

Post-Civil War Era

Segregation has existed all over the country, and it predated the Civil War. The Massachusetts supreme court in 1850 upheld Boston's system of segregated public schools. Congress mandated separate schools for blacks and whites in the District of Columbia during the Civil War. But segregation took root most strongly in the South after the end of Reconstruction. Southern states enacted a host of so-called Jim Crow laws that resulted in almost complete social, legal, and political segregation of whites and blacks.

In two important rulings the Supreme Court gave its approval to the practice.

In *The Civil Rights Cases* (1883) the Court, by a vote of 8 to 1, nullified an 1875 federal law that gave all persons, regardless of color, "the full and equal enjoyment" of public transportation, inns, theaters, and "other places of public amusement." (See PUBLIC ACCOMMODATIONS.) The Court held that the Fourteenth Amendment prohibited state-imposed DISCRIMINATION but did not apply to private discrimination or give Congress the power to pass laws reaching private conduct. (See CIVIL WAR AMENDMENTS.)

Thirteen years later the Court sanctioned the "separate but equal" doctrine developed to justify state-imposed racial segregation. In *PLESSY V. FERGUSON* (1896) the Court held, 8–1, that as long as the facilities provided to blacks were equal to those for whites, state laws requiring segregation did not violate the EQUAL PROTECTION or DUE PROCESS clauses of the Fourteenth Amendment. Nor did the Court view separation of the races as pinning on blacks a badge of slavery in violation of the Thirteenth Amendment.

The Little Rock Nine display their diplomas from Central High School in Little Rock, Arkansas. After Gov. Orval Faubus refused to allow these students to enroll, President Dwight Eisenhower enforced the Court's Brown *decision and sent federal troops to protect them as they entered the school.*   Source: Arkansas Gazette

Brown and After

Over the next sixty years the Court weakened the "separate but equal" doctrine but never directly questioned it. In 1914 the Court struck down an Oklahoma law because it did not provide blacks with the same train accommodations that whites had. In 1917 the Court struck down, on the basis of PROPERTY RIGHTS, a Louisville, Kentucky, ordinance that prohibited blacks from living on the same streets as whites. (See OPEN HOUSING.) In 1938 and 1948 it required Missouri and Oklahoma to admit blacks to the states' all-white law schools. In 1950 the Court rejected Texas's decision to create a separate law school for blacks, saying that the school did not provide blacks "substantial equality in . . . educational opportunities."

Four years later, in BROWN V. BOARD OF EDUCA-TION OF TOPEKA (1954), the Court unanimously declared that separation of the races in public schools was "inherently unequal." A year later, however, the Court softened the impact of the ruling by directing school officials to desegregate not immediately but with "all deliberate speed."

Many states began to comply with the Court's ruling, but others advocated "massive resistance" to the decision. Over the next decade, state and local officials devised a variety of "freedom of choice" plans that effectively preserved schools as racially separate. During this same decade, however, the Court cited *Brown* as precedent for rulings striking down other forms of segregation throughout the South, in parks and beaches, traffic courts and theaters, railroad cars and bus terminals.

Meanwhile, a growing civil rights movement was

engaging in boycotts, "sit-ins," "freedom rides," and other demonstrations to protest racial segregation and discrimination. In response, Congress in 1964 approved the most comprehensive civil rights act since Reconstruction. It barred discrimination in most public accommodations, prohibited JOB DISCRIMINATION on the basis of race, and established a procedure for withholding federal funds from any program, including schools, that continued to discriminate against blacks.

Four years later the Court strengthened the legal weapons against segregation in education and housing. It declared that state and local school officials had a duty to take affirmative steps to ensure effective SCHOOL DESEGREGATION. In another case, it reinterpreted an 1866 civil rights law as barring discrimination against blacks in the sale or rental of housing. The decision came just weeks after Congress had acted on the issue by approving a federal fair housing law.

With racial discrimination now clearly defined as illegal, the Court had the task of defining the scope of remedies available to victims of discrimination. The Burger Court approved a wide variety of measures to remedy school segregation, including BUSING, gerrymandered attendance zones, limited use of mathematical ratios, and compensatory education programs. The Court also extended the obligation to desegregate to nonsouthern school districts where existing segregation had been imposed not by law but by school board policy. In one major housing case the Court upheld an order to city and suburban officials to adopt an areawide plan to remedy segregation in public housing.

Integration, as distinct from desegregation, remained an elusive goal. The existence of racially separate neighborhoods slowed desegregation or contributed to "resegregation" of some school systems. But the Court said in 1977 that it would not strike down local ZONING plans that contributed to racial segregation unless there was proof of discriminatory intent. In two rulings in 1991 and 1992, the Court said that school districts could be freed from desegregation decrees once the effects of past discrimination had been eliminated.

Selective Service Rulings

The federal government first conscripted men into the army during the Civil War. Its authority to raise armies through a compulsory draft was not tested in the federal courts until after Congress during World War I adopted the Selective Service Act of 1917. The law was challenged on several grounds, including the charge that it violated the Thirteenth Amendment prohibition against involuntary servitude.

In 1918 the Supreme Court unanimously upheld the law in a series of cases known collectively as the *Selective Draft Law Cases.* Writing for the Court, Chief Justice Edward D. White said that the authority to institute a compulsory draft derived from the express war powers and the necessary and proper clause, strengthened by historical practice. He said the Thirteenth Amendment was intended to cover kinds of compulsory labor similar to slavery and not those "duties which individuals owe to the States, such as service in the army, militia, on the jury, etc."

Congress instituted the nation's first peacetime draft in 1940 as the country braced for possible entry into World War II. After the war ended, Congress in 1948 renewed the peacetime draft by passing the Universal Military Service and Training Act. The act provided authority for conscription for the Korean and Vietnam wars. The draft ended in 1975, after the end of the Vietnam War, and the nation returned to an all-volunteer army.

The Supreme Court has never ruled on the constitutionality of a peacetime draft. Lower federal courts, however, have upheld the draft in the absence of a declared war.

In 1980 Congress reinstituted peacetime draft registration, but not classification or conscription. President Jimmy Carter requested the action following the Soviet Union's invasion of Afghanistan.

Several men challenged Congress's decision to require registration of men but not women, claiming that the policy was unconstitutional SEX DISCRIMINATION. But the Supreme Court in *Rostker v. Goldberg* (1981) upheld the exclusion of women in a 6–3 decision. The Court held that because women were barred by law and policy from combat, they were "not similarly situated" with men for the purposes of draft registration.

Self-incrimination

The Fifth Amendment privilege against self-incrimination is stated clearly: no one "shall be compelled in any criminal case to be a witness against himself." But the Supreme Court has not construed this right literally. The Court has extended the privilege beyond the courtroom, most notably in the decisions, such as *MIRANDA V. ARIZONA* (1966), limiting police interrogation practices. (See CONFESSIONS.) The Court has also restricted the application of the privilege, however, by upholding immunity statutes that compel a witness to testify as long as the testimony itself cannot be the basis of a later criminal prosecution.

The Court's first major ruling interpreting the privilege prevented the government from requiring someone to turn over business records *(Boyd v. United States* [1886]). In *Counselman v. Hitchcock* (1892) the Court again gave the privilege a broad meaning by granting grand jury witnesses the right to refuse to answer incriminating questions. The Court extended the privilege to civil cases in 1924 and to legislative investigations in the 1950s.

Other rulings limited the Fifth Amendment protections. Twice, in 1908 and 1947, the Court refused to extend the privilege to state defendants. In both cases the Court permitted state officials to draw unfavorable inferences from a defendant's failure to testify in his own behalf. In addition, the Court in several cases held that the Fifth Amendment did not protect an individual from a state's use of testimony compelled by federal authority or from federal use of testimony compelled by state authority. The rulings were based on the "two sovereignties" doctrine.

The Court shifted its position in 1964. In *Malloy v. Hogan* it applied the privilege against self-incrimination to the states, overturning a contempt citation against a convicted gambler who had refused to testify before a state grand jury. On the same day the Court abolished the two sovereignties doctrine. In *Griffin v. California* (1965) it barred prosecutors from commenting on a defendant's silence or judges from instructing jurors that silence could be taken as evidence of guilt. In 1966 *Miranda* set out detailed guidelines for questioning of suspects in police stationhouses in order to protect the suspects' Fifth Amendment rights.

The Court extended the privilege against self-incrimination in other areas. Beginning with its decision in the Communist party registration case of *Albertson v. Subversive Activities Control Board* (1965), it struck down federal statutes requiring individuals to provide potentially incriminating information about group memberships, drug or firearms transactions, or gambling income.

In 1972 the Court significantly limited the privilege by upholding a new federal statute that gave only limited immunity from prosecution to someone compelled to testify before a court or grand jury.

Federal immunity statutes on the books since the mid-nineteenth century established procedures for requiring someone to testify provided he or she was granted "transactional immunity" (total exemption from prosecution for anything revealed in the testimony). The Court upheld such laws in 1896 and again in 1956 in a challenge brought by witnesses in government subversion inquiries.

In 1970 Congress included in the Organized Crime Control Act a provision giving immunized witnesses a limited grant of "use" immunity. The law simply forbade the use of any of the witness's compelled testimony or derivative evidence against him or her. A witness could still be prosecuted for crimes mentioned in his or her testimony if the evidence used in the prosecution was developed independently.

In *Kastigar v. United States* (1972) the Court found this narrower use immunity to be constitutional. Writing for the majority, Justice Lewis F. Powell, Jr., said the provision complied with the Fifth Amendment by affording "protection against being forced to give testimony leading to the infliction of [criminal penalties]." In a dissent, Justice William O. Douglas, joined by Justice Thurgood Marshall, wrote, "My view is that the Framers put it beyond the power of Congress to compel anyone to confess his crimes."

Four years later the Court restricted the Fifth Amendment protection for private papers, allowing the government to subpoena business records held by a person's lawyer or accountant. "The Fifth Amendment does not independently proscribe the compelled production of every sort of incriminating evidence but applies only when the accused is compelled to make a testimonial communication that is incriminating," the Court said in *Fisher v. United States* (1976).

Seniority

Many Supreme Court procedures are guided by the Court's long tradition of seniority. With the exception of the chief justice, who is "first among equals," justices participate in conference discussions, announce opinions, and take their seats in the courtroom on the basis of how long they have served on the Court. Adherence to the rules of seniority helps foster the Court's image of historic continuity.

During the Court's CONFERENCES, discussions of cases begin with the CHIEF JUSTICE and proceed down the line of seniority to the junior associate justice. It has frequently been said that the justices vote on cases in the reverse order, with the junior associate first and the chief justice last. Chief Justice William H. Rehnquist, however, has said that this is not true, at least not during his years on the Court. Typically, the justices indicate their position on the case during their turn for discussion.

Reverse seniority is followed when opinions are announced in the courtroom. The most junior of the justices who have written opinions that are ready to be announced goes first, followed by the next most junior, and so forth.

Office assignments, seating on the bench, and the justices' placement in official photographs are all determined by seniority. In the courtroom the chief justice is seated in the center behind the winged mahogany table. The senior associate justice is seated at the immediate right, and the second senior associate justice at the immediate left. The other justices take their places in alternating order of seniority, with the junior associate justice at the far left of the bench and the second newest appointee at the far right.

The order remains the same in official photographs, except that the four most junior members stand in the second row. Again, the junior associate is at the far left of this row, the second junior associate at the far right.

Seating in the conference room is also according to seniority. The chief justice sits at the east end of the table, the senior associate at the west end. The next three in order of seniority sit on one side of the rectangular table, while the four most junior share the opposite side.

Since the Court began barring anyone other than the justices from attending the conferences, the junior associate has been charged with sending for and receiving documents or other information the Court needs. Justice Tom C. Clark, who was the junior justice from 1949 until 1959, once referred to himself as "the highest paid doorkeeper in the world."

After conferences the chief justice used to tell the CLERK OF THE COURT which cases had been accepted for review or denied. Chief Justice Warren E. Burger, however, turned this task over to the junior associate.

Seniority also affects another important function of the Court—WRITING OPINIONS. The chief justice makes the assignment when in the majority. If the chief justice is not in the majority, the assignment task goes to the most senior associate justice in the majority.

Separate But Equal

See PLESSY V. FERGUSON.

Separation of Powers

The constitutional system of separation of powers is designed to protect individual liberties by dividing the functions of the federal government among three independent branches—legislative, executive, and judicial. Each branch exercises some control over the

George Washington, the hero of the Revolutionary War, presided at the Constitutional Convention of 1787. Alexander Hamilton (seated, foreground) and James Madison (seated, in front of Washington) played critical roles in organizing the convention and in securing ratification. Madison also drafted much of the document. Benjamin Franklin (seated, center foreground) acted as conciliator among the convention's factions.   Source: Library of Congress

others. Through shared powers and a network of checks and balances, the framers of the Constitution intended to prevent any single branch from dominating the government.

The president shares legislative power with Congress. The president can call Congress into session, recommend legislation, and veto any bill passed by Congress—subject to being overridden by two-thirds majorities in both houses. (See VETO POWER.)

The Senate must approve the president's appointment of executive branch officials and judges. (See APPOINTMENT AND REMOVAL POWERS OF THE PRESIDENT.) The president makes treaties, but the Senate must approve them. (See TREATY POWER.)

Through the process of IMPEACHMENT, Congress can even remove the president, executive branch officials, or judges.

Judicial power is shared through the provisions for presidential nomination and Senate confirmation of judges. (See CONFIRMATION PROCESS; NOMINATION TO THE COURT.) Congress also has the power to establish lower federal courts and, within limits, to determine the JURISDICTION of both the Supreme Court and the rest of the federal judiciary.

The Constitution's system of checks and balances gives each branch protections against the others. Each chamber of Congress has exclusive power to discipline its members. The president cannot adjourn Con-

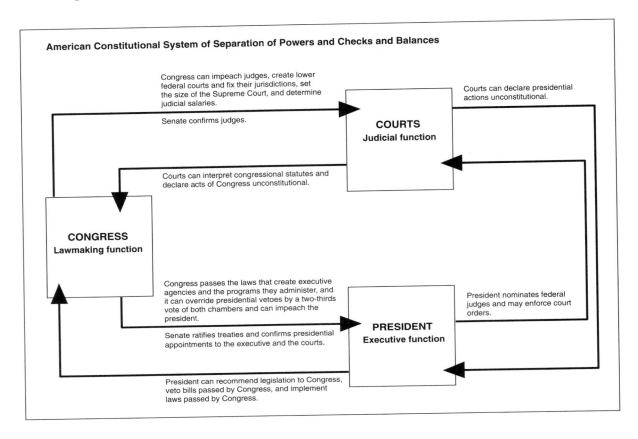

American Constitutional System of Separation of Powers and Checks and Balances

Congress can impeach judges, create lower federal courts and fix their jurisdictions, set the size of the Supreme Court, and determine judicial salaries.

Senate confirms judges.

Courts can declare presidential actions unconstitutional.

COURTS
Judicial function

Courts can interpret congressional statutes and declare acts of Congress unconstitutional.

CONGRESS
Lawmaking function

Congress passes the laws that create executive agencies and the programs they administer, and it can override presidential vetoes by a two-thirds vote of both chambers and can impeach the president.

President nominates federal judges and may enforce court orders.

Senate ratifies treaties and confirms presidential appointments to the executive and the courts.

PRESIDENT
Executive function

President can recommend legislation to Congress, veto bills passed by Congress, and implement laws passed by Congress.

gress unless the two chambers disagree about the adjournment date. No one can be a member of both the legislative and executive branch simultaneously. Congress cannot alter the president's compensation during the four-year term. Federal judges have life tenure as well as protection against pay reductions. By implication the courts have the power to declare unconstitutional an act of Congress or an action of the executive. (See JUDICIAL REVIEW.)

For the most part, the Constitution clearly outlines the powers of each branch of government. Still, some disputes have arisen. Can Congress limit the president's powers of appointment and removal? Can Congress delegate its power to the executive branch or to the courts? Can the president claim an executive privilege to withhold information from Congress or the courts? Can the president refuse to spend funds appropriated by Congress? Can Congress create

courts whose judges do not have the protections required by the Constitution?

Supreme Court rulings on such issues have special significance because they define the limits of the power that each branch of government can exercise. In the 1970s and 1980s the number of such cases brought to the Court increased. The disputes reflected tension between Congress and the president, but they also showed that both Congress and the president were trying to adapt constitutional structures to new problems.

The Court's decisions on issues of separation of powers reflect two different approaches, the formalist and the functional. In its formalist rulings, the Court has emphasized the need to draw sharp lines between the branches of government. The Court has often taken this view when one branch of government seemed to be seizing power at the expense of another.

An example is the Court's 1983 decision barring the use of the LEGISLATIVE VETO.

More often the Court has used the functional approach, allowing some flexibility in sharing powers as long as an arrangement does not threaten the essential attributes of the legislative, executive, or judicial function. An example is the Court's 1988 ruling upholding Congress's decision to provide for judicial appointment of an independent counsel to investigate and prosecute cases of misconduct in the executive branch.

On a few occasions the Court has tried to avoid refereeing disputes between the other two branches. The most conspicuous example is its refusal to draw lines between Congress's power to declare war and the president's power as commander in chief. (See WAR POWERS.)

Legislative Powers

The Court has adopted a pragmatic view toward the separation of powers issue that most affects Congress: the delegation of power doctrine. Since the early 1800s the Court has upheld laws passed by Congress that assign a role in law making to the executive or to the courts. The Court's legislative veto decision, however, bars Congress from retaining the right to veto a decision once it has made such a delegation of power. On another important separation of powers issue, the Court in 1975 supported Congress's spending power by refusing to recognize a presidential power to "impound" funds once Congress has appropriated them.

Delegation of Power

The Supreme Court has repeatedly said that Congress cannot delegate its legislative powers. In only two cases has the Court found laws to be in violation of the delegation of powers doctrine.

Congress can delegate decision-making functions in two ways. First, it can set an objective and then authorize an administrator or administrative body to adopt rules, within certain guidelines, to achieve the objective. Second, it can authorize an administrator to take a certain course of action if he or she determines that certain conditions exist. The Supreme Court has repeatedly supported both kinds of delegation.

Chief Justice John Marshall in 1825 explained the rationale for delegated rule-making power, in an opinion upholding a law giving federal courts broad authority to adopt rules of practice. Marshall wrote that Congress can establish "general provisions" and then authorize "those who are to act under such general provisions to fill up the details."

The Court's classic statement on so-called contingency delegations came in a 1928 decision upholding a law that authorized the president to raise or lower tariffs by as much as 50 percent to equalize production costs between the United States and competing countries. Writing for the Court, Chief Justice William Howard Taft said that as long as Congress laid down "an intelligible principle" for an administrator to follow, the act did not constitute an impermissible delegation of power.

The Court took a stricter view of the delegation doctrine in two cases in 1935 that struck down provisions of the National Industrial Recovery Act (NIRA), a key piece of President Franklin D. Roosevelt's economic recovery program.

Panama Refining Co. v. Ryan involved a provision of NIRA that authorized the president to ban "hot oil"—oil produced in violation of state limits on production—from interstate commerce. The company challenging the law contended that the delegation to the president was too broad. By an 8–1 vote, the Court agreed. "The Congress left the matter to the President without standard or rule, to be dealt with as he pleased," the Court said.

Four months later the Court handed Roosevelt another, broader defeat. *Schechter Poultry Corp. v. United States*—popularly known as the "Sick Chicken Case"—involved a challenge to the fair competition codes set for various industries under NIRA. The statute authorized the president to approve an industry code if requested by at least one association representing the industry.

The Schechters, poultry wholesalers in New York, contested a charge of violating the code by challenging the act, among other grounds, as an unconstitutional delegation of power. In a unanimous decision, the Court agreed. Chief Justice Charles Evans Hughes said the act left the president's discretion "unfettered." Justice Benjamin N. Cardozo, who had voted to uphold the "hot oil" provision, joined the Court this time, calling the industry code provisions a case of "delegation running riot."

The Court objected as well to the role that private associations played in recommending the industry codes. "Such a delegation of power is unknown to our law," Hughes wrote. The next year the Court used a similar flaw as one of several bases for striking down the Guffey Coal Act, which authorized the coal industry to establish mandatory wage and hour regulations for the industry.

The Court's strict enforcement of the delegation doctrine proved to be short-lived. The Court has never relied on *Schechter* to strike down a delegation by Congress. One reason is that Congress quickly grasped the need to provide some guidelines—however general—for administrators to follow in carrying out a law. The Fair Labor Standards Act of 1938, for example, authorized an administrator to set minimum wages for specific industries based on various factors and the recommendations of an industry advisory committee. The Court in 1941 upheld the law.

The Court's lax enforcement of the delegation doctrine has allowed Congress to create an array of regulatory agencies authorized to adopt rules to further policies set out in the most general terms. Although these general grants of regulatory power are often criticized, the Court has not used the delegation doctrine to require Congress to be more specific.

Legislative Veto

The legislative veto was a mechanism for one or both houses of Congress or one or more committees to block an administrative action or regulation. First used during the Hoover administration, the legislative veto became popular with Congress in the 1970s. In 1983, however, the Court sustained a challenge to the device, based on the separation of powers. The ruling in *Immigration and Naturalization Service v. Chadha* was seen as invalidating legislative veto provisions contained in more than 200 laws. The practical effect was less sweeping, because many agencies apparently continued to abide by formal or informal vetolike arrangements to avoid alienating members of Congress.

Impoundment

The Court's ruling on the impoundment issue came after a period of sharp disputes over spending between President Richard Nixon and the Democratic-controlled Congress. Nixon claimed a constitutional right to refuse to spend money appropriated by Congress—a claim that was strongly opposed by members of Congress. Between 1969 and 1973, Nixon impounded more than $15 billion in funds intended for more than one hundred domestic programs.

In *Train v. City of New York* (1975) the Court ruled one of those impoundments illegal. The decision, issued six months after Nixon had resigned, did not set limits for the president's impoundment power generally, but it appeared to cast doubt on any broad right of the president to withhold funds appropriated by Congress.

A year earlier Congress itself had moved to limit presidential impoundments by passing the Congressional Budget and Impoundment Control Act. The act requires the president to notify Congress of any impoundment and gives either house of Congress power to veto the impoundment. The Court's legislative veto ruling raises questions about the validity of the law, but it has not been tested in court.

Executive Powers

The Supreme Court has generally upheld broad assertions of presidential power. There have, however, been some dramatic exceptions. In 1952 the Court rejected President Harry S. Truman's wartime seizure of the nation's steel mills as an impermissible assertion of legislative power. (See *YOUNGSTOWN SHEET AND TUBE CO. V. SAWYER.*) In 1974 the Court rejected Nixon's plea of executive privilege in the Watergate tapes case—a decision that led to Nixon's resignation two weeks later. (See EXECUTIVE PRIVILEGE AND IMMUNITY.)

The Court has also permitted a major constitutional innovation that limits the president's power: the creation of "independent" regulatory agencies whose members cannot be removed by the president except for specified reasons. Although the Court endorsed this congressional limitation on the president's removal power, in later decisions it made clear that Congress cannot itself assume the power to appoint or remove officials who have executive functions.

Appointment and Removal

The Constitution specifies the president's power of appointment, and every president since George Washington has also assumed the implicit power to remove officials. The impeachment trial of President Andrew Johnson was based in part on Johnson's defiance of a law requiring that any official confirmed by the Senate could be removed only with the Senate's approval.

In *Myers v. United States* (1926) the Court invalidated an 1876 law that had similarly required Senate consent to the removal of postmasters. In the Court's opinion, Chief Justice Taft wrote that requiring Senate consent for removing executive officials would give it "the means of thwarting the executive in the exercise of his great powers."

Nine years later the Court agreed that Congress could limit the president's power to remove members of regulatory agencies. The decision in *Humphrey's Executor v. United States* (1935) prevented Franklin Roosevelt from replacing a member of the Federal Trade Commission. The Court explained that the earlier decision had been limited to "purely executive officers" and that Congress had the power "in creating quasi-legislative or quasi-judicial agencies, to require them to act independently of executive control."

The Court ruled in *Buckley v. Valeo* (1976) that Congress could not assume the power to appoint members of regulatory agencies. The ruling invalidated a provision of the Federal Election Campaign Act Amendments of 1974 that had provided for Congress to appoint four of the five members of the Federal Election Commission.

A decade later the Court again acted to protect presidential prerogatives. It struck down a provision of the Balanced Budget and Emergency Deficit Control Act of 1985 that gave the comptroller general, a legislative branch official, power to specify spending reductions for the president to carry out. "To permit the execution of the laws to be vested in an officer an-

swerable only to Congress would, in practical terms, reserve in Congress control over the execution of the laws," the Court declared in *Bowsher v. Synar* (1986).

Two years later the Court allowed Congress to grant the power to investigate executive branch misconduct to an independent counsel. The independent counsel was to be appointed by a three-judge panel and would be subject to removal only by the attorney general and only for good cause. In *Morrison v. Olson* (1988) the Court justified the decision in part on the constitutional provision for Congress to vest appointment of "inferior officers" in the courts. But the Court also considered whether the law interfered with the president's executive power. It concluded that the president still had sufficient powers to carry out constitutional duties.

Executive Privilege

Most disputes involving executive privilege have pitted Congress against the president or other executive branch officials, and most have been resolved by compromises without court action. The Supreme Court's two major rulings on the issue have upheld the power of Congress or the courts to override claims of executive privilege.

In *McGrain v. Daugherty* (1927) the Court upheld a Senate investigation into executive branch wrongdoing in the Teapot Dome oil lease scandal. In the Watergate tapes case *(United States v. Nixon* [1974]) the Court recognized a qualified privilege on the part of the president. Still, it upheld the subpoena against President Nixon for tapes of conversations relating to the Watergate break-in and cover-up to be used in the criminal trial of his former aides.

In the Nixon case the Court recognized the president's need for confidentiality to promote "complete candor and objectivity" from advisers. But it said that an absolute privilege to withhold evidence sought in a criminal case would "gravely impair the role of the courts under Article III."

Judicial Powers

The Supreme Court has generally prevented infringements on judicial powers since its earliest days.

In 1792 the justices refused to accept an assignment from Congress to make recommendations on pension claims by disabled veterans of the revolutionary war. The recommendations were to be reviewed by Congress or the president. Such an arrangement violated judicial independence, two of the justices explained in a letter to President George Washington, because it allowed the other branches to review court actions.

More recently, a 1978 bankruptcy reform act created a new corps of bankruptcy judges with broad powers but without the guarantees of life tenure and fixed compensation. In *Northern Pipeline Construction Co. v. Marathon Pipe Line Co.* (1982) the Court ruled that the law infringed on the independence of the judiciary.

The Court's 1989 decision upholding the U.S. Sentencing Commission shows a more flexible approach toward judicial power. The law created a seven-member commission, to be appointed by the president, that would include three judges as members and that would be designated as part of the judicial branch. The commission was to issue sentencing guidelines for federal judges to use in criminal cases.

In *Mistretta v. United States* (1989) the Court rejected several challenges to the law that were based on separation of powers. The Court upheld the innovative arrangement on the grounds that sentencing was a traditional function of judges and that the commission's powers did not contribute to a weakening of the judiciary.

Seventh Amendment

See JURIES.

Severability

Severability is the concept that allows part of a law to survive even after another part of the same statute has been held invalid. Without this device an entire statute would become void because of a single flawed provision.

Severability, which is also called separability, grows

out of the principle that the judiciary should uphold the constitutionality of legislative acts where possible. For a court to find a statute separable, the finding must coincide with legislative intent and the design of the law.

Congress commonly includes a severability, or saving, clause in its legislation. The clause declares that if one part of the statute is found unconstitutional, the rest of the act may still stand. The clause is a relatively modern element and is not critical to court determination of severability.

Legislative intent was one of the reasons the Supreme Court gave for striking down the general INCOME TAX in 1895. Having declared that the tax on income from property was unconstitutional, the Court said that would leave only taxes on income from occupations and labor, adding, "We cannot believe that such was the intention of Congress."

Despite a severability clause in the Bituminous Coal Conservation Act of 1935, the Supreme Court in 1936 ruled that the price-fixing provisions of the act were inseparable from the labor regulations provisions that it had declared unconstitutional.

To be severed, the valid portion of the law must be independent and complete in itself. If eliminating part of the law would defeat or change its purpose, the entire act should be declared void. The Court applied this principle in 1935 when it declared the Railroad Retirement Act of 1934 unconstitutional.

In a more recent case, the Court upheld the Balanced Budget and Deficit Reduction Act of 1985 after striking down one provision giving the comptroller general power to fix spending reduction targets for the president to follow. Congress had anticipated the problem and included an alternative process to replace the one that was struck down. The Court "severed" the unconstitutional provisions and left the remaining structure of the mechanisms intact.

Sex Discrimination

For nearly a century the Supreme Court rejected every effort to overturn sex-based classifications in the law. It began to apply the EQUAL PROTECTION clause to sex discrimination in the 1970s. In the process it adopted different tests that invalidated some gender-based classifications but upheld others. Meanwhile, Congress had passed several statutory prohibitions against sex discrimination. For the most part, the Court interpreted these strictly.

Romantic Paternalism

The Court's early refusals to outlaw sex discrimination reflected a narrow view of the Fourteenth Amendment and a paternalistic attitude toward women.

In *Bradwell v. Illinois* (1873) the Court upheld a state's refusal to let a woman practice law, saying that the Fourteenth Amendment did not affect a state's authority to regulate admission to the bar. In a concurring opinion, Justice Joseph P. Bradley added that women's "natural . . . delicacy" made them "unfit for many of the occupations of civil life." Two years later the Court refused to give women the right to vote under the privileges and immunities clause of the Fourteenth Amendment. (See VOTING RIGHTS.)

Romantic paternalism was more evident in the Court's later decisions upholding laws aimed at protecting women's health or morals. In 1904 the Court upheld a local ordinance barring the sale of liquor to women and preventing women from working in bars. Four years later, in *Muller v. Oregon* (1908), the Court upheld a law limiting the hours that women laundry workers could work. *Muller* came just three years after the Court had struck down a New York law limiting working hours for bakers.

This protective attitude survived at least until 1961, when the Court upheld an exemption for women from jury duty. "Woman is still regarded as the center of home and family life," the Court declared in *Hoyt v. Florida.* The ruling was overturned in 1975. (See JURIES.)

Search for a Standard

In its first decision striking down a state law because it discriminated against women, the Court adopted a rationality standard—the least stringent level of review. *Reed v. Reed* (1971) struck down an Idaho law giving men an automatic preference over women in court appointments to administer estates

Myra Bradwell, who lost her case in the Supreme Court.
Source: Library of Congress

of someone who died without a will. Writing for the unanimous Court, Chief Justice Warren E. Burger said a gender-based classification "must be reasonable, not arbitrary" and must reflect "a fair and substantial relation to the object of the legislation."

Using this standard the Court in several cases upheld gender-based classifications. For example, it upheld a property tax exemption for widows but not for widowers, stating that the exemption compensated for the "disproportionately heavy burden" women suffer from the loss of a spouse. But the Court did use the rationality standard to strike down a law that required divorced fathers to support their sons to age twenty-one but their daughters only to age eighteen.

As early as 1973 four members of the Court argued for a stricter test. In *Frontiero v. Richardson* the Court struck down, by a vote of 8 to 1, a military regulation that required husbands of military personnel, but not wives, to prove dependency status to receive certain benefits. In a plurality opinion Justice William J. Brennan, Jr., said that gender-based classifications were inherently suspect and had to be justified by a compelling government interest. Three other justices used the rationality standard to strike down the law, while Justice Potter Stewart concurred without joining either of the opinions. In three later cases the Court struck down other benefits provisions that were similarly based on the assumption that women depended on their husbands for support while men did not so depend on their wives.

In 1976 Brennan won majority support for an intermediate level of scrutiny for sex-based classifications. *Craig v. Boren* struck down an Oklahoma law that permitted the sale of low-alcohol beer to women at age eighteen but to men at age twenty-one. Four justices agreed with Brennan that gender-based classifications "must serve important governmental objectives and must be substantially related to achievement of those objectives."

In applying the standard the Court in 1981 upheld a state statutory rape law that punished males but not females for having sexual relations with someone under age eighteen. In the same year the Court nominally applied the standard when it decided, 6–3, that Congress could exclude women from the military draft. In 1992, the Court applied the intermediate test more strictly to strike down a women-only admissions policy at a state university school of nursing. The Court in 1994 ruled that lawyers cannot exclude potential jurors because of gender but left open the question of whether gender classifications are inherently suspect.

Statutory Protections

In 1963 Congress passed the first federal legislation against sex discrimination, the Equal Pay Act. Title VII of the CIVIL RIGHTS Act of 1964 more broadly prohibited employment discrimination on account of sex.

In its first Title VII sex discrimination case, the Court in 1971 struck down an employer's policy of refusing to hire women, but not men, who had preschool children. Six years later the Court barred the use of a minimum height and weight requirement for prison guards, saying the policy resulted in "a significantly discriminatory pattern." In *Los Angeles v.*

Manhart (1978) the Court said that requiring women to make higher contributions to an employee pension fund than men—based on their longer statistical life expectancy—also violated Title VII.

The Court in 1974 and 1976 refused to hold that health benefit plans of public or private employers that excluded coverage for pregnancy amounted to illegal sex discrimination. Congress responded by passing the Pregnancy Discrimination Act of 1978, requiring coverage of pregnancy in employee health plans.

With the exception of the pregnancy issue, the Court has given a broad construction to federal sex discrimination laws. In *Meritor Savings Bank v. Vinson* (1986) Chief Justice William H. Rehnquist wrote for a unanimous Court in applying Title VII to ban sexual harassment in the workplace. Five years later the Court again relied on Title VII to forbid so-called fetal protection policies that excluded women from jobs involving exposure to chemicals that might harm a developing fetus.

Shiras, George, Jr.

George Shiras, Jr. (1832–1924), is the only Supreme Court justice who had never engaged in any political or judicial activities before being appointed to the Court. In fact, he had never held any official position before he became a justice at age sixty.

Shiras was born into a prosperous family in Pittsburgh. He graduated from Yale in 1853 and, after studying law both privately and at Yale, was admitted to the bar in 1855. The West beckoned, and Shiras moved to Dubuque, Iowa, to practice law with his brother. After several years in Iowa, Shiras moved back to Pittsburgh to become the law partner of Judge Hopewell Hepburn, in whose office he had read law. Hepburn died in 1862, after which Shiras continued a successful independent practice. His clients included the Baltimore & Ohio Railroad and the major iron and steel companies of Pittsburgh.

Throughout his life Shiras, a moderate Republican, avoided political activity and the state political machine. In 1881 the Pennsylvania legislature offered Shiras the U.S. Senate nomination, but he declined.

Source: Library of Congress

As his legal practice prospered, Shiras developed a reputation for integrity, moderation, and good judgment. He was a quiet man who remained modest despite his accumulation of great wealth.

President Benjamin Harrison nominated Shiras for the Supreme Court in 1892. Harrison violated senatorial courtesy by not first consulting with Pennsylvania's two Republican senators, James Donald Cameron and Matthew S. Quay. The two men, who headed the state's political machine, forcefully opposed Shiras's appointment. But Shiras enjoyed strong support from the Pennsylvania bar, the iron and steel interests, and various other prominent people. When it became clear that the opposition was purely political, the Senate confirmed Shiras by a voice vote.

During his decade on the Court, Shiras was respected by his fellow justices for his analytical abilities and steadiness. However, he may have been the justice who switched his vote in *Pollock v. Farmers' Loan and Trust Company* (1895), resulting in a ruling that declared the income tax illegal. Most of the opinions he wrote dealt with procedural questions.

Shiras retired in 1903, as he had earlier decided to do, and spent the remaining two decades of his life shuttling between homes in Florida and northern Michigan. Shiras died in 1924 at age ninety-two.

Sixteenth Amendment

See INCOME TAX; REVERSALS OF RULINGS BY CONSTITUTIONAL AMENDMENT.

Sixth Amendment

See COUNSEL, RIGHT TO LEGAL; JURIES; TRIALS.

Size of the Court

Congress has increased or reduced the number of justices on the Supreme Court seven times in its 200-year history. Generally, laws decreasing the number of justices have been motivated by a desire to punish the president. Increases have been aimed at influencing the philosophical balance of the Court itself.

The Judiciary Act of 1789 set the number of Supreme Court seats at six. In the last days of John Adams's presidency, however, Congress reduced the number to five. Justice William Cushing was ill and not expected to live, and the outgoing Federalists wanted to deny the incoming Republican president, Thomas Jefferson, an opportunity to name Cushing's successor. The reduction in size never occurred. In 1802 the Republican-controlled Congress restored the number of justices to six.

In 1807 Congress increased the number of justices to seven, primarily because of the population growth in Kentucky, Tennessee, and Ohio, which was overloading the circuit courts over which Supreme Court justices presided. (See CIRCUIT RIDING.)

In 1837 Congress increased the Court to nine, again because of the increasing population and ex-

President Franklin D. Roosevelt's difficulty in getting a proposal to enlarge the Supreme Court through Congress is illustrated in this 1937 cartoon.   Source: Russell in the Los Angeles Times, *Brown Brothers, Sterling, Pa.*

pansion of the country into the West and Southwest. Presidents James Madison, James Monroe, and John Quincy Adams each had urged Congress to enlarge the Court so that the additional judges might ease some of the backlog of cases in the circuit courts, but Congress had refused because it did not want the sitting president to name the justices.

The next increase, to ten justices, came in the midst of the Civil War. On the surface the increase was again justified by the western expansion. The law created a tenth circuit composed of California and Oregon, and later Nevada. But the additional seat also gave President Abraham Lincoln an opportunity to appoint a justice who would decide issues in favor of the Union. Lincoln already had made three appointments in 1862, but his control of the Court still was not firm. Lincoln appointed Stephen J. Field to the seat, and Field did support the president on war issues.

Congress was not so accommodating of Lincoln's successor, Andrew Johnson. When Justice John

Catron died in 1865, Johnson nominated Attorney General Henry Stanbery, who was exceptionally well qualified for the position. The majority in Congress, however, was so opposed to Johnson's Reconstruction policies, and so fearful that his appointments to the Court might rule against Congress's Reconstruction programs, that it reduced the number of seats on the Court from ten to seven so that the next three vacancies on the Court would not be filled. The vacancy to which Stanbery had been nominated therefore no longer existed, and no action was taken on his appointment. The Court was reduced to eight members when Justice James M. Wayne died in July 1867.

No further vacancies occurred during Johnson's tenure. Little more than a month after Ulysses S. Grant was inaugurated in March 1869, Congress raised the number of seats on the Court to nine.

Congress has not changed the number of seats on the Court since 1869, although members of Congress frustrated by Court decisions have continued to propose such changes. The most serious of these proposals in the twentieth century came not from Congress but from the president, when Franklin Roosevelt proposed in 1937 that the number of justices be raised to fifteen. The increase ostensibly was to improve the efficiency of the Court. In reality it was designed to allow Roosevelt to appoint new justices who could be depended upon to support the constitutionality of his New Deal programs, several of which the Court had struck down.

The plan was unpopular with both the public and Congress and was not enacted. But the Court itself did a great deal to defuse the threat to its independence. Shortly after the proposal was made public, the Court in quick succession upheld a state minimum wage law and the National Labor Relations Act. Those rulings indicated that the Court was now willing to sanction broad government regulation of private enterprise.

Slaughterhouse Cases

The Fourteenth Amendment provides that the states shall not "abridge the privileges or immunities

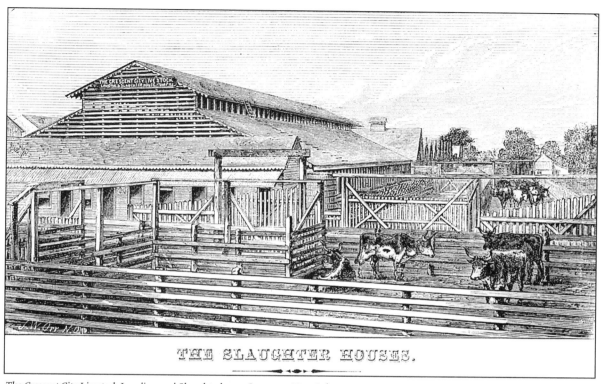

THE SLAUGHTER HOUSES.

The Crescent City Livestock Landing and Slaughterhouse Company, New Orleans. *Source: The Historic New Orleans Collection*

of citizens of the United States"; "deprive any person of life, liberty, or property, without due process of law"; or "deny to any person within its jurisdiction the equal protection of the laws." In an 1873 ruling, the Supreme Court gave the amendment a narrow interpretation that rendered it useless as legal protection for blacks or other disadvantaged groups for the next half century.

It was an occupational group, butchers, who brought the landmark cases under the Fourteenth Amendment. The cases are collectively called the *Slaughterhouse Cases.* New Orleans butchers charged that the state of Louisiana had violated the Fourteenth Amendment by granting to one company the exclusive right to operate a slaughterhouse in the city. This monopoly, they charged, deprived them of their right to carry on their business—a right included among the privileges and immunities guaranteed by the first section of the amendment.

The monopoly was granted in 1869, and the case reached the Supreme Court the next year. It was argued in 1872 and reargued in 1873. The Court announced its decision on April 14, 1873.

In a 5–4 ruling the Court rejected the butchers' claim. Writing for the majority, Justice Samuel Miller said that the monopoly did not forbid them from practicing their trade but only required them to do so at a particular slaughterhouse. Miller continued by construing the privileges and immunities clause to protect only the rights of U.S. CITIZENSHIP, not those of state citizenship. "It is only the former which are placed by this clause under the protection of the Federal Constitution," Miller wrote, "and . . . the latter, whatever they may be, are not intended to have any additional protection by this paragraph of the Amendment." A broader interpretation, he continued, would make the Court "a perpetual censor upon all legislation of the States."

Writing for the four dissenters, Justice Stephen Field argued that the amendment was intended to protect "the natural and inalienable rights which belong to all citizens." The majority's view, he said, rendered the amendment's first clause "a vain and idle enactment, which accomplished nothing."

Slavery and the Court

The issue of slavery came to the Supreme Court in its first decades only as a question of international or commercial law or of states' rights and federal power, not as a human rights issue. Only after the Civil War did the status of the nation's blacks become a question of individual rights rather than property rights.

The Constitution acknowledged slavery in several places, though without ever using the actual word. Importation of slaves could not be restricted before 1808 (Article I, Section 9). Runaway slaves had to be returned to their owners (Article IV, Section 2). And slaves were to be counted as three-fifths of a person for purposes of determining the number of a state's representatives in the House (Article I, Section 2).

In the face of those provisions, opponents of slavery had no success in using the Constitution to argue against the practice. Many abolitionists bitterly denounced the Constitution as a proslavery document and wanted to scrap it.

Slavery had a continuing impact upon pre–Civil War constitutional history. Concern about preserving slavery was the main impetus for theories of states' rights, which limited the expansion of federal power until after the Civil War.

In the decades leading up to the war the Supreme Court struggled to avoid entanglement in the issue. It gave firm support to federal power over the subject of fugitive slaves but left as much as possible to the states the question of the status of slaves who had spent time in both slave and free areas.

The Court departed from that line in 1857 with its decision in the Dred Scott case (*SCOTT V. SANDFORD*), which barred congressional control over slavery in the territories. The effort to resolve the slavery issue back-

fired, fueling the sectional conflict that burst out in civil war four years later.

International Law

In the first case involving slavery decided by the Court, *The Antelope* (1825), the justices held that the slave trade, even though illegal in the United States by that time, was not illegal under international law. The case involved slaves who arrived in the United States after being removed from a vessel captured by an American warship.

Chief Justice John Marshall made clear in his opinion that the legality of the situation alone, not its morality, was before the Court: "In examining claims of this momentous importance; claims in which the sacred rights of liberty and of property come in conflict with each other . . . this Court must not yield to feelings which might seduce it from the path of duty, but must obey the mandates of the law."

Commercial Law

Four years later, in *Boyce v. Anderson* (1829), the Court ruled that a slave who died in an abortive rescue attempt after a steamboat fire was a passenger, not freight, for purposes of his owners' damage suit against the vessels involved. "A slave has volition, and has feelings which cannot be entirely disregarded," Chief Justice Marshall wrote.

In 1841 the Court was faced with a case challenging Mississippi's ban on the importation of slaves. But the justices found a way to decide the case without ruling directly on the importation ban.

Fugitive Slave Laws

As the tension between slave and free states grew and the operations of the underground railway accelerated, an increasing number of cases challenged the federal fugitive slave law. The law had been enacted in 1793 to govern the return of runaway slaves from one state to another.

In *Prigg v. Pennsylvania* (1842) the Court affirmed the exclusive power of Congress to regulate disputes over fugitive slaves. The justices struck down a Pennsylvania law providing that before a runaway slave was returned to his or her alleged owner or the owners' representative, a hearing should be held before a

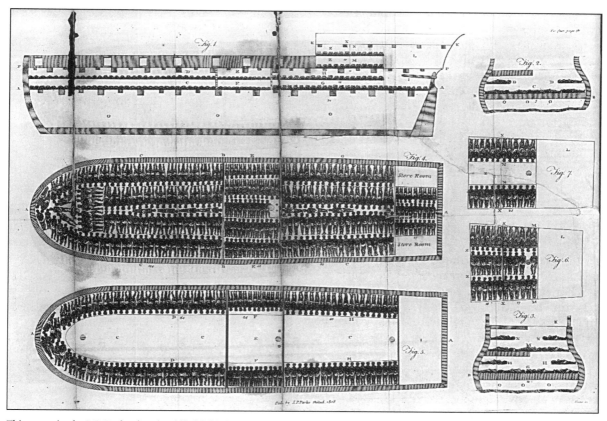

This engraving by J. P. Parke, done in Philadelphia in 1802, starkly depicts slaves as commodities, not human beings.
Source: Library of Congress

magistrate to determine the validity of the claim to the supposed slave.

In reaffirming the validity of the fugitive slave law six years later, the Court specifically disclaimed any power to interfere with the practice of slavery on its own. The Court called the issue "a political question" that had been left to the states as "one of [the Constitution's] sacred compromises."

On the eve of the Civil War the Court resolved the most famous of the fugitive slave cases, *Ableman v. Booth* (1859). Sherman Booth, an abolitionist editor, was prosecuted under the federal law for helping a fugitive slave to escape. The state courts of Wisconsin, where Booth lived, repeatedly issued writs of HABEAS CORPUS, ordering federal authorities to release him from custody. The orders were based on the view that the federal fugitive slave law was unconstitutional. The Court in March 1859 resoundingly defended the freedom of federal courts from such state interference and upheld Booth's conviction.

Slave or Free?

The first case in which the Court was asked to decide what effect residence in a free state or territory had on the status of a slave came in 1850. It was resolved with restraint and without incident.

The individuals involved were slaves in Kentucky who had worked for a time in the free state of Ohio but returned to Kentucky to live. The Court held that their status depended on the state where they were residing. No constitutional provision controlled state action on this matter, it held.

The Court reached a similar conclusion seven years later in the Dred Scott case. In *Scott* the Court went further, however, and held that slaves were not, and could become, citizens. The decision enraged many northerners but did not deflect the South from moving toward secession.

The issue of slavery was finally resolved on the battlefield. The Supreme Court did not speak again on the subject.

Solicitor General

The solicitor general is the attorney who represents the U.S. government before the Supreme Court. The solicitor general's office, which is part of the Justice Department, decides which cases the government should ask the Court to review and determines the government's legal position on any case in which it is involved.

The solicitor general has a staff of about two dozen attorneys who petition for hearings, prepare the government's briefs and supporting data, and argue the government's case before the Court. Sometimes the solicitor general argues before the Court. Most of the time the solicitor general is represented by one of the staff lawyers. The ATTORNEY GENERAL, the solicitor general's superior, may argue a case of particular importance.

In many cases in which the United States is not a party, the solicitor general participates, often at the Court's invitation, as an AMICUS CURIAE, or "friend of the court." In this capacity, the office submits a brief and sometimes participates in oral argument, stating the government's position on the issue at hand.

The solicitor general is under considerable pressure to limit the number of cases brought before the Court. The Court can hear only a limited number of cases each year, so it would be self-defeating for the solicitor general to petition for more hearings than the Court can be expected to handle. Furthermore, by restricting the number of cases brought, the solicitor general increases credibility with the justices, who can

be confident that the solicitor general is advancing only important cases.

As a result, the Court agrees to hear an exceptionally high percentage of the cases that the solicitor general's office asks it to review. According to one count, the Court accepted 76 percent of the federal government's petitions for certiorari during the 1984–1989 terms, and 77 percent of the petitions that the government supported as an amicus curiae. In contrast, the Court accepted only 2.5 percent of the petitions that were not brought or supported by the federal government.

The solicitor general's office is also involved in reviewing the federal government's position in the many court cases to which the government is a party in the lower courts. Each year the solicitor general's office reviews hundreds of briefs from government agencies. The briefs that are reviewed may be approved without change or totally rewritten. Most are revised and modified to some extent in collaboration with the author of the draft.

The post of solicitor general was created by Congress in 1870 when the Department of Justice was established. Before 1870 the functions of the solicitor general were carried out by the attorney general. Congress explained that it wanted to provide "a staff of law officers sufficiently numerous and of sufficient ability to transact" the government's legal business in all parts of the country.

As far as the general public is concerned, solicitors general are fairly anonymous figures, although several—William Howard Taft, Charles Evans Hughes, Stanley Reed, Robert H. Jackson, and Thurgood Marshall—later became justices of the Supreme Court. One solicitor general who became well known to the public was Robert H. Bork, who held the post from 1973 to 1977. Bork's notoriety had to do not with his Court-related duties but with his role in the infamous "Saturday night massacre." This incident occurred following President Richard Nixon's decision on October 23, 1973, to fire the special prosecutor in the Watergate affair, Archibald Cox, who was himself a former solicitor general. Attorney General Elliot Richardson and Deputy Attorney General William Ruckelshaus resigned rather than obey Nixon's order to fire Cox. The highest ranking official left in the Justice Depart-

Solicitors General, 1870–1994

Name	Term	State of origin	President
Benjamin H. Bristow	October 11, 1870–November 15, 1872	Kentucky	Grant
Samuel F. Philips	November 15, 1872–May 3, 1885	North Carolina	Grant
John Goode	May 1, 1885–August 5, 1886	Virginia	Cleveland
George A. Jenks	July 30, 1886–May 29, 1889	Pennsylvania	Cleveland
Orlow W. Chapman	May 29, 1889–January 19, 1890	New York	Harrison
William Howard Taft	February 4, 1890–March 20, 1892	Ohio	Harrison
Charles H. Aldrich	March 21, 1892–May 28, 1893	Illinois	Harrison
Lawrence Maxwell, Jr.	April 6, 1893–January 30, 1895	Ohio	Cleveland
Holmes Conrad	February 6, 1895–July 8, 1897	Virginia	Cleveland
John K. Richards	July 1, 1897–March 16, 1903	Ohio	McKinley
Henry M. Hoyt	February 25, 1903–March 31, 1909	Pennsylvania	Roosevelt
Lloyd Wheaton Bowers	April 1, 1909–September 9, 1910	Illinois	Taft
Frederick W. Lehman	December 12, 1910–July 15, 1912	Missouri	Taft
William Marshall Bullitt	July 16, 1912–March 11, 1913	Kentucky	Taft
John William Davis	August 30, 1913–November 26, 1918	West Virginia	Wilson
Alexander C. King	November 27, 1918–May 23, 1920	Georgia	Wilson
William L. Frierson	June 1, 1920–June 30, 1921	Tennessee	Wilson
James M. Beck	June 30, 1921–June 7, 1925	New Jersey	Harding
William D. Mitchell	June 4, 1925–March 5, 1929	Minnesota	Coolidge
Charles Evans Hughes, Jr.	May 27, 1929–April 16, 1930	New York	Hoover
Thomas D. Thacher	March 22, 1930–May 4, 1933	New York	Hoover
James Crawford Biggs	May 4, 1933–March 24, 1935	North Carolina	Roosevelt
Stanley Reed	March 23, 1935–January 30, 1938	Kentucky	Roosevelt
Robert H. Jackson	March 5, 1938–January 17, 1940	New York	Roosevelt
Francis Biddle	January 22, 1940–September 4, 1941	Pennsylvania	Roosevelt
Charles Fahy	November 15, 1941–September 27, 1945	New Mexico	Roosevelt
J. Howard McGrath	October 4, 1945–October 7, 1946	Rhode Island	Truman
Philip B. Perlman	July 30, 1947–August 15, 1952	Maryland	Truman
Walter J. Cummings, Jr.	December 2, 1952–March 1, 1953	Illinois	Truman
Simon E. Sobeloff	February 10, 1954–July 19, 1956	Maryland	Eisenhower
J. Lee Rankin	August 4, 1956–January 23, 1961	Nebraska	Eisenhower
Archibald Cox	January 24, 1961–July 31, 1965	Massachusetts	Kennedy
Thurgood Marshall	August 11, 1965–August 30, 1967	New York	Johnson
Erwin N. Griswold	October 12, 1967–June 25, 1973	Massachusetts	Johnson
Robert H. Bork	June 19, 1973–January 20, 1977	Connecticut	Nixon
Wade Hampton McCree, Jr.	March 4, 1977–June 30, 1981	Michigan	Carter
Rex Lee	August 6, 1981–June 1, 1985	Utah	Reagan
Charles Fried	October 23, 1985–January 20, 1989	Massachusetts	Reagan
Kenneth Starr	May 27, 1989–January 20, 1993	Virginia	Bush
Drew S. Days III	June 7, 1993–	Connecticut	Clinton

ment, Bork took command and fired Cox. Years later, in 1987, Bork was once again in the public spotlight when the Senate rejected his nomination to the Supreme Court. (See NOMINATION TO THE COURT.)

President Ronald Reagan's aggressive push to convince the Court to change its views on major social issues, such as abortion, affirmative action, and school prayer, thrust the solicitor general back into the national limelight. Solicitors general Rex Lee and Charles Fried drew public attention as they carried the president's arguments on these questions to the Court. The two men also drew criticism, both from those who thought they should do more to promote the president's policy positions before the Court and from those who thought they were doing too much. Kenneth Starr, solicitor general under President Bush, did not ask the Court to review as many cases as his two predecessors had.

Source: National Geographic Society

Souter, David H.

Despite intense investigation by interest groups and hearings by the Senate Judiciary Committee, the Senate knew relatively little about David H. Souter (1939–   ) when it considered his nomination to the Supreme Court in October 1990. Judiciary Committee chair Joseph R. Biden, Jr., said less was known about Souter than about any other Supreme Court nominee in the previous quarter-century.

A New Hampshire native, Souter received his law degree from Harvard Law School and then served as a state trial court judge for five years. From 1983 to 1990 Souter was a justice on the New Hampshire supreme court. In early 1990 President George Bush appointed him to the U.S. Court of Appeals for the First Circuit. By the time Bush nominated him to the Supreme Court just a few months later, Souter had not yet written an opinion as an appeals court judge.

More than any other Supreme Court nominee in modern history, Souter was a person without a past. Unlike many judges and legal scholars, he had written virtually nothing for legal reviews. His sole law article was a tribute to a state court justice published in the *New Hampshire Bar Journal.* As interest groups and

Senate staff investigated Souter, they found little to indicate how he would vote as a Supreme Court justice.

Souter took great pains not to enlighten them during three days of testimony before the Senate Judiciary Committee. While impressing the senators with his intelligence, Souter told them little about his views concerning the issues likely to come before the Court. The senators were particularly eager to learn Souter's view about abortion, but he continually sidestepped questions on the subject. At one point Souter said that while in college, he had counseled a friend and his pregnant girlfriend who wanted an abortion. However, Souter declined to say what he had advised the couple to do.

After Souter's testimony, the committee heard from witnesses who were split on whether Souter should be confirmed. He enjoyed bipartisan support from New Hampshire officials. Abortion rights groups and women's groups opposed his nomination, saying that he should have been forced to state his view about abortion. After hearing all the testimony, the Senate voted 90–9 to confirm Souter.

Speech, Commercial

Commercial speech—that is, advertising—was formerly considered unprotected by the First Amendment. Therefore, it was subject to regulation or even prohibition by Congress or the states. In a series of decisions in the 1970s the Supreme Court extended constitutional protection to commercial speech. It continued, however, to permit regulation to prevent the publication of false, deceptive, or misleading information. By the 1980s the Court had become more receptive to the notion of regulating or even banning some types of advertising.

The Court's early precedent in the commercial speech area was *Valentine v. Chrestensen* (1942), which upheld a local ordinance banning the distribution of commercial handbills. Two decades later the Court reached a landmark libel ruling, *NEW YORK TIMES CO. V. SULLIVAN* (1964). In that case the Court held that an advertisement seeking support for the civil rights movement "was not a commercial advertisement" in the same sense as in *Chrestensen* and did enjoy constitutional protection. The Court similarly cited the political nature of a commercial message in a 1975 decision that overturned the conviction of a Virginia newspaper editor for violating a state law prohibiting the advertising of abortion services.

The following year, in *Virginia State Board of Pharmacy v. Virginia Citizens Consumer Council, Inc.* (1976), the Court abandoned the distinction between advertising that conveyed important public information and advertising that dealt only with a commercial transaction. In striking down a ban on the advertisement of prices of prescription drugs, the Court said that commercial speech served important interests of consumers as well as the sellers of products or services. "The free flow of commercial information is indispensable to the proper allocation of resources in a free enterprise system," Justice Harry A. Blackmun wrote in his opinion for the Court.

State bar associations, which lay out rules of conduct for their members, prohibited the use of advertising. In Bates v. State Bar of Arizona *(1977) the Supreme Court ruled that such a ban violated the First Amendment.   Source:* Bates v. State Bar of Arizona

In later decisions the Court extended the doctrine into other areas, including advertising by lawyers. The Court also ruled that privately owned utilities could not be prohibited from promotional advertising or required to send out conservation messages with which they did not agree.

The expansion of the commercial speech doctrine appeared to halt in the 1980s. In 1986 the Court upheld, by a 5–4 vote, a Puerto Rico law that banned advertising of gambling within its borders even though gambling was legal there *(Posadas de Puerto Rico Associates v. Tourism Co. of Puerto Rico)*. Writing for the majority, Chief Justice William H. Rehnquist, who had been a dissenter in the early commercial speech rulings, said that since Puerto Rico could ban gambling altogether, it necessarily also enjoyed "the lesser power" to ban advertising of gambling.

Several commentators suggested that the ruling provided the basis for banning advertising of other legal products and services, including alcoholic beverages and tobacco. The dissenting justices said that the advertising ban did not satisfy First Amendment doctrines requiring that speech restrictions further a substantial public interest and use the least restrictive means in doing so.

Speech, Freedom of

The First Amendment states that "Congress shall make no law . . . abridging the freedom of speech, or of the press; or the right of the people peaceably to assemble, and to petition the Government for a redress of grievances." Along with the amendment's protections of religious liberty, these freedoms of expression are the most widely cherished of the liberties guaranteed by the Bill of Rights. (See ASSEMBLY, FREEDOM OF; PETITION, RIGHT OF; PRESS, FREEDOM OF; RELIGION, FREEDOM OF.)

Freedom of speech has never been held to be absolute. The Supreme Court has upheld many restrictions on free speech, based on national security, public safety, or protection of competing private interests. In the twentieth century, however, the Court has

gradually limited the power of the federal or state governments to regulate either pure speech or what it sometimes calls "speech plus"—that is, speech combined with conduct, such as parading, demonstrating, or picketing.

The Court has created various doctrines to limit government power to regulate speech. In 1919 the Court required that speech limitations be imposed only against a "clear and present danger." This doctrine held for fifty years until it was replaced by a stricter test. In the 1940s the Court said that First Amendment freedoms enjoyed a "preferred position" and were subject to restriction only after heightened judicial scrutiny. In the 1950s the Court more often used a "balancing doctrine" that weighed First Amendment rights against other public interests in reviewing regulation of speech, with unpredictable results. In more recent cases the Court has sometimes required a "compelling public interest" to justify government regulation, but again with unpredictable results.

Recognizing the inadequacies of these substantive tests, the Court has also used tests that focus on the challenged statute rather than the conduct or speech it regulates. These doctrines—statutory vagueness, facial overbreadth, and the least restrictive means test—are based on the premise that laws imposing broad restrictions may stop some people from exercising constitutionally protected freedoms. In several cases in the 1980s, however, the Court appeared to back away from the requirement that government regulation of speech should be no more restrictive than necessary.

National Security

The broadest official restrictions on pure speech have come during times of war or international tensions. The Court has sustained many federal and state controls on seditious or subversive speech, but its most recent decisions have either limited these laws or curtailed the government's ability to enforce them. (See SEDITION LAWS; COMMUNISM.)

The Sedition Act of 1798 was enacted when the nation was politically divided between pro-British and pro-French factions. The Court did not rule on

The Ku Klux Klan marches in Washington, D.C., 1926. In Brandenburg v. Ohio *(1969), which concerned the Klan, the Supreme Court held that it is unconstitutional to punish a person who advocates violence as a means of accomplishing political reform.*   *Source: Library of Congress*

the law before it expired in 1801. Similarly the Court was never asked to rule on the restrictions imposed on freedom of speech and press under martial law during the Civil War.

The Court first tried to establish a framework for balancing national security and free speech in the Sedition Act cases after World War I. In the first of the cases, *Schenck v. United States* (1919), Justice Oliver Wendell Holmes, Jr., created the most famous free speech doctrine: the clear and present danger test. In upholding convictions under the act, Holmes said that the First Amendment did not protect speech if the words raised a clear and present danger of bringing about evils that Congress had the constitutional authority to prevent. In later cases, Holmes often dis-

sented as the Court either applied his doctrine loosely or used a "bad tendency" test that required less proof of an imminent and probable danger.

In one of those rulings the Court laid the basis for expanding constitutional protections. In upholding New York's sedition law in *Gitlow v. New York* (1925), the Court for the first time held that the free speech and press clauses of the First Amendment applied to the states. As a result, the Court in the 1930s struck down some provisions of state laws restricting free speech rights.

The Court showed more deference to Congress with its Cold War rulings on federal antisubversive laws. "Overthrow of the Government by force and violence is certainly a substantial enough interest for the Government to limit speech," Chief Justice Fred M. Vinson wrote in the plurality opinion in *Dennis v. United States* (1951), upholding the 1940 Smith Act. The Court later narrowed the law, however, by requiring the government to prove advocacy of concrete action to overthrow the government—not merely advocacy of an abstract doctrine.

In 1969 the Court reinforced this distinction between advocacy and "incitement" in a decision overturning a state criminal syndicalism law. In *Brandenburg v. Ohio* the Court unanimously held that states had no authority to "forbid or proscribe advocacy except where such advocacy is directed to inciting or producing imminent lawless action and is likely to incite or produce such action."

Public Safety

Some laws restricting speech are enacted in the interest of protecting community peace and order. In reviewing such laws the Court has tried to find a balance between the rights of an individual to make a public speech and of an audience to hear that speech, and the government's obligation to maintain public order and safety.

In two key decisions, *Hague v. C.I.O.* (1939) and *Cox v. New Hampshire* (1941), the Court established the right of individuals to communicate ideas in public places subject to reasonable regulations concerning time, place, and manner. A related question was whether the First Amendment protected speech that sparked a breach of the peace or threatened to provoke violence.

In *Chaplinsky v. New Hampshire* (1942) the Court held that "fighting words"—words so insulting that they provoke violence from the person or persons to whom they are addressed—are not protected by the First Amendment. The ruling unanimously upheld the conviction of a Jehovah's Witness who provoked a public disturbance when he assailed another religion as "a racket" and called a police officer "a God damned racketeer" and "a damned Fascist."

In two later cases the Court issued seemingly contradictory rulings in cases where speakers were arrested and convicted for breach of the peace because of the unruly reactions that their speeches provoked from their audiences. In 1949 the Court reversed a

conviction by saying that the jury instructions in the case could have allowed the punishment of protected speech. Two years later the Court affirmed a conviction arising from a less serious disruption, ruling that police could arrest a speaker who refused a request to stop speaking, as long as the request was not a guise for suppressing speech.

More recent rulings appear to limit the discretion of law enforcement officials in dealing with potential disturbances. In 1969 the Court reversed convictions of civil rights protesters in Chicago whose march near the mayor's residence drew a hostile response from neighbors. In 1972 it reversed a Georgia man's conviction for calling a police officer a "son of a bitch," saying the law had been construed to cover more than "fighting words."

The Court has had less difficulty in dealing with efforts to place prior restraints on speech. In 1945 it overturned a citation for contempt of court against a union organizer who had refused to apply for the organizer's permit required by Texas law. In 1951 the Court overturned the conviction of a Baptist minister who conducted a worship service on a New York City street even though authorities had refused to issue him a permit because of his anti-Catholic and anti-Semitic remarks in previous appearances.

Offensiveness

Some laws have provided for punishing offensive speech even if it did not create or threaten a public disturbance. In a celebrated case in 1971, however, the Court declared that speech cannot be prohibited on the basis of offensiveness alone. In several cases, including the 1989 and 1990 flag-burning decisions and the 1992 "hate crimes" ruling, the Court has made clear that "symbolic speech" may be constitutionally protected even if it includes conduct defined as unlawful. Symbolic speech is the expression of ideas and beliefs through symbols rather than words.

In *Cohen v. California* (1971) the Court, by a vote of 5 to 4, reversed the conviction of a California man who entered a Los Angeles courthouse wearing a jacket inscribed with the slogan "Fuck the Draft." State law defined "offensive conduct" as a breach of the peace. In his opinion Justice John Marshall Harlan said the offending slogan was not conduct but speech and was protected unless it provoked or was intended to provoke a breach of the peace.

The Court first extended constitutional protection to symbolic speech in 1931. The decision reversed a conviction under a California law that prohibited raising a red flag as a symbol of opposition to organized government. In 1943 the Court issued one of its most eloquent defenses of free speech in the second of the FLAG SALUTE CASES, ruling that states could not compel schoolchildren to pledge allegiance to the flag. In three Vietnam War–era cases the Court reversed convictions of persons who used the flag to symbolize opposition to government policy—by flying the flag upside down, wearing pants with a flag sewn on the seat, or superimposing a peace symbol on a flag.

These rulings logically led to the Court's decision striking down state laws that prohibited the desecration of the American flag by burning or other means. But the Court's 5–4 ruling in *Texas v. Johnson* (1989) aroused a storm of protest that included calls for a constitutional amendment to reverse the decision. (See REVERSALS OF RULINGS BY CONSTITUTIONAL AMENDMENT.) Congress passed a federal flag protection act that supporters said would be upheld. In *United States v. Eichman* (1990), however, the Court by the same 5–4 majority struck down that law as well. Shortly after the second ruling, Congress rejected a constitutional amendment to overturn it.

In 1992 the Court again expanded free speech protections on a highly visible issue, hate crimes. Some states and localities had passed laws prohibiting displays of racial, religious, or gender prejudice, including such practices as cross burning or swastika displays. In *R.A.V. v. City of St. Paul* the Court struck down a hate crime ordinance enacted by St. Paul, Minnesota.

The vote in the case was unanimous, but the justices split 5–4 in their reasoning. Writing for the majority, Justice Antonin Scalia said the law improperly singled out "messages of racial, gender, or religious intolerance" on the basis of content. To fall within the fighting words doctrine, Scalia said, the law should have prohibited speech based on its threatening nature rather than the message it conveyed. The other four justices argued that the law should have been struck down as overly broad.

One year later, however, the Court unanimously

Gregory Johnson holds an American flag while another man sets it on fire. In 1989 the Supreme Court on First Amendment grounds overturned Johnson's conviction for flag burning. In 1990 the Court reaffirmed its decision by ruling the Flag Protection Act unconstitutional.   Source: Bill Pierce

ruled that states can impose additional penalties on criminals who select their victims on the basis of race, religion, ethnic origin, or other protected status. Rehnquist said that so-called hate crime penalty enhancement laws do not amount to punishment of speech.

The Court has allowed the government to punish symbolic speech when it includes conduct that the government has a strong interest in preventing. In *United States v. O'Brien* (1968) the Court said the government's interest in operation of the selective service system was strong enough to sustain the conviction of an antiwar protester for burning his draft card.

Private Interests

Some restrictions on speech are aimed at protecting private interests of individuals. These may include trespass laws allowing property owners to exclude free speech activities, limitations on door-to-door solicitation or canvassing, or noise control ordinances. The Court has sustained some such restrictions while striking down others.

The Court ruled in 1946 that the "company town" (a town wholly owned by the area's main employer) of Chickasaw, Alabama, could not prohibit distribution of handbills on the town's streets *(Marsh v. Alabama)*. In 1968 the Court, by a vote of 5 to 4, extended the decision to protect union picketing of a store in a shopping center. In two later decisions in 1972 and 1976, however, the Court first narrowed and then overruled the shopping center decision.

The Court has extended more protection to non-commercial, door-to-door solicitation and canvassing in the face of competing claims of residential privacy. The Court in 1943 overturned a local ordinance prohibiting door-to-door canvassing, but in later decisions it has upheld some regulations on time, manner, and place. More recently the Court has struck down some financial regulations affecting groups that raise funds through such solicitations. The Court in 1980 struck down an Illinois law denying the right to solicit funds door-to-door to any group that spent more than a certain percentage of income on its administrative costs. In 1984 and 1988 it struck down Maryland and North Carolina laws regulating the professional solicitation of funds.

Noise control ordinances were first questioned by the Court in a 5–4 decision in 1948 that struck down a law prohibiting use of sound trucks without permission of the local police chief. A year later, however, the Court sustained an ordinance prohibiting use of sound equipment that emitted "loud and raucous noise." In its most recent decision on the issue, the Court in *Ward v. Rock Against Racism* (1989) upheld a New York City regulation requiring all performers at its bandshell in Central Park to use the sound amplification system provided by the city. Writing for the Court, Justice Anthony M. Kennedy said the regulation furthered the city's interest in protecting residents from unwelcome noise.

Speedy Trial, Right to

The Sixth Amendment provides that "in all criminal prosecutions, the accused shall enjoy the right to a speedy and public trial." The Constitution, however, sets no definite time limits. The Supreme Court has used an ad hoc, balancing approach to evaluate pretrial delays resulting from government actions.

The Court explained its balancing approach in *Barker v. Wingo* (1972). In that ruling the Court said that it considers the conduct of the prosecution and the defense in examining four factors: length of delay, reason for the delay, the defendant's assertion of his or her right, and prejudice to the defendant. Delay may often be to defendants' advantage, but sometimes it can hamper their ability to defend themselves at trial.

The Court applied the speedy trial right to the states in *Klopfer v. North Carolina* (1967). (See INCORPORATION DOCTRINE.) The ruling struck down a North Carolina law that allowed indefinite postponement of a criminal prosecution without dismissal of the indictment. Even though the defendant was not in custody, the Court said the procedure "clearly denies [him] the right to a speedy trial."

Violation of the right requires dismissal of charges, the Court has ruled. In *Strunk v. United States* (1973) the Court said that reduction of sentence was an insufficient remedy for an impermissible delay.

The speedy trial right does not apply to delays before a person is accused of a crime. Explaining this conclusion in 1977, the Court said that requiring the government to bring charges prematurely "would increase the likelihood of unwarranted charges being filed, and would add to the time during which defendants stand accused but untried."

In *Barker* the Court said that a defendant's failure to demand a speedy trial did not necessarily preclude him from raising the issue in later legal challenges. The decision prompted Congress to pass the Speedy

Trial Act of 1974, setting a normal deadline of 100 days between arrest or indictment and trial in federal courts. Many states have passed similar laws, and these statutes now provide a concrete basis for defendants to assert their right to a speedy trial.

Spending Powers

The authority of Congress to appropriate and spend money, under the necessary and proper clause of the Constitution (Article I, Section 8), to carry out any of its enumerated powers has been broadly interpreted by the Supreme Court. From the early days of the Union, the power to spend money for internal improvements has been justified by the authority given to Congress over war, interstate commerce, territories, and the mails.

Use of the spending powers has been challenged only rarely, in part because of a ruling, *Frothingham v. Mellon* (1923), that limited the standing of taxpayers or state governments to bring suit contesting federal spending. In a series of decisions the Court has also upheld Congress's power to impose conditions on state and local governments to receive federal funds under grant-in-aid programs.

The Supreme Court's only major ruling questioning the broad spending powers of the federal government came in 1935, when it struck down the Agricultural Adjustment Act of 1933. This New Deal measure was designed to raise farm prices by taxing food processors and using the proceeds to pay benefits to farmers who reduced their production of commodities.

The Court's 6–3 ruling in the case, *United States v. Butler,* cited objections to both the taxing and spending components of the program. Writing for the Court, Justice Owen J. Roberts declared the crop benefit payments unconstitutional because they were part of an overall scheme that intruded on the states' authority over agricultural production.

In a pair of decisions two years later the Court effectively left the *Butler* decision a dead letter. Justice Roberts switched sides to form 5–4 majorities that sustained the unemployment compensation and old age benefits established by the 1935 Social Security Act. Writing for the Court in both cases, *Steward Machine Co. v. Davis* and *Helvering v. Davis* (both 1937), Justice Benjamin N. Cardozo said Congress's power to provide for the general welfare gave it the authority to tax employers to pay for the two benefit programs.

With the broad question of congressional authority settled, states protested the conditions Congress attached to federal funds. The Court rejected the states' challenges. In *Oklahoma v. Civil Service Commission* (1947) the Court upheld a provision of the Hatch Act that called for reducing federal highway funds if states failed to enforce the law's restriction against partisan political activity by state employees in federally funded programs. The Court declared that the federal government "has the power to fix the terms upon which its money allotments to States shall be disbursed." The Court reaffirmed the ruling in 1987 when it upheld a congressional provision that states raise the drinking age to twenty-one in order to receive the full allocation of federal highway aid.

Standing to Sue

Determination of standing involves the question of whether an individual has a sufficient personal interest at stake in a legal dispute to bring the matter into a court. The Supreme Court has developed complex rules to define standing. Some of the rules are based on the Constitution's CASE OR CONTROVERSY RULE, others on the concept of JUDICIAL RESTRAINT.

The standing doctrine determines how easy or difficult it is for plaintiffs to get into court, especially with suits that challenge laws or government policies as unconstitutional. During the 1960s and early 1970s, liberalized standing rules seemed to invite more litigation. Since that time the Supreme Court has tightened the standing rules in order to channel policy disputes away from the courts and back into the political process.

The Court has said that three elements are constitutionally required to establish standing:

The plaintiff must have suffered an "injury in fact"—that is, an invasion of a legally protected interest that is "concrete and particularized' and "actual or imminent" rather than "conjectural" or "hypothetical."

The conduct complained of must have caused the injury.

A favorable ruling must be "likely" to "redress" or relieve the injury.

The Court has developed three additional rules that focus on the legal basis for the suit. These self-imposed rules can be changed by Congress and are not consistently applied by the Court itself:

The plaintiff ordinarily must assert that the conduct complained of violates his or her own rights, not someone else's. (There are some important exceptions to this rule.)

The plaintiff must have an interest distinct from "the generalized interest of all citizens in constitutional governance."

The plaintiff must assert a legal interest that is "within the zone of interests to be protected or regulated by the statute or constitutional guarantee in question."

The standing doctrine poses a high barrier to so-called taxpayer suits—that is, suits based on a plaintiff's interest as a taxpayer in the expenditure of federal funds. A 1925 Supreme Court ruling was interpreted as barring virtually all taxpayer efforts to challenge the constitutionality of a federal law, unless the taxpayer could show some additional personal stake in the law's enforcement.

The case, *Frothingham v. Mellon*, stemmed from a challenge by a Massachusetts taxpayer to the use of federal grants-in-aid to states for maternal and child health programs. Frothingham asserted that the aid violated states' rights under the Tenth Amendment and her own PROPERTY RIGHTS under the Fifth Amendment. But the Court called her interest in the use of federal revenues "comparatively minute and indeterminable." The Court said further that the pos-

sible effect on her future tax burdens was "so remote, fluctuating, and uncertain" that she lacked adequate personal interest to bring suit.

In *Flast v. Cohen* (1968) the Court created a limited exception to the *Frothingham* doctrine for suits based on specific constitutional provisions restricting the federal SPENDING POWERS or TAXING POWER. The decision permitted a taxpayer's suit to block the use of federal funds to aid parochial schools. Writing for the Court, Chief Justice Earl Warren said that Flast had standing to challenge use of the funds as a violation of the First Amendment provision banning the establishment of religion. (See PAROCHIAL SCHOOLS, AID TO; RELIGION, FREEDOM OF.)

The Court later made it clear that the exception permitting taxpayer suits was very limited. In *United States v. Richardson* (1974) the Court barred a taxpayer suit challenging the secrecy of the Central Intelligence Agency (CIA) budget—a secrecy that allegedly conflicted with the constitutional provision for a public statement of all federal spending. But Chief Justice Warren E. Burger said the suit was not a challenge to Congress's power to tax or spend, as in *Flast*, but rather a challenge to the laws governing the CIA. In a series of rulings in the 1970s the Court barred other taxpayer suits challenging military surveillance programs, membership of some members of Congress in the armed forces reserves, municipal zoning ordinances, and the tax-exempt status of certain hospitals.

The Court has enlarged the categories of interests that may be asserted by citizens or taxpayers in federal cases. The asserted interest may be economic, constitutional, aesthetic, conservationist, or recreational. The interest must still be personal rather than general, but in some environmental and voting rights cases that requirement has been applied flexibly.

In situations where it appears unlikely that the people most directly affected by the challenged law will be able to bring their own legal action, the Court has allowed others to make the challenge. For example, white plaintiffs were allowed to challenge laws restricting the rights of blacks to live or buy property in certain neighborhoods. The Court has also permitted doctors to represent patients' rights to abortion, private schools to represent parents' rights to choose private education, and sellers to represent the rights of young consumers to buy contraceptives.

One unsettled question is the extent to which Congress can confer standing by including provisions in new laws permitting suits by any person. The issue was discussed in a 1992 decision, *Lujan v. Defenders of Wildlife,* which found no standing under such a provision in the Endangered Species Act. The suit was dismissed. In a plurality opinion three justices suggested that such broad standing provisions would not meet the case and controversy requirement of Article III and would also improperly intrude on the president's Article II power to faithfully execute the laws. But in a concurring opinion the two other justices who joined in the decision said Congress has the power "to define injuries and articulate chains of causation that will give rise to a case or controversy where none existed before."

Stare Decisis

Stare decisis is a Latin phrase meaning "let the decision stand." The phrase embodies the principle of adherence to settled cases. The Supreme Court generally operates under this doctrine, which provides that the principles of law established in earlier judicial decisions should be accepted as authoritative in similar later cases. (See PRECEDENT.)

States and the Court

The Constitution, written to create the national government, limits the powers and activities of the states. Yet it also assumes their continued operation as effective units of local government.

The Supreme Court has defined the limits of state power. Using its power of JUDICIAL REVIEW, the Court has time and time again struck down state action as being in conflict with the Constitution or with federal law. It has limited states' power over their economies and required them to protect individual rights in their courts, government programs, and political life. Through 1990 the Court had declared more than 1,200 state or local laws unconstitutional.

Under Chief Justice John Marshall the Court acted decisively to establish the supremacy of the new national government, although Congress and the president sometimes showed greater regard for states' rights. After Marshall's death the Court was more attentive to states' rights, but it had no power to contain the sectional rivalries or disputes over slavery that led to secession and Civil War. The Union victory was also the victory of national government and effectively ended the idea of the states as coequal sovereigns with the federal government.

Despite the Court's rulings limiting states' powers, the principle of FEDERALISM remains very much alive. States still manage their own social, economic, and political affairs unless Congress has acted to establish a uniform national rule or the Constitution requires one. And while the Court upholds federal supremacy, its rulings serve to legitimize as well as to limit states' powers.

States and Judicial Review

The states put up powerful resistance to the Supreme Court's power in the nation's early history. After the Court in 1793 upheld the right of a citizen of one state to sue another state in the Supreme Court, the states rose up in protest. Within five years Congress had approved, and the states ratified, the Eleventh Amendment to protect the states from being hauled into federal court. (See REVERSALS OF RULINGS BY CONSTITUTIONAL AMENDMENT.)

The states also resisted the Supreme Court's power—granted in Section 25 of the Judiciary Act of 1789—to review state court rulings and, by implication, to strike down state laws as contrary to the Constitution or federal law. When the Court in 1815 overrode a Virginia law barring landownership by foreigners, the Virginia supreme court responded by declaring Section 25 itself unconstitutional. Three months later the U.S. Supreme Court forcefully reaffirmed its power, saying Section 25 was "supported by the letter and spirit of the Constitution."

By 1825 the Court had invalidated, in whole or in part, statutes of ten different states. The states sought relief from Congress. Efforts were made to repeal Section 25, transfer the Court's jurisdiction over state court rulings to the Senate, or require more than a simple majority of the justices to nullify a state law. None succeeded, but the Court's power remained precarious.

The most dramatic clash of Court and state power involved a dispute between the state of Georgia and the Cherokee Indians in the early nineteenth century. In the 1820s the state sought to enforce increasingly stringent laws against the Cherokees. When the tribe asked the Court to bar enforcement of the laws, the state refused to appear and went ahead with the execution of an Indian who had been convicted of murder under the disputed laws.

Although the Court later decided it had no jurisdiction over the tribe's suit, there was soon a second challenge to the laws. Two missionaries had been convicted of violating a state law requiring white persons living on Indian territory to obtain a license. The missionaries appealed their convictions to the Supreme Court. In March 1832 the Court declared the state laws invalid because the federal government had exclusive jurisdiction over Indians.

Georgia, however, defied the Court by refusing to release the missionaries—with the tacit support of President Andrew Jackson. The dispute simmered for more than a year and cooled only because of other political developments. South Carolina protested a new federal tariff by claiming the right to nullify federal laws it viewed as unconstitutional; Jackson described the theory as treason. Having taken that stance, Jackson could not continue to sanction Georgia's defiance of the Court. Deprived of Jackson's support, Georgia officials pardoned the missionaries, ending the case.

There was sporadic state resistance to federal judicial power until the Civil War, but it largely disappeared with the war's end. Supreme Court decisions striking down state or local laws became more frequent; some 300 laws were struck down between 1914 and 1938. Still, the idea of judicial review was no longer seriously challenged. Much later, even the fierce opposition to the Warren Court's activist rulings on individual rights in the 1950s and 1960s failed to mount a broad attack against the Court's power.

States and the Economy

The framers of the Constitution sought to promote the creation of a national economy by giving Congress the power to regulate interstate and foreign commerce. (See COMMERCE POWER.) Supplementing that grant, the Constitution forbade states to tax imports or exports without congressional consent. (See TAXING POWER.)

In addition, the Constitution protected PROPERTY RIGHTS by prohibiting states from impairing the obligation of contracts. (See CONTRACT CLAUSE.) It also sought to guarantee the stability of commercial transactions by forbidding the states to coin money, issue bills of tender, or make changes in the legal tender. (See CURRENCY POWERS.)

The Marshall Court used these constitutional provisions to limit states' powers. In *GIBBONS V. OGDEN* (1824) it struck down New York's steamboat monopoly law under a broad interpretation of the federal commerce power. A Maryland tax on vendors of foreign goods was struck down in 1827. The Court invoked the contract clause several times to protect the rights of private corporations against encroachments by state legislatures.

Once these limits were established, the Court became more willing to acknowledge the states' power to regulate commerce within their own borders. Under Marshall's successor as chief justice, Roger B. Taney, the Court gave a broad approval to the states' POLICE POWER as the basis for a variety of state actions to protect citizens, public health and morals, and natural resources. On this basis, for example, the Court in 1847 upheld state laws requiring licensing to sell alcoholic beverages. In addition, the Court in 1852 adopted a rule recognizing concurrent federal and state power over commerce unless the subject required uniform national regulation *(Cooley v. Board of Wardens of the Port of Philadelphia)*.

In applying the *Cooley* rule in the decades after the Civil War, the Court put some subjects, such as immigration and railroad rates, under exclusive federal regulation. But the states were left in control of such major economic areas as manufacturing and agriculture.

The Court invoked this doctrine in the 1890s to narrow the reach of federal ANTITRUST law and in 1918 to overturn a federal CHILD LABOR law.

The Court in the late nineteenth and early twentieth centuries limited the states' regulation of economic affairs by construing the Fourteenth Amendment DUE PROCESS clause to protect private property rights and freedom of contract. This laissez-faire philosophy led the Court to overturn some state economic regulatory measures in the first third of the twentieth century—effectively creating a zone where neither the federal government nor the states could exercise authority.

The Court repudiated this substantive due process doctrine beginning in 1937. Since then the Court has been more tolerant of state regulation of business, even as it has upheld the extension of federal power into areas of the economy formerly left entirely to state control. It has continued to help preserve a national economy, however, by striking down state laws that impose undue burdens on interstate commerce or discriminate against commerce from other states.

For example, the Court has ruled that states impermissibly burdened interstate commerce by requiring specific kinds of mud flaps on trucks or by banning double-trailer trucks. In 1978 it ruled that New Jersey improperly discriminated against out-of-state commerce by prohibiting the importation of solid or liquid waste—that is, garbage—from another state. In several cases the Court has carefully scrutinized state tax measures to ensure that they treat out-of-state taxpayers the same as in-state taxpayers.

States and the Individual

The Supreme Court's decisions limiting state power to protect individual rights are of recent vintage. The Constitution imposes few restraints on how a state deals with an individual, and the Court initially interpreted the Bill of Rights to apply solely to the federal government and not to the states. Even after the adoption of the Civil War Amendments, the Court for decades ruled that most CIVIL RIGHTS questions remained within the purview of the states.

In the mid-1920s the Court began using the Fourteenth Amendment due process clause to protect certain individual rights against infringements by the states. (See INCORPORATION DOCTRINE.) First Amendment freedoms were the first to win protection, followed by due process rights of fair trial and fair treatment for persons suspected or accused of crimes. (See CRIMINAL LAW AND PROCEDURE.) Then, at mid-century, the Court adopted a stricter interpretation of the Fourteenth Amendment EQUAL PROTECTION clause to begin striking down legally mandated racial SEGREGATION.

Several landmark decisions were handed down by the Court under Chief Justice Earl Warren in these areas. *BROWN V. BOARD OF EDUCATION OF TOPEKA* (1954) barred racial segregation in public elementary and secondary schools. *BAKER V. CARR* (1962) subjected state REAPPORTIONMENT AND REDISTRICTING to federal court supervision. Decisions such as *GIDEON V. WAINWRIGHT* (1963) and *MIRANDA V. ARIZONA* (1966) brought about a revolution in state criminal justice systems and police stationhouses. All these decisions provoked strong protests from the states.

Many state and local governments engaged in what was called massive resistance to the *Brown* decision. Their actions were encouraged by a manifesto signed by more than one hundred southern members of Congress that called the ruling "a clear abuse of judicial power." After more than a decade of foot dragging in the states, the Court in 1965 declared that delay in desegregating public schools was "no longer tolerable." (See SCHOOL DESEGREGATION.)

On reapportionment, states lobbied Congress either to deny federal courts jurisdiction over such cases or to pass a constitutional amendment permitting one chamber of a state legislature to be apportioned on the basis of factors other than population. When those efforts failed, advocates of the constitutional amendment tried but failed to force Congress to call a constitutional convention to consider the measure.

Reaction to the criminal procedure rulings was less concerted, but the opposition from police, prosecutors, and other state officials helped make law and order a topic of national debate and a potent political issue in the 1968 presidential campaign. (See ELECTIONS AND THE COURT.)

With the appointment of more conservative justices, the Burger and Rehnquist courts eased some of

Despite the federal government's order to integrate schools and universities, Alabama governor George Wallace refused to comply until President John F. Kennedy federalized the National Guard. Wallace, a segregationist who ran for president in 1968 as an independent, was elected to four terms as governor.
Source: Library of Congress

states sharply restricted the states' sovereignty. The Court has cut less deeply into some other powers of the states, such as power over elections, the powers of their courts, the broad police power over their land and people, and the power to tax. Even these central areas of state sovereignty, however, are subject to limits.

Under the POLITICAL QUESTION doctrine, the Court has declined to rule on some questions of state political power. In 1912, for example, it avoided a direct ruling on a challenge to Oregon's adoption of the direct legislative devices of the initiative and referendum. But the Court's decisions permitting reapportionment challenges in federal courts were followed by rulings that subjected other state political issues to federal limits as well. The Court upheld the Voting Rights Act of 1965 against an argument that it invaded the reserved rights of the states to set voter qualifications. And it later struck down several state election laws on First Amendment or equal protection grounds. (See CAMPAIGNS AND ELECTIONS.)

The Court has similarly found limits on states' exercise of their police powers in such areas as public health and ZONING. It has limited states' taxing powers by prohibiting taxation for private purposes or direct taxation of the federal government. And it has created an opening, although a very narrow one, for federal courts to enjoin state courts to protect their own authority or to block enforcement of a flagrantly unconstitutional law. (See COMITY.)

Most significantly, the Court has narrowed the protection that the Eleventh Amendment established regarding federal court suits against the states. While adhering to the terms of the amendment, the Court in the nineteenth century allowed suits against state officials for carrying out an unconstitutional law or otherwise exceeding their lawful authority. In such circumstances, the Court has said, the official acts as an individual and can be sued as one.

Expanding this doctrine, the Court in *Ex parte Young* (1908) ruled that federal courts could issue INJUNCTIONS against state officials to block the enforcement of unconstitutional state laws. In 1918 the Court permitted private damage suits against state officials for injuries resulting from negligent or willful disregard for state laws.

the requirements on states in the areas of criminal procedure and desegregation. The decisions were not, however, the result of any special regard for state sovereignty. With only a few exceptions, the Court has held that the guarantees of the Bill of Rights apply equally to the federal government and the states. The states' powers in matters affecting individual rights thus depend on the Court's definition of those rights rather than on a balancing of the state interests.

The State as Sovereign

The Supreme Court's decisions establishing judicial review over the states, supporting broad application of Congress's commerce powers to state economies, and extending the Bill of Rights to the

In *Milliken v. Bradley* (1977) the Court went further in this direction. It ruled in a school desegregation case that federal courts could issue an affirmative injunction in such cases requiring a state to pay the cost of future constitutional compliance. The next year the Court, in a prison conditions suit, also upheld an award of attorneys' fees against a state. The combined effect was to open state treasuries to judicial decrees.

The Court has also sustained federal intrusions into state affairs under the guise of Congress's SPENDING POWERS. It has supported Congress's right to attach conditions to federal grants-in-aid, rejecting arguments that the financial penalties from noncompliance amount to federal coercion of the states.

The states were encouraged by a decision in 1976 that set some limit on federal power in the interest of states' sovereignty. In *National League of Cities v. Usery* the Court struck down, by a 5–4 vote, an act of Congress that had imposed federal minimum wage and overtime rules on state employees. Citing the Tenth Amendment, the Court declared, "There are attributes of sovereignty attaching to every state government which may not be impaired by Congress."

The states did not benefit from the promise of the *National League of Cities* ruling, for the Court first limited and then overruled it. Justice Harry A. Blackmun switched sides to form a new 5–4 majority in *Garcia v. San Antonio Metropolitan Transit Authority* (1985), saying the standard set in the earlier opinion had proved unworkable. States must rely on the political process rather than the Constitution to protect themselves from federal overreaching, the Court said.

In 1992 the Court itself found a case of congressional overreaching when it struck down a portion of a complex law regarding disposal of low-level radioactive wastes. The law provided financial incentives for the states to establish sites to dispose of such wastes within their own borders or in cooperation with other

One year after the Voting Rights Act of 1965 was passed, the Court upheld its constitutionality in South Carolina v. Katzenbach. *The act, which abolished literacy tests for voters and called for federal approval of state election laws, was challenged on the grounds that it violated states' rights to specify qualifications for voters. In ruling against discrimination, the Court paved the way for egalitarian polling procedures. Here, voters in Washington, D.C., cast their ballots in the 1992 presidential election.   Source: R. Michael Jenkins*

states. States that did not make such arrangements were required to "take title" to and assume liability for the wastes themselves.

In *New York v. United States* (1992) the Court, by a vote of 6 to 3, found the "take title" provision unconstitutional. While the monetary incentives were proper, Justice Sandra Day O'Connor wrote in her opinion for the Court, a direct command to regulate according to congressional dictates or take ownership of the radioactive wastes went too far. Congress could enact national regulations, O'Connor said, but it had no authority to "commandeer" the states' legislative processes.

Commentators were uncertain whether to view the ruling as heralding a possible revival of state sovereignty. In any case the decision showed that state prerogatives still had some role to play in the allocation of power between the states and the federal government.

Steel Seizure Cases

See YOUNGSTOWN SHEET AND TUBE CO. V. SAWYER.

Source: *Library of Congress*

Stevens, John P.

After being appointed to the Supreme Court in 1975, Justice John Paul Stevens (1920–   ) resisted efforts to peg him as either a liberal or a conservative. Overall, he took a centrist position and developed a reputation for writing scholarly opinions that made him a "judge's judge."

Stevens was born in Chicago. He graduated Phi Beta Kappa from the University of Chicago in 1941 and magna cum laude from the Northwestern University School of Law in 1947. In between receiving his degrees, Stevens served in the navy during World War II and earned a Bronze Star. After receiving his law degree Stevens served as a law clerk to Supreme Court justice Wiley B. Rutledge. He then left Washington to join a prominent Chicago law firm that specialized in antitrust law.

Stevens became an acknowledged expert in the field and in 1951 served as associate counsel to the House subcommittee on monopoly power. He then returned to Chicago to form his own law firm. From 1953 to 1955 Stevens was a member of the attorney general's National Committee to Study the Antitrust Laws. He continued practicing law and teaching part time at the law schools at Northwestern University and the University of Chicago until President Richard Nixon appointed him to the Seventh Circuit Court of Appeals in 1970. Stevens remained on the appeals court until President Gerald R. Ford nominated him in 1975 to replace Justice William O. Douglas on the Supreme Court.

One of Stevens's most important opinions for the Court came in *Wallace v. Jaffree* (1985). In that case the Court struck down an Alabama law allowing a moment of silence for prayer or meditation at the beginning of each school day. In the opinion for the 6–3 Court, Stevens wrote that it was "established principle that the government must pursue a course of complete neutrality toward religion."

Stevens frequently dissented from the most conservative rulings of the Burger and Rehnquist courts. He dissented when the Court sanctioned the search of a newspaper office for information about a demonstration, narrowed the circumstances in which state defendants have a right to counsel, and upheld a law restricting federal funding of abortions. He also dissented when the Court upheld a Georgia law against sodomy, allowed states to execute persons convicted of committing capital crimes when they were sixteen or seventeen, and upheld a Missouri law barring the use of public facilities to perform abortions.

had marched peacefully to protest racial discrimination, limited the area that police can search when they arrest a suspect, and ordered racially segregated private schools to admit blacks. But Stewart also dissented from many of the Court's liberal rulings. He dissented when the Court barred prayer in public schools, expanded suspects' right to legal counsel, and extended the protection against self-incrimination to defendants in state cases. He also dissented from Court decisions striking down loyalty oaths in Arizona and New York, requiring that criminal suspects be advised of their rights to remain silent and to have counsel, and overturning a state law barring anyone, including married couples, from using contraceptives.

In two cases involving the press Stewart found himself in the unusual position of joining the Court's most liberal justices on the losing side. In those cases the Court ruled that reporters do not have a constitutional right to protect sources and that the First

Stewart, Potter

Unlike many Supreme Court justices, Potter Stewart (1915–1985) was neither clearly liberal nor conservative. In his nearly twenty-three years as a justice, he wrote some of the Court's liberal opinions, but dissented from others.

Born in Jackson, Michigan, Stewart grew up in Cincinnati, Ohio. He received his undergraduate degree from Yale in 1937, spent a year in postgraduate study at Cambridge University in England, and graduated with honors from Yale Law School in 1941. He served in the navy during World War II. After the war Stewart joined a leading Cincinnati law firm. He served as a member of the Cincinnati city council from 1950 to 1953 and as vice mayor of the city from 1952 to 1953.

Stewart gained the attention of notable Republicans through his active involvement in Republican presidential campaigns. In 1954 he was appointed to the Sixth Circuit Court of Appeals, a position he held until President Dwight Eisenhower appointed him to the Supreme Court in 1958.

Liberal opinions that Stewart wrote for the Court overturned a state law making drug addiction a crime, struck down the convictions of students who

Source: Collection of the Supreme Court of the United States

Amendment does not bar police from searching newsrooms.

Stewart retired in July 1981 and died in 1985 following a stroke.

Stone, Harlan Fiske

When President Calvin Coolidge nominated Wall Street lawyer Harlan Fiske Stone (1872–1946) to the Supreme Court in 1925, Coolidge believed that Stone would be a conservative justice. Within a year of his appointment, however, Stone had aligned himself with the liberal wing of the Court.

Stone was born in Chesterfield, New Hampshire. He received his bachelor's and master's degrees from Amherst College, and graduated from Columbia University Law School in 1898. He then began practicing

Source: Library of Congress

law with the Wall Street firm of Sullivan and Cromwell. For the next twenty-five years Stone divided his time between practicing law and teaching law at Columbia.

In 1924 Coolidge appointed Stone attorney general. After serving only one year in the cabinet, Stone was nominated to the Supreme Court. Sen. Burton K. Wheeler, D-Mont., did his best to torpedo the nomination. At the time Stone was in the midst of prosecuting Wheeler for his participation in an oilfield fraud. (Wheeler was eventually acquitted.) Stone appeared before the Senate Judiciary Committee to defend himself, the first Supreme Court nominee to do so. He was successful in his defense, and the Senate confirmed him 71–6.

In *United States v. Carolene Products Co.* (1938) Stone set out a new standard for constitutional cases. He wrote that when a law is challenged for violating economic rights, the Court should presume the law is valid unless the plaintiff can prove otherwise. However, when the law infringes upon personal rights guaranteed by the Bill of Rights, the Court should take a much harder look at the statute. This new standard laid some of the groundwork for the later civil rights revolution.

In 1940 Stone was the sole dissenter when the Court upheld a state law requiring students to recite the pledge of allegiance even if doing so violated their religious beliefs. Three years later the Court reversed itself and adopted Stone's view that such a requirement is unconstitutional.

In 1941 President Franklin D. Roosevelt elevated Stone to chief justice. Roosevelt, a Democrat, actually wanted to appoint his attorney general, Robert H. Jackson, as chief justice. However, Jackson and Justice Felix Frankfurter convinced Roosevelt that appointing Stone, a Republican, would help draw the United States together as it approached entry into World War II. The United States entered the war only months after Stone became chief justice. Conflicts between personal liberty and governmental power dominated the court's docket while he presided.

Stone was not a gifted Court administrator. There was much personal bickering among the justices during his tenure, and Stone was either unable or unwilling to put aside his strongly partisan feelings to pull the Court together. This led to a Court that was frequently divided. On April 22, 1946, Stone was stricken ill while reading a dissent from the bench. He died later that day, having served twenty-one years on the Court.

Story, Joseph

At the age of thirty-two Joseph Story (1779–1845) was President James Madison's fourth choice to fill the Supreme Court seat vacated by the death of William Cushing. Story became one of the Court's most celebrated justices, and his Court opinions remain important documents in U.S. legal history.

Story was born in Marblehead, Massachusetts, six years after his father had taken part in the Boston Tea Party. He graduated second in his class from Harvard in 1798 and then began to read law for up to fourteen hours a day. A Republican-Democrat, he was the victim of prejudice when he began practicing law in Salem in 1801 because Federalists dominated the county bar.

Story was elected to the Massachusetts legislature in 1805 and served until his election in 1808 to the U.S. House of Representatives. He remained in Congress only one term. In 1811 he became Speaker of the House in the Massachusetts legislature. In November of that year Madison nominated him to the Supreme Court despite his lack of judicial experience. Madison had first asked Levi Lincoln and John Quincy Adams to accept the seat. Despite being separately confirmed by the Senate, both men declined. The Senate then rejected Madison's third choice, Alexander Wolcott, because of a belief that he was unqualified. Madison finally settled on Story, who became one of the two youngest justices ever to sit on the Court.

Story was actively interested in education for most of his life, and he supported higher education for women. He was elected to the Harvard board of overseers in 1819, became professor of law at Harvard in 1829, and helped found Harvard Law School. Story's reputation as a brilliant legal thinker grew at Harvard, where he wrote his famous nine commentaries on

Source: Collection of the Supreme Court of the United States

the law. He also wrote essays on the law for the *North American Review* and the *American Law Review,* as well as unsigned articles for the *Encyclopedia Americana.*

As a member of the Marshall Court, Story shared the chief justice's strongly nationalistic views. This viewpoint was expressed in Story's opinion for the Court in *Martin v. Hunter's Lessee* (1816), in which he wrote that the Supreme Court has the authority to hear appeals of state court decisions in civil cases involving federal statutes and treaties.

Story undoubtedly hoped to be named chief justice when Marshall died in 1835. However, President Andrew Jackson, who once called Story the "most dangerous man in America," nominated Roger B. Taney instead. As the Court gradually shifted from upholding federal supremacy to favoring states' rights, Story increasingly wrote dissenting opinions. During the Court's 1845 term, he began putting his affairs in order so he could resign. A sudden illness preempted his plans, however, and he died in September 1845.

Strict Construction

Strict construction is an imprecise term that originally meant a narrow view of the federal government's powers under the Constitution. More recently it has come to be a political slogan for a less activist federal judiciary, especially on CIVIL LIBERTIES issues. (See JUDICIAL ACTIVISM.) The opposite term, *broad construction,* is used less often. Broad construction has been the prevailing method of constitutional adjudication since 1937, especially on the scope of the federal government's powers.

Historically, the first great debate over how to interpret the Constitution centered on the powers granted to Congress under Article I, Section 8. Some of the nation's early leaders, including Thomas Jefferson and James Madison, wanted to "strictly construe" those powers. Others, most notably Alexander Hamilton, favored a broader construction.

The Supreme Court adopted the broader view in the landmark decision, *MCCULLOCH V. MARYLAND* (1819), upholding the chartering of the second Bank of the United States. The decision construed the necessary and proper clause of the Constitution as authorizing Congress to exercise "implied powers" in order to carry out the powers that were specifically enumerated.

The Court's decision did not end the debate. President Andrew Jackson cited doubts about the federal government's powers when he vetoed an internal improvements bill in 1830 and the rechartering of the national bank in 1832. In the late nineteenth and early twentieth centuries the Supreme Court itself adopted a strict construction of the federal COMMERCE POWER in some of its decisions striking down economic regulatory measures. In the 1930s the Court used a strict construction of the government's taxing and spending powers to strike down some major New Deal programs.

The Court effectively abandoned this narrow view of federal powers in 1937. Since then, with the growth of social services and the creation of an interdependent national economy, the debate over federal powers seems to have become a matter of historical interest.

The term *strict construction* resurfaced with a new meaning in the 1960s in response to the Warren Court's decisions safeguarding the rights of criminal suspects and defendants. Richard Nixon, both in his 1968 presidential campaign and in the White House, used the term *strict construction* to mean a philosophy of narrowly reading constitutional provisions that limited state criminal procedures.

Criminal procedure rulings by the Burger and Rehnquist courts have been less protective of defendants' rights than was true of the Warren Court. But the Court has not used the term *strict construction* as the basis for its decisions.

Critics of strict construction argue that its advocates use the term inconsistently. Nixon, for example, advocated—and acted upon—a broad construction of presidential power in foreign affairs and budget issues while urging strict construction on criminal procedure issues.

These critics make two more general points as well. First, they say that a strict or literal reading of many constitutional provisions would lead to absurd, or at least unacceptable, results. For example, the constitutional provision for granting copyright protection for "writings" has been broadly construed to apply to records and films. Freedom of "speech" extends to nonverbal expression. A strict construction of these terms would be counterproductive.

Second, critics maintain that many constitutional phrases have no strict or precise meaning. They point to such examples as the prohibition against "unreasonable" searches, the guarantee of "due process of law," and the ban on "cruel and unusual" punishment. These provisions and many others, the argument goes, cannot be defined from the constitutional text alone but require consideration of other factors, including changing social and political values.

These criticisms carry great weight among legal scholars, who generally view strict construction more as a political term than a legal theory. Nonetheless, as a political term, *strict construction* has strong appeal as a shorthand description of a legal philosophy that emphasizes JUDICIAL RESTRAINT and greater judicial deference to the political branches of government. (See also CONSTITUTIONAL LAW; ORIGINAL INTENT.)

Strong, William

When Justice Robert Grier announced his retirement in 1869, President Ulysses Grant's advisers recommended that he nominate William Strong (1808–1895), a justice on the Pennsylvania supreme court, to replace Grier. Many in Congress and across the nation wanted the nomination to go to Edwin M. Stanton, the former secretary of war. Members of Congress even circulated a petition for Stanton that was signed by large majorities in both houses. Grant bowed to the pressure and nominated Stanton. Four days after he was confirmed by the Senate, however, Stanton died suddenly. Grant then nominated Strong, who was duly confirmed in February 1870.

Strong was born in Somers, Connecticut, the son of a Presbyterian clergyman. He received both his undergraduate and graduate degrees from Yale College, after which he taught school in Connecticut and New Jersey and briefly attended Yale Law School. He was admitted to the bar in 1832 and established a legal practice in Reading, Pennsylvania. He quickly became a prominent citizen and was elected to the first of two terms in the U.S. House in 1847.

In 1857 Strong was elected to a fifteen-year term on the Pennsylvania supreme court. Citing a need to make more money, he resigned from the court in 1868. His absence from the bench lasted only two years before Grant named him to the U.S. Supreme Court in 1870.

A few hours after his nomination, Chief Justice Salmon P. Chase made public the Court's decision overturning the Legal Tender acts and holding that all debts had to be paid in coin instead of paper money. Grant was accused of nominating Strong and Joseph Bradley to fill two vacancies on the Court with justices who would overrule the decision, and in fact Strong did write the majority decision in 1871 upholding the legality of paper currency.

On the Court, Strong became known for his sharp intellect and eloquent arguments. He also became deeply involved in religious work while he was a justice. He served as vice president of the American Bible Society from 1871 to 1895 and as president of the American Tract Society from 1873 to 1895. Strong's

Source: Collection of the Supreme Court of the United States

devotion to religious work increased after he retired from the Court in 1880. Besides continuing his work with the bible and tract societies, Strong also served as president of the American Sunday School Union from 1883 until his death in 1895.

Students' Rights

See EDUCATION.

Subpoena

A subpoena is a court order to present oneself before a GRAND JURY or court to give testimony. A subpoena duces tecum (a Latin term meaning "bring with you") is a similar order to produce specified documents or papers. A legislative body may also issue a subpoena for a witness to appear before a legislative hearing.

Failure to comply with a subpoena without good cause may be punishable as CONTEMPT OF COURT or contempt of Congress. But a party may seek to quash a subpoena by asserting a privilege, such as the privilege against self-incrimination.

In COMMON LAW parties to civil suits and the prosecution in criminal cases had the right to obtain subpoenas to compel testimony. The Sixth Amendment extended this right to defendants in federal criminal TRIALS, stating that "in all criminal prosecutions, the accused shall enjoy the right . . . to have compulsory process for obtaining witnesses in his favor." The Supreme Court applied this provision to the states in *Washington v. Texas* (1967).

In its first major decision on the Fourth Amendment provision concerning search and seizure and the Fifth Amendment provision regarding self-incrimination, the Court in 1886 barred the government's use of a subpoena to obtain a business owner's records that could be used as evidence against him. Later decisions have undercut this ruling by narrowing the protection to purely personal papers.

The Supreme Court has never questioned the power of the House or Senate or their committees to issue subpoenas for legislative hearings. The Court reaffirmed a broad congressional subpoena power in 1975 when it rejected a First Amendment challenge to a subpoena issued by the Senate Judiciary Subcommittee on Internal Security for financial records of a group opposed to U.S. involvement in the Vietnam War.

In the case, *Eastland v. United States Servicemen's Fund,* the Court said that the subpoena on its face related to a legitimate legislative inquiry and that the congressional speech or debate clause barred any judicial inquiry into the subcommittee's motivation. In a concurring opinion three justices said, however, that they did not read the majority opinion to mean "that the constitutionality of a congressional subpoena is always shielded from more searching judicial inquiry."

Suffrage

See VOTING RIGHTS.

Summary Judgment

Summary judgment is a procedure in civil cases designed to avoid unnecessary trials. On a motion by either the plaintiff or defendant, the judge can decide that the parties to the suit do not disagree about the "material facts" in the case and that one side or the other is entitled to a judgment as a matter of law. The material facts are the facts the judge needs to decide the legal issues in the case.

Summary judgment is distinguished from pretrial motions for dismissal or for judgments on the pleadings because outside evidence is produced and considered by the court in making its decision. The evidence may be introduced in several forms, such as affidavits (sworn statements by the parties or witnesses) or depositions (sworn testimony given out of court under questioning by the lawyers for one or both parties).

In considering this evidence, the judge is not supposed to weigh the evidence or try to resolve any factual disputes between the parties. The judge is to grant summary judgment only if he or she finds that the parties are not in dispute about the "material facts."

Supremacy Clause

The major goal of the Constitutional Convention was to create a stronger national government than existed under the Articles of Confederation. Toward that end, the supremacy clause provides that the Constitution, "the Laws of the United States which shall be made in Pursuance thereof," and all treaties "shall be the supreme Law of the Land" (Article VI, Section 2).

The Supreme Court first invoked the supremacy clause in 1796 to strike down a state statute that conflicted with the provisions of the 1783 peace treaty with England. But it was Chief Justice John Marshall in the early nineteenth century who gave the most important early definitions of the clause in two rulings involving clashes between federal and state powers.

The Court's rulings in *MCCULLOCH V. MARYLAND* (1819) and *GIBBONS V. OGDEN* (1824) overturned state laws that respectively taxed the Bank of the United States and established a steamboat monopoly, by simply declaring each one to be in conflict with federal law. "In every such case," Marshall wrote in *Gibbons,* "the act of Congress . . . is supreme; and the law of the state . . . must yield to it."

Under Marshall's successor as chief justice, Roger B. Taney, the Court moved away from this expansive view of federal power and adopted instead a doctrine called dual federalism. Under this doctrine the states and the federal government were sovereign in their respective spheres, and states could exercise their PO-LICE POWER to limit the reach of national law. The Taney Court used this doctrine in 1837 to uphold a New York law regulating ships entering New York Harbor and in 1847 to sustain state laws requiring licenses to sell alcoholic beverages within the state.

In the first three decades of the twentieth century the Court used this broad view of the states' police power to strike down federal laws regulating various aspects of the economy. But the doctrine of dual federalism collapsed beginning in the late 1930s as the Court embraced a nearly unlimited view of the federal government's COMMERCE POWER over economic affairs. (See STATES AND THE COURT.)

Supreme Court Building

For the first 145 years of its existence, the Supreme Court was a tenant in buildings intended for other purposes. The Court did not move into its own building until 1935. Today, the Court is still housed in a single building, although one retired justice—Byron R. White—has chambers in the Federal Judicial Center building near the Court.

Between 1790, when the Court convened for the first time in New York City, and 1935 the justices met in nearly a dozen different places, many of them makeshift and cramped. (See HOUSING THE COURT.)

President William Howard Taft began promoting the idea of a separate building for the Supreme Court around 1912, near the end of his presidency. At the time the Court occupied the old Senate chamber on the first floor of the Capitol building. Taft continued to urge construction of a new building when he became chief justice of the Court in 1912. Taft's persistence proved successful. In 1929 Congress finally agreed to construct a permanent home for the Supreme Court and appropriated $9,740,000 for the project. Taft never saw the building; he died in 1930 before construction had begun.

The site chosen for the Court was One First Street, Northeast, across the plaza from the Capitol. It was the location of the "Brick Capitol," which Congress had used after the British burned the Capitol in 1814.

Architect Cass Gilbert was commissioned to design the building. Gilbert died in 1934, but the project was continued under Chief Justice Charles Evans Hughes and architects Cass Gilbert, Jr., and John R. Rockart. The project was supervised by David Lynn, who served as architect of the Capitol.

The architects chose the Corinthian style of Greek architecture to blend harmoniously with the congressional buildings on Capitol Hill. The building measures 385 feet by 304 feet and is four stories high.

The primary building material is marble, which cost more than $3 million—almost a third of the building's cost. White Vermont marble was used for the exterior. Georgia marble flecked with crystal was quarried for the four inner courts, while a creamy Alabama marble was used for most of the walls and floors of corridors and entrance halls.

Architect Gilbert insisted on Ivory Vein marble from Spain for the walls of the Court's great hall and the courtroom at its end. For the huge columns he used Light Sienna Old Convent marble from the Montarrenti quarry in Italy. The Italian marble was shipped to finishers in Knoxville, Tennessee, who made the blocks into thirty foot columns and shipped

An inner courtyard, one of four in the building.
Source: Lee Troell Anderson

them to Washington. Darker Italian and African marble was used for the floor.

Most of the floors are oak, and the doors and walls of most offices are American-quartered white oak. Bronze and mahogany were also used. The roof is made of cream-colored Roman tile set on bronze strips over lead-coated copper on a slab of watertight concrete. The building includes two self-supporting marble spiral staircases that rise from the garage to the top floor. The only other spiral staircases like them are in the Vatican and the Paris Opera.

Exterior

On the steps to the main entrance of the building is a pair of huge marble candelabra with carved panels representing Justice, holding sword and scales, and the Three Fates of Greek mythology, who are weaving the thread of life. On each side of the steps is a marble figure by sculptor James Earle Fraser. On the left is a female figure, representing the contemplation of justice; on the right, a male figure representing the guardian or authority of law.

Inscribed on the architrave above the entrance of the building is the motto "Equal Justice under the Law." Above the inscription is a pediment filled with sculptures representing Liberty enthroned, guarded by Authority and Order. On either side are groups depicting "council and research." Panels on the main door are the work of sculptor John Donnelly, Jr., and depict scenes in the development of the law.

Front view of the Supreme Court.   *Source: Congressional Quarterly*

profiles of lawgivers. From the great hall, oak doors open into the courtroom. Measuring 82 by 91 feet with a 44-foot-high ceiling, the room has twenty-four columns of Italian marble. Running along the upper part of the wall on all four sides of the room are marble panels sculpted by Adolph A. Weinman. Directly above the bench are two figures representing Majesty of the Law and Power of Government. Between these figures is a tableau of the Ten Commandments. At the far left is a scene representing "safeguard of the rights of the people" and "genii of wisdom and statescraft." At the far right is "the defense of human rights."

On the wall to the right of incoming visitors are figures of historical lawmakers of the pre-Christian era— Menes, Hammurabi, Moses, Solomon, Lycurgus, Solon, Draco, Confucius, and Augustus. To the left are lawmakers of the Christian era—Napoleon, Marshall, Blackstone, Grotius, Saint Louis, King John, Charlemagne, Mohammed, and Justinian.

The bench at which the justices sit extends across the room. The justices' chairs are black, but because each justice may choose his or her own chair, they are of different heights. The justices enter the courtroom from behind a red velvet curtain that hangs behind the bench.

Until 1970 there were only six suites inside the so-called "golden gates," the large bronze doors that seal the justices off from the public. The three justices with the least seniority occupied offices in the corridor just outside the gates. But in 1972 the space was redesigned, and the suites now stretch entirely around the first floor of the Court. All the old chambers had working fireplaces, so fireplaces were added to the redesigned offices, but the new fireplaces do not work.

The second floor contains the justices' dining room and library, the office of the reporter of decisions, the legal office, and the law clerks' offices.

On the third floor is the library, paneled in carved oak, and on the fourth floor is a gymnasium and storage area. The public is permitted to see only the ground floor and part of the first floor.

Interior

The basement contains the garage and also the offices of the facilities manager and a staff of electricians, plumbers, painters, air conditioning and heating specialists, and groundskeepers. The basement also houses a carpentry shop, laundry, and police roll-call room.

On the ground floor are the public information office, the clerk's office, publications unit, police "headquarters," and other administrative offices, in addition to the exhibit halls, cafeteria, and gift shop.

The first floor contains the great hall, the courtroom, the justices' chambers, and the conference room. Along both sides of the great hall are busts of former chief justices, heraldic devices, and medallion

Praise and Criticism

Since its completion in 1935, the Supreme Court building has been a subject of both outspoken praise and equally forthright criticism. It has been described

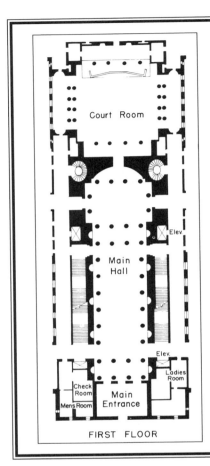

FIRST FLOOR

Visiting the Court

The Supreme Court is open for visitors year-round, Monday through Friday from 9 a.m. to 4:30 p.m. The Court is in session for oral arguments during two-week periods from the first Monday in October until the end of April or the beginning of May. ARGUMENTS are generally held from 10 a.m. to noon and 1 to 3 p.m. on Monday, Tuesday, and Wednesday. Visitors may attend oral arguments on a first-come, first-served basis. There are two lines to enter the courtroom, one for visitors who wish to hear only three minutes of argument and the other for visitors who wish to hear the entire argument.

During the weeks when the Court is not in session, lectures are given by the staff of the Curator's Office every hour from 9:30 a.m. to 3:30 p.m. On the ground floor are exhibits, portraits of all former justices, a gift shop, and a cafeteria. Visitors can also view a film about the Court.

Between 700,000 and 800,000 people visit the Court each year. Fewer visitors attend winter sessions than arguments in the spring.

---

as a "marble palace" and as a "marble mausoleum." Its admirers speak of its structural simplicity, austerity, beauty, and dignity. For them, the building is a fitting monument to the work of the Court.

Despite general public approval of the new building, it has had numerous critics, among them a few of the justices. One justice said that the Court would look like "nine black beetles in the Temple of Karnak."

When Congress appropriated the initial funds for the building in 1929, it was expected that additional funds would be needed for furnishings. The final cost of the building, including all the furnishings, was less than the authorized amount of $9.7 million, and

$94,000 was returned to the U.S. Treasury. It is estimated that replacing the building today would cost more than $100 million.

Sutherland, George

Justice George Sutherland (1862–1942) wrote the Court's first ruling guaranteeing the right to legal counsel in certain criminal cases. The decision came in *Powell v. Alabama* (1932), also known as the First Scottsboro Case. (See *SCOTTSBORO CASES*.)

The case involved nine young illiterate black men

Source: Library of Congress

who were charged with raping two white women on a freight train. Before the defendants' trial in Scottsboro, Alabama, a judge appointed all the members of the local bar as defense counsel. None of the attorneys appeared at the trial, however, so the judge appointed a local lawyer to represent the men. The lawyer had no time to prepare, and his clients were all convicted. They appealed, arguing that they were effectively denied the aid of counsel because they had no time to consult with their attorney and prepare a defense.

By a 7–2 vote, the Supreme Court agreed. In an opinion written by Sutherland, the Court said that in capital cases a court must appoint counsel for defendants who are unable to hire their own attorney or to represent themselves. Sutherland added that the duty "is not discharged by an assignment at such a time or under such circumstances as to preclude the giving of effective aid in the preparation and trial of the case."

Despite his speaking for the Court in this "liberal" ruling, Sutherland was basically a conservative justice.

Sutherland was born in 1862 in Buckinghamshire, England, and the following year his parents moved the family to the Utah Territory. Sutherland studied one year at the University of Michigan Law School in 1883 before returning to Utah, to begin practicing law in Provo. He helped found the Utah Bar Association in 1894, one year after he moved to Salt Lake City. In 1896, when the territory achieved statehood, Sutherland was elected to the first state senate.

Sutherland was elected to the U.S. House of Representatives four years later. In 1902 he decided against running for a second term in the House, and in 1904 he was elected to the first of two terms in the U.S. Senate. While in the Senate, Sutherland became good friends with Warren G. Harding. Sutherland wanted to run for a third Senate term in 1916, but failed to win renomination from the Utah Republican party. He remained in Washington, D.C., where he practiced law and became one of President Harding's key advisers.

In 1922 Harding appointed Sutherland to the Supreme Court. Sutherland later became a thorn in the side of President Franklin D. Roosevelt because he consistently voted to overturn many of Roosevelt's New Deal programs. Sutherland retired from the Court in January 1938, shortly after Roosevelt's Court-packing plan failed, and died in 1942.

Swayne, Noah H.

Shortly before Justice John McLean died in April 1861, he let it be known that he wanted his close friend, Noah Haynes Swayne (1804–1884), to succeed him on the Supreme Court. President Abraham Lincoln nominated Swayne, and the nomination was confirmed by the Senate. Nineteen years later, when Swayne's mental abilities had sharply declined, President Rutherford B. Hayes persuaded him to retire with the promise that his friend Stanley Matthews would succeed him in turn.

Although born in the slave-holding state of Virginia, Swayne grew up abhorring slavery. His parents were antislavery Quakers from Pennsylvania. When Swayne married a Virginia woman who owned slaves, he insisted that she free them. He was admitted to the bar in Virginia, but soon after left for the free state of Ohio because he didn't want to live in a state that allowed slavery.

Swayne became involved in politics shortly after arriving in Ohio. He was elected prosecuting attorney of Coshocton County in 1826 and served for three years before being elected to the Ohio legislature in 1829. In 1830 President Andrew Jackson appointed Swayne, a strong Jacksonian Democrat, U.S. attorney for Ohio. He served in that post until 1841 and simultaneously built a successful private legal practice. While serving as U.S. attorney, Swayne also served another term in the state legislature and a year on the Columbus city council.

In the 1850s Swayne's opposition to slavery forced him to abandon the Democratic party and join the new Republican party. Swayne had no judicial experience when Lincoln nominated him to the Supreme Court in 1862. Lincoln apparently chose him because of McLean's request and pressure from the Ohio governor and the state's congressional delegation.

On the Court Swayne generally expressed a strongly nationalistic viewpoint in his opinions. While a member of the Court Swayne also lobbied hard for

Source: Library of Congress

passage of the Fifteenth Amendment, which guaranteed voting rights for blacks. Swayne twice sought to become chief justice, in 1864 when Roger B. Taney died and again in 1873 when Salmon P. Chase died. He was not nominated either time. He retired in 1881 and died three years later.

T

Taft, William Howard

For much of his political life, William Howard Taft (1857–1930) actively lobbied and finagled for a seat on the Supreme Court. He finally got his wish in 1921 when President Warren G. Harding appointed him chief justice. With the appointment, Taft became the only person in U.S. history to have served as both president and chief justice.

Taft was born in Cincinnati. He attended Yale University and was named class salutatorian when he graduated in 1878. Two years later he received his law degree from Cincinnati Law School. While attending law school, he worked as a newspaper reporter. After being admitted to the bar in 1880, he embarked on a career of public service. He served as assistant prosecuting attorney for Hamilton County, Ohio (1881–1883), assistant county solicitor (1885–1887), and judge on the Ohio superior court (1887–1890).

Taft's career then continued on the federal level. He was U.S. solicitor general (1890–1891), judge on the Sixth Circuit (1892–1900), chairman of the Philippine Commission (1900–1901), civil governor of the Philippines (1901–1904), secretary of war (1904–1908), president of the United States (1909–1913), and joint chairman of the National War Labor Board (1918–1919).

After Taft became chief justice in 1921, he embarked on efforts to modernize the nation's judicial system. In fact, his legacy lies in his performance as an administrator rather than as a judge or legal scholar. A year after becoming chief justice, Taft persuaded Congress to create the Judicial Conference of the United States, the governing body that administers the federal judicial system. Even more important was his successful effort to convince Congress to pass the Judiciary Act of 1925. Taft asked for the law because the Court was becoming severely backlogged with cases. The law gave the justices virtually unlimited power to decide which cases they would review. Fi-

Source: Library of Congress

nally, years of lobbying by Taft helped convince Congress in 1929 to appropriate money for construction of a separate building to house the Supreme Court. Previously, the Court had been housed in the Capitol building.

Under Taft, the Court became even more conservative than it had been before. It repeatedly curtailed federal authority and restrained the states from regulating economic matters. Taft furthered the Court's conservatism by either selecting or approving three of

413

the four justices whom President Warren G. Harding appointed to the Court: George Sutherland, Pierce Butler, and Edward T. Sanford. In the case of Butler, Taft waged a letter-writing and lobbying campaign to ensure his nomination.

Although the Taft Court was undeniably conservative, it helped lay the groundwork for the "due process revolution" of the 1960s under which the Court extended the protections of the Bill of Rights against actions by states. Taft firmly believed in the power of judicial review and accepted the idea that the Court "made" law, a viewpoint generally considered liberal. Taft retired from the Court in February 1930 and died a month later.

Taney, Roger B.

After twice being rejected by the Senate, Roger Brooke Taney (1777–1864) was confirmed on his third nomination to federal office. The Senate rejected President Andrew Jackson's nominations of Taney to be secretary of the treasury and an associate justice of the Supreme Court, but finally confirmed him as chief justice in 1836. Taney served as chief justice for twenty-eight years.

Born on his father's tobacco plantation in Calvert County, Maryland, Taney attended local schools. After graduating first in his class from Dickinson College in Pennsylvania, Taney embarked on a career in law and politics. He was admitted to the bar in 1799, the same year he entered the Maryland house of delegates. He started a successful law practice in Frederick, Maryland, after being defeated for reelection.

Taney lost in another run for the Maryland house in 1803. His reputation in Frederick and Maryland continued to grow, however, and in 1816 he was elected to the state senate. He became Maryland's attorney general in 1827. Taney, a strong Jacksonian Democrat, directed Andrew Jackson's presidential campaign in Maryland in 1827 and 1828. Jackson rewarded Taney's hard work by naming him U.S. attorney general in 1831.

Taney was utterly loyal to Jackson. In 1832 he helped write the president's message vetoing the

Source: Collection of the Supreme Court of the United States

recharter of the second Bank of the United States. In one part of that message, Taney wrote that Jackson did not have to abide by the Supreme Court's interpretation of the Constitution. When Treasury Secretary William Duane refused Jackson's order to withdraw federal funds from the bank, Jackson fired Duane and replaced him with Taney. Taney quickly withdrew the money. Taney had to resign as treasury secretary after nine months when the Senate rejected his nomination.

In early 1835 Jackson nominated Taney to replace Gabriel Duvall on the Supreme Court. The Senate indefinitely postponed the nomination on a close vote. Jackson was undeterred, and late in 1835 he nominated Taney to be chief justice after the death of John Marshall. Daniel Webster and Henry Clay led the fight against Taney in the Senate, and the Whigs denounced him as a political hack. Nonetheless, the Senate confirmed Taney by a vote of 29 to 15.

In contrast to the Marshall Court, the Taney Court usually backed states' rights instead of federal supremacy. It was swept into sectional conflicts, including the struggle over slavery, that eventually exploded in the Civil War. Taney, who was born to a slaveholding family, personally accepted the idea of slavery. The Taney Court caused an uproar with its ruling in the Dred Scott case *(Scott v. Sandford* [1857]) that blacks could not become citizens and that Congress had no authority to stop the spread of slavery. Later, Taney wrote a private memorandum striking down Abraham Lincoln's Emancipation Proclamation, but he never released it because no case regarding the matter came before the Court. Taney died in 1864.

Taxing Power

Under the Articles of Confederation, Congress had no power to raise taxes; it could only request contributions from the states. To remedy this weakness, the framers of the Constitution gave Congress clear authority, as the first enumerated power in Article I, Section 8, "to lay and collect Taxes, Duties, Imposts, and Excises."

Congress's use of this power has always been controversial, from the tariffs passed in the nation's early years to the pervasive federal tax system of modern times. The Supreme Court balked at some expansive uses of the taxing power during its era of economic conservatism in the late nineteenth and early twentieth centuries. But the Court has now rejected or discarded its major barriers to congressional efforts to raise revenue or accomplish other goals through the tax code.

The Constitution places only one prohibition on the federal taxing power: Congress may not tax exports (Article I, Section 9, Clause 5). To ensure equal treatment for each state, the Constitution also requires all duties, imposts, and excises to be levied uniformly throughout the country and all direct taxes to be apportioned among the states on the basis of their

relative populations. The Court's most important ruling construing these limitations was its 1895 decision barring a federal INCOME TAX. That decision was nullified by adoption of the Sixteenth Amendment. (See REVERSALS OF RULINGS BY CONSTITUTIONAL AMENDMENT.)

For more than a century the Supreme Court also recognized an implied limitation on the federal power to tax state government. In 1988, however, the Court found no constitutional requirement for this limitation, while leaving it to Congress to maintain such exemptions as a political matter. On the other hand, the states are barred from taxing the operations of the federal government.

The Court has struggled to define the other limits that the Constitution places on the states' taxing power. The Constitution bans state duties on imports or exports or state-imposed tonnage duties without the consent of Congress (Article I, Section 10). The Court has construed the commerce clause to prohibit taxes that burden interstate commerce. The Court's rulings on these provisions have been complex and confusing, but over time they have tended to enlarge the states' taxing power as long as they treat in-state and out-of-state activities equally. (See STATES AND THE COURT.)

Direct Taxes

When delegates to the Constitutional Convention wrote that "capitation, or other direct Taxes" must be apportioned among the states by population, they seem to have had no clear idea what sorts of levies were "direct." In 1796 the government asked the Supreme Court to define the phrase in a test case concerning a federal tax on carriages. The Court upheld the carriage levy as an indirect use tax, declaring that only head taxes and taxes on land were direct taxes. Congress has never imposed either type of tax.

The Court's definition stood as valid until its 1895 ruling that taxes on income from land or income from personal property were also direct levies. The decision in *Pollock v. Farmers' Loan & Trust Co.* drew strong opposition and was overturned by the Sixteenth Amendment in 1913. Even before that, however, the Court had backed away from the ruling by sustaining taxes on certain kinds of incomes as "incidents of

In the past, young children often worked long hours in dangerous conditions. In an attempt to curb child labor, Congress in 1919 had passed the Child Labor Tax Law. In 1922 the Court deemed the law unconstitutional, declaring that the government's 10 percent excise tax on companies using child labor was a form of coercion.   Source: National Archives, Smithsonian Institution

ownership" and thus excise or indirect taxes rather than direct taxes. When it upheld the new federal income tax in 1916, the Court repudiated its 1895 ruling by saying that the income tax "inherently belonged" to "the category of indirect taxation."

Taxing as Police Power

Since the nation's earliest days, Congress has used the taxing power as a tool of regulation as well as a source of revenue. Protective tariffs were enacted to raise revenue and encourage domestic manufacture. Their validity was much debated, but the issue was settled in 1928 when the Court upheld a new tariff act. In its ruling the Court stated that a revenue-raising measure would not be invalidated by "the existence of other motives."

The Court has upheld use of the tax power as a regulatory tool to support another constitutional power. In 1869 the Court cited the federal government's currency power in sustaining a tax on state bank notes that had been passed in order to drive them out of the market in favor of untaxed national bank notes. In 1940 the Court cited Congress's commerce power in upholding a coal tax that fell only on producers who did not agree to price and competition regulations for the industry. Congress "may impose penalties in aid of the exercise of any of its enumerated powers," the Court declared. The decision effectively overturned a ruling four years earlier striking down a similar tax.

In cases where Congress used the taxing power on its own to achieve a desired social or economic goal, the Court developed two distinct lines of precedent. The first line held that if the tax produced some revenue, the Court would not examine the motives behind its imposition. In *McCray v. United States* (1904) the Court upheld a heavy tax placed on oleo that was colored yellow to resemble butter, but not on uncolored oleo. The tax was aimed at removing the competition to butter. But the Court said the levy was a permissible excise tax, whatever the real motive behind it. In *United States v. Doremus* (1919) the Court used similar reasoning to uphold, by a 5–4 vote, an antinarcotics act that imposed a registration fee on persons dealing in narcotics while making the sale or shipment of certain drugs illegal.

The dissenting view in *Doremus* became the majority position, beginning the second line of precedents, in the next major tax regulation case. This reasoning held a tax unconstitutional if its primary purpose was the punishment of a certain action and not the raising of revenue.

In *Bailey v. Drexel Furniture Co.* (1922) the Court struck down a 10 percent tax on the net profits of any company that employed children under a certain age. Writing for the eight-justice majority, Chief Justice William Howard Taft said that "the penalizing features" of a tax measure can so outweigh its revenue-raising effect that "it becomes a mere penalty with the characteristics of regulation and punishment." This line of cases culminated in two decisions in 1936 striking down major New Deal programs because of regulatory tax features: a coal industry labor code act and a law concerning agricultural production stabilization.

The next year the Court changed its view and upheld a license tax on firearms dealers and manufacturers that was designed to discourage the sale of weapons likely to be used by criminals. Directly contradicting Taft's opinion in the child labor tax case, the Court said a tax measure is not invalid "because the tax is burdensome or tends to restrict or suppress the thing taxed." Taxes on marijuana and gambling were upheld in 1950 and 1953 on similar reasoning.

Taxing Imports

The purpose of the constitutional ban on state taxes on imports was to prevent discrimination against imported goods and against interior states that had access to imports only if they first passed through coastal states.

The Court first enforced the clause in 1827 to strike down a state law requiring persons who sold imported goods to purchase licenses. In *Brown v. Maryland* Chief Justice John Marshall said the license fee was an indirect tax on imports that violated both the export-import clause and the federal regulation of foreign commerce. Imported goods were exempt from state taxation, Marshall explained, as long as they remained in their "original package" and thus not ready for sale.

Marshall suggested that this rule also applied to a tax on imports from other states. In 1869, however, the Court rejected Marshall's dictum, holding that a state could impose a general sales tax on goods from another state once interstate transportation had ended. Otherwise, the Court said, merchants could escape all state and local taxes.

Three years later the Court reaffirmed the original package doctrine to bar taxation of foreign imports stored in a warehouse and awaiting sale. This decision stood for more than a century. But in 1976 the Court overruled it, upholding a value-based property tax on imported goods awaiting sale. The export-import clause, the Court explained in *Michelin Tire Corp. v. Wages*, prohibits "discriminatory state taxation against imported goods as imports," not a uniform tax imposed on all goods regardless of origin.

Taxing of Commerce

States naturally look to tax commerce within their borders, as the Court explained in a 1959 decision, "to get some return for the substantial benefits they have afforded it." But efforts to define what kinds of levies do not unduly burden interstate commerce, the Court conceded, have yielded "little in the way of precise guides" for the states. The difficulties can be illustrated by three sets of cases involving common carriers, business "privilege" taxes, and sales of out-of-state goods.

In 1873 the Court on the same day struck down Pennsylvania's tonnage tax on freight that a railroad moved through the state while upholding a tax on the company's gross receipts. The tonnage tax unconstitutionally impeded interstate commerce, the Court said, but states could tax the company's property after the goods were no longer in transit. This rule still holds, but it poses the sometimes difficult question of defining when goods leave interstate commerce and become subject to state taxation.

The Court in 1891 took a less deferential view toward state business license fees, saying that a state could not impose a burden on the "privilege" of doing business within its borders. This rule stood for almost a century until the Court in 1977 dropped its opposition to all privilege taxes. In *Complete Auto Transit Inc. v. Brady* the Court said states could tax an interstate business if the levy was applied to an activity with a substantial connection to the state, was fairly apportioned, did not discriminate against interstate commerce, and was fairly related to the services provided by the state.

The sales tax cases began by distinguishing between "peddlers," who carry goods with them for sale, and "drummers," who take orders for future delivery. The Court in 1880 allowed states to require peddlers to pay for a license if the fee equally affected in-state and out-of-state peddlers. But in 1887 it barred a license requirement for out-of-state drummers, saying that a tax affecting goods not yet brought into the state was "a tax on interstate commerce itself." This distinction became more important as mail-order businesses grew. States responded by imposing a "use tax" on out-of-state goods equal to the sales tax. The Court in 1937 upheld this device. But the Court has continued to insist that out-of-state sales cannot be treated unequally. In 1977 it struck down a New York tax that burdened stock transactions taking place on out-of-state stock exchanges but not on the New York Stock Exchange.

Federal-State Tax Immunities

The doctrine of intergovernmental immunity dates to the Supreme Court's landmark decision in MCCUL-LOCH V. MARYLAND (1819), striking down a state tax on the federally chartered Bank of the United States. The decision was broadened over the next seventy years to bar the states from taxing government securities, federal lands, or the income of federal revenue officers. In *Collector v. Day* (1871) the Court similarly reasoned that the federal government could not infringe on the states' sovereignty by taxing their officers, property, or instrumentalities.

For more than a century these doctrines were applied extensively. In 1895, as part of the *Income Tax Cases,* the Court forbade federal taxation of state or municipal bonds. But gradually the Court limited the immunities granted to both the federal and state governments. State immunity from federal taxation was restricted to activities of a "strictly governmental nature." Federal contractors were much less often granted immunity from state taxation. Income tax immunity for state and federal officials was overturned in 1938 and 1939.

As the doctrine of immunity stood in the late 1970s, the federal government was prohibited from taxing state government property and instrumentalities. In 1988, however, the Court undercut the most significant of the prohibitions, which barred federal taxation of state and municipal bonds. In *South Carolina v. Baker* the Supreme Court held that nothing in the Constitution prevented Congress from taxing the interest paid on state and municipal bonds. Federally owned property, however, remains generally immune from state taxation. The states may not tax income from federal securities or tax-exempt bonds.

Temporary Restraining Order

A temporary restraining order (TRO) is a judge's order to a person to refrain from taking certain action before a hearing can be held on the question. It is distinguished from a temporary or preliminary INJUNCTION in that it may be issued on an EX PARTE basis, without written or oral notice to the party being restrained.

The Federal Rules of Civil Procedure require that a party applying for a temporary restraining order show that he or she will suffer "immediate and irreparable injury, loss, or damage" before a hearing can be held. The rules also specify that a TRO must expire within ten days, although a judge may decide to extend it.

The party against whom the TRO is issued may also file a motion for it to be dissolved or modified.

Tenth Amendment

See FEDERALISM; STATES AND THE COURT.

Term of the Court

By law the Supreme Court begins its regular annual term on the first Monday in October. Known as the October term, this session lasts about nine months. The summer recess, which is not determined by statute or Court rules, generally begins in late June or early July of the following year, when the Court has taken action on the last case argued before it during the term.

The Court's work does not end when the session is finished. During the summer recess the justices receive new cases to consider. About one-fourth of the applications for review filed during the term are read by the justices and their law CLERKS during the summer interval.

Until 1979 the Court adjourned its session when the summer recess began. If the Court needed to deal with any urgent matters that arose after the regular session had ended, it was permitted by statute to convene a special session.

Since 1979 the Court has been in continuous session throughout the year, taking periodic recesses. The October 1988 term, for example, did not adjourn until the first Monday in October 1989, when the new term began.

Over the years, the annual sessions of the Court have been changed several times. During its first decade the Court met twice a year, in February and August. The current opening date was set in 1917. The term has lengthened as the Court's caseload has grown.

The Court has held only four special sessions in its history. It has generally considered important cases that arose near the end of a term simply by delaying the end of the term until the matter was resolved. The four cases decided in special session were:

Ex parte Quirin, argued in July 1942, in which the Court upheld a military court's conviction of a group of Nazi saboteurs smuggled ashore from a German submarine.

Rosenberg v. United States, argued in June 1953, in which the Court vacated a stay of execution ordered by Justice William O. Douglas for Ethel and Julius Rosenberg, who had been convicted of revealing information about the atomic bomb to the Soviet Union.

Cooper v. Aaron, argued in August and September 1958, in which the Court unanimously upheld a lower court order enforcing a desegregation plan for Little Rock's Central High School.

O'Brien v. Brown, decided in July 1972, in which the Court allowed the Democratic national convention, rather than the Court, to determine which delegates from California and Illinois should be seated.

Among the decisions made by the modern Court after postponing adjournment of the regular term, the most famous is *United States v. Nixon* (1974). In that case, the Court on July 24, 1974, unanimously denied President Richard Nixon's claim of absolute executive privilege to withhold documents requested by the Watergate special prosecutor.

Test Case

A test case is a lawsuit that is planned and organized to gain a favorable ruling on a legal or constitutional issue from the Supreme Court. Many of the Court's most important rulings throughout its history have come in test cases. Examples include the SCHOOL DESEGREGATION ruling in *BROWN V. BOARD OF EDUCATION OF TOPEKA* (1954) and the ABORTION rights ruling in *ROE V. WADE* (1973).

There is no constitutional bar to test cases if they meet the requirement of the CASE OR CONTROVERSY RULE: a concrete, actual dispute between parties with adverse interests. But the Court has refused to rule on "friendly" or "collusive" suits. In a friendly suit, there is no real or substantial controversy; instead, each side agrees to pursue the suit to reach a mutually desired outcome.

The classic statement on friendly suits came in 1892 when the Court backed up a state court's refusal to declare unconstitutional a state law regulating railroad fares. "It never was the thought," Justice David J. Brewer wrote, "that, by means of a friendly suit, a party beaten in the Legislature could transfer to the courts an inquiry as to the constitutionality of the legislative Act."

Nonetheless, several landmark Court rulings have come in friendly cases. Among the cases that the Court could have rejected as friendly suits were the Dred Scott case (*SCOTT V. SANDFORD* [1857]) and the decision striking down the federal INCOME TAX *(Pollock v. Farmers' Loan and Trust Co.* [1895]).

An action for a declaratory judgment, authorized by the Federal Declaratory Judgment Act of 1934, may be viewed as a test case. But the act specifies that declaratory judgments can be issued only in "cases of actual controversy"—a provision that, as the Court ruled three years later, satisfied the Constitution's case or controversy rule.

Source: National Geographic Society

Thirteenth Amendment

See CIVIL WAR AMENDMENTS.

Thomas, Clarence

Charges of sexual harassment made the confirmation hearing for Supreme Court nominee Clarence Thomas (1948–), a prominent black conservative, one of the most tumultuous in the nation's history. The Senate finally confirmed Thomas by the narrowest margin in more than a century.

Thomas grew up in poverty in rural Georgia. After his parents split up, he was raised by his grandparents. His early education came in segregated Georgia schools run by white nuns. Thomas worked his way through college and received his law degree from Yale Law School.

During President Ronald Reagan's administration, Thomas served as head of the civil rights division in the Department of Education and then as director of the Equal Employment Opportunity Commission (EEOC). While at the EEOC, Thomas strongly opposed affirmative action programs, a stance that put him at odds with many black interest groups. In 1989 President George Bush appointed Thomas to the U.S. Court of Appeals for the District of Columbia Circuit. Two years later Bush nominated Thomas to the Supreme Court.

During his confirmation hearing Thomas, like Justice David Souter before him, sidestepped senators' questions about his personal views. He particularly avoided answering questions about abortion. Abortion was a critical issue in his confirmation hearing because many believed he would cast the fifth vote needed to overturn *Roe v. Wade,* the 1973 decision guaranteeing a woman's right to an abortion. The Senate Judiciary Committee deadlocked, 7–7, on whether to favorably recommend Thomas to the full Senate. It finally voted to send his name to the Senate without a recommendation.

Two days before the full Senate was scheduled to vote on Thomas's nomination, *Newsday* and National Public Radio reported that Anita Hill, a law professor at the University of Oklahoma, had told judiciary committee staff that Thomas had sexually harassed her when they worked together. Hill, a black woman, had worked with Thomas at both the Department of Education and the EEOC. It soon became clear that the committee had known about the allegations before it voted on Thomas but had done little to investigate them. This provoked a national uproar, particularly among women's groups. Hill was summoned to Washington for a new round of hearings on Thomas's nomination. In a clear, poised manner, she graphically described what she said were Thomas's advances and his comments to her at work about women's breasts, his own sexual prowess, and pornographic movies he had seen. Despite attempts by Republican senators to discredit Hill, she remained steadfast in her testimony. Thomas was equally poised and steadfast in denying her charges. He called the new hearing a "high-tech lynching for an uppity black." Ultimately, senators seemed unsure whom to believe, but a majority of them gave Thomas the benefit of the doubt and confirmed him, 52–48. Forty-one Republicans and eleven Democrats, primarily southerners, voted for Thomas and forty-six Democrats and two Republicans voted against him.

Thompson, Smith

Although he really wanted to be president, Smith Thompson (1768–1843) had to settle for a seat on the Supreme Court.

Thompson was born in Dutchess County, New York. After graduating from Princeton in 1788, he taught school and read law. In 1793 Thompson joined the law practice of James Kent and Gilbert Livingston, the latter a good friend of his father. The next year he married Livingston's daughter, Sarah, thus becoming a member of that prominent family.

Thompson was elected to the New York legislature in 1800, aligning himself with the Livingston wing of the anti-Federalist Republican party. An appointment to the New York supreme court came two years later. Two of his fellow justices were his cousins by marriage. One of them was Brockholst Livingston, whom Thompson later replaced on the U.S. Supreme Court. Thompson was elevated to chief justice of the New York court in 1814.

In 1819 President James Monroe appointed Thompson secretary of the navy. Thompson likely got the job through the influence of Martin Van Buren, a good friend from New York. The job of navy secretary carried few formal duties, leaving Thompson free to spend much of his time on New York politics. He sometimes joined with Van Buren in political maneuvers. Thompson also began to make it known publicly that he wished to become president.

Monroe nominated Thompson to the Supreme Court in December 1823. Thompson hesitated to ac-

Source: Collection of the Supreme Court of the United States

cept the seat, hoping he could instead run for president in 1824. When that was not possible, Thompson joined the Court. His political ambitions, however, did not end with his appointment. In 1828 he ran for governor of New York against his old friend Van Buren. Thompson lost in a bitter contest.

As a justice, Thompson joined with others who had begun to oppose the strong nationalism of Chief Justice John Marshall. His most important opinion came in *Kendall v. United States* (1838), when he wrote that federal courts had the power to review actions by the executive branch. Thompson served on the Court until his death on December 18, 1843, one day short of the twentieth anniversary of his confirmation by the Senate.

Three-Judge Court

A three-judge court is a special tribunal required by some federal statutes to try cases of special public importance. Congress created the procedure in the early twentieth century. It was intended as a way to give additional attention to and expedite Supreme Court review for specific categories of cases. The procedure burdened the federal judiciary and the Supreme Court, however, and was cut back by Congress in a 1976 court reform act.

The three-judge court included at least one judge from a federal circuit court of appeals and two from a federal district court. Appeals from the three-judge court went directly to the Supreme Court, which had to review the case.

Congress created the three-judge court for some antitrust and Interstate Commerce Commission cases. In 1910 Congress adapted the device to try to quell the controversy over a 1908 Supreme Court decision permitting federal courts to enjoin state officials from enforcing state statutes. Congress reasoned that public resentment over this new power of federal courts would be lessened if the power were exercised by three judges rather than by one and if any injunction could be directly appealed to the Supreme Court.

Congress in 1937 made similar provision for a three-judge court and direct review by the Supreme Court in actions for injunctions against acts of Congress claimed to be unconstitutional. Both the Civil Rights Act of 1964 and the Voting Rights Act of 1965 also required or permitted use of three-judge courts to enforce certain provisions.

The average number of cases heard by three-judge courts tripled from about 95 per year in the early 1960s to nearly 300 per year in the early 1970s. For the Supreme Court, the direct appeals meant that the justices had less control over the selection of cases to review.

Concern about these burdens led Congress in 1976 to all but abolish the use of three-judge courts. A three-judge court is still required in legislative or congressional apportionment cases and some other minor cases, but the number of such cases is very small.

Todd, Thomas

Although he served for nearly nineteen years as a Supreme Court justice, Thomas Todd (1765–1826) wrote just fourteen opinions. Only one of them was a dissenting opinion.

Todd was born in January 1765 in King and Queen County, Virginia. His father died when the boy was just eighteen months old. His mother died ten years later, and young Todd was then raised by a guardian. Todd used part of his inheritance to get a strong education in the classics. However, the guardian lost most of his charge's money through mismanagement.

When he was sixteen, Todd served for six months in the revolutionary war. He then returned home to attend Liberty Hall (now Washington and Lee University) in Lexington, Virginia. He graduated in 1783 and joined the household of Harry Innes, a distant relative and member of the Virginia legislature, to tutor Innes's daughters. He also began to read law under Innes's direction. He was admitted to the Virginia bar in 1788 and specialized in land law.

Todd embarked on a series of clerkships in 1792. He was clerk of the federal district for Kentucky

Source: Collection of the Supreme Court of the United States

(1792–1801), the Kentucky house of representatives (1792–1801), and the Kentucky court of appeals, the state's highest court (1799–1801). When a seat was added to the Kentucky appeals court in 1801, Governor James Garrard appointed Todd to the post. Todd became chief justice five years later. The court heard many land title suits during his tenure, and Todd became known for his fairness in settling the often complicated disputes.

In 1807 Congress amended the Judiciary Act of 1789 to create a new federal court circuit composed of Tennessee, Kentucky, and Ohio. President Thomas Jefferson asked members of Congress from the three states whom he should appoint to preside over the circuit as the sixth associate justice of the Supreme Court, and they suggested Todd. Jefferson nominated him, and the Senate confirmed the nomination in March 1807. During his nearly nineteen years as an associate justice, health and personal problems caused

Todd to miss five whole Court sessions. Most of his votes supported positions taken by Chief Justice John Marshall.

Traditions of the Court

Tradition plays a major role in the operations of the Supreme Court. The Court's insistence on the historic continuity of its procedures, and its strict adherence to conventions of secrecy and formal decorum, have yielded little to the changing moods and social patterns of the contemporary world outside its chambers.

At best this adherence to tradition gives the Court an aura of substance, dignity, and caution that befits the nation's highest institution of law. It also encourages public confidence in the integrity of the justices, their seriousness of purpose, and their independence from outside pressures. But to some critics the Court's formal traditions of procedure and behavior seem to reflect an old-fashioned and outmoded set of values that hamper the effective functioning of the modern Court.

Traditions affect justices' behavior outside the Court as well as on the bench. For example, justices seldom participate in Washington's cocktail party circuit, although this has long been a common practice for members of Congress, diplomats, and administration officials.

Some traditional aspects of the Court seem merely quaint, such as the white quill pens that are still placed at each chair at the attorneys' tables in the courtroom on argument days. Since attorneys no longer use quill pens for writing, the pens now serve as mementos instead.

Other traditions are much more substantive and more controversial. Proposed changes, such as the mandatory retirement of justices or the televising of Court sessions, continue to be debated.

The system of SENIORITY affects many Court procedures, such as conference discussions and voting, announcement of opinions, and seating in the courtroom. Two other traditions, secrecy and courtesy, are also important to the smooth operations of the Court.

Secrecy

Secrecy applies not only to formal deliberations but also to disclosure of personal disagreements and animosities among the justices. The unwritten code of secrecy has made the Court the most leakproof of governmental institutions. Nevertheless, there have been and continue to be occasional glimpses into the Court's inner workings and conflicts.

The practice of allowing no one except the justices in the conference room began years ago with the mistaken impression that pages had leaked a decision. Later leaks, including several instances in the 1970s, prompted the justices to take measures to prevent further premature disclosures or gossip.

Justices and their law clerks occasionally reveal something about the Court's operations in their writings and speeches. One of the best known examples was the papers of Chief Justice Harlan Fiske Stone.

When Chief Justice Stone died in 1946, his widow turned over all his papers and files to a writer, Alpheus T. Mason. In his biography of Stone, Mason revealed much of the Court's day-to-day operations, including feuds between liberal and conservative justices. More recently Chief Justice William H. Rehnquist wrote a book, *The Supreme Court: How It Was, How It Is,* that describes generally how the Court operates.

Justices have good reason to maintain the secrecy that surrounds their conference deliberations and their personal relations with other members of the Court. Widespread disclosure of what goes on in CONFERENCES could reduce public esteem for the Court and its rulings. When leaks occur, the Court refuses to confirm or deny their accuracy. The justices are extremely reluctant to reveal instances of conflict among themselves for fear that such information would damage the dignity of the Court and encourage further quarreling among the justices.

Courtesy

Both in and out of the courtroom the justices seek to present an image of formality and courtesy. Before they enter the courtroom and at the beginning of every private conference, they shake hands with one another. This practice began in the late nineteenth century when Chief Justice Melville W. Fuller decided that it was a good idea to remind the justices that differences of opinion did not preclude overall harmony.

The harmonious image is occasionally undermined by personal, ideological, and legal differences among justices with strong views and even stronger egos. Several justices are reported to have regarded some of their colleagues with distaste, disdain, or even hatred. Justice James C. McReynolds is often cited as someone whose lack of courtesy made life on the Court difficult for his fellow justices. A conservative appointed by Woodrow Wilson in 1914, McReynolds served until 1941. He showed great antagonism to the more liberal members of the Court and particularly to the two Jewish justices with whom he served, Louis D. Brandeis and Benjamin N. Cardozo. McReynolds is said to have once refused to sit next to Brandeis for a Court photograph.

Perhaps the most widely publicized airing of judicial animosities was the attack by Justice Robert H. Jackson against Justice Hugo L. Black in 1946. Jackson had wanted and expected to become chief justice when Harlan Fiske Stone died. Instead President Harry S. Truman nominated Fred M. Vinson. Jackson blamed Black for blocking his appointment as chief justice.

Jackson responded to the news of Vinson's appointment with an angry letter to the Senate and House Judiciary committees. In that letter Jackson denounced Black for participating in a case in which, Jackson charged, Black should have disqualified himself. The case involved the United Mine Workers, an organization that was being represented by Black's former law partner Crampton Harris.

Jackson failed to mention in his letter that Black and Harris had dissolved their partnership nineteen years earlier and had hardly seen each other since. Black did not reply to the charge, nor did he mention that he had disqualified himself in all cases involving the Federal Communications Commission because his brother-in-law was a member of the commission.

The desire of most justices to maintain mutually respectful and cordial relations with their colleagues has made outbursts like Jackson's rare. In several recent instances, however, individual justices have used stronger language than usual in referring to other justices in their written opinions. "Although Justice Kennedy repeatedly accuses the Court of harboring a 'latent hostility' or 'callous indifference' toward religion . . . nothing could be further from the truth, and the accusations could be said to be as offensive as they are absurd," Justice Harry Blackmun wrote in *County of Allegheny v. American Civil Liberties Union* (1989).

For the most part, disagreements are far more likely to be exhibited in subtler ways. A common method of criticizing another justice is to cite his or her words or previous opinions to show the inconsistency of that justice's views on a particular issue. Jackson, for example, was fond of quoting statements that Black had made when he was a senator from Alabama. Many of these criticisms are so subtle that they go unnoticed by everyone except those who are privy to the relationships between the justices.

Travel, Right to

The Supreme Court has repeatedly recognized an individual right to travel within the United States, though it has not settled on the precise constitutional basis for this right. The Court has also recognized a right to travel abroad. But it has allowed Congress and the executive branch to limit overseas travel on grounds of foreign policy, despite claims that the restrictions violated individuals' First Amendment rights.

The Court has struck down some restrictions on domestic travel as impermissible burdens on interstate commerce and others as violations of the privileges and immunities clause of the Fourteenth Amendment. Both arguments were endorsed in a unanimous decision, *Edwards v. California* (1941), which struck down a California law imposing penalties for bringing poor people into the state.

The five-member majority in *Edwards* held the law to be an unconstitutional interference with interstate commerce. The other four justices argued that the right to travel was a privilege of national citizenship

that states were prohibited from abridging under the Fourteenth Amendment.

The Court has never made a choice between these two lines of reasoning. In cases upholding the Civil Rights Act of 1964, it said that refusal of PUBLIC ACCOMMODATIONS to blacks traveling interstate was an unconstitutional burden on interstate commerce. In *Shapiro v. Thompson* (1969) the Court struck down a one-year residency requirement for receipt of state welfare benefits as a violation of the right to travel, adding that it saw no need to "ascribe the source of this right . . . to a particular constitutional provision."

The *Shapiro* decision said the right to travel was a fundamental interest that a state could impair only by showing a compelling reason for doing so. The Court invoked the doctrine in striking down a one-year state residency requirement for voting *(Dunn v. Blumstein* [1972]), though it upheld fifty-day residency requirements in two cases decided in 1973. The Court also relied on *Shapiro* in 1974 to strike down a one-year residency requirement to receive state-funded nonemergency medical care.

In 1974 the Court upheld, by a vote of 6 to 3, Iowa's one-year residency requirement to get a divorce in the state's courts *(Sosna v. Iowa).* Writing for the majority, Justice William H. Rehnquist said the law was justified because of the state's interest in protecting the rights of defendant spouses (that is, the spouse that did not file for the divorce) and of any minor children.

The right to international travel rests on the due process clause of the Fifth Amendment, but it is subject to broad regulation by Congress. The Passport Act of 1926, the basis for modern passport administration, authorized the State Department to deny travel documents to applicants with criminal records or to noncitizens. In addition, from 1917 to 1931, passports were generally denied to members of the American Communist party.

State Department policies restricting passports to known or suspected communists were struck down by the Supreme Court in two decisions in 1958 and 1964. The Court's 5–4 ruling in *Kent v. Dulles* (1958) held that Congress had not authorized the State Department to deny passports to persons based on their beliefs or associations. The second ruling, *Aptheker v. Secretary of State* (1964), invalidated provisions of the 1950 McCarran Act denying passports to members of communist organizations because they failed to distinguish between knowing and unknowing party membership.

In *Zemel v. Rusk* (1965) the Court upheld the State Department's power to bar use of U.S. passports for travel to specified countries, including Cuba. Later decisions made clear, though, that travelers could get around the ban by traveling first to another country.

In 1981 the Court again deferred to the State Department's power to restrict travel by U.S. citizens. The secretary of state had revoked the passport of a former Central Intelligence Agency (CIA) official, Philip Agee, on the ground that his actions in exposing CIA agents abroad caused serious damage to national security. Agee claimed the action violated his First Amendment right to criticize the government, but the Court in *Haig v. Agee* decided against him, 7–2.

Treaty Power

The Constitution gives the president the power to make treaties with foreign countries "by and with the Advice and Consent of the Senate . . . provided that two thirds of the Senators present concur" (Article II, Section 2). Although the clause is somewhat ambiguous, the Supreme Court said in *United States v. Curtiss-Wright Export Corp.* (1936) that it gives the president the sole authority to conduct negotiations with foreign governments. (See FOREIGN AFFAIRS.)

Beginning with the first treaty it approved—the Jay Treaty with Great Britain in 1795—the Senate has used its approval power to amend or modify the terms of international agreements. The Supreme Court upheld this power in *Haver v. Yaker* (1869). The House has no authority over treaties, although it may have to act to approve legislation or appropriate funds to carry out the terms of a treaty.

On a few occasions the Senate has rejected major treaties—notably, the 1919 Treaty of Versailles, which called for U.S. participation in the League of Nations after World War I. More often, the Senate has amended treaties in ways that made them unacceptable to the president or to the countries that were parties to the agreements.

The Supreme Court declared in the *Head Money Cases* (1884) that Congress has the power to pass legislation for the "enforcement, modification, or repeal" of a treaty. The Court's decision upheld a tax levied on immigrants despite earlier treaties with several nations guaranteeing immigrants free admission into the United States.

In a controversial decision in 1918 the Court suggested that the treaty-making power could give the federal government greater authority than Congress could exercise under domestic legislation. The case, *Missouri v. Holland,* concerned a treaty with Canada to protect migratory birds. The Court upheld the treaty despite lower federal court decisions several years earlier that had struck down similar congressional statutes as an intrusion on states' sovereignty. In *Reid v. Covert* (1957), however, the Supreme Court said that a treaty cannot override a specific provision of the Constitution.

The Supreme Court has held that the termination of a treaty requires an act of Congress. But the president may find that a treaty has been breached or determine that a treaty is no longer binding on the United States. The Court has stipulated that treaties may be abrogated by the president, Congress, or the president and the Senate acting together.

The congressional role in making and carrying out treaties has been diminished by the growing use of executive agreements. This practice, sanctioned by the Supreme Court, allows the president to negotiate agreements with foreign governments without submitting them to either house of Congress for approval.

Some executive agreements have been specifically authorized by acts of Congress—for example, the 1941 Lend-Lease Act that allowed President Franklin D. Roosevelt to help arm Britain before U.S. entry into World War II. Many others have resulted solely from presidential initiatives.

The Supreme Court first upheld the practice of bypassing congressional approval in *Tucker v. Alexandroff* (1902), which involved agreements with Mexico al-

Although the United States had promised immigrants free entry into the country, Congress in the 1800s passed laws taxing their admission. In 1884 the Court declared such taxes valid. Justice Samuel F. Miller stated in the Head Money Cases *that "a treaty made by the United States with any foreign nation . . . is subject to such acts as Congress may pass."*   Source: Library of Congress

lowing troops of both nations to cross the international border in pursuit of marauding Indians. The scope of executive agreements grew dramatically in the twentieth century.

President Theodore Roosevelt initialed what amounted to a secret treaty with Japan recognizing Japan's protectorate over Korea. President Woodrow Wilson's secretary of state, Robert Lansing, signed an agreement recognizing Japan's "special interest" in China. Franklin Roosevelt used executive agreements as a primary instrument of foreign policy both before and during U.S. involvement in World War II. And

presidents of both parties continued to make frequent use of executive agreements during the Cold War.

The Court has upheld this presidential prerogative in negotiating with foreign governments. In *United States v. Belmont* (1937) the Court supported Roosevelt's decision to extend diplomatic recognition to the Soviet Union. In 1981 the Court upheld the agreement that President Jimmy Carter negotiated to secure the release of fifty-two Americans who were being held hostage in Iran. The agreement established an international tribunal to resolve financial claims by U.S. citizens against the government of Iran. The

Court's decision in *Dames & Moore v. Regan* upheld Carter's action after noting that settlement of the claims was needed to resolve the dispute with Iran and that Congress had appeared to acquiesce in the agreement.

Trials

Trials are mentioned just once in the original Constitution. Article III, Section 2 requires jury trials for all crimes except in cases of IMPEACHMENT and specifies that trials be held in the state where the crime was committed. The BILL OF RIGHTS expanded the provisions concerning the right to trial. The Fifth Amendment provided that a criminal defendant could not be "compelled . . . to be a witness against himself." The Sixth Amendment created an array of other procedural rights in criminal trials, including the right to legal counsel. The Seventh Amendment protected the right to jury trials in civil cases. (See COUNSEL, RIGHT TO LEGAL; CRIMINAL LAW AND PROCEDURE; JURIES.)

State constitutions recognized most of these rights as well, but the provisions varied and many state courts were lax in enforcing them. In the 1920s the Supreme Court began to use the DUE PROCESS clause of the Fourteenth Amendment to correct some blatant injustices in state criminal trials. In the 1960s the Court made broader changes in state trial procedures by applying to the states most of the specific provisions of the Bill of Rights relating to criminal trials. (See INCORPORATION DOCTRINE.)

The Supreme Court had earlier brought about some important changes in civil and criminal trials by promulgating new rules of procedure for federal courts. Historically, federal courts had used a mix of state and federal procedural rules. In the 1930s concern about the lack of uniformity in federal courts led Congress to pass a law authorizing the Supreme Court to write new rules of civil procedure, subject to congressional veto. The Court issued the Federal Rules of Civil Procedure in 1938, and Congress allowed them to go into effect. Under a second authorizing act, the Court issued the Federal Rules of Criminal Procedure

in 1944. Both sets of rules modernized and simplified trial procedures in federal courts. States have also looked to the rules in revising their own trial procedures.

Criminal Trials

Two provisions of the Sixth Amendment give defendants specific rights regarding the presentation of evidence at trial. One requires that the defendant be "confronted with the witnesses against him." The other guarantees that a defendant have "compulsory process [that is, the use of the SUBPOENA] for obtaining witnesses in his favor."

Confrontation Clause

The Supreme Court has described the right of confrontation as a way to protect defendants' presumption of innocence by ensuring that they have the opportunity to cross-examine witnesses against them and to impeach the witnesses' testimony.

The Court applied this requirement to the states in 1965. In *Pointer v. Texas* the Court ruled that a defendant's rights had been violated when a state prosecutor introduced the transcript of a witness's testimony at a preliminary hearing, where the witness was not subject to cross-examination. Three years later, in *Bruton v. United States* (1968), the Court held that when two defendants are being tried together, the confrontation clause limits the prosecution's use of statements made by one defendant against the codefendant, since the statements could not be cross-examined unless the defendant took the stand.

State efforts to protect witnesses sometimes clash with the defendant's rights under the confrontation clause. In 1974 the Court ruled that a defendant's rights were violated by a state law that prevented him from cross-examining a juvenile witness about his delinquency record. But in 1990 the Court upheld a Michigan "rape shield" law that prevents a rape defendant from introducing evidence of a prior romantic relationship with the accuser unless he notifies the government of an intent to introduce such evidence within ten days after arraignment.

Several of the most recent cases concerning the confrontation clause have involved efforts to protect victims in child abuse cases from the additional trauma of testifying in the presence of the alleged attacker. The Court in 1988 said that states could not allow child abuse victims to testify behind a screen, but in 1990 it voted 5–4 to allow them to testify on closed-circuit television rather than in the courtroom *(Maryland v. Craig)*. On the same day in 1990 a different 5–4 majority ruled that a state could introduce hearsay statements from a child who was unable to testify in person only when the prosecution could show "particularized guarantees of trustworthiness" *(Idaho v. Wright)*.

Compulsory Process

The Court gave a broad meaning to the right of compulsory process in its decision extending the provision to the states. *Washington v. Texas* (1967) struck down a state rule of evidence that disqualified accomplices from testifying for one another in criminal cases. "The right to offer the testimony of witnesses, and to compel their attendance if necessary, is in plain terms the right to present a defense, the right to present the defendant's version of the facts," the Court declared.

Six years later the Court found a due process violation when a judge strictly enforced the rule against hearsay statements to prevent a defendant from offering testimony that another man had confessed to the crime with which he was charged. The Court has also relied on the right of compulsory process to prohibit a judge from silencing a defense witness by threatening him with prosecution for perjury and to bar use of a jury instruction generally casting doubt on the credibility of defense witnesses.

Disclosure Requirement

One of the Court's most important rulings supporting a defendant's rights at trial relied not on the specific provisions of the Sixth Amendment but on the more general due process clause. In *Brady v. Maryland* (1963) the Court held that prosecutors must disclose, upon request, any information in their possession that may be favorable to the accused. The ruling came in a murder case where a prosecutor had suppressed an out-of-court statement by the defendant's accomplice that he had actually committed the murder.

The Court in 1976 clarified and slightly expanded the ruling by requiring prosecutors to disclose any knowledge of perjured testimony given at trial and to turn over before trial—even without a specific request—any information that creates a reasonable doubt about the defendant's guilt.

Under the Fifth Amendment criminal defendants cannot similarly be required to provide information in their possession to the prosecution. But some states have adopted a limited form of discovery in criminal cases by requiring defendants to give notice of their intention to call expert witnesses or to rely on an alibi defense. The Court in 1976 upheld these so-called alibi notice requirements as long as the prosecution was similarly obliged to give the defendant pretrial notice of any rebuttal witnesses on the alibi issue.

Free Press and Fair Trial

As part of its increasing oversight of state criminal trials, the Supreme Court in the 1960s examined the issue of how to ensure that news coverage of criminal cases did not interfere with a defendant's right to a fair trial. The Court declared that judges have a responsibility to protect defendants from prejudicial publicity. But it later found that some of the procedures judges adopted, such as "gag rules" and closure of trials, were unconstitutional under the First Amendment.

In two early cases the Court in 1961 and 1963 overturned murder convictions because of pretrial publicity about the cases that was stimulated in large part by law enforcement authorities. In one case the police department had sent out press releases announcing that the accused had confessed to a series of six killings. In the other case the sheriff had allowed a local television station to film the interrogation during which the suspect confessed.

The Court's next two rulings on the free press/fair trial issue involved the effect of the presence of news reporters on the conduct of the trial itself. In 1965 the Court reversed the conviction of financier Billie Sol Estes because of the presence of television cameras, radio microphones, and newspaper photographers at his pretrial hearing and trial. The next year, in *Sheppard v. Maxwell* (1966), the Court overturned the conviction in one of the most notorious murder cases of the 1950s and used the ruling to lay out ground rules for judges, prosecutors, and law enforcement authori-

Dr. Sam Sheppard in September 1966 with his son and second wife. The Court decided that negative pretrial publicity had influenced the outcome of Sheppard's trial and overturned his conviction.   Source: The Cleveland Plain Dealer

ties to follow to ensure fair trials without restricting the press.

Sheppard involved the murder conviction of Dr. Sam Sheppard, a Cleveland physician, for the 1954 death by bludgeoning of his pregnant wife. There was extensive pretrial publicity, and news coverage of the trial was equally heavy. As the Court declared in its opinion, "newsmen took over practically the entire courtroom."

The Court blamed the trial judge for allowing "the carnival atmosphere" that prevented Sheppard from receiving a fair trial. The justices said that the judge should have considered a change of venue (change of location) or a continuance (postponement) to minimize the effects of pretrial publicity. Further, the judge

should have strictly controlled the conduct of reporters during the trial. And finally, the Court said the judge "might well have proscribed extrajudicial statements by any lawyer, party, witness or court official which divulged prejudicial matters," including any statement made by Sheppard and the identity or probable testimony of any witnesses.

An American Bar Association commission later adopted guidelines that largely followed the Court's recommendations for limiting the information about criminal cases that should be disclosed in advance of trial. The guidelines, which were opposed by press groups, reduced the amount of information released by police and prosecutors.

Some judges sought to go further either by closing

trials or preliminary hearings altogether or by forbidding news coverage of hearings that were open. In *Nebraska Press Association v. Stuart* (1976), however, the Court unanimously struck down a Nebraska judge's order preventing any coverage of a preliminary hearing in a highly publicized serial murder case. In a series of decisions beginning with *Richmond Newspapers Inc. v. Commonwealth of Virginia* (1980), the Court held that the press and public have a right of access to criminal trials and some pretrial hearings. (See PRESS, FREEDOM OF.)

The Court in 1981 allowed states to permit television coverage of criminal trials. Upholding Florida's decision in 1977 to experiment with televised trials, the Court said that its earlier decision in the Estes case had not been an absolute ban on photographic or broadcast coverage of criminal trials *(Chandler v. Florida).*

Civil Cases

The Supreme Court has had less to say about the procedures for civil trials than about those for criminal trials since there are fewer constitutional provisions regarding civil trials. The Seventh Amendment protects the right to jury trial in most civil suits, but the provision has not been extended to the states.

The Court has declined to recognize a right to counsel for poor people in civil cases, although it has done so under the Sixth Amendment in criminal cases. In *Lassiter v. Department of Social Services* (1981) the Court held that a state need not provide counsel for an indigent mother in a proceeding brought by the state to terminate her parental rights. While recognizing the severity of the potential sanction, the Court said that a lawyer was not necessary to ensure a fair hearing in such cases.

In 1981 the Court ruled in Chandler v. Florida *that allowing television coverage of criminal trials did not infringe upon a defendant's rights to due process and a fair trial. The controversial decision, in the fall of 1991, to broadcast the highly publicized rape trial of William Kennedy Smith brought the issue into the homes and workplaces of millions of Americans. To ensure privacy for Smith's accuser, Patricia Bowman, who remained unidentified until after the trial, television stations covered her face with a blurry circle on the screen. Smith, at far right of the table, was acquitted of the charge.   Source: Turner Broadcasting System, Inc.*

Trimble, Robert

Robert Trimble (1776–1828) resigned from one judgeship and declined another because they didn't pay enough to support his growing family, which eventually included at least ten children. After becoming wealthy through his private legal practice, however, he became a federal judge in 1817 and accepted an appointment to the Supreme Court in 1826.

Born in Virginia, Trimble spent most of his youth and adulthood in Kentucky. He is believed to have studied at the Bourbon Academy in Kentucky, and he next attended the Kentucky Academy (later Transylvania University). He set up a private law practice in Paris, Kentucky, in about 1800, and two years later he entered the Kentucky house of representatives.

In 1807 Trimble was appointed a justice on the Kentucky court of appeals. He lasted just one year before resigning, claiming he couldn't support his family on his annual salary of $1,000. In 1810 he declined the chief justiceship of Kentucky, again for financial reasons, and in 1812 he rejected a run for the U.S. Senate.

By 1817 Trimble had grown sufficiently wealthy that he decided he could accept an appointment by President James Madison to be the federal district judge for Kentucky. He served in that post until President John Quincy Adams nominated him to the Supreme Court in 1826. Trimble, Adams's only appointee to the Court, became the first federal judge to ascend to the Supreme Court. On the Court he joined with Chief Justice John Marshall in supporting national supremacy. He died in 1828 after serving as a justice for only two years.

Source: Library of Congress

Twenty-fourth Amendment

See VOTING RIGHTS.

Twenty-seventh Amendment

See AMENDING PROCESS.

Twenty-sixth Amendment

See REVERSALS OF RULINGS BY CONSTITUTIONAL AMENDMENT.

U

Unconstitutional Statutes

The Supreme Court has declared at least 128 acts of Congress unconstitutional in whole or in part. This power of JUDICIAL REVIEW, taken for granted today, is not explicitly established in the Constitution. But few scholars believe the omission means that the framers intended to deny the Court this authority.

Supreme Court decisions striking down acts of Congress are among the Court's most important and controversial rulings. The Court used the power to blunt civil rights laws in the Reconstruction era, thwart social and economic legislation in the Progressive and New Deal eras, throw out some antisubversive laws during the Cold War, and enforce the SEPARATION OF POWERS among Congress, the president, and the judiciary.

Alexander Hamilton anticipated the Court's power to invalidate acts of Congress during the debate over ratification of the Constitution. Writing in *The Federalist Papers,* No. 78, Hamilton reminded his readers that the Constitution limited legislative authority. Those limitations, he argued, "can be preserved in no other medium than through the medium of the courts of justice, whose duty it would be to declare all acts contrary to the manifest tenor of the Constitution void."

Early Rulings

Chief Justice John Marshall relied heavily on Hamilton's reasoning in his landmark opinion in *MARBURY V. MADISON* (1803), striking down a provision of an act of Congress for the first time. Like Hamilton, he stressed the Constitution's role of limiting the power of the legislature and the courts' role in enforcing those limitations. In the event of a conflict between a law and the Constitution, Marshall said, the court was bound to decide the case by applying the Constitution rather than "any ordinary act of the legislature." The ruling itself invalidated a minor pro-

vision of the Judiciary Act of 1789, but the principle it established was of historic significance.

The Court did not invalidate an act of Congress again until the so-called Dred Scott case (*SCOTT V. SANDFORD* [1857]). With the nation bitterly divided over slavery, the Court ruled that Congress had acted unconstitutionally in providing, in the Missouri Compromise of 1820, that slavery would be prohibited in the northern part of the Louisiana Territory. The ruling also declared blacks forever disabled from attaining citizenship. After the Civil War broke out, the Union government ignored the ruling. Congress voted to abolish slavery in the territories in 1862, and President Lincoln's attorney general recognized free blacks born in the United States as U.S. citizens.

Chief Justice Charles Evans Hughes described the Dred Scott case and two other nineteenth-century decisions invalidating congressional enactments as "self-inflicted wounds" by the Court. The others on Hughes's list were the first of the *LEGAL TENDER CASES* in 1870, barring use of paper money, and the 1895 decision overturning the federal INCOME TAX. All three decisions were later overturned. The Thirteenth and Fourteenth amendments abolishing slavery and guaranteeing citizenship to blacks overturned *Scott.* The Supreme Court reversed itself on the paper money issue just one year later. And the Sixteenth Amendment, ratified in 1913, authorized Congress to levy a federal income tax. (See REVERSALS OF EARLIER RULINGS; REVERSALS OF RULINGS BY CONSTITUTIONAL AMENDMENT.)

Reconstruction

After the Civil War the Supreme Court repeatedly used its power to declare acts of the Reconstruction-era Congress unconstitutional. In 1867 it barred LOYALTY OATHS for former Confederate supporters to practice law or serve in federal office as a violation of the Constitution's ban on EX POST FACTO laws and

Major Congressional Statutes Held Unconstitutional

(Case, date, law or provision held unconstitutional)

Marbury v. Madison (1803)   Judiciary Act of 1789 provision giving Supreme Court power to issue writs of mandamus in cases originating at the Court

Scott v. Sandford (1857)   Missouri Compromise provision barring slavery in northern part of Louisiana Territory; overturned by Fourteenth Amendment

Ex parte Garland (1867)   Test oath for former Confederate supporters

Hepburn v. Griswold (1870)   "Legal tender clauses" making paper money legal tender for all debts; overruled in 1871 *(Knox v. Lee)*

Civil Rights Cases (1883)   1875 civil rights act barring racial discrimination in public accommodations; five cases overturning Reconstruction-era civil rights provisions

Boyd v. United States (1886)   Provision of 1874 law allowing federal courts to require production of documents in forfeitures under revenue and customs laws

Pollock v. Farmers' Loan & Trust Co. (1895)   Income tax provisions of the tariff act of 1894; overturned by Sixteenth Amendment

The Employers' Liability Cases (1908)   1906 act imposing liability on railroads for injuries to employees

Newberry v. United States (1921)   Federal Corrupt Practice Act of 1911 provision limiting spending by senatorial candidate in party primary; overruled in 1941 *(United States v. Classic)*

Hammer v. Dagenhart (1918)   Original child labor law barring products made with child labor from interstate commerce; overruled in 1941 *(United States v. Darby Lumber Co.)*

Bailey v. Drexel Furniture Co. (Child Labor Tax Cases) (1922)   Child Labor Tax Act imposing 10 percent excise tax on goods manufactured with child labor; overruled in 1941 *(United States v. Darby Lumber Co.)*

Adkins v. Children's Hospital (1923)   District of Columbia minimum wage law for women; overruled in 1937 *(West Coast Hotel Co. v. Parrish)*

Myers v. United States (1926)   1876 law requiring "the advice and consent of the Senate" for removal of postmasters

Panama Refining Co. v. Ryan (1935)   National Industrial Recovery Act's "hot oil" provision penalizing interstate transportation of petroleum in excess of state production controls

Schechter Poultry Corp. v. United States (1935)   National Industrial Recovery Act provision for industry-written codes of fair competition; most important of several rulings striking down New Deal economic recovery legislation

United States v. Butler (1936)   Agricultural Adjustment Act providing for processing taxes on agricultural commodities and benefit payments to farmers

Carter v. Carter Coal Co. (1936)   Bituminous Coal Conservation Act of 1935 regulating prices and labor relations in coal industry and levying tax on coal to finance regulation scheme

Bolling v. Sharpe (1954)   1862 statute establishing segregated schools in the District of Columbia (companion case to *Brown v. Board of Education of Topeka*)

United States v. Brown (1965)   Labor-Management Reporting and Disclosure Act of 1959 provision barring current or former communists from labor union office

Shapiro v. Thompson (1969)   District of Columbia law establishing one-year residency requirement for welfare benefits

Oregon v. Mitchell (1970)   Voting rights for eighteen-year-olds; overturned by Twenty-sixth Amendment

Frontiero v. Richardson (1973)   Gender-based benefits provision for members of armed forces; first of several sex discrimination rulings in benefits cases

Buckley v. Valeo (1976)   Federal Election Campaign Act of 1974 provisions limiting spending by political candidates and establishing Federal Election Commission with congressionally appointed members

National League of Cities v. Usery (1976)   Fair Labor Standards Act provisions extending wage and hour coverage to state and local government workers; overturned in 1985 *(Garcia v. San Antonio Metropolitan Transit Authority)*

Immigration and Naturalization Service v. Chadha (1983)   Legislative veto provisions of Immigration and Nationality Act; ruling deemed to apply to similar provisions in as many as 200 statutes

Bowsher v. Synar (1986)   Gramm-Rudman-Hollings balanced budget act provision giving comptroller general, a congressional official, authority to set spending reduction figures

United States v. Eichman (1990)   1989 flag desecration statute

bills of attainder. (See ATTAINDER, BILL OF.) The ruling in *Ex parte Garland*—the first decision to strike down an act of Congress by a narrow 5–4 vote—provided a libertarian precedent for twentieth-century rulings restricting use of loyalty oaths to try to bar suspected communists from public positions.

The Court's rulings against Reconstruction-era CIVIL RIGHTS statutes proved less durable than its decision on loyalty oaths. In five rulings between 1876 and 1906 the Court struck down provisions of congressional statutes designed to guarantee civil rights to blacks. The most important ruling came in five companion cases, collectively called *The Civil Rights Cases* (1883). The Court's 8–1 decision struck down provisions of the Civil Rights Act of 1875 that made it a crime to deny anyone equal access to and enjoyment of public accommodations on account of race. The Court declared that the Fourteenth Amendment allowed Congress to forbid state action interfering with the rights of blacks, but that it did not permit legislation aimed at private racial DISCRIMINATION. On similar grounds, the Court in the same year overturned an anticonspiracy statute intended to protect blacks from retaliation by the Ku Klux Klan, lynch mobs, and the like.

Earlier, in 1876, the Court had overturned a VOTING RIGHTS provision of the Civil Rights Act of 1866, which had been reenacted in modified form in 1870, as an infringement on states' rights. The provision was intended to punish state officials for obstructing blacks from voting. In 1903 the Court struck down another provision of the act aimed at private conduct to discourage blacks from voting. Three years later, in *Hodges v. United States* (1906), the Court struck down another provision that targeted private racial discrimination: a section of the 1870 act giving blacks "the same right . . . to make and enforce contracts . . . as is enjoyed by white citizens."

These decisions helped allow racial segregation, both private and official, to take root in the South and elsewhere for nearly a century. But the force of the rulings evaporated in the civil rights revolution that began in the 1950s. Congress disregarded the precedents when it enacted the Civil Rights Act of 1964, including a PUBLIC ACCOMMODATIONS provision, and the Voting Rights Act of 1965. The Supreme Court, under Chief Justice Earl Warren, readily upheld both laws. In 1968 the Court expressly overruled *Hodges,* holding that the 1870 civil rights law could be invoked to bar private racial discrimination in housing. (See OPEN HOUSING.)

The Court and Business

The Court's narrow view of federal powers in the second half of the nineteenth century extended to other areas as well. In 1870 the Court struck down a congressional ban on the sale of inflammable naphtha as "a mere police regulation." In 1878 it threw out a provision against bankruptcy fraud on similar grounds. The Court's view represented the times. The nation was busy with the Industrial Revolution and westward expansion. For the most part, Congress maintained a hands-off attitude toward business, giving the Court few occasions to test the reach of federal legislative power.

By the turn of the century, Congress was being pressured by populists, progressives, and organized labor to take a more active role in regulating social and economic affairs. The Court, however, resisted. One example was its 5–4 decision in 1895 to overturn the new federal income tax, on the ground that it violated the constitutional requirement that direct taxes be apportioned among the states according to population. In 1908 the Court held unconstitutional two more laws backed by labor and opposed by business. An act enlarging the liability of railroads for injuries to their employees was thrown out, by a vote of 5 to 4, as extending beyond Congress's COMMERCE POWER. Three weeks later, the Court invalidated a law that outlawed "yellow dog" contracts, which railroads used to make their employees promise not to join labor unions. The Court found the law an undue restriction on freedom of contract. (See CONTRACT CLAUSE.)

A more dramatic conflict between Congress and organized labor on one side and the Court and business interests on the other arose over the issue of CHILD LABOR. Twice the Court struck down acts of Congress designed to restrict use of child labor in plants and factories. In *Hammer v. Dagenhart* (1918) the Court voted 5–4 to strike down a law barring from interstate commerce goods produced by child workers, on the grounds that it sought to regulate manufacturing rather than commerce. Congress responded in the same year with a 10 percent excise tax on goods manufactured with child labor. But in 1922 the Court, by a vote of 8 to 1, struck down the tax as an infringement of states' rights under the Tenth Amendment. Congress then approved a constitutional amendment to try to overturn the decisions, but it fell short of ratification.

Conflict with Congress over economic measures continued during the 1920s. In 1923 the Court threw out, by a vote of 5 to 3, a law establishing a minimum wage for women in the District of Columbia, basing its decision on freedom of contract. Twice the Court invalidated efforts by Congress to allow sailors and other maritime workers the benefits of state worker compensation laws, citing the constitutional mandate for uniform maritime laws. Twice the Court struck

down taxes on commodities futures trading. And in five cases the Court struck down expansive provisions for income, estate, or gift taxes.

The New Deal

The clashes over the federal government's power in economic affairs reached the point of constitutional crisis in the 1930s. To try to lift the country out of the Great Depression, President Franklin D. Roosevelt pushed a flurry of economic measures through a supportive Congress, only to find many of them overturned or restricted by the Supreme Court. Within a one-year period, the Court struck down three major pieces of the president's New Deal program, along with several lesser enactments.

The Court's most important ruling was the unanimous decision on May 27, 1935, in *Schechter Poultry Corp. v. United States*. The ruling held that the industry

The Court in 1936 overturned the Bituminous Coal Conservation Act, which Congress had passed to establish a regulatory commission for the depressed coal industry. Although Congress did not require compliance with the act, it offered as an incentive for participants a substantial rebate on the taxes it levied. The Court ruled that coal mining did not constitute interstate commerce and therefore that Congress could not regulate it.   Source: Utah State Historical Society

code provisions of the National Industrial Recovery Act amounted to an unconstitutional delegation of congressional power. On January 6, 1936, the Court cited the Tenth Amendment in striking down, by a vote of 6 to 3, the Agricultural Adjustment Act, designed to stabilize the agricultural market through crop controls and price subsidies. On May 18, 1936, the Court nullified, 5–4, a law designed to control the working conditions of miners and to fix prices for the sale of coal. The ruling called it an impermissible attempt to regulate manufacturing and struck down its industry funding scheme as an invalid tax.

Roosevelt responded, in his second term, with his infamous Court-packing plan to try to gain the power to make new appointments to the Court. The plan failed, but the justices had already begun to shift their position. Furthermore, retirements over the next several years allowed Roosevelt to reshape the Court more to his views. As a result the Court sustained several key New Deal enactments, including the Fair Labor Standards Act, the National Labor Relations Act, and revised versions of virtually all the major legislation it had struck down in 1935 and 1936. In the process the Court erased many of its restrictive precedents on economic measures, including the decisions barring the child labor and minimum wage laws.

Individual Rights

In the late 1930s the Supreme Court also began to adopt a more favorable attitude toward assertions of individual rights in such areas as freedom of speech, racial discrimination, and CRIMINAL LAW AND PROCEDURE. (See SPEECH, FREEDOM OF.) Over the next four decades the Court brought about what has been called a "rights revolution." That phase lasted until a conservative majority formed in the 1970s and solidified in the 1980s. While many of these rulings involved state laws, the Court's new attitude toward individual rights also led to conflicts with Congress in several areas.

Subversion

Congress and the executive branch established a web of antisubversive laws and regulations at the onset of the Cold War after World War II. (See COMMUNISM.) In the 1950s the Court generally upheld such

The majority in Jencks v. United States *(1957), in ruling that FBI reports of Clinton E. Jencks's communist activity should have been turned over to his defense attorneys when requested, established the policy that the prosecution in any legal case be required to submit to the defense any relevant statements by government witnesses. Dissenting opinion held that such a policy might allow the defense access to confidential files. Congress, urged by the FBI, the Justice Department, and the White House, passed a law restricting the impact of the Jencks decision. The law allowed only those pretrial statements signed or transcribed by a government witness to be requested at the time of the witness's testimony.* Source: The Los Angeles Examiner

laws, but a solid liberal majority struck down several provisions in the 1960s. In three rulings the Court invalidated sections of the 1950 Subversive Activities Control Act that barred members of Communist front organizations from obtaining a passport (1964) or working in defense plants (1967) and subjected Communist party members to prosecution for failure to register as members of a subversive organization (1965). The Court in 1965 also invalidated a law barring Communist party members from serving as union officers.

Civil Rights

The Court relied on the EQUAL PROTECTION clause of the Fourteenth Amendment in its historic ruling in *Brown v. Board of Education of Topeka* (1954) prohibiting racial segregation in public schools. But the Fourteenth Amendment applied only to the states, not to the federal government. A less well-known companion decision, *Bolling v. Sharpe,* interpreted the DUE PROCESS clause of the Fifth Amendment to contain an implicit equal protection requirement applicable to federal legislation. The ruling invalidated school segregation laws for the District of Columbia that dated from 1862. The legal principle provided the basis for the Court in the 1970s to strike down some provisions of federal benefits programs as illegal SEX DISCRIMINATION.

Criminal Procedure

On a handful of occasions before 1950 the Court had invoked the procedural protections for criminal defendants in the Fourth, Fifth, Sixth, and Seventh amendments to strike down provisions of federal laws. The Warren Court's criminal procedure revolution of the 1950s and 1960s resulted in several more such rulings. The Court limited the jurisdiction of military courts in half a dozen cases between 1955 and 1967. Three decisions in the late 1960s relied on the Fifth Amendment privilege against self-incrimination to restrict use of tax law provisions in prosecutions for gambling, firearms, and drugs. In 1968 the Court overturned the death penalty provision of the Lindbergh Kidnapping Act, saying that it penalized the right to jury trial by allowing imposition of the death penalty only if recommended by a jury.

The Court in 1978 also gave businesses new Fourth Amendment protections by limiting warrantless inspections of workplaces under the Occupational Safety and Health Act.

Sex Discrimination

The Court in the 1970s established restrictions against sex discrimination with rulings that invalidated gender-based provisions in federal benefits programs. The key ruling, *Frontiero v. Richardson* (1973), struck down a provision that made it harder for women than men in the military to gain dependent benefits for a spouse. The vote was 8–1, but the Court was divided in its reasoning. Although that division persisted, the Court in 1975 and 1977 struck down gender-based provisions for Social Security benefits and continued to expand sex discrimination protections in other areas as well.

Free Speech

A handful of federal provisions fell as the Court expanded free speech protections—a trend that continued into the 1980s. The Court struck down laws prohibiting demonstrations on the Capitol grounds (1972) or in front of the Supreme Court building (1983) or foreign embassies (1988). It overturned a ban on editorializing by public broadcasting stations (1984) and on "indecent" telephone messages (1989). In a dramatic confrontation with Congress and public opinion, the Court in 1990 struck down, by a vote of 5 to 4, a federal law against flag desecration, which Congress had passed four months after the Court's 1989 ruling overturning a similar state statute.

Political Speech

The Court in the 1970s and 1980s also created new First Amendment rights for political speech by striking down several key provisions of campaign finance reform laws. The key decision, *Buckley v. Valeo* (1976), struck down limits on campaign spending and on the amount of money that candidates could contribute to their own campaign. Later the Court also struck down limits on "independent" campaign expenditures by individuals or groups. (See CAMPAIGNS AND ELECTIONS.)

Separation of Powers

The end of the rights revolution under chief justices Warren E. Burger and William H. Rehnquist did not eliminate clashes with Congress. New conflicts arose as a result of the Court's strict interpretations of the Constitution's limitations on congressional power.

The most important ruling, *Immigration and Naturalization Service v. Chadha* (1983), struck down the so-called LEGISLATIVE VETO, a mechanism for blocking executive branch actions and regulations by a negative vote in just one chamber or one committee of

Specialist Theresa Pharms undertakes the "Green Hell" obstacle course in Panama in 1980 as part of her U.S. Army training. The controversy over allowing women to participate in military combat remains unsettled. In 1981 the Court affirmed Congress's right to ban women from the draft, a decision offensive to many women's rights advocates.
Source: U.S. Department of Defense

Congress. The Court's 7–2 decision, written by Chief Justice Burger, held that Congress could overturn regulatory actions only by a law passed by both the House and the Senate. More than 200 laws were said to be affected by the decision, including such major enactments as the War Powers Resolution of 1973, the Congressional Budget and Impoundment Act of 1974, and the Federal Election Campaign Act Amendments of 1979. In a 1987 decision, however, the Court limited the effect of the ruling by allowing such statutes to stand with the legislative veto provisions nullified.

Other decisions regarding the separation of powers were less sweeping. *Buckley v. Valeo* (1976) struck down a provision allowing Congress to name four members of the Federal Election Commission, on the grounds that it violated the president's appointment power. A 1982 decision overturned a provision of the 1978 Bankruptcy Reform Act creating a new corps of bankruptcy judges without the tenure and salary protections accorded other federal judges under Article III of the Constitution. In *Bowsher v. Synar* (1986) the Court struck down one provision of the Gramm-Rudman-Hollings balanced budget act giving the comptroller general, a congressional official, a role in enforcing the act's spending reduction requirements. Congress responded to all three decisions by revising the statutes to mend the constitutional defects.

V

Vacancy

A seat on the Supreme Court becomes vacant when a justice dies, resigns, or retires. On average, a vacancy on the Court has occurred about once every two years. How long the seat remains vacant depends on how quickly the president nominates a replacement and how long the Senate takes to act on the nomination. If the vacancy occurs during a presidential election year and the opposition party controls a substantial bloc of votes in the Senate, action on the nomination may be delayed until after the election.

That situation occurred in 1968 when Chief Justice Earl Warren announced his intention to retire. By the time President Lyndon Johnson nominated Justice Abe Fortas, Johnson was a lame-duck president, having announced that he would not seek reelection. Republicans, hopeful of winning the White House in 1968, wanted to "save" the seat for the Republican president-to-be to fill. Fortas's continuing role as an unofficial adviser to the president on policy matters while on the Court and his acceptance of fees for a series of university seminars had created doubts among enough senators to forestall confirmation. When Fortas's nomination finally reached the Senate floor, it was successfully filibustered, and Fortas asked the president to withdraw his name from nomination.

Richard Nixon, the Republican candidate, won election as president soon thereafter. In May 1969 he named Warren E. Burger as his choice for chief justice.

The longest vacancy in the Court's history lasted for two years, three months, and twenty-three days. The vacancy was created when Justice Henry Baldwin died April 21, 1844. During the vacancy the Senate refused to act on three nominations to the seat and rejected a fourth, and future president James Buchanan declined three invitations to take it. The first three nominations, all of which the Senate re-fused to consider, were made by President John Tyler. Tyler had been elected vice president on the Whig ticket in 1840 but had broken with the party—and lost his political base—when he succeeded to the presidency upon William Henry Harrison's death in 1841. Tyler had first offered the nomination to Buchanan, who declined it.

The vacancy was then left for Tyler's successor, James K. Polk, but the Senate rejected his first nominee on a 20–29 vote in January 1846. Polk's two attempts to convince Buchanan to take the job also failed. Finally, Polk turned to Robert C. Grier, a district court judge from Pennsylvania, who proved acceptable to almost everybody. The Senate confirmed Grier on August 4, 1846, the day after his nomination.

The second longest vacancy was only slightly shorter—two years, one month, and sixteen days. It occurred when Justice Peter V. Daniel of Virginia died on May 31, 1860. At this point four of the remaining justices were northerners, and four were from the South. Naturally, the South wanted President Buchanan to choose another southerner, while the North urged nomination of a northerner.

Nearly eight months after the vacancy had occurred, Buchanan in February 1861 nominated Secretary of State Jeremiah S. Black of Pennsylvania. If Buchanan had acted sooner, Black might well have been confirmed. He supported the Union but was not an abolitionist, and his nomination might have been acceptable to southern senators. But many of them had already resigned from the Senate to join the Confederacy. Moreover, Republicans wanted to hold the vacancy open for incoming president Abraham Lincoln to fill. Black's nomination was thus rejected by one vote, 25–26.

Buchanan made no further attempt to fill the vacancy. Lincoln, who was quickly presented with two more seats to fill, did not name anyone to the seat for more than a year, and then he chose Samuel F. Miller, a well-respected attorney from Iowa. The Senate confirmed Miller within half an hour of receiving his nomination on July 26, 1862.

Vacate

The term *vacate,* in its legal sense, means to rescind or cancel, to void an act such as a judgment. The Supreme Court, like other appellate courts, occasionally vacates, or voids, a judgment of a lower court that it finds to be in error.

Van Devanter, Willis

The retirement from the Supreme Court of Justice Willis Van Devanter (1859–1941) in June 1937 is one of the factors that helped avert a constitutional crisis over President Franklin Roosevelt's Court-packing plan.

In 1935 and 1936 the Court issued a series of 5–4 and 6–3 decisions that struck down the major provisions of Roosevelt's New Deal program. Van Devanter was a conservative justice who consistently voted against the president. Exasperated, Roosevelt responded by drafting a bill that would allow him to appoint a new justice for every justice over age seventy. The plan would have increased the Court's membership to fifteen justices, giving Roosevelt a chance to pack the Court with justices who supported the New Deal.

Within weeks after Roosevelt submitted the plan to Congress, the Supreme Court began to uphold portions of the New Deal, usually by 5–4 votes. The conservative Van Devanter still voted against the New Deal. But on June 2, 1937, just days before the Senate Judiciary Committee recommended rejection of Roosevelt's plan, Van Devanter retired. His action was prompted at least partly by a law passed in early 1937 that allowed justices to retire at full salary. To replace Van Devanter, Roosevelt nominated Hugo L. Black, a strong supporter of the New Deal. The crisis passed as the Court continued upholding the New Deal.

Source: Library of Congress

Van Devanter was born in 1859 in Marion, Indiana. He graduated from Indiana Asbury (now DePauw) University in 1878 and received his law degree from the University of Cincinnati Law School in 1881. After working three years in his father's law firm, Van Devanter moved to the Wyoming Territory and established a practice in Cheyenne. Shortly after arriving Van Devanter served on a commission that revised the territory's statutes. In 1888 he was elected to the territorial legislature, and two years later President Benjamin Harrison appointed him chief justice of the Wyoming Territory supreme court. Van Devanter was thirty when appointed. He served for only one year before resigning to return to his private practice.

Van Devanter was heavily involved in Republican politics, and in 1897 President William McKinley rewarded him with an appointment as assistant attorney general. President Theodore Roosevelt appointed him to the U.S. Court of Appeals for the Eighth Circuit in 1903, and President William Howard Taft nominated him to the Supreme Court in 1910. Many liberals strongly opposed the conservative judge. However, the Senate confirmed him by a voice vote. He served for twenty-six years before retiring in 1937, and died four years later, in 1941.

Veto, Legislative

See LEGISLATIVE VETO.

Veto Power

The veto power is the president's power to disapprove a bill passed by Congress, subject to being overridden in turn by Congress. It is one of the most important parts of the constitutional system of SEPARATION OF POWERS. The veto power has emerged since the Civil War as a major instrument of presidential power.

Under Article I, Section 7 of the Constitution, every bill passed by Congress must be presented to the president for approval or disapproval. The president can sign the bill into law or else veto it by returning the legislation to Congress, together with a message giving the reasons for disapproving it. Congress, in turn, can override the president's veto and enact a bill into law by a two-thirds majority vote in both the House of Representatives and the Senate.

Section 7 also gives the president the power to prevent a bill from becoming law by exercising a "pocket veto" after Congress has adjourned. If Congress is in session, the president has ten days (Sundays excepted) to act on a bill, or it becomes law without the presidential signature. If Congress adjourns before the expiration of the ten-day period, however, the president is not required to return the bill to Congress. The "pocket veto" kills the bill, since Congress then has no opportunity to vote to override the president's action.

The veto was used only sparingly in early U.S. history, but since the Civil War it has been a major weapon in political battles between Congress and the president. In all, presidents have vetoed 2,513 measures from 1789 through 1992, with all but 52 of the vetoes cast after 1860. Congress has overridden presidential vetoes only 104 times.

Early presidents used the veto only if they believed a bill was unconstitutional or defective in some manner. Andrew Jackson was the first president to use the veto to further his own legislative agenda. President Andrew Johnson's struggles with radical Republicans in Congress led him to use the veto twenty-nine times and resulted in 1866 in the first successful attempt by Congress to override a presidential veto.

President Grover Cleveland used the veto 584 times during his two terms in the White House. That record stood until the administration of President Franklin D. Roosevelt, who vetoed 635 bills during his twelve years in office. In more recent times, Democratic president Harry S. Truman used the veto to block bills opposed by organized labor, while Republican presidents Dwight Eisenhower, Richard Nixon, Gerald Ford, Ronald Reagan, and George Bush used the veto power extensively to thwart bills passed by Democratic-controlled Congresses.

Both Congress and the White House generally accept the politically determined outcome of veto battles. Perhaps for this reason, the Supreme Court has never been called upon to judge the validity of a direct veto. But legal disputes have arisen between Congress and the White House over what constitutes a congressional "adjournment" for purposes of exercising the pocket veto power.

In the *Pocket Veto Case* (1929) the Supreme Court ruled that President Calvin Coolidge had appropriately used the pocket veto to kill a bill that Congress had passed just before a four-month recess. Justice Edward T. Sanford's opinion for the Court concluded that an interim adjournment "prevents" the president from returning a bill to Congress within the time period specified in Section 7.

The Court soon limited the broad sweep of this ruling. In *Wright v. United States* (1938) the Court held that during a short recess of one chamber, an official of that chamber could receive a veto message to deliver to the chamber after the recess. Therefore, a pocket veto could not be used in those circumstances.

The question arose anew in 1970 when President Nixon vetoed a bill during a six-day Christmas recess.

In a suit brought by Sen. Edward M. Kennedy, D-Mass., a federal court of appeals held the veto invalid because the recess was not long enough to prevent Nixon from returning the bill to Congress with a direct veto message. A second case decided by the same court in 1976 broadened the ruling to prohibit the president from killing a bill by pocket veto during adjournments between the same session of Congress.

President Reagan sparked a new round in this debate by declaring that the pocket veto could be used whenever Congress recessed for longer than three days. During a brief recess he pocket-vetoed a bill barring aid to the U.S.-backed regime in El Salvador. This action was challenged by thirty-three House members, who won an appeals court ruling reaffirming the limit on pocket vetoes to periods following the final adjournment of Congress. The administration appealed the case of *Burke v. Barnes* to the Supreme Court, but the Court ruled that the dispute had become moot. The action left the lower court ruling in place, so that the issue was not definitively resolved.

President Bush exercised pocket vetoes twice in 1989, prompting two House committees to approve a bill in 1990 specifying that a pocket veto could be used only after Congress's final adjournment. But the bill was never brought to the House floor and died at the end of the 1990 congressional session.

Source: Library of Congress

Vinson, Frederick M.

As chief justice of the Supreme Court, Frederick Moore Vinson (1890–1953) had to be a peacemaker. The Court was seriously divided, and justices Hugo Black and Robert Jackson were having a very public and very bitter feud. Vinson succeeded in quieting the hostilities but was unable to resolve the conflicts. During his tenure there were proportionally more 5–4 decisions than under any other chief justice in the Court's history. Vinson died after serving seven years as chief justice, sorely disappointed that he had not been able to accomplish more.

Vinson was born in Louisa, Kentucky. After receiving his undergraduate and law degrees from Centre College in Kentucky, he passed the bar in 1911 at age twenty-one. He then served in several public positions. He was commonwealth attorney for the Thirty-second Judicial District of Kentucky (1921–1924), member of the U.S. House of Representatives (1924–1929, 1931–1938), judge on the U.S. Court of Appeals for the District of Columbia (1938–1943), director of the Office of Economic Stabilization (1943–1945), administrator of the Federal Loan Agency (1945), director of the Office of War Mobilization and Reconversion (1945), and secretary of the treasury (1945–1946).

When Chief Justice Harlan Fiske Stone died in 1946, Justice Robert Jackson expected to be promoted to chief justice. It was rumored, however, that if Jackson were appointed two justices would resign from the Court. President Harry S. Truman appointed

Vinson in an effort to calm the waters, thereby arousing the wrath of Jackson.

Vinson believed in a strong executive branch of government. When Truman ordered the government to take over the nation's steel mills the day before a threatened strike, the Court ruled 6–3 that Truman had unconstitutionally overstepped his powers. Vinson was one of the three justices who dissented from that decision.

Although Vinson was generally considered a liberal chief justice, some of his opinions were quite conservative. In 1950 the Court upheld the power of Congress to require that officers of labor unions sign statements that they were not members of the Communist party or other organizations that advocated overthrow of the government. Under the law, unions whose officers did not sign the statements became ineligible for protection by the National Labor Relations Board. In the opinion for the Court, Vinson wrote that the requirement did not violate union officers' First Amendment rights. Vinson died in September 1953.

Voting Rights

The right to vote, called suffrage, was limited to white male property owners when the United States was founded, but it has now been extended to virtually every adult American. The Supreme Court did not play a major role in enlarging the right to vote. The changes resulted instead from constitutional amendments and from the Voting Rights Act of 1965.

The Constitution left it to the states to define qualifications for voting. Early in the nation's history, popular pressure forced states to drop restrictive property qualifications for voting. But constitutional amendments were needed to extend the right to vote to blacks (1870), women (1920), and eighteen-year-olds (1970). (See CIVIL WAR AMENDMENTS; REVERSALS OF RULINGS BY CONSTITUTIONAL AMENDMENT.)

The issue of women's suffrage reached the Supreme Court in 1875 in a case brought under the privileges and immunities clause of the Fourteenth Amendment. In *Minor v. Happersett* the Court held that the right to vote was not a privilege of U.S. citizenship protected by the amendment. Women's suffrage groups worked for another forty-five years before winning ratification of the Nineteenth Amendment forbidding restriction of the suffrage on account of sex.

The Fifteenth Amendment expressly provides that the right to vote shall not be "denied or abridged" by the federal government or the states "on account of race, color, or previous condition of servitude." In a pair of decisions in 1876, however, the Court declared that the Fifteenth Amendment did not create a right to vote but only an "exemption from discrimination." On that basis the Court struck down voting rights provisions of an 1870 CIVIL RIGHTS enforcement act because they were not confined to racial DISCRIMINATION. The Court blocked the use of the act's conspiracy section against harassment or intimidation of blacks seeking to vote.

Exclusionary Devices

Encouraged by the Court's hands-off attitude, many southern states between 1890 and 1910 came up with devices to exclude blacks from voting. These included literacy tests, grandfather clauses, all-white primaries, and poll taxes. The Court held grandfather clauses unconstitutional in 1915 and finally ruled white primaries invalid in 1944. But the Court struck down the use of poll taxes and literacy tests only after Congress had acted.

Literacy Tests

The Court upheld the validity of literacy tests as a qualification for voting from 1898 *(Williams v. Mississippi)* until 1959. In 1965 the Court did strike down a Louisiana literacy test that required prospective voters to display a reasonable knowledge of any section of the state or federal constitution, calling it "not a test but a trap." But literacy tests were abolished only after passage of the federal Voting Rights Act.

Grandfather Clauses

Some states required potential voters either to pass a literacy test or else to show that their ancestors were entitled to vote in 1866; thus, most white males were

Despite such obstacles as an 1875 Supreme Court ruling that the right to vote was not guaranteed by the Fourteenth Amendment, women's suffrage groups in the nineteenth and early twentieth centuries persevered. Under the auspices of the National American Woman Suffrage Association, many women, like these on Pennsylvania Avenue in Washington, D.C., took to the streets to protest sex discrimination. In 1920 their efforts paid off when the Nineteenth Amendment, giving women the right to vote, was added to the Constitution.
Source: Library of Congress

exempt from the test. The Court in *Guinn v. United States* (1915) struck down the device as an evasion of the Fifteenth Amendment. The ruling was the first voting rights case in which the Court looked beyond the nondiscriminatory form of a law to scrutinize its discriminatory effect.

White Primaries

Several southern states excluded blacks from voting in Democratic primaries, which were tantamount to election in much of the Democratic-dominated South until the 1960s. The Court in 1927 and 1932 forbade such voting restrictions as discriminatory state action, whether they were imposed by state law or by the party's executive committee acting under state law. Texas Democrats responded by formally limiting membership to whites, and the Court in 1935 upheld that device. Nine years later the Court in *Smith v. Allwright* (1944) reversed itself and ruled that race-based voting qualifications set by a political party were state action subject to the Fifteenth Amendment.

Poll Taxes

Poll taxes were revived by southern states in the 1890s and were upheld by the Court in 1937 *(Breedlove v. Suttles)*. All but four states had abolished them by 1960, and in 1964 the states completed ratification of the Twenty-fourth Amendment abolishing the poll tax in federal elections. Two years later the Court in *Harper v. State Board of Elections* (1966) held the poll tax unconstitutional in state or local elections as a violation of the EQUAL PROTECTION clause of the Fourteenth Amendment.

Voting Rights Act

Large numbers of blacks were still shut out from voting. In 1965 Congress responded to a plea by President Lyndon B. Johnson to pass the federal Voting Rights Act. The law suspended literacy tests and provided for appointment of federal voting registrars in states with literacy tests and low voting rates, including six southern states and parts of a seventh. States or counties covered by the law were required to obtain federal approval before changing their voting laws or procedures.

The law represented a major intrusion on an area traditionally reserved to the states. Still, the Supreme Court in *South Carolina v. Katzenbach* (1966) upheld Congress's power to adopt the law under the Fifteenth Amendment. Since then, the act has been amended to cover additional areas and, in 1975, to abolish literacy tests nationwide. The Court, with one exception, has steadfastly upheld the act and interpreted it broadly.

The exception came in *Mobile v. Bolden* (1980), when the Court ruled, 6–3, that the act did not reach a voting system that had a discriminatory effect unless there was also evidence of a discriminatory intent. The ruling upheld an at-large system of electing city commissioners in Mobile, Alabama, which blacks claimed "diluted" their right to vote by effectively preventing the election of blacks to the city posts.

Congress responded in 1982 by amending the act to delete any requirement of discriminatory intent. (See REVERSALS OF RULINGS BY LEGISLATION.) In 1986 the Court applied the amended law to require the redrawing of six multimember legislative districts in North Carolina.

The Court has invoked the equal protection clause to strike down restrictive state voter qualifications in nonracial as well as racial contexts. In 1972 the Court struck down a one-year residency requirement for voting, though it later upheld a fifty-day waiting period. In four cases between 1969 and 1989 the Court said states could not limit voting in bond elections or school district elections to property owners or parents of schoolchildren in the district.

W

Waite, Morrison R.

Morrison Remick Waite (1816–1888) had no judicial experience and a limited record of public service when President Ulysses S. Grant nominated him as chief justice in January 1874. The nomination surprised Waite himself as much as it did the rest of the nation.

Waite was born into a prominent family in Lyme, Connecticut. He graduated from Yale College in 1837 and struck out for northwest Ohio the next year to seek his fortune. He studied law and was admitted to the bar in 1839. He practiced in Maumee City for just over a decade before moving to Toledo in 1850. In Toledo Waite built a strong practice specializing in railroad and business law.

Waite's first run for public office came in 1846 and ended in failure when he was defeated for Congress. He won a seat in the Ohio house in 1849 and served one term. A second run for Congress in 1862 also was unsuccessful. The next year Waite was offered a seat on the Ohio supreme court, but he declined in favor of serving as an informal adviser to the governor. Waite's big break on the national scene came in 1871 when he was appointed a member of the U.S. delegation that sought to settle the Alabama claims case. The United States wanted Great Britain to pay millions of dollars for allowing Confederate vessels to use British ports during the Civil War. Great Britain finally agreed to pay $15.5 million, and Waite's hard work during the negotiations drew national attention.

Waite was unanimously chosen president of the Ohio constitutional convention in 1873. While presiding there, he learned that Grant had appointed him chief justice. Waite actually was Grant's fourth choice for the job. Grant's first nominee turned down the job, and his next two withdrew when it seemed the Senate might reject them.

Under Waite's leadership, the Court had little sympathy for the rights of individuals. In 1875 Waite

Source: Collection of the Supreme Court of the United States

wrote an opinion for the Court stating that the right to vote was not a privilege of U.S. citizenship. Three years later the Court struck down a state law requiring that black and white passengers have equal access to trains. The Court said the law impermissibly interfered with interstate commerce. And in the *Civil Rights Cases* (1883) the Court ruled that Congress had no authority to protect blacks against private discrimination. Waite served as chief justice until his death in 1888.

War Powers

The Constitution divides war powers between Congress and the president. It gives Congress the power to declare war and to raise and maintain an army and navy (Article I, Section 8, Clauses 11–13). The president, as commander in chief, is given the power to conduct war (Article II, Section 2).

The sharing of power has resulted in frequent constitutional disputes between the legislative and executive branches. The Supreme Court has been reluctant to place any limits on the war-making power as exercised by either Congress or the president or to referee disputes between the two branches.

Congress has formally declared war in only five of the nation's conflicts: the War of 1812, the Mexican War, the Spanish-American War, World War I, and World War II. No formal declaration was made in the Naval War with France (1798–1800), the First Barbary War (1801–1805), the various Mexican-American clashes of 1914–1917, the Korean War, or the Vietnam War.

In addition, experts have counted more than 150 instances since 1789 when a president has authorized the use of armed forces abroad without congressional assent. Among the most recent examples are President Ronald Reagan's use of force against Libya, Grenada, and Nicaragua, and President George Bush's invasion of Panama. In 1991 Bush sought and obtained a resolution from Congress authorizing the use of U.S. troops to repel Iraqi forces from Kuwait.

The Supreme Court's first major pronouncement on the legal issues supported a broad view of the president's war-making power. The Court in the *Prize Cases* (1863) ruled, 5–4, that President Abraham Lincoln had acted lawfully in unilaterally declaring a blockade on southern ports at the outset of the Civil War in April 1861 while Congress was not in session.

The Court's next major ruling in this area came at the close of the Civil War. At the start of the war, Lincoln suspended the writ of HABEAS CORPUS, invok-

ing a provision of the Constitution (Article I, Section 9) that authorizes suspension of this form of judicial review "when in Cases of Rebellion or Invasion the public Safety may require it." Lincoln's use of military courts to try civilians accused of supporting the Confederate cause immediately stirred controversy in the North. Congress waited until 1863 to pass legislation authorizing Lincoln to suspend habeas corpus.

The Supreme Court avoided ruling on the issue during the war. But in 1866, the Court unanimously ruled in *Ex parte Milligan* that the president had no power to require civilians to be tried by military courts in an area where regular courts continued to function. By a 5–4 vote the Court ruled further that Congress also had no power to authorize military trials under such circumstances.

Congress and the White House united their efforts during World War I and World War II to exercise vast powers over the economy. The Supreme Court upheld these expansions of the federal government's wartime powers.

During World War I President Woodrow Wilson, acting with congressional approval, commandeered plants and mines; seized and operated the nation's transportation and communications systems; and managed the production and distribution of foods. The closest the Supreme Court came to questioning these actions was a 1921 decision that held unconstitutional a portion of the Lever Food Control Act. Section 4 of the act made it a criminal offense to charge excessive prices for food or fuel; the Court held the provision unconstitutional because it failed to define unjust or unreasonable prices.

President Franklin D. Roosevelt presided over a complex network of production and price controls during World War II, again with congressional approval. In the most important challenge to these measures, the Supreme Court upheld the Emergency Price Control Act of 1942 that created the Office of Price Administration (OPA). In *Yakus v. United States* (1944) the Court ruled that the act contained precise standards and permitted judicial review of administrative actions to enforce OPA regulations.

The Supreme Court also took a broad view of the government's wartime powers in controversial decisions that upheld Roosevelt's decisions to impose a rigid curfew on Japanese-Americans and to relocate more than 100,000 Japanese-Americans from their West Coast homes. (See *INTERNMENT CASES*.)

In *Hirabayashi v. United States* (June 1943) the Court unanimously upheld the curfew order as "within the boundaries of the war power." Eighteen months later the Court divided 6–3 in the case of *Korematsu v. United States* (December 1944), upholding the exclusion of Japanese-Americans from their homes. The Court relied heavily on the reasoning in *Hirabayashi* in concluding that it was not outside the power of Congress and the executive, acting together, to impose this exclusion. In a third decision, *Ex parte Endo* (1944), the Court avoided a direct ruling on the constitutionality of the detention of Japanese-Americans in internment camps, but it did order the release of a Japanese-American girl after her loyalty to the United States had been determined.

The Supreme Court rebuffed a broad assertion of presidential war powers during the Korean War. President Harry S. Truman, acting without congressional sanction, took over the nation's steel mills in order to prevent a strike. In the so-called *Steel Seizure Case* (*YOUNGSTOWN SHEET AND TUBE CO. V. SAWYER* [1952]), the Court voted 6–3 that Truman's action was unconstitutional. But the Court's majority recognized that Congress had power to authorize the taking of private property during wartime. In addition, several individual justices left open the possibility of upholding such actions by the president in some future emergency, such as an imminent invasion or threatened attack.

The Vietnam War, the nation's longest overseas conflict, was the subject of fierce debate between Congress and the White House under presidents Lyndon Johnson and Richard Nixon. Johnson claimed authority for waging the war under the Gulf of Tonkin Resolution, which he asked Congress to pass in 1964 after a reported attack on U.S. destroyers by North Vietnamese patrol boats. Some legislators disagreed with Johnson's broad view of the resolution, but Congress continued to appropriate funds for the conduct of the war even after repealing the measure in 1971 during Nixon's presidency.

Federal courts were asked repeatedly during the late 1960s and early 1970s to hold that U.S. involvement in Southeast Asia was unconstitutional because Congress had never declared war there. The Supreme Court steadily declined to hear cases that raised the issue.

In 1973 Congress passed the War Powers Act over Nixon's veto. The act was an effort by Congress to reassert its control over the decision to commit U.S. armed forces to combat overseas. The act authorizes the president to undertake limited military action in the absence of a declaration of war, but requires that the president consult with Congress in advance if possible. Further, it directs the president to submit a written report of such action to Congress within forty-eight hours. The act also stipulates that Congress may require the president to withdraw U.S. forces by adopting a concurrent resolution, not subject to presidential veto, within sixty days.

Every president from Nixon to Bush has refused to acknowledge the constitutionality of the War Powers Act. The provision for mandating withdrawal of U.S. forces by concurrent resolution was effectively nullified by the Supreme Court's 1983 decision on the LEGISLATIVE VETO. Congress did not move to replace the provision. In addition, the Supreme Court and lower federal courts have declined to enforce the act on the ground that it was up to Congress, rather than the courts, to decide whether a president had violated the law.

Warren, Charles

One of the most influential historians of the Supreme Court, Charles Warren had firsthand experience with the workings of the Court as an attorney who had argued several cases before it. A Boston native born in 1868, Warren was an assistant attorney general during Woodrow Wilson's administration.

In that position Warren was in charge of prosecuting German spies. He also drafted the Espionage Act and the Trading with the Enemy Act, both enacted in 1917, and the Sabotage Act of 1918. A memo he wrote for the State Department on neutrality became the basis for the Neutrality Acts of 1935, 1936, and 1937.

As a legal historian, Warren is best known for *The Supreme Court in U.S. History.* The work was published in 1922 and won the Pulitzer Prize in 1923. Among his other well-known books are *A History of the American Bar; A History of Harvard Law School; Congress, the Constitution, and the Supreme Court;* and *The Making of the Constitution.*

Warren, Earl

In its first major ruling under Chief Justice Earl Warren (1891–1974) in 1954, the Supreme Court unanimously struck down segregation in public schools. That was the beginning of a long string of liberal decisions that the Warren Court made over the next fifteen years.

Warren was born in Los Angeles. After receiving his undergraduate and law degrees from the University of California, he worked for a few years in private law offices in California. In 1919 he began an unbroken record of public service that stretched over half a century. His first public office was as deputy city attorney for Oakland, California. He then held a succession of local and state positions. Warren was deputy assistant district attorney for Alameda County (1920–1923), chief deputy district attorney for Alameda County (1923–1925), district attorney for Alameda County (1925–1939), attorney general of California (1939–1943), and governor of California (1943–1953).

In his early years as governor, Warren expressed conservative views. He denounced "communistic radicals" and backed the order during World War II to put all West Coast residents of Japanese ancestry into detention camps. As the war ended, however, Warren began proposing liberal programs, such as state-provided medical insurance and generous welfare benefits.

Warren twice tried unsuccessfully for national office. In 1948 he ran for vice president on the Republican ticket headed by Thomas E. Dewey. In 1952 he sought the Republican presidential nomination. When it became clear that he had little chance of winning the nomination, Warren threw his support be-

Source: Library of Congress

hind Dwight D. Eisenhower at a critical point and helped Eisenhower secure the nomination. Eisenhower repaid the political debt by appointing Warren chief justice in 1953.

Years later, after the Warren Court had firmly established its liberal record, Eisenhower called his appointment of Warren "the biggest damn-fool mistake I ever made." Under Warren's direction, the Court became the catalyst for the social revolution that swept across the United States in the late 1950s and 1960s.

The Warren Court's most important civil rights decision was *Brown v. Board of Education of Topeka* (1954), in which it ruled that separate schools for blacks and whites were inherently unequal. With *Brown* the Warren Court overruled more than a century of Court decisions upholding segregation and discrimination against blacks. In the years after *Brown* the Court supervised the desegregation of school systems across the country. In later civil rights decisions the Court barred discrimination in public accommodations, voting, and sale of real estate.

The Warren Court also brought about a "due process revolution" that vastly expanded the rights of criminals. Before the Warren Court, the due process guarantees of the Fourteenth Amendment primarily applied to persons arrested by federal law enforcement officers and tried in federal courts. By the time Warren retired in 1969, the Court had granted virtually all these rights to persons arrested and tried in state courts.

The due process revolution began in 1960 with a Court ruling that federal agents could not use evidence illegally seized by state agents. The Court then barred illegally obtained evidence from state trials, declared that criminal defendants in state courts had a right to an attorney even if they couldn't afford one themselves, and ruled that state suspects had a Fifth Amendment right against self-incrimination. The Court also said that state defendants had a right to cross-examine people who testified against them and that police could not question a suspect without first informing him or her of the rights to remain silent and to obtain legal counsel. It also ruled that states had to provide a speedy trial to defendants and to offer a jury trial to all persons charged with serious crimes. Finally, on Warren's last day as chief justice, the Court extended the guarantee against double jeopardy to state trials.

The Warren Court also substantially enlarged the constitutional protections afforded to individuals. It overturned a Connecticut law barring the use of contraceptives even by married couples, struck down a Virginia law prohibiting interracial marriages, and struck down prayer in public schools. It also overturned most state and local loyalty oaths and ruled that students could wear black armbands to school to peacefully protest the Vietnam War.

As part of its effort to guarantee the rights of individuals, the Warren Court took up the issue of legislative apportionment. In earlier years the Court had avoided such cases on the grounds that courts should not involve themselves in legislative issues. By the early 1960s legislative districts were badly unbalanced around the nation. In Tennessee, for example, slightly more than one-third of the state's voters elected two-thirds of the members of the state senate. In a pair of decisions in 1963 and 1964, the Warren Court ruled that the equal protection guarantee required that each person have an equal vote. By the end of the 1960s, this "one person, one vote" rule had resulted in the reapportionment of nearly every legislative and congressional district in the nation.

In the landmark case of *New York Times Co. v. Sullivan* (1964), the Warren Court issued one of the most important press decisions of the century. It ruled that public figures could recover damages for libel only if they could prove that an incorrect statement was published with the knowledge it was false "or with reckless disregard of whether it was false or not."

The Warren Court's liberal rulings angered conservatives and there was talk of trying to impeach the chief justice. The talk, much of it coming from the ultraconservative John Birch Society, never went anywhere. Besides serving as chief justice, Warren chaired the commission bearing his name that investigated the assassination of President John F. Kennedy. Warren retired from the Court on June 23, 1969, with his place firmly secured as one of the greatest chief justices in the nation's history. He died in 1974.

Washington, Bushrod

The nephew of George Washington, Bushrod Washington (1762–1829) served on the Supreme Court for nearly thirty-one years from 1798 until his death. Through all the years, he voted virtually in tandem with Chief Justice John Marshall. One colleague complained that the two "are commonly estimated as a single judge." The two men served on the Court together for twenty-nine years. During that period, Washington voted differently from Marshall in only three cases.

Washington was born in Westmoreland County, Virginia, and graduated from the College of William and Mary at age sixteen. He studied law for two years

Source: Library of Congress

ten, Washington nonetheless was responsible for the chief justice's only dissenting vote on a constitutional case, *Ogden v. Saunders* (1827). Washington's vote upholding state insolvency laws broke a tie and left Marshall in the minority.

One of his colleagues, Justice Joseph Story, said of Washington: "His mind was solid, rather than brilliant; sagacious and searching, rather than quick or eager; slow, but not torpid."

Wayne, James M.

When the Civil War broke out, James Moore Wayne (1790–1867), a Georgian, ignored calls from the South for him to resign from the Supreme Court and return home. For his loyalty to the Union, Wayne was disowned by Georgia and accused by a Confederate court of being an enemy alien.

Wayne was born in Savannah, Georgia, and en-

Source: Collection of the Supreme Court of the United States

after serving briefly as a private in the Continental Army. His law teacher was James Wilson, whom he later succeeded on the Supreme Court.

Washington drew the wrath of abolitionists in 1816 when he was elected first president of the American Colonization Society, which sought to send free blacks back to Africa. The criticism intensified in 1821 when he sold more than fifty of his late uncle's slaves, separating families with the sale. George Washington had left his Mount Vernon estate and his public and private papers to his nephew because he had no children of his own. He had left instructions that his slaves be freed when his wife Martha died. Bushrod ignored the instructions. In response to criticism of his action, Washington said the slaves were his property to do with as he liked.

On the Court, Washington was known as a methodical student of the law. Deferring to Marshall of-

tered the College of New Jersey (now Princeton University) at age fourteen. After graduation, Wayne read law under three different lawyers and established a private practice in 1810. The War of 1812 interrupted Wayne's legal career. During the war he served as an officer in the Chatham Light Dragoons, a volunteer militia unit from Georgia.

In 1815 Wayne was elected to the Georgia legislature, where he served two years. He became mayor of Savannah in 1817 at age twenty-seven and after two years resigned to return to his private legal practice. His respite from public service was brief. In late 1819 he was elected a judge on the Savannah court of common pleas, and he moved up to the Georgia superior court in 1822. Wayne served there until he entered the U.S. House of Representatives in 1829.

While in Congress, Wayne gained a reputation as a strong Unionist Democrat who was closely allied with the administration of President Andrew Jackson. Jackson nominated him to the Supreme Court in 1835. Despite his southern heritage, Wayne did not flinch from his strong support of the Union during the Civil War. Once the war ended, however, Wayne refused to hold circuit court in states under military Reconstruction rule because of his opposition to the punitive Reconstruction policies. He also voted to strike down the loyalty oaths required of former Confederates. He died of typhoid in 1867.

Source: Library of Congress

Webster, Daniel

One of the most powerful and persuasive orators in American history, Daniel Webster (1782–1852) was elected to both the House and the Senate, served as secretary of state in the Harrison and Tyler administrations, and ran a losing campaign for the presidency in 1836. He also argued more cases—and perhaps more important cases—before the Supreme Court than any other attorney in the nation's history. Because he was on one side or the other in so many cases in which the Court handed down decisions defining the scope of national powers for the first time, Webster became known as the "Expounder of the Constitution."

Webster argued his first case before the Supreme Court in 1814. In general he supported nationalism and broad powers for the national government, even if that meant limiting the rights of states in some instances.

Webster was able to advance these positions in several important arguments before the Court. In 1819 he argued on the winning side in two landmark cases. In *Dartmouth College v. Woodward* the Court upheld the federal Constitution's ban on state actions impairing contracts. For generations of loyal Dartmouth alumni, this case was immortalized by Webster's response to an inquiring justice: "It is, sir, as I have said, a small college, and yet there are those who love it."

In *MCCULLOCH V. MARYLAND*, decided the same year, the Court held that the Constitution gave Congress the power to enact all laws that are "necessary and proper" to carry out the responsibilities given the legislative branch by the Constitution. The Court also held that a state could not tax the national bank. It is said that Chief Justice John Marshall's famous statement that the "power to tax involves the power to destroy" was first spoken by Webster during the oral argument.

Five years later Webster was one of the winning attorneys in *GIBBONS V. OGDEN* (1824), the case in which the Court first began to define the reach of the federal power to regulate interstate commerce. Other significant cases followed, among them *Charles River Bridge v. Warren Bridge* (1837), another case involving contracts, which Webster lost.

In his later years, Webster continued to argue cases before the Court. But his eloquence was also heard from his desk in the U.S. Senate, where he served from 1827 to 1841 and from 1843 to 1850, and where he urged the states to remain unified. Perhaps the finest speech of his life was his 1830 reply to South Carolina senator Robert Y. Hayne on the issue of whether a state could nullify an act of Congress. Webster ended his oration with the stirring words, "Liberty *and* Union, now and forever, one and inseparable."

White, Byron R.

In 1946 Byron Raymond White (1917–   ) spent a year as a law clerk to Chief Justice Fred M. Vinson. Sixteen years later, he was appointed to the Supreme Court himself. White also has the distinction of being the only justice who ever played professional football.

White was born in Fort Collins, Colorado, and grew up in Wellington, Colorado. In high school and college White was an outstanding student-athlete who managed to rank first in his class while also excelling in football, basketball, and baseball. White earned the nickname "Whizzer" for his skills as a football player, skills that won him a one-year contract with the former Pittsburgh Pirates professional football team. After a year of playing pro ball White traveled to England to attend Oxford University on a Rhodes scholarship. While in England he met John F. Kennedy, whose father was the U.S. ambassador.

White returned to the United States in 1939 and enrolled at Yale Law School. During football season, he played professionally with the Detroit Lions. White served in the navy in the South Pacific during World War II and then returned to Yale, where he earned his law degree magna cum laude.

Fresh out of law school, White clerked for Chief Justice Vinson. He returned to Colorado in 1947 and for fourteen years practiced law with a prominent Denver firm. When Kennedy ran for president in 1960, White became a major figure in his campaign. Kennedy named White deputy U.S. attorney general and then chose him for the Court in 1962.

Upon joining the Warren Court, White became one of its more conservative members. He dissented from many of the liberal criminal procedure decisions, including the 1966 *Miranda* ruling on police interrogation. He was also one of two dissenters in the Burger Court's abortion rights ruling, *Roe v. Wade* (1973). White also took conservative positions on

Source: Collection of the Supreme Court of the United States

freedom of speech and freedom of press issues. In 1972, he wrote for a 5–4 majority that reporters have no constitutional right to withhold the identities of their confidential sources. On civil rights issues, however, White sided with liberals through most of his career.

White retired at the end of the 1992–1993 term. He announced his decision in March 1993 so that the new president, Bill Clinton, could select a successor in time for the Senate to complete confirmation before the Court's new term began in October.

White, Edward D.

From the very early years of the nineteenth century, there was a tradition of having a "New York" seat on the Supreme Court. When Justice Samuel Blatchford died in 1893, squabbles among New Yorkers ended the tradition. The disputes that ended the tradition, however, worked in favor of a southerner, Edward Douglass White (1845–1921), who succeeded Justice Blatchford on the Court.

President Grover Cleveland, a New Yorker himself, tried to appoint two different New Yorkers to replace Blatchford. However, New York senator David B. Hill, an old political enemy of the president, objected to the nominees. The Senate, which had a tradition of honoring a senator's objections to nominees of his own party from his home state, duly rejected both men. Cleveland then nominated White, the Senate majority leader, and the Senate immediately confirmed him.

White was born in the parish of Lafourche, Louisiana. The Civil War interrupted his studies at Georgetown College (now Georgetown University) in Washington, D.C. White left school in 1861 to return home to Louisiana and enlist in the Confederate Army. He was captured in 1863 at Port Hudson, Louisiana, and spent the rest of the war as a prisoner.

After the war White began reading law. He was admitted to the bar in 1868, established a prosperous practice in New Orleans, and jumped into Democratic politics. In 1874 he was elected to the state senate. Four years later, at age thirty-three, he was appointed

Source: Collection of the Supreme Court of the United States

to the Louisiana supreme court. White served on the court for three years, and in 1891 the legislature elected him to the U.S. Senate.

White served in the Senate for only three years before his surprise appointment to the Supreme Court in 1894. In an equally surprising move nearly seventeen years later, President William Howard Taft in 1910 named White chief justice, making White the first sitting justice to be elevated to chief justice.

Historians have suggested two explanations for Taft's selection of White as chief justice. One is that Taft chose White, a Catholic from the South, to boost his chances with southerners and Catholics in the next election. The other explanation is that the president, who had long sought the chief justiceship for himself, appointed White because of his age (White was sixty-five years old). According to this explanation, Taft hoped White would die or resign relatively soon so that he himself could be appointed chief justice after leaving the presidency. As it turned out, White died in 1921 and President Warren G. Harding did name Taft to replace him.

The Court became more liberal initially when White took over, but it resumed its conservative ways when World War I started. One of White's most important opinions as chief justice came in *Brushaber v. Union Pacific Railroad* (1916). In that case the Court upheld the constitutionality of a new law taxing incomes of more than $3,000 for single persons and more than $4,000 for married couples.

Whittaker, Charles E.

Charles Evans Whittaker (1901–1973) quit school after his mother died on his sixteenth birthday. Four years later he applied for admission to the University of Kansas City Law School. The school agreed to admit him, but only if he would seek private tutoring to complete his high school education. Whittaker raised the money for law school by selling pelts from animals he trapped and by working as an office boy in a law firm. He eventually became senior partner in that firm.

Whittaker was born in 1901 in Troy, Kansas. He grew up on a farm and to attend high school had to ride a pony through six miles of mud each way. A year after passing the Missouri bar exam in 1923, Whittaker received his law degree. He then joined the law firm he had served as an office boy and developed a prosperous practice. He represented many corporate clients, including Union Pacific and Montgomery Ward.

Whittaker was appointed to the U.S. District Court for the Western District of Missouri in 1954 and in 1956 moved up to the Eighth Circuit Court of Appeals. His judicial experience, along with his solid Republican party credentials, won him a Supreme Court

Source: Library of Congress

nomination from President Dwight Eisenhower in 1957.

Whittaker provided a conservative voice on the liberal Court headed by Chief Justice Earl Warren. After Whittaker had served only five years, his doctor recommended that he resign because overwork was exhausting him and compromising his health. Whittaker followed the advice and resigned in March 1962. He died in 1973.

Wilson, James

James Wilson (1742–1798) was one of the greatest legal minds in colonial America and an original nominee of President George Washington to the Court. Yet he was jailed in his later years when various investment schemes went sour.

Wilson was born September 14, 1742, in Caskardy, Scotland, into a farming family. The family was poor, but his devout Calvinist parents set aside money so he could be educated for the ministry.

Wilson studied in local grammar schools, and at fourteen won a scholarship to St. Andrews University. He entered the university's divinity school during his fifth year. However, his father's death forced Wilson to leave school and help support his family. He worked as a private tutor, but eventually sailed for America, where he tutored at the College of Philadelphia and began reading law in the office of John Dickinson, a prominent attorney. In 1768 he opened a private legal practice in Reading, Pennsylvania. Wilson moved to Carlisle in 1770, and his practice, specializing in land law, quickly grew to cover seven counties.

In 1775 Wilson was elected a delegate to the Continental Congress. He joined with other members of the Pennsylvania delegation in opposing separation from England. Eventually, however, he followed instructions from Pennsylvania's assembly and signed the Declaration of Independence.

Wilson gained a reputation as a conservative aristocrat with his opposition to the Pennsylvania constitution of 1776. Criticism by populists grew as his legal practice, now based in Philadelphia, was devoted increasingly to defending wealthy Tories and other businessmen. Wilson also spent considerable energy developing various business interests, notably land speculation schemes. In 1779 an armed mob angered by high inflation and food shortages attacked Wilson's home, and he had to erect barricades to keep them out. He was eventually forced into hiding.

Wilson served as a delegate to the Constitutional Convention in 1787 and was a member of the committee charged with writing the first draft of the Constitution. Although his populist opponents distrusted him, Wilson strongly believed that government should be created by the people and be subject to their will. Wilson was responsible for incorporating this idea of popular sovereignty into the Constitution.

Despite his earlier defense of Tories, Wilson fervently believed in democracy. He supported popular election of the president and members of Congress. He also fought to create a powerful national judiciary, and helped develop the principle of judicial review.

Wilson sought appointment by Washington as chief justice of the new Supreme Court. Washington chose John Jay instead and appointed Wilson an associate justice in 1789. His most famous opinion was in *Chisholm v. Georgia* (1793), when he argued that citizens of one state could sue another state. The Court's decision was later overturned by the Eleventh Amendment to the Constitution. Wilson was an accomplished legal scholar, and his views were cited as recently as 1964 by the Court in supporting the principle of "one person, one vote."

By about 1796 Wilson's investment empire had begun to crumble. Angry creditors chased him while he rode circuit, and they succeeded in having him jailed at least twice. He died in 1798 at a dreary inn next to the courthouse in Edenton, North Carolina.

Source: The Historical Society of Pennsylvania

Woodbury, Levi

Levi Woodbury (1789–1851) was the first Supreme Court justice to have attended law school. He primarily studied with practicing lawyers, as was common at that time, but he also briefly attended Tapping Reeve Law School in Litchfield, Connecticut.

Woodbury was born in Francestown, New Hampshire. After graduating with honors from Dartmouth College in 1809, he began studying law. He practiced in Francestown and Portsmouth after being admitted to the bar in 1812.

Politics soon caught the eye of the young attorney. In 1816 Woodbury became clerk of the state senate. His next step up the political ladder came the following year, when he was appointed to the New Hampshire superior court. After serving on the court for six years, he waged an insurgent campaign for New Hampshire governor and defeated an entrenched in-

Source: Library of Congress

cumbent. A reelection campaign failed, but in 1825 Woodbury won election to the New Hampshire house and was selected Speaker. Later that year the legislature elected him to the U.S. Senate.

President Andrew Jackson appointed Woodbury secretary of the navy in 1831 and made him secretary of the treasury in 1834. Woodbury's service as treasury secretary came amid the crisis over the Bank of the United States, during which he gained a reputation for following Jackson's orders. Woodbury continued as treasury secretary under President Martin Van Buren until 1841. In that year he was elected to the Senate once again. President James Polk nominated Woodbury to the Supreme Court in December 1845, and the Senate confirmed him in January 1846. Two years later Woodbury sought the Democratic nomination for president, but lost to Lewis Cass. He died in 1851 after having served less than six years on the Court.

Woods, William B.

As part of President Rutherford B. Hayes's effort to bring southerners back into the federal government after the Civil War, he nominated William Burnham Woods (1824–1887) of Georgia to the Supreme Court in 1880. Woods became the first justice from the South since Justice John Campbell was nominated in 1852.

Woods actually was a transplanted Yankee, having been born in Newark, Ohio. He attended Western Reserve College and graduated from Yale University in 1845, after which he studied law. Woods then formed a partnership with his law teacher in Newark that lasted until the Civil War. While building his law practice, Woods also sought public office. He was elected mayor of Newark in 1856 and ran a successful campaign for the state legislature the following year.

Woods, an ardent Democrat, initially opposed President Abraham Lincoln's war policy. He eventually became convinced, however, that the war was necessary. He joined the Union Army in 1862. Woods left the service a major general in February 1866 after having fought at Shiloh and Vicksburg and marched

Source: Collection of the Supreme Court of the United States

with Sherman through Georgia. Following the war Woods moved to Georgia to resume his law practice and become a cotton planter. Woods, by now a Republican, was elected chancellor of the middle chancery division of Alabama in 1868. The next year he was appointed U.S. circuit judge for the fifth circuit, a post he held until his nomination to the Supreme Court in 1880. As a judge, Woods gained the respect of his southern colleagues despite his service in the Union Army.

Woods served only six and a half years on the Supreme Court before his death in May 1887. Most of the opinions he wrote dealt with relatively routine legal matters rather than major constitutional issues. President Grover Cleveland continued the new tradition of having a southern seat on the Court by choosing Lucius Lamar of Mississippi as Woods's successor.

Workload of the Court

Throughout its history the Supreme Court has had to cope with a heavy and sometimes burdensome workload. In its early decades the Court heard few cases because appeals moved slowly through the new federal judiciary. The first case did not reach the court until 1791. The first formal opinion was not handed down until 1792, in the Court's third year of existence.

Despite the lack of casework, the justices had enough to do. The Judiciary Act of 1789 required them to travel around the country to preside over circuit courts. This practice, called CIRCUIT RIDING, was an exhausting and time-consuming task that was not finally abolished until 1891.

By that time the number of cases the Supreme Court was asked to review each year had increased markedly. Except for a few brief periods, the number has continued to grow ever since. As a result the Court declines to review many more cases than it accepts. This discrepancy between the number of cases that the Court is asked to review and the number that it actually reviews has given rise to concerns that the Court may be neglecting many important cases.

The Growing Workload

A glance at the number of cases on the Court's docket over the years illustrates the growing burden. In 1803, thirteen years after the Court first convened, there were only fifty-one cases on the docket. Seven years later, the number was ninety-eight.

The increasing population and expanding territory of the United States contributed to an ever increasing number of cases being filed not only with the Supreme Court but also with the circuit courts over which the justices presided. Congress in 1837 created two additional circuits and added two justices to the seven then on the Supreme Court.

The number of cases kept going up. There were 173 cases on the docket in 1845, 253 in 1850, 310 in 1860, and 636 in 1870. The creation of several more circuit judgeships in 1869 did little to stem the tide of cases flowing to the Court. In 1880 there were 1,212. By 1890 the number had jumped to 1,816.

Judiciary Acts of 1891 and 1925

The Court's workload was lightened, at least for a while, with passage of the Judiciary Act of 1891. Congress eliminated the justices' circuit-riding duties and set up a system of federal appeals courts between the old district and circuit courts, on one hand, and the Supreme Court on the other. (The old circuit courts were abolished in 1911.)

The decisions of these new courts were final in many cases. When a decision was appealed from one of these new courts, the Supreme Court had complete discretion in deciding whether to review it. The result was dramatic: the number of new cases on the Court's docket dropped to 379 in 1891 and to 275 in 1892.

In the years that followed, however, Congress passed many new laws creating opportunities for litigation, and the caseload again began to grow, to 723 cases in the 1900 term and 1,116 in the 1910 term.

The Judiciary Act of 1925 gave the Court considerably more room to decide which cases it would review, but the number of cases on the docket did not decline. There were 1,039 cases in 1930, 1,109 in 1940, 1,321 in 1950, 2,296 in 1960, 4,212 in 1970, 4,781 in 1980, and 5,502 in 1990. In the 1991–1992 term, there were 5,866 new cases on the Court DOCKET.

The dramatic rise in the Court's caseload, particularly after 1960, resulted from an increase in the number of criminal cases and from congressional enactment of legislation concerning civil rights, environmental, consumer, safety, and social welfare issues.

The number of cases on the Court docket filed by people too poor to pay the filing and docketing fees grew from about 500 in 1950 to nearly 3,800 in the 1991–1992 term. Many of these cases are filed by prisoners claiming that their due process rights under the Constitution have been denied. The great majority of the IN FORMA PAUPERIS cases are denied review, dismissed, or withdrawn. In the 1991–1992 term, the Court granted full review to only seventeen such cases.

While the number of cases on the Court's docket continues to go up, the number of cases that the Court actually schedules for full review has grown hardly at all. As Chief Justice William H. Rehnquist pointed out in 1986, the Court was hearing about 150 cases on the merits in 1935, and it was hearing about the same number in 1986. Recently the number of cases scheduled for argument actually declined, dropping from 146 in 1989 to 127 in 1991.

As the chief justice also noted, the difference between 1935 and 1986 was in the percentage of cases docketed that the Court actually reviews. In 1935 the Court was able to review roughly 20 percent of the cases on the docket. In the 1992–1993 term it gave full review to only about 3 percent of the 7,245 cases filed with the Court.

Studying the Problem

Two blue-ribbon panels examined the workload problem in the 1970s. One was the Study Group on the Caseload of the Supreme Court, set up by Chief Justice Warren E. Burger in the fall of 1971 and headed by Professor Paul A. Freund of Harvard Law School. The second was the Commission on Revision of the Appellate Court System, set up by Congress in 1972 and headed by Sen. Roman L. Hruska, R-Neb.

The Court's study group issued its report in December 1972. To ease the pressure of an overcrowded docket, the panel recommended the creation of a national court of appeals. The new court would be headquartered in Washington and would be able to consider all cases now within the Supreme Court's jurisdiction, except for cases involving its ORIGINAL JURISDICTION. The national court of appeals would screen all cases coming to the Supreme Court, denying review in some, deciding some itself, and sending the more important cases to the Supreme Court.

The Hruska commission in its 1975 report also endorsed the creation of a new national court of appeals. However, the new court was to decide cases of lesser importance referred to it by the Supreme Court instead of screening cases for the justices to decide.

In 1982 Chief Justice Burger proposed a third alternative, the creation of a special but temporary panel of the U.S. Court of Appeals for the Federal Circuit to hear and resolve cases in which two of the other federal circuit courts of appeals had disagreed. Like the earlier proposals, this idea represented a significant shift of responsibility from the Supreme Court to a lower court. Congress did not act on any of the proposals.

Beginning in the mid-1980s, the Court appeared to reduce its caseload on its own. The number of cases brought to the Court continued to increase but the justices granted review to fewer cases. In the 1970s the Court had averaged about 130 signed opinions per term. By the 1991–1992 term the number had fallen to 107, the lowest number since 1969.

Writing Opinions

The Supreme Court's written OPINIONS contain the Court's decision and also the Court's view of the legal issues that underlie the decision. They are the written record of the Court's work that guides future decisions in the lower courts as well as in the Supreme Court itself. The written opinions often affect national policy on major social and economic issues. They are read with close attention by judges, attorneys, lobbyists, news reporters, and policy makers.

The impact of a particular decision depends in part on who writes the opinion and how it is written. Once the justices vote on a case in conference, one of them is assigned to write the majority opinion. If the chief justice has voted with the majority, the chief justice makes the assignment. Otherwise the senior associate in the majority makes the assignment. (See ASSIGNING OPINIONS; CONFERENCES.)

Any justice, however, may decide to write a separate opinion. Justices who agree with the outcome of a case but not with the majority's reasoning may write CONCURRING OPINIONS. Justices who disagree with the outcome may write DISSENTING OPINIONS. Justices may concur with or dissent from all or only a part of the majority opinion.

Whether it is a majority, concurring, or dissenting opinion that is being written, the style depends primarily on the individual justice. In some cases the justice may prefer to write a restricted and limited opinion; in others he or she may take a broader approach to the subject. The decision of whether to write a narrow or broad opinion is likely to be influenced by the need to satisfy the other justices who voted with him or her in the majority while simultaneously trying to attract the support of justices who voted in the minority.

The time spent to prepare an opinion varies from justice to justice. Justice Oliver Wendell Holmes, Jr., was reportedly able to write an opinion over a weekend. Justices Hugo L. Black and Louis D. Brandeis were noted for reading widely on all aspects of a case before writing their opinions. Justice Felix Frankfurter was a perfectionist who often prepared as many as thirty or more drafts for each opinion.

Justices use their law CLERKS to obtain and sift through the material needed to write an opinion. Some justices—among them Chief Justice William H. Rehnquist—have their law clerks write the first draft of opinions. Other justices apparently reserve the writing for themselves. Justice William O. Douglas, for example, was said to give his clerks little or nothing to do in writing or organizing his written opinions.

When a justice is satisfied with a draft, it is circulated to the other justices. The justice who writes the majority opinion seeks to retain the support of the majority for the decision and also to obtain majority support for the legal reasoning supporting the decision. Often the author of an opinion must juggle opposing views and make major emendations to oblige justices who are unhappy with the initial draft. Some opinions have to be rewritten repeatedly before the majority is satisfied.

One illustration of the difficulty of writing a majority opinion is provided by Chief Justice Warren E. Burger's problems in the case of President Richard Nixon's White House tapes. In mid-1974 the Court voted unanimously that the president had to turn over the tapes, which were sought as evidence in the Watergate cover-up case. The Court rejected the president's argument that he could invoke executive privilege to withhold them.

Burger assigned the writing of the opinion to himself and, to save time, circulated the draft opinion piece by piece. The other justices were dissatisfied with what they were seeing. Many began writing their own version of the opinion. Burger was annoyed but was forced to compromise to maintain unanimity, which was considered extremely important to the effectiveness of the Court's ruling. As a result other justices wrote various parts of the final opinion, which was issued in Burger's name.

One reason for the secrecy surrounding the circulation of drafts is that some of the justices who voted with the majority may find the majority draft opinion so unpersuasive, or one of the concurring or dissenting draft opinions so convincing, that they change their vote. If enough justices alter their votes, the majority may shift, so that a dissenting position or the reasoning in a concurring opinion becomes the majority position. When a new majority emerges from this process, the task of writing and circulating a new draft begins all over again.

Before 1980 draft opinions were printed under rigid security in a print shop in the basement of the Court. Each copy was numbered to prevent extra copies from being removed from the premises. But after some experimenting in the late 1970s, the Court in 1980 began to use word processors to prepare draft opinions. Some of the justices—Byron R. White and John Paul Stevens among them—were using the machines themselves. Today the Court has replaced the old hot-lead typesetting machines with a computerized word-processing system.

X

XYZ Affair

The XYZ Affair was an incident provoked by tense relations between the United States and France in the late eighteenth century. The affair had its origins in the Jay Treaty of 1794. Negotiated by the chief justice of the United States, John Jay, and British foreign minister Lord Grenville, the Jay Treaty attempted to settle U.S. grievances with the British and establish a commercial treaty between the two nations. President George Washington's appointment of Jay to this political mission was criticized as inappropriate by some Americans who believed the chief justiceship should be nonpartisan and uninvolved with such matters. The mission created tension on the other side of the Atlantic as well because Britain at that time was at war with France, and because the French had established their own trade agreement with the United States in 1778.

The French reacted to the Jay treaty by harassing

The "Paris monster" here cries, "I must have money," while diplomat Charles Pinckney, on the left, retorts, "We will not give you six pence."
The French government refused to officially receive the American diplomats without a substantial payment.   Source: The Huntington Library

American ships. By the time John Adams became president in 1797, heightened tensions had created the possibility of war. In an attempt to improve the situation and restore friendly relations, Adams sent a three-person commission to meet with the French Directory. The team was Charles Cotesworth Pinckney, John Marshall (who later served as chief justice from 1801 to 1835), and Elbridge Gerry.

The diplomats were unofficially received by the French foreign minister, Charles Maurice de Talleyrand-Périgord, when they first arrived in Paris in October 1797. Then they waited for weeks with no word of a meeting with the Directory.

During this period French agents approached the emissaries. In return for obtaining negotiations, the agents demanded a payment of $250,000 to Talleyrand and a loan of several million dollars to France. The Americans refused to pay this blackmail. The United States, still hoping to avoid war, offered to extend to France the same privileges the British possessed under the Jay Treaty. Talleyrand, however, remained unsatisfied and stated that he would confer with none of the diplomats except Gerry.

On March 19, 1798, Adams presented his report on the ongoing affair to Congress. Two weeks later he explained it to the public, using the letters *X, Y,* and *Z* to represent the names of the French agents. Outraged at the French blackmail and at Talleyrand's abrupt dismissal of Pinckney and Marshall, Americans called for war. That summer Congress dissolved the 1778 treaty and halted commercial dealings with France.

Despite such warlike preparations, Adams continued to seek a peaceful end to the dispute. He made a new appointment of William Vans Murray as minister to France and sent another commission overseas. In spite of earlier protests over Chief Justice Jay's negotiations with the British, Adams named the new chief justice, Oliver Ellsworth, to the commission, along with Murray and William R. Davie. They successfully negotiated the Treaty of Mortefontaine, or the Convention of 1800, which reestablished friendly relations between France and the United States.

Y

Youngstown Sheet and Tube Co. v. Sawyer

President Harry S. Truman attempted to take over the nation's steel mills to avert a strike during the Korean War. His attempt led to a landmark Supreme Court decision in 1952 rejecting broad assertions of presidential power to take emergency action without express authority from Congress. (See WAR POWERS.)

The Court's 6–3 decision in *Youngstown Sheet and Tube Co. v. Sawyer* was a political setback for Truman as he presided over an unpopular, undeclared war on the Asian mainland. The ruling also held back, but did not stop, the growth of a constitutional doctrine concerning war powers: that the president possesses inherent power under Article II to take whatever steps are necessary to protect the nation during time of war or national emergency.

Truman feared that a steel strike would disrupt production and lead to ammunition shortages that would jeopardize the U.S. war effort in Korea. Bargaining sessions encouraged by the Wage Stabilization Board ended in failure when the plant operators rejected a wage settlement formula proposed by the board. The United Steel Workers of America announced an industrywide strike to begin April 9, 1952.

On April 8, Truman issued an executive order to Commerce Secretary William Sawyer, directing him to seize and operate the nation's steel mills. The order cited the state of national emergency proclaimed December 16, 1950, after the Chinese invasion of Korea. Truman explained his action as an exercise of general executive authority granted by Article II and his specific power as commander in chief.

The steel companies attacked the order as unconstitutional and obtained an injunction in the District of Columbia restraining Sawyer from carrying out the order. The Supreme Court set an expedited schedule for the case after the court of appeals stayed the district court injunction. The case was argued May 12 and 13 before a court that included four justices appointed by Truman, among them Chief Justice Fred M. Vinson.

Three weeks later, on June 2, the Court held that Truman's action was an unconstitutional exercise of power. In an opinion by Justice Hugo L. Black, the Court said that the president had no statutory authority for the seizure and that neither the power of commander in chief nor any inherent executive prerogative provided authority for it. "This is a job for the Nation's lawmakers, not for its military authorities," Black wrote.

The Court's opinion rejected Truman's assertion of power in part because Congress, just five years earlier, had refused to give the president the power to seize strike-bound industrial plants. The 1947 Taft-Hartley Act did authorize the president to keep plants operating during a sixty-day "cooling-off period" while labor and management kept bargaining, but Truman chose to bypass that procedure in the case of the steel mills.

The five other members of the Court's majority wrote concurring opinions, which showed a more tentative rejection of presidential powers than the outcome of the case suggested. Only justices Black and William O. Douglas said the president needed specific constitutional or statutory authority to sustain the seizure of private property. Four concurring justices did not rule out such emergency presidential actions in the future.

Justice Robert H. Jackson's concurring opinion has been particularly influential. He said the president enjoys greatest power when acting on the basis of express or implied congressional authorization, while presidential power is at its lowest when the president acts in a way incompatible with congressional policy. In between, Jackson said, is "a zone of twilight" in which president and Congress share authority. In that area, he said, congressional acquiescence or inaction might permit independent presidential action.

In dissent, Chief Justice Vinson criticized the majority for adopting a "messenger-boy concept" of the presidency. "Presidents have been in the past, and any man worthy of the Office should be in the future, free to take at least interim action necessary to execute legislative programs essential to survival of the Nation," Vinson wrote.

Z

Zoning

Zoning laws are now on the books in virtually every municipality. Such laws first appeared in the early twentieth century, as local governments sought to control urbanization and the encroachment of factories in residential areas. The Supreme Court upheld such ordinances against claims that they unconstitutionally interfered with private PROPERTY RIGHTS.

The landmark decision on the subject involved an ordinance enacted by the city of Euclid, Ohio, a suburb of Cleveland. The measure banned two-family dwellings and apartment houses, as well as commercial properties and public buildings, from an area of single-family dwellings.

In *Euclid v. Ambler Realty Co.* (1926) the Court voted 6–3 to uphold the ordinance. In his opinion for the Court, Justice George Sutherland found the measure to be a justifiable use of the POLICE POWER to prevent a local nuisance. "A nuisance may be merely a right thing in the wrong place—like a pig in the parlor instead of the barnyard," he wrote. As long as the classification for zoning purposes was "fairly debatable," he said, "the legislative judgment must be allowed to control."

With this approach the Court consistently rebuffed challenges to zoning ordinances. In 1954 the Court upheld the use of the federal police power in a slum-clearance project intended to result in a more attractive community. Twenty years later the Court upheld a zoning ordinance adopted by the village of Belle Terre, New York, that barred occupancy of houses by two or more unrelated persons. Justice William O. Douglas, who wrote for the Court in both cases, eloquently endorsed the Belle Terre ordinance as an effort to "lay out zones where family values, youth values, and the blessings of quiet seclusion and clean air make the area a sanctuary for people."

In 1977, however, the Court struck down, 5–4, a village ordinance that denied a grandmother the right to live in the same household with her sons and grandsons. Writing for the majority, Justice Lewis F. Powell, Jr., said the challenged ordinance "slice[d] deeply into the family itself" and was not entitled to the ordinary deference accorded zoning laws.

The Court's generally permissive attitude toward zoning laws has encouraged cities to use them in a variety of ways. In 1976 the Court upheld a Detroit ordinance requiring that adult movie theaters and bookstores be dispersed about the city. In 1978 it upheld New York City's historic preservation law, rejecting a claim that the city's refusal to allow construction of a tall office building on top of Grand Central Terminal amounted to an unconstitutional "taking" of the property without compensation.

When a more conservative Court returned to the issue in the late 1980s, it raised warning signs about the reach of land use restrictions. In a pair of California cases decided in 1987, the Court made clear that property owners might have a claim against regulating bodies for compensation if the regulation so curtailed their use of the land as to effectively take its value away from them. In 1992 the Court slightly strengthened protections for property owners with a ruling in a challenge to a South Carolina law controlling construction along the state's beachfronts. In *Lucas v. South Carolina Coastal Council* the Court held that a land use regulation denying an owner any economically beneficial or productive use of property amounted to a taking unless it could be justified by COMMON LAW principles relating to property and nuisance.

Reference Material

Appendixes

Supreme Court Nominations, 1789–1994

Name	State	Date of Birth	To Replace	Date of Appointment	Confirmation or Other Action *	Date Resigned	Date of Death	Years of Service
WASHINGTON								
John Jay	N.Y.	12/12/1745		9/24/1789	9/26/1789	6/29/1795	5/17/1829	6
John Rutledge	S.C.	9/1739		9/24/1789	9/26/1789	3/5/1791	7/18/1800	1
William Cushing	Mass.	3/1/1732		9/24/1789	9/26/1789		9/13/1810	21
Robert H. Harrison	Md.	1745		9/24/1789	9/26/1789 (D)		4/20/1790	
James Wilson	Pa.	9/14/1742		9/24/1789	9/26/1789		8/21/1798	9
John Blair	Va.	1732		9/24/1789	9/26/1789	1/27/1796	8/31/1800	6
James Iredell	N.C.	10/5/1751	Harrison	2/8/1790	2/10/1790		10/20/1799	9
Thomas Johnson	Md.	11/4/1732	Rutledge	11/1/1791	11/7/1791	3/4/1793	10/26/1819	1
William Paterson	N.J.	12/24/1745	Johnson	2/27/1793	2/28/1793 (W)			
William Paterson†			Johnson	3/4/1793	3/4/1793		9/9/1806	13
John Rutledge ‡			Jay	7/1/1795	12/15/1795 (R, 10-14)			
William Cushing ‡			Jay	1/26/1796	1/27/1796 (D)			
Samuel Chase	Md.	4/17/1741	Blair	1/26/1796	1/27/1796		6/19/1811	15
Oliver Ellsworth	Conn.	4/29/1745	Jay	3/3/1796	3/4/1796 (21-1)	12/15/1800	11/26/1807	4
ADAMS								
Bushrod Washington	Va.	6/5/1762	Wilson	12/19/1798	12/20/1798		11/26/1829	31
Alfred Moore	N.C.	5/21/1755	Iredell	12/6/1799	12/10/1799	1/26/1804	10/15/1810	4
John Jay ‡			Ellsworth	12/18/1800	12/19/1800 (D)			
John Marshall	Va.	9/24/1755	Ellsworth	1/20/1801	1/27/1801		7/6/1835	34
JEFFERSON								
William Johnson	S.C.	12/27/1771	Moore	3/22/1804	3/24/1804		8/4/1834	30
H. Brockholst Livingston	N.Y.	11/25/1757	Paterson	12/13/1806	2/17/1806		3/18/1823	16
Thomas Todd	Ky.	1/23/1765	New seat	2/28/1807	3/3/1807		2/7/1826	19
MADISON								
Levi Lincoln	Mass.	5/15/1749	Cushing	1/2/1811	1/3/1811 (D)		4/14/1820	
Alexander Wolcott	Conn.	9/15/1758	Cushing	2/4/1811	2/13/1811 (R, 9-24)		6/26/1828	
John Quincy Adams	Mass.	7/11/1767	Cushing	2/21/1811	2/22/1811 (D)		2/23/1848	
Joseph Story	Mass.	9/18/1779	Cushing	11/15/1811	11/18/1811		9/10/1845	34
Gabriel Duvall	Md.	12/6/1752	Chase	11/15/1811	11/18/1811	1/14/1835	3/6/1844	23
MONROE								
Smith Thompson	N.Y.	1/17/1768	Livingston	12/8/1823	12/19/1823		12/18/1843	20
J. Q. ADAMS								
Robert Trimble	Ky.	11/17/1776	Todd	4/11/1826	5/9/1826 (27-5)		8/25/1828	2
John J. Crittenden	Ky.	9/10/1787	Trimble	12/17/1828	2/12/1829 (P)		7/26/1863	

Name	State	Date of Birth	To Replace	Date of Appointment	Confirmation or Other Action *	Date Resigned	Date of Death	Years of Service
JACKSON								
John McLean	Ohio	3/11/1785	Trimble	3/6/1829	3/7/1829		4/4/1861	32
Henry Baldwin	Pa.	1/14/1780	Washington	1/4/1830	1/6/1830 (41-2)		4/21/1844	14
James M. Wayne	Ga.	1790	Johnson	1/7/1835	1/9/1835		7/5/1867	32
Roger B. Taney	Md.	3/17/1777	Duvall	1/15/1835	3/3/1835 (P)			
Roger B. Taney †			Marshall	12/28/1835	3/15/1836 (29-15)		10/12/1864	28
Philip P. Barbour	Va.	5/25/1783	Duvall	12/28/1835	3/15/1836 (30-11)		2/25/1841	5
William Smith	Ala.	1762	New seat	3/3/1837	3/8/1837 (23-18) (D)		6/10/1840	
John Catron	Tenn.	1786	New seat	3/3/1837	3/8/1837 (28-15)		5/30/1865	28
VAN BUREN								
John McKinley	Ala.	5/1/1780	New seat	9/18/1837	9/25/1837		7/19/1852	15
Peter V. Daniel	Va.	4/24/1784	Barbour	2/26/1841	3/2/1841 (22-5)		5/31/1860	19
TYLER								
John C. Spencer	N.Y.	1/8/1788	Thompson	1/9/1844	1/31/1844 (R, 21-26)		5/18/1855	
Reuben H. Walworth	N.Y.	10/26/1788	Thompson	3/13/1844	6/17/1844 (W)		11/27/1867	
Edward King	Pa.	1/31/1794	Baldwin	6/5/1844	6/15/1844 (P)			
Edward King †			Baldwin	12/4/1844	2/7/1845 (W)		5/8/1873	
Samuel Nelson	N.Y.	11/10/1792	Thompson	2/4/1845	2/14/1845	11/28/1872	12/13/1873	27
John M. Read	Pa.	2/21/1797	Baldwin	2/7/1845	No action		11/29/1874	
POLK								
George W. Woodward	Pa.	3/26/1809	Baldwin	12/23/1845	1/22/1846 (R, 20-29)		5/10/1875	
Levi Woodbury	N.H.	12/22/1789	Story	12/23/1845	1/3/1846		9/4/1851	5
Robert C. Grier	Pa.	3/5/1794	Baldwin	8/3/1846	8/4/1846	1/31/1870	9/25/1870	23
FILLMORE								
Benjamin R. Curtis	Mass.	11/4/1809	Woodbury	12/11/1851	12/29/1851	9/30/1857	9/15/1874	5
Edward A. Bradford	La.	9/27/1813	McKinley	8/16/1852	No action		11/22/1872	
George E. Badger	N.C.	4/13/1795	McKinley	1/10/1853	2/11/1853 (P)		5/11/1866	
William C. Micou	La.	1806	McKinley	2/24/1853	No action		4/16/1854	
PIERCE								
John A. Campbell	Ala.	6/24/1811	McKinley	3/22/1853	3/25/1853	4/30/1861	3/12/1889	8
BUCHANAN								
Nathan Clifford	Maine	8/18/1803	Curtis	12/9/1857	1/12/1858 (26-23)		7/25/1881	23
Jeremiah S. Black	Pa.	1/10/1810	Daniel	2/5/1861	2/21/1861 (R, 25-26)		8/19/1883	
LINCOLN								
Noah H. Swayne	Ohio	12/7/1804	McLean	1/21/1862	1/24/1862 (38-1)	1/24/1881	6/8/1884	19
Samuel F. Miller	Iowa	4/5/1816	Daniel	7/16/1862	7/16/1862		10/13/1890	28
David Davis	Ill.	3/9/1815	Campbell	12/1/1862	12/8/1862	3/4/1877	6/26/1886	14
Stephen J. Field	Calif.	11/4/1816	New seat	3/6/1863	3/10/1863	12/1/1897	4/9/1899	34
Salmon P. Chase	Ohio	1/13/1808	Taney	12/6/1864	12/6/1864		5/7/1873	8
JOHNSON								
Henry Stanbery	Ohio	2/20/1803	Catron	4/16/1866	No action		6/26/1881	

Name	State	Date of Birth	To Replace	Date of Appointment	Confirmation or Other Action *	Date Resigned	Date of Death	Years of Service
GRANT								
Ebenezer R. Hoar	Mass.	2/21/1816	New seat	12/15/1869	2/3/1870 (R, 24-33)		1/31/1895	
Edwin M. Stanton	Pa.	12/19/1814	Grier	12/20/1869	12/20/1869 (46-11)		12/24/1869	
William Strong	Pa.	5/6/1808	Grier	2/7/1870	2/18/1870	12/14/1880	8/19/1895	10
Joseph P. Bradley	N.J.	3/14/1813	New seat	2/7/1870	3/21/1870 (46-9)		1/22/1892	21
Ward Hunt	N.Y.	6/14/1810	Nelson	12/3/1872	12/11/1872	1/27/1882	3/24/1886	9
George H. Williams	Ore.	3/23/1823	Chase	12/1/1873	1/8/1874 (W)		4/4/1910	
Caleb Cushing	Mass.	1/17/1800	Chase	1/9/1874	1/13/1874 (W)		1/2/1879	
Morrison R. Waite	Ohio	11/29/1816	Chase	1/19/1874	1/21/1874 (63-0)		3/23/1888	14
HAYES								
John M. Harlan	Ky.	6/1/1833	Davis	10/17/1877	11/29/1877		10/14/1911	34
William B. Woods	Ga.	8/3/1824	Strong	12/15/1880	12/21/1880 (39-8)		5/14/1887	6
Stanley Matthews	Ohio	7/21/1824	Swayne	1/26/1881	No action			
GARFIELD								
Stanley Matthews †			Swayne	3/14/1881	5/12/1881 (24-23)		3/22/1889	7
ARTHUR								
Horace Gray	Mass.	3/24/1828	Clifford	12/19/1881	12/20/1881 (51-5)		9/15/1902	20
Roscoe Conkling	N.Y.	10/30/1829	Hunt	2/24/1882	3/2/1882 (39-12) (D)		4/18/1888	
Samuel Blatchford	N.Y.	3/9/1820	Hunt	3/13/1882	3/27/1882		7/7/1893	11
CLEVELAND								
Lucius Q. C. Lamar	Miss.	9/17/1825	Woods	12/6/1887	1/16/1888 (32-28)		1/23/1893	5
Melville W. Fuller	Ill.	2/11/1833	Waite	4/30/1888	7/20/1888 (41-20)		7/4/1910	22
HARRISON								
David J. Brewer	Kan.	6/20/1837	Matthews	12/4/1889	12/18/1889 (53-11)		3/28/1910	20
Henry B. Brown	Mich.	3/2/1836	Miller	12/23/1890	12/29/1890	5/28/1906	9/4/1913	15
George Shiras, Jr.	Pa.	1/26/1832	Bradley	7/19/1892	7/26/1892	2/23/1903	8/2/1924	10
Howell E. Jackson	Tenn.	4/8/1832	Lamar	2/2/1893	2/18/1893		8/8/1895	2
CLEVELAND								
William B. Hornblower	N.Y.	5/13/1851	Blatchford	9/19/1893	1/15/1894 (R, 24-30)		6/16/1914	
Wheeler H. Peckham	N.Y.	1/1/1833	Blatchford	1/22/1894	2/16/1894 (R, 32-41)		9/27/1905	
Edward D. White	La.	11/3/1845	Blatchford	2/19/1894	2/19/1894		5/19/1921	17
Rufus W. Peckham	N.Y.	11/8/1838	Jackson	12/3/1895	12/9/1895		10/24/1909	13
MCKINLEY								
Joseph McKenna	Calif.	8/10/1843	Field	12/16/1897	1/21/1898	1/5/1925	11/21/1926	26
ROOSEVELT								
Oliver W. Holmes	Mass.	3/8/1841	Gray	12/2/1902	12/4/1902	1/12/1932	3/6/1935	29
William R. Day	Ohio	4/17/1849	Shiras	2/19/1903	2/23/1903	11/13/1922	7/9/1923	19
William H. Moody	Mass.	12/23/1853	Brown	12/3/1906	12/12/1906	11/20/1910	7/2/1917	3

Name	State	Date of Birth	To Replace	Date of Appointment	Confirmation or Other Action *	Date Resigned	Date of Death	Years of Service
TAFT								
Horace H. Lurton	Tenn.	2/26/1844	Peckham	12/13/1909	12/20/1909		7/12/1914	4
Charles E. Hughes	N.Y.	4/11/1862	Brewer	4/25/1910	5/2/1910	6/10/1916	8/27/1948	6
Edward D. White ‡			Fuller	12/12/1910	12/12/1910		5/19/1921	10‡
Willis Van Devanter	Wyo.	4/17/1859	White	12/12/1910	12/15/1910	6/2/1937	2/8/1941	26
Joseph R. Lamar	Ga.	10/14/1857	Moody	12/12/1910	12/15/1910		1/2/1916	5
Mahlon Pitney	N.J.	2/5/1858	Harlan	2/19/1912	3/13/1912 (50-26)	12/31/1922	12/9/1924	10
WILSON								
James C. McReynolds	Tenn.	2/3/1862	Lurton	8/19/1914	8/29/1914 (44-6)	1/31/1941	8/24/1946	26
Louis D. Brandeis	Mass.	11/13/1856	Lamar	1/28/1916	6/1/1916 (47-22)	2/13/1939	10/5/1941	22
John H. Clarke	Ohio	9/18/1857	Hughes	7/14/1916	7/24/1916	9/18/1922	3/22/1945	6
HARDING								
William H. Taft	Ohio	9/15/1857	White	6/30/1921	6/30/1921	2/3/1930	3/8/1930	8
George Sutherland	Utah	3/25/1862	Clarke	9/5/1922	9/5/1922	1/17/1938	7/18/1942	15
Pierce Butler	Minn.	3/17/1866	Day	11/23/1922	12/21/1922 (61-8)		11/16/1939	17
Edward T. Sanford	Tenn.	7/23/1865	Pitney	1/24/1923	1/29/1923		3/8/1930	7
COOLIDGE								
Harlan F. Stone	N.Y.	10/11/1872	McKenna	1/5/1925	2/5/1925 (71-6)		4/22/1946	16
HOOVER								
Charles E. Hughes ‡			Taft	2/3/1930	2/13/1930 (52-26)	7/1/1941	8/27/1948	11‡
John J. Parker	N.C.	11/20/1885	Sanford	3/21/1930	5/7/1930 (R, 39-41)		3/17/1958	
Owen J. Roberts	Pa.	5/2/1875	Sanford	5/9/1930	5/20/1930	7/31/1945	5/17/1955	15
Benjamin N. Cardozo	N.Y.	5/24/1870	Holmes	2/15/1932	2/24/1932		7/9/1938	6
ROOSEVELT								
Hugo L. Black	Ala.	2/27/1886	Van Devanter	8/12/1937	8/17/1937 (63-16)	9/17/1971	10/25/1971	34
Stanley F. Reed	Ky.	12/31/1884	Sutherland	1/15/1938	1/25/1938	2/25/1957	4/2/1980	19
Felix Frankfurter	Mass.	11/15/1882	Cardozo	1/5/1939	1/17/1939	8/28/1962	2/22/1965	23
William O. Douglas	Conn.	10/16/1898	Brandeis	3/20/1939	4/4/1939 (62-4)	11/12/1975	1/19/1980	36 ‡
Frank Murphy	Mich.	4/13/1890	Butler	1/4/1940	1/15/1940		7/19/1949	9
Harlan F. Stone ‡			Hughes	6/12/1941	6/27/1941		4/22/1946	5 ‡
James F. Byrnes	S.C.	5/2/1879	McReynolds	6/12/1941	6/12/1941	10/3/1942	4/9/1972	1
Robert H. Jackson	N.Y.	2/13/1892	Stone	6/12/1941	7/7/1941		10/9/1954	13
Wiley B. Rutledge	Iowa	7/20/1894	Byrnes	1/11/1943	2/8/1943		9/10/1949	6
TRUMAN								
Harold H. Burton	Ohio	6/22/1888	Roberts	9/19/1945	9/19/1945	10/13/1958	10/28/1964	13
Fred M. Vinson	Ky.	1/22/1890	Stone	6/6/1946	6/20/1946		9/8/1953	7
Tom C. Clark	Texas	9/23/1899	Murphy	8/2/1949	8/18/1949 (73-8)	6/12/1967	6/13/1977	18
Sherman Minton	Ind.	10/20/1890	Rutledge	9/15/1949	10/4/1949 (48-16)	10/15/1956	4/9/1965	7
EISENHOWER								
Earl Warren	Calif.	3/19/1891	Vinson	9/30/1953	3/1/1954	6/23/1969	6/9/1974	15
John M. Harlan	N.Y.	5/20/1899	Jackson	1/10/1955	3/16/1955 (71-11)	9/23/1971	12/29/1971	16

Name	State	Date of Birth	To Replace	Date of Appointment	Confirmation or Other Action *	Date Resigned	Date of Death	Years of Service
EISENHOWER *(Continued)*								
William J. Brennan, Jr.	N.J.	4/25/1906	Minton	1/14/1957	3/19/1957	7/23/1990		33
Charles E. Whittaker	Mo.	2/22/1901	Reed	3/2/1957	3/19/1957	3/31/1962	11/26/1973	5
Potter Stewart	Ohio	1/23/1915	Burton	1/17/1959	5/5/1959 (70-17)	7/3/1981	12/7/1985	22
KENNEDY								
Byron R. White	Colo.	6/8/1917	Whittaker	3/30/1962	4/11/1962	7/28/1993		31
Arthur J. Goldberg	Ill.	8/8/1908	Frankfurter	8/29/1962	9/25/1962	7/25/1965	1/19/1990	3
JOHNSON								
Abe Fortas	Tenn.	6/19/1910	Goldberg	7/28/1965	8/11/1965	5/14/1969	4/5/1982	4
Thurgood Marshall	N.Y.	6/2/1908	Clark	6/13/1967	8/30/1967 (69-11)	6/27/1991	1/24/1993	24
Abe Fortas ‡			Warren	6/26/1968	10/4/1968 (W)			
Homer Thornberry	Texas	1/9/1909	Fortas	6/26/1968	No action			
NIXON								
Warren E. Burger	Minn.	9/17/1907	Warren	5/21/1969	6/9/1969 (74-3)	9/26/1986		17
Clement Haynsworth, Jr.	S.C.	10/30/1912	Fortas	8/18/1969	11/21/1969 (R, 45-55)		11/22/1989	
G. Harrold Carswell	Fla.	12/22/1919	Fortas	1/19/1970	4/8/1970 (R, 45-51)		7/31/1992	
Harry A. Blackmun	Minn.	11/12/1908	Fortas	4/14/1970	5/12/1970 (94-0)	8/3/1994		24
Lewis F. Powell, Jr.	Va.	9/19/1907	Black	10/21/1971	12/6/1971 (89-1)	6/26/1987		16
William H. Rehnquist	Ariz.	10/1/1924	Harlan	10/21/1971	12/10/1971 (68-26)			
FORD								
John Paul Stevens	Ill.	4/20/1920	Douglas	11/28/1975	12/17/1975 (98-0)			
REAGAN								
Sandra Day O'Connor	Ariz.	3/26/1930	Stewart	8/19/1981	9/21/1981 (99-0)			
William H. Rehnquist ‡			Burger	6/20/1986	9/17/1986 (65-33)			
Antonin Scalia	Va.	3/11/1936	Rehnquist	6/24/1986	9/17/1986 (98-0)			
Robert H. Bork	D.C.	3/1/1927	Powell	7/1/1987	10/23/1987 (R, 42-58)			
Anthony M. Kennedy	Calif.	7/23/1936	Powell	11/30/1987	2/3/1988 (97-0)			
BUSH								
David Hackett Souter	N.H.	9/17/1939	Brennan	7/23/1990	10/2/1990 (90-9)			
Clarence Thomas	Ga.	6/23/1948	Marshall	7/1/1991	10/15/1991 (52-48)			
CLINTON								
Ruth Bader Ginsburg	N.Y.	3/15/1933	White	6/22/1993	8/3/1993 (96-3)			
Stephen G. Breyer	Mass.	8/15/1938	Blackmun	5/17/1994	7/29/1994 (87- 9)			

SOURCES: Leon Friedman and Fred L. Israel, eds., *The Justices of the United States Supreme Court, 1789-1969, Their Lives and Major Opinions,* 5 vols. (New York and London: Chelsea House Publishers, 1969–1978); U.S. Senate, Executive Journal of the U.S. Senate, 1789–1975 (Washington, D.C.: Government Printing Office); Congressional Quarterly *Almanacs,* 1971, 1975, 1981, 1986, 1987 (Washington, D.C.: Congressional Quarterly, 1972, 1976, 1982, 1987, 1988); Clare Cushman, ed., *The Supreme Court Justices: Illustrated Biographies, 1789–1992* (Washington, D.C.: Congressional Quarterly, 1993).

NOTE: Boldface — Chief justice; Italics —Did not serve; *—Where no vote is listed, confirmation was by voice vote or otherwise unrecorded; † —Earlier nomination not confirmed. See above; ‡—Earlier court service. See above; W—Withdrawn; P—Postponed; R—Rejected; D—Declined.

Seat Chart of the Justices

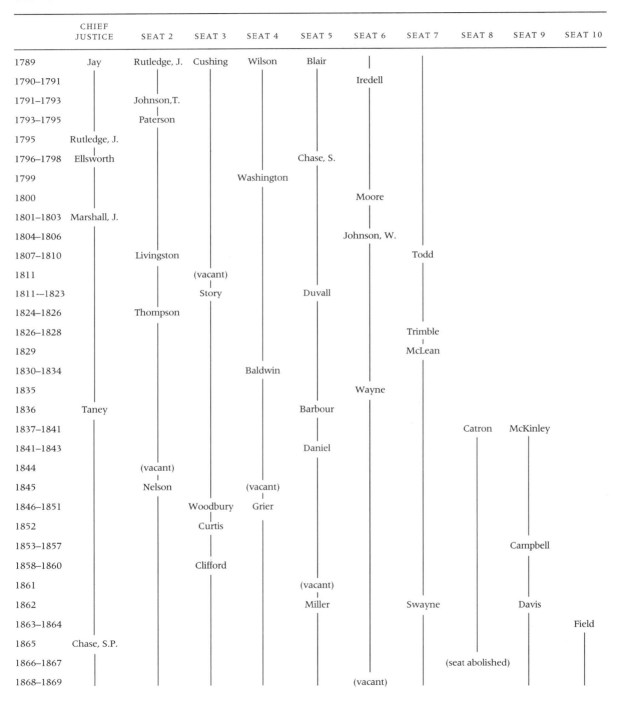

	CHIEF JUSTICE	SEAT 2	SEAT 3	SEAT 4	SEAT 5	SEAT 6	SEAT 7	SEAT 8	SEAT 9	SEAT 10
1789	Jay	Rutledge, J.	Cushing	Wilson	Blair					
1790–1791						Iredell				
1791–1793		Johnson, T.								
1793–1795		Paterson								
1795	Rutledge, J.									
1796–1798	Ellsworth				Chase, S.					
1799				Washington						
1800						Moore				
1801–1803	Marshall, J.									
1804–1806						Johnson, W.				
1807–1810		Livingston					Todd			
1811			(vacant)							
1811–1823			Story		Duvall					
1824–1826		Thompson								
1826–1828							Trimble			
1829							McLean			
1830–1834				Baldwin						
1835						Wayne				
1836	Taney				Barbour					
1837–1841								Catron	McKinley	
1841–1843					Daniel					
1844		(vacant)								
1845		Nelson		(vacant)						
1846–1851			Woodbury	Grier						
1852			Curtis							
1853–1857									Campbell	
1858–1860			Clifford							
1861					(vacant)					
1862					Miller		Swayne		Davis	
1863–1864										Field
1865	Chase, S.P.									
1866–1867								(seat abolished)		
1868–1869						(vacant)				

476

	CHIEF JUSTICE	SEAT 2	SEAT 3	SEAT 4	SEAT 5	SEAT 6	SEAT 7	SEAT 8	SEAT 9	SEAT 10
1870–1872				Strong		Bradley				
1873		Hunt								
1874–1877	Waite									
1877–1880									Harlan I	
1881				Woods			Matthews			
1882–1887		Blatchford	Gray							
1888				Lamar, L.						
1888–1889	Fuller									
1889–1890							Brewer			
1891					Brown					
1892						Shiras				
1893				Jackson, H.						
1894–1895		White, E.								
1896–1897				Peckham						
1898–1902										McKenna
1903–1906			Holmes				Day			
1907–1909					Moody					
1910				Lurton						
1910–1911	White, E.	Van Devanter			Lamar, J.		Hughes			
1912–1914									Pitney	
1914–1916				McReynolds						
1916–1921					Brandeis		Clarke			
1921–1922	Taft									
1922						Butler	Sutherland			
1923–1924									Sanford	
1925–1930										Stone
1930–1931	Hughes								Roberts	
1932–1937			Cardozo							
1937		Black								
1938							Reed			
1939			Frankfurter		Douglas					
1940–1941						Murphy				
1941–1942	Stone			Byrnes						Jackson, R.
1943–1945				Rutledge, W.						
1945–1946									Burton	

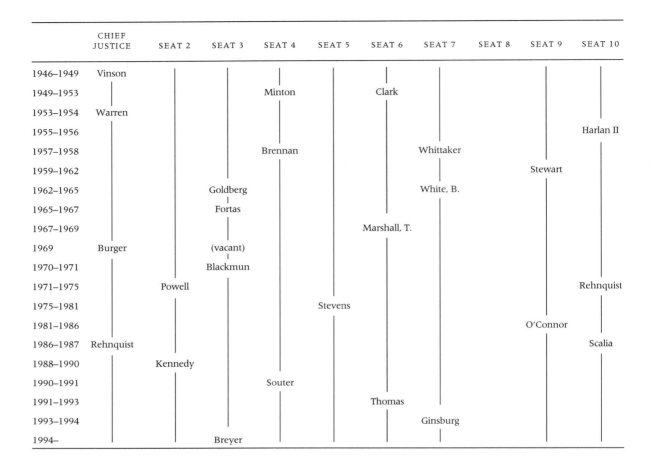

	CHIEF JUSTICE	SEAT 2	SEAT 3	SEAT 4	SEAT 5	SEAT 6	SEAT 7	SEAT 8	SEAT 9	SEAT 10
1946–1949	Vinson									
1949–1953				Minton		Clark				
1953–1954	Warren									
1955–1956										Harlan II
1957–1958				Brennan			Whittaker			
1959–1962									Stewart	
1962–1965			Goldberg				White, B.			
1965–1967			Fortas							
1967–1969						Marshall, T.				
1969	Burger		(vacant)							
1970–1971			Blackmun							
1971–1975		Powell								Rehnquist
1975–1981					Stevens					
1981–1986									O'Connor	
1986–1987	Rehnquist									Scalia
1988–1990		Kennedy								
1990–1991				Souter						
1991–1993						Thomas				
1993–1994							Ginsburg			
1994–			Breyer							

Government of the United States

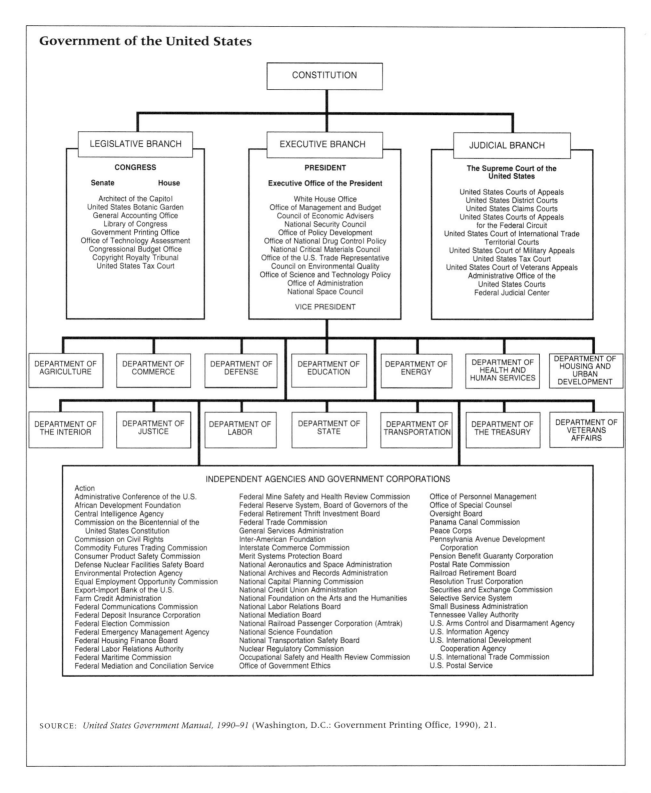

CONSTITUTION

LEGISLATIVE BRANCH

CONGRESS

Senate   **House**

Architect of the Capitol
United States Botanic Garden
General Accounting Office
Library of Congress
Government Printing Office
Office of Technology Assessment
Congressional Budget Office
Copyright Royalty Tribunal
United States Tax Court

EXECUTIVE BRANCH

PRESIDENT

Executive Office of the President

White House Office
Office of Management and Budget
Council of Economic Advisers
National Security Council
Office of Policy Development
Office of National Drug Control Policy
National Critical Materials Council
Office of the U.S. Trade Representative
Council on Environmental Quality
Office of Science and Technology Policy
Office of Administration
National Space Council

VICE PRESIDENT

JUDICIAL BRANCH

**The Supreme Court of the
United States**

United States Courts of Appeals
United States District Courts
United States Claims Courts
United States Courts of Appeals
for the Federal Circuit
United States Court of International Trade
Territorial Courts
United States Court of Military Appeals
United States Tax Court
United States Court of Veterans Appeals
Administrative Office of the
United States Courts
Federal Judicial Center

DEPARTMENT OF AGRICULTURE

DEPARTMENT OF COMMERCE

DEPARTMENT OF DEFENSE

DEPARTMENT OF EDUCATION

DEPARTMENT OF ENERGY

DEPARTMENT OF HEALTH AND HUMAN SERVICES

DEPARTMENT OF HOUSING AND URBAN DEVELOPMENT

DEPARTMENT OF THE INTERIOR

DEPARTMENT OF JUSTICE

DEPARTMENT OF LABOR

DEPARTMENT OF STATE

DEPARTMENT OF TRANSPORTATION

DEPARTMENT OF THE TREASURY

DEPARTMENT OF VETERANS AFFAIRS

INDEPENDENT AGENCIES AND GOVERNMENT CORPORATIONS

Action
Administrative Conference of the U.S.
African Development Foundation
Central Intelligence Agency
Commission on the Bicentennial of the
    United States Constitution
Commission on Civil Rights
Commodity Futures Trading Commission
Consumer Product Safety Commission
Defense Nuclear Facilities Safety Board
Environmental Protection Agency
Equal Employment Opportunity Commission
Export-Import Bank of the U.S.
Farm Credit Administration
Federal Communications Commission
Federal Deposit Insurance Corporation
Federal Election Commission
Federal Emergency Management Agency
Federal Housing Finance Board
Federal Labor Relations Authority
Federal Maritime Commission
Federal Mediation and Conciliation Service

Federal Mine Safety and Health Review Commission
Federal Reserve System, Board of Governors of the
Federal Retirement Thrift Investment Board
Federal Trade Commission
General Services Administration
Inter-American Foundation
Interstate Commerce Commission
Merit Systems Protection Board
National Aeronautics and Space Administration
National Archives and Records Administration
National Capital Planning Commission
National Credit Union Administration
National Foundation on the Arts and the Humanities
National Labor Relations Board
National Mediation Board
National Railroad Passenger Corporation (Amtrak)
National Science Foundation
National Transportation Safety Board
Nuclear Regulatory Commission
Occupational Safety and Health Review Commission
Office of Government Ethics

Office of Personnel Management
Office of Special Counsel
Oversight Board
Panama Canal Commission
Peace Corps
Pennsylvania Avenue Development
    Corporation
Pension Benefit Guaranty Corporation
Postal Rate Commission
Railroad Retirement Board
Resolution Trust Corporation
Securities and Exchange Commission
Selective Service System
Small Business Administration
Tennessee Valley Authority
U.S. Arms Control and Disarmament Agency
U.S. Information Agency
U.S. International Development
    Cooperation Agency
U.S. International Trade Commission
U.S. Postal Service

SOURCE: *United States Government Manual, 1990–91* (Washington, D.C.: Government Printing Office, 1990), 21.

Constitution of the United States

We the People of the United States, in Order to form a more perfect Union, establish Justice, insure domestic Tranquility, provide for the common defence, promote the general Welfare, and secure the Blessings of Liberty to ourselves and our Posterity, do ordain and establish this Constitution for the United States of America.

ARTICLE I

Section 1. All legislative Powers herein granted shall be vested in a Congress of the United States, which shall consist of a Senate and House of Representatives.

Section 2. The House of Representatives shall be composed of Members chosen every second Year by the People of the several States, and the Electors in each State shall have the Qualifications requisite for Electors of the most numerous Branch of the State Legislature.

No Person shall be a Representative who shall not have attained to the age of twenty five Years, and been seven Years a Citizen of the United States, and who shall not, when elected, be an Inhabitant of that State in which he shall be chosen.

[Representatives and direct Taxes shall be apportioned among the several States which may be included within this Union, according to their respective Numbers, which shall be determined by adding to the whole Number of free Persons, including those bound to Service for a Term of Years, and excluding Indians not taxed, three fifths of all other Persons.][1] The actual Enumeration shall be made within three Years after the first Meeting of the Congress of the United States, and within every subsequent Term of ten Years, in such Manner as they shall by Law direct. The Number of Representatives shall not exceed one for every thirty Thousand, but each State shall have at Least one Representative; and until such enumeration shall be made, the State of New Hampshire shall be entitled to chuse three, Massachusetts eight, Rhode-Island and Providence Plantations one, Connecticut five, New-York six, New Jersey four, Pennsylvania eight, Delaware one, Maryland six, Virginia ten, North Carolina five, South Carolina five, and Georgia three.

When vacancies happen in the Representation from any State, the Executive Authority thereof shall issue Writs of Election to fill such Vacancies.

The House of Representatives shall chuse their Speaker and other Officers; and shall have the sole Power of Impeachment.

Section 3. The Senate of the United States shall be composed of two Senators from each State, [chosen by the Legislature thereof,][2] for six Years; and each Senator shall have one Vote.

Immediately after they shall be assembled in Consequence of the first Election, they shall be divided as equally as may be into three Classes. The Seats of the Senators of the first Class shall be vacated at the Expiration of the second Year, of the second Class at the Expiration of the fourth Year, and of the third Class at the Expiration of the sixth Year, so that one third may be chosen every second Year; [and if Vacancies happen by Resignation, or otherwise, during the Recess of the Legislature of any State, the Executive thereof may make temporary Appointments until the next Meeting of the Legislature, which shall then fill such Vacancies.][3]

No Person shall be a Senator who shall not have attained to the Age of thirty Years, and been nine Years a Citizen of the United States, and who shall not, when elected, be an Inhabitant of that State for which he shall be chosen.

The Vice President of the United States shall be President of the Senate, but shall have no Vote, unless they be equally divided.

The Senate shall chuse their other Officers, and also a President pro tempore, in the Absence of the Vice President, or when he shall exercise the Office of President of the United States.

The Senate shall have the sole Power to try all Impeachments. When sitting for that Purpose, they shall be on Oath or Affirmation. When the President of the United States is tried, the Chief Justice shall preside: And no Person shall be convicted without the Concurrence of two thirds of the Members present.

Judgment in Cases of Impeachment shall not extend further than to removal from Office, and disqualification to hold and enjoy any Office of honor, Trust or Profit under the United States: but the Party convicted shall nevertheless be liable and subject to Indictment, Trial, Judgment and Punishment, according to Law.

Section 4. The Times, Places and Manner of holding Elections for Senators and Representatives, shall be prescribed in each State by the Legislature thereof; but the Congress may at any time by Law make or alter such Regulations, except as to the Places of chusing Senators.

The Congress shall assemble at least once in every Year, and such Meeting shall [be on the first Monday in December],[4] unless they shall by Law appoint a different Day.

Section 5. Each House shall be the Judge of the Elections, Returns and Qualifications of its own Members, and a Majority of each shall constitute a Quorum to do Business; but a smaller Number may adjourn from day to day, and may be authorized to compel the Attendance of absent Members, in such Manner, and under such Penalties as each House may provide.

Each House may determine the Rules of its Proceedings, punish its Members for disorderly Behaviour, and, with the Concurrence of two thirds, expel a Member.

Each House shall keep a Journal of its Proceedings, and from time to time publish the same, excepting such Parts as may in their Judgment require Secrecy; and the Yeas and Nays of the Members of either House on any question shall, at the Desire of one fifth of those Present, be entered on the Journal.

Neither House, during the Session of Congress, shall, without the Consent of the other, adjourn for more than three days, nor to any other Place than that in which the two Houses shall be sitting.

Section 6. The Senators and Representatives shall receive a Compensation for their Services, to be ascertained by Law, and paid out of the Treasury of the United States. They shall in all Cases, except Treason, Felony and Breach of the Peace, be privileged from Arrest during their Attendance at the Session of their respective Houses, and in going to and returning from the same; and for any Speech or Debate in either House, they shall not be questioned in any other Place.

No Senator or Representative shall, during the Time for which he was elected, be appointed to any civil Office under the Authority of the United States, which shall have been created, or the Emoluments whereof shall have been encreased during such time; and no Person holding any Office under the United States, shall be a Member of either House during his Continuance in Office.

Section 7. All Bills for raising Revenue shall originate in the House of Representatives; but the Senate may propose or concur with Amendments as on other Bills.

Every Bill which shall have passed the House of Representatives and the Senate, shall, before it become a Law, be presented to the President of the United States; If he approve he shall sign it, but if not he shall return it, with his Objections to that House in which it shall have originated, who shall enter the Objections at large on their Journal, and proceed to reconsider it. If after such Reconsideration two thirds of that House shall agree to pass the Bill, it shall be sent, together with the Objections, to the other House, by which it shall likewise be reconsidered, and if approved by two thirds of that House, it shall become a Law. But in all such Cases the Votes of both Houses shall be determined by yeas and Nays, and the Names of the Persons voting for and against the Bill shall be entered on the Journal of each House respectively. If any Bill shall not be returned by the President within ten Days (Sundays excepted) after it shall have been presented to him, the Same shall be a Law, in like Manner as if he had signed it, unless the Congress by their Adjournment prevent its Return, in which Case it shall not be a Law.

Every Order, Resolution, or Vote to which the Concurrence of the Senate and House of Representatives may be necessary (except on a question of Adjournment) shall be presented to the President of the United States; and before the Same shall take Effect, shall be approved by him, or being disapproved by him, shall be repassed by two thirds of the Senate and House of Representatives, according to the Rules and Limitations prescribed in the Case of a Bill.

Section 8. The Congress shall have Power To lay and collect Taxes, Duties, Imposts and Excises, to pay the Debts and provide for the common Defence and general Welfare of the United States; but all Duties, Imposts and Excises shall be uniform throughout the United States;

To borrow Money on the credit of the United States;

To regulate Commerce with foreign Nations, and among the several States, and with the Indian Tribes;

To establish an uniform Rule of Naturalization, and uniform Laws on the subject of Bankruptcies throughout the United States;

To coin Money, regulate the Value thereof, and of foreign Coin, and fix the Standard of Weights and Measures;

To provide for the Punishment of counterfeiting the Securities and current Coin of the United States;

To establish Post Offices and post Roads;

To promote the Progress of Science and useful Arts, by securing for limited Times to Authors and Inventors the exclusive Right to their respective Writings and Discoveries;

To constitute Tribunals inferior to the supreme Court;

To define and punish Piracies and Felonies committed on the high Seas, and Offences against the Law of Nations;

To declare War, grant Letters of Marque and Reprisal, and make Rules concerning Captures on Land and Water;

To raise and support Armies, but no Appropriation of Money to that Use shall be for a longer Term than two Years;

To provide and maintain a Navy;

To make Rules for the Government and Regulation of the land and naval Forces;

To provide for calling forth the Militia to execute the Laws of the Union, suppress Insurrections and repel Invasions;

To provide for organizing, arming, and disciplining, the Militia, and for governing such Part of them as may be employed in the Service of the United States, reserving to the States respectively, the Appointment of the Officers, and the Authority of training the Militia according to the discipline prescribed by Congress;

To exercise exclusive Legislation in all Cases whatsoever, over such District (not exceeding ten Miles square) as may, by Cession of particular States, and the Acceptance of Congress, become the Seat of the Government of the United States, and to exercise like Authority over all Places purchased by the Consent of the Legislature of the State in which the Same shall be, for the Erection of Forts, Magazines, Arsenals, dock-Yards, and other needful Buildings; —And

To make all Laws which shall be necessary and proper for carrying into Execution the foregoing Powers, and all other Powers vested by this Constitution in the Government of the United States, or in any Department or Officer thereof.

Section 9. The Migration or Importation of such Persons as any of the States now existing shall think proper to admit, shall not be prohibited by the Congress prior to the Year one thousand eight hundred and eight, but a Tax or duty may be imposed on such Importation, not exceeding ten dollars for each Person.

The Privilege of the Writ of Habeas Corpus shall not be suspended, unless when in Cases of Rebellion or Invasion the public Safety may require it.

No Bill of Attainder or ex post facto Law shall be passed.

No Capitation, or other direct, Tax shall be laid, unless in Proportion to the Census or Enumeration herein before directed to be taken.[5]

No Tax or Duty shall be laid on Articles exported from any State.

No Preference shall be given by any Regulation of Commerce or Revenue to the Ports of one State over those of another; nor shall Vessels bound to, or from, one State, be obliged to enter, clear, or pay Duties in another.

No Money shall be drawn from the Treasury, but in Consequence of Appropriations made by Law; and a regular Statement and Account of the Receipts and Expenditures of all public Money shall be published from time to time.

No Title of Nobility shall be granted by the United States: And no Person holding any Office of Profit or Trust under them, shall, without the Consent of the Congress, accept of any present, Emolument, Office, or Title, of any kind whatever, from any King, Prince, or foreign State.

Section 10. No State shall enter into any Treaty, Alliance, or Confederation; grant Letters of Marque and Reprisal; coin Money; emit Bills of Credit; make any Thing but gold and silver Coin a Tender in Payment of Debts; pass any Bill of Attainder, ex post facto Law, or Law impairing the Obligation of Contracts, or grant any Title of Nobility.

No State shall, without the Consent of the Congress, lay any Imposts or Duties on Imports or Exports, except what may be absolutely necessary for executing it's inspection Laws: and the net Produce of all Duties and Imposts, laid by any State on Imports or Exports, shall be for the Use of the Treasury of the United States; and all such Laws shall be subject to the Revision and Controul of the Congress.

No State shall, without the Consent of Congress, lay any Duty of Tonnage, keep Troops, or Ships of War in time of Peace, enter into any Agreement or Compact with another State, or with a foreign Power, or engage in War, unless actually invaded, or in such imminent Danger as will not admit of delay.

ARTICLE II

Section 1. The executive Power shall be vested in a President of the United States of America. He shall hold his Office during the Term of four Years, and, together with the Vice President, chosen for the same Term, be elected, as follows

Each State shall appoint, in such Manner as the Legislature thereof may direct, a Number of Electors, equal to the whole Number of Senators and Representatives to which the State may be entitled in the Congress: but no Senator or Representative, or Person holding an Office of Trust or Profit under the United States, shall be appointed an Elector.

[The Electors shall meet in their respective States, and vote by Ballot for two Persons, of whom one at least shall not be an Inhabitant of the same State with themselves. And they shall make a List of all the Persons voted for, and of the Number of Votes for each; which List they shall sign and certify, and transmit sealed to the Seat of the Government of the United States, directed to the President of the Senate. The President of the Senate shall, in the Presence of the Senate and House of Representatives, open all the Certificates, and the Votes shall then be counted. The Person having the greatest Number of Votes shall be the President, if such Number be a Majority of the whole Number of Electors appointed; and if there be more than one who have such Majority, and have an equal Number of Votes, then the House of Representatives shall immediately chuse by Ballot one of them for President; and if no Person have a Majority, then from the five highest on the list the said House shall in like Manner chuse the President. But in chusing the President, the Votes shall be taken by States, the Representation from each State having one Vote; A quorum for this Purpose shall consist of a Member or Members from two thirds of the States, and a Majority of all the States shall be necessary to a Choice. In every Case, after the Choice of the President, the Person having the greatest Number of Votes of the Electors shall be the Vice President. But if there should remain two or more who have equal Votes, the Senate shall chuse from them by Ballot the Vice President.][6]

The Congress may determine the Time of chusing the Electors, and the Day on which they shall give their Votes; which Day shall be the same throughout the United States.

No Person except a natural born Citizen, or a Citizen of the United States, at the time of the Adoption of this Constitution, shall be eligible to the Office of President; neither shall any Person be eligible to that Office who shall not have attained to the Age of thirty five Years, and been fourteen Years a Resident within the United States.

In Case of the Removal of the President from Office, or of his Death, Resignation, or Inability to discharge the Powers and Duties of the said Office,[7] the Same shall devolve on the Vice President, and the Congress may by Law provide for the Case of Removal, Death, Resignation or Inability, both of the President and Vice President, declaring what Officer shall then act as President, and such Officer shall act accordingly, until the Disability be removed, or a President shall be elected.

The President shall, at stated Times, receive for his Services, a Compensation, which shall neither be encreased nor diminished during the Period for which he shall have been elected, and he shall not receive within that Period any other Emolument from the United States, or any of them.

Before he enter on the Execution of his Office, he shall take the following Oath or Affirmation:—"I do solemnly swear (or affirm) that I will faithfully execute the Office of President of the United States, and will to the best of my Ability, preserve, protect and defend the Constitution of the United States."

Section 2. The President shall be Commander in Chief of the Army and Navy of the United States, and of the Militia of the several States, when called into the actual Service of the United States; he may require the Opinion, in writing, of the principal Officer in each of the executive Departments, upon any Subject relating to the Duties of their respective Offices, and he shall have Power to grant Reprieves and Pardons for Offences against the United States, except in Cases of Impeachment.

He shall have Power, by and with the Advice and Consent of the Senate, to make Treaties, provided two thirds of the Senators present concur; and he shall nominate, and by and with the Advice and Consent of the Senate, shall appoint Ambassadors, other public Ministers and Consuls, Judges of the supreme Court, and all other Officers of the United States, whose Appointments are not herein otherwise provided for, and which shall be established by Law: but the Congress may by Law vest the Appointment of such inferior Officers, as they think proper, in the President alone, in the Courts of Law, or in the Heads of Departments.

The President shall have Power to fill up all Vacancies that may happen during the Recess of the Senate, by granting Commissions which shall expire at the End of their next Session.

Section 3. He shall from time to time give to the Congress Information of the State of the Union, and recommend to their Consideration such Measures as he shall judge necessary and expedient; he may, on extraordinary Occasions, convene both Houses, or either of them, and in Case of Disagreement between them, with Respect to the Time of Adjournment, he may adjourn them to such Time as he shall think proper; he shall receive Ambassadors and other public Ministers; he shall take Care that the Laws be faithfully executed, and shall Commission all the Officers of the United States.

Section 4. The President, Vice President and all civil Officers of the United States, shall be removed from Office on Impeachment for, and Conviction of, Treason, Bribery, or other high Crimes and Misdemeanors.

ARTICLE III

Section 1. The judicial Power of the United States, shall be vested in one supreme Court, and in such inferior Courts as the Congress may from time to time ordain and establish. The Judges, both of the supreme and inferior Courts, shall hold their Offices during good Behaviour, and shall, at stated Times, receive for their Services, a Compensation, which shall not be diminished during their Continuance in Office.

Section 2. The judicial Power shall extend to all Cases, in Law and Equity, arising under this Constitution, the Laws of the United States, and Treaties made, or which shall be made, under their Authority; — to all Cases affecting Ambassadors, other public Ministers and Consuls; — to all Cases of admiralty and maritime Jurisdiction; — to Controversies to which the United States shall be a Party; — to Controversies between two or more States; — between a State and Citizens of another State;[8] — between Citizens of different States; — between Citizens of the same State claiming Lands under Grants of different States, and between a State, or the Citizens thereof, and foreign States, Citizens or Subjects.[8]

In all Cases affecting Ambassadors, other public Ministers and Consuls, and those in which a State shall be Party, the supreme Court shall have original Jurisdiction. In all the other Cases before mentioned, the supreme Court shall have appellate Jurisdiction, both as to Law and Fact, with such Exceptions, and under such Regulations as the Congress shall make.

The Trial of all Crimes, except in Cases of Impeachment, shall be by Jury; and such Trial shall be held in the State where the said Crimes shall have been committed; but when not committed within any State, the Trial shall be at such Place or Places as the Congress may by Law have directed.

Section 3. Treason against the United States, shall consist only in levying War against them, or in adhering to their Enemies, giving them Aid and Comfort. No Person shall be convicted of Treason unless on the Testimony of two Witnesses to the same overt Act, or on Confession in open Court.

The Congress shall have Power to declare the Punishment of Treason, but no Attainder of Treason shall work Corruption of Blood, or Forfeiture except during the Life of the Person attainted.

ARTICLE IV

Section 1. Full Faith and Credit shall be given in each State to the public Acts, Records, and judicial Proceedings of every other State. And the Congress may by general Laws prescribe the Manner in which such Acts, Records and Proceedings shall be proved, and the Effect thereof.

Section 2. The Citizens of each State shall be entitled to all Privileges and Immunities of Citizens in the several States.

A Person charged in any State with Treason, Felony, or other Crime, who shall flee from Justice, and be found in another State, shall on Demand of the executive Authority of the State from which he fled, be delivered up, to be removed to the State having Jurisdiction of the Crime.

[No Person held to Service or Labour in one State, under the Laws thereof, escaping into another, shall, in Consequence of any Law or Regulation therein, be discharged from such Service or Labour, but shall be delivered up on Claim of the Party to whom such Service or Labour may be due.][9]

Section 3. New States may be admitted by the Congress into this Union; but no new State shall be formed or erected within the Jurisdiction of any other State; nor any State be formed by the Junction of two or more States, or Parts of States, without the Consent of the Legislatures of the States concerned as well as of the Congress.

The Congress shall have Power to dispose of and make all needful Rules and Regulations respecting the Territory or other Property belonging to the United States; and nothing in this Constitution shall be so construed as to Prejudice any Claims of the United States, or of any particular State.

Section 4. The United States shall guarantee to every State in this Union a Republican Form of Government, and shall protect each of them against Invasion; and on Application of the Legislature, or of the Executive (when the Legislature cannot be convened) against domestic Violence.

ARTICLE V

The Congress, whenever two thirds of both Houses shall deem it necessary, shall propose Amendments to this Constitution, or, on the Application of the Legislatures of two thirds of the several States, shall call a Convention for proposing Amendments, which, in either Case, shall be valid to all Intents and Purposes, as Part of this Constitution, when ratified by the Legislatures of three fourths of the several States, or by Conventions in three fourths thereof, as the one or the other Mode of Ratification may be proposed by the Congress; Provided [that no Amendment which may be made prior to the Year One thousand eight hundred and eight shall in any Manner affect the first and fourth Clauses in the Ninth Section of the first Article; and][10] that no State, without its Consent, shall be deprived of its equal Suffrage in the Senate.

ARTICLE VI

All Debts contracted and Engagements entered into, before the Adoption of this Constitution, shall be as valid against the United States under this Constitution, as under the Confederation.

This Constitution, and the Laws of the United States which shall be made in Pursuance thereof; and all Treaties made, or which shall be made, under the Authority of the United States, shall be the supreme Law of the Land; and the Judges in every State shall be bound thereby, any Thing in the Constitution or Laws of any State to the Contrary notwithstanding.

The Senators and Representatives before mentioned, and the Members of the several State Legislatures, and all executive and judicial Officers, both of the United States and of the several States, shall be bound by Oath or Affirmation, to support this Constitution; but no religious Test shall ever be required as a Qualification to any Office or public Trust under the United States.

ARTICLE VII

The Ratification of the Conventions of nine States, shall be sufficient for the Establishment of this Constitution between the States so ratifying the Same.

Done in Convention by the Unanimous Consent of the States present the Seventeenth Day of September in the Year of our Lord one thousand seven hundred and Eighty seven and of the Independence of the United States of America the Twelfth. IN WITNESS whereof We have hereunto subscribed our Names,

George Washington,
President and deputy from Virginia.

New Hampshire: John Langdon, Nicholas Gilman.
Massachusetts: Nathaniel Gorham, Rufus King.
Connecticut: William Samuel Johnson, Roger Sherman.
New York: Alexander Hamilton.
New Jersey: William Livingston, David Brearley, William Paterson, Jonathan Dayton.
Pennsylvania: Benjamin Franklin, Thomas Mifflin, Robert Morris, George Clymer,. Thomas FitzSimons, Jared Ingersoll, James Wilson, Gouverneur Morris.
Delaware: George Read, Gunning Bedford Jr., John Dickinson, Richard Bassett, Jacob Broom.
Maryland: James McHenry, Daniel of St. Thomas Jenifer, Daniel Carroll.
Virginia: John Blair, James Madison Jr.
North Carolina:. William Blount, Richard Dobbs Spaight, Hugh Williamson.
South Carolina: John Rutledge, Charles Cotesworth Pinckney, Charles Pinckney, Pierce Butler.
Georgia: William Few, Abraham Baldwin.

[The language of the original Constitution, not including the Amendments, was adopted by a convention of the states on September 17, 1787, and was subsequently ratified by the states on the following dates: Delaware, December 7, 1787; Pennsylvania, December 12, 1787; New Jersey, December 18, 1787; Georgia, January 2, 1788; Connecticut, January 9, 1788; Massachusetts, February 6, 1788; Maryland, April 28, 1788; South Carolina, May 23, 1788; New Hampshire, June 21, 1788.

Ratification was completed on June 21, 1788.

The Constitution subsequently was ratified by Virginia, June 25, 1788; New York, July 26, 1788; North Carolina, November 21, 1789; Rhode Island, May 29, 1790; and Vermont, January 10, 1791.]

AMENDMENTS

AMENDMENT I
(First ten amendments ratified December 15, 1791.)
Congress shall make no law respecting an establishment

of religion, or prohibiting the free exercise thereof; or abridging the freedom of speech, or of the press; or the right of the people peaceably to assemble, and to petition the Government for a redress of grievances.

AMENDMENT II

A well regulated Militia, being necessary to the security of a free State, the right of the people to keep and bear Arms, shall not be infringed.

AMENDMENT III

No Soldier shall, in time of peace be quartered in any house, without the consent of the Owner, nor in time of war, but in a manner to be prescribed by law.

AMENDMENT IV

The right of the people to be secure in their persons, houses, papers, and effects, against unreasonable searches and seizures, shall not be violated, and no Warrants shall issue, but upon probable cause, supported by Oath or affirmation, and particularly describing the place to be searched, and the persons or things to be seized.

AMENDMENT V

No person shall be held to answer for a capital, or otherwise infamous crime, unless on a presentment or indictment of a Grand Jury, except in cases arising in the land or naval forces, or in the Militia, when in actual service in time of War or public danger; nor shall any person be subject for the same offence to be twice put in jeopardy of life or limb; nor shall be compelled in any criminal case to be a witness against himself, nor be deprived of life, liberty, or property, without due process of law; nor shall private property be taken for public use, without just compensation.

AMENDMENT VI

In all criminal prosecutions, the accused shall enjoy the right to a speedy and public trial, by an impartial jury of the State and district wherein the crime shall have been committed, which district shall have been previously ascertained by law, and to be informed of the nature and cause of the accusation; to be confronted with the witnesses against him; to have compulsory process for obtaining witnesses in his favor, and to have the Assistance of Counsel for his defence.

AMENDMENT VII

In Suits at common law, where the value in controversy shall exceed twenty dollars, the right of trial by jury shall be preserved, and no fact tried by a jury, shall be otherwise re-examined in any Court of the United States, than according to the rules of the common law.

AMENDMENT VIII

Excessive bail shall not be required, nor excessive fines imposed, nor cruel and unusual punishments inflicted.

AMENDMENT IX

The enumeration in the Constitution, of certain rights, shall not be construed to deny or disparage others retained by the people.

AMENDMENT X

The powers not delegated to the United States by the Constitution, nor prohibited by it to the States, are reserved to the States respectively, or to the people.

AMENDMENT XI (Ratified February 7, 1795)

The Judicial power of the United States shall not be construed to extend to any suit in law or equity, commenced or prosecuted against one of the United States by Citizens of another State, or by Citizens or Subjects of any Foreign State.

AMENDMENT XII (Ratified June 15, 1804)

The Electors shall meet in their respective states and vote by ballot for President and Vice-President, one of whom, at least, shall not be an inhabitant of the same state with themselves; they shall name in their ballots the person voted for as President, and in distinct ballots the person voted for as Vice-President, and they shall make distinct lists of all persons voted for as President, and of all persons voted for as Vice-President, and of the number of votes for each, which lists they shall sign and certify, and transmit sealed to the seat of the government of the United States, directed to the President of the Senate; — The President of the Senate shall, in the presence of the Senate and House of Representatives, open all the certificates and the votes shall then be counted; — The person having the greatest number of votes for President, shall be the President, if such number be a majority of the whole number of Electors appointed; and if no person have such majority, then from the persons having the highest numbers not exceeding three on the list of those voted for as President, the House of Representatives shall choose immediately, by ballot, the President. But in choosing the President, the votes shall be taken by states, the representation from each state having one vote; a quorum for this purpose shall consist of a member or members from two-thirds of the states, and a majority of all the states shall be necessary to a choice. [And if the House of Representatives shall not choose a President whenever the right of choice shall devolve upon them, before the fourth day of March next following, then the Vice-President shall act as President, as in the case of the death or other constitutional disability of the President. —][11] The person having the greatest number of votes as Vice-President, shall be the Vice-President, if such number be a majority of the whole number of Electors appointed, and if no person have a majority, then from the two highest numbers on the list, the Senate shall choose the Vice-President; a quorum for the purpose shall consist of two-thirds of the whole number of Senators, and a majority of the whole number shall be necessary to a choice. But no person constitutionally ineligible to the office of President shall be eligible to that of Vice-President of the United States.

AMENDMENT XIII (Ratified December 6, 1865)

Section 1. Neither slavery nor involuntary servitude, except as a punishment for crime whereof the party shall have been duly convicted, shall exist within the United States, or any place subject to their jurisdiction.

Section 2. Congress shall have power to enforce this article by appropriate legislation.

AMENDMENT XIV (Ratified July 9, 1868)

Section 1. All persons born or naturalized in the United States, and subject to the jurisdiction thereof, are citizens of the United States and of the State wherein they reside. No State shall make or enforce any law which shall abridge the privileges or immunities of citizens of the United States; nor shall any State deprive any person of life, liberty, or property, without due process of law; nor deny to any person within its jurisdiction the equal protection of the laws.

Section 2. Representatives shall be apportioned among the several States according to their respective numbers, counting the whole number of persons in each State, excluding Indians not taxed. But when the right to vote at any election for the choice of electors for President and Vice

President of the United States, Representatives in Congress, the Executive and Judicial officers of a State, or the members of the Legislature thereof, is denied to any of the male inhabitants of such State, being twenty-one years of age,[12] and citizens of the United States, or in any way abridged, except for participation in rebellion, or other crime, the basis of representation therein shall be reduced in the proportion which the number of such male citizens shall bear to the whole number of male citizens twenty-one years of age in such State.

Section 3. No person shall be a Senator or Representative in Congress, or elector of President and Vice President, or hold any office, civil or military, under the United States, or under any State, who, having previously taken an oath, as a member of Congress, or as an officer of the United States, or as a member of any State legislature, or as an executive or judicial officer of any State, to support the Constitution of the United States, shall have engaged in insurrection or rebellion against the same, or given aid or comfort to the enemies thereof. But Congress may by a vote of two-thirds of each House, remove such disability.

Section 4. The validity of the public debt of the United States, authorized by law, including debts incurred for payment of pensions and bounties for services in suppressing insurrection or rebellion, shall not be questioned. But neither the United States nor any State shall assume or pay any debt or obligation incurred in aid of insurrection or rebellion against the United States, or any claim for the loss or emancipation of any slave; but all such debts, obligations and claims shall be held illegal and void.

Section 5. The Congress shall have power to enforce, by appropriate legislation, the provisions of this article.

AMENDMENT XV (Ratified February 3, 1870)

Section 1. The right of citizens of the United States to vote shall not be denied or abridged by the United States or by any State on account of race, color, or previous condition of servitude.

Section 2. The Congress shall have power to enforce this article by appropriate legislation.

AMENDMENT XVI (Ratified February 3, 1913)

The Congress shall have power to lay and collect taxes on incomes, from whatever source derived, without apportionment among the several States, and without regard to any census or enumeration.

AMENDMENT XVII (Ratified April 8, 1913)

The Senate of the United States shall be composed of two Senators from each State, elected by the people thereof, for six years; and each Senator shall have one vote. The electors in each State shall have the qualifications requisite for electors of the most numerous branch of the State legislatures.

When vacancies happen in the representation of any State in the Senate, the executive authority of such State shall issue writs of election to fill such vacancies: *Provided,* That the legislature of any State may empower the executive thereof to make temporary appointments until the people fill the vacancies by election as the legislature may direct.

This amendment shall not be so construed as to affect the election or term of any Senator chosen before it becomes valid as part of the Constitution.

AMENDMENT XVIII (Ratified January 16, 1919)

Section 1. After one year from the ratification of this article the manufacture, sale, or transportation of intoxicating liquors within, the importation thereof into, or the exportation thereof from the United States and all territory subject to the jurisdiction thereof for beverage purposes is hereby prohibited.

Section 2. The Congress and the several States shall have concurrent power to enforce this article by appropriate legislation.

Section 3. This article shall be inoperative unless it shall have been ratified as an amendment to the Constitution by the legislatures of the several States, as provided in the Constitution, within seven years from the date of the submission hereof to the States by the Congress.][13]

AMENDMENT XIX (Ratified August 18, 1920)

The right of citizens of the United States to vote shall not be denied or abridged by the United States or by any State on account of sex.

Congress shall have power to enforce this article by appropriate legislation.

AMENDMENT XX (Ratified January 23, 1933)

Section 1. The terms of the President and Vice President shall end at noon on the 20th day of January, and the terms of Senators and Representatives at noon on the 3d day of January, of the years in which such terms would have ended if this article had not been ratified; and the terms of their successors shall then begin.

Section 2. The Congress shall assemble at least once in every year, and such meeting shall begin at noon on the 3d day of January, unless they shall by law appoint a different day.

Section 3.[14] If, at the time fixed for the beginning of the term of the President, the President elect shall have died, the Vice President elect shall become President. If a President shall not have been chosen before the time fixed for the beginning of his term, or if the President elect shall have failed to qualify, then the Vice President elect shall act as President until a President shall have qualified; and the Congress may by law provide for the case wherein neither a President elect nor a Vice President elect shall have qualified, declaring who shall then act as President, or the manner in which one who is to act shall be selected, and such person shall act accordingly until a President or Vice President shall have qualified.

Section 4. The Congress may by law provide for the case of the death of any of the persons from whom the House of Representatives may choose a President whenever the right of choice shall have devolved upon them, and for the case of the death of any of the persons from whom the Senate may choose a Vice President whenever the right of choice shall have devolved upon them.

Section 5. Sections 1 and 2 shall take effect on the 15th day of October following the ratification of this article.

Section 6. This article shall be inoperative unless it shall have been ratified as an amendment to the Constitution by the legislatures of three-fourths of the several States within seven years from the date of its submission.

AMENDMENT XXI (Ratified December 5, 1933)

Section 1. The eighteenth article of amendment to the Constitution of the United States is hereby repealed.

Section 2. The transportation or importation into any State, Territory, or possession of the United States for delivery or use therein of intoxicating liquors, in violation of the laws thereof, is hereby prohibited.

Section 3. This article shall be inoperative unless it shall have been ratified as an amendment to the Constitution by conventions in the several States, as provided in the Constitution, within seven years from the date of the submission hereof to the States by the Congress.

AMENDMENT XXII (Ratified February 27, 1951)

Section 1. No person shall be elected to the office of the President more than twice, and no person who has held the office of President, or acted as President, for more than two years of a term to which some other person was elected President shall be elected to the office of the President more than once. But this Article shall not apply to any person holding the office of President when this Article was proposed by the Congress, and shall not prevent any person who may be holding the office of President, or acting as President, during the term within which this Article becomes operative from holding the office of President or acting as President during the remainder of such term.

Section 2. This article shall be inoperative unless it shall have been ratified as an amendment to the Constitution by the legislatures of three-fourths of the several States within seven years from the date of its submission to the States by the Congress.

AMENDMENT XXIII (Ratified March 29, 1961)

Section 1. The District constituting the seat of Government of the United States shall appoint in such manner as the Congress may direct:

A number of electors of President and Vice President equal to the whole number of Senators and Representatives in Congress to which the District would be entitled if it were a State, but in no event more than the least populous State; they shall be in addition to those appointed by the States, but they shall be considered, for the purposes of the election of President and Vice President, to be electors appointed by a State; and they shall meet in the District and perform such duties as provided by the twelfth article of amendment.

Section 2. The Congress shall have power to enforce this article by appropriate legislation.

AMENDMENT XXIV (Ratified January 23, 1964)

Section 1. The right of citizens of the United States to vote in any primary or other election for President or Vice President, for electors for President or Vice President, or for Senator or Representative in Congress, shall not be denied or abridged by the United States or any State by reason of failure to pay any poll tax or other tax.

Section 2. The Congress shall have power to enforce this article by appropriate legislation.

AMENDMENT XXV (Ratified February 10, 1967)

Section 1. In case of the removal of the President from office or of his death or resignation, the Vice President shall become President.

Section 2. Whenever there is a vacancy in the office of the Vice President, the President shall nominate a Vice President who shall take office upon confirmation by a majority vote of both Houses of Congress.

Section 3. Whenever the President transmits to the President pro tempore of the Senate and the Speaker of the House of Representatives his written declaration that he is unable to discharge the powers and duties of his office, and until he transmits to them a written declaration to the contrary, such powers and duties shall be discharged by the Vice President as Acting President.

Section 4. Whenever the Vice President and a majority of either the principal officers of the executive departments or of such other body as Congress may by law provide, transmit to the President pro tempore of the Senate and the Speaker of the House of Representatives their written declaration that the President is unable to discharge the powers and duties of his office, the Vice President shall immediately assume the powers and duties of the office as Acting President.

Thereafter, when the President transmits to the President pro tempore of the Senate and the Speaker of the House of Representatives his written declaration that no inability exists, he shall resume the powers and duties of his office unless the Vice President and a majority of either the principal officers of the executive departments or of such other body as Congress may by law provide, transmit within four days to the President pro tempore of the Senate and the Speaker of the House of Representatives their written declaration that the President is unable to discharge the powers and duties of his office. Thereupon Congress shall decide the issue, assembling within forty-eight hours for that purpose if not in session. If the Congress, within twenty-one days after receipt of the latter written declaration, or, if Congress is not in session, within twenty-one days after Congress is required to assemble, determines by two-thirds vote of both Houses that the President is unable to discharge the powers and duties of his office, the Vice President shall continue to discharge the same as Acting President; otherwise, the President shall resume the powers and duties of his office.

AMENDMENT XXVI *(Ratified July 1, 1971)*

Section 1. The right of citizens of the United States, who are eighteen years of age or older, to vote shall not be denied or abridged by the United States or by any State on account of age.

Section 2. The Congress shall have power to enforce this article by appropriate legislation.

AMENDMENT XXVII *(Ratified May 7, 1992)*

No law varying the compensation for the services of the Senators and Representatives shall take effect, until an election of Representatives shall have intervened.

SOURCE: U.S. Congress, House, Committee on the Judiciary, *The Constitution of the United States of America, as Amended,* 100th Cong., 1st sess., 1987, H Doc 100–94.

NOTES

1. The part in brackets was changed by section 2 of the Fourteenth Amendment.

2. The part in brackets was changed by the first paragraph of the Seventeenth Amendment.

3. The part in brackets was changed by the second paragraph of the Seventeenth Amendment.

4. The part in brackets was changed by section 2 of the Twentieth Amendment.

5. The Sixteenth Amendment gave Congress the power to tax incomes.

6. The material in brackets has been superseded by the Twelfth Amendment.

7. This provision has been affected by the Twenty-fifth Amendment.

8. These clauses were affected by the Eleventh Amendment.

9. This paragraph has been superseded by the Thirteenth Amendment.

10. Obsolete.

11. The part in brackets has been superseded by section 3 of the Twentieth Amendment.

12. See the Nineteenth and Twenty-sixth amendments.

13. This Amendment was repealed by section 1 of the Twenty-first Amendment.

14. See the Twenty-fifth Amendment.

Selected Bibliography

Abraham, Henry J. *The Judicial Process*, 5th ed. New York: Oxford University Press, 1986.

———. *Justices and Presidents: A Political History of Appointments to the Supreme Court*. 2d ed. New York: Oxford University Press, 1985.

Agresto, John. *The Supreme Court and Constitutional Democracy*. Ithaca, N.Y.: Cornell University Press, 1984.

Alpert, Jeffrey P. *Legal Rights of Prisoners*. Beverly Hills, Calif.: Sage Publications, 1980.

Baker, Leonard. *Back to Back: The Duel Between F.D.R. and the Supreme Court*. New York: Macmillan, 1967.

———. *John Marshall: A Life in Law*. New York: Macmillan, 1974.

Baker, Liva. *Felix Frankfurter*. New York: Coward-McCann, 1969.

———. *The Justice from Beacon Hill: The Life and Times of Oliver Wendell Holmes*. New York: Harper Collins, 1991.

———. *Miranda: Crime, Law and Politics*. New York: Atheneum, 1983.

Ball, Howard. *Courts and Politics: The Federal Judicial System*. Englewood Cliffs, N.J.: Prentice-Hall, 1980.

———. *The Warren Court's Conceptions of Democracy: An Evaluation of the Supreme Court's Apportionment Cases*. Rutherford, N.J.: Fairleigh Dickinson University Press, 1971.

Barth, Alan. *Prophets with Honor: Great Dissents and Great Dissenters in the Supreme Court*. New York: Knopf, 1974.

Baum, Lawrence. *American Courts: Process and Policy*. Boston: Houghton Mifflin, 1990.

———. *The Supreme Court*. 4th ed. Washington, D.C.: CQ Press, 1991.

Becker, Theodore L., and Malcolm M. Feeley, eds. *The Impact of Supreme Court Decisions*. New York: Oxford University Press, 1973.

Belknap, Michael R., ed. *American Political Trials*. Westport, Conn.: Greenwood Press, 1981.

Benson, Paul R., Jr. *The Supreme Court and the Commerce Clause, 1937–1970*. New York: Dunellen, 1970.

Berger, Raoul. *Congress v. the Supreme Court*. Cambridge, Mass.: Harvard University Press, 1969.

———. *Government By Judiciary*. Cambridge, Mass.: Harvard University Press, 1977.

Berry, Mary Frances. *Stability, Security, and Continuity: Mr. Justice Burton and Decision-Making in the Supreme Court*. Westport, Conn.: Greenwood Press, 1978.

Beth, Loren P. *John Marshall Harlan: The Last Whig Justice*. Lexington, Ky.: University Press of Kentucky, 1992.

Beveridge, Albert J. *The Life of John Marshall*. 4 vols. Cambridge, Mass.: Houghton Mifflin, The Riverside Press, 1919.

Bickel, Alexander M. *The Least Dangerous Branch*. Indianapolis: Bobbs-Merrill, 1962.

———. *The Supreme Court and the Idea of Progress*. New Haven, Conn.: Yale University Press, 1978.

Bland, Randall Walton. *Private Pressure on Public Law: The Legal Career of Justice Thurgood Marshall*. Port Washington, N.Y.: Kennikat Press, 1973.

Blandford, Linda A., and Patricia R. Evans, eds. *Supreme Court of the United States, 1789–1980: An Index to Opinions Arranged by Justice*. Millwood, N.Y.: Kraus International Publications, 1983.

Blasi, Vincent, ed. *The Burger Court: The Counter-Revolution That Wasn't*. New Haven, Conn.: Yale University Press, 1983.

Blaustein, Albert P. *The First One Hundred Justices: Statistical Studies on the Supreme Court of the United States*. Hamden, Conn.: Archon Books, 1978.

Blue, Frederick J. *Salmon P. Chase, A Life in Politics*. Kent, Ohio: Kent State University Press, 1987.

Bond, James Edward. *I Dissent: The Legacy of Justice James Clark McReynolds*. Fairfax, Va.: George Mason University Press, 1992.

Brant, Irving. *The Bill of Rights: Its Original Meaning*. Indianapolis: Bobbs-Merrill, 1965.

Byrnes, James F. *All in One Lifetime*. New York: Harper, 1958.

Caldeira, Gregory A. "Neither the Purse nor the Sword: Dynamics of Public Confidence in the Supreme Court." *American Political Science Review* 80 (1986).

Cannon, Mark W., and David M. O'Brien, eds. *Views From the Bench: The Judiciary and Constitutional Politics*. Chatham, N.J.: Chatham House, 1985.

Caplan, Lincoln. *The Tenth Justice: The Solicitor General and the Rule of Law*. New York: Knopf, 1987.

Cardozo, Benjamin. *The Nature of the Judicial Process*. New Haven, Conn.: Yale University Press, 1921.

Carp, Robert A., and Ronald Stidham. *Judicial Process in America*. 2d ed. Washington, D.C.: CQ Press, 1993.

Casper, Gerhard, and Richard A. Posner. *The Workload of the Supreme Court*. Chicago: American Bar Foundation, 1976.

Chafee, Zechariah, Jr. *Free Speech in the United States*. Cambridge, Mass.: Harvard University Press, 1941.

Chase, Harold W. *Federal Judges: The Appointing Process*. Minneapolis: University of Minnesota Press, 1972.

Choper, Jesse H. *Judicial Review and the National Political Process*. Chicago: University of Chicago Press, 1980.

———. *The Supreme Court and Its Justices*. Chicago: American Bar Association, 1987.

Claude, Richard. *The Supreme Court and the Electoral Process*. Baltimore: Johns Hopkins University Press, 1970.

Corwin, Edward S. *The Constitution and What It Means Today*. 12th ed. Princeton, N.J.: Princeton University Press, 1958.

———. *Liberty Against Government: The Rise, Flowering and Decline of a Famous Judicial Concept*. Baton Rouge: Louisiana State University Press, 1948.

Cover, Robert M. "The Origins of Judicial Activism in the Protection of Minorities." 91 *Yale Law Journal* 7 (1982).

Cox, Archibald. *The Court and the Constitution*. Boston: Houghton Mifflin, 1987.

———. *The Role of the Supreme Court in American Government*. New York: Oxford University Press, 1976.

Curtis, Charles P. *Lions Under the Throne*. Fairfield, N.J.: Kelley Press, 1947.

Dahl, Robert. "Decision-Making in a Democracy: The Role of the Supreme Court as a National Policy-Maker." 6 *Journal of Public Law* 279 (1957).

Danelski, David J. *A Supreme Court Justice Is Appointed*. New York: Random House, 1964.

Davis, Sue. *Justice Rehnquist and the Constitution*. Princeton, N.J.: Princeton University Press, 1989.

"Dedication to Justice Harry A. Blackmun on the Occasion of His Twenty-fifth Year as a Federal Judge." *Hamline Law Review* 8 (1985).

Dershowitz, Alan. *Taking Liberties: A Decade of Hard Cases, Bad Laws, and Bum Raps*. Chicago: Contemporary Books, 1988.

Dewey, Donald O. *Marshall versus Jefferson: The Political Background of Marbury v. Madison*. New York: Knopf, 1970.

Dolbeare, Kenneth M., and Phillip E. Hammond. *The School Prayer Decisions*. Chicago: University of Chicago Press, 1971.

Dorsen, Norman. *Discrimination and Civil Rights*. Boston: Little, Brown, 1969.

Douglas, William Orville. *The Court Years, 1939–1975: The Autobiography of William O. Douglas*. New York: Random House, 1980.

———. *Go East, Young Man: The Early Years: The Autobiography of William O. Douglas*. New York: Random House, 1974.

Dumbauld, Edward. *The Bill of Rights and What It Means Today*. Norman: University of Oklahoma Press, 1957.

Dunham, Allison, ed. *Mr. Justice*. Chicago: University of Chicago Press, 1964.

Dunne, Gerald T. *Justice Joseph Story and the Rise of the Supreme Court*. New York: Simon and Schuster, 1970.

Ellis, Richard E. *The Jeffersonian Crisis: Courts and Politics in the Young Republic*. New York: Oxford University Press, 1971.

Ely, John Hart. *Democracy and Distrust: A Theory of Judicial Review*. Cambridge, Mass.: Harvard University Press, 1980.

Emerson, Thomas I. *The System of Freedom of Expression*. New York: Random House, 1970.

Epstein, Lee. *Conservatives in Court*. Knoxville: University of Tennessee Press, 1985.

Ervin, Sam J., Jr. "The Exclusionary Rule: An Essential Ingredient of the Fourth Amendment." *Supreme Court Review* 283 (1983).

Estreicher, Samuel, and John Sexton. *Redefining the*

Supreme Court's Role. New Haven, Conn.: Yale University Press, 1986.

Fairman, Charles. "Does the Fourteenth Amendment Incorporate the Bill of Rights?" 2 *Stanford Law Review* 5 (1949).

Farrand, Max. *The Records of the Federal Convention of 1787*. 4 vols. Rev. ed. New Haven, Conn.: Yale University Press, 1966.

Fellman, David. *The Constitutional Right of Association*. Chicago: University of Chicago Press, 1963.

———. *The Defendant's Rights Today*. Madison: University of Wisconsin Press, 1976.

Fisher, Edward C. *Search and Seizure*. Evanston, Ill.: Northwestern University Press, 1970.

Fisher, Louis. *Constitutional Dialogues: Interpretation as Political Process*. Princeton, N.J.: Princeton University Press, 1988.

Frank, Jerome. *Courts on Trial: Myth and Reality in American Justice*. Princeton, N.J.: Princeton University Press, 1973.

Frank, John P. *Marble Palace: The Supreme Court in American Life*. New York: Knopf, 1958.

Frankfurter, Felix, and James M. Landis. *The Business of the Supreme Court: A Study in the Federal Judicial System*. New York: Macmillan, 1928.

Freund, Paul A. *On Understanding the Supreme Court*. Boston: Little, Brown, 1949.

Freund, Paul A., and Stanley N. Katz, gen. eds. *History of the Supreme Court of the United States*. 9 vols. New York: Macmillan, 1971–1984.

Friedman, Stephen J., ed. *An Affair with Freedom: Justice William J. Brennan, Jr.*. New York: Atheneum, 1967.

Gal, Allon. *Brandeis of Boston*. Cambridge, Mass.: Harvard University Press, 1980.

Garraty, John A. *Quarrels That Have Shaped the Constitution*. New York: Harper & Row, 1964.

Gerber, Scott D. "The Jurisprudence of Clarence Thomas." *Journal of Law and Politics* 8 (Fall 1991).

Gerhart, Eugene C. *America's Advocate: Robert H. Jackson*. Indianapolis: Bobbs-Merrill, 1958.

Glazer, Nathan. "Should Judges Administer Social Services?" 50 *The Public Interest* (1978).

Glendon, Mary Ann. *Rights Talk*. New York: Free Press, 1991.

Glick, Henry R. *Courts in American Politics*. New York: McGraw-Hill, 1990.

Goldman, Robert L. *Thurgood Marshall: Justice For All*. New York: Carroll & Graf, 1992.

Goldman, Sheldon, and Thomas Jahnige. *The Federal Courts as a Political System*. New York: Harper & Row, 1976.

Goldman, Sheldon, and Austin Sarat, eds. *American Court Systems: Readings in Judicial Process and Behavior*. 2d ed. New York: Longman, 1989.

Graglia, Lino A. *Disaster by Decree: The Supreme Court's Decisions on Race and the Schools*. Ithaca, N.Y.: Cornell University Press, 1976.

Graham, Fred P. *The Due Process Revolution: The Warren Court's Impact on Criminal Law*. Rochelle Park, N.J.: Hayden, 1979.

Greenawalt, Kent. *Discrimination and Reverse Discrimination*. New York: Knopf, 1983.

Grossman, Joel B. *Lawyers and Judges: The ABA and the Politics of Judicial Selection*. New York: Wiley, 1965.

Guggenheim, Martin, and Alan Sussman. *The Rights of Young People*. New York: Bantam Books, 1985.

Hall, Kermit L. *The Magic Mirror: Law in American History*. New York: Oxford University Press, 1989.

Halpern, S.C., and C.M. Lamb, eds. *Supreme Court Activism and Restraint*. Lexington, Mass.: Lexington Books, 1982.

Hand, Learned. *The Bill of Rights*. New York: Atheneum, 1964.

———. *The Spirit of Liberty*. New York: Vintage, 1959.

Harrell, Mary Anne, and Burnett Anderson. *Equal Justice Under Law: The Supreme Court in American Life*. Washington, D.C.: Supreme Court Historical Society with National Geographic, 1982.

Haw, James A., et al. *Stormy Patriot: The Life of Samuel Chase*. Baltimore: Maryland Historical Society, 1980.

Henkin, Louis. *Foreign Affairs and the Constitution*. New York: Foundation Press, 1972.

Highsaw, Robert Baker. *Edward Douglass White: Defender of the Conservative Faith*. Baton Rouge: Louisiana State University Press, 1981.

Hodder-Williams, Richard. *The Politics of the U.S. Supreme Court*. London: Allen & Unwin, 1980.

Hofstadter, Richard, ed. *Great Issues in American History*. 2 vols. New York: Random House, 1969.

Holmes, Oliver Wendell. *Collected Legal Papers*. New York: Harcourt Brace, 1920.

———.*The Common Law*. Boston: Little, Brown, 1881.

Howard, A.E. Dick. "The States and the Supreme Court." 31 *Catholic University Law Review* 380 (1982).

Howard, J. Woodford, Jr. *Courts of Appeals in the Federal Judicial System*. Princeton, N.J.: Princeton University Press, 1981.

———. *Mr. Justice Murphy: A Political Biography*. Princeton, N.J.: Princeton University Press, 1968.

Hughes, Charles Evans. *The Supreme Court of the United States: Its Foundations, Methods and Achievements, An Interpretation*. New York: Columbia University Press, 1928.

Hyman, Harold M., and William M. Weicek. *Equal Justice Under Law*. New York: Harper & Row, 1982.

Irons, Peter. *The Courage of Their Convictions: Sixteen Americans Who Fought Their Way to the Supreme Court*. New York: Free Press, 1988.

Jackson, Robert H. *The Struggle for Judicial Supremacy: A Study of Crisis in American Power Politics*. New York: Random House, 1941.

Jacobs, Roger F., comp. *Memorials of the Justices of the Supreme Court of the United States*. Littleton, Colo.: F.B. Rothman, 1981.

Jacobstein, J. Myron, and Roy M. Mersky, eds. *Fundamentals of Legal Research*. Mineola, N.Y.: Foundation Press, 1985.

Johnson, Herbert Alan. *John Jay, Colonial Lawyer*. New York: Garland, 1989.

"The Jurisprudence of Justice Antonin Scalia." *Cardozo Law Review* 12 (June 1991).

Katzmann, Robert A. *Judges and Legislators: Toward Institutional Comity*. Washington, D.C.: Brookings, 1988.

Kelly, Dean M. *Government Intervention in Religious Affairs*. New York: Pilgrim Press, 1982.

King, Willard L. *Lincoln's Manager, David Davis*. Cambridge, Mass.: Harvard University Press, 1960.

———. *Melville Weston Fuller*. New York: Macmillan, 1950.

Kluger, Richard. *Simple Justice: The History of Brown v. Board of Education and Black America's Struggle for Equality*. New York: Knopf, 1976.

Krislov, Samuel. *The Supreme Court in the Political Process*. New York: Macmillan, 1965.

Kurland, Philip B. *Politics, the Constitution, and the Warren Court*. Chicago: University of Chicago Press, 1970.

———. *Religion and the Law: Of Church and State and the Supreme Court*. Chicago: Aldine, 1962.

Kurland, Philip B., and Ralph Lerner, eds. *The Founders' Constitution*. 5 vols. Chicago: University of Chicago Press, 1987.

Lamb, Charles M., and Stephen C. Halpern, eds. *The Burger Court: Political and Judicial Profiles*. Champaign: University of Illinois Press, 1991.

Landynski, Jacob W. *Search and Seizure and the Supreme Court*. Baltimore: Johns Hopkins University Press, 1966.

Lasky, Victor. *Arthur J. Goldberg, the Old and the New*. New Rochelle, N.Y.: Arlington House, 1970.

Lasser, William. *The Limits of Judicial Power: The Supreme Court in American Politics*. Chapel Hill: University of North Carolina Press, 1988.

Lawhorne, Clifton O. *The Supreme Court and Libel*. Carbondale: Southern Illinois University Press, 1981.

Leonard, Charles. *A Search for Judicial Philosophy: Mr. Justice Roberts and the Constitutional Revolution of 1937*. Port Washington, N.Y.: Kennikat Press, 1971.

Lerner, Max. *The Mind and Faith of Justice Holmes*. Boston: Little, Brown, 1943.

Levy, Leonard. *Against the Law: The Nixon Court and Criminal Justice*. New York: Harper Torchbooks, 1976.

———. *Constitutional Opinions*. New York: Oxford University Press, 1986.

———. *Emergence of a Free Press*. New York: Oxford University Press, 1985.

———. *Original Intent and the Framers' Constitution*. New York: Macmillan, 1988.

Lewis, Anthony. *Gideon's Trumpet*. New York: Vintage, 1964.

Lewis, Walker. *Without Fear or Favor: A Biography of Chief Justice Roger Brooke Taney*. Boston: Houghton Mifflin, 1965.

Lieberman, Jethro K. *The Litigious Society*. New York: Basic Books, 1981.

Louthan, William C. *The United States Supreme Court: Lawmaking in the Third Branch of Government*. Englewood Cliffs, N.J.: Prentice-Hall, 1991.

Luker, Kristin. *Abortion and the Politics of Motherhood*. Berkeley: University of California Press, 1984.

Magee, James J. *Mr. Justice Black, Absolutist on the Court*. Charlottesville: University of Virginia Press, 1979.

Magrath, C. Peter. *Morrison R. Waite: The Triumph of Character*. New York: Macmillan, 1963.

Marcus, Maeva. *Truman and the Steel Seizure Case: The Lim-*

its of Presidential Power. New York: Columbia University Press, 1977.

Marke, Julius J. *Vignettes of Legal History*. South Hackensack, N.J.: F.B. Rothman, 1965.

Martin, Fenton S. *How to Research the Supreme Court*. Washington, D.C.: Congressional Quarterly, 1992.

Mason, Alpheus Thomas. *Brandeis: A Free Man's Life*. New York: Viking, 1946.

———. *Harlan Fiske Stone: Pillar of the Law*. New York: Viking, 1956.

———. *The Supreme Court From Taft to Burger*. Baton Rouge: Louisiana State University Press, 1979.

———. *William Howard Taft: Chief Justice*. New York: Simon & Schuster, 1965.

McCloskey, Robert G. *The American Supreme Court*. Chicago: University of Chicago Press, 1960.

McCune, Wesley. *The Nine Young Men*. New York: Harper and Brothers, 1947.

McRee, Griffith John. *Life and Correspondence of James Iredell*. New York: D. Appleton, 1857.

Medalie, Richard J. *From Escobedo to Miranda: The Anatomy of a Supreme Court Decision*. Washington, D.C.: Lerner Law Book Co., 1966.

Meltsner, Michael. *Cruel and Unusual: The Supreme Court and Capital Punishment*. New York: William Morrow, 1974.

Miller, Arthur Selwyn. *The Supreme Court and American Capitalism*. New York: Free Press, 1968.

Morgan, Richard E. *The Law and Politics of Civil Rights and Liberties*. New York: Knopf, 1985.

Morris, Richard B. *John Jay, the Nation, and the Court*. Boston: Boston University Press, 1967.

Murphy, Bruce Allen. *The Brandeis/Frankfurter Connection: The Secret Political Activities of Two Supreme Court Justices*. New York: Oxford University Press, 1982.

———. *Fortas: The Rise and Ruin of a Supreme Court Justice*. New York: Morrow, 1988.

Murphy, Paul L. *The Constitution in Crisis Times, 1918–1969*. New York: Harper & Row, 1972.

Murphy, Walter F. *Congress and the Court: A Case Study in the American Political Process*. Chicago: University of Chicago Press, 1962.

———. *Elements of Judicial Strategy*. Chicago: University of Chicago Press, 1964.

Murphy, Walter F., and C. Herman Pritchett, eds. *Courts, Judges, and Politics*. New York: Random House, 1986.

Nagel, Stuart S. "Court-Curbing Periods in American History." 18 *Vanderbilt Law Review* 925 (1965).

Nelson, Harold L., ed. *Freedom of the Press: From Hamilton to the Warren Court*. Indianapolis: Bobbs-Merrill, 1967.

Novick, Sheldon M. *Honorable Justice: The Life of Oliver Wendell Holmes*. Boston: Little, Brown, 1989.

O'Brien, David M. *Storm Center: The Supreme Court in American Politics*. 2d ed. New York: Norton, 1990.

O'Brien, Francis William. *Justice Reed and the First Amendment: The Religion Clauses*. Washington, D.C.: Georgetown University Press, 1958.

Olson, Walter K. *The Litigation Explosion*. New York: Plume, 1991.

Paschal, Joel Francis. *Mr. Justice Sutherland, A Man Against the State*. Princeton, N.J.: Princeton University Press, 1951.

Peltason, Jack. *Federal Courts in the Political Process*. New York: Random House, 1955.

Perry, Michael J. *The Constitution, the Courts, and Human Rights*. New Haven, Conn.: Yale University Press, 1982.

Pfeffer, Leo. *This Honorable Court: A History of the United States Supreme Court*. Boston: Beacon Press, 1965.

Phelps, Glenn A., and Robert A. Poirer. *Contemporary Debates on Civil Liberties: Enduring Constitutional Questions*. Lexington, Mass.: Lexington Books, 1985.

Pollak, Louis H., ed. *The Constitution and the Supreme Court: A Documentary History*. 2 vols. New York: World Publishing, 1966.

Posner, Richard A. *Cardozo: A Study in Reputation*. Chicago: University of Chicago Press, 1990.

Post, Robert C. "Justice William J. Brennan and the Warren Court." *Constitutional Commentary* 8 (Winter 1991).

Pringle, Henry F. *Life and Times of William Howard Taft*. New York: Farrar and Rinehart, 1939.

Pritchett, C. Herman. *The American Constitution*. 3d ed. New York: McGraw-Hill, 1977.

———. *Civil Liberties and the Vinson Court*. Chicago: Viking, 1954.

———. *The Roosevelt Court: A Study in Judicial Politics and Values, 1937–1947*. New York: Macmillan, 1948.

Provine, Doris Marie. *Case Selection in the United States Supreme Court*. Chicago: University of Chicago Press, 1980.

Pusey, Merlo F. *Charles Evans Hughes.* 2 vols. New York: Macmillan, 1951.

Rehnquist, William H. *Grand Inquests: The Historic Impeachments of Justice Samuel Chase and President Andrew Johnson.* New York: Morrow, 1992.

———. *The Supreme Court: How It Was, How It Is.* New York: Morrow, 1987.

Rodell, Fred. *Nine Men: A Political History of the Supreme Court of the United States from 1790–1955.* New York: Random House, 1955.

Rohde, David W., and Harold J. Spaeth. *Supreme Court Decision Making.* San Francisco: Freeman, 1976.

Ross, Susan Deller, and Ann Barcher. *The Rights of Women.* New York: Bantam Books, 1983.

Rubin, Eva. *Abortion, Politics, and the Courts: Roe v. Wade and Its Aftermath.* New York: Greenwood Press, 1987.

Rudko, Frances H. *Truman's Court: A Study in Judicial Restraint.* Westport, Conn.: Greenwood Press, 1988.

Savage, David G. *Turning Right: The Making of the Rehnquist Supreme Court.* New York: Wiley, 1992.

Scheingold, Stuart. *The Politics of Rights.* New Haven, Conn.: Yale University Press, 1974.

Schlesinger, Steven R. *Exclusionary Injustice.* New York: Marcel Dekker, 1977.

Schmidhauser, John R. *Judges and Justices: The Federal Appellate Judiciary.* Boston: Little, Brown, 1979.

———. *The Supreme Court as Final Arbiter in Federal-State Relations, 1789–1957.* Chapel Hill: University of North Carolina Press, 1958.

Schnayerson, Robert. *The Illustrated History of the Supreme Court of the United States.* New York: Harry N. Abrams with the Supreme Court Historical Society, 1986.

Schwartz, Bernard. *Inside the Warren Court.* Garden City, N.Y.: Doubleday, 1983.

———. *Super Chief: Earl Warren and His Supreme Court.* New York: New York University Press, 1983.

Schwartz, Herman. *Packing the Courts: The Conservative Campaign to Rewrite the Constitution.* New York: Charles Scribner's Sons, 1988.

Scigliano, Robert. *The Supreme Court and the Presidency.* New York: Free Press, 1971.

Segal, Jeffrey A., and Albert D. Cover. "Ideological Values and the Votes of U.S. Supreme Court Justices." *American Political Science Review* 83 (1989).

Shapiro, Martin. *Freedom of Speech: The Supreme Court and Judicial Review.* Englewood Cliffs, N.J.: Prentice-Hall, 1966.

Shogan, Robert. *A Question of Judgment: The Fortas Case and the Struggle for the Supreme Court.* Indianapolis: Bobbs- Merrill, 1972.

Sickels, Robert J. *John Paul Stevens and the Constitution: The Search for Balance.* University Park: Pennsylvania State University Press, 1988.

Simon, James F. *The Antagonists: Hugo Black, Felix Frankfurter and Civil Liberties in Modern America.* New York: Simon & Schuster, 1989.

———. *Independent Journey: The Life of William O. Douglas.* New York: Harper & Row, 1980.

Smith, Christopher E. *Courts and the Poor.* Chicago: Nelson-Hall, 1991.

Spaeth, Harold J. "Justice Sandra Day O'Connor: An Assessment," in *An Essential Safeguard: Essays on the United States Supreme Court and Its Justices.* Edited by D. Grier Stephenson, Jr. New York: Greenwood Press, 1991.

———. *Supreme Court Policy Making: Explanation and Prediction.* San Francisco: Freeman, 1979.

"Special Issue: Justice Byron R. White: On the Twenty-fifth Anniversary of His Accession to the Supreme Court of the United States." *University of Colorado Law Review* 58 (Summer 1987).

Steamer, Robert J. *The Supreme Court in Crisis.* Amherst: University of Massachusetts Press, 1971.

Steiner, Gilbert. *The Abortion Dispute and the American System.* Washington, D.C.: Brookings, 1983.

Stephenson, D. Grier. *The Supreme Court and the American Republic: An Annotated Bibliography.* New York: Garland, 1981.

Stern, Robert L., Eugene Gressman, and Stephen M. Shapiro. *Supreme Court Practice.* Washington, D.C.: Bureau of National Affairs, 1986.

Stites, Francis N. *John Marshall, Defender of the Constitution.* Boston: Little, Brown, 1981.

Strong, Frank R. *Substantive Due Process of Law: A Dichotomy of Sense and Nonsense.* Durham, N.C.: Carolina Academic Press, 1986.

Supreme Court. *Rules of the Supreme Court of the United States.* Rev. ed. Washington, D.C.: Clerk, U.S. Supreme Court, 1980.

Swindler, William F. *Court and Constitution in the Twentieth Century: The Old Legality, 1889–1932*. Indianapolis: Bobbs- Merrill, 1969.

———. *Court and Constitution in the Twentieth Century: The New Legality, 1932–1968*. Indianapolis: Bobbs-Merrill, 1970.

Swisher, Carl Brent. *Stephen J. Field, Craftsman of the Law*. Chicago: University of Chicago Press, 1930.

Temple, Larry. "Mr. Justice Clark: A Tribute." *American Journal of Criminal Law* 5 (October 1977).

Tribe, Laurence H. *God Save This Honorable Court*. New York: Random House, 1985.

"A Tribute to Chief Justice Warren E. Burger." *Harvard Law Review* 100 (March 1987).

"A Tribute to Justice Lewis F. Powell, Jr." *Harvard Law Review* 101 (December 1987).

Urofsky, Melvin I. *Felix Frankfurter: Judicial Restraint and Individual Liberties*. Boston: Twayne, 1991.

Vose, Clement E. *Constitutional Change: Amendment Politics and Supreme Court Litigation Since 1900*. Lexington, Mass.: D.C. Heath, 1972.

Walker, Samuel. *In Defense of American Liberties: A History of the ACLU*. New York: Oxford University Press, 1990.

Walker, Thomas G., and Lee Epstein. *The Supreme Court of the United States: An Introduction*. New York: St. Martin's, 1993.

Warner, Hoyt Landon. *The Life of Mr. Justice Clarke: A Testament to the Power of Liberal Dissent in America*. Cleveland, Ohio: Case Western Reserve University Press, 1959.

Warren, Charles. *The Supreme Court in United States History*. 2 vols. Rev. ed. Boston: Little, Brown, 1926.

Wasby, Stephen L. *The Supreme Court in the Federal Judicial System*. New York: Holt, Rinehart and Winston, 1978.

Westin, Alan F., ed. *An Autobiography of the Supreme Court: Off-the-Bench Commentary by the Justices*. New York: Macmillan, 1963.

———. *The Supreme Court: Views from Inside*. New York: Norton, 1961.

White, G. Edward. *The American Judicial Tradition: Profiles of Leading American Judges*. New York: Oxford University Press, 1988.

———. *Earl Warren, A Public Life*. New York: Oxford University Press, 1982.

Wilkinson, J. Harvie, III. *From Brown to Bakke: The Supreme Court and School Integration*. New York: Oxford University Press, 1979.

———. *Serving Justice: A Supreme Court Clerk's View*. New York: Charterhouse, 1974.

Williams, Charles F. "The Opinions of Anthony Kennedy: No Time for Ideology." *ABA Journal* 74 (1 March 1988).

Witt, Elder. *A Different Justice: Reagan and the Supreme Court*. Washington, D.C.: Congressional Quarterly, 1986.

———. *Guide to the U.S. Supreme Court*. 2d ed. Washington, D.C.: Congressional Quarterly, 1990.

Wolfe, Christopher. *The Rise of Modern Judicial Review*. New York: Basic Books, 1986.

Woodward, Bob, and Scott Armstrong. *The Brethren: Inside the Supreme Court*. New York: Simon & Schuster, 1979.

Yarbrough, Tinsley E. *John Marshall Harlan: Great Dissenter of the Warren Court*. New York: Oxford University Press, 1992.

———. *Mr. Justice Black and His Critics*. Durham, N.C.: Duke University Press, 1988.

Index

PRODUCTION NOTES

The Supreme Court A to Z

was designed, composed, and paged by Kachergis Book Design,

Pittsboro, North Carolina. The text type is 9.5/12 Meridien,

with Centaur display type. Using word-processing files supplied

by CQ Books and illustrations scanned by R. R. Donnelley, page

layouts were prepared in QuarkXPress 3.1 on a Macintosh IIFX,

and files were output to imposed negatives by R. R. Donnelley.

The book was printed on #50 Finch Opaque paper and bound

in Kivar 6 by R. R. Donnelley, Harrisonburg, Virginia.

John Jay

J. Rutledge

Oliv Ellsworth

J Marshall

R. B. Taney

S. P. Chase

M. R. Waite

Melville W. Fuller